WOMEN, HEALTH, AND NATION

McGill-Queen's/Associated Medical Services (Hannah Institute) Studies in the History of Medicine
Series Editors: S.O. Freeman and J.T.H. Connor
Volumes in this series have financial support from Associated Medical Services, Inc., through the Hannah Institute for the History of Medicine Program.

Women, Health, and Nation

Canada and the United States since 1945

Edited by

GEORGINA FELDBERG,
MOLLY LADD-TAYLOR, ALISON LI,
AND KATHRYN MCPHERSON

McGill-Queen's University Press
Montreal & Kingston · London · Ithaca

© McGill-Queen's University Press 2003
ISBN 0-7735-2500-9 (cloth)
ISBN 0-7735-2501-7 (paper)

Legal deposit second quarter 2003
Bibliothèque nationale du Québec

Printed in Canada on acid-free paper that is 100% ancient forest free
(100% post-consumer recycled), processed chlorine free.

This book has been published with the help of a grant from York University through the Burroughs-Wellcome Fund.

McGill-Queen's University Press acknowledges the support of the Canada Council for the Arts for our publishing program. We also acknowledge the financial support of the Government of Canada through the Book Publishing Industry Development Program (BPIDP) for our publishing activities.

National Library of Canada Cataloguing in Publication

Women, health, and nation: Canada and the United States since 1945/edited by Georgina Feldberg ... [et al.].

Includes bibliographical references and index.
ISBN 0-7735-2500-9 (bound). – ISBN 0-7735-2501-7 (pbk.)

1. Women – Health and hygiene – Canada – History – 20th century.
2. Women's health services – Canada – History – 20th century. 3. Women – Health and hygiene – United States – History – 20th century. 4. Women's health services – United States – History – 20th century. I. Feldberg, Georgina D., 1956–

RA564.85.W644 2003   362.1'082'097109045   C2002-904593-2

This book was typeset by Dynagram Inc. in 10/12 Baskerville.

Contents

Acknowledgments

The editors would like to thank the Burroughs Wellcome Fund 40th Anniversary Award for the History of Medicine and Science for its generous funding of our collaborative research project, "Women, Science and Medicine in Post-War North America: Canadian-American Comparisons, 1940–1980." Burroughs Wellcome, the Social Sciences and Humanities Research Council of Canada, and York University provided funding support for the 1998 conference that inspired this volume. We extend our warm thanks to the conference participants. We appreciate the expert research assistance provided by Joseph Tohill, Kristin Burnett, and especially Lisa Rumiel. We also wish to thank Judith Turnbull for her excellent copy editing and Wendy Winters for her skilful and good-natured assistance in the final stages of preparing the manuscript.

WOMEN, HEALTH, AND NATION

Introduction

North Americans often tell stories and anecdotes about their health-care experiences. Some emphasize the benefits of Canada's "social-ized" national health-insurance program, while others praise the American system for giving insured patients quick and easy access to costly high-tech treatments. Policy analysts frequently compare the two countries' health-insurance systems; indeed, popular opinion and the press often link Canada's health-care system to the very fabric of Canadian national identity. Feminist scholars investigate and critique the biomedical orientation that both countries share.

Yet there have been few scholarly analyses of how national health-care differences have shaped women's lives, and studies that address the historical dimensions of those national differences are fewer still. The twenty essays and documents in *Women, Health, and Nation* bring national politics, and the question of health-care access, to bear on the social history of Canadian and American women's health. They explore Canadian and American women's medical care and health activism in order to show how, and to what extent, national citizenship has helped to shape women's health.

Since the 1970s, feminists have interrogated nearly every aspect of women's health and medical care. They have criticized women's secondary status within the medical system and noted how supposedly natural bodily experiences, such as menstruation and childbirth, have changed over time. Historians have illuminated the processes whereby "regular" medical doctors, dedicated to scientific thought and practice, came to dominate health services, often marginalizing female

practitioners in the process. Most histories of women's health focus on
the nineteenth and early twentieth centuries, when the scientific and
medical framework known as biomedicine established its authority in
North America.[1] This volume extends the historical analysis into the
understudied post-1945 era, when medicalization was largely complete
but Canadian and American health-insurance systems diverged.

As a starting point for what we hope will be an ongoing dialogue,
our volume considers five themes in the postwar history of women and
health: the power of the nation-state, the authority of Western biomedicine, diversity, women's agency, and reproduction. Our foremost
theme concerns the power of the nation-state and its constitutive institutions, structures, entitlements, and values, but we also explore citizen engagement with government policies. The concept of nation-
state is complicated, however, by the existence of "nations" within
Canada and the United States; in Quebec and among Native North
Americans – known in Canada as First Nations – a separate national
identity is embraced.

The federal governments of both Canada and the United States
expanded dramatically in the prosperous years after the Second World
War, and both countries made substantial investments in hospital construction, medical research, and social services. Yet, although an orientation towards biomedicine crossed the border, the two countries'
health-care systems evolved in very different ways. After Canada introduced its national health-insurance program, Medicare, in 1968, Canadian women's health-care experiences and activism, and even their
health expectations, were shaped by the confidence gained from their
medical entitlements. By contrast, American women's private lives and
public actions were shaped by the absence of national health insurance. Most women in the United States had to pay substantial out-of-
pocket costs and negotiate with private insurance companies or public
agencies for medical expenses. Since their health insurance was likely
tied to marriage or employment, fear of losing coverage was always in
the back of American women's minds.

Nationality mattered to women's health in a myriad of ways. For one
thing, governments had the power to limit, if never fully impede, the
flow of pharmaceuticals. For another, Canadian and American regulatory and research institutions sometimes responded differently to the
same research. Although the idea that pregnancy and menopause were
treatable diseases freely crossed the border, Barbara Clow's analysis of
the thalidomide crisis (Chapter 2) and Alison Li's study of the development of Premarin (Chapter 5), an estrogen replacement therapy, show
that government regulatory agencies wielded significant power in sometimes different ways. For example, while Canadian regulators approved

the sale of thalidomide, a tranquilizer that turned out to cause fetal deformities when taken early in pregnancy, American women were spared by the delaying tactics of Dr Frances Kelsey, an official at the U.S. Food and Drug Administration who refused to permit the sale of thalidomide in the United States.[2]

National governments, along with professional associations, also had the power to deny or legalize abortion services, to prohibit or force women to be sterilized, and to set the standards of medical practice. Georgina Feldberg's assessment (Chapter 6) of the impact of national and international accreditation policies on medical care at Toronto Women's College Hospital and the articles by Leslie Reagan (Chapter 18) and Elena Gutiérrez (Chapter 19) on California women's lack of reproductive rights expose the state's multifaceted power over women's bodies. When Gutiérrez points out that the forced sterilization of Mexican immigrant women had much to do with citizenship and language, she – like Karen Flynn in her essay on Afro-Caribbean immigrant nurses in Canada (Chapter 12) – underscores the importance of national, as well as racial, categories of difference. Whether they sought legal abortions or higher wages, women who physically crossed national borders knew only too well the power of the nation-state and of federal authorities.

The burgeoning welfare state of the postwar era also had a significant impact on women's health. Hospital construction, the expansion of medical and social services, and better housing, transportation, and working conditions led to substantial improvements in women's health in the 1950s and 1960s. Yet the repercussions of federal power were mixed. Even during the heyday of the Canadian welfare state, as Kathryn McPherson observes in Chapter 11, Aboriginal women had to contend with impure water and other environmental hazards, as well as with the ideologies of colonialism that underpinned government health services. Federal intervention into health care also had an ambiguous effect on female health practitioners. As Aline Charles points out in Chapter 13, although national health insurance benefited women by extending coverage to all female citizens regardless of income or marital status, it eroded the long-standing influence of nuns in Catholic hospitals in Quebec and throughout Canada.

A second theme of this collection is the authority of biomedicine, a subject that has received much critical attention from feminist scholars since the 1970s. Unnecessary hysterectomies and Caesarean sections, like the over-prescription of addictive tranquilizers, confirm that biomedicine has often been used to the detriment of women's mental and physical health and to the exclusion of other ways of healing. Gutiérrez's account of the sterilization of Mexican immigrant women

represents a classic example of the white medical establishment misus-
ing its power, but Michele Landsberg's essay (Chapter 16), reprinted
from 1973, shows that gynaecology also felt oppressive to relatively
privileged women. Yet, as several essays show, the medical profession
was not homogeneous or all-powerful, and women's relationship to
biomedicine was complex. Heather Munro Prescott's analysis of gynaecological care for adolescent girls in the 1950s (Chapter 10)
reveals a medical specialty that was deeply divided over gender norms
and the growing independence of adolescent girls. In Chapter 3,
Molly Ladd-Taylor argues that the emergence of genetic counselling
in the 1950s was due more to patient demand and popular ideas
about family psychology than to scientific developments or "male
medical control." In a similar vein, Georgina Feldberg observes that
female physicians frequently used middle-class hospital patients for
surgical trials and that most patients genuinely welcomed the experiments. Patients' ambivalence towards biomedicine is poignantly illustrated in Maureen McCall's account of her experience with in vitro
fertilization (Chapter 9) and Ann Starr's reflections on her stay in a
Boston psychiatric hospital (Chapter 14).

Throughout the years covered by this volume, patients and activists
wrestled with the utility of the biomedical framework in an attempt to
understand, and resolve, their health concerns. Some women felt empowered when conditions like pregnancy and menopause were medicalized, since doctors were then forced to take women seriously and
recognize their symptoms as "real." Others resented the depiction of
their normal bodily experiences as pathologies requiring treatment.
Michelle McClellan, in her sensitive portrayal of alcoholism reformer
Marty Mann and her campaign to get alcohol addiction recognized as
a medical disease (Chapter 4), shows how the "medical model" could
be used to try to liberate women from negative images of moral or
sexual failing. As McClellan points out, however, the openings presented by medicalization were limited at best. Lesbians, like alcoholics,
faced the ire of religious moralists in the 1950s, but they fought vigorously against the depiction of homosexuality as a disease. For them,
medicalization meant danger, not deliverance.

As the varied responses to medicalization suggests, the diversity of
women's experiences and health-care needs is a third theme of this
volume. Early studies of racism in the U.S. health-care industry documented the job discrimination faced by African-American nurses and
doctors and the abuse of non-white patients who were exploited as
test subjects. In recent years, scholars such as Vanessa Northington
Gamble and Susan Smith have complicated the narrative of victimization by uncovering the histories of black women physicians, nurses,

and lay activists who were the central health-care providers in their communities.[3] In Chapter 15 of this volume, Gamble reflects both on the insensitivity and racism that black women physicians still face and on the inspiration to be found in their foremothers. Several essays build on Gamble's and Smith's work and take it to Canada, where, as the two articles on Aboriginal health show, racial cleavages did not run strictly along black-white lines. Karen Flynn's research on skilled Afro-Caribbean nurses who immigrated to Canada reveals the differences and similarities between Canadian and American racial politics. Although Flynn's nurses had to contend with the racism of government and medical authorities, their nursing skills – in contrast to those of African-Americans – were both needed and valued by hospital administrators. Moreover, Flynn points out, Canadian authorities privileged some black nurses over others, treating nurses from English-speaking Commonwealth countries, such as Trinidad, better than French-speaking Haitians. In addition to racism, Haitian nurses had to contend with a linguistic and cultural discrimination that reflected the historic tension between English- and French-speaking Canadians. Other essays in this volume point to the ways in which differences in ability, sexuality, and class shaped women's experience of biomedicine.

Several essays point out the importance of adding region and religion to our analysis of diversity. North Americans living and working in large urban centres had very different health-care experiences from those in more remote areas. While Gutiérrez's sterilization survivors were mistreated by Los Angeles doctors who had inordinate power, the power of individual physicians was almost inconsequential for Inuit and First Nations women in the Canadian North. In some places, the power of biomedicine was established by its absence. Judith Zelmanovits points out in Chapter 8 that patients often had to leave their isolated communities to receive medical treatment. Moreover, in Canada and the United States, federal Indian Health programs set Western biomedicine in opposition to Native traditions, giving outpost medical services a colonizing function that weakened Native healing traditions. In response, Aboriginal Canadians demanded that they, and not Ottawa, control basic services.

Religious healing practices persisted off as well as on the reserves, and several essays in this volume challenge the conventional opposition between religion and medical science. Aline Charles's study of nuns in Quebec hospitals (Chapter 13) and Laura Ettinger's research on a Catholic maternity centre in New Mexico (Chapter 7) remind us of the ongoing spiritual and health-care work of Catholic religious orders. Their local studies illuminate patterns of health-care provision that are often overlooked when the focus is on the "male medical system." Although feminist health activists of the 1970s sought to restore "women's culture" to health care, in many ways it had never left.

Women's agency is a fourth theme of *Women, Health, and Nation*. Women's active role in establishing public health services for women and children in the first half of the twentieth century has been well documented, and it is not surprising that women continued to play a key role in the expansion and delivery of health care in the postwar period. The work of nurses was especially significant, as the six essays on that profession show. Public health nurses often served as "medical missionaries," bringing medical services to remote communities in Canada and the United States for the first time. They had a great deal of professional autonomy and often did the jobs reserved for doctors elsewhere. Bedside nurses were equally active in health-care reform, as Susan Smith and Dawn Nickel's study of the changing care of the dying shows (Chapter 17). Frustrated with the limits of biomedicine when it came to helping patients who could not be cured, nurses joined other female professionals in mounting a continent-wide campaign for palliative care. Several of this volume's essays demonstrate that lay activists also helped to shape the provision of services and even – as in the case of alcoholism reformer Marty Mann – concepts of health and disease.

Grassroots activists played an exceptionally prominent role in the feminist health movement of the 1970s. We discuss the national differences and similarities in Canadian and American women's activism in our essay (Chapter 1) and we have reprinted in Chapter 16 three examples of women's health movement propaganda. "Show Me a Gynecologist and I'll Show You a Male Chauvinist (Even If She's a Woman)" and "(Not Just) Another Day at the Gynecologist," both written in the 1970s, illustrate feminist anger at the power and insensitivity of gynaecologists. "Mom's Secret," by Chuck Conconi, is both a sober reflection on the stigma of breast cancer in the 1940s and a son's moving tribute to his late mother's determination and courage. Together with the personal narratives we have included from Gamble (Chapter 15), Starr (Chapter 14), and McCall (Chapter 9), these documents remind us of the important role that feminists and other writers have had in bringing women's personal experiences with health and illness into public view.

Two essays address, from different vantage points, the best-known example of women's health activism in the 1960s and 1970s: the campaign for reproductive rights. In Chapter 18, Leslie Reagan recounts how American women seeking abortions in the 1960s often went to Mexico, a move that radicalized many and fuelled a national campaign for abortion on demand. A few years later, Elena Gutiérrez adds (Chapter 19), Mexican-American women mounted a legal challenge to coercive sterilization and built a very different movement for reproductive rights. Because both essays focus on Los Angeles, they raise fascinating questions about abortion-rights activism, sterilization abuse, and the Mexican-American border.

Reagan's and Gutiérrez's essays on California also point to the final theme of our volume: the role of reproduction in women's health activism and history. Nearly half of the essays in *Women, Health, and Nation* focus on maternity care or reproductive rights, themes common to feminist activism in the 1970s but at odds with the more recent orientation towards the "whole" woman and the social and environmental determinants of health.[4] Our emphasis on reproduction reflects both its central place in the historical literature and the fact that reproductive politics have been at the foundation of women's health activism since the 1940s. Efforts to safeguard the health of mothers and babies formed a crucial part of nation-building in the early twentieth century, as many scholars have shown, and they have continued to do so in the postwar years. Maternity care was often the first medical service remote communities got. Even when providers offered much more than reproductive health – as was the case with Toronto's Women's College Hospital and the outpost nurses in the Canadian North – it was their gynaecological and obstetrical work that captured the attention of politicians, donors, and the general public. Reproductive issues, from legal abortion to midwifery services to the debate over infertility technologies, have also been central to recent feminist activism. Because reproduction has long been considered the key to women's health needs, it can be a lens through which we can analyse a wide range of social, cultural, and political factors that shaped the history of women's health.

In the concluding essay of this collection (Chapter 20), historian-activist Susan Reverby reflects on the past four decades of feminist health activism and on her own political work within – and sometimes against – the U.S. health-care system. Reverby stresses the diversity of the women's health movement and highlights the tension between the individual body and the body politic. This tension can be seen, on the one hand, in activists' efforts to provide information and improve medical care for individual women and, on the other, in their struggle to change the medical system. Yet it is expressed most clearly in the movement for reproductive rights, where each woman's right to control her body and choose any infertility procedure, regardless of cost, can conflict with society's obligation to ensure prenatal care to all women by lowering costs.

The tension Reverby observes between the body and the body politic is precisely why a national comparative framework is important: it places the body politic – that is, the nation-state – at the core of the analysis. Thus, while American women theoretically can choose any medical treatment they can afford, Canadians are guaranteed the right to basic health care, though not to every high-tech procedure or technique. However, recent fiscal concerns and political pressures (for example, to enhance the health-care "choices" available to Canadians or to make health-care access universal in the United States) may lead the two systems to converge. A historical perspective is crucial if we are to make sense of the current debates, for it reveals not just the differences, but the similarities and interconnections between the two countries' health-care systems. It shows that, just as the inequitable, market-driven American medical system was the product of concrete political choices, Canada's universal health-insurance program, a creation of the recent past, may not endure. History reminds us that both countries' health-care systems, for all their virtues and all their flaws, were shaped by ordinary men and women who, as patients, providers, policy-makers, and grassroots activists, kept pressing for change. Those who want a better future can find guidance from the past.

NOTES

1 See, for example, Wendy Mitchinson, *The Nature of Their Bodies: Women and Their Doctors in Victorian Canada* (Toronto: University of Toronto Press 1991); and Judith Walzer Leavitt, ed., *Women and Health in America: Historical Readings*, 2nd ed. (Madison: University of Wisconsin Press 1999).
2 Barbara Clow in this volume; William G. Rothstein, "Pharmaceuticals and Public Policy," in *Readings in American Health Care: Current Issues in Socio-Historical Perspective*, ed. William G. Rothstein (Madison: University of Wisconsin Press 1995), 375–91.
3 Jerry L. Weaver and Sharon D. Garrett, "Sexism and Racism in the American Health Care Industry: A Comparative Analysis," *International Journal of Health Services* 8, no. 4 (1978): 677–701; James Jones, *Bad Blood: The Tuskegee Syphilis Experiment* (New York: Free Press 1981); Darlene Clark Hine, *Black Women in White: Racial Conflict and Cooperation in the Nursing Profession, 1890–1950* (Bloomington: Indiana University Press 1989); Vanessa Northington Gamble, *Making a Place for Ourselves: The Black Hospital Movement, 1920–1945* (New York: Oxford University Press 1995); and Susan L. Smith, *Sick and Tired of Being Sick and Tired: Black Women's Health Activism in America, 1890–1950* (Philadelphia: University of Pennsylvania Press 1995).

See also Susan Reverby, ed., *Tuskegee Truths: Rethinking the Tuskegee Syphilis Study* (Chapel Hill: University of North Carolina Press 2000).

4 Baukje Miedema, Janet M. Stoppard, and Vivienne Anderson, eds, *Women's Bodies, Women's Lives: Health, Well-Being and Body Image* (Toronto: Sumach Press 2000).

PART ONE

Why Borders Matter

1

Comparative Perspectives on Canadian and American Women's Health Care since 1945

Georgina Feldberg, Molly Ladd-Taylor,
Alison Li, and Kathryn McPherson

In September 1993 U.S. president Bill Clinton presented his comprehensive Health Security Plan to Congress, unleashing an enormous backlash, not just against health-care reform, but against government in general. As Americans battled over the very idea of national health insurance, many Canadians watched with amusement. Only two years earlier, the prestigious *New England Journal of Medicine* had praised the economic efficiency of Canada's comprehensive, government-funded health-insurance system, popularly known as Medicare. By the end of the decade, however, Canadians were themselves engaged in a passionate debate over the merits of their health-care system. As it became clear that Canadians were unable to access quickly the range of services available to well-insured Americans, some physicians, politicians, and patients advocated privatization of some, if not all, sectors of health services. Others argued vociferously against the introduction of "American-style" health care; for them, Medicare was a key part of Canadian national identity. These national comparisons were not new. Since the 1940s, when Western governments began to establish health and welfare services, Canadian and American doctors and pundits have kept a watchful eye on each other, offering periodic appraisals of why one system or the other was better for the health of their respective nations.[1]

Women's health concerns have been conspicuous in their absence from most of these national comparisons, and women's voices are seldom heard in health-policy debates. Yet women – as patients, providers, researchers, and policy-makers – played an important role in all of

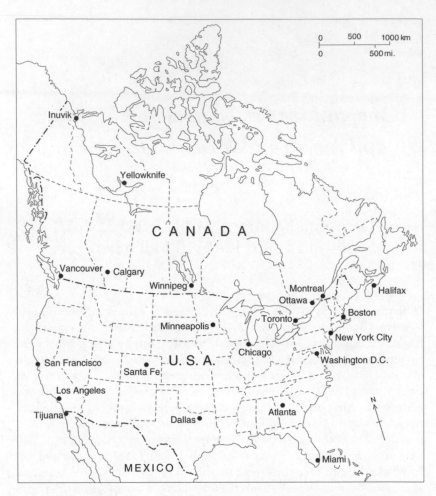

the developments we associate with the post–Second World War medical system: the breathtaking advances in biomedical science, the growing demand for up-to-date technologies, and the improved access to
health-care services. We need only think of Hillary Rodham Clinton or
Canadian health minister Monique Bégin, who was responsible for the
1984 Canada Health Act, for examples of high-profile political leaders
who tried to reshape health policy. We need only think of palliative
care and breast cancer treatment to see the impact that physician-
reformers, such as Elisabeth Kubler-Ross and Susan Love, have had on
patient care. And we need only think of legalized abortion and the
changing management of childbirth to see the impact that ordinary
women have had on the shape of the post-1945 health-care system.
As the major users and employees of the medical system, women have

experienced its problems and benefits most acutely. It is not surprising, then, that in the 1970s women's political activism created dynamic women's health movements on both sides of the border. Although far from homogeneous, these movements have had a powerful influence on North American health-care systems and definitions of health.

Women's historians contributed to health activism by charting patterns of women's health and health care. Some of the earliest work emerged in the 1970s with a critique of the gender asymmetry of modern medicine, known colloquially as the "male medical model." Classic works such as Barbara Ehrenreich and Deirdre English's influential pamphlets *Complaints and Disorders: The Sexual Politics of Sickness* and *Witches, Midwives and Nurses: A History of Women Healers* analysed the development of a system of male control over female healers that seemed to transcend national borders. They portrayed Western medicine as male dominated and oppressive to women, and they assumed the universality of women's bodily experiences, particularly when it came to sexuality and reproduction. This is not to say that race and class were ignored. Ehrenreich, English, and Linda Gordon (Gordon wrote an influential 1976 history of the American birth control movement) were deeply concerned with these divisions among women; yet for the most part, they saw race and class oppression as barriers to the underlying unity of the female experience.[2]

By the 1980s, the majority of feminist scholars had rejected the earlier emphasis on a common – or potentially common – "female" experience. Instead, they emphasized the ways that race, class, ethnicity, and sexual orientation intersect with gender to produce profound differences in women's bodily experiences of health and illness. In the classic example, reproduction, middle-class white women sought greater access to birth control, abortion, and contraceptive sterilization, while poor and non-white women were forcibly sterilized or compelled to use the contraceptive Norplant. Both groups of women sought reproductive rights and "control" over their bodies, but they had very different relationships with both doctors and the state.[3]

Despite their increasing focus on diversity and the power of the state, feminist historians have rarely considered national citizenship as an example of "difference" among women. Citizenship, however, along with national differences in health-care financing and delivery, provides a powerful illustration of one of the most important points made by recent feminist scholars: that the public and private spheres are not truly separate, since public policies profoundly affect women's private lives. Continuing with the sterilization example, it is worth noting that although the sterilization of Canadian women deemed mentally retarded continued into the late twentieth century, women of colour in Canada, unlike their counterparts in the United States, were not forcibly sterilized in large numbers in the 1970s. Whether this was because of national health insurance, Canada's more extensive welfare state, dissimilarities in medical education, or different racial ideologies we do not know. Indeed, we know little about how national differences in funding and access to medical services affected women, or how nationally specific political structures and cultural values shaped women's experiences of illness or health. We do not know how (or if) national identity influenced Canadians' and Americans' employment in, experiences with, or activism around health care. This essay begins a dialogue on these questions. It argues that while national differences have played out unevenly and speaking of a "Canadian" or an "American" female health experience obscures important disparities like class, race, and region, the nation-state has nevertheless been an important force in shaping women's health.

CANADIAN AND AMERICAN HEALTH CARE BEFORE 1945

Surprisingly little historical scholarship contrasts the medical pasts of North America's two largest and most prosperous nations, and studies that focus specifically on women and health are fewer still.[4] Yet it is because Canada and the United States are so similar but have developed dramatically different health-financing systems that they provide a rich opportunity for comparison. Former colonies of Britain, the two countries are both relatively young nations with large immigrant populations, enormous regional differences, decentralized political structures, and federal systems of government. The similarities between the United States and Canada appear even greater when their medical systems are compared to those of Europe. Most European nations, including England, had highly centralized national governments and established some form of health insurance by 1913. By contrast, in both Canada and the United States, the national health-insurance campaigns of the early twentieth century failed. Instead, commercial insurance companies, military organizations, religious orders, and charities moulded North American health-care institutions and women's access to them.[5]

The many cultural values and beliefs shared by Americans and Canadians, and especially by their English Protestant elites, also helped to shape the two countries' medical systems. By the early twentieth century, most middle-class North Americans had abandoned fatalistic religious beliefs about the inevitability of sickness or early death and placed their faith in science – and medical doctors – instead. Male doctors in both Canada and the United States dominated the provision of health services. They used the cultural authority of medical science, organizations like the Canadian and American Medical Associations, and state or provincial licensing bodies to weed out competitors such as midwives and chiropractors. Women entered the medical profession in this period, but their numbers were small and the difficulties they faced were enormous. Discrimination within medical schools, together with the hostility women physicians faced as they tried to secure residencies or set up private practices, reinforced a powerful gender hierarchy. Especially in hospitals, which became the major site of medical practice and education in the twentieth century, male doctors typically dictated the pace and content of patient care, while female nurses monitored its daily application.[6]

A few women did manage to carve out successful careers in medicine and hospital administration. The growing field of public health provided rewarding career opportunities for the largest number of female physicians and nurses, although many also found meaningful careers in the voluntary health sector and worked for agencies like the Red Cross. Some cities had hospitals specifically for women that employed female doctors and lay administrators to oversee their daily operations, and Catholic institutions often relied on the administrative skills of nun-nurses. By contrast, most traditional non-Catholic hospitals reserved formal authority for their male medical superintendents and boards of directors, although they often vested a great deal of power in the hands of nursing superintendents who ensured that hospitals functioned smoothly.[7]

The cross-border travel of doctors, nurses, administrators, funding, and ideas fostered the development of what was essentially a North American medical-nursing system. Canada's pioneering female doctors, Jennie Trout and Emily Howard Stowe, received their medical education in the United States, and the prominent doctor and medical reformer William Osler travelled freely between his home in Montreal and his work at Baltimore's Johns Hopkins Medical School. Abraham Flexner's famous 1910 report on medical education included both Canadian and American medical schools in its mandate, and American philanthropic organizations like the Rockefeller Foundation made significant financial contributions to Canadian institutions. Canadian hospitals regularly recruited American women as superintendents of nursing, while a Canadian, Isabel Maitland Stewart, ran the prestigious nursing program at Columbia University Teacher's College. In both Canada and the United States, hospital administrators endeavoured to secure and maintain their hospitals' accreditation from the American

College of Surgeons, a fact that reflects their shared preoccupation with their hospitals' reputations as "modern" medical institutions.[8]

Given this steady exchange of personnel, money, and ideas – and the decentralized political systems both countries shared – it is not surprising that public health programs in Canada and the United States developed along a similar course. By the early twentieth century, most cities had water and sewage systems, and state and provincial governments had health departments responsible for food inspection, health education, and the control of infectious diseases.[9] Women played important and well-documented roles in developing these programs, especially those intended to protect maternal and infant health. Prominent physicians such as S. Josephine Baker, director of the New York Bureau of Child Hygiene, and Helen MacMurchy, chief of the Child Welfare Division of Canada's Department of Health, worked with public health nurses, social workers, and grassroots activists in a continent-wide campaign against infant and maternal mortality.[10] In the United States, their efforts culminated in the 1921 passage of the Sheppard-Towner Maternity and Infancy Protection Act, the country's first federal social welfare measure. Although no comparable nationwide initiative was undertaken in Canada, most provinces established public health nursing programs to improve maternal and child health care in rural areas. Still, government support for these health services was tenuous at best. The Sheppard-Towner Act fell victim to medical opposition and was repealed in 1929, and many of the Canadian initiatives collapsed during the Great Depression.[11]

The crises of depression and war revitalized the debates over national health insurance. The economic despair of the 1930s seemed to shatter the promise of modern medicine, for it put medical and nursing care out of reach of many families and left practitioners hard-pressed to collect fees. Doctors, like midwives and nurses, were often paid "in kind" with pigs, poultry, or garden produce. Even so, organized medicine continued to oppose national health insurance; it considered voluntary health-insurance plans, such as Blue Shield, preferable to "socialized medicine." Political support for national health insurance, however, increased during the Second World War, partly because war mobilization and the expansion of federal power demonstrated the ability of government to organize the national economy and protect the populace. While Britons discussed the 1942 Beveridge Report and its sweeping recommendations for a cradle-to-grave welfare state, Canadian and American policy-makers debated how North American governments could – and should – improve health coverage. In 1943 the Canadian Parliament established the Special Committee on Social Security to consider, among other things, a federally funded universal health-

insurance system. In the same year, New York senator Robert Wagner
introduced a bill modelled on the Beveridge Report into the U.S. Congress. North America appeared to be on the verge of a revolution in the
provision and funding of health care.[12]

MEDICAL EXPANSION IN THE POSTWAR YEARS

Both Canada and the United States emerged from the Second World
War with buoyant economies and popular support for increased government involvement in health care. With a watchful eye on Britain,
then in the process of developing its National Health Service, both governments announced national health-insurance plans in 1945. Prime
Minister Mackenzie King laid out his plan at the Dominion-Provincial
Conference on Reconstruction. A few months later, President Harry
Truman presented Congress with a dramatic proposal for massive investment in hospital construction, medical education and research,
and universal health insurance. Although his hospital construction and
research-funding laws passed easily, Truman's health-insurance plan
fell victim to a vicious Cold War conservatism that linked socialized
medicine to an international Communist conspiracy.[13] National health
insurance also stalled in Canada. There, the problem was not right-
wing opposition, but disagreement between the federal and provincial
governments. Several Canadian provinces objected to King's proposed
funding mechanisms and to Ottawa's encroachment into health care,
defined in the Canadian constitution as a provincial responsibility. Despite the failure of Ottawa's health-insurance plan, the creation of the
Department of National Health and Welfare and a program of federal
grants for hospital construction signalled the federal government's new
presence in the health-care field.[14]

Although both countries failed to institute national health insurance,
they poured public dollars into medical research, hoping to develop
more drugs as wondrous as insulin, penicillin, and the polio vaccine.
The budgets of the U.S. National Institutes of Health and the Medical
Research Council of Canada swelled, yet vestiges of the older system remained and philanthropic foundations and profit-minded pharmaceutical companies continued to finance a significant portion of medical
research.[15] In this era, new voluntary organizations began to take an
active role in shaping the direction of medical research, creating a complex set of relationships among public, private, and non-profit sector
groups. Charities such as the American and Canadian Cancer Societies
and the March of Dimes ran fundraising campaigns for specific diseases
and then lobbied governments for additional monies. In making granting decisions, charitable organizations relied on professional advisory

boards or on cooperation with government agencies to ensure proper peer review of scientific proposals. However, their support base remained the individual citizen, and thus their focus stayed on simple and saleable concepts, like "finding the cure," that would appeal to the public. Such methods of research funding had long-term implications for women's health, not just because they stressed cure over prevention, but because they constructed a hierarchy among diseases, with "men's" concerns, such as lung cancer and heart disease, at the top. It was not until the 1980s that a handful of ostensibly "women's" diseases, like breast cancer and osteoporosis, broke through the funding barrier.[16]

The massive postwar investment in biomedical services and research had considerable cultural implications, as medical authority seeped into all aspects of daily life. Forms of behaviour once understood in a moral or religious context, such as alcoholism, juvenile delinquency, and homosexuality, were redefined as medical issues to be treated by drug regimens and psychotherapy. At the same time, a growing number of medical specialties, including psychiatry, gynaecology, and paediatrics, expanded their practices to include the "not yet sick." Psychiatry, for example, once concerned primarily with the institutional care of the mentally ill, became a high-status specialty that treated a variety of arguably less ill patients in private practice settings.[17] The cultural emphasis on mental health and treating the not yet sick had the greatest impact on mothers, who were now held responsible for the present and future problems of their children.[18]

The expanding authority of biomedicine also strengthened the position of male doctors within an increasingly complex health-care system. As new layers of subsidiary workers, such as licensed practical nurses, laboratory technicians, dietitians, and physiotherapists, were incorporated into the medical industry, physicians retained their place at the top of the hierarchy. At the same time, medical specialization created a more finely graded hierarchy among doctors themselves. Women and minorities, uncommon enough in the medical profession as a whole, were still rarer in its most prestigious specialties, such as surgery. As late as 1976, only 8.3 per cent of physicians practising in the United States (but 97 per cent of nurses) were women. The greatest numbers of women doctors were in paediatrics or psychiatry; only 8.5 per cent specialized in gynaecology.[19] This meant that most women saw only male doctors, a fact that surely contributed to the anger at "male medicine" that exploded in the 1970s.

Despite the growing power of the medical profession, the white male medical model was never hegemonic, as the essays in this volume show. Throughout the postwar period, prayer and religious instruction

were combined with modern medical techniques; the blending of faith
and medicine was represented architecturally by the chapel in every
hospital. In Catholic hospitals, nuns placed prayer cards on meal trays,
said the rosary with their patients, and called on St Jude, the patron
saint of hopeless causes, to respond to patients' distress. Protestant
faith healers cured the sick, and health providers working in rural
communities learned to combine medical techniques with folk practices, such as putting a knife under the bed to cut childbirth pains.
Racial and ethnic minorities, effectively excluded from the mainstream medical profession until the 1960s, built and provided financial support for medical institutions of their own. Boston's Beth Israel
and Toronto's Mount Sinai are just two of the best-known Jewish hospitals.[20] Although most black hospitals have now disappeared, largely because of racial integration and government-funded health programs,
they provided opportunities for African-American doctors and nurses
and much-needed clinic care for the African-Americans who were
denied entry to white institutions.[21]

Still, many women were too poor or geographically isolated to experience either the benefits or shortcomings of biomedicine. In the
United States, where health coverage was especially sporadic, many
families received no medical care at all. Likewise, rural and Aboriginal
Canadians were often at too great a distance from modern services.
They were further disadvantaged by social factors such as poverty, inadequate housing, environmental degradation, violence, and substance
abuse, which many studies now confirm are important determinants of
health. Despite the economic and cultural power of the biomedical industry, many North Americans remained under-served, rather than
overpowered, by modern medicine.[22]

Both the United States and Canada dramatically expanded medical
insurance coverage in the postwar years. The first stage of this expansion came in the late 1940s and 1950s, when job-based health-
insurance plans, a rise in real income, and (in Canada) national
hospitalization insurance brought medical care within reach of the
majority of working-class families for the first time. Still, coverage remained uneven and incomplete. Even after Canada established national hospitalization insurance in 1957, only one-half of Canadians
had insurance covering other medical expenses. The situation was
not dissimilar in the United States. Nearly two-thirds of the population had some insurance coverage for hospital costs, mostly through
veterans' or union-won employee benefits, yet health coverage in the
United States was highly inequitable. According to one study, 91 per
cent of workers in the highly unionized manufacturing sector, but

just 41 per cent of agricultural workers, had hospitalization insurance. Moreover, the fact that health insurance was tied to employment or military service reinforced conventional family norms and women's economic dependence on men. Since part-time and low-paying "women's" jobs generally carried no health insurance, single women and lesbians often found themselves without coverage and working wives depended on their husbands' insurance.[23] For example, as late as the 1980s, Molly Ladd-Taylor's mother was forced to stay in a hurtful marriage because she had a chronic disease and could not risk losing her husband's health plan.

The second stage of expansion came in the 1960s, when Canada instituted universal health insurance and the United States extended federally funded medical coverage to senior citizens and the poor. Canada's western province of Saskatchewan, led by its dynamic social democratic premier Tommy Douglas, enacted a comprehensive medical-insurance plan in 1961. Doctors responded by going on a twenty-one-day strike. Although Douglas's government prevailed, the memorable "Doctors' Strike" led to a momentous compromise. The province agreed not to put doctors on salary and to maintain the traditional fee-for-service payment structure, but with the government, instead of patients or private insurance companies, now paying the bill. Saskatchewan's plan became the prototype for the federal government's 1968 Medical Care Act, popularly known as Medicare. According to Medicare's terms, the provinces would administer their own health-insurance plans (since health care is a provincial responsibility), but the federal government would pay part of their costs. To qualify for federal funds, provinces had to agree to four guiding principles: (1) universality – all Canadian citizens and permanent residents were entitled to health coverage; (2) comprehensiveness – all "medically necessary" services were covered; (3) portability – Canadians were entitled to care wherever in Canada they lived or travelled; and (4) public administration. By 1971, all ten provinces and two territories had agreed to these principles and Canada's socialized medical system was in place.[24]

While Canada moved to universal health-care access by insuring medical *services*, the United States expanded access by insuring targeted *populations*.[25] The 1962 Migrant Health Act and the War on Poverty provided federal funds for rural health clinics, community mental health services, and neighbourhood health centres. In 1965 two amendments to the Social Security Act, Medicare and Medicaid, extended health insurance to senior citizens and the poor. There was an enormous disparity between the two programs, however. Medicare, a national entitlement program associated with the popular Social Security old age insurance system, had uniform standards for eligibility and benefits; it covered hospital costs and some physician services for Americans over sixty-five and for some younger people with disabilities. By contrast, Medicaid was a joint federal-state program; it provided federal grants to the states to reimburse hospitals and doctors who cared for medical indigents. Medicaid, associated with Aid to Families with Dependent Children, carried the stigma of public assistance. Coverage thus varied widely from state to state.[26] The inequities between the two programs both reflected and reinforced the gendered, two-track American welfare system that has been eloquently critiqued by feminist scholars.[27]

Even though Medicare and Medicaid dramatically increased health coverage, they paid less than half the medical expenses incurred by senior citizens and just one-third the health costs of the poor. Like private insurance plans, Medicare limited coverage of hospital stays to a set number of days and paid only part of approved physicians' fees. As a result, many recipients had to purchase private insurance to cover the remaining costs. Seniors who could not afford co-payment, either because they were already poor or because a long illness had drained their bank accounts, wound up on Medicaid. Yet despite their many limitations, the health reforms of the 1960s made health services accessible to impoverished Americans for the first time. According to one study, non-poor people went to the doctor 20 per cent more often than poor people in 1964 but the poor visited the doctor 18 per cent more often than the non-poor ten years later.[28]

If the United States and Canada travelled down very different health-care roads in the 1960s and 1970s, the consequences did not initially seem very great. In 1971 the two countries spent essentially the same percentage of their gross national product (GNP) on health care, 7.6 and 7.4 per cent respectively. Five years later, nearly 90 per cent of Americans had either public or private health insurance, a rate not so very different from that in Canada.[29]

Within a decade, however, the divergence between the two countries was stunning. Canada strengthened its commitment to universal health insurance in the Canada Health Act of 1984 (which prohibited additional billing, or "extra-billing," for medically insured services), but the United States took a sharp turn to the right, freezing Medicare and drastically reducing funding for Medicaid. By the end of the 1980s, virtually all Canadians had access to medical services, while the proportion of Americans without health insurance was on the rise. And the American medical system was growing more expensive. While Canada spent 8.6 per cent of its GNP on health care, the United States spent an astonishing 11.4 per cent.[30]

THE POLITICAL CONTEXTS OF WOMEN'S
HEALTH ACTIVISM

The feminist health movement that exploded in the 1970s was bound up with the postwar expansion of health-care coverage and the growth of the biomedical industry. The 1950s and 1960s saw the medicalization of many aspects of women's lives, from puberty and menopause to depression and weight control, and an increase in aggressive medical treatments delivered in large, impersonal institutions. Women's experience of childbirth provides a telling example. In the 1950s, although "family togetherness" was the cultural ideal, birthing women in the United States and Canada were typically separated from their families and sent to labour in a sterile hospital room. Their pubic hair was shaved, they were strapped to a table with their feet in stirrups, and they were given drugs to speed up, or slow down, the course of labour. Proponents of "natural childbirth" challenged these conventions in the late 1960s and 1970s, and by the 1980s hospitals had abandoned the worst of them. Even so, medical interventions in the rising number of "high risk" births continued to grow.[31]

The number of women subjected to invasive medical treatments was shockingly high. By the 1970s, American women had surgery two and a half times more often than men. The vast majority of these surgeries were gynaecological – Caesarean sections, hysterectomies, and D&Cs – and far too many were medically unnecessary. One critic calculated that as many as seven out of thirteen Caesarean sections were probably unneeded, while another study, published in 1978, estimated that 62 per cent of American women would have their uterus removed if trends continued.[32]

Unnecessary operations were not the only problem. Many patients found the insensitivity of their doctors – and of the medical system as a whole – equally upsetting. The treatment of breast cancer patients was particularly distressing. Radical mastectomies were performed immediately following a biopsy, while the woman was still under anaesthesia. Well into the 1970s, a woman would go into the operating room not knowing if she would still have her breast when she woke up. In the United States, women's anger at such insensitive practices was heightened by their cost. As the feminist sociologist Sheryl Ruzek wrote sardonically, "When one is forced to pay a large proportion of one's income for services which are humiliating, hazardous and ineffective, resentment is certain to exist."[33]

Many women suffered from callous medical treatment, but prior to the women's health movement, most felt powerless to affect the medical care they received. A few openly expressed dissatisfaction with medical care. In an article in *McCall's*, for example, actress Julie Harris admitted having a frustrating birth experience, while editor Doris Anderson used the pages of *Chatelaine*, Canada's foremost woman's magazine, to speak out.[34] Grassroots groups like La Leche League, which promoted breast-feeding on demand at a time when most doctors advised bottle-feeding according to a set schedule, challenged doctors' authority over infant feeding – and the medicalization of infant care – by drawing on traditional ideas about women's natural maternal role.[35]

These sporadic challenges to medical authority gained momentum in the 1960s. The widely publicized thalidomide tragedy, mounting concerns about addiction to prescription tranquilizers, and the 1969 publication of Barbara Seaman's exposé, *The Doctor's Case against the Pill*, raised troubling questions about the safety of prescription drugs and the failure of pharmaceutical companies and doctors to inform women of the risks. Feminists in both the United States and Canada urged women to "take control" of their bodies and stand up to medical mistreatment.

Feminist health activists engaged in three main strategies: education, self-help, and political reform. In both countries, women who were frustrated with their doctors' unhelpful explanations and condescending behaviour turned to education. Painfully aware of their own ignorance about medicine and their bodies, women throughout North America gathered in small consciousness-raising groups to discuss health issues from anatomy to birth control to the structure of the health-care system. The renowned *Our Bodies, Ourselves*, by the Boston Women's Health Book Collective, grew out of these discussions. The book began as mimeographed notes for a small discussion group in 1969 and was first published as a pamphlet in 1973; by 1996, a much-revised version had sold more than four million copies worldwide. The best-known Canadian publication was the *McGill Birth Control Handbook*, published illegally in Montreal in 1968 and distributed on university campuses throughout Canada and the United States. Most early feminist health publications were highly political, combining practical information about menstruation, yeast infections, and birth control with a vocal critique of how corporate and medical elites determined the national health agenda, often in opposition to the needs of women.[36]

Self-help was the second major feminist health initiative, and activists endeavoured to increase women's control over health care by establishing services that provided an alternative to male medicine. Often framing their efforts in terms of recovering the lost traditions of women healers, North American women established Feminist Women's Health Centers and promoted a "self-help gynaecology." Staffed mostly by female volunteers, including doctors, nurses, and lay activists, women's clinics provided routine gynaecological care, birth control information, and abortion referrals and counselling at a low cost. Patients were encouraged to take an active role in their own care: they didn't have to just lie back with feet in the stirrups and submit passively to a doctor's exam, but could use a speculum to look at their own cervixes. "Something revolutionary" was happening at women's clinics, feminist health critic Gena Corea reflected, and it raised the ire of some medical practitioners. In 1972 police raided the Los Angeles Feminist Women's Health Center, arrested two clinic workers for practising medicine without a licence, and confiscated patient records, instruments, examining tables, and even the yogurt used to treat yeast infections. Although clinic founder Carol Downer was eventually acquitted, her trial was a political sensation that drew the attention and support of women across the continent.[37]

Political change was a third goal of women's health activism, although critical differences in their relationship to the state distinguished the efforts of Canadians and Americans. Because the "free" market dominated health-care delivery in the United States, concepts of consumerism shaped the actions and political rhetoric of American reformers. Health activists advised women to be better consumers, to know the side effects of the drugs they were taking, to shop around for an obstetrician or gynaecologist, and to get a second opinion. They also campaigned to increase women's choices in medical care by expanding the available medications, services, and therapies. Americans used the language of political liberalism and civil rights; they asserted women's right to medical information and adapted the Patient's Bill of Rights devised by consumer advocate Ralph Nader to women's specific needs. The rhetoric of consumerism and civil rights could be in conflict, since the former aimed only to improve medical services for consumers, while the latter asserted that all citizens had a right to adequate medical care.[38] Both, however, drew largely on the language of individualism. For the most part, feminist health activists in the United States conceived of medical care within an individualistic framework, as either a consumer choice or a personal right. Such rhetoric was by no means absent in Canada, but there, health care was viewed primarily within a community or welfare-state context, as a benefit of citizenship; Canadian feminists did not have to defend women's right to adequate health care. Consequently, they placed their emphasis on improving the existing system by extending coverage to new services, such as abortion and midwifery, and by changing how other services were provided.[39]

While American feminists who came of age during the Vietnam War tended to define themselves in opposition to their nation's policies, Canadians had considerable confidence in their government or at least in the federal welfare-state apparatus that had developed since the Second World War. Women's different perspectives on their national governments also had a material basis: Canadian feminists had access to the apparatus of the state to an extent unimaginable in the United States. Even the most mainstream American groups, such as the National Organization for Women, relied entirely on private donations. By contrast, the National Action Committee on the Status of Women (NAC) was a federally funded watchdog agency devoted to improving government services for women. Through NAC, an alternative feminist health magazine called *Healthsharing* was started in 1979. *Healthsharing* served as a focal point for Canadian women's health activism for the fifteen years it received federal funds.[40]

National differences in women's activism are clearly evident in the feminist campaign for legal abortion, perhaps the most important issue of the early 1970s. Prior to *Roe v. Wade*, the 1973 Supreme Court decision that legalized abortion in the United States, most American states and all Canadian provinces prohibited abortion unless the procedure was approved by a committee and performed in a hospital. "Abortion on demand" symbolized women's desire for social roles other than motherhood and became the rallying cry of a young feminist movement. As the American feminist Lucinda Cisler wrote in 1969, "Without the full capacity to limit her own reproduction, a woman's other 'freedoms' are tantalizing mockeries that cannot be exercised."[41] Radical feminists in both countries organized demonstrations and speak-outs, telling publicly their stories of illegal abortions and demanding that women – not doctors or hospital committees – be the ones to decide when abortion was necessary. In Canada the most dramatic challenge to abortion policy was the 1970 Abortion Caravan. A group of Vancouver women demanding "abortion on demand" journeyed across the country to the nation's capital in Ottawa, stopping in towns and cities along the way to rally support. When federal officials would not meet with the women, they chained themselves to the visitors' gallery in the House of Commons, an act that revealed not only their militancy, but also their belief that radical change could occur within the existing government-funded health-care system.[42] Significantly, there was no Canadian equivalent to "Jane," the Chicago abortion collective that dramatically defied the law (and the medical profession) by performing approximately 11,000 illegal abortions between 1969 and 1973.[43] Indeed, the most powerful symbol of Canadian abortion-rights activism came, not from a feminist collective, but from the combative male physician Henry Morgentaler, who went to jail in the 1980s for the right to perform abortions outside of hospitals.

Only in 1988, fifteen years after *Roe v. Wade*, did the Supreme Court of Canada decriminalize non-hospital abortions.

American and Canadian women's health activists had many successes. They increased the numbers of women physicians, raised doctors' awareness of patients' rights, successfully pressed researchers and pharmaceutical companies to improve drug testing and research protocols, and prompted dramatic changes in the management of pregnancy, childbirth, and other health conditions affecting women. However, their movements were not without tensions. Three issues – working within the medical system, racism, and technology – were particularly divisive. The first conflict to emerge was over women's place in the medical system. Many nurses felt alienated from feminists who sought to increase the numbers and enhance the authority of women doctors but paid little attention to the largely female nursing workforce. The provocative article title " 'Why doesn't a smart girl like you go to medical school?' The women's movement takes a slap at nursing" captured the resentment felt by many white-collar health-care workers.[44] Women physicians, too, felt under fire from feminists who saw the entire medical system as oppressive. As Georgina Feldberg's essay in this volume shows, many doctors were stung by the charge that "feminist physician" was an oxymoron; political, and often generational, tensions existed between women working within the medical system and those seeking more radical change.

Race and racism represented another source of friction among women activists. By the late 1970s, African-American (and some white) activists outspokenly criticized the women's health movement for its white, middle-class orientation, reflected in its focus on the doctor-patient relationship and a narrow, almost exclusively gynaecological definition of women's health. Not surprisingly, tensions exploded first in the United States in the campaign for reproductive rights, as black women urged "pro-choice" feminists to consider the impact of their demands on poor women of colour, who were often denied the choice to have children because of forced sterilization or poverty. How, they asked, could white, middle-class feminists claim to support abortion rights but remain virtually silent when the 1977 Hyde Amendment essentially eliminated Medicaid funding for abortion? How could the National Organization for Women, the largest feminist organization in the United States, claim to be pro-choice but testify against regulations intended to prevent sterilization abuse?[45]

Furthermore, black feminists pointed out, white feminists' narrow understanding of women's health obscured many of the most important health issues affecting women of colour, including poverty, stress, and the lack of health insurance. Continuing the long tradition of health activism in the black community, African-American women set up their own health organizations. The best known was the Black Women's Health Project, founded by Byllye Avery in 1983. Its community-based self-help programs combined medical information, spiritual traditions, and alternative therapies to address a wide range of health and wellness issues, including substance abuse, weight control, and cancer.[46]

The need for feminists to address women's diverse health needs was also an issue in Canada, where Aboriginal and immigrant women faced significant linguistic, cultural, and geographic barriers to securing appropriate medical care in spite of national health insurance. Like Americans, Canadian feminists initially assumed white women's experience to be the norm. However, by the 1980s they endeavoured to address the unique health needs of immigrants and women of colour. Yet the resources available to Canadian activists were far greater than those to women in the United States. While American women's health organizations struggled to stay afloat, Toronto feminists received $1.5 million in government and private funds to establish culturally sensitive health services for immigrants, women with disabilities, teenagers, and older women.[47]

Lesbians added another dimension to the need for culturally sensitive health care in both countries. Rejecting the homophobia of the medical and nursing professions and the persistent belief that homosexuality was a disease (two problems that crossed the border), lesbians played a major role in the self-help health movement of the 1970s. They emphasized the interconnections between physical and mental health, called attention to the ways that homophobia aggravated and even caused disease, and vigorously criticized the medical profession for demeaning lesbian patients, thereby stopping them from seeking basic services.[48] Similarly, disability activists in both countries pressed feminist health critics to analyse concepts of health and ability that limited the access that people with disabilities had to appropriate services. However, while Canadians generally worked to improve access and cultural sensitivity within existing welfare-state services, activists in the United States (where there was no guarantee of basic health coverage) built their campaign around civil rights. Their efforts culminated in the 1990 passage of the Americans with Disabilities Act, which protected the civil rights of Americans with physical and mental disabilities.[49]

The willingness of government and private agencies to fund some women's health initiatives contributed to a third tension among women's health activists, this one over the merits of science and technology. Here again, the differences are best illustrated through the

issue of reproduction – in this case, infertility treatments and the debate over new reproductive technologies. The extraordinary advances
in medical technology, from ultrasound and amniocentesis to in vitro
fertilization, set the background for the conflict, which erupted in the
mid-1980s. Many feminist health activists considered genetic tests and
infertility treatments an ineffective and even dangerous example of
an overly commercial medical science, one that panders to false
hopes for a cure and would lead to a new trade in women's bodies
and women's further loss of control to male-dominated biomedicine.
Other activists, however, emphasized the real pain of infertility; they
criticized what they considered anti-technology feminists' romanti-
cized construction of "natural" motherhood and demanded that in
vitro and fertility treatments be made more accessible. While American feminists debated, Canada set up the Royal Commission on New
Reproductive Technologies. As the commission crossed Canada, consulting with citizens and lobby groups, some feminist commissioners
became disillusioned with the process, claiming that feminist insights
into the potential dangers of reproductive technology were being
ignored or downplayed. When the commission issued its very moderate final report in 1993, the same activists who had entrusted their
cause to the state decried the result.[50] This prompted the American
reproductive-rights activist Rosalind Petchesky to retort that, compared to the "dreary picture in the U.S.," the "de-commercializing
thrust" of the commission's final report seemed, "from a U.S. feminist's vantage point, nearly utopian."[51]

HEALTH SYSTEMS IN CRISIS

Ironically, the medical industry began to pay more attention to
women's health needs just as North American health-care systems were
coming under stress. Rising health-care costs and disappointment with
biomedicine provided the backdrop for the changes to health care in
the 1970s and 1980s. Exposés of unnecessary medical procedures and
other abuses of medical power, many of them brought to public attention by feminist health activists, contributed to a disillusionment with
medical science.[52]

    In the United States, a new method of health-care delivery, called
Health Maintenance Organizations (HMOs), was a major source of dissatisfaction. HMOs grew out of a 1973 effort to encourage prepaid
health plans, but they became a significant part of the U.S. health-care
scene only in the 1980s. The advantage of HMOs, at least from the perspective of the insurer, was that they carried less economic risk than
traditional fee-for-service financing, where there was an economic

incentive to over-treat. Although insurance companies had little control over treatment costs or medical fees when the physicians were in private practice, HMOs prepaid a fixed sum per patient, often adding a financial incentive if actual costs turned out to be lower than expected. As they became more common, HMOs shifted the economic impetus of America's market-driven health-care system from over-medicalization to under-treatment.[53] Whereas doctors in the 1960s made money by keeping patients in hospital and ordering lots of medical tests, the HMOs employing them in the 1980s made money when doctors did less.[54] The implications for women's health were enormous. On the positive side, because HMOs had no incentive to over-treat, they encouraged preventive health measures, such as Pap smears, and relied on nurse practitioners, who, for routine care, used fewer tests and less invasive procedures than specialists. More negatively, HMOs often restricted patients' access to specialists and costly medical tests and treatments. In 1994 a California court awarded $89 million in damages to the family of Nelene Fox, who died of breast cancer after her HMO refused to pay for the high-dose chemotherapy and bone-marrow transplant her doctors recommended.[55]

The growing proportion of families without health insurance was even more troubling than the problems with HMOs. Because health benefits could consume more than half of pre-tax corporate profits in the 1980s, many companies reduced their employees' health coverage or employed "part-time" workers with no benefits at all. By 1992, the situation was so bad that some 38.9 million Americans (17.4 per cent of the population under sixty-five) were uninsured. Another 40 million were under-insured. The vast majority of the uninsured were the working poor: office workers, factory operatives, saleswomen, farm and domestic workers, and housewives. Women of colour lacked health insurance at significantly higher rates than non-Hispanic whites, although Hispanics were more likely to be uninsured than any other racial or ethnic group. For poor mothers, no health insurance meant anguished calculations: how high a fever or how deep a cough before a doctor's visit was necessary? Medical care could cost a month's rent or more, so poor women treated themselves and their children with black market drugs or home remedies – or let health problems go. And, increasingly, even middle-class Americans felt that health care was becoming unaffordable. Two-thirds of those surveyed in one poll worried that they would have financial difficulty paying for the costs of a major illness or that they would be unable to cope at all.[56]

While U.S. health coverage deteriorated, Canada strengthened its popular universal health-insurance system. The 1984 Canada Health Act, guided into law by Minister of Health Monique Bégin, made

Medicare more truly universal by prohibiting direct charges to patients, such as user fees or extra-billing, and making it illegal for obstetricians, gynaecologists, and other specialists to bill patients above the government rate. Most Canadians were proud of their health-care system and considered it a key part of their national identity, a crucial distinction between their country and its powerful neighbour to the south. Unlike in the United States, Canadians boasted, no one in their country would be denied medical treatment or hospital admission because of inability to pay.

By the end of the 1980s, however, fissures had emerged in Canada's health-care system. Economic recession and rising medical costs put Medicare under severe financial pressure and exacerbated long-standing regional tensions. The economic crisis augmented the disparity between rich and poor provinces and made it more difficult for provinces to provide health care in remote areas. Rural Canadians simply did not have access to the medical specialists and high-tech services available in cities, and it was often difficult to recruit physicians to work in their communities. The increasing number of homeless Canadians, including women, also found themselves without adequate access to care. When federal transfer payments to the provinces were reduced, provincial governments were forced to find new ways to stretch diminishing dollars. Several provinces "de-listed" (refused to pay for) "non-essential" treatments, such as in vitro fertilization and cosmetic surgery, and imposed caps on the amount physicians could bill in any given year. Some provinces, most notably Quebec, explored alternative forms of service delivery, such as community health centres. Most tried to restructure their hospital systems in order to reduce expenditures on costly hospital services and shift care into the community. A few provincial leaders with strained budgets questioned whether new immigrants should be eligible for coverage and denied insurance to those who entered with pre-existing illnesses. Even so, health-care spending jumped to a high of 10 per cent of the gross domestic product by 1992.[57] Some Canadians, frustrated by what seemed to be longer waits for medical tests and treatments, began seeking care abroad. Politicians, physicians, and economists charged that Medicare costs were spiralling out of control while the quality of the system declined. While there was no consensus on the source of increased costs (some argued that it was driven by over-medicalization; others, by consumer abuse) or on the solutions (some proposed a transfer to preventive, community-based services, while others argued for increased private spending), many Canadians believed something needed to be done.[58]

In both Canada and the United States, attempts at fiscal restraint intersected with the feminist critique of biomedicine in complicated ways. Maternal hospital stays provide a nice illustration. Women's health activists had forcefully criticized the medicalization of birth; new mothers and babies in the 1950s and 1960s, for example, might have spent as many as ten days in the hospital after an uncomplicated birth. By the 1990s, however, budget cuts had converged with feminists' insistence that birth should not be medicalized, and many new mothers were sent home after twenty-four hours. Hospital readmissions for infant jaundice and dehydration escalated, and "drive-through deliveries" became a major political issue. In 1996 the U.S. Congress passed legislation requiring insurers to pay for at least forty-eight hours in hospital following a normal delivery.[59]

The reformist spirit of new U.S. president Bill Clinton and rising fears of a health-care crisis prompted new Canadian-American comparisons in the early 1990s. While American liberals looked to Canada's single-payer system as a way to make coverage universal and reduce administrative costs, Canadian conservatives became more vocal in their praise of America's free-market system and its promise of speedy access to medical tests and services for which Canadians sometimes had to wait. Most Canadians, however, strenuously opposed the introduction of a two-tier, "American-style" medical system. Defenders of Canada's Medicare pointed out that Americans spent 10–15 per cent more than Canadians on health administration alone, and called for better funding of Canada's universal health-insurance system.[60]

In both countries, discussions of health reform prompted medical attention to "women's health" concerns. Hospitals opened home-like birthing rooms and special women's health units; governments ran educational campaigns about prenatal care and osteoporosis prevention; and magazines and television shows dramatically increased their coverage of women's health issues. The U.S. National Institutes of Health established the Office of Women's Health Research and the Women's Health Initiative to ensure that women were included in medical research and clinical trials. Health Canada poured funds into the Canadian Women's Health Network and five Centres of Excellence for Women's Health Research. In 1996 the bilateral Canada-U.S.A. Women's Health Forum sought to establish a transnational women's health agenda.

The new investments in biomedical research on women often came at the expense of other initiatives, however. For example, Health Canada funded the Centres of Excellence at the same time that it reduced funding to grassroots women's health groups. This led many feminists to worry that the new attention to women's health would strengthen the biomedical model – and the biomedical industry – at the expense of a more political and social analysis. While applauding the inclusion of women in a greater range of research protocols, such as drug trials to control hypertension, critics observed that most biomedical researchers failed to investigate the gendered, social determinants of illness, such as stress, domestic violence, and poverty.[61] Furthermore, Canadian health critics pointed out, many health "reforms," like the shift to non-hospital and outpatient care, often led to layoffs or wage reductions for nurses and hospital workers – most of them female – while increasing the unpaid caregiving work of family and friends – again, most of them female. Even in today's more "woman friendly" policy environment, feminists have had to struggle to place the needs of female employees and caregivers, as well as patients, on the policy agenda.[62]

These recent developments have raised the stakes for women's health activists, forcing us to confront what scholar-activist Susan Reverby, in her essay in this volume, identifies as a fundamental tension between the "body" and the "body politic." In the past, the competition between addressing the health needs of the individual body and working to change the body politic was sometimes muted. For example, feminists' individualistic demand for control over our bodies brought once-secret suffering into public view, leading to legalized abortion, a transformation in the treatment of breast cancer, and new research on women's health needs. In recent years, however, that same call for control has contributed to a consumerist mindset that presumes the individual's "right to choose" any biomedical procedure, regardless of cost. Yet it is simply not possible to guarantee individual choice in medical treatment while ensuring broad access to health care, the American feminist sociologist Sheryl Ruzek points out, and feminist health advocates must rethink some of our most basic assumptions about individualism and choice.[63]

The urgency of this rethinking was made stunningly clear in the months after 11 September 2001, for the terrorist attacks and economic collapse in the United States left many millions of Americans, especially immigrants, without jobs or health care. Although unemployment has little effect on health coverage in Canada, the combination of rising costs, reduced government spending on everything but security, and new pressures to expand heath-care "choices" is placing unprecedented demands on Medicare. In both countries, the war on terrorism has thrown women's health issues far off the national agenda. If we are to improve health care for women amidst these unprecedented political and economic challenges, we must sustain the efforts of generations of activists to render women's health issues visible, be attentive to the diversity of women's needs, and push national governments to make adequate health care accessible to all.

NOTES

1 Steffie Woolhandler and David Himmelstein, "The Deteriorating Administrative Efficiency of the U.S. Health Care System," *New England Journal of Medicine* 324 (May 1991): 1253–8. See also Daniel Drache and Terry Sullivan, eds, *Health Reform: Public Success, Private Failure* (London: Routledge 1999).

2 Barbara Ehrenreich and Deirdre English, *Complaints and Disorders: The Sexual Politics of Sickness* (Old Westbury, N.Y.: Feminist Press 1973), and *Witches, Midwives, and Nurses: A History of Women Healers* (Old Westbury, N.Y.: Feminist Press 1973); Linda Gordon, *Woman's Body, Woman's Right: Birth Control in America*, 2nd ed. (New York: Penguin 1990).

3 Angela Davis, *Women, Race and Class* (New York: Random House 1981).

4 Comparative works on the history of North American medical systems include Terry Boychuk, *The Making and Meaning of Hospital Policy in Canada and the United States* (Ann Arbor, Mich.: University of Michigan Press 1999); Antonia Maioni, *Parting at the Crossroads: The Emergence of Health Insurance in the United States and Canada* (Princeton, N.J.: Princeton University Press 1998); and Carolyn Hughes Tuohy, *Accidental Logics: The Dynamics of Change in the Health Care Arena in the United States, Britain and Canada* (New York and Oxford: Oxford University Press 1999).

5 Maioni, *Parting at the Crossroads*; George Torrance, "Socio-Historical Overview," in David Coburn, Carl D'Arcy, George Torrance, and Peter New, eds, *Health and Canadian Society: Sociological Perspectives*, 2nd ed. (Richmond Hill, Ont.: Fitzhenry & Whiteside 1987); Paul Starr, *The Social Transformation of American Medicine* (New York: Basic Books 1982).

6 See, for example, Charles Rosenberg, *The Care of Strangers: The Rise of America's Hospital System* (New York: Basic Books 1987); James Connor, *Doing Good: The Life of Toronto's General Hospital* (Toronto: University of Toronto Press 2001); Regina Morantz-Sanchez, *Sympathy and Science: Women Physicians in American Medicine* (New York: Oxford University Press 1985); Susan Reverby, *Ordered to Care: The Dilemma of American Nursing, 1850–1945* (New York: Cambridge University Press 1987); and Kathryn McPherson, *Bedside Matters: The Transformation of Canadian Nursing, 1900–1990* (Toronto: Oxford University Press 1996).

7 Morantz-Sanchez, *Sympathy and Science*; Aline Charles's and Laura Ettinger's contributions to this volume.

8 Michael Bliss, *William Osler: A Life of Medicine* (Toronto: University of Toronto Press 1999); Howard Berliner, *A System of Scientific Medicine:*

Philanthropic Foundations in the Flexner Era (New York: Tavistock 1985); Rosemary Stevens, *In Sickness and in Wealth: American Hospitals in the Twentieth Century* (New York: Basic Books 1989).

9 Judith Leavitt, *The Healthiest City: Milwaukee and the Politics of Health Reform* (Madison: University of Wisconsin Press 1996); Heather MacDougall, *Activists and Advocates: Toronto's Health Department, 1883–1983* (Toronto: McClelland and Stewart, 1993).

10 Dianne Dodd, "Advice to Parents: The Blue Books, Helen MacMurchy, M.D., and the Federal Department of Health, 1920–34," *Canadian Bulletin of Medical History* 8, no. 2 (1991): 203–30.

11 Nancy Tomes, *The Gospel of Germs: Men, Women and the Microbe in American Life* (Cambridge: Harvard University Press 1998); Molly Ladd-Taylor, *Mother-Work: Women, Child Welfare and the State* (Urbana: University of Illinois Press 1994); Cynthia Commachio, *Nations Are Built of Babies: Saving Ontario's Mothers and Children* (Montreal and Kingston: McGill-Queen's University Press 1993); Karen Buhler Wilkerson, *False Dawn: The Rise and Decline of Public Health Nursing, 1900–1930* (New York: Garland 1989); Meryn Stuart, "Shifting Professional Boundaries: Gender Conflict in Public Health, 1920–1925," in Dianne Dodd and Deborah Gorham, eds, *Caring and Curing: Historical Perspectives on Women and Healing in Canada* (Ottawa: University of Ottawa Press 1994); Kathryn McPherson, "Nurses and Nursing in Early Twentieth Century Halifax, 1900–1925" (MA thesis, Dalhousie University 1982).

12 Maioni, *Parting at the Crossroads*; C. David Naylor, *Private Practice, Public Payment: Canadian Medicine and the Politics of Health Insurance, 1911–1966* (Montreal and Kingston: McGill-Queen's University Press 1986).

13 Ronald Numbers, *Almost Persuaded: American Physicians and Compulsory Health Insurance, 1912–1920* (Baltimore: Johns Hopkins 1978).

14 Naylor, *Private Practice, Public Payment*; Starr, *Social Transformation of American Medicine.*

15 Between 1962 and 1972 the research funding provided by the Medical Research Council of Canada grew by 774 per cent, from $4,083 to $35,664. See Ann Crichton, David Hsu, and Stella Tsang, *Canada's Health Care System: Its Funding and Organization*, rev. ed. (Ottawa: Canadian Hospital Association 1994), 174; and Terrie Romano and Alison Li, *Celebrating the Medical Research Council of Canada: A Voyage in Time, 1960–2000* (Ottawa: Medical Research Council [Canada] 2000).

16 Amy Sue Bix, "Disease Chasing Money and Power: Breast Cancer and Aids Activism Challenging Authority," *Journal of Policy History* 9 (1997): 5–32; James Patterson, *The Dread Disease: Cancer and Modern American Culture* (Cambridge, Mass.: Harvard University Press 1987).

17 Gerald Grob, *The Mad among Us: A History of the Care of the Mentally Ill* (New York: Free Press 1994).

18 Mona Gleason, *Normalizing the Ideal: Psychology, Schooling and the Family in Postwar Canada* (Toronto: University of Toronto Press 2000).

19 Helen I. Marieskind, *Women in the Health System: Patients, Providers, Programs* (St Louis: C.V. Mosby 1980), 132; Deborah Gorham, " 'No Longer an Invisible Minority': Women Physicians and Medical Practice in Late Twentieth-Century North America," in Dodd and Gorham, eds, *Caring and Curing.*

20 Robert Orsi, *Thank You, St. Jude: Women's Devotion to the Patron Saint of Hopeless Causes* (New Haven: Yale University Press 1996), 160–2.

21 Vanessa Gamble, *Making a Place for Ourselves: The Black Hospital Movement, 1920–45* (New York: Oxford University Press 1995); Susan L. Smith, *Sick and Tired of Being Sick and Tired: Black Women's Health Activism in America, 1890–1950* (Philadelphia: University of Pennsylvania Press 1995).

22 Catherine McBride and Ellen Bobet, "Health of Indian Women," QASR (Quantitative Analysis and Socio-demographic Research) Working Paper Series 91–1, Indian and Northern Affairs Canada 1991. On American Indian health services, see Robert A. Trennert, *White Man's Medicine: Government Doctors and the Navajo, 1863–1955* (Albuquerque: University of New Mexico Press 1998).

23 Government of Canada, *Preserving Universal Medicare: A Government of Canada Position Paper* (Ottawa: Health and Welfare Canada 1984), 8; Starr, *Social Transformation of American Medicine,* 334.

24 Monique Bégin, *Canada's Right to Health* (Westmount, Que.: Optimum Publishing 1984); see also Monique Bégin, *The Future of Medicare: Recovering the Canada Health Act* (Ottawa: Canadian Centre for Policy Alternatives 1999).

25 Tuohy, *Accidental Logics,* 30–4, 47–61; Jaap Kooijman, *And the Pursuit of National Health: The Incremental Strategy toward National Health Insurance* (Amsterdam/Atlanta: Rodopoi 1999).

26 For discussions of the genesis of the U.S. system, see Starr, *Social Transformation of American Medicine,* 370–4; David Rothman, *Beginnings Count: The Technological Imperative in American Healthcare* (New York: Oxford University Press 1997), 67–86; Theodore Marmor, *The Politics of Medicare* (New York: Aldine-Atheson 1973); Daniel Fox, *Health Policies, Health Politics: The British and American Experience 1911–1965* (Princeton, N.J.: Princeton University Press 1986); Michael D. Reagan, *The Accidental System: Health Care Policy in America* (Boulder, Colo.: Westview Press 1999), 73–88; Antonia Maioni, "Divergent Paths, Convergent Futures? The Politics of Health Care Reform in Canada and the United States," *Canadian-American Public Policy* 18 (1994): 1–34; and Maioni, *Parting at the Crossroads.*

27 Linda Gordon, ed., *Women, the State, and Welfare* (Madison: University of Wisconsin Press 1990).

28 Starr, *Social Transformation of American Medicine,* 373.

29 U.S. Bureau of the Census, *Statistical Abstract of the United States, 1980* (Washington: Government Printing Office), 109.

30 Perrin Beatty, "A Comparison of Our Two Systems," in Arnold Bennett and Orvill Adams, eds, *Looking North for Health: What We Can Learn from Canada's Health Care System*, (San Francisco: Jossey-Bass 1993), 33; Theda Skocpol, *Boomerang: Health Care Reform and the Turn against Government* (New York: Norton 1996), 23; Maioni, "Divergent Paths"; Maioni, *Parting at the Crossroads*.

31 Gena Corea, *The Hidden Malpractice: How American Medicine Mistreats Women* (New York: Harper & Row 1985).

32 Sheryl Ruzek, "Feminist Visions of Health: An International Perspective," in Juliet Mitchell and Ann Oakley, eds *What Is Feminism?* (New York: Pantheon 1986), 184–207; Marieskind, *Women in the Health System*, 19.

33 Ruzek, "Feminist Visions of Health," 194–5.

34 Shannon Stettner, "From Abortion Reform to Abortion Repeal: The Role of Doris Anderson's *Chatelaine* in the Lives of Women Readers" (MA thesis, University of Waterloo 2000).

35 Lynn Y. Weiner, "Reconstructing Motherhood: The La Leche League in Postwar America," *Journal of American History* 80 (1994): 1357–81.

36 Barbara Seaman, *The Doctors' Case against the Pill* (Alameda, Calif.: Hunter House 1969); Ruzek, "Feminist Visions of Health"; Carol Weisman, *Women's Health Care: Activist Traditions and Institutional Change* (Baltimore: Johns Hopkins University Press 1998), 73.

37 Corea, *The Hidden Malpractice*, 302; Sheryl Ruzek, *The Women's Health Movement: Feminist Alternatives to Medical Control* (New York: Praeger 1978).

38 Georgina Feldberg and Robert Vipond, "The Virus of Consumerism," in Drache and Sullivan, *Health Reform*.

39 Sheryl Burt Ruzek, "Rethinking Feminist Ideologies and Actions: Thoughts on the Past and Future of Health Reform," in Adele E. Clarke and Virginia L. Olesen, eds, *Revisioning Women, Health, and Healing: Feminist Cultural, and Technoscience Perspectives* (New York: Routledge 1999), 303–23.

40 Enakshi Dua, Maureen Fitzgerald, Linda Gardner, and Darien Taylor, eds, *On Women Healthsharing* (Toronto: Women's Press 1994).

41 Lucinda Cisler, "Unfinished Business: Birth Control and Women's Liberation," in Robin Morgan, ed., *Sisterhood Is Powerful* (New York: Vintage 1970), 274–322.

42 Frances Wasserlein, "'An Arrow Aimed at the Heart': The Vancouver Women's Caucus and the Abortion Campaign, 1969–1971" (MA thesis, Simon Fraser University 1990).

43 Weisman, *Women's Health Care*; Ruzek, *The Women's Health Movement*.

44 Janet Muff, "'Why doesn't a smart girl like you go to medical school?' The women's movement takes a slap at nursing," in Janet Muff, ed., *Socialization, Sexism, and Stereotyping: Women's Issues in Nursing* (St Louis: C.V. Mosby 1982).

45 Davis, *Women, Race and Class*; see also Sheryl Burt Ruzek, Adele E. Clarke, and Virginia L. Olesen, "What Are the Dynamics of Differences?" in their

Women's Health: Complexities and Differences (Columbus: Ohio State University Press 1997), 51–95.

46 See Evelyn C. White, ed., *The Black Women's Health Book* (Seattle: Seal Press 1990).

47 Vijay Agnew has traced the tremendous conflict that erupted within this centre between the predominantly white board of directors and the predominantly non-white staff. See Vijay Agnew, *Resisting Discrimination: Women from Asia, Africa, and the Caribbean and the Women's Movement in Canada* (Toronto: University of Toronto Press 1996); Dua et al., *On Women Healthsharing.*

48 Jennifer Terry, "Agendas for Lesbian Health: Countering the Ills of Homophobia," in Clarke and Olesen, *Revisioning Women, Health and Healing,* 324–42.

49 Joseph P. Shapiro, *No Pity: People with Disabilities Forging a New Civil Rights Movement* (New York: Times Books 1994); Paul K. Longmore and Lauri Umansky, eds, *The New Disability History: American Perspectives* (New York: New York University Press 2001).

50 *Proceed with Care: Final Report of the Royal Commission on New Reproductive Technology* (Ottawa: Minister of Supply and Services 1993); M. Eichler "Frankenstein meets Kafka: The Royal Commission on New Reproductive Technologies," in G. Basen, M. Eichler, and A. Lippman, eds, *Misconceptions: The Social Construction of Choice and New Reproductive and Genetic Technologies* (Hull, Que.: Voyageur Publications 1993).

51 R. Petchesky, "Rethinking Reproductive Freedom," in L. Weir, ed., *Governing Medically Assisted Human Reproduction* (Toronto: University of Toronto Press 1997), 7.

52 For example, works by Corea, *The Hidden Malpractice,* and Seaman, *The Doctor's Case against the Pill.*

53 Jonathan Lomas, Catherine Fooks, Tom Rice, and Roberta J. Labelle, "Paying Physicians in Canada: Minding our P's and Q's," *Health Affairs* 8 (Spring 1989): 80–102; Jonathan Lomas, Julia Abelson, and Brian Hutchison, "Registering Patients and Paying Capitation in Family Practice: Lessons from Canada," *British Medical Journal* 311 (November 1995): 1317–18.

54 Reagan, *The Accidental System,* 21–4, 107–26.

55 Reagan, *The Accidental System,* 37–38; Weisman, *Women's Health Care,* 134–40; "Not My Health Care: Consumers Sue Insurers over Denial of Care," *Newsweek* 123 (10 January 1994), 36–8.

56 "Number of Insured Americans Up for First Time Since '87," *New York Times,* 29 September 2000; "No Health Insurance: A Parent's Nightmare," *Los Angeles Times,* 7 December 1997; "Many Latinas Lack Health Insurance, Study Finds," *Los Angeles Times,* 28 January 1999; Skocpol, *Boomerang,* 25; Rothman, *Beginnings Count,* 134–5.

57 Government of Canada, *Preserving Universal Medicare*, 12; Robert G. Evans, "Two Systems in Restraint: Contrasting Experiences with Cost Control in the 1990s," in D. Thomas ed., *Canada and the United States: Differences that Count*, 2nd ed. (Peterborough, Ont.: Broadview Press 2000); Canadian Institute for Health Information, *The Evolution of Public and Private Health Care Spending in Canada, 1960 to 1997* (Ottawa: Canadian Institute for Health Information 1999), 12.

58 Nicholas Regush, *Condition Critical* (Toronto: Macmillan 1987); Michael Rachlis and Carol Kushner, *Strong Medicine: How to Save Canada's Health Care System* (Toronto: HarperCollins 1994).

59 "Drive-Through Deliveries Leave Hit and Run Babies," *Physician's Weekly*, 28 October 1996, http://www.physweekly.com/archive/.

60 Evans, "Two Systems in Restraint," 35, 45; Michael Rachlis, Robert G. Evans, Patrick Lewis, and Morris L. Barer, *Revitalizing Medicare: Shared Problems, Public Solutions* (Vancouver: Tommy Douglas Research Institute 2001).

61 Sue V. Rosser, *Women's Health – Missing from us Medicine* (Bloomington: Indiana University Press 1994); Clarke and Olesen, *Revisioning Women, Health, and Healing.*

62 "What's Policy Got to Do with It?" *Health Canada – Centres of Excellence for Women's Health Research Bulletin* 2, no. 1 (Summer 2001).

63 Ruzek, "Rethinking Feminist Ideologies and Actions," 303–23.

PART TWO

The Ironic Promise of Biomedicine

The rise of biomedicine in the years after 1945 dramatically reshaped the way women experienced health, illness, and medical care in Canada and the United States. The tremendous achievements of biomedicine included the extension of the fundamental understanding of life (for example, in the discovery of the structure of DNA), the creation of powerful new technologies and therapies (such as antibiotics), and the application of systematic, experimental methods to clinical research. Perhaps as significant was the expansion of the scope of what physicians and patients deemed appropriate subjects for scientific scrutiny and medical intervention. The essays in this section probe the impact of an intensifying medical interpretation of virtually every facet and stage of women's lives.

In the early postwar years, the growth of biomedical institutions and approaches was buoyed by the general expectation that progress in biomedicine was an unquestionable good. In the decades that followed, this assumption was increasingly challenged both within and without medicine.

This shift in attitude forms the background for this section's four chapters. The authors explore the personal and societal costs and gains of our increasing tendency to frame in biomedical terms such experiences as alcoholism, pregnancy, menopause, and even the decision to conceive a child. The expansion of this biomedical viewpoint can be seen most strikingly in the way the language of statistics, probability, and risk assessment has come to inform our interpretation of what had previously been considered natural events or moral choices (for example, the emergence of genetic counselling). This broadened view was accompanied by a heightened expectation that science would bring clearer understanding and more perfect control of women's physical, mental, and emotional well-being.

Another issue that these chapters examine is the way that "science" has been invoked for its rhetorical value, as shorthand for all that is rational, modern, and forward thinking. The invocation of the authority of science has not always been matched with actual scientific knowledge or the availability of scientific treatments, as can be seen in the medicalization of alcoholism.

A third motif that emerges is the way in which women have made sense of the explosion of scientific information and have faced the complex new choices arrayed before them. While physicians, professional health-care workers, and new professionals such as genetic counsellors guided women through the maze of facts, private industry, popular media, government, non-profit organizations, and activists – with all their divergent interests and aims – also played significant roles in presenting and interpreting science for women.

While in theory scientific knowledge is in the public domain and should therefore freely transcend national and cultural boundaries, in practice the picture is much more complicated. For example, large national and multinational drug companies have actively defended their intellectual property rights against infringement worldwide, a practice that has created particularly heated debate with respect to the patenting of human genes, some of which are potential keys to the diagnosis and treatment of diseases such as breast cancer, osteoporosis, and Alzheimer's disease. Biomedical knowledge also has distinct national characteristics, since the size and scope of public funding for medical research are governed by political considerations.

These essays raise important questions for future research. How have the direction and content of scientific research been shaped by commercial interests, public policy considerations, and patient activism? How has the emergence of systematic clinical research, including double-blind experiments, affected the decision-making of physicians and patients in the individual therapeutic encounter? How has the introduction of the language of science and probabilities changed women's experience and expectations of health and medicine?

2

"An Illness of Nine Months' Duration": Pregnancy and Thalidomide Use in Canada and the United States

Barbara Clow

In the summer of 1962, Sherri Chessen Finkbine was living in Scotts-dale, Arizona, a suburb of Phoenix.[1] Mother of four, married to a high school teacher, she starred in *Romper Room*, a popular television pro-gram for children. She was also expecting her fifth baby. In the early weeks of her pregnancy, Finkbine took some sedatives to "quiet her nerves" as well as her stomach, both of which were apparently in a state of turmoil. Her husband, Robert, had purchased the pills in England the previous year while leading a group of high school students on a tour of Europe. When the news of thalidomide's teratogenic proper-ties surfaced in the American press, Finkbine immediately checked the label on the medication, discovering, to her horror, that the three-dozen pills she had ingested contained the noxious drug. The couple feared for the health of their baby and dreaded the prospect of giving birth to a disabled child.

When Finkbine was a little over two months pregnant, she and her husband consulted her physician about the possibility of a therapeutic abortion. A panel of doctors, including two psychiatrists, examined her and agreed that the birth of a physically disabled child would "cause grievous mental and emotional trouble for the mother." These medi-cal experts recommended abortion and immediately scheduled the surgery. But a storm of controversy made the Finkbines hesitate to pro-ceed. Local religious leaders openly opposed the couple's decision, and the legality of the procedure was in doubt. As elsewhere in the United States, Arizona law sanctioned abortions only when pregnancy jeopardized the life of the mother. In rare instances, the courts also allowed women at risk of mental illness to terminate their pregnancies. Sherri Finkbine, however, did not appear to be in imminent physical or psychological danger, at least not by the standards of the Arizona statute. Although she and her family would undoubtedly suffer enormous emotional and economic hardship if their child had congenital malformations, Finkbine's pregnancy did not threaten her mental stability or her physical well-being. When the couple, in conjunction with hospital officials, petitioned the courts to indemnify them against legal action, the judge refused to grant them blanket immunity for an abortion. If Finkbine's life was in peril, he reasoned, she need not fear the law; if she was not in danger, then the terms of the statute were clear.

Unwilling to risk criminal prosecution and lacking the time to mount a challenge to existing abortion laws, the Finkbines cast about for alternatives. Discovering that some other countries, including Japan and the Scandinavian nations, had more lenient abortion policies, the couple flew to Sweden. Sherri underwent physical and psychiatric evaluation and then submitted her request for abortion to the Swedish Medical Board. On 18 August 1962, two weeks after their arrival in Stockholm, the couple received permission for the procedure. A therapeutic abortion took place without incident the following morning.

Although their fight to terminate the pregnancy had succeeded, it had also been costly in a number of ways. By making her situation public, for example, Sherri sacrificed her career in children's television. "The station would be in a precarious position if I returned," she acknowledged. Notoriety proved unpleasant as well, even for a television celebrity accustomed to public scrutiny. In the wake of the abortion, doctors appealed to the media and the public to give Sherri the rest and privacy she needed to recover. The trip to Sweden was also expensive. With four children at home and a single salary to draw on, the Finkbines could ill afford the $4,000 they had spent to procure an abortion. Nonetheless, the couple felt vindicated by the outcome of the procedure, having learned from the surgeon that thalidomide had affected the development of the fetus. Robert Finkbine subsequently told reporters, "We felt we were doing the right thing all along for Sherri's mental health … Now we know we were right for the baby as well. The last thing we wanted to do was to bring a deformed youngster into the world if it could be prevented."

Sherri Finkbine's story gave impetus to the burgeoning movement for women's reproductive rights in the United States. As Linda Gordon has argued, "Popular awareness of medical, even eugenic, reasons for abortion grew in 1962 as a result of an epidemic of influenza … and the favorable press given to Sherri Finkbine."[2] While mental anguish or physical suffering were often not enough to convince the public of the need for more liberal abortion laws, birth defects worked powerfully on the popular imagination. Finkbine's experience also highlighted the suffering of women who had taken thalidomide. Months of anxiety about the health of their babies plagued these mothers, relieved only by an abortion or the arrival of a healthy infant. Moreover, women who bore disabled children faced years, perhaps even a lifetime, of unremitting demands upon their physical and psychological resources. Intensive media coverage of the Finkbine saga also contributed to a growing sense of public, professional, and political outrage. How, everyone wondered, had a powerful teratogen like thalidomide made its way into the hands of pregnant women?

INTRODUCING THALIDOMIDE

Thalidomide first appeared in West Germany in 1957, under the trade name Contergan. It was synthesized in 1953 by Chemie Grünenthal and then tested on animal and human subjects before being released for general consumption. These early experiments suggested that Contergan was not only a highly effective sleeping aid, but also an exceptionally safe one. In contrast to other sedatives popular in the 1950s, such as barbiturates, thalidomide could be ingested in large quantities without causing permanent injury or death.[3] The manufacturer and the government consequently felt confident that the drug could be sold without a prescription. By 1959, thalidomide was the most popular sleeping pill in West Germany; it was also an ingredient in a dozen other medicines sold over-the-counter for the treatment of colds, flu, headaches, neuralgia, and asthma.[4]

While Contergan swept the West German market, Chemie Grünenthal licensed pharmaceutical firms in other countries to manufacture and/or distribute thalidomide.[5] In North America, two manufacturers cornered the thalidomide market, the Cincinnati-based firm Richardson-Merrell and a Montreal pharmaceutical company, Frank W. Horner Limited. In September 1960 Richardson-Merrell submitted a New Drug Application to the United States Food and Drug Administration (FDA) and the following month made a similar application to the Canadian Food and Drug Directorate (FDD).[6] While U.S. officials refused to approve the drug for sale because they were dissatisfied with the details of toxicity studies, Canadian regulators apparently felt that the safety of thalidomide had been well established by European experience and the five hundred pages of documentation submitted by the company. On 1 April 1961 Richardson-Merrell's brand of thalidomide, Kevadon, went on sale in Canada, and six months later Frank W. Horner joined the competition with its product, Talimol.[7]

Although pharmaceutical manufacturers harped on the safety of thalidomide, as early as 1956 doctors conducting clinical trials in Hamburg, West Germany, noticed dizziness and loss of balance among elderly patients treated with Contergan. Moreover, as sales of thalidomide skyrocketed, so too did reports of other disturbing side effects, which included severe constipation, hangover, loss of memory, hypotension, petechial hemorrhages, trembling, incoordination, numbness, and even partial paralysis.[8] Officials at Chemie Grünenthal insisted that these noxious side effects developed only with overdosing or extended treatment, and they claimed that symptoms subsided with the cessation of thalidomide therapy.[9] But as pharmaceutical preparations containing thalidomide flooded world markets, doctors also began to notice a disturbing increase in phocomelia, an unusual congenital anomaly involving the absence or shortening of the arms and/or legs due to the malformation of the long bones, with associated abnormalities of the hands, feet, fingers, and/or toes. No one connected thalidomide with this epidemic of birth defects until 1961, when a West German physician, Widukind Lenz, and an Australian practitioner, William McBride, independently reached the conclusion that the drug was a powerful teratogen.[10] Chemie Grünenthal continued to insist on the safety of the drug, but mounting pressure from the public, the medical profession, and the state finally convinced the company to recall the drug on 27 November 1961. Distillers Company (Biochemicals) Limited in Great Britain followed suit the same day, and the Swedish manufacturer Astra withdrew its product two weeks later.[11]

Meanwhile, Canadians continued to enjoy access to thalidomide until the spring of 1962. Although federal regulators learned about the possible connection between the drug and congenital malformations in December 1961, they were lulled into a false sense of security by the fact that Kevadon and Talimol were available only by prescription. Government officials were satisfied that warning letters issued to physicians by the manufacturers would "in effect, withdraw it from the market insofar as pregnant women are concerned."[12] Through the winter, both Richardson-Merrell and Horner kept in regular contact with the FDD, assuring the Canadian government that evidence implicating thalidomide as the cause of birth defects was "inconclusive." Late in February 1962, however, a damning report on thalidomide appeared in *The Lancet* and three days later the government finally removed the drug from the Canadian market "pending clarification." For months afterwards, officials in the FDD worked to trace and retrieve supplies of thalidomide lurking on the shelves of pharmacies and in medicine cabinets or squirrelled away in doctors' desk drawers.

Although these efforts probably saved some children from exposure, more than four million tablets had made their way into Canadian homes and hospitals during eleven months of legitimate sales and at least another million pills had been distributed as samples. By 1962, countless Canadian infants and their families had already suffered the devastation wrought by thalidomide, joining the ranks of thousands upon thousands of victims around the world.[13]

Against this backdrop of international shock and anguish, American consumers and regulators had cause to celebrate. Frances Kelsey, a physician recently hired by the FDA, had resisted enormous pressure from Richardson-Merrell to approve thalidomide for sale in the United States.[14] As a result, comparatively few American children were born with phocomelia or other congenital malformations associated with exposure to the drug. Kelsey was lionized by the media and the public for her role in averting a national disaster, and President Kennedy awarded her a medal for distinguished federal civilian service.[15] Since the 1960s, authors have continued to praise Kelsey's foresight and intelligence. "Her criticisms of thalidomide," wrote a group of reporters for the London *Sunday Times*, "were so basic, so persistent, and so scrupulously scientific that any charges ... that her actions were merely lucky or marked by excessive bureaucratic caution can be dismissed as ludicrous."[16]

While it is not my intention to trivialize Frances Kelsey's achievement, neither do I want to encourage the belief that Americans escaped exposure to thalidomide because they had more enlightened attitudes and practices or more progressive policies. Popular and professional discourse from the 1950s and 1960s demonstrates that Canadians and Americans shared convictions about pregnancy management and the use of tranquilizers that rendered them equally vulnerable. On the one hand, doctors in both countries regularly concluded that pregnancy demanded medical intervention. In the 1950s, for example, two physicians – one Canadian and one American – independently quoted the same telling aphorism: "Pregnancy is an illness of nine months' duration."[17] Doctors who endorsed this view of gestation, whether practising in Canada or the United States, tended to prescribe tranquilizers on the grounds that many of the common "complaints" of pregnancy could be attributed to psychological disturbance. Medical enthusiasm for sedatives and tranquilizers also led hundreds of American doctors to participate in clinical trials of thalidomide; some physicians even imported private supplies of the drug while it was still under review by the Food and Drug Administration.[18] On the other hand, popular discourse supports the conclusion that thalidomide would have found favour with the U.S. public if the drug had been approved for sale. Like

Canadians, Americans were already consuming huge quantities of mood-altering drugs, and there is no reason to suspect that they would have ignored the newest tranquilizer, thalidomide. Indeed, neither FDA restrictions nor Kelsey's heroic efforts were entirely effective in curtailing access to the drug; many people living in the United States still managed to obtain thalidomide from doctors, family, and friends or, like Robert Finkbine, while travelling and living abroad. In 1960 North America stood poised to embrace thalidomide.

PREGNANCY AND THE MEDICAL PROFESSION IN THE 1950S

Today, at the beginning of the twenty-first century, many North Americans are keenly aware of the need to safeguard the prenatal environment. Pregnant women often renounce alcohol, for example, or sip wine furtively, expecting at any moment to be accosted by family, friends, or even strangers concerned about fetal alcohol syndrome. Moreover, gravid women sometimes find themselves under intense pressure to adjust not only their alcohol intake but every habit that might detract from the quality of the in utero experience of their children. One of the most popular advice manuals on pregnancy today urges prospective mothers to monitor and evaluate every morsel they consume. "Before you close your mouth on a forkful of food," the authors admonish readers, "consider, 'Is this the best bite I can give my baby?' If it will benefit your baby, chew away. If it'll only appease your appetite, put your fork down."[19] Prescriptive literature is thus infused with the alarming message that unborn babies are desperately vulnerable to harm or neglect.

In the 1950s the medical profession took a rather different view of pregnancy, regarding the average fetus as a fairly robust creature. Doctors and educators did, though, repeatedly urge women to eat well during pregnancy, recognizing that problems could arise from a deficient diet. According to a 1956 article in *McCalls* magazine, "research has shown that there is a definite relationship between what the expectant mother eats and both her health and that of her baby."[20] Aside from this emphasis on nutrition, however, educational literature stressed the safety of the womb rather than the potential dangers facing the unborn child. On the one hand, it was believed that dense layers of abdominal muscle, strong ligaments supporting the uterus, and a warm cushion of amniotic fluid protected the fetus from physical insult. One practitioner reported the case of a pregnant woman involved in a serious car accident: "She broke both legs, both arms and suffered a brain concussion. [But] her baby was unharmed."[21] On the other hand, the medical profession rejected the notion that maternal attitudes or experiences could influence the fetus, either for good or evil. Cravings for strawberries would not result in birthmarks, doctors insisted, any more than hours of reading "highbrow" literature would enhance the intellectual abilities of the developing child. "During the nine months between conception and birth," concluded one American specialist, "the baby is completely oblivious to what his mother sees, does, thinks or dreams ... His basic characteristics were endowed him by his parents' genes at the most critical moment of life, when his father's sperm cell curtsied to his mother's egg cell."[22] As further proof of the hardiness of the human embryo, doctors and educators pointed out that the vast majority of infants emerged from the womb without serious complications. As a 1950 article in *Better Homes and Gardens* concluded, "Contrary to old wives' tales, the little rascals are pretty rugged."[23]

Although many practitioners regarded the human fetus as sturdy and well protected, they were not unmindful of environmental hazards, such as radiation.[24] During this period, doctors increasingly became concerned about all manner of threats to the developing embryo, including maternal illnesses, such as rubella, and maternal stresses, such as grief.[25] Nevertheless, a growing appreciation of the diverse causes of birth defects did not fundamentally alter the professional perception that the fetus could and usually did resist noxious influences. One of the clearest examples of this view can be found in the pages of *Williams Obstetrics*, a medical text popular in the 1950s. According to the eleventh edition, published in 1956, moderate tobacco use provoked "no physiological alteration" in the mother or her baby. As a result, the manual recommended only that women limit their smoking to six cigarettes a day, or about a third of a pack.[26] The next edition of the text, published five years later in 1961, reported that babies born of smoking mothers typically weighed less than the offspring of non-smoking women. Nonetheless, the authors continued to advise moderation rather than abstinence because marked differences in birth weight did not seem to translate into serious problems for the newborn.[27] Indeed, both editions of the text expressed greater concern about intercourse in the final weeks of pregnancy than about smoking, alcohol consumption, or the use of prescription drugs. From the perspective of the medical profession, detrimental influences in the environment represented the exception rather than the rule of embryology.

Experimental evidence offered doctors few compelling reasons to avoid prescribing medication to women during pregnancy, and clinical experience with pregnant patients promoted the liberal use of drugs.

Doctors and educators touted motherhood and child-bearing as natural functions – the essence of womanhood – but they regarded gestation itself as a profoundly unsettling experience, psychologically as well as physically. As one practitioner concluded, "The fundamental viewpoint, which has been molded by our experience, is that pregnancy is to be regarded as a period of increased susceptibility to crisis."[28] During the early months of pregnancy, women were seen as especially prone to emotional and mental instability. Indeed, husbands might find their wives' personalities altered beyond all recognition by the impending birth of a child. The happy, relaxed woman could become morose, while the sexually reserved woman might suddenly find herself amorous.[29] "No one," wrote a prominent Canadian physician, "can predict which mood will devour a woman for her nine months as a perambulating incubator."[30] Although doctors recognized an organic basis for the emotional turmoil of pregnancy, most agreed that the mental health of the gravid woman determined the nature and degree of disruption.[31] Childhood experiences, for example, could leave a woman ill-prepared for motherhood. According to a 1950 article in the *Journal of the American Medical Association,* women who had been overly indulged or protected in childhood became "parasites" in adulthood, drawing "on the mental and moral strength of others."[32] At the same time, the personal context of pregnancy could precipitate a psychological crisis. Unwed mothers, unhappy wives, and impoverished women might well regard pregnancy as an unmitigated disaster.[33] As one doctor observed, "The psychological changes which form part of any pregnancy process can set in motion pathological amounts of anxiety and activate a variety of personality disturbances."[34] In other words, pregnancy represented an emotional challenge for any woman, but those unprepared for or unable to accept motherhood could become unhinged by the experience.

Medical reactions to the "symptoms" of gestation, particularly gastric upset, mirrored professional perceptions of pregnancy. As with other aspects of pregnancy, doctors appreciated that nausea and vomiting might have an organic basis, but many felt that "morning sickness" could be traced to psychological maladjustment.[35] "The preponderance of women," concluded one obstetrician, "have vomiting of pregnancy because of psychogenic components ... A great proportion of them did not want to become pregnant for various reasons."[36] Observation of pregnant patients seemed to justify medical theories about the causes of gastric upset. Doctors reasoned that if physiological factors alone explained pregnancy nausea, then all women would exhibit symptoms, but only about half of all gravid women endured nausea and vomiting, while the other half enjoyed pregnancies free of these discomforts. Moreover, practitioners noted that nausea usually subsided by the end of the first trimester, by which time most women had allegedly accepted or become resigned to their pregnancies.[37] Cessation of somatic symptoms seemed to coincide with the resolution of psychic conflict. Further evidence of the psychosomatic nature of morning sickness came from clinical experiments. In a 1955 study, pregnant women complaining of nausea were given an anti-nausea drug, a mood-altering drug, or a placebo. Clear patterns of relief did not emerge from these tests, leaving the investigator to conclude that many treatments would improve pregnancy nausea, provided they were administered with "sympathy, understanding, and assurance of success."[38]

A psychosomatic explanation for nausea and vomiting profoundly influenced the medical management of pregnancy. In some cases, professional convictions that hysteria or anxiety provoked nausea encouraged doctors to ignore the suffering of their patients. According to one practitioner, "experienced obstetricians ... quite understandably felt that such manifestations although temporarily uncomfortable were not deserving of serious consideration."[39] Other physicians seemed to believe that nausea demanded treatment, but in the absence of a satisfactory physiological explanation for morning sickness, many advocated some form of emotional support or psychological treatment. "Some type of therapy for the nauseated pregnant woman is essential," concluded one doctor, "but until physiologic research points out specific therapy the *woman* rather than the *nausea* must be treated."[40] Although this approach to treatment seemed sound, given the assumptions of the medical profession, most obstetricians and family practitioners had neither the time nor the training to evaluate the mental health of their pregnant patients. A 1950 survey of prenatal care in New York, for instance, revealed that doctors spent no more than a couple of minutes with each woman.[41] Perhaps as a result of such constraints, many practitioners supplemented or simply replaced emotional support with drugs – lots of drugs. In this period, medical practitioners prescribed all manner of chemotherapeutic agents for gravid women experiencing nausea and vomiting: vitamins, antacids, antihistamines, antiemetics, anticholinergics, and hormones. Stimulants, such as amphetamines, sometimes helped alleviate the discomfort of pregnant patients, but more often doctors relied on a vast repertoire of depressants, such as chlorpromazine.[42] Sedatives and tranquilizers, in particular, represented a logical treatment choice for physicians who believed that morning sickness began with emotional distress or psychological disturbance; drugs that calmed the nerves, they reasoned, would also soothe the roiling stomachs of anxious expectant mothers.

Medical perceptions of fetal development and gestation thus set the stage for the introduction of thalidomide to North America. Some practitioners were lulled into a false sense of security by promotional literature that described thalidomide as "atoxic," even for children and gravid women.[43] But professional discourse in this period suggests that doctors routinely prescribed dozens of dangerous drugs for their pregnant patients on the grounds that gestation could and should be treated. In 1956, for example, the author of *Williams Obstetrics* recommended steady doses of phenobarbital for pregnant women unable to eat.[44] Many practitioners relied on sedatives and tranquilizers specifically because they regarded pregnancy as a time of emotional instability and morning sickness as a psychosomatic symptom. In this context, thalidomide was unusual only in its teratogenic effects; in all other respects, the drug was simply the latest addition to a fast-growing pharmacopoeia of drugs prescribed for pregnant women in the 1950s.

PREGNANCY AND THE PUBLIC IN THE 1950S

As with professional perceptions, lay attitudes and experiences facilitated the use of drugs like thalidomide during gestation. Although many women in postwar North America looked forward to parenting, pregnancy could evoke considerable ambivalence. Single women, for example, often took pains to deny that they were pregnant because of the social stigma associated with illicit sex and illegitimate births. In 1950 *Chatelaine* magazine ran a story entitled "Unwed Mother," in which a young, unmarried woman suspected that she was pregnant after repeated bouts of morning sickness. She tried to reassure herself – and her roommate – that she had the flu, but when her nausea persisted, she "kept saying to herself: 'I'm not pregnant. It's just my nerves. I'm upset.'"[45] Wanting desperately to escape a shameful pregnancy, these women may have hoped that treatment would eliminate their worries along with their discomfort. Moreover, those who attributed their symptoms to tension rather than to pregnancy were especially likely to ask for medication that would calm their nerves.

During this period, some married women took an equally dim view of pregnancy. One mother wryly described her feelings upon realizing that she was expecting another baby. "It all begins," she observed, "when you wake up with a nasty touch of the twenty-four-hour flu, and it ends some eight months later in the maternity wing of your friendly neighborhood hospital. Sandwiched in between is a lot of rich, emotional experience of the sort said to build character. Like the day you stop taking your temperature and relinquish all hopes of its being a virus that bit you. Of course, it *couldn't* be possible ... but there it is: you must be pregnant. It's as welcome as the income tax."[46] Many of these unwilling mothers balked not at the prospect of children, as psychologists believed, but at the prospect of *unexpected* children. Unplanned babies threatened to rob young parents of the chance to build careers and a healthy relationship, and they strained the emotional or financial resources of many couples who already had children.[47] "I'm desperate," one woman told her doctor, "We simply can't manage another child."[48] Probably the vast majority of women eventually accepted their pregnancies, learning to cherish the new or latest addition to the family. But in the early weeks of gestation, when pregnancy seemed like "a fate worse than death," these dismayed women often turned to the medical profession for help.[49] Doctors, confronted by distressed and desperate women, doled out support or sedatives – or both.

Whether or not women hoped or planned for pregnancy, whether or not they welcomed it, many found the experience rife with anxiety. Fear of pain and even death plagued pregnant women, despite the relatively low incidence of maternal mortality and the variety of analgesic options available in this period.[50] New mothers probably endured the most acute distress because they did not know what to expect from pregnancy or childbirth, but even experienced mothers harboured fears. One doctor was puzzled by the distress of a woman in the midst of her fourth pregnancy, until a nurse pointed out that the patient feared her child would be disabled in some way. "They're scared that their luck will run out," she said.[51] Moreover, both new and experienced mothers found gestation trying because it transformed them into public property. Strangers stroked their bulging abdomens at parties, while friends, family, the neighbours, the druggist, and even the butcher inundated them with advice or tales of horror.[52] "There's magic in the words, 'I'm going to have a baby,'" observed one obstetrician, "more magic than you'd think. Those words apparently have the power to transform nice people into ghouls; a woman can scarcely get the words out of her mouth before otherwise intelligent people are telling her of Mongolian idiots, three-day labors, varicose veins, false pregnancies and hospitals which make a habit of mixing up babies."[53] Impatient with this deluge of advice, one woman brandished the latest book on prenatal care at her tormentors.[54] But other gravid women suffered considerably as a result of these well-meaning efforts, and their heightened anxiety made them prime candidates for calming medication.

In addition to the emotional strains of pregnancy, gestation exacted a physical toll from many women, leaving them nauseated, depressed, and exhausted. Despite the demands on their bodies, however, pregnant women were under considerable pressure to remain active, even-tempered, and attractive. A prominent Canadian physician reported that most men had a limited appreciation of and therefore little sympathy with the physical trials of pregnancy. "Husbands have a habit of assuming," she wrote, "that because childbearing is a natural function for women some internal arrangement absorbs all the discomfort. Many of them thinly veil their suspicions that their wives are complaining about trivia."[55] One man apparently responded to his wife's requests for unusual midnight snacks with the observation that she craved attention more than food.[56] At the same time, pregnancy did not excuse women from their domestic responsibilities. One mother noted that a husband "is likely to prove difficult about the dust on the piano, the wrinkled mountain of unironed clothes, the unbrushed children in their buttonless overalls, and his canned and freezer dinner."[57] Magazine articles also urged women to make extra efforts to remain appealing to their spouses during pregnancy. One author suggested that expectant mothers might like to adopt "the lovely habit of putting on a 'new face' and dressing in one of your prettiest dresses before your husband comes home every evening."[58] Other writers recommended a variety of strategies to guard the figure, complexion, and hair: exercises, foundation garments, flattering clothes, perfumes, and cosmetics could offset the less attractive aspects of pregnancy.[59] According to an editor at *Mademoiselle* magazine, "there are two kinds of pregnant women, those who grow prettier and those who grow frowzy and ugly. I do believe the choice is up to oneself, a matter of point of view."[60] Expecting a child herself, this woman concluded, "I will not look like a sweet potato with poison oak ... Richard [her husband of course] is far too nice to have to come home to a sweet potato."[61]

Although these tactics promised to boost the morale of pregnant women and promote marital harmony, both radiance and serenity were difficult to achieve or simulate with a sour stomach poised for action. Working women found nausea and vomiting especially disruptive. Imagine Sherri Finkbine struggling with this problem before an audience of parents and children during regular tapings of *Romper Room.* Under pressure of all kinds, battling the unpleasant side effects of pregnancy, many of these women gladly accepted drugs that offered relief. Given the psychosomatic interpretation of nausea that prevailed in the medical community, it is not clear that every pregnant woman who was taking sedatives knew it. What does seem certain, however, is that many expectant mothers demanded treatment for debilitating symptoms. As one physician remarked, "Nothing so irritates the average pregnant woman or so alienates her from her obstetrician as to be told that her nausea and vomiting are completely psychologic."[62]

Experience and expectations thus encouraged gravid women to solicit medical and medicinal aid for the stresses and strains of pregnancy. In some cases, reassurance from a knowledgeable and sympathetic practitioner worked wonders, helping patients to deal with their fears as well as their nausea, but harried doctors and miserable women frequently relied on drugs to alleviate the discomforts of gestation. Sherri Finkbine was a perfect example of this phenomenon. Although it seems she would have welcomed another baby, perhaps even planned for it, there is little doubt that pregnancy strained her body and her life. We will never know whether or not her doctor would have recommended sedatives or tranquilizers because Finkbine circumvented the medical encounter by dosing herself with her husband's sleeping pills. As with many other women, a combination of emotional stress and physical distress prompted her to seek relief.

"ASPIRIN FOR THE SOUL": TRANQUILIZERS, SEDATIVES, AND THALIDOMIDE

Although popular and professional attitudes help to explain thalidomide use among pregnant women, we cannot fully understand this historical episode without an appreciation of the pharmaceutical prescribing and consuming habits of North Americans in the 1950s. In the immediate aftermath of the Second World War, doctors relied mainly on narcotics, such as phenobarbital, to sedate troubled or troublesome patients, but during the 1950s, the pharmaceutical industry kicked into high gear, producing a bewildering array of sedatives and tranquilizers. Miltown, Equanil, Compazine, Thorazine, and Librium, to name a few, made their debut in the postwar era,[63] and North Americans literally ate them up. According to one report, American druggists sold $150 million worth of tranquilizers in 1956 alone.[64] Miltown and Equanil proved so popular in Canada that more than a billion tablets were purchased in the first year of sales. "They make me feel as if I'd had a second highball," patients reported.[65] In the midst of this tranquilizer mania, thalidomide was just the newest choice among a rich selection of "happy pills" available to the North American public. Popular and professional enthusiasm for mood-altering drugs, like popular and professional perceptions of pregnancy, helped to create an environment conducive to the use of thalidomide.

CONCLUSION: TOWARDS A SOCIAL HISTORY OF THALIDOMIDE

In the years since the withdrawal of thalidomide, we have generally blamed the tragedy on the pharmaceutical industry and the political authorities. In the early 1960s, scientists and business officials at Chemie Grünenthal faced a long list of criminal charges and civil suits that revolved around issues of inadequate testing, misleading marketing, and failure to apprise doctors and patients of the dangers of thalidomide. Although company owners and employees escaped jail terms as well as punitive fines, the firm itself paid more than a million Deutsche marks in out-of-court settlements with the families of thalidomide victims. Other pharmaceutical manufacturers, such as Distillers Company (Biochemicals) Limited in Britain and Richardson-Merrell in the United States, faced similar suits and paid large sums in fines and compensation. In some cases, the state also acknowledged its complicity in the pharmaceutical disaster; months after the teratogenic properties of thalidomide became known, regulatory agencies in many countries failed to withdraw the drug or warn the public. Japanese women, for instance, could obtain thalidomide without prescription for more than a year after the drug had been recalled elsewhere. Many governments, including those of Canada, Sweden, and Britain, eventually accepted responsibility for the victims of thalidomide, setting up special programs of care and/or creating compensation packages.[66]

The considerable attention paid to commercial malfeasance and governmental indifference or ineptitude has diverted our attention from the *social* history of thalidomide. Although pharmaceutical companies and regulatory agencies were undoubtedly culpable in this medical disaster, they were not alone. In clinics and homes throughout much of the world, doctors and patients made the final decision to use the drug, often with devastating consequences for the unborn. As a result, we need to consider not only the political and business factors that facilitated the thalidomide tragedy, but also the cultural conditions that generated widespread enthusiasm for the drug in the late 1950s and early 1960s. The social history of thalidomide suggests that popular and professional attitudes set the stage for disaster as surely as did the greed of drug companies and the deficiencies of state regulation. Medical convictions about the robustness of the fetus and the psychological origins of pregnancy symptoms encouraged doctors to prescribe a host of sedating drugs for gravid women. Popular expectations of the medical profession in combination with a variety of personal circumstances similarly encouraged women to try to manage their pregnancies through the use of drugs. For both prescribers and consumers, thalidomide offered an apparently safe and satisfactory solution to the problems of pregnancy.

Since the 1960s, social historians have laboured to recapture the experiences of "ordinary" people and "oppressed" minorities overlooked by previous scholars. Many of the earliest social histories, in addition to elaborating upon the vibrancy of subcultures and countercultures, emphasized the effects of discrimination in the lives of workers, immigrants, and women. Historians of women's health zeroed in on the pernicious effects of scientific discourse and medical practice: doctors ignored and trivialized women's health concerns, invoking biology to justify the social, economic, and political subordination of women. Searching for social justice in their own time, many of these ground-breaking scholars emphasized the victimization of men and women in the past. Subsequent generations of historians took a broader view, exploring not only injustices and prejudices, but also the creativity and determination of people confronted by rigid expectations and limited horizons. Women and workers alike developed complex strategies to manage and challenge inequity. With this new view of the "victims" of history came a revised interpretation of the "oppressors." Feminist scholars, for example, began to argue that modern medicine might be an instrument of liberation for women rather than simply a tool of oppression.[67] Only in the movies, it seems, do the good guys still wear white hats.

The social history of thalidomide similarly complicates our understanding of women and health because it exposes the tensions between agency and responsibility. If we accept that women have the right and power to make health-care choices, we run the risk of blaming them for their ill health or, in the case of thalidomide, for the suffering of their children. But if we hold doctors responsible for the tragedy or accuse drug manufacturers and government officials of impropriety, we run the risk of disenfranchising women and providing a rationale for the revival of paternalism. Popular and professional discourse around the thalidomide episode seems to exacerbate rather than resolve the contradictions implicit in many discussions of women's health. Can we absolve women of responsibility for the outcome of health-care choices and at the same time defend and advance their right to make those choices? Given these implications and the nature of the thalidomide tragedy, it is not surprising that most authors have chosen to focus on the inadequacies of drug regulation, the dangers of capitalism, or even the plight of infants rather than confront the convictions of the people who dispensed the pills and the women who swallowed them.[68]

Although the history of thalidomide in North America offers no comfortable lessons about women's health, we cannot ignore the social and cultural dimensions of the episode without fostering serious misapprehensions about the past. For example, many people today believe that thalidomide was prescribed by doctors and ingested by women primarily as a treatment for morning sickness. Indeed, it was this assumption that first led me to investigate popular and professional perceptions of pregnancy. As we have seen, medical ideas about the origins of pregnancy symptoms as well as personal anxieties about childbirth and parenting undoubtedly contributed to the use of thalidomide. But not all practitioners or patients used the drug to treat morning sickness. In the years after the withdrawal of thalidomide, investigators discovered that women who ingested the drug late in pregnancy usually bore healthy children, while those who took it in early pregnancy had babies with profound, often life-threatening complications. Eventually, researchers concluded that thalidomide had its greatest impact on the fetus in the two to four weeks following the first missed menstrual period, when many women might not realize that they were pregnant. A Montreal study of mothers whose babies were affected by thalidomide confirmed this pattern of exposure: more than one-third had taken the drug as a routine sedative rather than as a treatment for morning sickness.[69] The social history of thalidomide thus serves to refine our perceptions of women's health history by exposing the spectrum of women's experiences. While the medicalization of pregnancy in the twentieth century undoubtedly contributed to the tragedy, a pervasive postwar confidence in modern medicine also encouraged the use of a drug that proved deeply noxious to the human fetus.

At the same time, the social history of thalidomide provides important insights into current health-care concerns, particularly in this era of retrenchment and restructuring. Emphasis on the ineptitude of governmental agencies or the rapaciousness of the pharmaceutical industry has obscured the central role played by consumers in the thalidomide episode. As a result, in the wake of the tragedy, we have instituted salutary changes in the policing of new therapeutic products in order to better protect the public but we continue to ignore the perspectives of consumers. Not surprisingly, the North American public is far from content. Although Canadians and Americans enjoy much better protection than they did in the 1950s, they are frequently distrustful of the state and discontented with decisions about specific diagnostic and therapeutic products. Some patients demand access to products that the government or the medical profession has deemed unsafe; others demand stricter regulation of procedures that have contentious ethical dimensions. Workable, sustainable reform of the health-care system cannot be accomplished without a fuller appreciation of the evolving needs and expectations of health-care consumers.

Finally, the social history of thalidomide raises interesting questions about the significance of nation in postwar North America. On the surface, national frameworks would appear to be absolutely crucial to the story because the experiences of thalidomide differed dramatically in the two countries: Canadians suffered the consequences of massive exposure to the drug; Americans did not. At least one pair of authors explained this difference by reference to the regulatory systems of Canada and the United States, contrasting the "vigilance" of the FDA with the "negligence" of the FDD.[70] This argument is hardly credible because it ignores the international scope of the thalidomide tragedy. By the early 1960s, the drug was available in forty-six countries around the world – "eleven European, seven African, seventeen Asian, and eleven North and South American."[71] Each of these nations, with its own distinctive set of regulatory practices and policies, approved thalidomide for sale and suffered, to a greater or lesser degree, the same consequences. Moreover, an explanation based on national differences ignores important affinities between the Canadian and American approach to health in the years after the Second World War. Standards of regulation, research, and practice were not sufficiently different in the two countries to account for their divergent experiences with thalidomide. Moreover, popular and professional discourse reveals that Canadians and Americans shared perceptions of pregnancy that rendered them equally vulnerable to the suffering caused by thalidomide. That the United States largely escaped the tragedy owes less, I think, to a distinctive national character or a superior regulatory system than to Frances Kelsey, a woman born in Canada.

Many other currents in the social history of thalidomide remain to be explored, from the role the tragedy played in the abortion- and the disability-rights movements to its impact on popular perceptions of the fetus and prenatal advice literature. With a fuller appreciation of the cultural legacy of thalidomide as well as its political and medical implications, we can hope to better understand the challenges facing contemporary and future systems of health care in North America.

NOTES

1 Sherri Finkbine's story is drawn from the following newspaper reports: Bill Becker, "Abortion to Bar Defective Birth Is Facing Legal Snag in Arizona," *New York Times* (25 July 1962): 22; "Mother Loses Round in Legal Battle for Abortion," *New York Times* (31 July 1962): 9; "Mother, Rebuffed in Arizona, May Seek Abortion Elsewhere," *New York Times* (1 August 1962): 19; "U.S. Mother Seeks Aid from Sweden," *New York Times* (5 August 1962): 64; Werner Wiskari, "Mother Awaits Swedish Verdict," *New York Times* (13 August 1962): 16; Werner Wiskari, "Sweden Accedes to Abortion Plea," *New York Times*, 18 August 1962, 43; "Mrs Finkbine Undergoes Abortion in Sweden," *New York Times* (19 August 1962): 69.

2 Linda Gordon, *Woman's Body, Woman's Rights: Birth Control in America* (New York: Penguin 1990), 408.

3 Richard E. McFadyen, "Thalidomide in America: A Brush with Tragedy," *Clio Medica* 11 (1976): 79.

4 Henning Sjöström and Robert Nilsson, *Thalidomide and the Power of the Drug Companies* (Middlesex, U.K.: Penguin 1972), 38–9.

5 Ibid., 136–47, 39–40; Insight Team of the *Sunday Times* of London, *Suffer the Children: The Story of Thalidomide* (New York: Viking Press 1979), 29; Ethel Roskies, *Abnormality and Normality: The Mothering of Thalidomide Children* (Ithaca, N.Y.: Cornell University Press 1972), 1–2.

6 McFadyen, "Brush with Tragedy," 80; "Chronology Re Thalidomide," 17 August 1962, Health Protection Branch, Health Canada (HPB).

7 Jean F. Webb, "Canadian Thalidomide Experience," *Canadian Medical Association Journal* 89 (1963): 987–92.

8 Insight Team, *Suffer the Children*, 30–2; Sjöström and Nilsson, *Power*, 46–59.

9 "Chronology re Thalidomide," 5.

10 Sjöström and Nilsson, *Power*, 97–104; Insight Team, *Suffer the Children*, 86–107; William McBride, *Killing the Messenger* (Cremorne, Australia: Eldorado 1994), 52–69.

11 Sjöström and Nilsson, *Power*, 94–104.

12 "Chronology re Thalidomide," 9.

13 June Callwood, "The Unfolding Tragedy of Drug-Deformed Babies," *Maclean's* (19 May 1962): 13; "Survey of Effects of Thalidomide," Charles B. Walker, Officer-in-Charge, Biostatistics Section, 18 June 1962, HPB. The language of victimization, suffering, and tragedy is used here because it is characteristic of both contemporary and current discourse on thalidomide. Although disability studies and some disability communities have eschewed the language of victimization, thalidomiders have not, as evidenced by organization names such as TVAC, Thalidomide Victims Association of Canada. The choice of terms is undoubtedly tied to the search for political redress and legal compensation, but it may also serve other personal and social functions that have yet to be fully explored.

14 Sjöström and Nilsson, *Power*, 115–22; Insight Team, *Suffer the Children*, 64–85.

15 See, for example, "Heroine of FDA Keeps Bad Drug off Market," *Washington Post* (15 July 1962), and "Dr Kelsey Receives Gold Medal from Kennedy at White House," *New York Times* (8 August 1962): 19.

16 Insight Team, *Suffer the Children*, 81. See also Sjöström and Nilsson, *Power*, 128.

17 Attributed to De Lee by Daniel Cappon, "Some Psychodynamic Aspects of Pregnancy," *Canadian Medical Association Journal* 70 (February 1954): 149; attributed to Mariceau by Bernard I. Coopersmith, "Thorazine-Dexedrine Combination in Treatment of Nausea and Vomiting in Pregnancy," *Obstetrics and Gynecology* 8 (August 1956): 235.

18 "Deformed Baby Dies Here," *New York Times* (31 July 1962): 9; "More Pills Traced Here," *New York Times* (4 August 1962): 20.

19 Arlene Eisenberg, Heidi E. Murkoff, and Sandee E. Hathaway, *What to Expect When You're Expecting* (New York: Workman Publishing 1996), 81.

20 Amy Selwyn, "How Tough Is an Unborn Baby," *Better Homes and Gardens* 29 (September 1950): 172; "What to Eat If You Are Pregnant," *Parents Magazine* 28 (July 1953): 63; Fredrick J. Stare and Mary B. McCann, "If You're Eating for Two," *McCalls* 83 (March 1956): 106, 108; Icie G. Macy, "Diet for Mothers-to-Be," *Today's Health* 36 (August 1958): 37+.

21 Selwyn, "How Tough," 173; Alan F. Guttmacher and Grace Hechinger, "Don't Believe Those Old Wives' Tales about Having a Baby," *Parents Magazine* 36 (October 1961): 185–6.

22 Alan F. Guttmacher with Mary Scott Welch, "How True Are Those Old Wives' Tales about Pregnancy?" *Colliers* 129 (21 June 1952): 73. See also Nathan Fasten, "The Myth of Prenatal Influences," *Today's Health* 28 (October 1950): 27, 43; Elizabeth Chant Robertson, "Can a Scare Deform Your Baby?" *Chatelaine* 23 (January 1957): 54–5; Joan S. Pollack, "Why All These Myths about Pregnancy?" *Today's Health* 37 (August 1959): 26–8.

23 Selwyn, "How Tough," 172; Fasten, "The Myth of Prenatal Influences," 27, 43; Guttmacher and Scott Welch,"How True Are Those Old Wives' Tales," 18–19+; Robertson, "Scare," 54–5; Pollack, "Why All These Myths," 26–8; Guttmacher and Hechinger, "Don't Believe Those Old Wives' Tales," 82–3+.

24 Ehtel Strattan, "X-rays and Pregnancy," *Today's Health* 32 (June 1965): 27+.

25 Edward T. Wilkes, "Your Baby Can Be Perfect Too," *Woman's Home Companion* 77 (October 1950): 78–9; Murray H. Bass, "Diseases of the Pregnant Woman Affecting the Offspring," *Advances in Internal Medicine* 5 (1952): 15–58; Carol Buck, "Exposure to Virus Diseases in Early Pregnancy and Congenital Malformations," *Canadian Medical Association Journal* 72 (15 May 1955): 744–6; Alison D. McDonald, "Maternal Health and Congenital Defects," *New England Journal of Medicine* 258 (17 April 1958): 767–73; Alton L. Blakeslee, "Stress and Abnormalities," *Today's Health* 34 (November 1956): 14; Theodore H. Ingalls, "Causes and Prevention of Developmental Defects," *Journal of the American Medical Association* 161 (14 July 1956): 1047–51; "Expectant Mother's Fear May Affect Baby," *Science News Letter* 71 (27 April 1957): 267; Albert S. Norris, "Prenatal Factors in Intellectual and Emotional Development," *Journal of the American Medical Association* 172 (30 January 1960): 413–16; Sidney Tobin, "Emotional Depression during Pregnancy," *Obstetrics and Gynecology* 10 (December 1957): 677.

26 Nicholson J. Eastman, *Williams Obstetrics*, 11th ed. (New York: Appleton-Century-Crofts 1956), 341.

27 Nicholson J. Eastman and Louis M. Hellman, *Williams Obstetrics*, 12th ed. (New York: Appleton-Century-Crofts 1961), 348. See also Guttmacher and Hechinger, "Don't Believe Those Old Wives' Tales," 186.

28 Gerald Caplan, "Psychological Aspects of Maternity Care," *American Journal of Public Health* 47 (January 1957): 25; H.B. Atlee, *The Gist of Obstetrics* (Springfield, Ill.: Charles C. Thomas, Publisher 1957), 20–1, 69.

29 Maxine Davis, "Psychology and Nutrition of Pregnancy, Part One," *Good Housekeeping* 137 (October 1953): 198–98+; M. Straker, "Psychological Factors during Pregnancy and Childbirth," *Canadian Medical Association Journal* 70 (May 1954): 510–14; Herbert Thoms and Bruce Bliven, Jr, "Emotional Problems of Pregnancy," *McCalls* 86 (January 1959): 28.

30 Marion Hilliard, "Your First Baby," *Chatelaine* 23 (January 1957): 46.

31 George J. Wayne, "Depressive Reactions during Gestation and the Puerperium," *American Journal of Obstetrics and Gynecology* 64 (December 1952): 1282; Eastman, *Williams Obstetrics*, 11th ed., 678.

32 James Ramsdell Bloss, "Causes of Fear among Obstetric Patients," *Journal of the American Medical Association* (hereafter *JAMA*) 144 (16 December 1950): 1358; Wayne, "Depressive Reactions," 1282–7; Daniel Cappon, "Some Psychodynamic Aspects of Pregnancy," *Canadian Medical Association Journal* 70 (February 1954): 147; Marion Hilliard, "The Four Fears That Prey on Women," *Chatelaine* 21 (July 1955): 16, 40; Carl L. Kline, "Emotional Illness Associated with Childbirth," *American Journal of Obstetrics and Gynecology* 69 (April 1955): 748–52.

33 John Parks, "Emotional Reactions to Pregnancy," *American Journal of Obstetrics and Gynecology* 62 (August 1951): 339–42; Leo Kanner, "Psychiatric Aspects of Pregnancy and Childbirth," in Eastman, *Williams Obstetrics*, 11th ed., 346–55.

34 Straker, "Psychological Factors," 513.

35 R.D. Anspaugh, "Effects of Dexedrine Sulfate on Nausea and Vomiting of Pregnancy," *American Journal of Obstetrics and Gynecology* 60 (October 1950): 888; Henry P. Wager, "Emesis Gravidarum: Mechanism and Control," *Obstetrics and Gynecology* 6 (July 1955): 99–100; "Current Status of Therapy in Nausea and Vomiting of Pregnancy," *JAMA* 160 (21 January 1956): 208.

36 Leonard H. Biskind, "Emotional Aspects of Prenatal Care," *Postgraduate Medicine* 24 (December 1958): 636.

37 "Pregnancy Illness Relief," *Science News Letter* 56 (3 September 1949): 148; Wager, "Emesis," 99; Eastman, *Williams Obstetrics*, 11th ed., 354–5; Thoms and Bliven, "Emotional Problems," 99–100; Caplan, "Psychological Aspects," 27–8; Vivian Cadden, "The Unplanned Baby," *Parents Magazine* 33 (February 1958): 88.

38 Arthur G. King, "The Treatment of Pregnancy Nausea with a Pill," *Obstetrics and Gynecology* 6 (September 1955): 336.

39 Caplan, "Psychological Aspects," 26.

40 King, "Pill," 337–8 (emphasis added).

41 Edwin M. Gold, Margaret A. Losty, and Helen M. Wallace, "Blueprint for Changing Concepts in Antepartum Care," *American Journal of Public Health* 40 (July 1950): 792. See also Ann Oakley, *Captured Womb: A History of the Medical Care of Pregnant Women* (Oxford: Basil Blackwell 1984), 134–5, 150.

42 M.H. Bertling and John C. Burwell, Jr, "Diethylstilboestrol in Nausea and Vomiting of Pregnancy: A Preliminary Report," *American Journal of Obstetrics and Gynecology* 59 (February 1950): 461–2; Wager, "Emesis Gravidarum," 101–4; Eastman, *Williams Obstetrics*, 11th ed., 682; "Current Status of Therapy," 209.

43 Sjöström and Nilsson, *Power*, 43–5.

44 Eastman, *Williams Obstetrics*, 11th ed., 682.

45 Wallace Reyburn, "Unwed Mother," *Chatelaine* 16 (June 1950): 57.

46 Shirley Wright, "Confessions of an Unwilling Mother," *Chatelaine* 23 (October 1960): 25 (original emphasis).

47 Cadden, "Unplanned Baby," 37: Wright, "Unwilling Mother," 25–6.

48 Hilliard, "Four Fears," 40.

49 Ibid., 16, 40; Wright, "Unwilling Mother," 25;

50 Bloss, "Causes of Fear," 1358–61; Hilliard, "Four Fears," 9, 40; Thoms and Bliven, "Emotional Problems," 99–101; Norman Pleshette, "A Study of Anxieties during Pregnancy, Labor, the Early and Late Puerperium," *Bulletin of the New York Academy of Medicine* 32 (1956): 436–42; Eastman, *Williams Obstetrics*, 11th ed., 349; Judith Walzer Leavitt, *Brought to Bed: Childbearing in America, 1750–1950* (Oxford: Oxford University Press 1986), 28.

51 Hilliard, "Four Fears," 40; Hilliard, "First Baby," 9+; Maxine Davis, "Psychology and Nutrition of Pregnancy, Part One," *Good Housekeeping* 137 (October 1953): 197–8.

52 Peter Rabe, "Who's Having This Baby?" *McCalls* 81 (September 1954): 15; Pollack, "Why All These Myths," 26–8; Guttmacher and Hechinger, "Don't Believe Those Old Wives' Tales," 82–3, 182.

53 Guttmacher and Scott Welch, "How True Are Those Old Wives' Tales," 18.

54 Pollack, "Why All These Myths," 27.

55 Marion Hilliard, "First Baby," 47.

56 Pollack, "Why All These Myths," 27.

57 Wright, "Unwilling Mother," 26; Anspaugh, "Effects of Dexedrine," 890.

58 Lucile D. Kirk, "Good Looks: Keep Attractive While Pregnant," *Parents Magazine* 32 (February 1957): 96.

59 Anne Holden Braden, "Prescription for Pregnancy," *Today's Health* 29 (March 1951): 40–4; Guttmacher and Scott Welch, "How True Are Those Old Wives" Tales," 19, 77; Vivian Wilcox, "Pretty as a Picture All Around the Clock," Robert Turnbull, "There's a Wonderful Glow about You," and June Werker, "You Can Have Your Baby and Your Figure," *Chatelaine* 26 (January 1960): 54–61; "How to Look Your Best during Pregnancy," *Redbook* 118 (January 1962): 54–5+.

60 Bernice Peck, "Career Babies," *Mademoiselle* 46 (March 1958): 142–5.

61 Ibid., 145.

62 King, "Pill," 332.

63 Insight Team, *Suffer the Children*, 53–4; Sangster, "Happy Pill," 60, 63; Joel Lexchin, *The Real Drug Pushers: A Critical Analysis of the Canadian Drug Industry* (Vancouver, B.C.: New Star Books 1984), 19.

64 Dorothy Sangster, "Should You Take a Happy Pill?" *Chatelaine* 23 (April 1957): 21+; "A New Doctor Disease: Prescribing Tranquilizers," *Science Digest* 47 (May 1960): 35.

65 Sangster, "Happy Pill," 61.

66 Sjöström and Nilsson, *Power*, 196–270; Ralph Adam Fine, *The Great Drug Deception: The Shocking Story of MER/29 and the Folks Who Gave You Thalidomide* (New York: Stein and Day 1972), 167–81; Insight Team, *Suffer the Children*, 1–4, 122–223.

67 For an interesting review of historical, sociological, and feminist theory on women and medicine, see Deborah Lupton, "Feminisms and Medicine," *Medicine as Culture: Illness, Disease and the Body in Western Society* (London: Sage Publications 1994), 131–60.

68 Ethel Roskies is a notable exception. A doctoral candidate in psychology at the Rehabilitation Institute of Montreal during the 1960s, Roskies developed a tremendously subtle and sensitive analysis of the experiences of mothers of "thalidomide babies" treated at the institute.

69 Roskies, *Abnormality and Normality*, 2–3, 30–1; Monica O'Neill, "A Preliminary Evaluation of the Intellectual Development of Children with Congenital Limb Malformations Associated with Thalidomide" (thesis, licentiate in philosophy, psychology, Université de Montréal, April 1965), 35; Webb, "Canadian Thalidomide Experience," 987–92.

70 Sjöström and Nilsson, *Power*, 112, 131.

71 Insight Team, *Suffer the Children*, 29. See also Yoichiro Yamakawa, "The Legal Settlement of Thalidomide Cases in Japan," in T. Soda, ed., *Drug-Induced Sufferings: Medical, Pharmaceutical and Legal Aspects* (Amsterdam: Excerpta Medica 1980), 365; Sjostrom and Nilsson, *Power*, 39–40, 147; Roskies, *Abnormality and Normality*, 1–2.

3

"A Kind of Genetic Social Work": Sheldon Reed and the Origins of Genetic Counselling

Molly Ladd-Taylor

Over forty and surprised to find myself pregnant with my third child, I did not hesitate to have amniocentesis, a prenatal test where the amniotic fluid is extracted to check for chromosomal anomalies, including Down's syndrome. This was not the first time I had had amniocentesis, but it was my first time in Canada, and the experience felt dramatically different from the one I had had in the United States just three years before. In Minneapolis the amnio was done at a small private clinic, and the few people I saw were much like myself – white, middle-class or affluent, and over thirty-five. In Toronto the test was done in a large urban hospital, and the women in the waiting room reflected the tremendous racial and linguistic diversity of the city's population. In Minneapolis the amnio process started at a meeting in a private office with a thirty-something white woman who showed my husband and me diagrams of chromosomes and asked us about our genetic background; in Toronto it began with dozens of expectant mothers (and a few fathers) watching a film. After the film, I had a short interview at a counter with a South Asian man who told me I was lucky to be Caucasian because I had a lower risk for genetic disease. The test results from the American clinic came in less than ten days; I waited three very long weeks in Toronto. In the United States I was able to "choose" amniocentesis because it was covered by my private health insurance; by contrast, in Canada, where health coverage is universal and the government pays for most prenatal tests, amnio is available and advised (though not required) for "high-risk" women of every race and class.

Although I initially felt overwhelmed by my different experiences in Canada and the United States, upon closer reflection I became increasingly impressed by their similarities. Despite significant disparities between Canada and the United States in funding and access to health care, genetic tests are rapidly becoming routine in both countries; scientific research and medical conventions do not stop at the border. Canadians and Americans share many cultural values that contribute to our governments' support for genetic research and the routine use of amniocentesis today: a faith in biomedicine, an infatuation with testing and measurement, and a strong belief in the possibility – and desirability – of controlling human events through science and technological innovation. Other shared values – about gender, disability, and what constitutes a happy family life – have added to the appeal of genetic services, both today and in the past.

The routinization of prenatal diagnosis in North America and Europe and the enormous resources poured into the mapping of the human genome have made amniocentesis and other "new" reproductive technologies the subject of heated debate in recent years. While many scientists and consumers welcome prenatal testing (and biomedicine generally) as a means of increasing women's control over reproduction, helping to ensure the health of their unborn children, others – most notably feminists and disability-rights activists – have raised important concerns. Feminist critic Barbara Rothman worries that prenatal testing has led to the concept of the "tentative pregnancy": women dismiss their bodily experiences and consider themselves not "really pregnant" until the tests results come through. In a tentative pregnancy, she points out, even a wanted fetus may be aborted if it is found to be imperfect. Prenatal tests offer the "illusion of choice" but may actually heighten the social, perhaps even economic, pressures to make the "right" choice and abort a fetus with a genetic anomaly. Some feminists also fear that new reproductive technologies and the cultural imperative to use them tighten male doctors' control of reproduction and women's bodies and thus pose a serious threat to women's procreative freedom.[1]

The most widely discussed reservations about prenatal testing concern its eugenic implications. Critics argue that amniocentesis, because its very existence presumes a willingness to abort a "defective" fetus, operates as a form of "quality control" for human life – and a highly flawed quality control at that. As numerous authors have pointed out, the mindset behind genetic tests ignores the economic and social discriminations that constrain the lives of people with disabilities and wrongly sees all forms of disability as equally incapacitating. One's quality of life cannot be determined from a prenatal test.

Warning of the slippery slope from routine amniocentesis to eugenics extremism, critics of the new reproductive technologies remind us that forced eugenic sterilization, "euthanasia" of people with mental and physical disabilities, and Nazi genocide against the Jews were all part of medically sanctioned programs involving the destruction of "lives not worth living." Although few think that the state-directed horrors of the Second World War will recur, given scientists' greater understanding of the complexities of genetics and the current emphasis on individual choice, scholars warn that a consumer-driven market for genetic services poses dangers of its own.[2] The eugenic implications of my own decision to have a prenatal test were brought home to me in Toronto, where a eugenic-era pedigree chart sat conspicuously on the back of my amniocentesis consent form.

This essay, inspired partly by the jolt of seeing that pedigree chart and partly by my resistance to the view that my decision to have an amnio test reinforced eugenic inequities, interrogates the relationship between eugenics and reproductive choice. My specific focus is on the early years of genetic counselling and the writings of one of its founders, Minnesota geneticist Sheldon Reed. Reed's early career is a useful place to begin a historical analysis of the tangled relationship between eugenics and genetic counselling, for although he sat on the board of the American Eugenics Society and published regularly in eugenics journals, Reed was the principal advocate of non-directive, or client-centred, genetic counselling. Reed coined the term "genetic counselling" in 1947 in order to remove "genetic social work" from the shackles of eugenics. For thirty years he was the director of the University of Minnesota's Dight Institute for Human Genetics, an organization that exemplified the "eugenic origins of medical genetics," to quote the title of a marvellous essay by science historian Diane Paul. The Dight Institute was established in 1941 by a bequest from the idiosyncratic physician (and socialist) Charles Fremont Dight, who was the president of the Minnesota Eugenics Society and the chief architect of Minnesota's eugenic sterilization law. (Dight's contribution to that law brought him the honour of a special invitation to observe, in January 1926, the state's first six legal sterilizations of women.)[3]

Reed, a Harvard PhD who taught at both Harvard and McGill University, Canada's leading genetic research institute, before moving to Minnesota in 1947, served as the Dight Institute's second director until he retired in 1977. According to the terms of Dight's will, the Dight Institute was obliged to work for "race betterment" through three programs: popular and academic instruction in human genetics and eugenics; the collection of family histories of hereditary traits; and the provision of genetic services to people with specific questions

or concerns.[4] In his first report as director, Reed wrote that promoting the "eugenic standpoint" to Minnesotans was the "most important function" of the Dight Institute.[5] His subsequent career would
reflect Dight's race-betterment strategy exactly. Reed lectured widely
on genetic science and counselling before popular and scientific audiences; published studies of heredity, such as *Mental Retardation: A
Family Study* (1965), a follow-up of an investigation begun in 1911 by
field workers from the Eugenic Record Office at Cold Spring Harbor;
and helped to establish genetic counselling as a reputable field distinct from eugenics. His readable *Counseling in Medical Genetics* (first
published in 1955, but revised and updated in 1963 and 1980),
though directed mainly at family physicians, was written in non-
scientific language and distributed to a wider audience. It established
Reed as a leading authority on genetic counselling.

Most histories of the genetic counselling profession acknowledge its
eugenic origins but then describe its evolution away from those unfortunate roots. According to the standard narrative produced by genetic
counselling professionals, the profession developed in three stages.
The first, from the late 1800s to the 1930s, was the period of the
eugenics movement. Charles Davenport and his staff at the Eugenic
Record Office filled out pedigree charts and did some counselling, but
they focused most of their attention on reducing the "unfit" part of the
population through coercive measures such as immigration restriction
and sterilization. The second stage, which lasted from the mid-1930s
until the late 1960s, was one of transition. During this stage, the
eugenics movement declined and heredity counselling moved into the
medical world. Most genetic counsellors were university- or hospital-
based research scientists who understood their work in terms of public
health and preventive medicine; only a few, like Reed, also thought of
"heredity counselling" in psychological or therapeutic terms. It was
not until the third stage of professionalization, which occurred in the
late 1960s and the 1970s, that genetic counselling emerged as a profession with its own educational requirements, organizational structures, and ethical code. Now women with master's degrees in the field,
rather than male physicians and researchers, constituted the majority
of practitioners. This new generation of genetic counsellors was committed to the value-neutral, non-directive methods associated with psychotherapist Carl Rogers, understanding the purpose of genetic
counselling as helping families at risk for genetic anomalies to sort out
their feelings and find emotional support. Because the counsellors'
chief concern was the psychological happiness of their clients, and not
the "racial" or public health interests of the larger society, genetic
counselling was believed to enhance an individual's reproductive

choice. While its social-control dimensions did not completely evaporate, on the whole, "at least in North America, the shift in ethos was dramatic."[6]

Recent research has emphasized the continuities in twentieth-century eugenics, suggesting that the shift to non-directive genetic counselling was not as dramatic as the profession's narrative suggests. For one thing, critics of genetic testing point out, class and cultural biases persist; the possibility of eugenic abuse remains ever-present in America's highly stratified, market-driven society. For another, as this essay shows, the therapeutic orientation of modern genetic counselling began well before the 1970s. Although more research is needed to determine the extent of Sheldon Reed's influence on counselling practice, a study of his early writings reveals a medical genetics driven as much by family ideals as by eugenics, that is, as much by patients' demands as by technology.[7] Reed's career helps to illuminate the powerful appeal of genetic services by shifting our attention away from scientific advances and new technologies towards older (and more familiar) concepts of health and family happiness. It is significant that Reed outlined the contours of non-directive, client-centred genetic counselling in the late 1940s and early 1950s, twenty years before abortion was legalized in the United States and Canada, more than ten years before the routine use of amniocentesis and other new reproductive technologies, and several years before geneticists understood the workings of human chromosomes. Indeed, the first edition of *Counseling in Medical Genetics* was published four years before Jerome Lejeune discovered (in 1959) that Down's syndrome was caused by an extra chromosome.[8] Clearly, the scientific and technological breakthroughs in genetic testing followed the development of genetic counselling, and not the other way around.

The rise of a eugenics-inspired therapeutic counselling directed at people of "normal" intelligence (that is, of the middle class) has received surprisingly little scholarly attention. Most historical analyses of eugenics in the postwar years focus on population control or the rise of genetic science, and although the "psychologization" of North American society has been the subject of many excellent studies in recent years, it has rarely been considered from the perspective of eugenics or the expanding purview of modern medicine.[9] Yet counselling was crucial to the reconfiguration – and medicalization – of eugenics in the postwar era. Reed's writings reveal the deep ideological affinities between eugenics-based concerns with improving the population and the pronatalist domesticity of the baby boom. In contrast to the 1920s and 1930s, when educated middle-class women had substantially fewer children than their uneducated low-income counterparts, white-collar couples bore an increasing proportion of the nation's children during the pronatalist 1950s. Eugenics-inspired marriage counsellors, like *Ladies' Home Journal* columnist Paul Popenoe and University of Pennsylvania professor Emily Mudd, promoted the view that people of normal intelligence were most likely to be happy if they had large families. In so doing, they helped to redirect eugenics away from politically unpopular state policies aimed at reducing the numbers of the unfit and towards therapeutic counselling, which was supposed to ensure individual happiness and higher fertility rates in the "superior" part of the population. Reed, who called genetic counselling the "modern way of carrying on a program in eugenics" in 1950, adopted the same strategy. "It is my impression that my practice of divorcing the two concepts of eugenics and genetic counseling contributed to the rapid growth of genetic counseling," he reflected in 1974. "Genetic counseling would have been rejected, in all probability, if it had been presented as a technique of eugenics."[10]

Of course, the move to disassociate the whole of eugenics from its more coercive manifestations did not originate in the postwar period. As early as the 1920s, reform eugenicists (to use historian Daniel Kevles's term) began to dispute simplistic associations between race, class, and intelligence, and to distance themselves from eugenics-based racism and the coercive sterilization and immigration policies espoused by hard-liners like Davenport. Deciding for oneself whether or not to have children was a right that must be safeguarded in a democracy, Frederick Osborn, secretary of the American Eugenics Society, proclaimed in 1940; eugenic mating should not be forced. Osborn proposed a eugenics program that bypassed the law and used propaganda, the mass media, and therapeutic family counselling to reinforce the "social and psychological pressures" on families to have more, or fewer, children (depending on their level of intelligence and achievement). Reed, twenty years younger than Osborn, shared his therapeutic orientation; his term "genetic counselling," which superseded "genetic hygiene," "heredity counselling," and similar phrases associated with a bygone era, reflects Reed's sensitivity to an increasingly therapeutic American culture.[11]

Despite postwar efforts to cloak eugenics in therapeutic terms, it is difficult to reconcile the Dight Institute's explicitly eugenic program with Reed's assertion in the 1970s that genetic counselling was "a kind of genetic social work without eugenic connotations." This difficulty can be explained partly by the variable definition of eugenics: the term can refer to anything from innocuous efforts to "improve" the population by providing better health care to coercive policies to eliminate those considered unfit. In the years following the Holocaust, the association between eugenics and Nazi Germany and an increased sensitivity to racism and human rights destroyed popular support for "eugenics," even though scientific discoveries about DNA, wonder drugs such as the polio vaccine, and greater access to medical care led to greater scientific and popular support for its fundamental presupposition: that the human population can be improved. The relationship between eugenics and genetic science grew increasingly complex when nuclear-era concerns about radiation disassociated, to some degree, genetic mutation from "bad heredity" and treatments for some genetic diseases, such as phenylketonuria, were found.[12]

Reed's views on the relationship between eugenics and genetic counselling reflect the same ambiguity. On the one hand, he was well aware that coercive eugenics policies were counterproductive. "It would seem clear from the whole of our cultural experience that people do not wish to be *told* how many children they can have," he remarked. "... Decisions regarding reproduction must be made by the couples themselves." On the other hand, Reed consistently espoused genetic counselling, with family physicians playing the principal advisory role. While Reed insisted that the purpose of medical genetics was to help individual patients rather than to support a population policy, he also expressed the belief, one that was increasingly common in the 1950s, that modern medicine could solve both personal and societal problems. Although Reed admitted that the impact of genetic counselling would occasionally be dysgenic, in the sense that couples with a family history of disability might be encouraged to have more children, he wrote that while it might be "dysgenic in regard to a particular gene, it should be remembered that those who are sufficiently concerned to come for counseling have commendable concepts of their obligations as parents and these laudable characteristics should be transmitted to the next generation."[13]

Reed's client-centred (as opposed to strictly eugenic) approach to genetic counselling suggests the limitations of a top-down analysis that sees genetic services as imposed on women by male doctors; his therapeutic orientation may in fact have been partly a response to patient pressure. In a 1974 reflection on the history of genetic counselling, Reed described his first days at the Dight Institute. On the morning of his arrival, he had given genetic advice to a family in which four out of five children had a blood condition, and the next day, he had advised a family where five of the eight children had an heredomacular (skin) degeneration. Reviewing his daily log, he wrote, "I could not see that these consultations had much to do with eugenics, at least not in the case of individual families."[14] But they had a lot to do with families and medicine.

Two assumptions about human nature guided Reed's medical genetic counselling: (1) that if properly informed, most people of normal intelligence (and middle-class status) would make rational and responsible decisions that coincided with the interests of society; and (2) that personal happiness was bound up with a "normal" family life. "The desire for a happy family of normal children is one of the strongest human motivations," he reflected. "In civilized countries responsible parents no longer leave reproduction to the vagaries of chance." These guiding assumptions are especially striking because from today's perspective geneticists in Reed's time had little scientific information to offer. Prior to a full understanding of chromosomes and before prenatal diagnosis and legalized abortion permitted couples to terminate a particular pregnancy, geneticists could offer only the vaguest estimate of risk, on the basis of which couples had to decide whether or not to try to have children at all. Reed candidly told his audience of doctors that the main goal in assessing the "risk" of disability was therapeutic: to calm down expectant couples who feared having a second or even third child with a disability, to quell shame and maternal guilt, and to alleviate tensions between parents about who was to blame (in practice, apparently, this usually meant defending the mother). "Our serious clients come to us because they are troubled," Reed observed. "They show great affection for their abnormal child and give it more than its ordinary share of attention, but the parents are unhappy both for the defective child and for themselves." But the chief advantage to parents of knowing the risk of a genetic anomaly was emotional. Parents would be "psychologically forearmed" if their baby was affected and would experience "mental uplift" if he or she was not. In most cases, the risk of repeated disability was small, and counselling revived "flagging spirits" and established hope for better luck.[15]

In promoting medical genetic counselling as a means to help patients achieve individual and familial happiness, Reed made liberal use of personal case histories intended to prove the usefulness of medicine's increasing role in both the physical and mental aspects of family life. Each chapter of the 1955 and 1963 editions of *Counseling for Medical Genetics* ended with "illustrative examples" that underscored both the uniqueness and the commonalities of such cases. The cases were not narrowly focused on symptoms; rather they reflected the wide range of physical and mental health concerns addressed by family physicians. Despite the different genetic issues each case raised, however, Reed's patients were remarkably similar: they were implicitly white, middle class, and responsible, and they all desired a "normal" family life.

Reed's discussion of the cases reveals his medical-scientific approach to the vagaries of human reproduction and disability. He consistently used his scientific authority to combat common "superstitions," such as the belief in marking the baby, and to disparage reproductive decisions based mainly on religious beliefs. Surely, he maintained, if clients were properly informed about genetics, they would show "common sense" and make rational, planned decisions about parenthood regardless of their religious background. Scientific knowledge could heal the mind as well as the body. As an example, Reed referred to the father of a Down's syndrome child, a war veteran who wasn't sure whether his child's disability was caused by his own masturbation or by the bad heredity of his wife. This father's experience typified the relief and "washing away of guilt feelings" parents felt once they understood the significance of chromosomes.[16]

Although Reed's wife, Elizabeth, had a doctorate in genetics, his writing, like that of most of his contemporaries, presumed that mothers would stay home to care for their children. At the same time, he expressed great concern about married women's state of mind, and he frequently involved himself in marital conflicts, almost always in defence of the wife. For instance, Reed recommended family counselling to a "most attractive and capable" mother of five whose first husband was schizophrenic and whose second had a violent disposition and an "unwholesome" attitude towards her daughter by the first husband. Although the client had consulted with Reed to find out if future children were likely to inherit her husband's mental difficulties, the geneticist made it clear that "heredity was not the primary problem." Similarly, he expressed sympathy for a pregnant woman with three children, two of whom had bilateral clubfeet, because her husband wanted even more kids. After reassuring the exhausted mother that the odds were "with her" because each birth carried only a 25 per cent risk of the disability, Reed advised the following "cure": Take to bed with a feigned illness just as your husband is about to leave for a two-week fishing vacation, and remain sick – especially at night – so that your husband will have to care for you night and day until his vacation is over. "This is a most educational experience beneficial for all males who are overly eager for the women to produce and care for large families," he explained.[17]

Despite taking it for granted that most women wanted children, Reed was a staunch advocate of planned parenthood for social, economic, and eugenic reasons. Describing the "slavery involved in taking physical care of young children" as a major reason that "responsible persons" refused to have large families, he depicted genetic counselling as a way to assist married women to gain control over their reproduction. "Few women think of themselves as slot machines in which a chance is taken every time something is inserted in the slot," he remarked. "They are not neutral about their fertility. Either they want a baby or they do not. If they want one, they want to be sure that it has a high chance of being normal." Geneticists and family doctors in general could be women's allies in negotiations with their husbands over child-bearing, thereby enhancing women's reproductive rights.[18]

Because surgical sterilization is the most effective way to prevent reproduction over an extended period of time and because it is so closely associated with coercive eugenics, it is worth noting that Reed often described sterilization as psychologically beneficial to the individual. The story he told of a twenty-four-year-old Catholic mother of four was especially poignant. She had lost one child to fibrocystic disease of the pancreas and had another who was gravely ill. Medical expenses had eaten up the family's savings, but although the couple was determined to have no more children, they believed that birth control was a sin. Their priest advised abstinence, but the couple felt that this was not a viable option, so the mother decided on sterilization (which meant sinning once, rather than continuously). In addition, Reed reported, "she considered it an even greater sin to risk having further defective children who would suffer and die, while also depriving their normal brothers and sisters of their rightful socio-economic positions in the community." The counsellor's sympathy was clear. Confident that most Catholics would make a "rational" decision about birth control and reproduction if armed with scientific information, he concluded that "anyone can appreciate her dilemma, but no one can decide for her which alternative to accept."[19]

In fact, Reed and his wife had made exactly the same decision a few years earlier, when they had decided that Elizabeth Reed should have her tubes tied during a Caesarean section to avoid potential damage to future babies from rhesus factors. Reed told his story to show that every individual has some "bad" genes: "The geneticist, of all people, should not knowingly take a large chance of producing a defective child."[20] But his personal tale also illustrates another point: counselling was directed mainly at middle-class couples who (like the Reeds) could be expected to make rational decisions about their personal situations and responsible decisions for society. When it came to the properly informed and counselled "normal" population, there was no need for coercive eugenics.

Despite Reed's confidence that non-directive counselling would suffice for "normal" people, old eugenics habits persisted in his approach to mental illness and disability. In 1965, two years after President John F. Kennedy increased government support for non-profit facilities for people with intellectual disabilities, Sheldon and Elizabeth Reed published *Mental Retardation: A Family Study*, a seven hundred–page tome that resembled the family studies of the eugenics era more than his own writing on genetic counselling. The Reeds' project, sponsored by the Minnesota Human Genetics League, a eugenics advocacy organization, was widely publicized in Minnesota, for it was based on research at the State School and Hospital (formerly the School for the Feeble-minded), located in the town of Faribault. The Reeds' longitudinal study, which was initiated in 1949, followed up on pedigree charts and family histories of 549 patients that had been compiled by Eugenic Record Office fieldworkers who visited Faribault between 1911 and 1918. Tracking the descendants of 289 of the original patients, whom they categorized according to etiology (primarily genetic, probably genetic, environmental, and unknown), the Reeds eventually gathered information on more than eighty thousand people. In the end, they found – not unlike their eugenicist forebears – that mental retardation ran in families. The greatest predisposing factor for mental retardation was a mentally retarded relative, regardless of whether the cause of disability was primarily genetic or environmental. Like eugenicists in the past, they found a solution in reducing the fertility of those considered unfit. "When voluntary sterilization becomes a part of the culture of the United States," the Reeds concluded, "we should expect a decrease of about 50 per cent per generation in the number of retarded persons." While some Minnesotans expressed doubts about their state's "voluntary" eugenic sterilization law, Reed remained a strong supporter.[21]

Reed's support for eugenics and sterilization should not be confused with simple racism, however. In fact, he was a racial liberal who denounced the "pernicious perversion" of Darwin's ideas by "Nazi criminals" and maintained repeatedly that racial differences are, "like beauty, only skin deep … All men are brothers under the skin!" As a prominent geneticist, Reed was often asked to comment on racial difference; he always responded that genetic differences were trivial and could never be properly measured given the absence of any "pure" races in America and the "incomparably bad" environment in which African-Americans were forced to live. In his view, racial inequality was a sociological problem rooted in a struggle over economic resources; racial prejudice was learned behaviour, the result of ignorance and a misunderstanding of science. Years before the furor over Arthur Jensen's claim that lower test scores among African-Americans reflected their lesser intelligence, Reed maintained that the racial variation in test results was exclusively sociological. For that reason, he hailed the 1954 Supreme Court decision in *Brown v. Board of Education*, which declared racially segregated schools to be unconstitutional, and urged northerners to make financial contributions to southern black schools.[22]

As a racial liberal, Reed was best known for his strong support of transracial adoption. Adoption agencies inquiring into the suitability of a particular child for placement in an adoptive home had long been among the most regular clients of the Dight Institute, and skin colour was one of their principal concerns. Reed used that concern to strongly and consistently urge white parents – if they were free of racial prejudice – to adopt light-skinned black or mixed-race children who could "pass for white." In his view, biracial children made the best genetic risk of all potential adoptees. Reed's advocacy of transracial adoption only for light-skinned black children, which seems so problematic today, must be understood in the context of the highly segregated midwestern society of the early 1950s. Minnesota's black population was small, and most white Americans had yet to become aware of the civil-rights cause. Reed's ideas about race reflect both his commitment to the liberal political ideals of equal opportunity and a colour-blind America and his understanding of genetic science. In his view, centuries of racial intermingling in America had made a "hybrid race of the first order," superior to both blacks and whites. However, his insistence on the adoptive value of biracial children reveals his beliefs about gender and normality as well as race: he was convinced that a nuclear family of healthy and normal children was the key to adult happiness. "Normal" children included those who were biracial but not those who were developmentally disabled.[23]

The value Reed placed on having a "healthy" and "normal" child is key to his – and our – world view. These concepts were in flux in the postwar years as the accomplishments of biomedicine expanded North Americans' expectations for health while narrowing the bounds of the normal. Rosemarie Garland Thomson has shown how the economic and social changes associated with modernization reshaped and standardized the physical body, defining it, machine-like, in terms of efficiency and value. While genetic science recast "freaks" of old as biological errors, preventable by a complicated set of risk assessments and reproductive controls, mass IQ testing, schools that were compulsory and organized by grade, and the fast pace of factory work marked the "slow" student or worker as subnormal. This standardization reached a peak at mid-century, when psychologist Arnold Gesell and his collaborators established and publicized age-specific stages of a child's "normal" development based on the cultural and behavioural norms of the white middle class.[24]

The pronatalist domesticity of the baby boom era surely added to the pressure to have a "normal" child. Family togetherness and companionship lay at the heart of the postwar domestic ideal, a prerequisite for the happy family life that was considered necessary to the self-fulfilment and social success of adults. As adult contentment became more tied to family togetherness and as children's problems, from autism and schizophrenia to trouble in school, were increasingly attributed to inadequate mothering, parenting children with disabilities became more problematic. There were no disabled children in *Leave It to Beaver.*

Middle-class parents of developmentally delayed children were determined to make a place for themselves and their families in the domestic culture of the postwar period. Trying to normalize their imperfect families, they strove to redefine mental retardation as a children's issue through organizations such as the National Association for Retarded Children, founded in Minneapolis in 1950, and through personal narratives or "confessions" in the popular press. In campaigning for better awareness of disability issues, greater funding for research, and improved conditions in state institutions, they constructed a view of people with developmental disabilities as permanent children. In 1950 Nobel prize–winning author Pearl Buck told the long-secret story of her daughter Carol's mental retardation in *The Child Who Never Grew,* which was widely excerpted in the *Ladies' Home Journal* and similar magazines. A few years later, television celebrities Dale Evans and Roy Rogers recounted the short life of their daughter, who had had Down's syndrome and had died of encephalitis at the age of two. The story of President Kennedy's sister Rosemary also became widely known. Clearly, if such illustrious Americans as Pearl Buck, Dale Evans, and the Kennedys could have mentally retarded children, the long-held view of mental retardation as a lower-class phenomenon no longer sufficed.[25] As Sheldon Reed reminded his readers, bad genes could happen to good people.

Despite these efforts, it remained nearly impossible to reconcile the real-life issues of raising a developmentally delayed child with the ideal of family togetherness. Most experts, including Arnold Gesell and Benjamin Spock, advised institutionalizing children with severe disabilities, and many parent-activists concurred. Although Pearl Buck's daughter lived at home until she was ten, by the time her mother's book appeared in 1950 she had lived in an institution "with her own kind" for more than twenty years. The middle-class families that chose to institutionalize their disabled children felt that they were acting selflessly in providing a safe and non-competitive environment for their children. In addition, the removal of disabled children from the home enabled their parents and their non-disabled siblings to lead a "normal" family life and live up to the companionate family ideal.[26]

As a genetic counsellor, Reed supported – and advised his physician-readers to support – the dominant view about institutionalization.

Consider, for example, his advice to a couple who had two severely disabled children, one of whom died in infancy. Feeling a "great need
and desire for a normal family," the couple had tried to adopt, but
their application was rejected because their surviving son lived at
home (as opposed to in an institution). They consulted the geneticist
only after their efforts to adopt had failed. Reed informed the couple
of the 1-in-4 odds that another child would have the same disability,
but then urged them to reconsider institutionalization, even if they decided to have another child. Too often, he told readers, parents centred their attention on a disabled child to the detriment of his normal
siblings. After pointing out the psychological damage they might in-
flict on their child, Reed told the couple that "this decision is yours to
make, not ours." But he left little doubt that they would make the
"right" decision.[27]

The context for genetic counselling changed in the 1970s. Several
emerging factors, such as the dramatic increase of married women in
the workforce, feminism, and the concept of reproductive choice, led
people to place individual happiness above eugenic, societal, and familial concerns. Nevertheless, although legalized abortion and more
accurate prenatal testing rendered Reed's early methods of risk assessment obsolete, his basic philosophy of genetic counselling remained
much the same. In the 1980 edition of *Counseling in Medical Genetics*, as
in the 1955 edition, Reed's racial liberalism, concern with a happy
family life, and insistence on the value of scientific knowledge – even
when it did not lead to "control" over the outcome – shaped his
approach to genetic services. This is why Reed recommended amniocentesis in high-risk cases, even if the parents were unwilling to abort.
Parental anxiety would be allayed if the results were normal, and if the
fetus was affected, the family would be prepared. There would be
certainty, if not control.[28]

Reed's faith in scientific knowledge and his privileging of the normal are poignantly illustrated in his 1980 discussion of Huntington's
chorea. Writing when the test for the Huntington's gene was still in development, Reed said he would urge everyone with a family history of
Huntington's to take the test (while defending their right to refuse).
While individuals who would develop the disease would suffer with
that knowledge, he conceded, those without the gene would rejoice;
the "real benefits" to the healthy overcame the "damage and distress"
to the diseased. "My value judgment is that release should be provided
for those without the gene at the expense of those who have it," he
wrote. "The affected should make the sacrifice rather than the unaf-
fected." In the genetic counsellor's world view, genetic science was
valued for the relief it provided to the "innocent."[29]

At the turn of the twenty-first century, the mapping of the human genome and the cloning of human embryos have raised the hopes of many North Americans about the possibility of treating or even eliminating most genetic disease. At the same time, sensationalist news stories about post-menopausal mothers and test-tube babies heighten popular anxieties about individualism run rampant and intensify fears that even affluent people of normal intelligence cannot be trusted to make the right or responsible choice. Ironically, Sheldon Reed's early advocacy of non-directive genetic counselling, together with the connection he hammered home between personal fulfilment and a happy family of normal children, helped to lay the foundation for the individualistic, market-driven, and seemingly irresponsible genetic services we have today.

This is not, however, a simple story that sets an enlightened feminist "us" against a controlling and prejudiced "them," for the development of genetic services cannot be attributed to "male" medicine alone. Geneticists like Sheldon Reed were responding, at least in part, to the difficulty women had raising children with disabilities in a society that offered them few resources. It is for very similar reasons that many feminists who deplore the eugenic abuses of the past choose amniocentesis in the present. But the demand for genetic services is cultural as well as economic. Many North American women of child-bearing age, raised in a prosperous era of astonishing advances in science and biomedicine, have infinitely high expectations for health and for our ability (indeed, right) to control our bodies, careers, and reproduction. At the same time, we still live in a society where child rearing is a private responsibility and the costs of disability are borne largely by individual women and families. Many feminists today hold beliefs not so very different from Sheldon Reed's. Personal fulfilment is tied to a happy family life, liberal views on race are accompanied by discomfort with developmental disability and other forms of difference, and the ability to plan, control, and choose reproduction is a valued goal. It is an illusion of choice, to be sure, but it is one we savour nonetheless.

NOTES

1 Barbara Katz Rothman, *The Tentative Pregnancy: Prenatal Diagnosis and the Future of Motherhood* (New York: Penguin 1997), 14; Gena Corea et al , *Man-Made Women: How New Reproductive Technologies Affect Women* (Bloomington: Indiana University Press 1997).
2 Ruth Hubbard, *The Politics of Women's Biology* (New Brunswick, N.J.: Rutgers University Press 1990), 197. See also Robert Proctor, "The Destruction of

'Lives Not Worth Living,'" in Jennifer Terry and Jacqueline Urla, eds, *Deviant Bodies* (Bloomington: Indiana University Press 1995), 170–96.

3 Diane Paul, "The Eugenic Origins of Medical Genetics," in Diane Paul, *The Politics of Heredity: Essays on Eugenics, Biomedicine and the Nature-Nurture Debate* (Albany: SUNY Press 1998), 133–56.

4 Clarence P. Oliver, *A Report on the Organization and Aims of the Dight Institute* (Minneapolis: University of Minnesota Press 1943).

5 "The Biennial Report of the Dight Institute for 1946–48," box 1, Dight Institute Records, University of Minnesota Archives.

6 Paul, "Eugenic Origins," 148. Histories of genetic counselling include James Sorenson, "Genetic Counseling: Values That Have Mattered," and Barbara Bowles Biesecker, "Practice of Genetic Counseling," both in *Prescribing the Future: Ethical Challenges in Genetic Counseling*, ed. Dianne Bartels et al. (New York: Aldine de Guyer 1993); Ian Porter, "The Evolution of Genetic Counseling in America," in *Genetic Counseling*, ed. H.A. Lubs and F. de la Cruz (New York: Raven Press 1977); Diane Paul, "From Eugenics to Medical Genetics," in *Health Care Policy in Contemporary America*, ed. Alan I. Marcus and Hamilton Cravens (Pennsylvania State University Press 1997); Rayna Rapp, *Testing Women, Testing the Fetus: The Social Impact of Amniocentesis in America* (New York: Routledge 1999).

7 Molly Ladd-Taylor, "Eugenics, Sterilisation and Modern Marriage: The Strange Career of Paul Popenol," *Gender and History* 13 (August 2001): 298–327; Diane Paul, *Controlling Human Heredity, 1865 to the Present* (N.J.: Humanities Press 1985).

8 Sheldon C. Reed, *Counseling in Medical Genetics* (Philadelphia: W.B. Saunders 1955).

9 Ellen Herman, *The Romance of American Psychology: Political Culture in the Age of Experts* (Berkeley: University of California Press 1995); Elaine Tyler May, *Homeward Bound: American Families in the Cold War Era* (New York: Basic Books 1988).

10 Reed, quoted in Paul, "Eugenic Origins," 134; Sheldon C. Reed "A Short History of Genetic Counseling," *Social Biology* 21 (1974): 332–9 (quotation on 135).

11 Daniel Kevles, *In the Name of Eugenics* (New York: Knopf 1985); Frederick Osborn, *Preface to Eugenics* (New York: Harper 1940), 297.

12 Reed, "A Short History," 335; Kevles, *In the Name of Eugenics*, 238–90.

13 Sheldon Reed, "Heredity Counseling," *Eugenics Quarterly* 1–2 (1954–56): 89.

14 Reed, "A Short History," 334–5.

15 Reed, *Counseling in Medical Genetics*, 225–6, 14; Sheldon C. Reed, "Counseling the Parents of the Retarded," lecture typescript, n.d., box 12, Dight Institute Records.

16 Reed, *Counseling in Medical Genetics*, 51; Sheldon C. Reed, *Parenthood and Heredity* (New York: John Wiley & Sons 1964), 58.

17 Reed, *Parenthood and Heredity*, 203–4; Reed, *Counseling in Medical Genetics*, 70.

18 Sheldon C. Reed, "A Eugenics Program for the Future," lecture typescript, n.d., box 8, Dight Institute Records; Reed, *Parenthood and Heredity*, 143.

19 Reed, *Counseling in Medical Genetics*, 133.

20 Ibid., 143–4.

21 Elizabeth W. Reed and Sheldon C. Reed, *Mental Retardation: A Family Study* (Philadelphia: W.B. Saunders Company 1965), 77–8.

22 Sheldon Reed to Roscoe Brown, 3 November 1952, Dight Institute Records; Sheldon C. Reed, "Color of the U.S.A. – 3000 A.D.," lecture typescript, n.d.; "All Men Are Brothers under the Skin," address before the Minneapolis Urban League, 11 February 1951, box 12, Dight Institute Records.

23 Reed, *Counseling in Medical Genetics*, chap. 20.

24 See Rosemarie Garland Thomson, ed., *Freakery: Cultural Spectacles of the Extraordinary Body* (New York: New York University Press 1996).

25 James W. Trent Jr., *Inventing the Feeble Mind: A History of Mental Retardation in the United States* (Berkeley and Los Angeles: University of California Press 1994), 226–68; Kathleen Jones, "Education for Children with Mental Retardation," unpublished paper in author's possession.

26 Ibid.

27 Reed, *Counseling in Medical Genetics*, 63.

28 Sheldon C. Reed, *Counseling in Medical Genetics*, 3rd ed. (New York: Alan Liss 1980), 50.

29 Reed, *Counseling in Medical Genetics*, 3rd ed., 22.

4

Marty Mann's Crusade and the Gendering of Alcohol Addiction

Michelle L. McClellan

INTRODUCTION

One of the most influential yet least studied figures of twentieth-century public health was Margaret "Marty" Mann (1904–80), the founder of the National Committee for Education on Alcoholism and the leading popularizer of the disease model of alcoholism. A central player in the "modern alcoholism movement," a loosely affiliated group of scholars and advocates who formulated and disseminated a medicalized view of problem drinking, Mann crafted a unique position as a result of her gender and her status as a self-acknowledged alcoholic. The ways in which the media and Mann herself portrayed her alcoholism and recovery illustrate the complicated process by which alcoholism, especially in women, came to be defined as a medical problem. By insisting that alcoholism constituted a disease rather than a sin or a lack of will power, Mann sought to remove the stigma, shame, and silence associated with problem drinking. Hoping that a medical model would eliminate the double standard of judgment that was applied to alcoholic women, Mann endeavoured to include women in a disease paradigm that often excluded them or rendered them invisible. Operating within the constraints of resonant historical associations among alcohol, gender, medicine, and religion, Mann sought to cast herself as "modern" and "scientific" even though she had achieved her own recovery through the spiritually based program of Alcoholics Anonymous (AA).

In 1944 Mann founded the National Committee for Education on Alcoholism (NCEA), an educational and public health organization designed to publicize and popularize the disease model of alcoholism.[1] (This organization still exists as the National Council on Alcoholism and Drug Dependence.) Her campaign received considerable press coverage, and her persona as a recovering alcoholic became an inextricable part of her crusade. Like many alcoholics, Mann offered her experience as a conversion narrative: from a life of privilege and success she had been brought by alcoholism into suffering and despair before finding recovery and redemption through Alcoholics Anonymous. She clearly shaped her story to advance the agenda of the NCEA, offering herself as living proof of the NCEA doctrine that alcoholics can be helped and are worth helping.

Yet Mann's life story, formulaic in some ways, could never be typical; as a woman, she represented the exception among alcoholics. Mann's dual identity as a woman alcoholic and a woman reformer captures and reflects, on the one hand, many of the tensions that accompanied the ongoing transformation of "womanhood" in twentieth-century America and, on the other, the gendered nature of the disease of alcoholism. Even as she publicized the modern alcoholism paradigm, which considered alcoholism a disease and emphasized the difference between the alcoholic and the "normal" drinker for whom moderate recreational drinking was perfectly acceptable, her very identity as a *female* alcoholic posed an implicit challenge to the gendered nature of that paradigm. This paradigm reflected the wider cultural view of drinking as a male prerogative and alcoholism as a disease of men. Further, Mann's campaign contributed to and reflected discourses of race/ethnicity and class. Mann was not only white, she was an upper-class, native-born Protestant, and the class and ethnic elements of her identity underscored her exceptionality along gender lines. Finally, the very fact that alcoholism had struck a woman like her served as a reminder of the insidious nature of the disease; her own case demonstrated that alcoholism did not respect boundaries of class, ethnicity, or gender.

Mann's efforts to popularize the modern alcoholism paradigm and to include women under its rubric achieved mixed results. She served as the executive director of the NCEA until 1968, by which time the modern alcoholism movement had accomplished many of its goals. By the late 1950s, the American medical establishment had officially endorsed the definition of alcoholism as a disease, and treatment in hospitals and clinics had become more widely available. In 1963 a sympathetic profile of Mann's life and career in *Reader's Digest* illustrated the extent to which alcoholism had become normalized. Mann's courage in coming forward, combined with her shrewd marketing of her life story, contributed to the growing acceptance of the disease model.

Yet Mann's hope that medicalization would eliminate the special hurdles faced by alcoholic women has not been realized. American society underwent significant transformations in the 1960s and afterwards, not least in attitudes towards mood-altering substances. At the same time, the modern women's movement challenged conventional gender roles. As a result of both these developments, women's addiction to alcohol and other substances has attracted increasing attention from the medical establishment and a less judgmental attitude from the general public. However, the persistent association of women's drinking with their social and reproductive roles has resulted in a continuing stigmatization of women with drinking problems, as well as a double standard in treatment.[2] Mann played a pivotal role in reshaping American attitudes towards alcoholism, demonstrating in her own life the liberating potential of the disease model but also the double standard by which alcoholic women were judged through the end of the twentieth century.

DEFINING A DISEASE THROUGH AUTOBIOGRAPHY

Central to Mann's campaign was the redefinition of alcoholism as a disease, a medical condition divorced from moral judgments and articulated in the language of modern medical science rather than temperance rhetoric. To this end, she sought parallels with health problems that had followed a similar trajectory. Tuberculosis seemed a perfect example, one that also allowed Mann to inject her own life story into her campaign. In all her public health efforts, Mann shrewdly depicted her own experiences to advance her alcoholism campaign, packaging her autobiography to further her agenda.

Born in 1904 to a wealthy Chicago family, Mann enjoyed a privileged childhood until, as a teenager, she contracted tuberculosis during the late 1910s.[3] While her parents had the resources to send her to California to be treated by a well-known specialist, they did not inform her of the nature of her illness, fearing that she would reveal her condition to her friends. Mann recalled, however, that she only cooperated with the treatment regimen when her doctor, breaking his promise to her parents, told her that she had tuberculosis.

Mann thus drew a number of parallels between tuberculosis and alcoholism: ignorance, stigma, and secrecy, which could literally kill people who suffered from the disease; the consequent need for frank discussion and openness regarding treatment; and her own status as an atypical victim of both conditions.[4] A privileged debutante, Mann had nevertheless contracted tuberculosis, a disease associated with filth and poverty. As a young professional woman, she would become a chronic alcoholic, even though she seemed far removed from the stereotype of the Skid Row bum. Mann offered herself as living proof that alcoholism, like tuberculosis, could strike anyone, regardless of race, gender, or class advantage; she insisted that victims should not be prisoners of silence and shame, but should be able to find medical care as easily as people suffering from any other medical condition.

Following the interlude for tuberculosis treatment, Mann returned to the typical activities of a young woman of her social position, activities that apparently included considerable recreational drinking. In her later descriptions of this period, Mann emphasized how widespread drinking was among her social set, despite the fact that Prohibition was in effect across the country. Alcohol consumption was clearly part of heterosexual socializing and courtship. Mann recalled, "Every boy in our crowd carried a flask and every girl drank from it. Drinking was a matter of pride with us."[5] In fact, Mann gained a reputation for her ability to drink others under the table; apparently neither she nor anyone else was concerned about her drinking habits during this period.

Shortly after this carefree era, Mann's drinking pattern changed fundamentally. A brief marriage during the 1920s ended in divorce as a result, she later explained, of her husband's alcoholism. She failed to learn from this experience, however, and she herself continued to drink.[6] Soon after her divorce, her father suffered business reversals and Mann had to find a job. She worked in a series of positions over the next decade and a half, primarily in journalism, public relations, and the arts, first in New York and then in London.[7] Heavy drinking continued to be a part of her social and professional life during the 1930s. She slowly lost control, later recalling, "My degeneration to complete loathsome drunkenness came so gradually that it is difficult to describe."[8] Returning to the United States in the belief that a change of scenery could solve her problem, Mann, now unable to hold a job, found herself dependent on the largesse of her sister for a place to live and on strangers in bars for her liquor. She recalled, "I had no money but that didn't matter. By then I had learned that a woman needs to finance only that first drink. The rest I cadged like an expert."[9] This image stands in sharp contrast to that of the carefree young debutante who sipped from the flasks of her dancing partners; it indicates what could happen to a woman whose drinking violated proper boundaries.[10]

Mann's accounts of this period show how far she had "fallen" in both class and gender terms, reflecting the stereotypical link between alcohol consumption, especially public drinking by women, and problematic sexuality. One encounter marked the nadir of her drinking career:

At one bar a drunken Irish bartender of 60, who knew how a drunk felt in the morning minus a shot, would stand treat when she was broke.

One night he invited her to accompany him to a drinking party. An Irish bartender date a debutante? She told him she wouldn't fit in.

"Shure, ye'll fit. Anyone can look at ye an' see a drinkin' woman."

That hurt. She went home to a mirror, saw bags under her eyes, bloat under her jowls and a woman 55 at 32. So began innumerable trips to psychiatrists.[11]

This experience demonstrated the extent to which Mann had lost her position in terms of class and ethnicity; an upper-class Protestant whose family claimed seventeenth-century New England origins, she was now reduced to relying on the generosity of an Irish bartender for drinks. The Irish, of course, were the ethnic group most closely associated with alcoholism in both medical literature and the popular imagination. This episode also symbolized the magnitude of her "fall" in terms of gender, reflected both in the bartender's presumption in asking her out, which might have indicated an implicit obligation she owed because of the drinks, and in the deterioration of her appearance.

Mann found the encounter with the bartender sufficiently humiliating to prompt her to seek help for her drinking problem. Her search illustrates the limited range of treatment opportunities at mid-century, the complicated nexus of medical and spiritual approaches to alcoholism, and the ultimate success, in her case as in many others, of the Alcoholics Anonymous program. As she later outlined the story of her recovery, Mann first sought help from a doctor. Her decision to turn to the medical rather than the religious establishment demonstrates both her own "modernity" and the success of doctors, particularly psychiatrists, in claiming jurisdiction over problem drinking. Yet the medicalization of alcoholism was a complex and contested process, and Mann, like many other alcoholics, found that physicians had promised more than they could deliver. Mann had to face the ignorance of doctors regarding alcoholism and endure their contempt for alcoholics; the refusal of hospitals and sanitaria to accept alcoholic patients; and the failure of medical treatment, when she did receive it, to "cure" her drinking problem. Mann was hospitalized first at Bellevue, a municipal hospital in New York City, and then at a private sanitarium in Connecticut, but she showed little improvement until a physician at the sanitarium introduced her to Alcoholics Anonymous.

The accounts Mann offered of her introduction to Alcoholics Anonymous varied over the years, but all identified her encounter with the

AA program as the key moment in her recovery, an almost mystical turning point. To heighten the drama, Mann often hinted that her psychiatrist in the Connecticut sanitarium had been about to give up on her case when, as a last resort, he had suggested that she read an early manuscript copy of the AA "Big Book," which outlined the AA program and included autobiographical accounts by alcoholics who had stopped drinking. She was initially resistant to AA because of the spiritual elements in its philosophy, but at a critical moment in her life she found herself transformed by the AA message. Faced with a personal crisis, upset and desperate for a drink, she noticed a sentence in the open book on her bed: "We cannot live with anger." She described this experience as a liberation: "The walls crumbled – and the light streamed in. I wasn't trapped. I wasn't helpless. I was *free*, and I didn't have to drink to 'show them.' This wasn't 'religion' – this was freedom! Freedom from anger and fear, freedom to know happiness and love."[12] When she attended her first AA meeting shortly after this revelation, Mann felt that she had "come home at last." Depictions of her experience in the popular media cast it as a happy ending: "Five years have passed since then – years in which Marty Mann has neither had a drink nor wanted one."[13] This rosy picture did not accurately reflect the reality; in other accounts, Mann called her rehabilitation process "long and arduous" and acknowledged that she had suffered one or two "slips" – episodes in which she drank again.[14] Despite these early difficulties, however, Mann achieved lasting sobriety through her membership in the AA fellowship, according to all accounts.

Along with the spiritual message and the acknowledgment of a "Higher Power," the AA program promoted the "scientific" view that alcoholism is a disease, not a sin or a sign of moral weakness.[15] For Mann, AA's Big Book provided answers that all the doctors she had consulted could not. When she read the book, Mann recalled, "I grasped the clear picture and accepted the fact that I was the victim of a progressive and often fatal disease known as alcoholism. That book made me understand that I could never again safely touch liquor if I wanted to be well."[16] Mann embraced the explanation for her drinking problem that AA provided, and then promoted that definition of alcoholism through the NCEA. She used her own life story to illustrate this model of alcoholism. She did not attempt to provide personal reasons why her drinking patterns had changed so radically; indeed, she believed that defining herself as an alcoholic was explanation enough. In identifying herself as an alcoholic, Mann was saying that she suffered from a disease, that she had been "allergic" to alcohol from the very beginning, and that the years of apparently controlled drinking were but the preview to an inevitable descent into alcoholism.

· If the definition of alcoholism as a disease and an allergy was one fundamental component of the AA program, the emotional and psychological support of other alcoholics was another. Mann was frequently the only woman at the meetings she attended, yet she always emphasized how comfortable she felt there. Because Mann was single and had no children, her treatment was not complicated by family responsibilities as was that of many other women. While she surely had to cope with other issues of gender and sexuality, she has left no evidence of this, only insisting, even as she took pride in her status as the "first woman member" of AA, that she always felt totally at home among the men. Constructing a gender-neutral identity as an alcoholic, she explained this essential aspect of the AA fellowship to a reporter, who offered this observation: "Being able to talk plainly with no shame to others who have been through the same distress means a lot [to her]. For, she says, no one except an alcoholic can truly understand the feelings of one."[17]

Describing her early adulthood – a period in which she lost control of her drinking, unsuccessfully sought help from the medical and psychiatric establishment, and eventually achieved recovery through Alcoholics Anonymous – Mann cast her life as a conversion narrative, emphasizing the social, economic, and emotional costs of her drinking to underscore the magnitude of her recovery. Like many other alcoholics who gained sobriety through AA, Mann considered her initial attempts to find a cure through medical treatments to have been "false starts" at recovery, a preview to her recovery and awakening through AA. She had an additional reason to construct the narrative of her recovery in this way, of course: by emphasizing doctors' ignorance and the general lack of treatment facilities for alcoholics, Mann hoped to elicit support for NCEA information centres and clinics. Since a psychiatrist had encouraged her to try AA, Mann perhaps did not feel as much conflict between medical and spiritual approaches to alcoholism treatment as other problem drinkers might have experienced. In public pronouncements, however, she subsumed the religious aspects of her recovery under the modern, scientific language of her public health campaign.

THE NATIONAL COMMITTEE FOR EDUCATION ON ALCOHOLISM

While her recovery had not been easy, by the early 1940s Mann was able to return to full-time employment. However, a series of jobs in her former fields did not satisfy her; as she explained later, she felt that she needed to devote herself to something more meaningful.[18] Drawing on her formidable skills in public relations and journalism, she deter-

mined to spread the message of the modern alcoholism movement –
that alcoholism was a disease – to still-suffering alcoholics and their
families.

To that end, with the financial backing of the Yale Center for Alcohol Studies, the leading centre for research on alcoholism, and the
support of Bill Wilson, a co-founder of Alcoholics Anonymous, and of
a number of leading scientists, Mann established the National Committee for Education on Alcoholism. She served as executive director
of this organization from its founding in 1944 until 1968 (by which
time it had been renamed the National Council on Alcoholism). The
NCEA philosophy, as defined by Mann, contained three key elements:
(1) alcoholism is a disease and should be understood as a public
health problem; (2) the alcoholic can be helped; and (3) the alcoholic
is worth helping. To spread this message, the NCEA helped establish
information centres around the country where alcoholics and their
families could learn about alcoholism and the disease model. The
NCEA also sponsored clinics for alcoholism treatment, and through
advocacy and lobbying, it improved access to medical care for alcoholics in hospitals.[19] Through these activities and Mann's lecture tours,
interviews, and other publicity, the NCEA popularized the research
conducted by the Yale Center for Alcohol Studies and created a wider
awareness of the Alcoholics Anonymous fellowship and other treatment options among the American public. Directly and indirectly,
then, the NCEA provided much-needed assistance for alcoholics and
their families. Further, while debate remains regarding the precise nature of alcoholism as a clinical entity, Mann's efforts clearly transformed American attitudes towards problem drinking.

Mann deliberately modelled the NCEA on other public health organizations, maintaining that alcoholism was a disease like any other. She
insisted that alcoholism was a public health issue, not a moral question, frequently comparing it with tuberculosis and other illnesses. She
declared in 1946: "At the present time there are but two clinics for
drunkenness in the entire country; yet alcoholism is as prevalent a disease as either tuberculosis or cancer and one that, rightly handled, is
more easily treated. Our committee proposes to play the same part in
fighting the disease as the tuberculosis committee does in its field. We
are certain that when people in general become aware of the true state
of affairs they will help in stamping out this evil."[20]

Mann's fundamental goal was to lift the stigma that surrounded
alcoholism, so that the alcoholic would not be ashamed to seek help.
She offered herself as living proof of the NCEA message that alcoholics
can be helped and are worth helping. She insisted that she had come
forward to help others. As she explained in a 1946 radio address,

"Naturally I don't enjoy airing my personal life, but in this work it seems an important way of helping other people. Some of them might find hope thru my experience."[21] Indeed, much of the power of Mann's image came from her own identity as an alcoholic; she was seen as a living embodiment of the NCEA's message. As one newspaper account presented it, "Her mission is to drive into the public mind the scientific fact that alcoholism is not a vice or a sin but a disease; that the drinking habit is but a symptom of the disease; that this symptom can be overcome and its victims rehabilitated. There is no better example of how this can be done than Marty Mann, herself."[22] Cognizant of the importance of her image to the cause, Mann deliberately shaped her persona, especially with respect to issues of modernity, respectability, and sexuality, to advance her public health crusade.

As a number of scholars have shown, the medicalization of alcoholism in the United States occurred within a specific social, cultural, and political climate, shaped largely by Prohibition and its repeal. The cultural politics around alcohol in the United States were significantly gendered,[23] and Mann found that she needed to differentiate herself from the familiar image of the self-righteous and overly zealous temperance campaigner. For example, Carry Nation, a woman who had achieved notoriety through her turn-of-the-century "hatchetation" campaign to close saloons, was frequently evoked in newspaper stories about Mann.[24] One reporter wrote, "No Carri [sic] Nation, Mrs Mann, who is an ex-drinker herself, believes that a helping hand can do more to help alcoholics than all the axes in the country."[25] Similarly, a 1946 profile of Mann in the Dayton, Ohio, *Daily News* asked in its headline, "Prudish and Self-Righteous?" but replied with evident relief: "Nope, Reformed Drunk Is O.K."[26] Mann herself evoked Nation's crusade in order to distance herself from it, projecting instead a "rational," "scientific," and "modern" approach. She urged readers not to confuse her campaign with that of earlier temperance advocates: " 'But please don't get the idea that our committee is a crusading outfit that is going around the country with hatchets trying to smash up gin mills.' "[27]

In addition to differentiating her from temperance crusaders, Mann's self-consciously modern attitude towards social drinking simultaneously challenged social conventions that identified drinking as a masculine prerogative. A central tenet of the modern alcoholism paradigm was that alcoholics were fundamentally different from normal drinkers, for whom recreational drinking posed no threat to physical or psychological health. Yet gendered social customs continued to restrict this normalization of moderate drinking, in effect excluding women from the modern alcoholism paradigm. In discussing recreational drinking, Mann attempted, consciously or not, to remedy this imbalance. As she explained in the *New York Times Magazine* in 1946, "Those of us who are alcoholics are personal drys because we realize that we can't take liquor in moderation. But this does not mean that we believe that those who can should be deprived of it. For us it is drunkenness or dryness. For those who are not afflicted as we are, to drink or not to drink is not such as important question."[28] Here, Mann makes no reference to gender, presenting herself as simply another alcoholic and implying in the process that recreational drinking would be fine for her, even as a woman, if only she were not an alcoholic.

On the other hand, even as Mann sought to separate herself from earlier temperance crusaders, she took advantage of the traditional image of women as health educators that had been shaped to a significant extent by women's role in the temperance campaign – only now, according to Mann, rather than spreading propaganda against liquor, she was making use of scientific knowledge to eliminate the stigma surrounding the disease of alcoholism.[29] Mann even suggested that women were especially suited to such a campaign. Further, while the NCEA publicly touted its connection with the Yale Center (and the work of its male scientists), Mann drew heavily on established networks of club women in getting the NCEA off the ground. She explained her strategy thus: "With the help of a friend of mine who is the head of the Club Women's Service Bureau of the New York Herald-Tribune, I plan to speak to women's groups all over the country, wherever I can get a hearing." With the help of influential friends, Mann planned to create a "committee of women of standing, who are connected with all the leading women's organizations of the country, to start the ball rolling."[30] Mann did not restrict herself to women, even "women of standing," in her search for support. She addressed mixed-gender groups and welcomed the financial and practical support of male health-care professionals, scientists, and civic leaders. Yet her reliance on women is striking, especially given that alcoholism was viewed as a predominantly male affliction.

Building on networks of club women who could work behind the scenes while distancing herself from the likes of Carry Nation, Mann avoided one tactic that her prohibitionist predecessors had chosen – turning to the government for help. It may seem surprising that Mann, while urging Americans to take responsibility for alcoholism as a public health problem, did not seek government funding or support. This was perhaps because she modelled the NCEA after public health groups working on tuberculosis and cancer, where she found little precedent for seeking federal funding.[31] Some alcoholism treatment centres, especially by the 1950s, sought and received local and state support, but while the NCEA encouraged the establishment of clinics, the central focus of Mann's efforts remained educational – through lectures and information centres, to spread the word that alcoholism was a disease, to alleviate the stigma associated with the condition, and to urge problem drinkers to seek help.

There was an additional reason for Mann to avoid the question of government support. Temperance crusaders had achieved the ultimate government sanction in the form of a constitutional amendment, yet the "noble experiment" had ended, according to most observers, in fiasco. Most of the individuals involved in the modern alcoholism movement had no desire to repeat the experience. Indeed, during the immediate post-repeal years, the medical and scientific establishment sought to reclaim alcohol-related problems from the political and legal realm. The political legacy of Prohibition made government support for Mann's cause less likely; it also made her reluctant to identify too closely with the temperance campaign. She assumed that her role should be voluntary and educational, consistent with the female reform tradition and perhaps more agreeable to the wealthy women whose patronage she sought.

Clearly, gendered associations regarding women, alcohol, and reform persisted in American society during the twentieth century, and Mann used them to her advantage. In fact, in another illustration of Mann's complicated and contradictory identity as a modern woman, her very role as a woman reformer served to undercut any accusation of deviance that might have been made against her because of her alcoholism. According to the dominant psychiatric interpretation of the period, alcoholism in women – and in men – was the result of inadequate gender-role adjustment, with patterns of problematic sexuality frequently evident as well. In some ways, Mann seemed to fit this profile. She was, after all, a divorced "career girl" with no children. While her childlessness could have underscored her "deviance" in the midst of the reproductive consensus of mid-twentieth-century America, it also worked to make her status as an alcoholic more palatable. Observers might have viewed Mann's childlessness and her alcoholism as but two manifestations of underlying gender-identity deficiencies, but they could at least note with relief that however irresponsible and selfish Mann might have been when she drank heavily, she had not neglected children into the bargain. In fact, Mann's agitation for openness regarding alcoholism and for more facilities for alcoholism treatment was reminiscent of the efforts of women reformers of an earlier age who had directed what might have been viewed as their "maternal" energies towards social problems. Mann's campaign, considered in this tradition, looks like a form of social motherhood. While she was a career woman, Mann became a career woman with a cause, which made all the difference. Even as she sought to distance herself from women who had advocated temperance and prohibition, Mann was able to build on their legacy as a woman reformer, casting her activism as a campaign for public health. Her brand of social motherhood could be viewed as compensation for her biological childlessness.

SEXUALITY, SECRETS, AND SHAME

One issue that perhaps could not have been finessed so easily was Mann's sexuality, yet here too various elements of her public persona, combined with such circumstances as her position of class privilege and the simple passage of time, muted potential accusations of deviance. By the time she became a public figure, Mann's divorce was almost twenty years in the past, and it could easily be explained away as a result of her husband's alcoholism. Similarly, her "cause" could have been read as an appropriate substitute for marriage. Nevertheless, despite such mitigating factors, Mann's single status could have raised questions about her, given the common association between women's drinking and problematic sexuality. Revealingly, Mann's choice of title of address might have been an attempt to minimize her divorce and single status. "Mann" was her maiden name (she never publicly revealed her husband's name), to which she returned following her divorce, but she continued to use the title of "Mrs." In a letter, an old friend (who apparently had been long out of touch) expressed surprise over this version of her name and asked if Mann found it better in her work to be a Mrs; unfortunately, Mann's answer has not come to light.[31] Mann's silence regarding her sexuality and any relationships she might have had following her divorce contrasts with her almost belligerent outspokenness regarding her alcoholism, suggesting the limits of the disease model for issues involving sexuality and revealing much about stigma and shame, about gender and sexuality in mid-twentieth-century America.

According to mid-twentieth-century psychiatrists, male alcoholics frequently displayed homosexual leanings; lesbianism among female alcoholics, on the other hand, was rarely discussed in the psychiatric literature. Although it would be unwise to draw a firm conclusion from the available documents and rumours, some evidence does suggest that Mann enjoyed romantic, and possibly even sexual, relationships with women.[33] If this was indeed the case, the lack of attention to the sexual orientation of women alcoholics in the professional literature would have made it easier for Mann to deflect attention from this realm of her life. If she had such relationships, Mann's silence about her romantic life stands in contrast to her attempts to alleviate the stigma attached to alcoholism. On one level, the frankness of her private communications and public pronouncements about alcoholism and shame could have applied to homosexuality as well. Consider, for example, her declaration that "I have no more reason to be ashamed of having been a victim of alcoholism than I am ashamed of having once had tuberculosis."[34] The disease model of alcoholism, however, had a crucial limitation that prevented its application to homosexuality, a limitation that may suggest why Mann, even if she did have relationships with women, may not have considered herself a lesbian (or been able to claim such an identity).[35] Mann argued that her alcoholism should be viewed as a disease that was not her fault, not as a sinful behaviour wilfully chosen; but a woman who loved other women would not want to make a similar argument regarding lesbianism. In claiming an alcoholic identity, she also committed herself to abstinence from drink. In one newspaper profile, for example, she explained, " 'I am not ashamed of being an alcoholic ... I am proud to know that, being one, I have been given the power and the strength to give up drinking. I know it is forever.' "[36] If lesbianism were to be considered a disease like alcoholism, "recovery" would have to mean restraint.

In any case, the much more familiar stereotype about alcoholic women held that they were heterosexually promiscuous. Except for her failed marriage, Mann provided no information about any relationships with men. Her class privilege cushioned her, during her drinking years, from the kinds of problematic and even dangerous sexual experiences that befell many alcoholic women. The experience with the Irish bartender was in this context the exception that proved the rule, and it reveals that a woman could more easily claim recovery from alcoholism than from heterosexual promiscuity. Mann embraced the disease model of alcoholism because it alleviated the shame and stigma associated with excessive drinking. In sexual matters, however, redemption was more difficult, especially for women. Mann offered the incident with the Irish bartender as an illustration of the degradation she suffered as a result of her drinking, but she was careful to indicate that she had only skirted the edge of a sexual "fall." Indeed, as she portrayed the episode in the media, the encounter had inspired her to seek help while she could still be redeemed, before she took any sexual step that would have ruined her reputation irrevocably.

CONCLUSION

Marty Mann's experiences as an alcoholic and her public health campaign illuminate the complicated gendered processes involved in the medicalization of alcohol addiction. Mann had to negotiate persistent and sometimes conflicting social and cultural associations regarding gender and alcohol, religion and medicine, as she endeavoured to redefine alcoholism, holding that it was not a moral weakness but rather a disease. Assuming that a definition of alcoholism articulated in the language of modern medical science would alleviate the stigma that alcoholic women in particular faced, Mann fought to include women under the rubric of the disease model. Achieving her own recovery through Alcoholics Anonymous, Mann constructed for herself a gender-neutral identity as "alcoholic." With considerable bravery and savvy, she then offered her story as proof that alcoholics can be helped and are worth helping; she also provided a constant, if frequently implicit, challenge to the gendered nature of the disease model. Mann's campaign succeeded in reshaping American views regarding alcoholism. By the end of the twentieth century, the majority of Americans, including the medical establishment, had accepted the disease model of addiction, at least in some form. Yet alcoholic women continue to face a double standard, associated largely with reproductive roles. For them, the liberating potential that Mann envisioned as inherent in the modern alcoholism paradigm has not yet been realized.

NOTES

1 For more on the modern alcoholism movement and the modern alcoholism paradigm, see Ronald Roizen, "The American Discovery of Alcoholism, 1933–1939" (PHD dissertation, University of California at Berkeley, 1991); Bruce Holley Johnson, "The Alcoholism Movement in America: A Study in Cultural Innovation" (PHD dissertation, University of Illinois, 1973).

2 Consider, for example, media accounts of fetal alcohol syndrome and attempts to incarcerate pregnant addicts.

3 *Current Biography,* 1949, 37–9; "Biographies – Mrs Mann," Marty Mann Papers, Department of Special Collections, Syracuse University Library (hereafter referred to as MMP). Mann's father was the general manager of Marshall Field's department store. For overviews of Mann's life, see Floyd Miller, "What the Alcoholic Owes to Marty Mann," *Reader's Digest* 82 (January 1963): 173–80; "The Birth of the National Committee on Alcoholism," *Guideposts,* n.d., MMP.

4 "Transcript of Keynote Address," MMP. For more on tuberculosis during the early twentieth century, see Sheila M. Rothman, *Living in the Shadow of Death: Tuberculosis and the Social Experience of Illness in American History* (Baltimore: Johns Hopkins University Press 1994), especially Part 4.

5 Marty Mann, "Alcoholics Anonymous Official Tells of Life Plagued by Liquor," *Washington, D.C., Times-Herald,* 22 May 1945, MMP. See also

S.J. Woolf, "The Sick Person We Call an Alcoholic," *New York Times Magazine*, 21 April 1946, MMP; newspaper clipping from Wilmington, Del., *Daily Journal*, 22 February (no year), MMP; and "Nancy Craig Program – WJZ," MMP. For more on courtship rituals during this period, see Beth Bailey, *From Front Porch to Back Seat: Courtship in Twentieth-Century America* (Baltimore: Johns Hopkins University Press 1988). The dances and parties Mann described were clearly influenced by the conventions of her socio-economic class. See Mann, "Alcoholics Anonymous Official Tells of Life Plagued by Liquor." The implementation of Prohibition in 1920 brought no appreciable changes in the drinking habits of Mann and her family and friends, showing the differential impact of Prohibition by socio-economic class.

6 Woolf, "The Sick Person." See also " 'We the People,' CBS (May 1946)," MMP.

7 Mann, "Alcoholics Anonymous Official," for "sudden and shocking bankruptcy." For Mann's career/occupations, see *Current Biography*, 1949, which lists interior decorating, photography, freelance writing, and public relations (p. 37). See also program for Detroit Economic Club speech, 25 November 1946, MMP.

8 Marty Mann, "Mrs Mann Tells of Cheap Bar Life," *Washington, D.C., Times-Herald*, 23 May 1945, n.p., MMP.

9 Ibid.

10 Ibid. "Ex-Bar Roamer Warns Women," *Detroit Times*, 25 January [1948], MMP.

11 Kenneth Foree, "Woman Pioneer, but No Prairie Schooner," *Dallas News*, 7 February (no year), MMP. Another account of the incident appears in Alvin H. Goldstein, "Now She Can Leave It Alone," *St. Louis Post-Dispatch*, 26 November 1944, MMP.

12 The book that Mann saw was published as *Alcoholics Anonymous: The Story of How More Than One Hundred Men Have Recovered from Alcoholism* (New York: Works Publishing 1939). Mann's own story, from which this account is taken, appeared anonymously in the revised edition published in 1955 as *Alcoholics Anonymous: The Story of How Many Thousands of Men and Women Have Recovered from Alcoholism* (New York: Alcoholics Anonymous World Services, Inc. (1955), 227–8. Note that the revised subtitle in the 1955 edition included women. In other versions Mann described an even more turbulent scene. See Sidney Fields, "The Birth of the National Committee for Education on Alcoholism, Part 1: The Search," *Guideposts*, n.d., MMP. "Poison for Ladies," undated clipping, MMP; and Woolf, "The Sick Person We Call an Alcoholic."

13 "Poison for Ladies."

14 Marty Mann, "Mrs Mann Tells about Final Victory over Alcoholism," *Washington, D.C., Times-Herald*, 24 May 1945, MMP.

15 It is worth noting that AA thus challenges the divide that many alcoholism scholars have constructed between those who advocate "medical" and those who advocate "moral" (read "religious") models of alcoholism. See Ernest Kurtz, *Not-God: A History of Alcoholics Anonymous* (Center City, Minn.: Hazelden Educational Services 1979).

16 Mann, "Mrs Mann Tells about Final Victory over Alcoholism."

17 Woolf, "The Sick Person We Call an Alcoholic."

18 *Current Biography*, 1949, 38; program for Detroit Economic Club speech, 25 November 1946.

19 "NCA: History," "NCA–Historical," and "NCA–Constitution and By-Laws," MMP. "Committee for Education on Alcoholism Historic Event, Says Dwight Anderson," *AA Grapevine* 1, no. 5 (October 1944): n.p., MMP. See also Kurtz, *Not-God*, 117–19; and Johnson, "The Modern Alcoholism Movement," 266–75.

20 Woolf, "The Sick Person We Call an Alcoholic."

21 "Nancy Craig Program – WJZ," MMP.

22 "Poison for Ladies."

23 See Catherine Gilbert Murdock, "Domesticating Drink: Women and Alcohol in Prohibition America" (PhD dissertation, University of Pennsylvania 1995); Kenneth D. Rose, *American Women and the Repeal of Prohibition* (New York: New York University Press 1996).

24 For more on Nation, see Ernest H. Cherrington, *Standard Encyclopedia of the Alcohol Problem* (Westerville, Ohio: American Issue Publishing Co. 1928), 4: 1850–2; D. Leigh Colvin, *Prohibition in the United States* (New York: George H. Doran Co. 1926), 321–2; Herbert Ashbury, *The Great Illusion: An Informal History of Prohibition* (New York: Greenwood Press, 1968), 117–20. Many recent writers who regard Prohibition as a failure, even a tragic mistake, depict Nation with condescending language – for example, "Motivated by prurience and sexual nausea, she was part fraud, part fanatic, but not a total fool." Sean Dennis Cashman, *Prohibition: The Lie of the Land* (New York: Free Press 1981), ix.

25 Dorothy Jones, "500,000 U.S. Women Victims of Alcoholism, Speaker Says," *Detroit News* (25 November 1946), MMP; "Women Drinkers," *Erie Times*, 2 December (no year), MMP.

26 Newspaper clipping, Dayton, Ohio, *Daily News*, 30 April 1946, MMP.

27 Woolf, "The Sick Person We Call an Alcoholic."

28 Ibid.

29 "Memo on: National Committee for Education on Alcoholism," MMP.

30 Typed fragment and "Memo on: NCEA," MMP.

31 Barron Lerner, MD, PhD, personal communication with author.

32 NR to Mann, n.d. [1948], MMP.

33 See, for example, J to Mann, 15 August 1959, reference to Mann living with a woman friend with whom she owned a summer home ("Mrs Marty

Mann, Ex-Alcoholic"), MMP; references to "Priscilla" throughout personal correspondence, all in MMP; and Ron Roizen, PhD, personal communication with author, May 1997.

34 Mann to NR, 21 January 1947, MPP.

35 Of course, the question of labelling women who had relationships with other women is extremely complicated and has attracted significant attention in the secondary literature. See, for example, Lillian Faderman, *Odd Girls and Twilight Lovers: A History of Lesbian Life in Twentieth-Century America* (New York: Columbia University Press 1991); Leila J. Rupp, "Imagine My Surprise: Women's Relationships in Historical Perspective," *Frontiers* 5 (Fall 1980): 61–70; and especially the classic essay by Carroll Smith-Rosenberg, "The Female World of Love and Ritual," in her *Disorderly Conduct: Visions of Gender in Victorian America* (New York: Oxford University Press 1985): 53–76.

36 "Poison for Ladies."

5

Marketing Menopause: Science and the Public Relations of Premarin

Alison Li

One of the top-selling prescription drugs in the United States and Canada at the close of the twentieth century was Premarin, the trade name of a blend of estrogens used to treat the symptoms of menopause. The Montreal drug company Ayerst, McKenna and Harrison first introduced Premarin to the market in 1942. Although the drug is more than sixty years old and its patent expired over thirty years ago, it is the flagship product of Wyeth-Ayerst, a subsidiary of American Home Products (Ayerst merged with Wyeth in 1986), and possesses some two-thirds of the market share in menopausal drugs in the United States.[1] In 2000 the Premarin family of drug products brought Wyeth-Ayerst close to $1.9 billion in global sales.[2]

In their studies of medical technologies, sociologists Susan Bell and Nelly Oudshoorn challenge the traditional linear model of drug development in which it is assumed that a new drug is tested and its purpose defined before it is taken to the marketplace. Instead, they suggest that technologies are often still undergoing the process of definition as they are adopted.[3] Over the past half-century, the manufacturers of Premarin (first Ayerst, then Wyeth-Ayerst) have displayed a remarkable ability to refashion the product, adapting it to changing scientific evidence, social and political contexts, and regulatory environments.

Scholars such as Susan Bell and anthropologist Margaret Lock have mapped the historically and culturally contingent constructions of menopause. They have critiqued the medical characterization of menopause as a "deficiency disease," one caused by failing ovaries and requiring hormone replacement therapy.[4] This medical construction has,

however, taken on different shadings in different periods. In the 1940s
and 1950s, Premarin suited the medical model of menopause as a deficiency disease requiring hormone replacement therapy. In the 1960s
and 1970s, such books as *Feminine Forever*[5] promoted estrogen as a way
to smooth out the physical and psychic bumps of the "change of life."
By the late 1980s, sales of Premarin soared when it began to be pitched
as a preventive treatment for osteoporosis, thus becoming part of a
healthy woman's lifestyle not only during menopause but also potentially for the remainder of her life. In the 1990s, the rationale for its use
grew to include prevention of heart disease and possibly Alzheimer's
disease. In recent years, health-care policy analysts began to consider estrogen replacement therapy (ERT) in socio-economic terms, evaluating
the cost-effectiveness of widescale estrogen use.

The manufacturer of Premarin has endured challenges from many
directions. It has met with difficult scientific questions regarding the
link between estrogen use and cancer; in the 1940s, it faced competition from its successful rival, the synthetic estrogen DES; and beginning in the 1960s and 1970s, feminist health activists challenged the
characterization of menopause as a medical condition requiring pharmaceutical intervention. In recent years, the voices of animal-rights
activists have been added to the mix; in a well-publicized campaign,
celebrities such as Mary Tyler Moore have charged cruelty in the treatment of the horses used in the production of Premarin. The drug company has also fought the encroachment of generic drug manufacturers
into its lucrative market. While it is important to emphasize the agency
of women as patients and the reciprocal nature of the interactions
between patients and physicians, laboratory researchers, and drug
companies, it is also imperative that we take into account the increasing sophistication and breadth of the drug-promotion techniques employed by the pharmaceutical industry, an industry that has
successfully adopted, perhaps even subverted, the language and forums of women's self-empowerment.

In this paper, I explore the interrelation of scientific evidence and
the commercial promotion of Premarin and examine the shaping
and reshaping of the drug's profile and public relations over the
course of its more than fifty years of history. In the early period, the
image of dispassionate science served as a general source of authority.
Later, scientific information was framed in terms of personal empowerment and responsibility. More recently, the model of scientific
thinking is introduced through the language of statistics, probability,
and risk assessment. Ironically, Wyeth has also come to argue that
the key to the safety and efficacy of Premarin is hidden in ambiguous
scientific data.

"A REMEDIAL AGENT FOR CERTAIN FEMININE DISORDERS"

From the very beginning, scientific credentials were key to the promotion of Premarin. Premarin first emerged out of the collaboration between Ayerst, McKenna and Harrison, a Montreal firm founded in 1925, and J.B. Collip, a leading biochemist and hormone researcher at McGill University in Montreal.[6] Collip and his group were engaged in a broad-based program of research into hormones during the 1930s, a period that has been characterized as an endocrine "gold rush," as many groups of investigators hurried to isolate and describe the products of the glands.[7]

Premarin's predecessor was a hormone substance known as "Emmenin," first extracted by Collip and his group in 1930 and described as "a remedial agent for certain feminine disorders."[8] Emmenin became popular because it was shown to be effective in the treatment of several types of menstrual disorder (menopause was only one of several conditions for which it was used) and because it was one of the first orally active estrogens, distributed in the palatable form of sugar-coated tablets.[9] (Although other forms of estrogen had some degree of oral activity, most were administered by injection.)[10] In 1934 Ayerst entered the much larger U.S. market, the company's competitive edge provided by the fact that it had been able to overcome the prohibitive price of raw placentas, having developed a good supply of them in Montreal.[11]

By 1939, the advent of an inexpensive new synthetic estrogen – Diethylstilbestrol (DES) – challenged Emmenin's dominance. In the early days of its existence, DES seemed a remarkable boon. It was some twenty times more potent and much less expensive to produce than natural estrogens, and it became the first product widely used for estrogen replacement therapy in the treatment of menopause and a variety of other gynaecological conditions.[12] Spurred to search for a cheaper source for estrogens, Ayerst developed a method of extracting a potent, orally active blend of estrogens from pregnant mare urine, giving rise to the name PREgnant MARe urINe. Introduced into the market in 1942, Premarin quickly became many times more profitable than Emmenin and catapulted Ayerst to the status of a large, successful company. Ayerst was purchased by the large U.S. firm American Home Products the following year.[13]

Invoking the authority of science and the credibility of academic research, Emmenin and Premarin bottles bore labels indicating that they had been standardized in Collip's laboratory. The Ayerst management credited the collaboration with Collip with "creating a confidence in

our firm that we would not have otherwise enjoyed." They acknowledged their debt to the scientist with life-long royalty payments not
only on Emmenin, but interestingly, on Premarin as well, a product in
which he had had no direct role.[14]

"FEMININE FOREVER"

In the 1920s, science-based pharmaceutical companies promoted female sex hormones for a wide range of indications, starting from a restricted group of menstrual disorders and extending, by the late 1920s,
to include the treatment of menopause, infertility, problems of the
genitals, psychiatric conditions such as schizophrenia and depression,
dermatological diseases such as eczema, and even diseases of the joints.
By the early 1930s, some pharmaceutical firms, such as the Dutch company Organon, were actively seeking to establish female sex hormones
as a specific treatment for menopause by instigating large clinical trials
involving older women and examining the effect of therapy on the
cluster of symptoms associated with menopause, including high blood
pressure, increased heart rate, headaches, and depression.[15]

After its introduction in 1942, Premarin was taken up by researchers
and clinicians as "a dependably helpful agent in giving complete relief
from the common autonomic, emotional and mental complaints of the
menopausal syndrome."[16] Most gynaecologists, however, did not interpret menopause itself as a disease state. Susan Bell examined question-
naires sent by pharmaceutical manufacturers of DES in 1941 to clinical
investigators during the period before the drug was released for sale. In
replying to the question "In treating the menopause, do you consider
the control of symptoms the objective desired?" some physicians
seemed to challenge the assumption that menopause was pathological.
One answered: "I do not treat menopause. I do treat the patient with
menopausal syndrome. Hormone therapy is only adjunctive in our re-
gime. Only about 35–40% need it!" Another replied: "The control of
symptoms is the objective desired by the patient and since the menopause is not a disease the physician need not go further in providing
adequate treatment."[17] Gynaecology textbooks popular into the 1950s
continued to indicate that menopause was a normal phase of life and
advised that most women required no treatment at all. Margaret Lock
argues, however, that "the acceptance by a good number of physicians
of an apparently simple idea, namely, that the unpleasant symptoms of
a minority of menopausal women could be eliminated by boosting
their declining estrogen levels for a few months or at most for a year or
two," resulted in the reconceptualization of menopause as a deficiency
disease, something that was to have powerful ramifications.[18]

Authors Kathleen MacPherson, Barbara Seaman, and Gideon Seaman have traced Ayerst's skilful deployment of resources in promoting Premarin to professionals and potential customers during the 1960s and 1970s. In addition to targeting physicians and nurses through established educational and promotional channels, the company reached out to the general public. From the 1960s to 1970, Ayerst funded the Information Center on the Mature Woman in New York City, whose director was Sandra Gorney, author of *After Forty* (1973). The centre provided information to magazines and newspapers and supplied speakers for radio and television, all promoting estrogen replacement therapy. MacPherson notes that Gorney's words were widely used but "rarely with any indication that the source was a drug company."[19]

In the 1960s, one of the most vocal proponents of estrogen therapy was gynaecologist Robert Wilson. He and his wife, Thelma Wilson, a nurse, co-authored "The Fate of the Nontreated Postmenopausal Woman: A Plea for the Maintenance of Adequate Estrogen from Puberty to the Grave," a research article that described in extremely colourful terms the experience of the aging woman. They characterized menopausal women as sad, miserable creatures, no longer whole women. Ayerst set up the Wilson Foundation, which supported research into aging, and funded Robert Wilson's research. As part of the foundation's work, Wilson published *Feminine Forever*, a popular book that argued that all menopausal women, except possibly those with breast cancer, should be treated with estrogen and progestogens for the rest of their lives.[20]

The sales of estrogen therapy drugs almost quadrupled between 1963 and 1973, making estrogen one of the top five prescription drugs in the United States with annual sales figures of nearly $70 million. A survey in Washington in 1973 estimated that 51 per cent of women had taken estrogen for at least three months and that the median use was ten years. According to Kaufert and McKinlay, prior to the early 1970s, neither physicians nor epidemiologists had shown much interest in menopause or estrogen therapy, there were no specific government guidelines for its use, and the pharmaceutical industry had more or less had a free hand in promoting the drug directly to physicians or indirectly to consumers through popular media.[21]

Examining the *New England Journal of Medicine* and the *Journal of the American Medical Association*, Kaufert and McKinlay note that by the early 1970s the "whiff of quackery" associated with the Wilsons' over-enthusiastic endorsement of estrogen had been dispelled and there was a general tone in these journals that estrogen was both safe and legitimate. Menopause was defined as a deficiency disease with potentially serious health implications, and estrogen treatment was the physician's logical choice for therapy. True, it was implied, patients sometimes foolishly demanded estrogen, stimulated by its character-ization in popular media as a "youth drug," but physicians could be sure that hormone therapy was a reasonable option.

This situation changed when laboratory researchers began report-ing a possible link between estrogen and endometrial cancer and breast cancer. Their findings were vigorously debated within the clini-cal and research communities, and these debates, were quickly picked up by the press.[22] The U.S. Food and Drug Administration deter-mined that the evidence implicating estrogen as a carcinogen seemed strong, and it thus ruled in 1976 that manufacturers of estrogen had to include a package insert warning of the risks. This requirement had a marked impact on the sales of estrogen: they declined by 18 per cent in 1975–76 and a further 10 per cent in 1976–77. Ayerst at-tempted to counter the effect of the insert by issuing a circular that advised physicians that Premarin was safe, and the pharmaceutical in-dustry asserted that the requirement for the package insert was un-constitutional. A stream of pro-estrogen articles, moreover, appeared in the free medical press, which was controlled by the pharmaceutical industry.

Kaufert and McKinlay demonstrate that clinicians joined the phar-maceutical industry in their battle. The American College of Obstet-rics and Gynecology, with the formal support of the American Cancer Society and the American College of Internal Medicine, contended that the release of information to patients contravened the medical profession's right to control access to medical knowledge. The ability of patients to have access to risk information – particularly the risk of an iatrogenic illness (an illness inadvertently caused by a medical treat-ment) – challenged the physician's authority to decide what to disclose to a patient and how to balance risks and benefits.

Kaufert and McKinlay argue that the debate over estrogen points out the differences in the perspectives of laboratory researchers and clinicians: to the researchers, estrogen was of interest as a potential cause of cancer; to clinicians, not only was estrogen a legitimate ther-apy and one demanded by their patients, but, "once menopause was defined as a deficiency disease … it became an obligation."[23]

"LIVING SMART"

Estrogen therapy began to be rehabilitated in the 1980s. The connec-tion between estrogen replacement therapy and the prevention of osteoporosis had begun to be demonstrated in the 1970s through a se-ries of decisive clinical trials. This opened huge new markets to Ayerst, since Premarin use would no longer be limited to women undergoing menopause; it could potentially be prescribed to post-menopausal women for the remainder of their lives. In 1989 the U.S. FDA approved Premarin as a preventive for osteoporosis.[24] In the late 1980s, as medical protocol for osteoporosis began to focus on prevention, Premarin became one of Ayerst's best-sellers. In the 1990s, additional clinical trials indicated that estrogen could be used in the treatment as well as in the prevention of osteoporosis.[25]

The public campaign became increasingly insistent in the United States, where direct-to-consumer (DTC) advertising has grown at a tremendous rate since 1985.[26] DTC advertising expenditures for prescription drugs were about $90 million in 1990, more than $200 million by 1994, and more than $700 million in 1996. It is noteworthy that advertisements are generally directed at the large market of healthy people. In 1998 drug companies spent more on advertising to consumers than on promoting drugs to health professionals – $665 million versus $462 million.[27] In that year, American Home Products spent $37 million in direct-to-consumer advertising for Premarin, making it the ninth most advertised prescription drug. Antihistamines such as Claritin and Allegra, the smoking-cessation drug Zyban, Propecia for hair loss, and Pravachol and Zocor for lowering cholesterol commanded more advertising dollars, but Premarin ranked right behind Eli Lilly's Evista (osteoporosis) at $38.9 million and Prozac at $37.5 million in consumer advertising expenditures.[28]

Joel Lexchin, physician and drug industry critic, argues that there are two reasons for the shift to DTC advertising in the United States: first, consumers are increasingly demanding access to medical information, and second, more U.S. patients are receiving care through managed-care organizations. In managed-care organizations, there is an overall budget ceiling. Physicians' options for prescribing treatments are often limited by organizational rules about how certain conditions are to be managed and by restricted access to certain drugs. The managers of pharmaceutical benefits in these organizations generally try to contain drug costs by negotiating substantial discounts with manufacturers, limiting access to new and potentially expensive drugs, and requiring mandatory generic substitutions. In the earlier model of health delivery in which physicians operated on a fee-for-service basis and were essentially small businesses, drug companies found it adequate to market directly to physicians. In this new health-care delivery system, manufacturers have resorted to DTC advertising to stimulate demand and to bypass the power of the managed-care organizations. Lexchin cites studies that demonstrate that consumer behaviour is altered by DTC advertising; certain DTC advertising is shown to be effective because it increases demand for a drug by driving patients to doctors' offices.[29] In Canada, patients do not pay for the drugs they use while in hospital but most pay at least a part of the cost of the pharmaceuticals they use outside the hospital, the actual amount depending on whether they are covered through private drug plans through their employers or (in the case of seniors and people on public assistance) through provincial drug benefit plans. In many cases, private and provincial drug plans specify that generic rather than brand name versions be used if they are available.

By the early 1990s, competition in the industry had resulted in an increase in both the sophistication of promotional techniques and the sheer quantity of promotional activities engaged in by pharmaceutical firms. Barbara Mintzes identifies a number of important trends in pharmaceutical promotional spending, including the sponsorship of professional medical seminars and the formation of non-profit patient advocacy groups, where the fact (and potential influence) of pharmaceutical funding is not always made transparent.[30] According to Gilbert and Chetley, the funding of patient groups is favoured by drug firms for a number of reasons: companies can spread awareness of, and create demand for, a new drug at the pre-launch stage through these groups; an endorsement by a patient group is perceived to be more credible than one coming directly from a company; patient groups can pave the way for drugs by lobbying government for fewer controls on drug licensing and pricing; and patient groups are able to reach consumers directly.[31] An important intermediary in this process is the public relations firm. PR firms can serve as matchmakers, helping drug industry personnel form and make use of partnerships with patient groups.[32]

In 1982 Ayerst began a new public relations campaign – run by the public relations firm Burston-Marsteller – aimed at promoting public awareness of osteoporosis among the 77 per cent of women who, according to the PR firm's survey, had never heard of the disease. Within three years, the campaign had succeeded in meeting its stated goals. Burston-Marsteller had launched an extensive media effort through radio, television, and popular magazines. It had selected a national women's health association, the Nurses Association of the American College of Obstetricians and Gynecologists, as a way to educate health professionals and the public. The PR firm offered two tiers of seminars, one for the association's nurse members and the second for consumer education. Finally, the public relations firm successfully lobbied in the U.S. Congress for a bill to create an Osteoporosis Awareness Week; the bill was passed in Congress and the Senate in 1984. Burston-Marsteller also paid for a multi-city tour by three of the medical experts who had contributed to the key report on osteoporosis issuing from the

National Institutes of Health Consensus Development Conference. The report was of critical importance in that it included osteoporosis within the menopausal syndrome and identified hormone replacement therapy and calcium as the two treatments of choice.[33]

In the early 1990s, scientific and media attention moved to focus on the link between estrogen replacement therapy and the reduction of the risk of heart disease in women. Later in the decade, the connection between estrogen and Alzheimer's disease began to attract interest as well. Some clinical trials showed a 53 per cent lower incidence of Alzheimer's disease among estrogen users than among non-users, and others showed some short-term improvement in dementia or the slowing of cognitive decline.[34]

By the mid-1990s, lower and lower age groups of women began to be portrayed as potential subjects of hormone replacement therapy. Official recommendations for hormone replacement therapy in perimenopausal women were limited and generally restricted to the use of progesterone. A Health Canada committee in 1995 advised that hormone replacement therapy might be considered appropriate in some very limited cases of perimenopausal women (defined as aged 45–55, before the onset of menopause) who were experiencing specific symptoms, namely chronic failure to ovulate, possibly resulting in periods that were irregular in duration and flow.[35]

In the popular press, however, the net was cast far more widely. In the late 1990s, a number of popular health books turned to the subject of perimenopause, characterizing it as a stage in life that should be of concern to women as young as thirty-five and warning, "Menopause begins silently, before its symptoms." New York Times health columnist Jane Brody advised women to watch for symptoms that they might not associate with menopause, such as insomnia, difficulty in concentrating, poor memory, reduced stamina, itchy or dry skin, wrinkling, urinary incontinence or frequency, vaginal dryness, headaches, declining libido, and mood swings. Pointing out the risk of heart disease and osteoporosis if the condition were left untreated, Brody contended, "During the approximately 15 years of perimenopause, you have a good shot at averting the adverse changes these two conditions can wreak on your body later in life." She noted that a growing number of gynaecologists believed that women should begin hormone replacement years before they cease to have regular menstrual periods.[36]

In 1996 Wyeth-Ayerst hired the public relations firm Yecies Associates to develop a campaign called "Living Smart" to promote the message that hormone replacement therapy should be considered part of a smart woman's healthy lifestyle. This campaign, as described in the language of public relations, was "a combination of specifically-targeted,

hard-hitting corporate and community outreach programs and ancil-
lary materials" to raise visibility and increase usage of Premarin as a
preventive and prescriptive treatment for osteoporosis. The target audience was women over thirty-five who could be reached through a
campaign directed at "large corporations with mixed gender emphasis,
alumni associations, and women's organizations." The Living Smart
campaign was intended to erase some of the negative issues associated
with aging and focus on what women could do to stay healthy after age
thirty-five. Yecies reported that the outreach programs attracted large
audiences of women in peer-group situations, and claimed that by targeting peer groups, the PR firm had been able to overcome "the denial
and resistance usually associated with health problems." So that the
promotion of Living Smart would continue after the sessions, Yecies
made free exercise videos available at every conference and offered opportunities to win sessions with nutritionists or personal trainers. The
campaigners developed mailing lists from the programs and sent every
program attendee a booklet on osteoporosis. The campaign objective
was to set the stage for the women to ask their physicians about estrogen replacement therapy. The firm was able to report that it had
exceeded its expectations: 80 per cent of the participants went on to
request further information from their physicians, surpassing the campaign goal of 50 per cent.[37]

Television advertising for prescription drugs grew by 107.6 per cent
between 1994 and 1998 compared with a 28.7 per cent increase in
print advertising.[38] In the United States, DTC advertising is regulated
under section 9(1) of the U.S. Food and Drug Act, which states: "No
person shall label, package, treat, process, sell or advertise any drug in
a manner that is false, misleading or deceptive or is likely to create an
erroneous impression regarding its composition, merit or safety."[39]
Wyeth-Ayerst has been among the firms found in violation of the code.
In 1999 the FDA demanded that Wyeth-Ayerst withdraw a television ad-
vertisement that, in the FDA's judgment, presented the risks and benefits of Premarin in a misleading manner. According to FDA advertising
standards, risks and benefits are to be presented in a "reasonably comparable" and balanced way. The FDA charged Wyeth-Ayerst with making "broad and ambiguous health claims for Premarin" and suggesting
benefits that had "yet to be substantiated or even identified." In the
television ad, the risks of Premarin were presented against a visual
background of multiple, distracting images and activities, while the
benefits were presented clearly and against a background without any
distractions.[40]

In Canada, direct-to-consumer advertising has been prohibited under the Food and Drugs Act since 1949. The Pharmaceutical Manufacturing Association of Canada (PMAC) Code of Marketing Practices

covers most forms of drug promotion aimed at doctors, including the activities of sales representatives who pay personal visits to doctors to promote drugs. Included as well are conferences and continuing medical education sponsored by companies. In Canada, industry sponsors are allowed to be involved in developing the agenda for educational symposia and choosing speakers. A 1997 FDA guideline no longer allows this in the United States.[41] Joel Lexchin argues that there are serious weaknesses in the way that the PMAC Code is enforced because of the potential for conflict between the commercial objectives of the industry and ethical and scientific goals.[42]

A new public relations battle facing Wyeth in recent years is the animal-rights campaign against the manufacture of Premarin. The pregnant mares' urine (PMU) is today produced from an estimated seventy-five thousand horses at some five hundred PMU farms in North America, with the vast majority located in the Prairie provinces of Western Canada. There are about thirty PMU farms in North Dakota, near the Canadian border, and several more have recently been established in Minnesota. Almost all PMU farms are under an exclusive contract to provide pregnant mares' urine to Wyeth-Ayerst Laboratories.[43] In their vocal campaign, animal-rights groups, including People for the Ethical Treatment of Animals (PETA), have made use of the Internet to condemn the treatment of the mares and their foals on these farms. The agribusinesses have refuted these charges on their own websites. The North American Equine Ranching Information Council website provides an online slideshow of life on a PMU ranch, highlighting the "unique relationship between agriculture and medicine for over 58 years" and describing Premarin as a "medication developed by a Canadian pharmaceutical company in collaboration with McGill University." Emphasis is placed on the fact that many of the horse farms are independent and belong to second- and third-generation horse ranchers.[44]

"THE RIGHT TO ASK FOR THE BRAND NAME"

In the late 1980s and 1990s, Wyeth-Ayerst began deploying scientific evidence in its competition with generic drug manufacturers. Ironically, here it was the ambiguity in experimental evidence – the fact that the function of Premarin was not precisely known – that became the company's key argument for Premarin's superiority to generic drugs. The regulatory situation in the United States diverged from that in Canada.

In the United States, a month's supply of .625 mg doses of Premarin costs $16.54, and the generic manufacturer Duramed argues that the cost of the generic drug would be about 30 per cent less.[45] A

Wyeth-Ayerst Canada brochure, produced for distribution to patients who've been prescribed Premarin, carries this warning: "Depending on which province you live in, a pharmacist may substitute it with a generic synthetic alternative … without telling you. *You have the right to ask for the brand name.* Premarin costs under $1.35 a month more than the synthetic generic alternative – that's less than the cost of a large coffee!" In explaining that women should ask for Premarin, the brochure stresses terms like "original" and "natural" (as opposed to the generics, which are described as synthetic) and emphasizes the over fifty-year history of Premarin use.[46]

When Premarin was first introduced to the market in 1942, it was approved for treating menopausal symptoms and related conditions. It was known to contain two estrogens – estrone and equilin. The only requirement for drug approval was that the drug be shown to be safe and that its promotion not be misleading. In 1970 the U.S. Pharmacopeia set out compendial standards for conjugated estrogens, describing Premarin as containing two forms of estrogen: sodium estrone sulfate and sodium equilin sulfate.

Amendments to the Food, Drug and Cosmetics Act in 1962 required that manufacturers demonstrate that their products were effective as well as safe. The FDA published a Federal Register notice announcing that Premarin and a number of other estrogen products approved before the 1962 amendments were shown to be effective in the treatment of menopausal symptoms. At the time, there was little information on the detailed composition of Premarin or the pharmacological activity of its components. Instead, the standards were set on the assumption that the different forms of estrogen had a similar effect and the potency of the overall mixture was a sum of the activity of all its estrogens. Therefore, the identity of any particular ingredient, particularly those present in trace quantities, was not considered critical. It was also believed that small differences in estrogenic potency between Premarin and generic copies would not be clinically meaningful when it came to the effect that they had on bone mineral density.[47]

In the 1980s and 1990s, Wyeth-Ayerst began to argue against the licensing of generic versions of Premarin in the U.S. market, marshalling scientific evidence (often ambiguous) of Premarin's superiority. Wyeth-Ayerst pulled together a strong lobby in its effort to keep the generics out, and it included a number of women's groups. The Business and Professional Women/USA acknowledged that it had received $65,000 for its foundation from the company.[48]

The firm challenged the U.S. FDA's approval of its generic competitors, Duramed Pharmaceuticals and Zenith Laboratories, in 1988, submitting data indicating that the generics were not "bioequivalent" to

Premarin, a natural substance. This led in 1991 to the complete withdrawal of generic forms of conjugated estrogens in the United States, leaving Premarin the only version available.

The dispute focused on two issues: the composition of Premarin and the dissolution characteristics. The claim was made that the generic products, synthetic estrogens made from plant sources, were in a sense "too" pure. Premarin, a natural animal product, contains a blend of five different estrogens, plus a number of trace ingredients. The synthetics, the firm argued, might contain the two ingredients that are deemed "active" – sodium estrone sulfate and sodium equilin sulfate – but lacked many other trace ingredients (delta [8,9] dehydroestrone sulfate [DHES], for example) that Wyeth-Ayerst contended *might* be essential to Premarin's action. They also argued that the generics were absorbed into the bloodstream faster and therefore might not be as effective. Furthermore, Premarin had been widely used for over fifty years. The company claimed that millions of women might be put at risk if allowed to take a generic that was not identical and did not have the same long history.[49]

Behind this argument was a purported ambiguity about how Premarin works. Since generic drug manufacturers do not have to repeat the same clinical tests that the innovator drug companies do, they have to demonstrate that their products contain the same active ingredients. But if the identity of these active ingredients is in dispute, it might be argued that generic manufacturers cannot fulfil this requirement.

Part of the dispute was based on emerging scientific evidence that not all estrogens have the same effect on the same tissues. Some are more active in specific tissues and organs, such as breast, uterus, or bone. New analytic techniques had also allowed the further characterization of the chemical components of Premarin. The component in dispute, delta (8,9) dehydroestrone sulfate, identified in 1975, was found to make up only about 4.4 per cent of the estrogens in Premarin. However, more recent pharmacokinetic studies provided the unexpected result that the metabolites of DHES were in a significant concentration in blood plasma – they made up about 34 per cent of the concentration of estrone and equilin together – opening up the possibility that DHES, while making up only 4.4 per cent of the estrogens in the tablet, might generate a significant pharmacological effect.[50]

The FDA's Fertility and Maternal Health Drugs Advisory Committee deliberated in 1989–90 but was not able to arrive at a consensus about whether any substances other than the two main estrogens were to be considered active ingredients. In 1991 the FDA's Generic Drugs Advisory Committee endorsed the proposal to include three additional estrogens in Premarin as concomitant components, and in 1992 the U.S. Pharmacopeia monograph was amended to reflect this recommendation. In 1994 Wyeth-Ayerst filed a citizen petition requesting that delta (8,9) dehydroestrone sulfate be designated a concomitant component and that no generic versions lacking this substance be approved. In July 1995 the Fertility and Maternal Health Drugs Advisory Committee again concluded that there was not enough data to determine whether components other than the first two active ingredients must be present to ensure the same level of efficacy and safety. The FDA's Center for Drug Evaluation and Research (CDER) Ad Hoc Working Group on Conjugated Estrogens deliberated on the composition and clinical effects of conjugated estrogens in 1996–97 and filed a report in May 1997. It argued that newer clinical studies indicated that it was crucial that the active components of Premarin be adequately characterized, especially in relation to the effect of Premarin on bone mineral density. A CDER document explains: "For approval of a generic product, the legal and scientific test is not whether the generic product would result in the same clinical effects as the innovator, but rather *whether the active ingredients in the generic product are the same.*"[51]

The director of the CDER, Dr Janet Woodcock, commented, "For a drug used by this many American women for this amount of time, it's shocking how little is known about it."[52] CDER announced that it would not approve synthetic generic forms of Premarin because "the active ingredients in Premarin have not yet been confidently defined" and therefore synthetic generic versions could not be shown to have the same active ingredients.[53]

When Wyeth-Ayerst took this argument to Canada's drug regulatory body, however, it backfired. Following the withdrawal of generic conjugated estrogens in the United States, Wyeth-Ayerst raised similar concerns about the sale of generics in Canada, arguing that since there was a potential for lack of efficacy and an increased risk of endometrial cancer, the continued marketing of generics posed a potential health hazard for Canadian women. The company contended that generic manufacturers should be required to conduct clinical studies on the safety and efficacy of their projects and to submit a New Drug Submission.[54]

The Ad Hoc Advisory Committee on Conjugated Estrogens, formed by the Therapeutic Products Directorate, deliberated on the issue through 1991. ICN Canada Limited, a Montreal generic drug manufacturer, pointed out that the version of Premarin marketed in Canada differed from that sold in the United States in an important regard: the Canadian version had almost the same absorption rate as the generics called into question by Wyeth-Ayerst in the United States. One

financial analyst commented that if Wyeth-Ayerst's claims against the
U.S. generics were correct, then in fact Premarin had "been producing
unsafe plasma levels in [Canadian] women for years ... The Canadians
called their bluff." The committee rejected Wyeth-Ayerst's claim and
allowed the generics to remain on the market in Canada.[55]

In contrast to the U.S. situation, generic conjugated estrogens had
been on the Canadian market since 1963, establishing a long history
of safety and efficacy. Health Canada's Therapeutic Products Directorate issued a statement calling for the establishment of a "uniquely
Canadian Standard with Canadian specifications." Since 1982, the
CSD (Canadian Standard Drug) has required a third component,
17-dihydroequilin, which had not been required in the U.S. Pharmacopeia. In 1997 the directorate proposed an amendment to the Food
and Drug Regulations that would see the continuation of the requirement of the three components and the adoption of the more modern
analytic methods required in the U.S. Pharmacopeia. The directorate
noted that "because the rate of release of estrogen does not appear to
be significant for safety and efficacy effects," Canadian standards for
these tests would continue to apply.[56]

THE ECONOMIC VALUE OF PREVENTION

The newest sphere in which drug manufacturers are supporting research is the socio-economic impact of hormone replacement therapy.[57] As Margaret Lock points out, menopause in the late twentieth
century became linked with the expensive diseases of later life, the
ones that account for the bulk of health-care expenditures in industrial societies and are thus of greatest concern for public policy.[58]

Lock reports that in the early 1990s the pharmaceutical industry was
lobbying the U.S. government to consider estrogen replacement therapy necessary for the health of all women forty years of age and over.
The analogy it used in justifying ERT (and its use for the duration of a
woman's life) was no longer the analogy of insulin and diabetes.
Instead, the industry compared ERT with compulsory vaccination,
though with the key difference that this treatment was not a one-time
affair, but rather one that had to be maintained for decades.[59]

The interest that the drug industry has in this new direction might
be indicated by an international workshop sponsored by Ciba-Geigy in
Basel in March 1993 on the medical-economic aspects of hormone replacement therapy. Ciba-Geigy was a competitor of Wyeth-Ayerst's in
the estrogen market, introducing the hormone in a transdermal patch
that provides a steady low dose of the hormone through the skin.[60] Ar-
gentinian clinical researcher J.A. Tieffenberg, a participant in the Basel

workshop, argued that the social and economic impact of menopause was largely underestimated. He contended that menopause could no longer be considered "a minor problem affecting women for a few years only, controlled easily with symptomatic treatment." Furthermore, it could not be considered a problem only in the developed world, as contemporary projections estimated that by the year 2000, 12 per cent of the world population would be women aged forty-five and over and that 300 million of these women would be from less-developed countries. He concluded there could be a number of economic justifications for the use of estrogen in transdermal patch form.[61]

CONCLUSION

Almost sixty years after Premarin's introduction, Wyeth-Ayerst has proven itself capable of great agility in its deployment of the evidence, the ambiguities, and the aura of science, beginning with Ayerst's close association with Collip's laboratory in the 1940s. The product was first framed as a boon to sufferers of specific menopausal symptoms but was later portrayed as a tool of femininity and then as a preventive health measure. Its potential market expanded from the relatively small group of women experiencing menopausal symptoms over the course of four to five years to the vast market of peri- and post-menopausal women who might potentially take the drug from age thirty-five until the end of their lives. Through several decades, Wyeth-Ayerst has been able to rally to its cause the support of laboratory researchers, clinicians, and women's groups, and in a number of hard-fought campaigns, it has succeeded in winning both policy decisions and public support.

Premarin's sales in 2000 were up 5 per cent over those in 1999, and it continued to be the single best-selling prescription drug in the United States.[62] Hormone replacement therapy sales will grow from $2.7 billion in 1998 to $5.9 billion by 2008 in seven major markets around the world, according to a 1999 estimate.[63] As the market for these drugs continues to swell with the population of women of menopausal age, we might expect the selling of science to become even more intense.

NOTES

1 Pamela Sherrid, "Will boomer women defy menopause? The drug industry is betting they will try," *U.S. News Online*, 11 September 2000, http://www.usnews.com/usnews/issue/000911/boomer.htm.
2 *American Home Products Annual Report 2000*, 12.

3 Susan Bell, "A New Model of Medical Technology Development: A Case Study of DES," *Research in the Sociology of Health Care* 4 (1986): 1–32; Nelly Oudshoorn, *Beyond the Natural Body: An Archaeology of Sex Hormones* (London and New York: Routledge 1994), 82–111.

4 Margaret Lock, *Encounters with Aging: Mythologies of Menopause in Japan and North America* (Berkeley: University of California Press 1993); Susan Bell, "Changing Ideas: The Medicalization of Menopause," *Social Science and Medicine* 24 (1987): 535–42.

5 Robert A. Wilson, *Feminine Forever* (New York: Evans and Company 1966).

6 Alison Li, *Extracts and Enterprise: J.B. Collip, A Life in Medical Research* (forthcoming from McGill-Queen's University Press); Murray Llewellyn Barr and R.J. Rossiter, "James Bertram Collip, 1892–1965," *Biographical Memoirs of Fellows of the Royal Society* 19 (1973): 235–67; *Thirty-Five Years in the Pharmaceutical Manufacturing Industry in Canada* (Montreal: Ayerst, McKenna and Harrison Ltd. 1961), 3–4.

7 Barr and Rossiter, "James Bertram Collip"; Li, *Extracts*; Robert L. Noble, "Memories of James Bertram Collip," *Canadian Medical Association Journal* (hereafter *CMAJ*) 93 (1965): 1356–64.

8 "Important Discovery at McGill University," press release, 12 February 1930, Principal's Papers, RG 2, container 6, file 1259, McGill University Archives.

9 J.B. Collip, "The Ovary Stimulating Hormone of the Placenta," *Nature* 125 (1930): 444; A.D. Campbell and J.B. Collip, "On the Clinical Use of the Ovary-Stimulating Hormone of the Placenta, Preliminary Report," *CMAJ* 22 (1930): 219–20.

10 D.L. Thomson, "Editorial: Emmenin," *CMAJ* 32 (June 1935): 670–80.

11 J.C. Simpson to F. Cyril James, 13 December 1940, Faculty of Medicine, RG 38, container 6, file 133, McGill University Archives.

12 There is an extensive literature on the tragic consequences of DES use for the children who were exposed to the drug in utero. DES was widely used until 1970, when it was discovered that daughters with a history of in utero exposure suffered from a rare cancer of the vagina and genital-tract abnormalities. See Roberta J. Apfel and Susan M. Fisher, *To Do No Harm: DES and the Dilemmas of Modern Medicine* (New Haven: Yale University Press 1984; and David A. Edelman, *DES/Diethylstilbestrol – New Perspectives* (Lancaster: MTP Press 1986). In a sociological study of the early history of DES, 1938–41, Susan Bell examines the role of DES in the medicalization of menopause and analyses the interactions among the medical community, the pharmaceutical industry, and government in the development of the drug. Bell, "Changing Ideas," 535–42; Bell, "A New Model," 1–32.

13 Elmer Severinghaus and Ruth St John, "Oral Use of Conjugated Estrogens-Equine," *Journal of Clinical Endocrinology* 3 (1943): 98–100; *Thirty-five Years*, 4–6.

14 Oudshoorn, *Beyond the Natural Body*, 84–5; "McGill University Summary
   Statement of Endocrinology Royalty Funds at March 31, 1947," RG 2, container 136, file 3881, Principal's Papers, McGill University Archives.
15 Oudshoorn, *Beyond the Natural Body*, 97–8.
16 Severinghaus and St John, "Oral Use," 98–100.
17 Susan E. Bell, "Gendered Medical Science: Producing a Drug for Women,"
   Feminist Studies 21, no. 3 (Fall 1995): 469–500.
18 Lock, *Encounters with Aging*, 342–4.
19 Kathleen MacPherson, "Feminist Praxis in the Making: The Menopause
   Collective" (PHD thesis, Brandeis University 1986), 117–18; Barbara
   Seaman and Gideon Seaman, *Women and the Crisis in Sex Hormones*
   (New York: Bantam 1977).
20 Robert Wilson and Thelma Wilson, "The Fate of the Nontreated Postmenopausal Woman: A Plea for the Maintenance of Adequate Estrogen from
   Puberty to the Grave," *Journal of the American Geriatrics Society* 11 (1963):
   347–62; Wilson, *Feminine Forever.*
21 Patricia A. Kaufert and Sonja M. McKinlay, "Estrogen-Replacement
   Therapy: The production of Medical Knowledge and the Emergence of
   policy," in *Women, Health and Healing: Toward a New Perspective*, ed. Ellen
   Lewin and Virginia Olesen (New York: Tavistock Publications 1985),
   113–38.
22 Ibid., 125.
23 Ibid., 125–6.
24 "Learning to Spend at American Home," *Business Week*, 11 June 1990:
   80–81; "The Politics of Generics," *Business Week*, 3 February 1997: 128.
25 Bruce Ettinger, "Overview of Estrogen Replacement Therapy: A Historical
   Perspective," *Proceedings of the Society for Experimental Biology and Medicine* 217,
   no. 1 (January 1998): 2–5. See also Elaine S. Berman, "'Too Little Bone':
   The Medicalization of Osteoporosis," *Journal of Women's Health and Law* 1,
   no. 3 (October 2000): 257–77.
26 Direct-to-consumer advertising has been used in the United States since
   the early 1980s except during the period 1983–85, when the FDA called a
   moratorium in response to severe adverse effects and some deaths associated with benoxaprofen (Oraflex), an anti-arthritis drug, one of the
   first drugs to be heavily advertised to the public in the early 1980s. This
   moratorium was lifted in 1985.
27 "Direct-to-Consumer Advertising of Prescription Drugs – Discussion
   Paper," 6 April 1999, Health Canada.
28 Henry. J. Kaiser Family Foundation, *Prescription Drug Trends: A Chartbook*
   (July 2000), 58, http://www.kff.org/content/2000/3019/PharmFinal.pdf.
29 Joel Lexchin, "Direct-to-Consumer Advertising: Impact on Patient Attitudes and Behaviour and Doctors' Responses," submission to the Consultation on Direct-to-Consumer Advertising of Prescription Pharmaceuticals

Workshop, 14 April 1999, http://www.hc-sc.gc.ca/hpb-dgps/therapeut/
zfiles/english/consult/dtca/99-04-14_14_e.html.

30 In the U.K., the ratio of private to public spending on drug information
was estimated to be 50 to 1 in 1997. Barbara Mintzes, *Blurring the Boundaries: New Trends in Drug* (HAI-Europe, 1998). Available at Health Action
International website, http://www.haiweb.org/pubs/blurring/
blurring.intro.html.

31 D. Gilbert and A. Chetley, "New Trends in Drug Promotion," *Consumer
Policy Review* 6, no. 5 (1996): 165.

32 Erica Johnson, producer/reporter, "Promoting Drugs through Patient
Advocacy Groups," *CBC Marketplace,* 14 November 2000. Available at
CBC website, http://www.cbc.ca/consumers/market/files/health/
drugmarketing/index.html.

33 MacPherson, *Feminist Praxis in the Making,* 162–71.

34 Ettinger, *Overview of Estrogen Replacment Therapy,* 3.

35 Special Advisory Committee on Reproductive Physiology to the Drugs
Directorate, Health Protection Branch, Health Canada, *Menopause*
(Ottawa: Minister of National Health and Welfare, Canada, 1995), 88.

36 Jane Brody, "Personal Health; Menopause Begins Silently, before Its
Symptoms," *New York Times,* 27 January 1998, citing James E. Huston and
L. Darlene Lanka, *Perimenopause: Changes in a Woman's Health after 35* (Oak-
land, Calif.: New Harbinger 1997); and Nancy Lee Teaff and Kim Wright
Wiley, *Perimenopause: Preparing for the Change* (Rocklin, Calif.: Prima 1996).

37 "Living Smart with Premarin", PR Central website, http://www.
prcentral.com/c96premarin.htm (March 1998).

38 Kaiser Family Foundation, *Prescription Drug Trends – A Chartbook,* 56.

39 Working Group on Women and Health Protection, "To Do No Harm:
Direct-to-consumer advertising of prescription drugs," submission to the
Consultation on Direct-to-Consumer Advertising of Prescription Pharmaceuticals Workshop, 12 April 1999, at http://www.hc-sc.gc.ca/hpb-dgps/
therapeut/zfiles/english/consult/dtca/99-04-14_15_e.html.

40 "Drug Companies Getting F.D.A. Reprimands for False or Misleading
Advertising," *New York Times,* 28 March 1999: 28.

41 Working Group on Women and Health Protection, "To Do No Harm."

42 Joel Lexchin, "Enforcement of Codes Governing Pharmaceutical Promotion: What Happens When Companies Breach Advertising Guidelines?"
CMAJ 156, no. 3 (1997): 351–6.

43 "The Truth about Premarin"website, http://athena.athenet.net/
~nrsprntg/stpindex.html (March 2001).

44 North American Equine Ranching Information Council website,
http://www.naeric.org (March 2001).

45 Judy Mann, "The Politics of Pharmaceuticals," *Washington Post,* 2 April
1997: E13.

46 "Free menopause information and support programme for women taking Premarin," Wyeth-Ayerst Canada brochure.

47 U.S. Food and Drug Administration, Center for Drug Evaluation and Research (hereafter U.S. FDA, CDER), "Synthetic Generic Conjugated Estrogens: Timeline," 5 May 1997, http://www.fda.gov/cder/cetimeline.htm; U.S. FDA, CDER, "Backgrounder on Conjugated Estrogens: Timeline," 5 May 1997, http://www.fda.gov/cder/cebackground.htm.

48 Mann, "The Politics of Pharmaceuticals," E13.

49 "The Politics of Generics," 128–32.

50 U.S. FDA, CDER, "Backgrounder on conjugated estrogens."

51 Ibid.

52 "The Politics of Generics," 132.

53 U.S. FDA, CDER, "Synthetic Generic Conjugated Estroges."

54 Health Canada, "Background to Schedule 873 – Conjugated Estrogens," http://www.hc-sc.gc.ca/hpb-dgps/therapeut/zfiles/english/schedule/gazette.i/sch-0873b_e.html.

55 "The Politics of Generics," 128, 130, 132.

56 Health Canada, "Publication of Schedule of Amendments, Food and Drug Regulations – Amendment (Schedule No. 873)," 29 November 1997, http://www.hc-sc.gc.ca/hpb-dgps/therpeut/zfiles/english/schedule/gazette.i/sch-0973_3.html.

57 This is not entirely novel. Oudshoorn shows that the board of directors of the drug company Organon polled the management of major Dutch industries to inquire about the economic implications of the menopausal symptoms of their female employees in 1938. They did this in a bid to argue the importance of female sex hormone therapy to the Health Financing Institution. Oudshoorn, *Beyond the Natural Body*, 95–6.

58 Lock, *Encounters with Aging*, 350–1.

59 Ibid.

60 Ibid., 359.

61 J.A. Tieffenberg, "Socioeconomic Analysis of Hormone Replacement Therapy in Postmenopausal Women," in J.-M. Cossery, ed., *Medical-Economic Aspects of Hormone Replacement Therapy* (Carnforth: Parthenon Publishing Group 1993), 17.

62 *American Home Products Annual Report 2000*, 12. It is the second most dispensed drug in Canada with 4,872,000 prescriptions dispensed in 1999. IMS Health, "Baby-boomers responsible for more than half the growth in visits to Canadian doctors in 1999," Canada Newswire, May 2000, http://www.newswire.ca/releases/May2000/04/c1491.html.

63 According to a report by Decision Resources, a Waltham, Massachusetts-based consultancy. Jim Papanikolaw, "Hormone Replacement Therapy Set for Growth in Developed Nations," *Chemical Market Reporter*, 20 December 1999.

PART THREE

Transforming Childbirth

Since 1945, the vast majority of babies in both Canada and the United States have been born in hospital. Some observers hail the medicalization of birth for reducing serious complications and easing anxiety. Others sharply criticize medical interventions into what they see as a natural event. Feminist health activists have been especially critical of male-dominated hospital birth, painting a powerful picture of postwar obstetrical patients plied with drugs, isolated from their families, and alienated from their bodies and babies. By the 1970s, they had brought about a modest revival of midwifery and "natural childbirth." Nevertheless, the number of high-tech interventions into pregnancy and birth has continued to grow.

The essays and the personal narrative in this section challenge the linear narrative of male medical control. They show that women – as nurses, midwives, and doctors – have played a continuous role in maternity care since 1945. Women and biomedicine do not always appear in opposition here, for women – physicians and patients alike – embraced invasive procedures like Caesarean sections, infertility treatments, and surgical sterilization if these promised to enhance women's control of reproduction. Medicalized birth has not only been the result of doctors' preferences and patients' desires, however. In Chapter 6 Georgina Feldberg shows that at Toronto's Women's College Hospital medicalized birth was also a consequence of health insurance and hospital accreditation policies. Health financing and administrative imperatives played significant roles in determining obstetrical practice and "cutting-edge" care.

A second theme of this section, expressed most forcefully by Laura Ettinger in Chapter 7, concerns the relationship of science and religion. Ettinger's study of the efforts of nun-nurses to bring modern medicine and Catholic religious values to Latinas in New Mexico, like Maureen McCall's narrative (Chapter 9), in which she admits that she concluded her high-tech infertility treatments with an acceptance of "fate," challenges the conventional scholarly opposition between biomedicine and religious faith. As these essays demonstrate, women often combined confidence in medical science with spirituality and enthusiasm for "natural" birth.

A third theme is the importance of region to women's health. Patients in big cities like Toronto had relatively easy access to medical technologies in the 1950s, but as late as the 1990s, Maureen McCall had to travel to another city for her infertility treatments. Access to medical care was even more limited for the rural Latina and Aboriginal women described by Ettinger and Zelmanovits in chapters 7 and 8. There were few doctors of either sex in the rural American Southwest or Canadian North; birthing women there were cared for by nurses and nurse-midwives – medical missionaries, to use Ettinger's apt phrase – who were outsiders to the region. Yet the years under study were ones of transition, for by the 1980s almost all babies in these remote regions were delivered in hospital, even when it meant an extended stay away from home.

Many questions remain, and much more research is needed on the birth cultures and experiences of women from different regions, cultures, and economic backgrounds. What was lost and what was gained for each group as birth was medicalized and moved to hospital? What role has health insurance played in determining obstetrical interventions? Did national health insurance change the management and experience of childbirth?

6

On the Cutting Edge:
Science and Obstetrical Practice in a
Women's Hospital, 1945–1960

Georgina Feldberg

North American hospitals changed dramatically in the atmosphere of scientific enterprise that followed the Second World War, and they acquired diverse goals, staffing structures, and standards for care (cf. Ettinger, Chapter 7; Charles, Chapter 13; and Li, Chapter 5). Amidst these scientific and institutional changes, Toronto's Women's College Hospital (WCH), Canada's foremost and first training ground for women physicians, sought new ways to build and consolidate its status as a hospital that provided services for women, by women. This strategy included formal certification of its teaching opportunities in obstetrics and gynaecology, so in 1950, the secretary of the medical advisory committee wrote to the Royal College of Physicians and Surgeons of Canada as follows: "We are anxious, that the Service of Obstetrics and Gynaecology shall be recognized as suitable experience for post-graduate work toward the fellowship exam."[1] For almost four decades, WCH had produced some of Canada's first women obstetricians. It offered them numerous opportunities. Between July 1949 and July 1950 alone, the WCH resident in obstetrics and gynaecology had performed "herself, with supervision by the staff ... a range of procedures on the uterus, tubes and cervix," including five Caesarean sections, thirteen total hysterectomies, and two subtotal hysterectomies.[2] Thus, WCH had already earned its professional stripes, but in the era of postwar scientific medicine, the hospital's merit needed to be measured, counted, and regularized. As hospitals became more institutional and medical specialties more powerful, WCH sought formal university affiliation, "approval as a hospital for advanced graduate training," and the standing of an accredited institution.[3]

To qualify as a post-graduate training site, Women's College Hospital had also to pass and receive the approval seal of the Joint Commission on Hospital Accreditation, a transborder regulatory body comprised of members from the American College of Physicians, the American College of Surgeons, the American Hospital Association, the American Medical Association, and the Canadian Medical Association. The joint commission represented the power of institutions and science in the post-1945 period. It aimed to ensure that hospitals conformed to a universal, professional standard of administration and performance.[4] Its assessors visited and reviewed hospital operations.

Women's College Hospital, the commission judged, had several strengths but also critical weaknesses. The hospital's administration and methods for selecting members of the governing board, to ensure representation, received full marks. Staff appointments and training also scored highly. But the assessor noted overcrowded facilities, inappropriate committee structures, and inadequate record keeping as general deficiencies, and he identified deficiencies in several clinical services, especially obstetrics and gynaecology. In 1949, the year under review, he assigned that department a score of only 44/75, which reflected more general concerns about physical layout and hospital organization. "Patients coming to the laboratory must walk or pass through the obstetrical service area," the assessor observed. "Records are exceedingly poor."[5]

A still more significant concern was that the "Caesarean section rate is rather high, no indications on records."[6] In 1949 at WCH, doctors delivered 4.2 per cent of the viable infants born (88 of 2,104) by c-section. This rate was almost double the "national average" and "expected normal rate" of 2.3.[7] Through the 1950s, c-section deliveries at WCH climbed. By 1960 the rate was 154 per 2,967 births, or 5.1 per cent; by 1967 it was at 7.2 per cent; and by 1970 it had hit 8.4 per cent. Repeatedly, accreditation committees chastised hospital staff for deviating from surgical and national norms.[8]

The evidence that women physicians practising at Toronto's preeminent women's hospital performed "too many" Caesarean sections complicates standard historical accounts of women's medical work. Reproduction and reproductive concerns have dominated women's health history for almost three decades. Rates of c-sections have served as a particular flashpoint for late twentieth-century women's health activists, who decried these surgical interventions as unnecessary interference with the natural birth process. Yet, the Canadian women doctors who worked at WCH in the postwar era relied heavily on such surgical interventions. In one of the most contested areas of gynaecologic practice, they apparently exceeded both the national

norm and the expected rate derived from more traditional male institutions, and traditional medical authorities reprimanded them. The
transnational committee's concern with the practices and outcomes at
a woman's hospital, together with the complex process by which
Women's College Hospital's programs in obstetrics and gynaecology
negotiated accreditation, reflected intersecting tensions between gender, science, nation, and professional medicine in the post–Second
World War era. This chapter makes use of institutional reports and papers, oral histories provided by women who gave birth at WCH after
1945, and patient case histories created by nurses and physicians, to
explore those tensions.

WOMEN, SCIENCE, AND MEDICINE: THE HISTORICAL CONTEXT OF CANADIAN WOMEN'S MEDICAL WORK

In Canadian medical lore, Women's College Hospital occupies the special place of a pioneering institution.[9] WCH is celebrated for at least
two kinds of contributions: it educated aspiring women physicians who
had nowhere else to study, and it afforded women patients the opportunity to be treated by a "lady doctor." The hospital evolved from one
of the first Canadian female medical colleges. Prior to 1900, women's
access to Canadian medical schools was extremely limited. Canada's
first women physicians, Emily Stowe and Jennie Kidd Trout among
them, had to travel to the United States to receive their degrees. When
they returned to Ontario, legal and institutional barriers further im-
peded their ability to practise. The women doctors had no hospital
privileges, and they were initially denied medical licences.[10] Consequently, by the 1880s, Canadian women had decided to mobilize a
campaign for a local female medical college. Two opened soon thereafter, one in Kingston, Ontario, and the other in Toronto. These later
amalgamated into a single institution, the Ontario Medical College for
Women, which operated until the University of Toronto and other
Canadian institutions allowed co-education.[11]

The Women's College, as it was known, instructed students in all the
standard medical sciences. As the college's announcements made clear,
it also prepared graduates to care for the needy in Asia, as missionaries,
or to tend to poor women at home.[12] The college's goals of training
and service merged in 1898, when students opened the Dispensary and
Clinic of the Women's Medical College in a few basement rooms.[13]
This precursor to Women's College Hospital offered women the opportunity to develop clinical skills, build up a clientele, and serve the
poor. The dispensary began to metamorphose into a teaching hospital

in December 1911, when it opened its first beds in a small house in Cabbagetown, the eastern core of old Toronto. Renamed the Women's College Hospital, it outgrew that space within a decade and relocated to a larger residential building on Rusholme Road, in Toronto's newly emerging west end.

The hospital's continued growth reflected the achievements of singular women who, "despite the odds," battled discrimination to take their place as professionals and astutely recognized the special needs of female patients. While other hospitals excluded women medical graduates from fellowships and residencies, WCH created opportunities for them. When men went off to serve overseas, the hospital carved out a special niche. It marketed the concept of "women's work for women's needs," and in annual reports and general publicity proposed that "the women of Toronto and the Province of Ontario deserve a special hospital of their own in which they may be treated by physicians and surgeons of their own sex."[14]

By 1930 the hospital had outgrown its residential location and its image as an informal facility. Responding to scientific and demographic changes, the WCH board launched a campaign for a new, high-rise, institutional structure. The chosen site was directly across from Queen's Park, seat of the provincial legislature. The prime minister, the Honourable R.B. Bennett, laid the cornerstone in 1934. Now situated in the downtown core within walking distance of the University of Toronto and its teaching hospitals, WCH acquired a new professional image. However, the urban growth and the scientific impulse to hospital expansion that had inspired the board also created financial and professional pressures. Soon WCH found itself in competition for patients and government grants. Pressures increased following the Second World War when, fuelled by the successes of biomedicine and strong private and public investment in scientific research, the North American economy boomed. As WCH lost patients and standing in the climate of postwar Canada, obstetrics and birthing provided new opportunities.

OBSTETRICS AND WOMEN'S MEDICINE

Women's College Hospital was not a traditional lying-in or maternity hospital. From its earliest days, it functioned as a general hospital, ensuring that a wide-ranging visiting and regular staff provided services that included general medicine and surgery, ear-nose-and-throat, x-ray, and orthopaedics. Later, WCH also created a number of pioneering clinics in dermatology, diet, and cancer detection. A breast cancer program, opened in 1948, drew women from across Ontario. Obstetrics was but one part of what WCH did. During the 1920s, approximately 300 women gave birth there each year. While the number rose to between 500 and 600 a year during the 1930s and to just over 1,000 a year by 1945, birthing mothers and their infants consistently accounted for only a quarter to a third of the WCH in-patient census.[15] Compared to other Toronto hospitals, for example the Wellesley and the General, the proportion of births to total admissions at WCH was high and, at a time when hospital birth was not the norm, even exceptional. Still, at other women's hospitals, such as Toronto's Salvation Army Women's Hospital, and more formal maternity units, such as the Burnside Lying-In, births accounted for more than 90 per cent of hospital stays.[16]

After the Second World War, although the proportion of births remained constant, WCH became recognized as Toronto's premier obstetrical site. Three factors – hospital-driven initiatives, science, and the growth of suburbia – facilitated this transformation. WCH actively promoted diverse medical services designed to attract and retain obstetrical patients. In 1935, after staff delivered the hospital's first set of triplets, WCH developed nurseries and nursing care for premature infants. By the early 1970s, the hospital's neonatal intensive-care unit was at the forefront of North American medicine. As early as 1960, WCH recognized the problem of infertility and created special programs that provided integrated care for women who wanted children but were having difficulty conceiving or sustaining pregnancies. Shortly after the legalization of birth control in Canada, WCH opened a pioneering, off-site, birth control clinic, the Bay Centre for Birth Control, to promote family planning and help ensure that children born were wanted.[17]

Alongside these efforts, WCH reconstructed its historical role. The hospital's obstetrical and gynaecological services came to figure prominently in its efforts to mark its historical significance and justify its continued existence. Annual reports and hospital histories repeatedly emphasized the unique care that the hospital offered, celebrating the delivery of the hospital's first baby, on Christmas Day, 1911, as the starting point of a long tradition of special and specialized medicine.[18]

Rhetoric aside, the proportion of obstetrical work undertaken at WCH did not change dramatically after 1945. Throughout the baby boom, obstetrical patients continued to make up about a quarter of the patient census. Moreover, the ratio of births to other admissions became more like that at other hospitals.[19] However, science and the growth of Toronto's suburbs helped to shape a different patient demographic. New patients came to the hospital, and they came because of the lure of a different kind of care.

During the early decades of wCH's existence, obstetrical patients reflected the hospital's more general concern for women in economic as well as medical need. Consistent with the mores of their time, the hospital founders believed that the health of the nation depended on the well-being of mothers. At a time when hospital births were not the norm, they actively drew working-class women into the clinics, noting that "this class is perhaps the most important in the country as regards to the next generation of labouring citizens ... If the mother's health fails, what is to become of the family?"[20] They admitted these women at the charity rate, so that during the 1920s wCH received about one-fifth of its operating expenses from public sources, falling again midway between the parochial and general hospitals and the more charitable enterprises.[21]

wCH also provided a haven for single women and others in distress. In key years, often corresponding to those when soldiers came to or left town, unwed mothers comprised as much as 20 per cent of obstetrical cases.[22] Some came directly from farming communities outside Toronto or even from other provinces. Many came from shelters or homes, like the Industrial Refuge, Victor Home, and Presbyterian Home, which routinely sent their "girls" to wCH for both obstetrical and gynaecologic care.[23] Other patients entered the obstetrical service via the "special" – or venereal disease – clinic that the hospital had opened following the First World War with a grant from the Provincial Board of Health. The clinic, operated by Drs Guest and Kerr, treated the infected wives of soldiers alongside others in need, and ensured that there was follow-up care for the women and their children.[24]

The hospital's clientele shifted after 1945. Initially, patients had come primarily from the urban core, which by the 1930s included in its population immigrants from Eastern Europe. Following the Second World War, new immigrants from southern Europe moved into the downtown and the older immigrants moved north. So did the Anglo-Canadian middle classes.[25] Although they now lived further from the hospital, these middle-class, suburban mothers came to rely increasingly on the authority of scientific advice and institutions.[26] Patients in search of scientific maternity now came to wCH from bungalows in the north, east, and west of the city.

Both informal and formal initiatives contributed to the hospital's changing reputation. Networks of friends and family sustained suburban mothers of the postwar era, and these networks promoted the hospital. In interviews and oral histories, the women who gave birth at wCH during the 1950s and 1960s speak of the communications chains that led and influenced them.[27] Some followed their mothers, and daughters born at wCH returned to have their own babies. Others, like

Mary, who was a patient during the 1960s, heard about WCH from neighbours and friends: "It was known to be the maternity hospital so any of the girls who had their babies wanted to go to Women's College because they knew it specialized in maternity."[28] While some spoke of WCH as part of a family tradition, others saw the hospital as a solution to isolation. Immigrants, alone in Toronto or even Canada, sought the advice of friends and neighbours as a replacement for the wisdom of family. Dorothy, who lived in North Toronto and had no family close by, exemplified their concerns. She had come to Canada from wartorn Europe and had begun her married life in a room in the downtown core, where immigrants and refugees settled. By the early 1950s, Dorothy's husband had prospered, and they bought their own home, a smallish bungalow in the new northern suburbs. Dorothy wanted to begin a family but had no familial support. Having left home as a teenager, she describes herself as "clueless" about the basics of family life. The doctors and nurses at WCH became surrogates for sisters and other female relatives; it was from them that she learned how to feed, bathe, and clothe her baby. It was from them that, in her words, she also learned how to adjust and cope.[29]

The female physicians who practised at WCH were another draw. Marion Hilliard, in particular, became a guiding influence for women of all ages. Born in 1902 in rural Ontario, Hilliard received her MD from the University of Toronto in 1927. In 1926, while still a student, she assisted in births at WCH, and she formally joined the hospital staff in 1928. Her early cases were gynaecologic, but in February 1929 Hilliard delivered her first baby and she maintained an obstetrical practice thereafter. Hilliard became chief of obstetrics and gynaecology in 1947, and by the 1950s, she had become an icon for both the individual patients she cared for and the public at large. In popular magazines and on the radio, she proffered the advice about sex, childbirth, and general reproductive health that would become the foundation for her best-selling book *A Woman Doctor Looks at Love and Life*. Hilliard established a standard for medical practice that women from across Canada sought.[30]

Women doctors appealed to patients for several reasons. For some, they provided the connection between new scientific expertise and older, informal women's networks; they offered a kind of psychological solidarity to mothers who were alone and isolated in the suburbs, with no familial elders to turn to. Janet, who had her babies at WCH during the 1960s, spoke of this womanly connection: "A woman doctor who had had children of her own," she noted, "would know more of what it felt [like] ... She had had a baby and understood how you felt."[31] Other women reflected on their growing awareness of the limitations of hospital births. Looking back, some commented on their dissatisfaction with the traditional hospital-birth experience and their hope that a hospital run by women for women would provide better care.

There was still another reason to have babies at WCH: the hospital's extremely low rates of maternal and infant deaths. Throughout the 1950s, these rates fell well below the national norm. In 1949 the hospital reported "3 maternal deaths for 2294 obstetrical admissions." This statistic was calculated as a rate of ".13%" or .13 deaths per 100 patients, about half the national average of .25 per cent.[32] In 1952 the hospital reported "1 maternal death for 2497 admissions," a rate of ".04%." This rate fell well below the national average of .25 per cent. In 1953 there were 2,800 births and no maternal deaths at WCH.[33] Infant mortality rates were similarly low and through the 1950s stayed well below average. In 1949 the infant mortality rate at WCH was 1.5 per cent (31 deaths for 2,104 viable births) compared to the national norm of 2 per cent. By 1952 infant deaths dropped to 1.27 per cent, while the national rate remained 2 per cent. Many women who gave birth in the post-1945 era knew of mothers and babies who had died. They feared maternal and infant death and expressed confidence in WCH as a "good and safe" facility.

ON THE CUTTING EDGE: SCIENCE AND FEMINIST MEDICAL PRACTICE

By the time the Joint Commission on Hospital Accreditation arrived, WCH had gained the reputation of an exemplary obstetrical institution. The hospital had worked hard to build this image, through its work, its formal and informal publicity campaigns, and its efforts to construct a unique history. Its desire for accreditation in obstetrics and gynaecology reflected this larger effort. However, the hospital's obstetrical practices did not conform neatly with the expectations of the joint commission. Despite their achievements, WCH and its staff were asked to justify and reform their practices.

The joint commission's concern about c-section rates serves as a lens through which the historian can view the hospital's struggles. The commission's judgment that c-sections at WCH exceeded the national norm was based on data collected for and interpreted by a group that was ostensibly joint and transnational but was in actuality dominated by representatives of U.S. institutions. The commission's norms were consequently American, shaped by the vision of Abraham Flexner. Flexner sought to make medical education and practice more scientifically acceptable, and he produced a report that transformed twentieth-century American medicine.[34] Hence, the tools used to measure and rate the

Canadian women physicians' practice were part of a much larger set of standards, none of which necessarily applied to any Canadian hospital, let alone to a maverick women's facility.

Canadians recognized this cultural divide. In May 1965, when Dr Kenneth Hodgins presented an address on hospital accreditation to the medical staff of WCH, he noted the hospital's long record of accreditation and asked, "Why am I taking your time to discuss this subject?"[35] Accreditation, Hodgins explained, was a relative thing, varying from time to time according to the standards of the assessors and rising expectations of practice. It was also, he suggested, largely an "American thing." In Canada "[we] hear very little about Accreditation except when the survey of a particular hospital is coming up. You seldom if ever have a patient ask if the hospital is accredited."[36] The difference could be attributed almost entirely to insurance. In the United States "such diverse organizations as private insurance companies and labour unions are taking a greater interest in the public hospitals. For years, Blue Cross subscribers in large cities such as New York and Chicago have been told, they will receive full benefits only when cared for in an accredited hospital."[37] Canadian hospitals, Hodgins argued, were different; accreditation primarily served the needs of aspiring physicians, the students whose residency and training requirements would be recognized and evaluated. Hodgins promoted accreditation for the merit badge it symbolized.

Accreditation provided a widely recognized standard for administration and operations that, for many reasons, WCH sought. But there were costs to accreditation, one of which was conformity to an American medical norm, which in the post-1945 era was increasingly scientific and bureaucratic. For WCH, much of the cost associated with accreditation was administrative. To receive accreditation, the hospital needed to address the commission's concerns about the number of beds in hallways, the structure of hospital advisory committees, and above all the state of patient records. The latter were too scanty and too unstructured for the examiners' taste.[38] Accreditation required more frequent meetings, more committees, "regulations around attendance" for medical staff and departmental meetings as well as for doctors' rounds, and improved record keeping.[39]

Accreditation also required conformity to standards of clinical practice in ways Hodgins did not perceive. When the commission deemed the rate of c-sections at WCH "in excess" of the national norm, it did not define the normal population. Was the standard Canadian? Was it adjusted to reflect WCH's small size? Was it corrected for its particular patient population?[40] WCH had a reputation for accepting difficult cases and catering to women's diverse reproductive needs. The hospital staff routinely tested limits. They offered birth control advice and, at a time when abortion was neither legally nor medically sanctioned, terminated pregnancies. In 1954 the staff reported performing eight therapeutic abortions.[41] A decade earlier Dr Kerr, a long-standing member of the obstetrical staff and co-founder of the VD clinic, had ordered a therapeutic abortion for Mrs C., who at twenty-two had an acute nervous disorder, resulting in physical shakes, that her pregnancy aggravated. "I believe that the pregnancy endangers her life and should be terminated," Dr Kerr wrote. Her colleague who reviewed the order agreed.[42] At the other end of the reproductive spectrum, WCH operated an infertility clinic that assisted women who had difficulty conceiving. Mrs S.V., an Estonian woman who had immigrated to Canada from Sweden in 1948, sought help from Dr Hilliard. She was thirty-three but had not conceived. In 1949 she saw Dr Hilliard for "sterility."

The high rate of C-sections reflected, and needed to be assessed in, these contexts of care. Moreover, though rates of C-sections at the hospital were apparently high, rates of maternal and infant mortality were very low. However, no assessor commended WCH for its high scores or questioned whether the two phenomena – a high rate of C-sections and low rates of infant and maternal mortality – were connected. Nor did the assessors ask whether WCH physicians used surgery as a means of saving a life when either the mother or baby was in distress.

Case records for the years 1945–60 provide the context; they give a sense of the special needs of patients who came to WCH and shed light on when and why C-sections were performed. The complaint that the medical staff at WCH kept deficient records – that "obstetrical records are exceedingly poor"[43] – was justified. Feminist historians of science have sometimes argued that meticulous record keeping and attention to detail are female virtues,[44] but if so, WCH doctors once again deviated from the norm. The small, overworked staff spent more time on patient care than on meetings and note taking. Records and registers from 1921 onward are complete, but microfilm case histories are less illuminating than historians might wish. Beyond the usual problems of physician handwriting and poor-quality film, the historian interested in these materials encounters a frustrating inconsistency. At first the hospital assigned patients a new number on each admission; later, it consolidated the charts, but by number rather than name. Sometimes the case includes a full medical record but little patient history; sometimes the patient history is complete but there are few clinical details. The structure of the patient chart changed often, sometimes yearly. Despite these limitations, the charts provide rich information about the patients and the care they received. They include demographic information (age, marital status, address, and often occupation, ethnicity, and religion) and sometimes nursing notes, patient histories, family histories, outpatient visits, laboratory records, and consent forms.

The patient files indicate that WCH doctors sometimes performed a c-section when a labour went unduly long or other complications occurred. Mrs F.H. came to WCH in 1949 to have her second child. Her first baby, a son, was born in 1946. The delivery had been long and had required surgical interventions and forceps. Her infant had stopped breathing following delivery and had required artificial resuscitation. Mrs F.H.'s emotional state is not described in the chart, but the medication orders indicate that Phenobarbital was prescribed for sleep, suggesting distress. Three years later, Mrs F.H. returned to the hospital with labour pains. When a day later she still had not delivered her child, the house surgeon began a medical induction. Several hours later, Dr Hilliard was called in to perform a c-section.[45]

Fear of losing an infant provided another reason for ordering a c-section. For example, Mrs A.D., who immigrated to Canada from southern Europe, was thirty-two years old when she came to WCH. During the course of her marriage, she had become pregnant nine times and had miscarried eight times, so she had had only one living infant. Mrs D. badly wanted her baby. Her chart records that from the second month of her pregnancy, she received prenatal care that included daily injections of vitamin E and corpus luteum – an early form of hormonal supplements. Atypically, the chart also includes the results of pregnancy tests, suggesting that Mrs D. sought medical care before conceiving. Mrs D. underwent a c-section, but despite the care she received prior to and during delivery, she lost her child. It is not clear whether her past history was a reason for surgical intervention, but her case suggests that c-sections were used to prevent stillbirths generally, since one was used to save this baby specifically.[46]

The opportunity to perform a sterilization was another rationale for c-sections. By 1952, the accreditation survey form that staff were required to complete inquired about both the number of c-sections performed during the review period *and* the number of sterilizations (primarily tubal ligations) and therapeutic abortions. An on-paper connection between c-sections and these methods of limiting births was made explicit when the 1960 accreditation survey unambiguously asked which tubal ligations were associated with c-sections and which were independent. That year, fully half of the sterilizations performed at WCH occurred as part of a c-section, suggesting a strong relationship between these procedures.

Sterilization has a complicated North American history (cf. Gutierrez, Chapter 19; Ladd-Taylor, Chapter 3). Like other forms of obstetric and gynaecologic surgery, it is associated with exploitative medical practice. It is also associated with eugenic practices and the involuntary termination of disabled and minority women's reproductive ability. Canada, like the United States, has a history of forcibly sterilizing those seen to be "feeble-minded" or otherwise unsuited for motherhood.[47] Through the period 1920–40, physicians associated with WCH used common eugenic language when referring to patients, whose intelligence and competence they often measured. Nonetheless, patient records do not suggest that the hospital's physicians routinely practised involuntary sterilization. Rather, they suggest that obstetrical practices acknowledged patients' varied physical and psychological responses to pregnancy and sought to meet these with a wide range of procedures – abortion, c-section, and infertility treatment among them – that, at least on paper, had the patient's consent.

At a time when birth control was limited, sterilization in conjunction with a c-section was part of a range of options WCH could offer. Mrs S., another patient of Marion Hilliard's, delivered a baby through a c-section in 1944. Twenty-two years old, white, and Canadian of Scots-Presbyterian origin, Mrs S. was newly married. Her pregnancy had been difficult, and she had become dangerously anaemic, requiring a transfusion. Prior to surgery, she signed a consent for the c-section and "to be operated on for the purpose of rendering me sexually sterile because I have been competently advised and believe that a pregnancy would endanger my life."[48] Her husband's signature appeared alongside hers. Mrs K. had a similar history. White, Canadian of Scots descent, married, and a member of the United Church, Canada's largest Protestant denomination, Mrs K. was thirty-seven. She, too, had a difficult pregnancy. Her blood pressure had been persistently high, and during the sixth month she was confined to hospital for a week. Dr Hilliard noted: "It was a question of whether she could continue her pregnancy in view of this. I believe any further pregnancy would be dangerous to her life." Like Mrs S., Mrs K. signed a consent indicating that she had been competently advised and agreed that another pregnancy would be risky.[49]

Concern that another pregnancy would be physically dangerous offered one rationale for combining a c-section with surgery; fear of future unwanted pregnancies another. Women in their thirties with three or more children at home sometimes became candidates for a c-section with sterilization. Their previous deliveries had been routine and the current pregnancy without complications. White, Anglo-Saxon, and middle class, they appeared to be of means. Often they were private patients with private or semi-private rooms and some form of insurance coverage. They had signed consents to surgery that would render them "permanently sexually sterile." These women formed a significant percentage of those who underwent c-sections in the period 1945–60; for them, surgery appeared to provide the only reliable method of contraception. The surgical artifice of the c-section was consequently, at least in part, an emancipatory choice in that it gave women access to an effective from of family planning at a time when alternatives were limited. It represented a strategic alliance between medical women, their patients, and surgical science.

CARING AND CUTTING: HISTORICAL IMAGES OF WOMEN'S MEDICAL WORK

The argument that women physicians strategically used science and the scalpel in their patients' interest stands in contrast to much historical scholarship. A vilification of scientific medicine and the portrayal of women as at odds with science characterized women's health histories written in the 1970s and 1980s. A historical tradition, upon which much Canadian women's health activism built, underscored traditional female methods of healing and explored the ways in which the changing power and prestige of science displaced and delegitimized women's practices or restricted women's access to essential services, such as birth attendants or abortion.[50]

   Lesley Biggs notes the historical contingency of this scholarship. Reproduction and reproductive concerns came to dominate women's health history during the 1970s and 1980s, she suggests, because "women's right to control their own bodies became a focus of struggle while at the same time it provided women with an issue which could unite women (or so it seemed at the time)."[51] Activism and the academy joined in an effort to make a place for traditional female practitioners and patients, to underscore the importance of women's experience of birth and to explicate the complex social, cultural, economic, and political factors that had allowed male physicians to usurp female midwifery and steal a unique and universalizing female experience. While traditional medical historians chronicled the battles that brave physicians fought to ensure that pregnant women had access to anaesthesia, hospital birth, and other measures believed to reduce infant and maternal mortality, new scholars critiqued the introduction of hospital birth, the development of birth control measures, and other medical interventions as embodiments of a male technological impulse to control female sexuality and suppress female rituals of healing.[52] They struggled, as well, to move "beyond the Great Doctors"[53] and capture the contributions that large numbers of non-professional and untrained women made to birthing.

However, as Biggs's brilliant review and rethinking of the historical writing on women and reproduction suggests, the effort to reclaim women's health history created a universalized female norm that underplays particular historical contexts and obscures differences among varied groups of women. Too often, the histories overlooked nation and particular configurations of race, colonialism, class, economic development, and regional politics.[54] They also overlooked women doctors, whose work did not fit neatly within any critical tradition. While recent scholarship confronts differences among women and forces us to contend with the ways in which race, class, gender, sexual orientation, and other particularities of experience intersect,[55] there is still little attention paid to the ways in which women's relationships and access to the authority of science shape and create marginality. Yet, women's diverse relationships to the power of science are a critical point of difference, especially where health and medicine are concerned. As Canadian women's health activism grew during the 1970s and 1980s, and as medicine came to be constructed as scientific and male and at odds with "real women's" or "true feminist" interests, the relationship of women to science could be as divisive as the chasms of class and race.

Those chasms characterize the studies of women doctors. Minorities and mavericks who struggled to make a unique place for women in the world of medical science, the pioneering women physicians are difficult to categorize. Gender essentialism and appeals to a special female affinity to healing have shaped some analyses; these portray women physicians as engaged in a kind of medical work that served female patients better.[56] The historical affirmation of a different, female medicine sat well with efforts to recruit women doctors, so that by the late 1980s and early 1990s, newspapers and popular magazines such as *Canadian Living* and *Chatelaine* extolled the advantages of female medical practice.[57] Canadian surveys also purported that women physicians spent more time with their patients, prescribed fewer drugs, and recommended surgery less quickly.[58]

At the same time, some practitioners, patients, activists, and academics (such as Michelle Landsberg, whose critique of gynaecology is included in this volume) rejected the idea of an inherently female, feminine, or feminist style of medical practice. The classic Canadian work, Veronica Strong-Boag's "Canada's Women Doctors, Feminism Constrained," suggested that several cohorts of Canadian doctors avoided feminist causes.[59] Still others, committed to gender neutrality, contested doctrines of separate spheres and maintained that women physicians grounded their practice as solidly in scientific knowledge and technologic intervention as did their male peers.

The history of WCH echoes these debates. In June 1971, when Canada's prime minister, Pierre Elliott Trudeau, laid the cornerstone for the new wing and proudly pronounced that "the hospital has been organized by some of the most remarkable activists of their time in the face of extreme adversity," a group of female demonstrators contemptuously dismissed his naïveté. "Tell it like it is, sister,"[60] they exhorted, for from the perspective of the street, a medical institution neither could nor did represent the community of women. WCH patients expressed some of the same apprehensions, and when interviewed in the 1990s, they spoke of the contradictions found in the woman doctor's medical practice. The faith that women doctors would have learned from their personal experience was peculiarly misplaced, since many of the leading female obstetricians were single, and even when married, childless. Reality sometimes contradicted expectation, and women doctors were not always gentler and more sympathetic. Grace, who gave birth during the 1950s, described her much-beloved obstetrician as "very protective of her patients – she expected her patients to be tough, not to moan and groan after the first pregnancy."[61] Like others, Grace suggested that some of the women doctors provided tough love and, instead of pampering, encouraged young mothers to be stalwart and keep a stiff upper lip. Others were blunter. Emily described Hilliard, who delivered her babies in the 1950s, as a "battle axe" whom she feared and later loathed.

Women's College Hospital itself also responded to the historical trend. Through the 1980s and 1990s, as different Ontario governments reviewed the public health insurance scheme, argued that spending reductions were necessary to reduce escalating medical expenditures, and embarked upon a plan for restructuring, WCH became a public symbol of women's distinct needs.[62] Government recommendations that the hospital merge with other Toronto institutions in order to enhance efficiency and reduce costs were hotly decried. WCH dominated the news as loyal patients and alumni rallied behind the affirmation that this was a unique institution founded as the "union of those who love on behalf of those who suffer."[63] This campaign emphasized a history of caring and extolled the hospital's holistic approach. Thus, for example, the cover of the annual report for 1986 features a picture of one of the early hospital nurses.

However, as the accreditation process and the exploration of explanations for the number of c-sections demonstrate, critical negotiations between science, gender, and feminism framed women's medical practice in post-1945 Ontario. In addition to caring, the doctors at WCH strategically applied science and the scalpel. To the physicians who practised obstetrics at WCH, science was instrumental. From the moment the Women's Medical College was established, in 1883, women physicians had appreciated the power of science; college announcements and reports boldly laid claim to the rigorous "scientific" training that enabled women physicians to practise at the highest medical standard. Canada's female physicians struggled at once to stand on an equal footing with their professional colleagues and meet the needs of their particular patients. After 1945, when the contexts of institutional growth and state investment in research complicated the lives of smaller, non-research-oriented hospitals, WCH physicians allied themselves strategically with science to serve their own professional ends and meet the needs they perceived their patients to have. Elite women, they fell outside the community that is normally labelled activist. Yet, until the very end of the twentieth century, they dominated women's organizing around health and forged its successes.

By virtue of their gender, these women physicians were marginal. Their appeal to the Joint Commission on Hospital Accreditation betrayed that marginality and institutional vulnerability. Like other activists, they worked outside the mainstream of power and operated independently of political institutions and lobbies. Nevertheless, unlike other activists, these women enjoyed a very different relationship to science, which they succeeded in moulding to their own and their female patients' interests.

NOTES

Author's Note: This essay is based on papers and letters, including a complete series of patient registers and case files dating from 1917, housed at Women's College Hospital, Toronto. I thank Miss Robbins of the library and archives and the staff of the health records unit, particularly Allyson Nichols and Matija Misetich, for their assistance.

1 Secretary Medical Advisory Committee WCH to John E. Plunkett, Honorary Secretary, Royal College of Physicians and Surgeons of Canada, series 9, container 20, file 1 (undated but presumed 1950–51 because of dates of procedures given), Women's College Hospital Archives (hereafter WCHA).

2 Ibid.

3 Application for Approval of a Hospital for Advanced Graduate Training, Women's College Hospital to Royal College of Physicians and Surgeons of Canada (1950), series 9, container 20, file 1, WCHA.

4 Bylaws, Joint Commission on Accreditation of Hospitals, reprint from *Bulletin*, American College of Surgeons, September–October 1952, series 9, container 20, file 4, WCHA.

5 Accreditation Survey 1949, p. 12, series 9, container 20, file 4, WCHA.

6 Ibid.

7 Accreditation Survey 1960, p. 12, series 9, container 20, file 4, WCHA.

8 Ibid, Accreditation Surveys 1950–59, series 9, containes 20, file 4, WCHA.

9 Few formal histories of women's medical education in Canada, the Ontario Medical College for Women, or Women's College Hospital exist. See Augusta Stowe Gullen, *A Brief History of the Ontario Medical College for Women* (Toronto, 1906); Martin Kendrick and Krista Slade, *Spirit of Life: The Story of Women's College Hospital* (Toronto: Women's College Hospital 1993); Lykke De La Cour and Rose Sheinin, "The Ontario Medical College for Women, 1883–1906: Lessons from Gender Separatism in Medical Education," in Marianne Ainley, ed., *Despite the Odds: Essays on Canadian Women and Science* (Montreal: Vehicule Press 1990), 112–120; Veronica Strong-Boag, "Canada's Women Doctors: Feminism Constrained," in Linda Kealey, ed., *A Not Unreasonable Claim: Women and Reform in Canada, 1880s–1920s* (Toronto: Women's Press 1979); and Anne Rochon Ford, *A Path Not Strewn with Roses: One Hundred Years of Women at the University of Toronto, 1884–1984* (Toronto: University of Toronto Press 1985). See also Sheryl Stotts McLaren, "Becoming Indispensable: A Biography of Elizabeth Smith Shortt" (PHD dissertation, York University 2001).

10 Jacalyn Duffin, "The Death of Sarah Lovell and the Constrained Feminism of Emily Stowe," *Canadian Medical Association Journal* (hereafter CMAJ) 146, no. 6 (15 March 1982): 881–8; Constance Backhouse, *Petticoats and Prejudice: Women and Law in Nineteenth-Century Canada* (Toronto: Women's Press 1991), 112–41.

11 Peter Dembski, "Jenny Kidd Trout and the Founding of the Women's Medical Colleges of Kingston and Toronto," *Ontario History* 77, no. 3 (1985): 183–206; De La Cour and Sheinin, "Ontario Medical College", McLaren, "Becoming Indispensable."

12 See, for example, Ontario Medical College for Women, *Annual Report, 10th Session* (1892–93): 11. See also Ruth Compton Brouwer, *New Women for God: Canadian Presbyterian Women and the India Missions, 1876–1914* (Toronto: University of Toronto Press 1990).

13 Ontario Medical College for Women, Annual Announcement (1898), 6; see also Kendrick and Slade, *Spirit of Life.*

14 Women's College Hospital Campaign Fund, "How Long Shall They Be Turned Away," flyer (1928), WCHA.

15 Statistics are taken from WCH, Annual Reports, 1920–26, and from the Province of Ontario, Reports of the Inspectors of Prisons and Public Charities upon the Hospitals and Charitable Institutions of the Province of Ontario (hereafter Report of Inspector), 1920–30.

16 Percentages are derived from a review of Reports of the Inspector. For discussions of childbirth in early twentieth-century Canada, see Jo Oppen-

heimer, "Childbirth in Ontario: The Transition from Home to Hospital in the Early Twentieth Century," *Ontario History* 25, no. 1 (March 1983); and Katherine Arnup, Andree Levesque, and Ruth Roach Pierson, eds, *Delivering Motherhood: Maternal Ideologies and Practices in the 19th and 20th Centuries* (London and New York: Routledge 1990). Earlier periods are discussed in Wendy Mitchinson, *The Nature of Their Bodies: Women and Their Doctors in Victorian Canada* (Toronto: University of Toronto Press 1991).

17 Kendrick and Slade, *Spirit of Life*, 54; Laurie Bell, *A History of the Bay Centre for Birth Control* (Toronto: Women's College Hospital n.d., [ca. 1990]).

18 Kendrick and Slade, *Spirit of Life*, 29; WCH, Annual Reports.

19 The data come from Hospital Accreditation Surveys; WCH, Annual Reports; and Reports of Inspectors.

20. Repeated often in annual reports and histories, this claim originated with Dr Jennie Gray, WCH, "Report and History of the Women's College Hospital Dispensary," *Annual Report of the Women's College Hospital Dispensary* (1911), 4.

21 Reports of Inspectors, 1920–29.

22 The percentage is based on a review of the patient registers housed at WCH.

23 Carolyn Strange, *Toronto's Girl Problem: The Perils and Pleasures of the City, 1880–1930* (Toronto: University of Toronto Press 1995).

24 Jay Cassell, *The Secret Plague: A History of Venereal Disease in Canada* (Toronto: University of Toronto Press 1989).

25 Veronica Strong-Boag "Home Dreams: Women and the Suburban Experiment in Canada, 1945–1960," *Canadian Historical Review* 72 (1991): 471–504.

26 Katherine Arnup, *Education for Motherhood: Advice for Mothers in Twentieth Century Canada* (Toronto: University of Toronto Press 1994); Veronica Strong Boag, "Intruders in the Nursery: Childcare Professionals Reshape the Years One to Five," in Joy Parr, ed., *Childhood and Family in Canadian Society* (Toronto: McClelland and Stewart 1982).

27 The words of these women come from a series of taped oral histories conducted in 1993–94 with women who had experiences as patients at WCH. The sample was recruited through a newspaper ad and a snowball technique. All identifying information has been changed or removed.

28 Oral history, Mary

29 Oral history, Dorothy.

30 Rose Sheinin and Alan Bakes, *Women and Medicine in Toronto Since 1883: A Who's Who* (Toronto: University of Toronto Press 1987); Wendy Mitchinson, "Marion Hilliard," in J. Dicken and E. Cameron, *Great Dames* (Toronto: University of Toronto Press 1997); Marion Hilliard, *A Woman Doctor Looks at Love and Life* (New York: Permabooks 1953).

31 Oral history, Janet.
32 Accreditation Report, 1949, 12, WCHA.
33 WCH, Annual Report, 1953.
34 Rosemary Stevens, *In Sickness and in Wealth: American Hospitals in the Twentieth Century* (New York: Basic Books 1989); Daniel Fox, *Health Policies, Health Politics: The British and American Experience* (Princeton, N.J.: Princeton University Press, 1986).
35 Kenneth Hodgins, "Hospital Accreditation," address to the medical staff of Women's College Hospital, May 1965, typescript, s9, C20, file 1B, 1, WCHA.
36 Ibid.
37 Ibid.
38 Accreditation Surveys, 1949 and 1955, WCHA.
39 Hodgins, "Hospital Accreditation."
40 The Canadian context for obstetrical interventions is described in V. Strong-Boag and Kathryn McPherson, "The Confinement of Women: Childbirth and Hospitalization in Vancouver, 1919–1939," *BC Studies* 69–70 (1986): 147–74.
41 Accreditation Report, 1954, section 18, WCHA.
42 The aggregate and individual information is drawn from a review of a random series of patient case files for the period following the Second World War. The cases have been coded according to a system developed to track the work, and all identifying information has been removed or modified so as to protect the individual identities. Patient record code 1425, Health Records Unit, Sunnybrook and Womens College Hospital.
43 Accreditation Report, 1949, 12, WCHA.
44 Evelyn Fox Keller, *A Feeling for the Organism: The Life and Work of Barbara McKlintock* (San Francisco: W.H. Freeman 1983).
45 Patient record code 1479.
46 Patient record code 1367.
47 Angus McLaren, *Our Own Master Race: Eugenics in Canada, 1885–1945* (Toronto: McClelland and Stewart 1985). See also Angus McLaren and Arlene Tigar McLaren, *The Bedroom and the State: A History of Birth Control in Canada* (Toronto: McClelland and Stewart 1986); cf. Ladd-Taylor in this volume.
48 Patient record code 1457.
49 Patient record code 7555.
50 Historical critiques of medical dominance in childbirth in Canada can be found in Catherine L. Biggs, "The Case of the Missing Midwives: A History of Midwifery in Ontario from 1795–1900," *Ontario History* 65 (1983); and Suzanne Buckley, "Ladies or Midwifes? Efforts to Reduce Infant and Maternal Mortality," in Linda Kealey, ed., *A Not Unreasonable*

Claim: Women and Reform in Canada, 1880–1920s (Toronto: Women's Press 1976), 131–49.

51 C. Lesley Biggs, "Fragments from the History of Midwifery in Canada: A Reconsideration of the Historiographic Issues," in Ivy Bourgeault, Cecilia Benoit, and Robbie Davis-Floyd, eds, *Reconceiving Midwifery: The New Canadian Model of Care*, forthcoming.

52 For an example of traditional approaches, see Edward Shorter, *The History of Women's Bodies* (New York: Basic Books 1982). The classic critiques include Barbara Ehrenreich and Dierdre English, *For Her Own Good* (New York: Anchor Press 1979); Gena Corea, *The Hidden Malpractice: How American Medicine Mistreats Women* (New York: Harper & Row 1985); Barbara Katz Rothman, *In Labour: Women and Power in the Birthplace* (New York: Norton 1982); and Ann Oakley, "Wisewoman and Medicine Man: Changes in the Management of Childbirth," in J. Mitchell and A. Oakley, eds, *The Rights and Wrongs of Women* (London: Penguin 1976). Historical studies of birthing in Canada include J.T.H. Connor, "Larger Fish to Catch Here Than Midwives: Midwifery and the Medical Profession in Nineteenth-Century Ontario," in Diane Dodd and Deborah Gorham, eds, *Caring and Curing: Historical Perspectives on Women and Healing in Canada* (Ottawa: University of Ottawa Press 1994), 103–34; and Mitchinson, *Nature of Their Bodies*.

53 Susan Reverby and David Rosner, "Beyond the Great Doctors," in Reverby and Rosner, eds, *Health Care in America: Essays in Social History* (Philadelphia: Temple University Press 1979).

54 Biggs, "Fragments."

55 For example, see Catherine Biggs, Brian Burtch, and Farah Schroff, eds, *Health and Canadian Society/Santé et Société Canadienne, Special Issue on Midwifery* 4, no. 2 (1996–97).

56 Regina Morantz-Sanchez, *Sympathy and Science: Women Physicians in American Medicine* (New York: Oxford 1985); Virginia Drachman, *Hospital with a Heart: Women Doctors and the Paradox of Separatism at the New England Hospital, 1862–1969* (Ithaca and London: Cornell University Press 1984); Dodd and Gorham, *Caring and Curing*.

57 "Why Women Prefer Female Doctors," *Toronto Star*, 18 November 1989: 32.

58 A. Paul Williams et al., "Women in Medicine: Practice Patterns and Attitudes," CMAJ 143, no. 3 (1990): 194–201.

59 Strong-Boag, "Canada's Women Doctors." See also Dianne Dodd, "Helen MacMurchy: Popular Midwifery and Maternity Services for Canadian Pioneer Women," in Dodd and Gorham, *Caring and Curing*; and McLaren, "Becoming Indispensable."

60 *Toronto Star*, 23 June 1971; *Globe and Mail*, 24 June 1971.

61 Oral history, Grace.

62 Feminist columnists such as Doris Anderson, the former editor of *Chatelaine*, and Michele Landsberg took up WCH as a cause and wrote frequent articles in the *Toronto Star*. Doris Anderson, "Is Pioneering Hospital Facing a Hostile Takeover," *Toronto Star*, 23 October 1989.

63 The phrase, borrowed from an early WCH annual report, is featured in Kendrick and Slade, *Spirit of Life*.

7

Mission to Mothers: Nuns, Latino Families, and the Founding of Santa Fe's Catholic Maternity Institute

Laura E. Ettinger

In 1948 Rosita and José, a poor Latino couple living just outside of Santa Fe, New Mexico, began preparing for the birth of their first child.[1] During the early stages of her pregnancy, Rosita saw the nurse-midwives at Catholic Maternity Institute's clinic once a month. As she entered her seventh month, her visits increased. Recognizing that "motherhood is more than a physical experience," Rosita sought to gain a "richer and fuller appreciation of what it means to be a mother" by attending the institute's classes for prospective mothers. José also attended "special classes for fathers so that he [would have] some idea what to expect." When Rosita's labour began, José rushed to the local grocery store to call Sister Theophane, the attending nurse-midwife. Sister Theophane then joined José and Rosita's mother, offering Rosita support and praying for her. Carefully, Sister Theophane watched the progress of Rosita's labour, trying to interfere as little as possible. She encouraged Rosita to relax, gave her no anaesthetic, and did not restrain her in any way. Eventually they all welcomed a new healthy baby into the world. Sister Theophane's services did not end with the delivery; she visited the baby and family every other day for the first twelve days. After that, Rosita and her newborn went to the clinic for checkups.[2]

Catholic Maternity Institute (CMI), founded in 1944 in Santa Fe, New Mexico, by the Medical Mission Sisters, trained nuns and lay women to become nurse-midwives, and then provided prenatal, labour and delivery, and postnatal care to poor Latina women. CMI represents a blending of public and private sector health initiatives. It developed in cooperation with the Archbishop of Santa Fe, the New Mexico State Department of Health, and the United States Children's Bureau, but was staffed and maintained by the Medical Mission Sisters, a Philadelphia-based order with mostly foreign missions.

This chapter uses CMI to challenge the false opposition between science and religion. Despite the scholarly emphasis on the triumph of the "male medical model" of science and expertise after the Second World War, my study of CMI, like Aline Charles's essay on nuns in Quebec hospitals (Chapter 13), demonstrates the continuing importance of faith and religion in medicine. It shows the error of equating religion with tradition and science with modernity (since CMI nurse-midwives valued both religion and professionalism) and emphasizes the role of religious orders in the provision of modern health services.[3] Finally, by demonstrating that there were female medical experts who rejected the medicalization of motherhood before the women's movement in the late 1960s and 1970s, this essay challenges the conventional understanding of natural childbirth. Religion – not simply women's frustrations with depersonalized hospital births, psychological theories, and feminism – stimulated natural childbirth's popularity.[4]

CMI was the fifth nurse-midwifery service and school founded in the United States. Nurse-midwives (registered nurses with training in midwifery) first practised in the United States in the mid-1920s, constituting a new female occupation. They hoped to improve obstetrical and health care for women who would not otherwise be served by general practitioners or obstetricians. They provided their patients with prenatal, labour and delivery, postpartum, and general nursing services.

CMI was founded for two major reasons. First, the Catholic Church wanted to reduce the influence of Protestant missionaries, government agents, and family-planning advocates at Santa Fe's Maternal Health Center, a clinic founded by nationally known birth control activist Margaret Sanger. Second, the Medical Mission Sisters wanted to perform useful and professional work in accordance with their beliefs. By establishing CMI in 1944, the sisters created the first Catholic obstetrical educational program, training sister-nurse-midwives to serve patients in New Mexico and in missions around the world. Prior to 1936, the Catholic Church had prohibited nuns from engaging in surgery and obstetrics or performing any medical work that was deemed harmful to chastity. The Medical Mission Sisters was the first order to minister officially to child-bearing women and infants. CMI filled a need felt by medical missionary women who wanted to serve poor patients but could not go to distant lands such as India because of travel restrictions imposed by the Second World War.[5] In addition to providing opportunities for education and satisfying work, CMI gave nuns an opportunity to promote Catholic family values through family-centred, natural childbirth. While increasing numbers of North American women gave birth in isolated and sterile hospital rooms and received expensive and increasingly technological obstetrical care, the staff at CMI viewed birth as a natural, normal family event, requiring few, if any, medical or surgical interventions.

Northern New Mexico provided the perfect site for the mission for several reasons. First, the area's high rates of maternal and infant deaths already concerned the state health department, the federal Children's Bureau, the local Catholic Church, and medical missionary women. New Mexico had the highest infant mortality rate and the second highest maternal mortality rate in the United States.[6] The death rate among Latino infants and children was almost three times that of the Anglo population in this area.[7] Latinos made up 60.4 per cent of the population of Santa Fe County in 1950 and 54.3 per cent in 1960.[8] Low-income Latinas, who made up the majority of CMI's patients, had little or no access to professional health care and tended to use *parteras* (local midwives). Missionaries, like New Mexico public health authorities, saw *parteras* as unprofessional and even dangerous, and efforts to improve and regulate midwifery before and during the time CMI was in operation helped to bring a statewide decline in the number of *parteras*. However, many families in northern New Mexico, the area with the state's largest Latino population, continued to seek out traditional Latino birth attendants.[9] Although many poor Native Americans lived in the area CMI served, they did not need CMI because they received health-care services from a government-sponsored Indian hospital in Santa Fe.[10]

Another factor that made this site ideal was the perception in the area that Catholic views of religion and family were being threatened. Historically, Protestant and Catholic missionaries had competed throughout the American Southwest. Protestants had been more successful than Catholics in proselytizing after the Civil War and had developed a separate women's missionary movement in the Southwest. Protestant women sought to Americanize and convert Latino Catholics in northern New Mexico and southern Colorado, first through their schools and later through their health-care programs. While most Latino Catholics did not convert to Protestantism, they did take advantage of the education, health care, and other services the Protestants provided.[11] Although the Protestant threat may have lessened by the postwar period, it encouraged the church to provide Latino Catholics with health care within a Catholic setting.[12]

The church also wanted to offer an alternative to the Santa Fe Maternal Health Center. When the Maternal Health Center opened in 1937, Santa Fe's Archbishop denounced its distribution of birth control information and devices and warned his flock to stay away from the new clinic. The opposition of the Catholic Church, along with other needs of the Maternal Health Center's poor patients, caused the centre to de-emphasize its contraceptive services and focus more on providing comprehensive maternal and infant health care and social services.[13]

Condemnation of birth control was a major impetus for CMI's maternity work. Sister Catherine Shean, a CMI nurse-midwife, argued that CMI's creation was necessary more to combat "those who desire race suicide" than to provide birth attendants or lower the high maternal and infant mortality rates.[14] CMI nurse-midwives praised Latino Catholic families who "seem[ed] to achieve far greater success in rearing large families, and in trying to live according to the laws of God and Church, than many families in the middle and high income brackets in the large cities."[15] A Catholic magazine article on the Medical Mission Sisters' work at home and abroad argued: "Limiting the family to a few children, as advocated by Mrs Sanger and her ilk, may seem the obvious path to better health all around, more prosperity, easier living and less unhappiness. Strangely enough, it doesn't work out that way."[16]

The expansion of government-run maternal and child health services may have provided another impetus for CMI's creation. In the 1920s and 1930s, county, state, and federal health-care personnel, workers from New Deal agencies, agricultural and home demonstration agents, and literacy program teachers visited northern New Mexico to help poor Latino villagers.[17] These secular missionaries – social workers, teachers, and government agents – seemed to threaten the Catholic welfare programs. As the founder of the Medical Mission Sisters explained about the mission in Santa Fe, although "the Government has inaugurated rehabilitation and housing projects and the Public Health Department has given its services, ... there is plenty of room for improvement, and what is more important, opportunity and urgent need for Catholic initiative to extend the Church's social program to these peoples."[18]

To understand CMI's work, it is necessary to explore the role of nuns in health care and the history of the Medical Mission Sisters. Within the Catholic Church, this work was innovative. Until 1936 the Catholic Church prohibited nuns from providing for "the immediate care of children in the cradle or of women who ... have children in the houses called maternities and all other works of charity which do not seem fitting for virgins consecrated to God."[19] Although a few nuns worked in obstetrics and surgery despite the church's prohibition, none publicly challenged the canon law.[20] However, nuns had cared for the sick since ancient times. Women religious established the first Catholic hospital in the United States in 1820 and administered at least 265 hospitals during the nineteenth century. Nuns nursed soldiers, new immigrants, and victims of cholera, smallpox, and yellow fever. Nevertheless, papal prohibition forbade them to work in obstetric units – "*even assisting* at obstetrical cases" – or to work in nurseries, venereal wards, and other places where their sexual purity could be threatened. It also discouraged women religious from learning anatomy and surgical procedures.[21]

Changes to papal law came after much prodding. Agnes McLaren, an older Scottish physician and Catholic convert, and her protegé, Anna Dengel, a young Austrian physician, wanted nuns to staff a new Catholic hospital in India, where Muslim rules prohibited male doctors from attending women in childbirth. However, they encountered continual resistance from papal authorities. In 1925 Dengel finally decided to circumvent the canon law on women religious and medicine by founding the Medical Mission Sisters; its members would take private rather than conventional vows.[22]

In 1936, after McLaren's and Dengel's repeated requests for a change in the papal rules and after eleven years of the Medical Mission Sisters bringing medical aid to mission countries, Pope Pius XII allowed nuns to work in obstetrics. According to the papal instruction, mission lands needed nuns to provide "more suitable safeguards for the health of mothers and infants." In places such as Africa, mothers and babies were dying in large numbers, yet only "the civil authorities and non-Catholic sects are giving closest attention to these conditions." The instruction encouraged the development of new congregations of women religious devoted "to help[ing] both mothers and infants whose lives are endangered." It explained that "these new tasks demand both an adequate knowledge of the medical art and special training of the soul." Thus, nuns should obtain medical or nursing degrees from Catholic hospitals and universities, and receive special spiritual training as well.[23]

Catholic Maternity Institute responded to the 1936 papal instruction directly. CMI provided maternity services in homes and local clinics and established a school of nurse-midwifery, "*the only Catholic school of this kind in the United States.*"[24] Affiliated with the Catholic University of America in Washington, D.C., the CMI School of Nurse-Midwifery filled a real need by offering sister-nurse-midwives and other interested women clinical instruction and fieldwork in nurse-midwifery. After six months, students received a certificate in nurse-midwifery.[25] Not only did "they save the baby" in New Mexico – as the title of one article in the Catholic press claimed – students also saved souls in impoverished areas throughout the world. Although the school admitted women who were not nuns and not Catholic, many of those trained at CMI were sister-nurse-midwives who lived and worked in medical missions in developing countries.[26]

Catholic writers, pleased that the Catholic Church's long-standing prohibition against nuns working in obstetrics was lifted, had high hopes for the sister-nurse-midwives. As one Catholic writer explained, "Catholic Medical Missions could not develop because there were no Catholic doctors for the missions. The care of the sick for the most part was in the hands of Religious Sisterhoods, who were not allowed to study and practice medicine, surgery and obstetrics until recently."[27] A sister-physician writing in the Catholic medical press argued that "professional medical aid in Catholic missions has been, and still is, singularly backward." On the other hand, Protestants, she noted, had a long history of trained physicians, nurses, and midwives doing mission work.[28] With the advent of the Medical Mission Sisters, Catholics could now compete with Protestants in the growing area of professional health care; they could also compete for the bodies and souls of their patients. As one sister-nurse-midwife argued, "Medical work in the missions makes Christ's love for the sick a visible, tangible action that even the most ignorant can understand and appreciate."[29] For this nun, medical missionary work was a wedge into the culture and religion of the people she served.[30] In addition, in an era of medical professionalization, both the church and its nuns wanted the opportunity to offer health care based on scientific training to Catholic patients and potential converts.

CMI sisters combined religion and science. For the nuns, family-centred, natural childbirth reflected Catholic values. Thus, Sisters M. Theophane Shoemaker and M. Helen Herb, two of the first nurse-midwives to work at CMI, had trained at the Maternity Center Association, a New York nurse-midwifery school that helped to pioneer the natural childbirth method. Supporters of natural childbirth advocated minimal use of drugs, arguing that this allowed women to participate fully in the central event of their lives. According to its promoters, natural childbirth was an ecstatic experience requiring education and preparation. Developed in Britain in the early 1930s and popularized in the United States during the mid-1940s, natural childbirth depicted a woman's happiness in childbirth as the basis for a happy family and society. Informed by a postwar emphasis on motherhood, family, and home and by new psychological theories, natural childbirth advocates argued that labouring women who used this new method could feel pleasure and a sense of accomplishment, in addition to happiness. Many advocates saw natural childbirth as suitable for only some women, those with no medical or psychological complications and, equally importantly, those who asked for natural childbirth in advance; this latter group was usually limited to the upper and middle classes.[31] The select group of women who used natural childbirth often also chose to "room-in" with their newborns, rather than allow their babies to be separated from them during the postpartum period, as was the norm at American hospitals. Both rooming-in and natural childbirth were attempts to make hospital childbirth more personalized for child-bearing women.[32] Unlike most natural childbirth advocates, CMI also saw religion as a crucial element of family-centred and natural childbirth. These approaches to childbirth fit with CMI's desire to promote birth as both a manifestation of God and the most important event in a woman's life, to be shared by the whole family. According to CMI staff and students, witnessing and participating in the miracle of birth drew the Catholic family closer together.

For CMI nurse-midwives, birth was a moment of exhilaration, the revelation of God's work. A woman who accompanied a CMI nun on a delivery explained: "At the moment of birth of a baby (of a new soul) every woman is exalted. Feeling herself closer to creation, she remembers her secret pact with God somewhere in the depths of her spirit. All I can say, is that the feeling at that time was akin to joy and yet was above joy. Perhaps it was a sort of ecstasy which comes with the completion of birth – at the end of creation as at the beginning."[33] One Catholic magazine told the story of Mrs Adalina Montano, "a typical patient at the Catholic Maternity Institute," who was expecting her sixth child. Mrs Montano used the techniques she learned in CMI classes and thus "suffered no fear or tension during labor, but simply worked calmly to bring forth her child. During the whole time, her husband stood by, occasionally speaking softly to her and joining her in the Rosary. This seemed to give her a great deal of comfort. In a very short while, she gave birth to a healthy, beautiful little boy. After the baby was laid in his tiny bed, everyone joined together around Mrs Montano's bed to offer a simple prayer of thanks."[34] In a family-centred home delivery, God and family came together beautifully. As Sister Paula D'Errico remembered, "With home deliveries, I was always deeply impressed when the family got together bedside after birth. And mom and junior were at center stage. All the family knelt down and said a prayer of welcome to the baby and thanksgiving to God."[35]

CMI nurse-midwives' approach to childbirth challenged the distant professionalism common to modern medical practice.[36] Both CMI nurse-midwives and writers in the Catholic press favourably compared CMI's approach to childbirth with the approach found in more technological settings. After attending a home birth with one of the nuns, a CMI student-nurse-midwife "could not help marveling at the wonderful occurrence we had just witnessed. What a remarkable difference in this type of warm, personal consideration of the total family health picture, to the usual hospital delivery of a large city, with its marked impersonal professional team, its expensive equipment, and scientific explanations for 'rigid procedures, surgery, analgesia, anesthesia, and technique.' "[37] Another person who witnessed a CMI home birth maintained that "I was seeing what birth was meant to be – a family affair – not just another late night for an obstetrician, a headache for an overworked student-nurse, and the pacing of ether-smelling halls for the father, with nothing to do. No, this father had plenty to do and might still have. He had an important part in this lovely, mysterious drama. Thank God! I thought to myself, Christ was not born in a modern hospital. Could anything have been more horrible!"[38] For CMI's nuns, even a manger was preferable to the bleak, sterile hospital bed.

Prior to 1950, almost all CMI deliveries were conducted in patients' homes. This differed dramatically from national trends in childbirth; by 1950, 88 per cent of all American births took place in hospitals.[39] In 1951 CMI opened La Casita, the nation's first out-of-hospital birth centre, a maternity in-patient unit with a home-like atmosphere, to provide for patients who lived far from Santa Fe or whose homes would not be adequate for deliveries. As a result, home births declined. Despite the attempts of CMI staff to present "an adequate home environment as the ideal setting for a normal delivery," increasing numbers of women asked to be delivered at La Casita rather than at home. Patients argued that they received more adequate rest at La Casita, but CMI staff suspected that giving birth at La Casita might have represented status to some women.[40]

The evidence suggests that patients liked what CMI had to offer. Whether deliveries occurred at La Casita or in their homes, CMI's patients seemed to appreciate the nurse-midwives' commitment to personalized home (or home-like) care, as well as CMI's low price for that care. The patient caseload grew by word of mouth. In fact, CMI nurse-midwives often delivered the babies of several generations in one family.[41] Women who chose CMI could not have afforded maternity care in Santa Fe's only hospital, St Vincent's Hospital, run by the Sisters of Charity, or from Santa Fe's limited number of general practitioners, but beyond the consideration of prohibitive cost, CMI's patients may have avoided physician and hospital care because of a preference for female birth attendants.[42]

Catholic Maternity Institute seems to have provided a middle ground between scientific male medicine and the traditional *partera*. Not formally educated, *parteras* learned mostly from other *parteras*, often older female relatives and neighbours, as well as through occasional contact with physicians and the classes for midwives arranged by the New Mexico Department of Public Health. Highly esteemed in their own communities, *parteras* performed their work as neighbours and friends, not only as wage labourers. The care they provided varied, depending on their skills and experience, as well as on their knowledge of and access to scientific medicine. Some knew safe hygienic practices, while others did not. Many used folk practices passed down through generations. Traditionally, *parteras* provided no prenatal care; many Latinas, like other lower-class women, did not see the necessity of prenatal care because they viewed pregnancy and childbirth as natural states. *Parteras* delivered babies in the mothers' homes using medicinal plants to hasten the delivery or deal with problems, such as postpartum hemorrhage. They also provided a comfortable environment for birth and said prayers as part of their services. In the postpartum period, *parteras* advised new mothers to stay in bed for eight days and to eat a special *dieta* for forty days following the birth. After taking health department midwives' classes and receiving a midwifery licence, some *parteras* became well respected in both Latino and Anglo communities. They mixed Latino and Anglo healing practices and worked with local nurse-midwives, public health nurses, and physicians.[43]

Unlike many *parteras*, CMI nurse-midwives placed great emphasis on prenatal care. Months before her delivery, the patient registered with CMI, where a nurse-midwife took her medical history and the medical director, a certified obstetrician, performed a complete medical examination. Thereafter, the patient visited the prenatal clinic once a month through the seventh month and then every two weeks until the ninth month, when she was examined weekly by the nurse-midwives. Pregnant women also attended six mothers' classes, which included instruction on normal childbirth; those who could not attend received individual instruction. In the last month, the medical director performed another medical examination. As a CMI nurse-midwife explained, "When a patient is in labor and a normal delivery is anticipated, she calls the Institute and a certified nurse-midwife attends her in her home, giving support, maintaining nutrition, coaching her through the labor and, ultimately, delivering the infant." The nurse-midwives prepared patients for natural childbirth, but gave analgesics, such as Demerol, when necessary. If complications arose, patients were sent to CMI's medical director or to nearby St Vincent's Hospital. The nurse-midwives also made postpartum and newborn visits on the first, third, fifth, seventh, ninth, and twelfth days after the birth.44 As stated earlier, the nurse-midwives, like the *parteras*, spent extensive time with patients and their families, and they supported the families' emphasis on prayer and religious ritual.45

Unlike *parteras*, CMI nurse-midwives did not share their patients' ethnicity. They did, however, have a common religion. The fact that many CMI nurse-midwives were nuns surely helped CMI to attract and retain patients. CMI's mostly Catholic patients seem to have felt an immediate trust in the sister-nurse-midwives because they were nuns. The patients even transferred that trust to any lay students accompanying the nuns.

The religious, ethnic, class, and regional backgrounds of the nurse-midwifery students at CMI varied; included among the students were nuns from different religious communities as well as lay people from throughout the United States and abroad. Despite these internal differences, CMI's approach and its association with nuns continued to dominate, indicating that the commitment to natural childbirth and the shared religion created a powerful bond among the diverse staff, students, and patients.46

The language barrier was undoubtedly a problem. Few nurse-midwives or nurse-midwifery students spoke Spanish, although they generally learned some Spanish words along with way. In the prenatal clinic, CMI used volunteers to translate. When the nurse-midwives assisted at home deliveries, they found that many of the men spoke English and most of the women knew at least some English. Reflecting on the attitudes she and her fellow CMI staff members held in the mid-twentieth century, Sister Catherine Shean explained: "The thinking [at the time CMI opened] was that the Spanish-American people were American citizens and so they should learn to speak English ... Looking back now, I think it would have been wonderful if we'd all spoken Spanish."47

Clearly, CMI's patients preferred nurse-midwives over healers within their own communities.48 CMI's nurse-midwives offered patients an opportunity to combine their own view of birth, as a natural, religious event occurring in the home, with the promise and status of safe, modern, scientific, and professional care. The sisters also believed that natural childbirth appealed to their patients and was one of the reasons they chose to use CMI. CMI nurse-midwife Sister M. Michael Waters argued that an emphasis on "the *mother's own idea*, that childbirth is a natural function of the body, normally uncomplicated," helped convince Latina women of the need for medical supervision during pregnancy.[49]

Catholic Maternity Institute closed in 1969 because of financial problems and the Medical Mission Sisters' commitment to foreign populations. As the number of sister-nurse-midwives declined, CMI was forced to pay an expanding lay staff modest salaries. The sisters, who had always focused on foreign missions, decided to place their limited resources in areas outside the United States that had greater needs and fewer health professionals. The Medical Mission Sisters considered CMI to be a luxury service. While the sisters at CMI might have seen thirty to fifty patients each day, those working in India might have seen five hundred patients each day. In addition, by the late 1960s, with CMI's help, mothers and children in the region CMI served enjoyed more health-care options than they had in 1944. In Santa Fe County, the infant death rate per 1,000 live births had decreased from 87.6 in 1939 to 15.1 in 1967, compared with an overall decline in the United States from 48.0 to 22.1. The maternal death rate per 1,000 live births in Santa Fe County decreased from 4.67 to zero.[50] Low-income families could now choose hospital care for their deliveries because New Mexico had passed a bill paying for hospital service for the medically indigent and Santa Fe's St Vincent's Hospital had expanded to service all of the area's maternity needs. CMI also faced increasing opposition from local physicians and decreasing enthusiasm from the School of Nursing at the Catholic University of America. As a consequence of all these factors, the Medical Mission Sisters decided to turn their program over to the community.[51]

In August 1969 responsibility for CMI was transferred to a local lay board of directors and the institute became the Community Maternity Institute – still CMI. Investigations in 1968 and 1970 concluded that CMI had "serious financial troubles," since it generally served low-income families unable to pay their bills. The investigations indicated further that CMI did not have enough local financial support and needed outside funds to continue. In addition, they found that CMI lacked support from Santa Fe's medical profession. Despite these problems, the investigations noted "enthusiastic endorsement" of CMI's work from patients and a continuing need for the maternity services CMI provided. Between late 1969 and June 1970, Community Maternity Institute operated a limited program, with prenatal and postnatal care performed by its staff and the actual deliveries done by physicians at a local hospital. However, after investigating several possible roles for CMI, the board of directors voted to close existing services in June 1970.[52]

At the time of its closure, CMI had satisfied the missionary goals of the Catholic Church and the Medical Mission Sisters. First, through its work, CMI had offered an alternative to the services of Protestant missionaries, government agents, and family-planning advocates in the area. Second, CMI's nurse-midwifery staff had reinforced Catholic family values through its personal, family centred, and natural approach to childbirth. Although similar to that of other nurse-midwifery services, this approach differed from the care most American women received in hospitals. Finally, CMI allowed nuns, for the first time, to receive an obstetrical education in a Catholic setting. Thus, CMI provided a place for the Catholic Church to do good work, provide health care within a Catholic environment, and keep Catholic families in its fold. CMI also offered the Medical Mission Sisters an opportunity to serve the poor, promote their values regarding childbirth, birth control, and the family, and openly do work that until then had been forbidden to Catholic nuns.

CMI, then, forces us to reassess the dominance of the male medical model in the years following the Second World War. It demonstrates that the bureaucratization found in twentieth-century hospitals and childbirth was not all-pervasive and did not go unchallenged. Drawing on their deep commitment to both religion and science, CMI nurse-midwives offered their patients the advantages of medical science without the disadvantages of depersonalized, assembly-line care. The history of CMI clearly proves that health-care providers and patients sought to mix faith in religion with faith in science. It thus shows the importance of considering faith and religion when writing the history of maternity care.

NOTES

Author's note: The author wishes to thank the following people for their help in the development of this essay: Theodore Brown, Carol Coburn, Lynn Gordon, Molly Ladd-Taylor, Judith Walzer Leavitt, Alexandra Lord, and Kathleen Mahoney.

The chapter's title comes from a *Time* article on Catholic Maternity Institute: "Mission to Mothers," *Time*, 9 December 1946.

1 Debates abound over the appropriate terminology to use for people of Mexican origin. I have chosen to use the broad term, Latino, when discussing Catholic Maternity Institute's patients.

According to Felipe Gonzales, director of the Southwest Hispanic Research Institute and associate professor of sociology, University of New Mexico, it is safe to assume that the Latino population in Santa Fe County and surrounding areas has roots going back to the nineteenth century. Although New Mexico is at the Mexican border, it has received the smallest amount of modern Mexican immigration of all the border states with a large Mexican immigrant and/or Mexican-American population. In addition, the fact that Catholic Maternity Institute nurse-midwives described their patients as "Spanish-American" gives more credence to the argument that Mexican-Americans, not Mexican immigrants, populated the area. Gonzales says that Anglos would have been even more likely than Latinos to distinguish between different Latino populations, and would have called their patients "Mexicans" if they had been Mexican immigrants. Felipe Gonzales, personal communication with the author, 15 February 2001.

2 This story comes from Pauline E. King, producer, "Nurse-Midwife," film (Santa Fe: Catholic Maternity Institute 1948), Medical Missions Sisters Archives (hereafter MMSA), Philadelphia, Pa. The film shows this family and the birth of their baby. Some women did not receive prenatal care as often as the nurse-midwives recommended. However, all received much more care than they would have had otherwise.

3 See Robert A. Orsi, *Thank You, St. Jude: Women's Devotion to the Patron Saint of Hopeless Causes* (New Haven, Conn.: Yale University Press 1996), 182–3.

4 See Helen Wessel, *Natural Childbirth and the Christian Family* (New York: Harper & Row 1963), for a popular discussion of the connections between natural childbirth and Christianity. Wessel's book is currently in its fifth edition (1994).

5 The Medical Mission Sisters opened two "home missions" during the Second World War, one in Santa Fe and another in Atlanta. See "Catholic Colored Clinic, Atlanta, Ga.," *Medical Missionary Magazine*, September-October 1955: 115, MMSA; Medical Mission Sisters, *History of the Society of Catholic Medical Missionaries, Pre-Foundation to 1968* (London: Medical Mission Sisters 1991): 182–4, MMSA; Rita McInerney, "DeGive Family Colorful in City, Catholic History," *Georgia Bulletin: The Official Newspaper of the Archdiocese of Atlanta* 31, no. 20 (20 May 1993): 4–5.

6 "Many Mothers and Babies Saved by Medical Mission Sisters," *Santa Fe New Mexican*, 8 March 1945, MMSA.

7 "Great Progress Made by Maternity Institute Nuns," *Register, Santa Fe, New Mexico*, 15 July 1945, MMSA.

8 The 1950 Latino population statistic is from census statistics included in City Planning Commission, City of Santa Fe, *General Characteristics, City of Santa Fe, New Mexico* (Santa Fe: Urban Planning Assistance Program of the New Mexico State Department of Finance and Administration 1960): 21. The 1960 statistic is from census statistics included in Bureau of Business Research, Institute for Social Research and Development, *New Mexico*

Statistical Abstract, 1970 (Albuquerque: University of New Mexico 1970),
1:16. The statistic from both decades includes "white persons of Spanish
surname."

9 Sandra Schackel, *Social Housekeepers: Women Shaping Public Policy in New
Mexico, 1920–1940* (Albuquerque: University of New Mexico Press 1992),
50.

10 Although CMI served mostly poor Latinas, it was open to anyone. Shortly
before it closed in 1969, CMI served several Anglo women who had come
there specifically for an alternative to hospital care. Telephone interview by
the author with Sister Catherine Shean, 18 August 2000; telephone interview by the author with Rita Kroska, 24 July 2000.

    Although located in an urban area, CMI served women in an area of
2,827 square miles within a radius of 30 miles from Santa Fe. Elinor Miller,
"Grand Multiparas: A Ten-Year Study," *Obstetrics and Gynecology* 4, no. 4
(October 1954): 419.

11 Sarah Deutsch, *No Separate Refuge: Culture, Class, and Gender on the Anglo-
Hispanic Frontier in the American Southwest, 1880–1940* (New York: Oxford
University Press 1987); Susan M. Yohn, *A Contest of Faiths: Missionary Women
and Pluralism in the American Southwest* (Ithaca, N.Y.: Cornell University Press
1995); Gilberto M. Hinojosa, "Mexican-American Faith Communities in
Texas and the Southwest," in *Mexican Americans and the Catholic Church,
1900–1965*, ed. Jay P. Dolan and Gilberto M. Hinojosa (Notre Dame, Ind.:
University of Notre Dame Press 1994), 26–45.

12 Sister Catherine Shean, a nurse-midwife who worked at CMI from 1945
until its closing in 1969, does not think that the Protestant missionaries
posed a problem for the Medical Mission Sisters. She argued that the sisters
always tried to work in cooperation with others, helping their patient populations. She also explained that in the early 1960s CMI had a short-lived
arrangement with Presbyterian-Embudo Hospital, north of Santa Fe, that
involved providing the nurse-midwifery students with hospital experience.
St Vincent's Hospital, a Catholic hospital in Santa Fe, refused to allow the
nurse-midwifery students to deliver babies there. Telephone interview by
the author with Sister Catherine Shean, 18 August 2000.

13 Michael Anne Sullivan, "Walking the Line: Birth Control and Women's
Health at the Santa Fe Maternal Health Center, 1937–1970" (MA thesis,
University of New Mexico 1995).

14 Article in *El Paso News*, 27 October 1947, MMSA.

15 Rose Gioiosa, "Life Begins in an Adobe: Home Maternity Service of the
Medical Mission Sisters," *Child-Family Digest*, October 1953: 56 (reprinted
from the *Grail*), MMSA.

16 Mary Zook, "Sister-Doctor," *Extension*, November 1955: 68, MMSA.

17 Deutsch, *No Separate Refuge*, 183.

18 Anna Dengel, *Mission for Samaritans: A Survey of Achievements and Opportunities in the Field of Catholic Medical Missions* (Milwaukee: Bruce Publishing Company 1945), 113.

19 Quoted from the Sacred Congregation of Bishops and Regulars, 1901, in Sister M. Bonaventure Beck, "The Society of Catholic Medical Missionaries: Origin and Development" (MS thesis, Catholic University of America 1955), 20.

20 See, for example, a photograph of nuns in an operating room at the turn of the twentieth century in Kathy Smith Franklin, "'A Spirit of Mercy': The Sisters of Mercy and the Founding of Saint Joseph's Hospital, Phoenix, 1892–1912," Twenty-ninth Annual Conference of the Western Association of Women Historians, San Marino, California, 17 May 1998. Carol K. Coburn's research on nuns at the Troy Maternity Hospital in 1909 and 1910 indicates that Catholic sisters did obstetric work. Carol K. Coburn, personal communication with the author, 17 May 1998.

21 Jo Ann Kay McNamara, *Sisters in Arms: Catholic Nuns through Two Millennia* (Cambridge, Mass.: Harvard University Press 1996), 622–6. For the statistic on nuns administering hospitals in the nineteenth century, see Mary Ewens, "The Leadership of Nuns in Immigrant Catholicism," in *Women and Religion in America*, vol. 1: *The Nineteenth Century*, ed. Rosemary Radford Ruether and Rosemary Skinner Keller (San Francisco: Harper & Row 1981), 102. On the prohibition of "*even assisting* at obstetrical cases," see "First Medical Mission Sisterhood," *Catholic Missions* 27, no. 6 (August-September 1950): 6, MMSA.

22 Zook, "Sister-Doctor," 32–3; Medical Mission Sisters, *History of the Society of Catholic Medical Missionaries, Pre-Foundation to 1968*, chaps 1–3.

23 Quoted from Instruction, Issued by the Sacred Congregation for the Propagation of the Faith to the Religious Institutes of Women, 11 February 1936, in Beck, "The Society of Catholic Medical Missionaries," 145–6.

24 "First Medical Mission Sisterhood," 12 (emphasis in original).

25 Sister Rosemary Smyth, "History of the Catholic Maternity Institute from 1943 to 1958" (MS thesis, Catholic University of America 1960), 44–53. Starting in 1947, CMI also offered a master's program with a major in maternity nursing, designed to "give a broad professional background to graduate nurses who intended to do administration, teaching, supervision, or consultation in the field of obstetric nursing." In 1954 CMI extended the work for the certificate program from six months to one year.

26 I interviewed several sister-nurse-midwives who trained at CMI. The work of Sister Paula D'Errico seems typical. After receiving her nurse-midwifery certificate in 1952, Sister Paula D'Errico went on to medical missions in Venezuela, Ghana, Kenya, South Africa, and Ethiopia. Interview by the author with Sister Paula D'Errico, Philadelphia, Pa., 6 September 1995.

27 "First Medical Mission Sisterhood," 5.

28 Sister M. Elise Wynen, "The Society of Catholic Medical Missionaries," *Catholic Medical Quarterly*, January 1949: 45–6, MMSA.

29 Beck, "The Society of Catholic Medical Missionaries," 6.

30 See E. Richard Brown, "Public Health Programs in Imperialism: Early Rockefeller Programs at Home and Abroad," *American Journal of Public Health* 66, no. 9 (September 1976): 897–903, for an argument about how philanthropies set up health-care programs as a way to introduce a wedge into the native cultures.

31 Margarete Sandelowski, *Pain, Pleasure, and American Childbirth: From the Twilight Sleep to the Read Method, 1914–1960* (Westport, Conn.: Greenwood Press 1984), chaps 4 and 5.

32 Sara Lee Silberman, "Pioneering in Family-Centered Maternity and Infant Care: Edith B. Jackson and the Yale Rooming-In Research Project," *Bulletin of the History of Medicine* 64, no. 2 (Summer 1990): 262–87. Judith Walzer Leavitt describes women's alienating experiences of hospital births in *Brought to Bed: Childbearing in America, 1750–1950* (New York: Oxford University Press 1986), 171–95.

33 Sally Green, "Lo! A Child Is Born: The Ever-Wondrous Miracle of the Birth of a Baby," *Rosary*, December 1957: 13, MMSA.

34 Jacques and Jillen Lowe, "Nurse-Midwives of Santa Fe," *Sign*, April 1955: 52, MMSA.

35 Rita A. Kroska, executive producer, "50th Celebration Reunion, Remembering CMI Santa Fe," video (Tucson: Medical Mission Sisters/Catholic Maternity Institute Historical Project 1994).

36 On Catholic sister-nurses and the struggles they faced trying to reconcile their profession and their vocation, see Christopher J. Kauffman, *Ministry and Meaning: A Religious History of Catholic Health Care in the United States* (New York: Crossroad Publishing Company 1995), 154–81, 238–44.

37 Gioiosa, "Life Begins in an Adobe," 55.

38 Green, "Lo! A Child Is Born," 11.

39 Neal Devitt, "The Transition from Home to Hospital Birth in the United States, 1930–1960," *Birth and the Family Journal* 4, no. 2 (Summer 1977): 56.

40 Smyth, "History of the Catholic Maternity Institute," 27–9.

41 Telephone interview by the author with Sister Catherine Shean, 18 August 2000.

42 On Latina women's preference for female attendants, see Sister M. Lucia van der Eerden, *Maternity Care in a Spanish-American Community of New Mexico*, Catholic University of America Anthropological Series, no. 13 (Washington, D.C.: Catholic University of America Press 1948), 54–5.

43 Van der Eerden, *Maternity Care in a Spanish-American Community*, 8–19; Fran Leeper Buss, *La Partera: Story of a Midwife* (Ann Arbor: University of Michigan Press 1980), 7, 65–6; transcript of interview by Jake Spidle with

Anne Fox, in 1986, p. 11, University of New Mexico Medical Center Library, New Mexico Medical History Project, Oral History Collection, Albuquerque, N.M.; telephone interview by the author with Sister Catherine Shean, 18 August 2000.

44 Miller, "Grand Multiparas," 418–19; Cecilia Buser, "How I Came to Become a Nurse-Midwife and Came to Love It," in *CMI Graduates and Faculty Remember Nurse-Midwifery in Santa Fe, New Mexico*, ed. Rita A. Kroska and Catherine Shean (Tucson, 1996), 12–17.

45 Catholic nurses and nuns also supported Catholic patients' emphasis on prayer and religious rituals in hospitals. Orsi, *Thank You, St. Jude*, 166–7, 177–82.

46 Interview with Sister Catherine Shean, in Rita A. Kroska, executive producer, "CMI: In-Depth Interviews with the Foundresses," video (Tucson: Medical Mission Sisters/Catholic Maternity Institute Historical Project 1996); telephone interview by the author with Sister Catherine Shean, 18 August 2000; telephone interview by the author with Rita Kroska, 24 July 2000.

47 Telephone interview by the author with Sister Catherine Shean, 18 August 2000.

48 Most patients who registered with CMI for maternity care ultimately delivered with CMI's nurse-midwives or, in the case of problems, with the help of CMI's medical director. However, a few CMI patients who registered with CMI delivered their babies with a traditional midwife or a private physician. See book #1, Delivery Records, December 1943–April 1963, CMI, MMSA.

49 Sister M. Michael Waters, "Culture in Relation to a Maternity Service," *Public Health Nursing* 42 (1950): 70 (my emphasis).

50 U.S. Public Health Service Bureau of Health, Manpower Education, Division of Nursing, "A Study to Determine the Need and Scope for Educational Programs in Nurse-Midwifery and/or Continuing Education for Maternity Nursing in New Mexico and the Direction Each Should Take," *Final Report*, 1 October 1970–31 December 1971, 10, personal files of Ruth Watson Lubic [former director of Maternity Center Association].

51 Telephone interview by the author with Sister Catherine Shean, 18 August 2000; telephone interview by the author with Rita Kroska, 24 July 2000.

52 U.S. Public Health Service Bureau of Health, "A Study to Determine the Need and Scope for Educational Programs in Nurse-Midwifery," 14–16.

8

"Midwife Preferred": Maternity Care in Outpost Nursing Stations in Northern Canada, 1945–1988

Judith Bender Zelmanovits

When nurse Jean Goodwill was hired by the Department of National Health and Welfare [DNHW] to work in an Arctic nursing station in the 1950s, the Canadian government was in the process of expanding the services it provided to northern Aboriginal[1] communities. One of the reasons underlying the expansion was a concern in the postwar period about infant mortality rates, purportedly disproportionately higher in the North than in southern areas of the country.[2] The other main factor cited was high rates of tuberculosis.[3]

Goodwill had no special training in midwifery or advanced obstetrics, but she was assured that a nurse with midwifery training would join her within six months. However, the nurse-midwife never arrived, leaving Goodwill and a nursing assistant to deliver fifty babies in her first year of service.[4] This experience is similar to that of many of the nurses who graduated from Canadian hospital and university schools of nursing and were hired during the period under study – 1945 to 1988 – and her story points to two of the issues that will be explored in this chapter. First, while the government recognized the need to provide obstetrical services to northern communities, its intentions were constantly undermined by its inefficiencies in staffing the nursing stations with sufficient appropriately qualified personnel. The second issue, a consequence of the first, was that, in the North, nurses had an opportunity to expand their skills in maternity care in an environment where they had greater autonomy and professional authority than they would have had in nursing positions in the south.

In this exploration of the role played by non-Aboriginal "southern" nurses in the provision of maternity care to Aboriginal women in northern Canada in the decades following the Second World War, the focus is on *station* or *outpost* nurses, those women who, alone or with another nurse,[5] were charged with providing primary care in nursing stations established and maintained by DNHW. Some attention is paid as well to nurses who worked in the small hospitals established in the zones,[6] administrative units created by the Department of Indian Affairs; these nurses cared for parturient Aboriginal women who had been evacuated from their communities and they also provided escort duty on "medivac" missions to transport high-risk mothers or mothers and premature babies from their remote communities to southern hospitals.[7]

While traditional research methods based on archival sources are used in this study, the insights of nurses, as recorded in unpublished sources, such as diaries, letters, and field reports, and in published accounts, including articles from professional journals and memoirs in book format, and the recollections they shared in personal and telephone interviews provide the centre of focus.[8] Their voices reflect their personal stories, which differ according to their training and experience, the time frame and geographic location of their service to DNHW, and their personal world view. Perspectives also differ according to whether their stories were written at the time of their sojourn in the North or were filtered by time. All interviews took place after a lapse of time; for some, this was almost half a century. Many of the interviewees refreshed their memories by looking at slides, photos, souvenirs, and government correspondence and by rereading letters and diary entries, materials often shared with me at the time of the interview or subsequently. Although the narratives offer an incomplete story, shaped as they are by nostalgia, selection, and self-censorship, they point clearly to overriding commonalities of theme.

The vast northern regions to which Canadian nurses were posted included Arctic and Subarctic areas. The Arctic extended from the 60th parallel north to Ellesmere Island and from Yukon Territory in the west to Baffin Island in the east,[9] and the Subarctic consisted of the northern areas of the provinces whose communities were distant from provincial health facilities. Many of the settlements were – and are at present – accessible only by plane and by season. The majority of the inhabitants were Aboriginal people, but there were also non-Aboriginals, including teachers, Royal Canadian Mounted Police (RCMP), and store managers.[10] The nurses provided primary health care and, in many cases, they also made regular visits to small surrounding settlements that did not have a nurse. While most of the patient care was done on

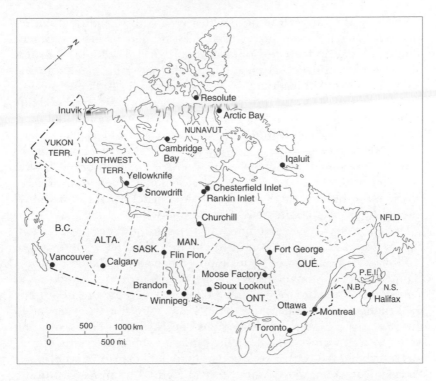

an outpatient basis, the nursing stations in which the nurses lived and worked included beds for short-term live-in patients, such as parturient women.

As will be shown in this chapter, the role of region is important, as it shapes the work performed by the nurses. There is a strong body of critical literature that explores the class, race, and gendered dimensions of various types of public health work, including service to Indian reservations.[11] While northern nurses are not public health nurses per se (in fact, few among those included in the study had official training in public health when they accepted their initial posting), many of the themes that emerge from their accounts are similar to those in the public health literature. A major factor that differentiates their experience from that of nurses in southern Canada is the geographic and social isolation of the communities they served.[12] Their responsibility was significant, as they were forced to make diagnostic and prescriptive decisions often without benefit of advice from colleagues. They had to perform procedures that were outside their usual scope because transport of patients to the nearest hospital was not expedient, and they worked with little supervision, since those to whom they reported were in distant offices in zone headquarters or Ottawa.

Responsibility for providing health care to Aboriginal people has historically been a controversial issue, as attested to in government documents dating back to Confederation in 1867. While the British North America (BNA) Act charged the federal government with the responsibility for "Indians and the lands reserved for Indians," the government acknowledged a moral but not a legal or treaty responsibility to provide health services.[13] Little interest in the development of medical services was demonstrated by the Department of Indian Affairs (DIA), which waited until 1904 to appoint its first medical superintendent. Responsibility changed hands when DIA was absorbed by the Department of Mines and Natural Resources in 1936, and its medical division, the Indian and Northern Health Service (INHS), was subsequently transferred to the newly formed DNHW in 1945.[14]

Dr Percy Moore, superintendent of INHS at the time of expansion, clearly expressed the position of the branch when he wrote in 1946, "Although neither law nor treaty imposes such a duty, the Federal government has, for humanitarian reasons, for self-protection, and to prevent spread of disease to the white population, accepted responsibility for health services to the native population."[15] At this time, service to the vast area of the northern regions consisted of twenty-seven full-time physicians and twenty-four field nurses, whose professional care was supplemented by the work of part-time field matrons and dispensers, many of whom were without formal medical training.[16] Until the mid-1970s, there was a steady increase in the number of nursing stations, and these became, as described by J.B. Waldram, "the backbone" of the Medical Services Branch (MSB), the branch that replaced INHS in 1962.[17]

State medical service to Inuit communities developed much more slowly than that provided to Indian communities. In their study of the Inuit people of Arctic Canada, Tester and Kulchyski refer to "an era of neglect of Inuit affairs on the part of the state"[18] in the first half of the century, a situation that slowly began to change with respect to medical services when the federal government established its first nursing station at Port Harrison in the Eastern Arctic in 1947. By the mid-1960s, there were twenty-five stations.[19]

Since the graduate nurse force was, according to annual reports from the ministry, "at the heart of the field service,"[20] responsibility for maternity care was considered one of the most important aspects of northern nurses' jobs; yet, for many reasons, it was one of the least clearly defined. Most of the nurses working in the North were prepared through their training and experience in southern Canadian hospitals to give some perinatal care, but not to perform deliveries, a task that was the prerogative of doctors.[21] No provision was made for advanced obstetrical training before the nurses took up their posts in remote communities, and once they were in the field, DNHW turned a blinkered eye to the work they were doing. Thus, for a period of several decades, the work of providing maternity care to Aboriginal women in some of Canada's isolated northern communities involved expanded scope and authority for nurses from the south. These nurses often functioned as midwives, an occupation that held an "alegal"[22] status in the country at the time, and many provided a type and quality of care that was consistent with the cultural norms of the communities in which they were working.[23]

In the sources surveyed and in nurses' oral accounts, there is ample evidence of the tasks they performed. Maternity service in the nursing stations was divided into three stages: antenatal, perinatal, and post-natal care. In all stages, because station nurses were the only caregivers in communities, they assumed many of the responsibilities generally undertaken by physicians in southern, urban areas of the country. Elements of prenatal and postnatal care are clearly recorded in the 1971 *Report of Special Project Nursing*[24] and attested to by nurses in their interviews. Prenatal care consisted of monthly checkups. At the first appointment, the nurse confirmed the pregnancy, took a history, and did a complete physical, which included urinalysis, abdominal examination, Pap smear, and examination for sexually transmitted diseases (STDs). At subsequent appointments, the nurse monitored blood pressure, hemoglobin, weight, and fetal heart rate. She also counselled her patient about confinement, prescribed vitamins and iron, and offered support. If an expectant woman showed any unusual symptoms, she might be kept in the nursing station overnight. Nurses often gave prenatal talks on subjects such as pregnancy, childbirth, diet, and budgeting time for the new baby and other children. During delivery, which was often performed by the nurse, in addition to her regular tasks, she might have checked the baby for phenylketonuria[25] and applied silver nitrate to the baby's eyes.[26] In the postnatal period, nurses saw new mothers weekly up to six weeks, checking breasts and perineum (especially if there was a tear during delivery), checking for bleeding or infections, offering advice on feeding the baby, and providing information about immunization and birth control. A complete physical was done at six weeks. For the baby, temperature, pulse, and respiration were checked, height and weight were recorded, and the cord was checked and cleaned.

There is no doubt that DNHW officials preferred to hire nurses with midwifery training for positions at northern nursing stations. This sort of hiring, with precedent in Canadian history,[27] seemed advantageous from three perspectives: it demonstrated that the government was attempting to deal with the high infant mortality rate; it spoke to the problem that the few doctors with the Indian and Northern Health Service were geographically scattered across the North and only visited certain communities once or twice yearly; and perhaps most importantly, it had economic benefits. A nurse-midwife within a community meant that doctors could make fewer visits to it and fewer women had to be transported out to zone hospitals or southern cities to deliver their babies. As transportation in and out of isolated settlements was by air and hence often difficult and always expensive, nursing station deliveries would save money; as well, they would lessen the problem caused by the interruption in health-care service to the community that resulted when a nurse had to accompany a woman on her trip out of the settlement.

However, in Canada during most of the period under study, there was no training for or official recognition of midwifery as a separate discipline and very few women were trained as nurse-midwives. The University of Alberta School of Nursing began offering an advanced practical obstetrics course for graduate nurses in 1943, but its graduates seldom numbered more than ten per year.[28] It was not until 1967 that Dalhousie offered an outpost nursing program that featured training in midwifery.[29] This shortage in Canada of nurses trained in midwifery meant that nurses had to be imported from abroad, particularly from Great Britain and Australia, where their training included practical experience in midwifery. Dr John Read, professor of preventive medicine at Queen's University, provided evidence of this in his report on his visit to the Moose Factory region in 1965: "My initial impression was that all the nurses had 'accents.' I subsequently learned that only one of the 'outpost' nurses was from Canada, most of them being from the Commonwealth countries. There seemed to be two main reasons for this, the one being the pioneering attitude of these girls and the second related to their training and experience in midwifery."[30]

An ideal applicant was nurse Anna Chan, who left her home and family in Hong Kong to train in nursing and midwifery in London, England.[31] Her practical experience prior to migrating to Canada included the delivery of some two hundred babies[32] and extensive public health work in South London. On immigrating to Canada, she was employed for five years at Doctor's Hospital in Toronto, where she soon found that she missed the opportunity to use her midwifery skills. Thus, in 1970, she acted on a colleague's suggestion to apply for work in the Canadian North. Within two weeks, DNHW responded to her letter of inquiry, acknowledging that "her qualifications were perfect" and offering her a position in the East Arctic settlement of Arctic Bay, situated on the northern shore of Baffin Island. Anna provided references, but no interview was requested. When Sue Pauhl applied in 1971, she was immediately hired, too, and placed in the northern Ontario community of Moose Factory.[33] In fact, when the employers read her application, they asked her to begin work the next week. Although she was not a registered nurse (RN), in her position as a registered nursing assistant (RNA), she had eleven years of experience in labour and delivery and in emergency OR (operating room). These women were the ideal nursing recruits, but they seem to have been the exception among applicants.

Lois Chételat reports that, as a new graduate from a hospital school of nursing in London, Ontario, in 1961, she was not so readily placed. After being hired by INHS, she was informed that there was no position for her. Then, six weeks later, she was rehired to work at the new zone hospital in Inuvik, N.W.T.[34] She had no special training in obstetrics or public health, but once she assumed her duties on the maternity and surgical ward of the hospital, she learned practical midwifery skills from the Irish head nurse. This training stood her in good stead when, a few months later, she was called upon to "assist" a medical student in delivering a baby. The student had never performed a delivery, and as Chételat explains, "although he knew generally what to do, I knew the routine step by step and had to tell him what to do."[35] In 1963, while on duty at the Aklavik nursing station, which she had joined "with no formal training but with much enthusiasm to learn," Chételat performed a successful breech delivery. Describing the success of this experience, she wrote in a letter to her family, "I was thrilled to death."[36]

The Department of National Health and Welfare was of the opinion that the hiring of nurse-midwives would help to decrease the rate of infant mortality. It is likely that DNHW encountered little resistance to this idea from the medical community, since medical practitioners did not, in general, object to midwives practising in remote, sparsely populated areas of the country where they did not offer the physicians competition for patients.[37] Yet, despite the apparent desirability of midwifery qualifications, there was no official government support for the policy; in fact, there is clear evidence that the state was not prepared to pay for what they deemed to be better care. Recognition of midwifery skills and special obstetrical training was not reflected in nurses' earnings. This can be seen, for example, in a salary chart in a 1952 *Regional Superintendent's Letter*. Nurses were graded according to experience and special training. While those with public health training were compensated for their expertise, there was no category for qualifications in midwifery.[38] Similarly, in the late 1950s, when DNHW began a program entailing leaves of absence at half pay to nurses wanting to upgrade their skills, the program supported enrolment in public health courses but not midwifery or obstetrical training.[39] While this was consistent with a general policy shift in northern health care from an emphasis on treatment to an emphasis on prevention,[40] it also reflected the pattern of maternity care in southern hospitals, where the state supported a hierarchical, gendered division of labour in which the task of delivering babies was reserved for members of the male-dominated medical profession, while antenatal and postnatal care was provided by the overwhelmingly female nursing force.

With no policies designed to attract specially trained nursing staff and no support for Canadian-trained nurses to gain midwifery training (midwifery was not recognized by the state),[41] the federal government was unable to adhere to its "preference" for midwives. Moreover, it continued to be plagued with the problem of a shortage of personnel, including adequately trained nurses. Thus, in the 1970s, MSB collaborated with various universities to set up programs to provide health-care services to particular northern communities.[42] As schools of nursing were drawn into the programs, the training of field nurses became a topic of concern, and as a result, courses for specialized training were developed.[43] But even these programs failed to provide enough nurses to staff all the stations, and the government increasingly adopted a policy of evacuating women to zone or southern hospitals for delivery.

Initially, it was women deemed "high risk" who left their communities for two to twelve weeks to give birth in hospital. High risk was always medically defined, and its definition included, for example, most primigravida and multiparous women, an anticipated multiple birth, and women with chronic medical problems such as diabetes. The evacuation practice varied according to the charge nurse, the community, and the time period. For example, Anna Chan, who delivered more than forty babies during the two years she spent in Arctic Bay in the late 1960s, usually delivered the first babies of low-risk mothers herself at the nursing station, although occasionally a mother requested to go out because she saw this as the "modern way." Of the six women that Chan sent out, one was deemed at risk because of her age, recorded in her file as sixty-eight years.[44]

The evaluation of patient risk did not take into consideration the social and emotional aspects related to lengthy periods of absence from family and community. As Nancy Menagh, who nursed at the Yellowknife Hospital in the 1970s explained in an interview, "It was terrible for them. They didn't have family with them and they were worried all they time about who was looking after the family, what the husband was doing and such. I think that was a terrible strain for them."[45] Inuit midwife Nellie Kusugak expressed a similar point of view on a CBC Radio N.W.T. phone-in show on the topic of birthing in 1988: "The ones I had the most concern for were the children and the family left behind by the mother. You can really notice that the children really miss their mother. Most were looked after by their family and some [were left] with grandparents. They all had others to feed besides the ones left behind ... They also had to send money to the mother and feed the children. Most husbands thought this was an added burden to them."[46]

By the late 1970s, almost all women from remote communities were sent out to hospitals or birthing centres for delivery.[47] This meant changes in the station nurses' responsibilities in perinatal care, although they were still called upon to deliver the babies of those mothers whose gestational period had been miscalculated, whether by accident or intention. Nurse Sue Pauhl told the story of a woman who went into labour some six weeks ahead of her estimated delivery time. She gave birth to a nine-pound baby who was clearly not a "preemie." Nurses report that women sometimes avoided visiting the station in the early prenatal period so that they could falsify their anticipated date of delivery and thus avoid having to leave their community.[48] Other expectant mothers could not be evacuated because of weather conditions; there was no transportation, for example, in or out of some communities for several weeks at a time during spring breakup and fall freeze-up. In the years prior to mass evacuation, the vague guidelines controlling nursing practice and a lack of communication between outpost nurses and program administrators in zone offices and Ottawa were factors that shaped both the work done in maternity care by the nurses and the relationship between the nurses and the women and families served by the outpost stations.

There is no question that the placement of southern nurses in northern communities in the postwar period was a reflection of the government's efforts to structure Aboriginal health according to colonialist policies – that is, to impose southern medical practices on Aboriginal peoples with little thought about their traditions, values, and beliefs.[49] This is but another aspect of the patriarchal, patronizing, and assimilatory policies articulated in the Indian Acts of 1876 and 1880, which made "Indians" wards of the Canadian state,[50] and extended into the area of health-care provision in the twentieth century.[51] This attitude is seen, for example, in the annual reports of the late 1940s and through the 1950s, which all included the same sentence: "A health service for native Indian and Eskimo was developed as a voluntarily assumed moral obligation on the part of the government to provide assistance to a more primitive people."[52]

While the ministry's position was clearly stated, there is some question about the extent that the actions and attitudes of nurses reflected government policy, especially in the early years of expansion. Nurses write and speak of the fact that they were offered little or no formal preparation for their postings in the form of literature, orientation, and pre-service or in-service training programs.[53] Dorothy Knight, en route to her post at Frobisher Bay [Iqaluit] in 1957, wondered what she should really know about the Arctic. "Ottawa had sent her no literature about the North. She had received no information about the people she was being sent to work with. She knew nothing about their way of life. Come to think of it, Health and Welfare had forwarded no further instructions about what they wanted her to do."[54] That same year, Kathleen Dier was hired to open a nursing station in Cambridge Bay, Northwest Territories. She noted that she was sent off with a copy of *The Canadian Mother and Child,* a widely distributed government publication. It is likely that this would have been the 1953 edition of the book,[55] which contained the potentially useful section "A Chapter for the Midwife"; however, the rest of the book, in its illustrations, substance, and language, was clearly intended for the dominant group in Canadian society and hence was culturally inappropriate as a teaching aid for the Inuit mothers in the High Arctic community.[56] Literature that was available in the stations, such as the "black book," produced by MSB in the mid-1960s, dealt specifically with medical and surgical procedures; Anna Chan referred to the manual as her bible.[57] Jan Stirling and others noted that the most useful reference for maternity was British author Margaret Myles's *A Textbook for Midwives,* which also served as a practical text.[58] Sue Pauhl reported that even in the mid-1970s she received no literature prior to departure. In her first placement at the Moose Factory Hospital, her orientation consisted of a tour, after which she immediately set to work; in a later placement on Baffin Island, as her orientation, the charge nurse read the manual to her page by page.[59] Lois Chételat, who went north as a new graduate, only realized how much a good orientation program would have helped her in dealing with some of the situations she faced in Inuvik when she participated in an orientation program in preparation for a CUSO (Canadian University Services Overseas) posting in India.[60]

Once nurses were at their posts, communication was limited and frequently hindered by weather conditions that restricted mail delivery (in some instances, to twice a year), by radio-phone systems that storms rendered useless, by interference from the northern lights, and by the often considerable distance between the transmitter and the nursing station. Further, they experienced problems when administrators failed to respond to questions posed in the monthly reports they submitted. In Knight's memoirs from the mid-1950s we read: "Nothing in her mail from Health and Welfare, she noted with disappointment. Did her employers know she existed?"[61]

Documented references to rules and regulations were often vague and open-ended. A 1950 *Regional Superintendent's Letter* admits to a lack of regulations as it asks outpost nurses, "Do you deliver your maternity cases in the nursing station? We do not lay down rules for you to follow. We leave it to you to decide what to do. If possible you should have [the patients] in the nursing station for confinement."[62] Thus, in many instances, field nurses were likely influenced less by directives from or the philosophy of their employers than by their own development and experience as nurses.

The basic tenets of nurses' training and the nurses' place in the medical hierarchy of southern hospitals significantly influenced the way nurses approached maternity care. In the southern, urban hospital setting during this period, there was, in the perception of many, a demarcation between the "caring" role of the nurse and the "curing" role of the doctor.[63] In traditional health-care delivery in northern communities, this caring/curing dichotomy stood in sharp contrast to the holistic notion of healing espoused by Aboriginal people.[64] Since the nurse was the primary, and often the only, trained medical person in the community, the boundaries between the caring and curing aspects of her work were blurred most of the time. However, it was the caring role of the nurse that emerged clearly when juxtaposed with the role of the doctor and other health professionals who made irregular, usually rushed, visits to northern communities. These rare visitors saw and treated patients requiring medical attention in a clinical setting, whether the nursing station or a community building, such as a school or church. Often, by the time of the next scheduled visit, there would have been a change in personnel. By contrast, the nurse was a familiar and regular presence in the community, someone who visited homes and schools and provided immediate and ongoing medical care as required to all members of the family. She was also the one who offered prenatal and postnatal care in her clinic and in the mothers' homes. This was a role that was more consistent with Aboriginal healing traditions than that of the doctor.

In a study comparing traditional Cree healing with "Western" health care,[65] the researchers suggest that there are similarities between the curing activities of the (Cree) healer and the caring tasks performed by nurses in the Western health-care system.[66] While Aboriginal groups differ in their healing traditions, there are many shared and similar characteristics; this is evident in maternity practices. Thus, it seems likely that the findings of this study would apply, at least in part, to other Aboriginal groups. These similarities, then, would have helped shape the nurse's role in community maternity care.

In their positions in southern hospitals, nurses were taught to follow orders given by doctors. Dorothy Knight recalled her nursing supervisor in Sarnia saying in the early 1950s, "Nurses do not, repeat, do not make independent decisions."[67] Sue Pauhl remembers that in the urban hospital where she worked in the 1960s, a certain protocol was in place for labour and delivery that included procedures such as sterile draping and strapping the mother's arms down. At the time, she firmly believed in the necessity of these practices and would not have thought of questioning either the procedures or the doctor's orders. However, in the North, the outpost nurses found themselves in positions where necessity demanded that they make independent decisions and perform tasks beyond the traditional scope of their work, without the technical aids of southern hospitals and with no possibility of conferring with professional colleagues. For some, their own nursing philosophies and practices changed over time and as their confidence in their skills increased. Sue Pauhl notes that in her later placements in the North (in the 1980s and 1990s), the only equipment she needed for a delivery was a pair of gloves.[68]

Since babies did not always conveniently arrive when the doctor was making his daily or twice-yearly visit to the community, nurses such as Mary Hope, who wrote a book about her work in northern British Columbia in the early 1950s, would perform deliveries, a task Hope had previously considered the responsibility of doctors. The official position articulated by health department officials was that nurses would be guided in such circumstances by a doctor who was only a telephone call away.[69] This points to a reluctance on the part of the state to interfere with the conventional division of labour in maternity care. As well, it was an optimistic assumption given the weather conditions and difficulties of communication and transportation.[70] As Hope writes, "If I couldn't get the doctor, I delivered the baby myself. After midnight, I could not call Outside as Central closed up shop."[71]

Following a special project nursing seminar in northern Alberta in 1970, Helen Taylor, president of the Quebec Association of Nurses, described the confinement of an "Eskimo" woman at an outpost nursing station. She reported: "It was the most normal,[72] best managed delivery I ever saw. The woman was a cooperative patient, it was her sixth baby, so it turned out to be a truly good experience." Taylor assisted in the delivery.

I suppose I played the role of the nurse and the station nurse played the traditional role of the doctor. The delivery was without sedation or medication and it was perfect. I think the mother was geared to have a more normal delivery than perhaps some of the inhabitants of the south. We communicated with simple words or gestures, as the woman did not speak English and the interpreter often used by the nurse was not available. Really without a word spoken, the communication was very close. The mother thanked us by smiling and squeezing our arms.[73]

While Taylor's report offers the somewhat idealized view of a southerner who, in her brief visit to the northern nursing station, is witness to one birth, it does give a sense of the expansion of the traditional role of the nurse in the birthing process. Excluded at the point of delivery from maternity service in southern hospitals, not only is she included in nursing station births, but she assumes a position of authority usually reserved for the medical practitioner. Even nurses with midwifery training experienced a wider scope of practice. Accustomed for the most part to performing low-risk deliveries, in the North they sometimes dealt with the complexity of the high-risk patients for whom, in other locations, they would have called in a doctor.

Nurses participated in birthing in their communities at different levels. Some kept a respectful distance, a reflection of their recognition of their own lack of training and experience in obstetrics. As Dorothy Knight admitted to herself in the 1950s, "The most sensible way of handling the kind of ignorance you've brought to the Arctic, Dorothy, ... is to impose it on others as little as possible."[74] In the Eastern Arctic Inuit settlement where she worked, there were two official midwives, and in the early days, she was relieved that she was not asked to help. While she "worried about faulty hygiene, she felt it was wise to leave the Inuit to deal with childbirth as they had always done."[75] Working on the Pacific coast about the same time, Bessie Banfill noted that she was advised "to stand by for abnormal maternity cases but was warned against interfering with Indian deliveries."[76]

Other nurses delivered babies, some working on their own or with family members in the nursing station, some working cooperatively with the midwife and women of the community in the home of the parturient mother. It is clear that gender was important in the role that a nurse played in a community birth, whether as an observer, an assistant, or the main attendant. Birth in Aboriginal communities was a women-centred ritual. Amy Wilson, who "attended births when asked," relates that in the early 1950s, "when an Indian woman goes into labor her favorite midwife comes to help her. Often it is her mother or mother-in-law. If there are no complications, no one else is called. If it is a difficult birth all the old women come."[77] Other women often came to watch and offer support. Even when the birth took place in the nursing station rather than in the home, most nurses invited family members and the community midwife to participate. Kay Semple tells of sitting in the delivery room of her Resolute Bay station following a birth that she had facilitated in 1977: "Mum, Dad, granny midwife, and I had toast and tea together."[78]

Such a harmonious scene was not always the case. Anna Chan points out that in some communities there was conflict between the midwives and the medical people. This often happened, she suggests, when there were several midwives in a community vying for patients. In Anna's case, there was only one old woman, and she was glad to have the nurse take over the work. She advised Anna that "so and so is pregnant" and encouraged women to go to the nursing station for prenatal care.[79]

Since the sources I have surveyed offer no evidence that nurses took part in other Aboriginal healing rituals, it seems possible that some were included in birthing not because of their professional qualifications but because they were women who had established a relationship with the family through their public health activities. Irene Culver was the sole nurse in the tiny Hudson Bay settlement of Fort George for a period of six months in 1955, and she did not officially take part in the few births that occurred during that time. However, when the wife of the handyman at the station gave birth, she was invited to join the women in the tent where the birth took place.[80]

These examples suggest that nurses hesitated to interfere in the birthing practices of the local caregivers and the women they were attending. They also demonstrate that in the northern communities birthing was viewed as a natural occurrence, not a medical problem, and that because many southern nurses came to their positions without a strong biomedical model of birthing, they were able to accommodate this notion. Nurses may also have been influenced by the international interest, beginning in the 1950s, in "natural" or alternative forms of childbirth, concepts popularized by the writing and work of men such as Grantly Dick-Reed in Britain and Ferdinand Lamaze and Frédéric LeBoyer in France. Their methods eschewed the use of medications such as anaesthesias and analgesics during labour and delivery as well as technological "aids" such as continuous electronic fetal monitoring. They recommended instead the use of exercise regimes and relaxation techniques.

Nurses show in their writing that they were trying to come to terms with the concept of birthing as a natural process that did not necessarily have to be medically managed, as was the custom in the south. Accounts in nurses' reports offer descriptions of so-called natural births in the communities in which the nurses worked. In 1951 Nurse

Aylsworth reported to her professional journal, *Canadian Nurse,* from her post in northern Saskatchewan: "Abnormalities in obstetrics are rare in this part of the country, due, in part, to the fact that the people live simple lives, get plenty of exercise and are of a placid nature. Dr Read [*sic*], in his 'Natural Childbirth,' can teach them nothing for they already know the art of relaxation. We do not perform epi- siotomies and rarely do we get a tear. I had the thrill of delivering an 11-pound baby without any injury to the mucous membrane."[81]

In a similar vein, an unnamed nurse working at Chesterfield Inlet offered the following comments in a 1952 *Regional Superintendents' Newsletter:* "Generally speaking, the Eskimo mother-to-be does not ben- efit from the attention and medical care that white women receive. She travels by dog team and works hard till the last day. However, strange as it may seem, miscarriages seldom occur ... The coming of the baby is usually quick and simple and in no time the mother is well again."[82]

A link is posited between Aboriginal women and nature in descrip- tions of certain maternity practices that occur repeatedly in the writing and words of outpost nurses. While on the one hand nurses worried about the standards of hygiene in the homes of their patients, on the other they commented on the low rate of perinatal infection. Accord- ing to Amy Wilson, "Nothing particularly clean is used, yet it is surpris- ing how few die. It is the infant mortality rate that soars."[83] Concerns that nurses expressed in relation to hygiene were often followed by descriptions of the salubrious effect of natural substances used by women in their communities. Banfill, commenting that in their quest for cleanliness, white women may have infected babies, adds, "Nature provides certain types of moss and reed that seem to be germ proof and the only antiseptic measures needed. For instance moss bags into which babies were placed may have provided some sort of antisepsis. [When moss was] used as a cord dressing, no more infections were encountered than when sterile gauze dressings are applied."[84]

"Soft, clean, muskeg moss" had other uses. As Amy Wilson de- scribes, "[The moss] had been gathered by the mother, washed and dried and stored for this occasion. A bit of it was tucked under the baby. It is very absorbent, and when soiled is thrown away and fresh moss used. One seldom sees a baby with sore buttocks if moss has been used as a diaper."[85]

Nurses also wrote in positive terms about the "mothering" qualities that they observed in their communities. Nurse Aylsworth notes in her report to DNHW: "The Indian women cuddle their baby almost con- stantly from the time they are born ... When she takes her baby any- where, she bundles it in a mossbag and ties it to her back."[86] Banfill, describing the mother/baby relationship, writes: "Indian mothers ... cuddled satisfied babies." She compares this with the "motherless nurseries of city hospitals."[87] As is evident in these examples, maternity practices in Aboriginal communities were often the subject of nurses' comments because they were at odds with the practices of the bio-medical model with which they were familiar, with the advice offered by doctors and so-called baby experts to mothers in the south at the time, and also with the recommendations offered in *The Canadian Mother and Child*. Some of the practices mentioned included taking a kneeling[88] or support-standing[89] position during labour and delivery, having the support of female friends and relatives during birthing,[90] nursing on demand,[91] and carrying the baby close to the body instead of leaving her in the crib.[92]

The segments cited are representative of extant 1950s to 1980s pieces written by nurses from outpost stations across the country and of nurses' recollections of their northern experiences. In their descriptions, they focus on birthing traditions quite different from what they had experienced in the context of the southern classroom and hospital. Can we interpret the apparent respect for and willingness to understand Aboriginal birth customs expressed by non-Aboriginal nurses as female cross-cultural bonding? Read on a literal level, the narratives and reports suggest an admiration for the Aboriginal woman's ability to give birth without medical assistance and a respect for her nurturing skills. Viewed metaphorically, however, some of their depictions have other connotations. There is a suggestion on the part of some nurses, more evident in published accounts, of an objectification of their Aboriginal patients, of the perception that they were "primitive" exotics who, being closer to nature, were able to birth naturally with less pain than non-Aboriginal women in southern hospitals.[93] Some of the writings suggest a tendency to essentialize Aboriginal women's bodies and their birthing experiences. The fact that Nurse Aylsworth rarely saw tears may be more a reflection of the pace of labour and delivery than of common physical characteristics in her patients. A more general example of this tendency to essentialize, as reflected in references to their "simple lives," points to the fact that some nurses brought from the south as part of their baggage a sense of cultural superiority. The ambiguities evident in written texts suggest that nurses who came to the North ill-prepared professionally and culturally to provide maternity care to Aboriginal women were grappling with the notion of gender identity and how it was played out in northern birthing traditions. The assumptions they brought with them about the responsibilities of women in the birthing process – as caregivers and as those giving birth – were clearly brought into question in the North. As they became more familiar with the birthing rituals of the northern communities, some of the nurses seem to have moved towards accommodation of the notion of birthing as a natural process. Thus, in claiming what is natural in women's bodies, they were joining the women of the community across racial and cultural boundaries.

The oral testimonies of nurses who were not merely observers of birthing traditions in the North but also participants in the process suggest that the myth of pain-free, natural parturition among Aboriginal women has a solid physiological basis rooted in perinatal traditions, traditions that were not part of the nurses' southern experience during the period under study. These traditional practices include, for example, the position assumed during labour. Lesley Paulette, a member of the Native Women's Association of the Northwest Territories, explains that in traditional deliveries "women generally give birth in a squatting or kneeling position never lying on their backs."[94] Nurses speak of women standing while giving birth, supported on each side or leaning on a stick. All these positions aid the baby in its movement through the birth canal.[95] As well, absent from northern birthing traditions are pain-easing medications, sedatives that slow the pace of labour, and episiotomies that delay postpartum recovery. The traditional model of birthing also differs from the medical model in its inclusion of family and community members, who offer the mother physical and emotional support during labour and delivery and through the postpartum period. According to Sue Pauhl, reflecting on her almost three decades of northern nursing service, these practices, strengthened by the attitude that birth is a normal and natural event, tend to result in shorter labour and less intense contractions.[96] Nurses also referred to the Aboriginal custom, particularly of the Inuit, of bearing pain in silence. This custom was evident in childbirth as well as in other usually painful procedures, such as dental extraction and suturing.[97]

In the postwar period, the federal government established nursing stations in remote northern communities in order to provide better health services to Aboriginal people. One of the purposes of the stations was to reduce high infant mortality rates. While no specific statistics for the perinatal mortality rate were gathered by the state at the time, other sources suggest that perinatal mortality was in fact not the problem, rather that most deaths occurred during the first year of a child's life.[98] The government, however, anticipated that medicalization of maternity care would help to reduce high infant mortality rates. Nurses, taking their positions at isolated posts, were agents of the medicalization process and hence, in the long term, an integral part of the process that led to changes in traditional birthing practices and a subsequent loss of self-responsibility for health on the part of Aboriginal families. With the general movement in the south towards greater medicalization of childbirth in the postwar period,[99] an era when the biomedical model was a powerful determinant of how and where birth should take place, the gap between the customs of northern Aboriginal people and non-Aboriginals in southern, urban areas of the country initially widened. By the 1970s, however, the steady incursion of southern maternity procedures had become evident. An example of this trend was the increased number of evacuations of Aboriginal women to southern centres for hospital deliveries, a process that disrupted family life, contributed to the process of acculturation, since women were absent from their communities for extended periods of time and exposed to the southern culture,[100] and led to the deskilling of Aboriginal midwives.[101] Ironically, even as this encroachment into the North peaked in the 1980s,[102] many women in the south were rejecting the medically managed, highly technologized model of birthing that had become the norm, opting instead for a more natural form of childbirth.

In the short term, however, the situation had a unique impact on two groups of women. While government officials tried to hire nurses with midwifery or special obstetrical training, they often failed to do so. As has been shown, some outpost nurses, aware of their lack of direct experience with the delivery of babies, kept a respectful distance from birthing women or joined other relatives and neighbours to support the mother simply by being there through labour and delivery. As such, they were part of the community of women participating in an important event. Other nurses built upon their experience by attending births if called upon and often working alongside the community midwife, particularly if the birth was a complicated one, sharing the authority. Some among this group, such as Lois Chételat, expanded her knowledge by learning practical midwifery skills from a co-worker. For those nurses who did have midwifery or advanced obstetrical experience – Anna Chan and Sue Pauhl, for example – northern nursing offered the opportunity to expand the scope of their practice beyond what was permitted in southern hospitals, since from time to time they had to deal with higher-risk patients.

Another way in which some nurses expanded their authority was through their writing. As they became familiar with Aboriginal birthing customs, they interpreted them through their reports and narratives to the "outside" world, that is, to their employers, other nurses, their families, and the readers of their published narratives. DNHW encouraged the nurses to write on specific topics for internal distribution. A letter from Director Moore to the regional superintendent, Saskatchewan Region, on 21 January 1963 outlines plans for a series of articles on maternal and child care: "They will cover prenatal, delivery, infant and preschool. There will be one special on breast feeding. Would [nurses] Miss Belfry and Miss M. Ragolsky have time to write one or two typed pages on 'Continuity of Patient Care' for the mother and baby? They did so much work on their presentation at Coqualeetza."[103] Other materials were used for external publications such as the *Indian and Northern Health Services Newsletter* in order to enhance the profile of the department or to assist in recruitment.

For Aboriginal women, the less-intrusive approach of the early decades of service resulted in prolonging the use of traditional birthing practices, practices that seem to have served the communities better, particularly for low-risk births. If complications occurred, the nurse could be called upon for assistance. It is likely that the mother would know the nurse and would feel more comfortable with a female caregiver, the customary attendant during childbirth, than she would have felt with a male doctor. Even as more women began giving birth in the nursing station, the environment was more home-like than a distant hospital, as they had the support and comfort of their family and community. It is this model that many women in the North advocate as they seek to bring birthing back to their communities. In a workshop on childbirth in the North held in 1988, Martha Greig called for a return to teamwork, "a collaboration of the Inuit midwives and the health care givers because we need both."[104]

Over the period under study, a change in the pattern of birthing is evident. While Anna Chan delivered more than forty babies during her two-year mandate in the 1960s, by the 1990s a delivery by a nurse in the nursing station was an unplanned occurrence, since all mothers were going out.[105] In the interim, state policy shaped maternity care provided to Aboriginal women in the North, both for the caregivers and for those giving birth. The form that this care took reflected the absence of a clearly articulated policy. For nurses, whatever their training or prior experience, this absence of policy provided an opportunity to expand their practical experience and authority in maternity care.

INTERVIEWEES

Arlene Aish, 1970s: accompanied student nurses from Queen's University to Moose Factory.

Barbara Bromley, 1960s: Yellowknife Health Centre; covered Ndhilo, Detta, Rae Edzo, Lac La Martre, Holman Island, Fort Rae, and Snowdrift.

Dr Alex Bryans, 1960s, 1970s: a founder of Queen's University/Moose Factory partnership.

Anna Chan, 1970–72: Pond Inlet and Arctic Bay.

Lois James Chételat, 1961–63: Inuvik Hospital and Aklavik station.

Sheila Clark, 1989 to present: Sioux Lookout, Ont.; Fond du Lac, Sask.; St Theresa Point, Garden Hill, and Red Sucker Lake, Man.; Rankin Inlet, Cambridge Bay, Gjoa Haven, Pelly Bay, Holman Island, Coppermine, Pangnirtung, Clyde River, and Grise Fiord.

Irene Culver, 1950–76: Fort George station, Moose Factory Hospital, and reserves on Manitoulin Island.

Gloria Lynn, 1970–72: Moose Factory Hospital; locums to Great Whale River and Paint Hills.

Nancy Menagh, 1973: Yellowknife Health Centre; 1984–87: Inuvik.

Sue Pauhl, 1971 to present: Moose Factory, Faro, Hall Beach, Pangnirtung, Gjoa Haven, Rankin Inlet, and Inuvik.

Sharon Richardson, 1968–70: Grise Fiord.

Kathlyn Semple, 1976–1987: Rae Edzo, Snow Drift, Resolute Bay, Grise Fiord, and Bearskin Lake.

Jan Stirling, 1971 to present (post-retirement): public health work at Yellowknife, which included Ndhilo, Detta, Rae Edzo, Lac La Martre, Fort Rae, and Snowdrift; relief work at Cambridge Bay, Coppermine, Holman Island, and Fort Resolution.

Anne Wieler, 1954–86: Nelson House, Frobisher Bay, Baker Lake, and Fort Smith; administrative positions in Keewatin Zone and Yukon Zone; and senior nurse advisor, MSB.

NOTES

Author's Note: The research for this essay has been completed with support from the Kitty Lundy Memorial Grant.

1 Although terminology used in the printed sources shifts, for consistency in this essay, I use the term "Aboriginal" to refer to people of Indian, Inuit, and Métis heritage. The Inuit were formerly commonly known by the pejorative Indian term "Eskimo." Where this term occurs in direct quotes, I have used single quotation marks.

2 Brooke Claxton, "Submission to the Special Joint Committee to Examine and Consider the Indian Act. By the Minister of National Health and Welfare," in Joint Senate/House of Commons Committee to Investigate the Indian Act, *Minutes of Evidence and Proceedings*, no. 3 (Canada: Parliament 6 June 1946), 61–98. Claxton's report includes the following chart:

Mortality Rate from Diseases Peculiar to the First Year of Life
(rate per 100,000 of live population)

	Indians	*Whites*
1942	156.5	50.8
1943	153.8	56.4
1944	159.1	54.7

3 This is discussed extensively in many government reports, including George Graham-Cumming, "Health of the Original Canadians, 1867–1967," *Medical Services Journal*, February 1967: 29–142.

4 Jean Goodwill, Editorial, *Canadian Nurse* 80 (January 1984).

5 Due to chronic shortages of staff, a nurse was often on her own. This occurred even if there were two nurses at the station, since one nurse would have to make visits to satellite communities, or go out on medivac or leave.

6 Federal Indian Health Services were administered through zones created by the Canadian government. The number of zones varied, and while boundaries were not clear-cut, they tended to conform to geographic and population disparities. For example, zone hospitals were established in Frobisher Bay (Iqaluit) in the Eastern Arctic, Moose Factory in northeastern Ontario, and Yellowknife and Inuvik in the Northwest Territories.

7 "Medivac" is the term used for a medical evacuation mission. Lois Chételat recounted the story of her trip between Fort McPherson and the zone

hospital at Inuvik, describing how she had sat on the floor of a small draughty Beaver aircraft beside a woman who was in premature labour and about to deliver a baby in a footling breech position. Telephone interview, 24 August 1999.

8 Testimonies from Aboriginal women are limited to proceedings of a 1988 workshop funded by a branch of DNHW as reported in John D. O'Neil and Penny Gilbert, eds, *Childbirth in the Canadian North: Epidemiological, Clinical and Cultural Perspectives* (Winnipeg: Northern Health Research Unit, University of Manitoba 1990). This is an area that would benefit from further research.

9 Since 1988, health services to communities in the N.W.T. have been provided through the government of the N.W.T. in Yellowknife.

10 In Resolute Bay, nurse Kay Semple looked after the medical needs of researchers working at the nearby meteorological station. Interview, Aurora, Ont., 19 July 2000.

11 This essay builds on studies such as Kari Dehli, "Health Scouts for the State? School and Public Health Nurses in Early 20th Century Toronto," *Historical Studies in Education* 2, no. 2 (Fall 1990): 247–64; Kathryn McPherson, *Bedside Matters: The Transformation of Canadian Nursing, 1900–1990* (Don Mills, Ont.: Oxford University Press 1996), 57–63; Susan L. Smith, *Sick and Tired of Being Sick and Tired: Black Women's Health Activism in America, 1890–1950* (Philadelphia: University of Pennsylvania Press 1995), chap. 5; and Emily K. Abel and Nancy Reifel, "Interactions between Public Health Nurses and Clients on American Indian Reservations during the 1930s," in J. Walzer Leavitt, ed., *Women and Health in America: Historical Readings*, 2nd ed. (Wisconsin: University of Wisconsin Press 1999), 489–506.

12 The impact of psycho-social isolation is discussed in Brenda Canitz, "A Study of Turnover in Northern Nurses: Isolation, Control and Burnout" (MSc thesis, University of Toronto 1991).

13 This statement appeared in annual reports written by all the superintendents from Dr P. Bryce to Dr P.E. Moore. However, as noted in James B. Waldram, D. Ann Herring, and T. Kue Young, *Aboriginal Health in Canada* (Toronto: University of Toronto Press 1995), 146, certain Indian organizations have claimed that medical services are a treaty right but court challenges have upheld the position of the federal government.

14 All other aspects of Indian administration remained with the Indian Affairs Branch (IAB) and were transferred to the newly created Department of Indian Affairs and Northern Development (DIAND) in 1966. Some analysts of Aboriginal health policy claim that this split in jurisdiction did not serve Aboriginal people well.

15 P.E. Moore, "Indian Health Services," *Canadian Journal of Public Health* 37 (1946): 140–2.

16 In many communities, the Indian agent, the priest, or the RCMP officer served as dispenser.

17 Waldram et al., *Aboriginal Health in Canada*, 164.

18 Frank James Tester and Peter Kulchyski, *Tammarniit (Mistakes): Inuit Relocation in the Eastern Arctic 1939–63* (Vancouver: University of British Columbia Press 1994), 5.

19 Waldram et al., *Aboriginal Health in Canada*, 172. The nursing stations were supported by hospitals in Inuvik and Frobisher Bay.

20 Department of National Health and Welfare, *Annual Report* (1952).

21 This is discussed, for example, in McPherson, *Bedside Matters*, 96. McPherson states that "what was missing in nurses' education was training in the actual delivery."

22 Defined as "having no clear status in law." Brian Burtch, *Trials of Labour: The Re-emergence of Midwifery* (Montreal and Kingston: McGill-Queen's University Press 1994). See also John D. O'Neil and Penny Gilbert, *Childbirth in the Canadian North: Epidemiological, Clinical and Cultural Perspectives* (Winnipeg: Northern Health Research Unit, Manitoba 1990), 41. A participant in a discussion group at the 1988 DNHW-funded workshop ("Cultural Perspectives on Pregnancy and Childbirth") on the topic of childbirth in the Canadian north explains: "I think this [midwifery] is an issue that is muddy for a lot of people ... In Canada it is not illegal to be a midwife. It is in some provinces alegal, which means it has not really been defined."

23 In this period, Aboriginal people were largely unrepresented among the trained nurses in the field. The one exception noted in the literature is Jean Goodwill, who is of Cree background. Other staff associated with the nursing station – assistant, housekeeping staff, cook, driver, janitor, interpreter – were Aboriginal.

24 *Report of Special Project Nursing: Northern Seminars* (Ottawa: DNHW 1971). These seminars were sponsored and conducted by MSB, DNHW, in cooperation with the University Schools of Nursing, and the Canadian Nurses' Association, in January, February, and March 1971.

25 National Archives of Canada (hereafter NA RG 29, file 820-2-2-4, vol. 2698 (5 September 1962), letter from Dr P. Moore to Chief, Child and Maternal Health Division, Department of National Health and Welfare (hereafter DNHW).

26 Interview with Kathlyn Semple, Brampton, Ont., 19 July 2000.

27 Mary-Ellen Kelm, *Colonizing Bodies: Aboriginal Health and Healing in British Columbia 1900–50* (Vancouver: University of British Columbia Press 1998), 148. Kelm states that "the work of field matrons in midwifery [in the first half of the twentieth century] seems to have been the main money-saver."

28 Helen K. Mussallem, *Nursing Education in Canada* (Ottawa: Royal Commission on Health Services 1965), 110. Nurse Barbara Bromley, who worked for DNHW MSB in Yellowknife, was a 1948 graduate of the University of

Alberta program. In her fifth year she specialized in public health. Telephone interview, 10 January 2000.

29 Lois James-Chételat, "Reclaiming the Birth Experience: An Analysis of Midwifery in Canada from 1788 to 1987" (PhD thesis, Carlton University 1989), 282.

30 NA, RG 29, file 850-3-6 (3 June 1965).

31 Interview with Anna Chan, Toronto, 11 June 1999.

32 Chan notes proudly that none of these babies died.

33 Interview with Susan Pauhl, Colgan, Ont., 16 September 1999.

34 Lois Chételat, telephone interview, 24 August 1999; repeated in chap. 2 of Chételat's unpublished manuscript, "Alice's Daughters: A Social History of Three Generations of Women in One Family." The hospital at Inuvik, completed in 1960, was the first fully staffed and equipped hospital north of the Arctic Circle.

35 Chételat. The incident was recorded at the time in her letters home, then repeated to me in a telephone conversation on 24 August 1999.

36 Chételat, in a letter to her family dated 3 January 1963 and quoted in her manuscript, "Alice's Daughters," 50. Chételat chose to work in the Arctic for the adventure and experience that it promised. Her experiences in perinatal care are among the most memorable for her.

37 Discussed in Chételat thesis, "Reclaiming the Birth Experience."

38 DNHW, Indian and Northern Health Services (hereafter INHS), Regional Superintendent's Letter (1 October 1952): 2.

39 Interview with Irene Culver, Manitoulin Island, Ont., 8 July 1998. Culver, an outpost nurse at Fort George, attended the University of Toronto for ten months in 1956 to earn a public health certificate.

40 This was stated regularly in annual reports issued by DNHW.

41 This is evident in published and unpublished government documents, in published narratives and reports in the professional journal *Canadian Nurse* written by nurses who served in the field, and in interviews. While DNHW had neither requirements nor provisions for midwifery training, nurses hired for northern nursing with the Grenfell Mission were required to complete a twelve-month midwifery training course, usually in England (Lesley Diak, *Labrador Nurse* [London: Victor Gollancz 1963]) and some provincial health departments providing northern service sent hirees to the United States (Gladys Aylsworth, "An Outpost Nurse in Saskatchewan," *Canadian Nurse* 47 [September 1951]: 640; Donalda McKillop Copeland, *Remember Nurse* [Toronto: Ryerson Press 1960]).

42 University of Toronto established its Sioux Lookout Project in north western Ontario and Queen's University was linked with Moose Factory in northeastern Ontario. Interview with Dr Alex Bryans, one of founders of Moose Factory program, Kingston, Ont. 14 April 1999.

43 NA RG 29, file 820-2-24, pt 2, Kergin Report, "Clinical Training of Nurses for Northern Medical Services" (1970).

44 Chan, 11 June 1999.

45 Telephone interview with Nancy Menagh, 20 September 1999.

46 Voice of Nellie Kusugak from transcript of CBC Radio N.W.T. phone-in show, 16 December 1988 (translated from Inuktitut by Nellie Kusugak), in O'Neil and Gilbert, *Childbirth in the Canadian North*, 53.

47 Figures vary from community to community, but all reflect changes in traditional patterns as childbirth was removed from the smaller communities and from the context of the family. For example, Elizabeth Robinson reports that among the James Bay Cree, 7% had their babies in hospital in the 1940s; in the 1960s it was 91%. "Pregnancies, Deliveries, and Perinatal Mortality in the James Bay Cree Area, Quebec, 1975–1984," in O'Neil and Gilbert, *Childbirth in the Canadian North*, 13.

48 Pauhl, 16 September 1999.

49 Aboriginal people were not involved in any discussions related to the expansion of medical services, nor was there any suggestion on the part of the state that Aboriginal people be trained as health-care professionals. Task Force on Community Health Auxiliaries, *Report* (Ottawa: MSB 1973).

50 The Indian Act, 1876, as reprinted in Dave De Brou and Bill Waiser, eds, *Documenting Canada* (Saskatoon: Fifth House Publishers 1992), 95–102. For the purposes of northern health care, the term "Indians," as used in the act, referred to groups now known as Indian (Native, First Nations) and Inuit.

51 Discussed extensively in texts such as Waldram, Herring, and Young, *Aboriginal Health in Canada*.

52 DNHW, INHS, *Annual Report* (1948).

53 In 1950, while awaiting transportation to her nurse-in-charge position at the outpost station at Fort George on the east coast of James Bay, Irene Culver spent a week in Moose Factory, where she "became aware that outpost nursing was extremely different from hospital nursing where patients' treatment is prescribed by a doctor. At the nursing station I would be doctor, nurse, administrator, stenographer, engineer." Irene Culver, *Intukweensquaw of James Bay* (Cobalt: Highway Book Shop 1986), 7.

54 Betty Lee, *Lutiapik* (Toronto: McClelland and Stewart 1975), 19.

55 *The Canadian Mother and Child* (Ottawa: Department of National Health and Welfare 1953).

56 Kathleen Dier, "Early Days at Cambridge Bay NWT," *Canadian Nurse* 80 (1984): 19.

57 Chan, 11 June 1999.

58 Telephone interview with Jan Stirling, 29 November 1999. See also "Margaret Myles Demonstrates Art of Midwifery to Nurses of the North," a photo in *Canadian Nurse* 66 (1970): 10.

59 Pauhl, 16 September 1999.

60 Chételat, 24 August 1999.

61 Lee, *Lutiapik*, 147.

62 NA, RG 29, vol. 2697, file 802-2-2, pt. 1, Regional Superintendent's Letter (May 1950). In a 1963 letter, Superintendent Otto Rath encouraged nurses to train Aboriginal midwives in the ways of birthing practised in the south; this suggests an attempt to colonize the practices of traditional healers. NA, RG 29, vol. 2698, file 802-2-4.

63 The problems in the care/cure dichotomy as it relates to the work of nursing have been clearly demonstrated by writers such as K. McPherson, who argues that for the women in her study, caring *was* curing. McPherson, *Bedside Matters*, chap. 6.

64 Lesley Malloch, "Indian Medicine, Indian Health: Study between Red and White Medicine," *Canadian Woman Studies* 10, nos 1 and 2 (Summer/Fall 1989).

65 Equivalent to what has been referred to as "southern" or "Euro-Canadian" health system in this paper.

66 Janice Morse et al., "Cree Indian Healing Practices and Western Health Care," *Social Science and Medicine* 32, no. 12 (1991): 1361–6.

67 Lee, *Lutiapik*, 126.

68 Pauhl, 16 September 1999.

69 In the early years covered by this study, communication was by radio-telephone, a system largely replaced by the more efficient telephone via satellite in the mid-1970s.

70 Many northern communities were closed to the "outside" for several weeks during spring thaw and autumn freeze-up as the mode of transportation shifted from sled/Bombardier to boat. Culver, 8 July 1998.

71 Mary E. Hope, *Northward My Calling* (Toronto: Ryerson Press 1954), 56.

72 Taylor uses the term "normal" to describe a delivery that did not require medication or technological aids. Nurses tend to use the term "natural."

73 In 1970 the Medical Services Branch sponsored a project that provided an orientation for nursing leaders in the work of MSB in remote nursing stations. It was intended to promote recruitment and retention of northern nurses and to improve and expand their educational level. *Report of Special Project Nursing: Northern Seminars*. Helen Taylor's report was reprinted in "Nurse Educators Travel to North on Seminars" (report by Helen Taylor, president of Association of Nurses, Quebec) *Canadian Nurse* 67 (March 1971): 8.

74 Lee, *Lutiapik*, 101.

75 Ibid.

76 B.J. Banfill, *With the Indians of the Pacific* (Toronto: Ryerson 1966), 96.

77 Amy Wilson, *A Nurse in the Yukon* (Sidney, B.C.: Gray's Publishing 1966), 48–9.

78 Semple, 9 June 1999.

79 Chan, 11 June 1999.

80 Culver, 6 July 1998.

81 Aylsworth refers to Grantly Dick-Reed, whose ideas on childbirth inspired the founding of the Natural Childbirth Association in the 1950s. Aylsworth, "An Outpost Nurse in Saskatchewan," 640. Dick-Reed's writing focused on the theme of childbirth without fear; Lamaze advocated using "psychoprophylactic" techniques of relaxation and controlled breathing; and Leboyer's theme was birth without violence *(Pour une naissance sans violence)*.

82 NA, RG 29, file 802-2-2, vol. 2697, pt. 3, Regional Superintendent's Newsletter 29 (November 1952).

83 Wilson, *A Nurse in the Yukon*, 47. Perinatal mortality rate is calculated by adding the number of stillbirths to the number of baby deaths within seven days of a live birth. One of the problems with government statistics at the time is that separate figures were not kept for the perinatal period; they were included in the infant mortality rate.

84 Banfill, *With the Indians of the Pacific*, 97.

85 Wilson, *A Nurse in the Yukon*, 47. A renewed interest in the use of moss diaper bags by groups such as Wapekeka First Nations is documented in a 2001 video entitled *The Shibogama Project 11*.

86 Aylsworth, "An Outpost Nurse in Saskatchewan," 640.

87 Banfill, *With the Indians of the Pacific*, 94.

88 Copeland, *Remember Nurse*, 60; Lee, *Lutiapik*, 102.

89 Wilson, *A Nurse in the Yukon*, 48.

90 Culver, 9 July 1998; Wilson, *A Nurse in the Yukon*, 48.

91 Aylsworth, "An Outpost Nurse in Saskatchewan," 640.

92 NA, RG 29, file 802-2-2, vol. 2697, pt. 3 (November 1952); Aylsworth, "An Outpost Nurse in Saskatchewan," 640.

93 The romanticizing of childbirth among Aboriginal women is a pattern seen both in fictional accounts and in texts such as Egbert H. Grandin, and George W. Jarman, *A Textbook on Practical Obstetrics*, 3rd ed. (Philadelphia: F.A. Davis Company 1900), 245. Grandin and Jarmen write: "The Indian squaw, in the early history of this country, gave birth to her child without delaying her companions when on the march and was able at once to join them in their journey."

94 Lesley Paulette, "The Changing Experience of Childbirth in the Western N.W.T.," in O'Neil and Gilbert, *Childbirth in the Canadian North*, 45.

95 For hospital deliveries, women were in the lithotomy position, necessary when the mothers' legs were numbed by epidural anaesthesia.

96 Pauhl, 16 September 1999.

97 I posed a question about pain to all the interviewees, one based on my personal experience of working as a physiotherapist with Inuit children at the Montreal Children's Hospital. These children were evacuated from Frobisher Bay for orthopaedic surgery to reduce congenitally dislocated hips. I was struck by the stoic manner in which most of them did their post-operative exercises.

98 As Dr Sabean told Nurse Knight, "The high infant mortality rate among Inuit had little to do with problems at birth. Most often [it was of] pneumonia or of burns and scalds once they can move around." Lee, *Lutiapik*, 10.

99 In 1939 less than half of Canadian women delivered in hospitals; however, by the 1970s the figure was 99%. See A. Prentice et al., *Canadian Women: A History* (Harcourt Brace Jovanovich 1988), 321.

100 C. Higgins et al., "Mother-Child Separation: A Study in a Remote Health Care Setting," *Canadian Medical Association Journal* 125 (1981): 1114–17.

101 Discussed on the CBC Radio phone-in show.

102 J.D. O'Neill, "The Politics of Health in the Fourth World: A Northern Canadian Example," *Human Organization* 45, no. 2 (1986): 119–28. O'Neil states that in the 1970s 70% of deliveries were done in communities, while by the mid-1980s all Inuit women were evacuated to southern transient centres up to six weeks prior to parturition and local involvement of lay midwives had essentially disappeared.

103 NA, RG 29, vol. 2698, file 8202-2-4, letter from Dr Percy Moore to Regional Superintendent.

104 Martha Greig's voice as recorded in the DNHW-funded workshop "Cultural Perspectives on Pregnancy and Childbirth," 39.

105 Interview with Sheila Clark, Uptergrove, Ont., 25 May 2000. Clark offers evidence that such an event occurred when she was working on Holman Island in the early 1990s. She and another nurse, neither of whom had midwifery training, delivered twins who had been undiagnosed by ultrasound. The mother was admitted at 4:30 p.m.; they had delivered the babies by 7:30; and the medical team arrived only at 11:30 p.m.

9

Pursuing Conception: A Physician's Experience with In Vitro Fertilization

Maureen McCall

My husband and I have lived with infertility for years now, and living with it is like living with an invisible disability.

In the first years of waiting for what most couples expect will be the natural and relatively easy consequences of a loving marriage, the constant questions from others about our reproductive intentions were embarrassing and difficult to answer. We've now heard them for nine years.

Judgmental warnings not to put career before family and about growing old without children, and comments about the selfishness of childless couples hurt terribly and were almost impossible to answer. As a female physician with a very busy obstetric practice, I learned to expect the inevitable questions about when it would be "my turn." I usually made a joke about how it would never happen unless patients quit keeping me up all night in the case room, but it was harder to take the thoughtless questions from colleagues who should know that there are myriad medical and personal reasons why a couple might choose, or be forced, to remain childless.

Like most infertile couples, we felt uncomfortable sharing our burden, even with our closest friends and family. Why does infertility so often remain a secret? There is the embarrassment associated with any issue that involves sex, feelings of inadequacy, and fear of criticism or lack of understanding, and this is particularly true if a couple is seeking treatment such as artificial insemination or in vitro fertilization (IVF).

We felt the pain of revealing our problems only to have friends, family, and even physicians trivialize its significance. We heard all the clichés: "Relax!" "Take a vacation." "Don't work so hard." "Apply for adoption and before you know it you'll be pregnant." In the first couple of years we even listened to some of this advice. Today, many years and vacations later, we have nothing but a great collection of fertility symbols to show for it.

After multiple surgeries, blood tests, semen analyses, and biopsies it became clear that IVF was our last and most appropriate option. At first I felt compelled to chronicle this experience for myself; now I realize how therapeutic my IVF diary has been. It has helped us work through difficult feelings and make important decisions. We hope that sharing our experience will help other couples and the physicians who counsel them.

WAITING OUR TURN

Once we decided to try IVF, my life began to revolve around the calendar and the telephone. I say "my life" rather then "our lives" because it is a biologic fact that the initial phase of IVF treatment involves the woman almost exclusively. Although my husband was interested and supportive, biologic reality made me feel more acutely the burden of the success or failure of this endeavour. In order to plan an IVF cycle, I had to phone the "period hot line" answering machine and leave a message about the starting day of my period for each of the next few months – it was like playing a role in a spy movie as I closeted myself away from prying ears to leave coded messages at the fertility headquarters.

Eventually, we were "offered" a treatment cycle. This momentous phone call came in the middle of a busy day at the office, a day when I knew that I would not be able to discuss things with my husband before a response was needed. I signed on and hoped that we would be able to rearrange our lives without too much difficulty. With about three weeks' notice I had to plan for a ten- to twelve-day absence from work. Everyone was most interested in what exotic vacation we were planning. Had we found a great deal on a scuba package to Mexico or a London show tour? The excuse I chose, "unexpected family problems," was partly true; it put a stop to prying questions and helped explain the uncertainty of my return to work. Had I lived in the same city as the fertility clinic I might have been able to work half days, as many working women try to do, but I was glad to have the forced leave from work so that I could focus all of my physical and emotional energy on this experience.

THE BIG TURNOFF

The first phase of the treatment cycle began on day 21 of my menstrual cycle with five-a-day inhalations of a hormone medication. Fourteen days later I had to have a pelvic ultrasound. Wanting to be an ideal patient, I drank the prescribed amount of water to fill my bladder and chugged down a few more glasses for good measure. The technician advised me that she was getting excellent pictures and that to date only two of her patients had voided on the examining table. I was about to be number three when she told me that I could go to the bathroom and empty "just one cupful" into the toilet. When I successfully completed this almost-impossible feat, I felt only marginally better physically, but psychologically I was confident that if I could do this, I had what it takes to complete the rigours of IVF treatment.

Having committed the result of my ultrasound report to memory, I made another surreptitious phone call to the IVF clinic and then anxiously awaited the return call later that morning to discuss the next phase of treatment.

THE HUMAN PIN CUSHION

The ultrasound report was okay, so now it was time to dig for the additional $1,000 to $1,500 it would cost for the injectable menotropins treatment. I did not want to purchase this ahead of time in case the ultrasound report was unfavourable, but now that the green light had been given I only had a few hours to track down a pharmacy that carried the drugs and would be willing to ignore the limit on my credit card. The clinic advises patients to check their private health plans for coverage of the cost of infertility drugs, to find which local pharmacies carry them, and to compare costs – good advice that I had been too busy to take. Luckily, I found what I needed at my neighourhood drugstore, where the pharmacist kindly and quietly asked if I was Dr U.R. Childless, then gave me the physician's discount. If everything worked out, she would have the discount returned many times over in diaper and baby powder purchases. As I looked at the big price tag on the little bag, a curious piece of medical school trivia about one source of this drug came back to me: I pictured the collection of this precious commodity made from the urine of post-menopausal Italian nuns.

Finally, my husband would begin to take an active role. Because our infertility problems included concerns about antisperm antibodies produced by my husband, he started a course of prednisone. His cast-iron stomach held up well to the assaults and his good humour never wavered, even in the face of my admonitions to avoid hot baths, alcohol, and excess caffeine – and to wear his boxer shorts.

While most women would have to go to a clinic or hospital, I was fortunate to be able to do the injections myself. Injecting my alternating hips was not difficult, but ferreting away syringes and needles in my desk drawer and mixing, drawing up, and injecting the drug behind the locked office door made me feel a bit like a criminal. By week's end, my hips were sore, my nose was irritated and bleeding from the frequent inhalations of another preparation used to turn my normal cycles off, and I had a constant heavy and slightly uncomfortable feeling in my pelvis.

I generally felt much more tired than usual, but emotionally I was very positive that the treatment was working. Whether it was a direct effect of the menotropins or a result of the abdominal bloating associated with the ovarian stimulation, I noticed a decrease in my appetite, particularly for the evening meal; unfortunately, there was no noticeable weight loss.

INTENSIVE MONITORING

On the seventh day of the menotropins treatment, I arrived at the clinic for the "intensive monitoring and treatment phase." Laboratory staff conducted the first of a number of early-morning blood tests, and then I filled my bladder for another ultrasound to count and measure the developing follicles and measure the length of my uterus. From this point on, the daily dose depended on my blood work and ultrasound results; when it was calculated, by ten or eleven in the morning, I presented my hip for injection. The routine was dehumanizing; I felt as though I were a collection of parts to be measured, analysed, and injected, not a woman hoping to conceive.

Thankfully, the rest of the ultrasounds to monitor the growth of the ovarian follicles were done transvaginally, a method that is much less uncomfortable and more accurate than the transabdominal technique. Although I had no problems with these exams, other patients expressed extreme distaste about the use of the vaginal probe. Clinic staff always tried to preserve modesty and dignity, but there is no way to make some people comfortable with this procedure. Maybe it is the ceremonial draping of the transducer with a condom and then coating it with conduction jelly that makes it seem just a little obscene! By noon each day, the visits to the labs and clinic were over and I had the rest of the day to explore the "big city." My expeditions were considerably shorter and more sedate than I had planned because my oversized ovaries complained about being jostled by every step.

EGG RETRIEVAL — "OUCH!"

Having safely and relatively quickly reached the point where we were ready for egg retrieval, we now began to hope that the retrieval would be a success, that lots of healthy eggs would be recovered.

I had spoken with women who had undergone egg retrieval under both light sedation and general anesthetic, and I had seen a film about a woman's terrible experience when only sedation was used. I was nervous but decided that light sedation would be a good chance to practise the breathing techniques I had seen my patients use in labour; if all else failed, I could scream until they knocked me out.

Yes, it hurt. There was a brief sharp pain as the retrieval needle went through the vaginal vault and into my ovary, then a kind of burning and pressure-like pain as the follicles were drained. I wiggled my toes, concentrated on my breathing, and sang to myself between short gasps of pain and a few moans and groans. All in all it wasn't nearly as bad as the gum surgery that I'd had six months earlier, and it was over in less than fifteen minutes.

The final count was seventeen eggs retrieved! I was extremely proud of my ovaries for the remarkable job they had done, and felt sure that with that many targets to hit we would get at least a few bull's eyes.

FERTILIZATION AND EMBRYO TRANSFER

Then, more waiting. If things were going well, we wouldn't get a phone call until late the next morning to tell us the embryo count and arrange for embryo transfer. If things were not going well, we would be called first thing in the morning. Our hearts sank when the phone rang at 9 a.m., but the news was not so bad – two eggs had been fertilized and the technician was calling to ask my husband to come down to the lab and donate again right away. The final count by the time of embryo transfer the next day was nine! We had a definite biologic possibility of parenthood and began to hope that this would become a reality.

The embryo transfer the next morning was a breeze. The technician showed me the tiny four- and six-cell embryos on a monitor before drawing them up into a catheter for transfer. In less time and with less discomfort than it takes to have a Pap smear, the transfer was complete. For the next hour I rested in a reclining chair with my feet up, trying to send messages about healthy implantation to my uterus.

The nurse gave me instructions for the next two weeks until we knew if I was pregnant: "Don't get overtired, no strenuous exercise, no heavy lifting, no vacuuming, no swimming, no sex, and no hot tubs or saunas." I knew, and they agreed, that none of these things were proven to make any difference, but they would at least give me something to do (or *not* do) while I hoped. For the following two weeks I tried to hug as many babies as possible, walked slowly and carefully everywhere I went, tried not to cough or sneeze, continued to take my daily dose of folic acid, and ate more fruits and vegetables. It couldn't hurt – we knew that any one cycle of IVF treatment at our centre had about a 25 per cent chance of achieving a pregnancy and about a 20 per cent chance of resulting in a birth nine months later – about the same odds as any normal fertile couple might expect after one month of trying the good old natural way. After 0 per cent success in sixty-one months of trying, our odds were definitely looking up.

THE PRICE TAG

What costs were involved in one cycle of IVF treatment? They included the drugs, the clinic's medical fees, clinic overhead, monitoring, surgery, anaesthesia, and my motel accommodation. After subtracting tax-deductible treatment costs and our private insurer's reimbursement of drug expenses, out-of-pocket expenses were only a few hundred dollars.

Still, the emotional costs were huge. Compressed within a few weeks were all the hopes and dreams of five years of seeking parenthood. With these strong positive feelings were normal ones of ambivalence that were hard to cope with after all we had gone through; we worried about the changes in our lives if this really were to succeed, about the risk of a multiple pregnancy and miscarriage.

Two weeks of excitement, worry, and hope passed while we paid attention to any tiny physical sign of success or failure. Just one day before the scheduled pregnancy test, a few drops of blood announced our failure and I was left sobbing behind the bathroom door. We were crushed. Later I was angry at the clinic for building up our hope, only to let us lose it once again.

A few weeks later, when my mind and body were out of the hormonal fog of IVF treatment, we called to request that our names be added to the waiting list for an embryo-transfer cycle. We had enough embryos to try one or two of these cycles, during which frozen embryos are thawed and transferred into the womb. A "cryocycle" – my husband suggested that they give this procedure a more positive name, like "laughocycle" – has a lower overall success rate than an IVF cycle, but we felt that it would be preferable to more drugs and surgery. We also wouldn't be left wondering what to do with our potential offspring sitting in liquid nitrogen in a city many miles away.

CRY-OCYCLES

Months later a cryocycle failed and I was surprised to find that I was more depressed then the first time. I was angry with my body for letting us down, even angry with the clinic staff for their encouraging words and smiles. Nearly a year has passed since we began the IVF and embryo-transfer treatments. As I sit down to make another entry in this sporadic journal, I am resigned to report another embryo-transfer failure. We may have one more try at it if our two remaining embryos survive a thaw cycle. We are not at all hopeful that it will succeed this time, but neither are we too worried. After much introspection, tears, and conversations late into the night, we have begun to consider a childless future acceptable.

We are lucky to have had the resources to undertake IVF treatment. Whether or not we have a child, it has helped us to know that we took the chance we had. Now we can feel more comfortable with whatever fate hands us. As much as we have been angry with the treatment failures, the reality is that it was just a bad roll of the dice – not our fault and not the fault of the clinic staff, who were caring and supportive. We know the smiling baby pictures on the wall of the clinic waiting room have helped to make many dreams come true, and we can feel happy for those parents instead of cheated and sorry for ourselves.

My diary will end here, no matter how many more treatments we pursue, I don't feel like I need to focus so much on our infertility anymore, and that feels good.

Excerpted from the *Canadian Medical Association Journal* 154 (1 April 1996): 1075–9. Reprinted with permission.

PART FOUR

Patients and Providers

When the women's health movement emerged in the 1960s and 1970s, one of the first issues raised was the inordinate power of the male-dominated medical profession. Indeed, throughout the post–Second World War decades, doctors enjoyed unprecedented cultural authority. Biomedical science bolstered the social legitimacy of physicians and surgeons, while the extension of insurance programs offered doctors a financial stability they had never before enjoyed.

Yet, as the essays in this section show, not every practitioner experienced medicine's new cultural authority in the same way. Many physicians struggled to make scientific knowledge useful and relevant to new generations of patients, while some medical specialists – like gynaecologists – found they had to compete for scientific legitimacy with new groups of sub-specialists, all carving out their own spheres of authority. Meanwhile, women and non-white practitioners continued to confront sexism and racism on the wards and in their professional associations.

For all the influence that doctors have had in shaping patients' experiences with medical care, the chapters that follow remind us that, for many patients, encounters with other health professionals and workers have been equally important. Nurses, dieticians, physiotherapists, laboratory workers, and ward aides – many of them women – have provided the day-to-day labour that has kept health institutions and agencies running smoothly. In fact, the expansion of the health-care sector in the 1950s and 1960s was so dramatic that married women and non-white workers were recruited for the first time into many health-care jobs.

The presence of so many female health-care workers has influenced the relationship between patients and providers in complex ways. Many North American women have sought out female doctors or midwives, and these health professionals have in turn tried to offer a more patient-centred style of care. Likewise, patients often appreciated the attention and concern expressed by female nurses, aides, and attendants. Although many female attendants occupied the lower echelons of the institutional or organizational hierarchies of the health-care system, they were not all – or always – without authority. Medical hierarchies found room for nuns to wield tremendous power in Catholic institutions; they put public health nurses in positions of authority over working-class, poor, or Amerindian women; and they often ensured that non-white caregivers were subordinate to white supervisors.

The essays presented here explore how these tensions played out in diverse social and historical settings between 1945 and the 1980s. They consider how federal agencies entrusted some female health providers with substantial social and cultural authority even while trying to reduce the social influence of others.

10

"Guides to Womanhood":
Gynaecology and Adolescent Sexuality in the Post–Second World War Era

Heather Munro Prescott

Today, the pelvic exam appears to be a straightforward, routine medical procedure, one that most contemporary textbooks recommend be performed on all age groups, not just on adult women. Until the mid-twentieth century, however, it was extremely unusual for adolescent girls to receive a pelvic exam from a physician. This essay charts the changes in medicine and society that transformed gynaecology for adolescents in the post–Second World War era.

Prior to the war, most gynaecology textbooks recommended that vaginal examinations of girls should be avoided, and many even advised against pelvic examinations for any unmarried woman. These views were based on Victorian views about young women, which held that girls should remain chaste and pure until marriage. Many physicians believed that a vaginal exam would not only damage the hymen, the physical proof of a young woman's virginity, but could also arouse sexual passions in the patient by drawing unnecessary attention to this area of the anatomy.[1] Medical texts advised physicians to substitute a rectal examination for a pelvic exam; they could receive all the information they needed from a rectal examination, which – the textbooks claimed – would be far less upsetting to the patient and would have the added benefit of preserving the young patient's hymen. Textbooks recommended that in the rare cases when a vaginal exam needed to be performed for accurate diagnosis, it could be performed with the young patient under anaesthesia so that she would not be traumatized.[2]

To be sure, some physicians recognized that this reluctance to examine young women's pelvic anatomy could lead to the misdiagnosis of gynaecological conditions and a failure to detect and treat disease in a timely manner. As Dr Herman E. Hayd of Buffalo, New York, argued in a 1901 paper presented before the American Association of Obstetricians and Gynecologists, the "popular disbelief that so-called womb trouble exists only in married women" had permitted numerous young girls and maiden women "to go on suffering for years and often into chronic invalidism without relief." Nevertheless, even though Hayd argued that "it is a crime to permit young girls to go on suffering ... without proper diagnosis being made of their troubles," he also agreed that vaginal examinations could "not only shock the highly sensitive nature of a modest young girl, but direct her mind to her genital organs." Hayd therefore recommended that diagnosis be made by the rectum or under anaesthesia whenever possible.[3]

This attitude towards pelvic examinations for virgins persisted even in the face of the changing behaviour of adolescent girls and young women during the late 1910s and 1920s. As several historians have argued, the First World War and the following decade constituted the first "sexual revolution" in American society; in these years, young women abandoned Victorian reticence and became more frank and open in their sexual behaviour. Although most adolescents stopped short of intercourse during this period, petting and necking became so acceptable, even among girls from "respectable" families, that Victorian notions of female sexual purity were seriously called into question.[4]

These changes in female adolescent behaviour prompted new views about the psychological development of adolescent girls. Before the 1920s, most writers on adolescent female psychology argued that healthy female development involved protecting the young girl from the premature awakening of sexual instincts and longings. This view was revised somewhat in the early 1900s by the noted child psychologist G. Stanley Hall, who considered uncontrolled sexual passion to be a natural part of female adolescence. Hall, too, however, recommended that young women needed to be protected from their desires and channelled into "wholesome" activities such as art, music, and literature. Under this view, only delinquent girls succumbed to their sexual instincts.[5]

By the 1920s, it had become increasingly obvious that this view had to be revised, as growing numbers of "respectable" girls engaged in what had previously been regarded as delinquent behaviour. Rather than label these girls as delinquents, experts in adolescent mental hygiene revised their views of female adolescent psychology and interpreted sexual curiosity and a certain degree of sexual experimentation to be a normal part of healthy female development. In fact, mental hygiene experts worried more about girls who did not adopt an avid interest in the opposite sex by the middle years of adolescence. Mental hygienists argued that such girls might become lesbians or otherwise fail to attain a normal adult feminine role.[6]

The new female psychology of the post–First World War years led to significant changes in the gynaecological treatment of adult women. Marriage manuals from the 1920s stated that sexual attraction and gratification were essential to a healthy marriage. As a result, young women began to expect sexual compatibility in marriage and would consult gynaecologists before marriage to ensure that there were no "barriers" to successful intercourse. In response to these requests, some gynaecologists would stretch the hymen for their patients or instruct young women in how to do it themselves. Others developed the pre-marital hymenectomy, a surgical operation that cut an opening in the hymen or removed it altogether prior to first intercourse.[7]

However, hymenectomy was never recommended for adolescents, except when an imperforate hymen obstructed menstrual flow. More importantly, although gynaecologists increasingly used the premarital examination as a means of ensuring marital compatibility, this did not accompany a recognition of women's rights to sexual autonomy out-side of marriage. Gynaecological textbooks recommended that proof of betrothal – as well as the permission of the groom – be obtained before a hymenectomy was performed on an adult woman, and they continued to argue that the primary purpose of the premarital exami-nation was to ensure sexual compatibility within, not outside of, mar-riage. In the case of adolescent girls, psychologists and other mental health professionals claimed that this age group was psychologically unready for "going all the way." Mental health experts therefore argued that gynaecologists should refuse to perform any procedure on adolescent girls that might make premarital intercourse easy to perform.[8]

These views on adolescent sexuality were strongly shaped by racial biases. Physicians attributed unwed pregnancy among black teenagers either to the innate "moral incapacities" of black women or to an alleg-edly greater tolerance of illegitimacy among African-Americans. White girls who became pregnant out of wedlock, in contrast, were depicted as neurotic or maladjusted, particularly if they insisted on keeping their babies without marrying the father. The "cure" for a white unwed mother's maladjustment, therefore, was to convince her either to legit-imize her pregnancy by marrying the child's father or to give up the baby for adoption and prepare for a "normal" path to marriage and motherhood.[9]

Thus, the issue of pelvic exams for adolescent girls, especially those who were white and from the middle class, remained controversial well into the 1940s and 1950s. Although a small number of gynaecologists performed pelvic examinations on girls during the 1930s, most believed that girls who were not psychologically ready for intercourse were equally unprepared for physical examination of the vagina. Most gynaecologists therefore recommended that this procedure be avoided except in cases of gross physical disease, and even then should only be performed under anaesthesia. By adopting such a course, noted one gynaecology textbook from the 1930s, "there will be less danger of inducing morbid introspection and of engendering psychosis that cannot fail to have an unfavorable effect on the patient."[10]

After the Second World War, several factors led some gynaecologists to begin modifying their attitude towards adolescent gynaecological examinations. First, between 1945 and 1965 the number of teenagers in the general population doubled and over half of these young people were female.[11] As the number of teenagers in the general population grew, gynaecologists naturally became interested in teenagers as a potential market for their services.

Second, gynaecologists became increasingly concerned about competition from other medical specialists during the late 1940s, and this anxiety prompted them to expand the professional boundaries of their field. Gynaecologists were particularly concerned about the expanding field of endocrinology, since endocrinologists had begun to offer treatments for adolescent and adult menstrual difficulties during the 1930s. As one gynaecologist from this period observed, gynaecologists' "false modesty" had opened up "the whole field of menstrual disorders as a happy hunting ground for the empiric endocrine-enthusiast under the not wholly disinterested guidance of the manufacturing chemist."[12] Similar concerns were expressed about other specialties, particularly general medicine and paediatrics; one president of the American Gynecological Society exclaimed that the problem of "threatened encroachments of other medical disciplines … has seemed to me one of the most important that face our specialty."[13]

To protect themselves from competition from other medical specialties, gynaecologists in the postwar years began to adopt what Pamela S. Summey and Marsha Hurst have referred to as an "expansionist view" of their specialty, in which the gynaecologist was responsible for "caring for women's entire reproductive system in all its physical and psychological aspects."[14] This new view was in part an attempt to move beyond the profession's surgical focus of the early twentieth century, when surgical intervention was frequently used to solve even minor gynaecological problems. As Somers Sturgis, chief of gynaecology at the Brigham and Women's Hospital in Boston, argued, gynaecologists at this time wanted to reorient gynaecology "towards the total picture of problems of the reproductive system in the female" and to encourage physicians to "take care of their gynecologic patient as a woman rather than a case with a 'potentially surgical' condition."[15] Sturgis was particularly concerned about adolescent patients and whenever possible wanted to protect them from "unrewarding surgical exploration" and intervention.[16]

Finally, gynaecologists' interest in adolescents was intimately intertwined with controversies about gender roles in the aftermath of the Great Depression and the Second World War. As women began to take on jobs and responsibilities that had formerly been the province of men, and as men faced "emasculation" by the crippling psychological effects of depression and war, the meaning of "masculine" and "feminine" was constantly under question. During the postwar years, a variety of experts in psychology, medicine, and social science worked to shore up American gender roles, using their clear distinctions as a means of compensating for the social disruptions caused by the difficult years just passed. According to the historian Elaine Tyler May, rigidly defined gender roles served as a "psychological buffer" against the political and social uncertainties of the postwar years. Thus, much of the intellectual, scientific, and political activity of this period was devoted to a strategy of "domestic containment" that reinforced traditional beliefs about what constituted "masculine" and "feminine." Even when these experts recognized significant dissatisfaction with postwar domestic ideology, particularly among women, they did not challenge the system. Instead, they adopted a therapeutic approach to personal problems, one "geared at helping people feel better about their place in the world rather than changing it." In the process, experts "undermined the potential for political activism and reinforced the chilling effects of anticommunism and the cold war consensus."[17]

Therefore, a combination of market interests and concern over gender roles led some gynaecologists to re-examine their policies on adolescent girls. One of the leaders in this area was Dr Goodrich C. Schauffler of the University of Oregon Medical School. Through his textbooks on paediatric and adolescent gynaecology, his column for mothers in the *Ladies' Home Journal,* and other popular advice literature, Schauffler led something of a crusade during the 1940s and 1950s to encourage gynaecologists, as well as mothers, to abandon their cautious approach towards the adolescent pelvis. Schauffler's justification for this move was partly pragmatic: he believed that prudish attitudes towards the adolescent girl's genitals led to lack of basic knowledge, "not only of the pathologic conditions in this field, but also

of normal anatomy and physiology and developmental processes." Such
ignorance, noted Schauffler, resulted in vast amounts of undiagnosed
and untreated disease in young girls and adolescents.[18]

For Schauffler and other advocates of adolescent gynaecological
exams, more was involved than accurate diagnosis of gynaecological
disease; they were also worried that many of the adolescent girls they
saw in their practices had an "unhealthy" attitude towards their genitals, expressed in excessive modesty or anxiety in regard to this area of
their body. Whereas nineteenth- and early twentieth-century physicians had viewed modesty as one of the cornerstones of adolescent
female identity, by the 1940s physicians had begun to claim that a girl
who found gynaecological examinations distasteful had a "morbid"
attitude towards this area, which indicated an underlying ambivalence
towards the feminine role. If this attitude was allowed to persist into
adulthood, these physicians argued, then the woman would encounter
a host of sexual problems once she married, including frigidity,
dyspareunia (painful intercourse), sterility, and hostility towards her
spouse. Needless to say, such a woman would be unwilling or even inca-
pable of bearing healthy, well-adjusted children. To prevent such problems, a "gentle, unprejudiced physician" could help young women to
accept their femininity by eliminating the fears and anxieties they had
about their genitals. In fact, some even suggested beginning routine
pelvic exams during infancy so that girls would become as accustomed
to this procedure as to examinations of their teeth and toes. The result
of this "scientific" attitude, they claimed, would be the elimination of a
host of marital and social problems that arose out of a young woman's
"pathological" reaction to her developing body.[19]

In elevating their own competence in the treatment of adolescents,
gynaecologists blamed the mother for a girl's failure to adjust to normal femininity. They suggested that mothers who protected their
daughters from sexual knowledge and refused to educate them properly about female sexual development did their daughters no favour
but were actually thwarting their daughters' acquisition of a healthy
attitude towards the feminine body. As Schauffler put it, "the fact that
so many women do not understand these rudiments of sex is responsible for much unnecessary personal and parental trouble." The solution, said Schauffler and others, was for mothers to reject the "many
old wives' tales about the impropriety, impracticality, and even inde-
cency of doctors' examinations in the genital area," and to allow physicians to provide their daughters with a thorough understanding of the
female pelvic anatomy.[20]

Support for gynaecological examinations for adolescents did
not necessarily entail support for teenage sexual activity. In fact,

Schauffler and other proponents of adolescent gynaecological examinations were opposed in principle to intercourse among teenagers. However, proponents also claimed that extramarital sexual activity was the result of an earlier ignorance about and unhealthy adaptation to the developing sexual organs, not a consequence of premature sexual awakening caused by a pelvic examination. Schauffler even suggested that girls who adopt a "conscious-virginal or adult attitude of self-protection" during a pelvic examination were probably guilty of masturbation, petting, or even intercourse. In contrast, girls who became accustomed to the gynaecologist's touch before puberty would gain a "sensible" attitude towards these body parts and would not be tempted to engage in such "aberrant" behaviour as masturbation and premarital intercourse.[21]

To further placate concerned parents, proponents of gynaecological examinations for adolescents were careful to point out that the procedure would not pose a risk to the young woman's virginity. Some proponents claimed that the examination would not damage the hymen, and some even designed special instruments for adolescents and girls that could be inserted through an intact hymeneal membrane. The inventor of one of these devices, Dr John W. Huffman of Northwestern University Medical School, was especially adamant that his device would allow examination of adolescent and even prepubertal girls without threatening their anatomical virginity.[22] Other proponents argued that using the intact hymen as a criterion of virginity was outdated and that "hymeneal worship" by parents and physicians posed a serious threat to the health of young women. Edward D. Allen of the University of Illinois College of Medicine, for example, argued that the "aura of protection and perfection" that parents and doctors alike threw about the young girl's hymen posed a "grave risk to her psychic and physical well-being." Rather than avoiding the young girl's genitals "under the guise of protecting her virginity," physicians must realize that "virginity is a state of mind and not an anatomic condition" and not hesitate to perform pelvic exams on both adolescent and prepubescent girls.[23]

Despite these reassurances, a significant number of gynaecologists remained skeptical about pelvic examinations for young girls and adolescents. Although they agreed that in theory too much caution could result in undetected disease, they also believed that unbridled use of the procedure could psychologically traumatize young girls and turn them off the profession of gynaecology altogether. Somers Sturgis warned, for example, that "an attempt to explore the vagina digitally will generally stir up extreme resentment and hostility" in the adolescent patient, making her reluctant to return to the gynaecologist for advice.[24] Advocates of gynaecological exams, of course, also recognized this problem, arguing that insensitive examinations of the young girl and adolescent could "make the child antagonistic to necessary gynecologic examinations in later life."[25]

Opponents, however, argued that rather than helping girls adjust to their feminine role, premature gynaecological examinations could actually thwart healthy female development. Dr J. Roswell Gallagher, director of the Adolescent Unit at Boston Children's Hospital, warned that "these young girls are going through a period in their emotional development which involves their attempting to discard their tomboyishness and to accept a feminine way of life; at this particular time a maneuver such as a vaginal examination may represent a sexual attack and have a regrettable emotional effect."[26] According to this viewpoint, rather than guiding girls towards healthy womanhood, overzealous gynaecologists would stunt young girls' adaptation to the feminine heterosexual role.

Physicians on both sides of the pelvic exam controversy participated in the process of "domestic containment" during the postwar period. Opponents believed that performing gynaecological exams on adolescents would inhibit healthy female heterosexual development. Although they abandoned the older Victorian rhetoric that a pelvic exam would physically "ruin" a young girl by destroying the hymen, opponents did believe that a girl could be psychologically "ruined" by the probing hands of the gynaecologist and come to reject anything that had to do with femininity, including marriage and motherhood. Proponents of gynaecological examinations for adolescents operated within a similar conception of women's proper roles, arguing that familiarity with the gynaecologist's touch was a necessary prelude to healthy attitudes towards the developing female body and normal sexual adjustment within marriage.

Gynaecologists tended to be silent on issues of race and class, except when discussing pregnancy rates among black and lower-class white teenagers. In fact, some gynaecologists at this time suggested that encouraging these girls to adopt white, middle-class attitudes and values would help alleviate the problem of teenage pregnancy in these groups.[27] Middle-class blacks also believed that emphasizing female purity would help counteract white prejudices about the alleged sexual depravity of black women, thereby contributing to their larger program of racial uplift. Overturning white stereotypes became especially important during the Civil Rights Movement of the 1950s.[28] In theory, then, this could mean that gynaecologists who supported adolescent pelvic examinations were interested in promoting the health of all adolescent girls, regardless of race or class. However, given gynecologists' interest in expanding their paying clientele at this time, it is likely that they were directing their messages about regular pelvic examinations primarily towards a white, middle-class clientele.

Proponents of adolescent pelvic examinations presented a potentially radical challenge to traditional thinking about the adolescent pelvis. Proponents rejected the notion that the adolescent pelvis was a sacred territory that should remain uncharted until marriage, arguing instead that familiarity with pelvic anatomy and physiology was an essential part of normal adolescent female development. Although the ultimate goal of this familiarity was to help young women adapt to their future roles as wives and mothers, proponents did at least recognize that young women were entitled to knowledge about their reproductive organs.

Similar concerns about women's proper roles emerged in discussions about the treatment of adolescent menstrual disorders during the 1940s and 1950s. These discussions were part of a larger movement to redefine menstruation as a normal, as opposed to pathological, physiological process. As numerous historians have argued, most nineteenth-century physicians tended to portray menstruation as a potentially dangerous, even life-threatening, condition that required constant vigilance throughout a woman's reproductive life. George Englemann, president of the American Gynecological Society, summed up this position best in a statement he made in 1900: "Many a young life is battered and forever crippled in the breakers of puberty; if it crosses these unharmed and is not dashed to pieces on the rock of childbirth, it may still ground on the ever-recurring shallows of menstruation, and lastly, upon the final bar of the menopause where protection is found in the unruffled waters of the harbor beyond the reach of sexual storms."[29] Because of the alleged perils of puberty, menstruation, and menopause, physicians advised women to avoid strenuous mental and physical activities during their periods. These prescriptions were in turn used to restrict women's opportunities in employment, higher education, and the professions.[30]

Since menstruation and reproduction were considered potentially pathological processes, nineteenth-century gynaecologists argued that they required careful supervision by medical experts and radical intervention in cases of gross physical abnormality and disease. Because the specialty of gynaecology was founded in part on the basis of surgical treatments developed in the mid-nineteenth century, many of the solutions to female troubles were surgical in nature. For example, the common treatment for dysmenorrhea (excessive menstrual pain) and menorrhagia (excessive bleeding) was dilation and curettage, and in extreme cases, removal of the ovaries and/or uterus.[31]

Gynaecologists' views of menstruation gradually changed during the first half of the twentieth century, as growing numbers of women entered higher education and the new "pink collar" occupations without any apparent ill effects. Although some physicians undoubtedly clung to the notion of menstruation as pathology, this view gradually disappeared from mainstream medical opinion. In particular, the need to encourage women to enter the war production industries during the Second World War made the notion of menstrual debility increasingly untenable. Gynaecologists combatted the problem of "menstrual absenteeism" by emphasizing the normality of menstruation and stating that most women did not need to rest during their monthly courses. Although liberal attitudes towards women workers dissipated shortly after the war ended, the notion that menstruation need not be considered a "disease" did not.[32]

Popular knowledge appears to have lagged behind medical views, however, for the medical advice literature from the 1940s and 1950s is full of complaints that women were continuing to view menstruation as a "sickness" and "scaring their daughters to death" with lurid tales of the trials and tribulations women endured because of "the curse." Schauffler, for example, warned mothers of "the possible harmful effect that your own repeated complaints about your menstrual problems may have upon your daughters," attributing many menstrual complaints such as dysmenorrhea and amenorrhea (absences of menses) to a young girl's fears about menstruation.[33] Of course, gynaecologists may have been exaggerating the extent to which mothers failed to prepare their daughters in order to exalt their own medical expertise. However, Joan Jacobs Brumberg's work indicates that as late as the 1960s, a significant number of girls felt ill-prepared for menstruation.[34]

Some physicians went even further and argued that girls who experienced menstrual difficulties were confused about their femininity. This perspective on adolescent female sexuality drew upon the work of the Viennese psychoanalyst Helene Deutsch. Like her mentor Sigmund Freud, Deutsch believed that the central task of female psychological development was the resolution of penis envy. According to Deutsch, girls who identified too closely with their fathers and refused to accept the feminine role of wife and mother should be considered psychologically disturbed or immature in their psychological development. "True motherliness," wrote Deutsch, "is achieved only when all masculine wishes have been given up or sublimated into other goals. If 'the old factor of lack of a penis has not yet forfeited its power,'" warned Deutsch, "complete motherliness remains still to be achieved."[35]

Likewise, physicians who treated adolescent gynaecological problems frequently attributed these complaints to psychological conflicts
about feminine role identity. This concept was best expressed in a
paper presented by J. Roswell Gallagher before the New England
regional meeting of the American College of Physicians in 1954. Physicians who encountered young women with menstrual problems in
their practices, said Gallagher, should consider the following questions: "Is it worry about school, or confusion about death or a conflict
in her home? Does her poor relationship with her mother make her
unwilling to become more feminine? Does menstruation disturb her
because it means an end of childhood? Does it gripe her that she isn't
a boy? Does she resent being treated like a baby? Is she afraid of the
consequences of growing up? Do boys and sex alternately frighten and
intrigue her?"[36]

Gynaecologists frequently used psychodynamic explanations for all
adolescent gynaecological complaints, even those caused by chromosomal or hormonal defects. This view was particularly apparent in
Sturgis's research on Turner syndrome, a genetic condition in which
females have only one x chromosome and hence altered ovarian function, little or no estrogen production, amenorrhea, and extremely
short stature. Although Sturgis acknowledged the need to give these
patients estrogen supplements to prevent osteoporosis, he also believed that simply giving estrogen would not change these "neuters"
into "little girls interested in boys and dating and all." Instead, their
gender identity was determined by "the mature adult figure that they
have identified with, whether it is a father in one case and they're little
tomboys, or whether it's a warm, feminine mother or mother figure in
the other case where they are 'little girls.'" To illustrate this point,
Sturgis gave an example of two Turner patients. One was an xx-xo
mosaic, which meant she had some estrogen production. Despite the
presence of female hormones, this patient was a "tomboy" because her
mother "was out working all day, paying no attention to this youngster,
but she was very close to her father." The girl seldom wore dresses and
"had a couple of brothers and she loved to play sports with them." The
other patient was a "doll-like" girl who liked to wear frilly dresses and
hair-ribbons, even though she produced no estrogen whatsoever. The
feminine behaviour in the second patient, Sturgis argued, was due to a
mother who gave the girl an appropriate role model by choosing to
stay at home and be a housewife rather than pursue a career outside
the home.[37]

Clearly, like the debates about adolescent gynaecological examinations, discussions of adolescent gynaecological problems contained
mixed messages about the proper place of women in American society.

On the one hand, gynaecologists tried both to eliminate the notion that menstruation was a "sickness" requiring extensive medical attention and to reduce the use of surgery as a means of dealing with female reproductive problems; on the other hand, they tended to reinforce postwar views about female roles.

The debates over adolescent gynaecological examinations and menstrual difficulties were accompanied by an intense controversy about the growing use of intravaginal tampons by adolescent girls. The invention of tampons was the result of a combination of female ingenuity and medical expertise. Women first began to experiment with homemade versions of "internal protection" as early as the fifteenth century BC. This method of menstrual hygiene was particularly appealing to actresses, burlesque performers, and professional models, who wanted to avoid unsightly bumps and bulges caused by external menstrual guards.[38] At the same time, physicians began to use tightly wound pieces of surgical cotton that they called "tampons" or "tamponades" to control various hemorrhages, discharges, inflammations, and infections, not only in the vagina, but also in other orifices such as the nose, ear, and rectum.[39] In 1933 Earle Cleveland Haas obtained the first patent for a vaginal tampon designed specifically for menstruation, and in 1936 the first mass-produced tampons appeared on the market, under the brand name Tampax. The product was an immediate sensation; working women and athletes in particular liked the product because it was less cumbersome and conspicuous than sanitary napkins. The popularity of tampons received an added boost during the Second World War, as women and doctors alike recognized the advantages of internal protection for female war workers and military personnel.[40]

Use of tampons by adolescent girls remained controversial well into the 1960s, and this issue revealed some of the same anxieties that surrounded other discussions about gynaecological services for this age group. Many parents believed that using the product would corrupt their daughters by damaging or destroying the hymen and making it easier for girls to engage in premarital intercourse. Others believed that tampons caused "erotic stimulation" in the genital area, which, like masturbation, could cause nervous instability in young women.[41]

Despite these objections, adolescent girls continued to use tampons with or without parental knowledge or approval. According to Joan Jacobs Brumberg, tampons gradually became part of adolescent girl culture in the years following the Second World War, as young women learned how to "put it in" from friends and older siblings. Brumberg demonstrates that using tampons allowed adolescent girls to become better acquainted with their bodies and their own sexuality in a context that was separate from either professional or parental control.[42] The sanitary products industry responded to this growing teen market by offering "small"- or "junior"-size products designed especially for the adolescent vagina. Manufacturers of tampons also expanded their market by providing consumer education programs in public schools, guided by the philosophy that if "you sold them younger, you sold them longer," for you would have developed product loyalty at an early age.[43]

This tension between parental disapproval of tampons and adolescents' growing enthusiasm for the product placed gynaecologists in something of a professional bind: should they endorse tampon use by adolescents and risk the moral disapproval of parents and religious leaders; or should they advise against internal protection for adolescents and risk alienating a potential market for their services?

Until the 1960s, most gynaecologists took the former course and advised against adolescent use of tampons on both moral and hygienic grounds. Given the recent controversy about toxic shock syndrome, concerns about the health problems associated with tampon use were not entirely without merit. In other words, doctors did not simply "invent" these problems to prevent women from using tampons. Yet the medical argument against tampon use went beyond issues of hygiene to incorporate larger cultural views about the moral virtue of adolescents. A survey conducted by J. Milton Singleton and Herbert F. Vanorden of the University of Kansas Medical School in 1943 indicated that out of a sample 250 physicians, only 4 supported use of tampons by virgins, and only 25 supported tampon use by married women. The most common reason given for objecting to tampon use by virgins was that it "brings about pelvic consciousness and undue handling, may cause eroticism and masturbation." Others objected to tampon use by all women because of potential health problems; some claimed that it was "unhygienic, unscientific, [and] distinctly unphysiological to dam up blood in the genital tract." Others argued that the tampon cord acted as a wick that drew urine and other contaminants into the genital tract, while some warned of the dangers of tampons that were "lost" in the vagina or cervix. Singleton and Vanorden concluded that physicians should recommend against the use of tampons by all women, particularly virgins, and help protect gullible young women from "attractive advertising" and free samples distributed in schools by the sanitary products industry.[44]

A small number of gynaecologists in the 1940s and 1950s supported tampon use by adolescents; yet they too were forced to address concerns about morality and safety of the product. The sex researcher Robert Latou Dickinson was a particularly ardent supporter of tampon use by both adult women and adolescents. Dickinson was also involved in research to discern the anatomical differences between heterosexual women and lesbians. He believed that lesbians had abnormally large external genitalia, caused in part by the erotic stimulation of the clitoris during homosexual practices, and that the vaginal stimulation provided by the tampon was more conducive to fostering heterosexuality in young women than were sanitary napkins, which stimulated the clitoris. He wrote that "the tampon has a caliber that does not impede standard anatomic virginity" and was considerably "smaller than the average penis." Although Dickinson acknowledged that there was a "momentary" stimulation of the vagina during the insertion of a tampon, he argued that this posed far less of a problem than the external menstrual guard, which "in addition to applying some degree of heat within a confined space, is responsible for rhythmic play of pressure against surfaces uniquely alert to erotic feeling."[45]

Supporters of adolescent tampon use also argued that opponents based their claims on an outmoded view of female adolescence. As in the case of pelvic examinations, tampon proponents argued that forbidding girls to use tampons encouraged them to develop an unhealthy attitude towards their genitals. Schauffler, for example, wrote in the 1958 edition of his textbook *Pediatric Gynecology* that while "the status of vaginal tampons remains controversial," he nevertheless supported their use by adolescents, since "in this practice a girl learns sensible familiarity with her own anatomy which is of value to her later sex practice."[46]

To be sure, supporters recognized the health risks associated with tampon use, but instead of condemning the product altogether, they made use of these problems to bolster their own professional authority in the area of menstrual hygiene. Dickinson summed up the professional interests behind this issue, claiming that just as surgical tampons "used to pay the office rent" so too could expert advice on menstrual tampons help assure gynaecologists a steady clientele.[47] Dickinson and other gynaecologists realized that women liked the convenience and security that tampons offered and were not likely to stop using them even in the face of medical warnings. Yet these gynaecologists also argued that many women – particularly adolescents – did not have adequate knowledge of the anatomy and physiology of the vagina and that they eagerly succumbed to slick advertising copy without being properly informed of the dangers of tampon use. In addressing this problem, gynaecologists argued that women needed expert medical instruction in how to use a tampon properly; they claimed that gynaecologists were the ones best qualified to teach women about tampons and advised all women to consult their gynaecologist to see if they were anatomically suited to using the product.[48]

As in the case of pelvic exams, supporters claimed that tampon use gave a young woman familiarity with her body, a familiarity that was essential to healthy adaptation to their future roles as wives and mothers; yet these supporters also claimed that gynaecologists were the only ones qualified to instruct girls in the use of this product. In the process, gynaecologists enhanced their professional authority in the area of menstrual hygiene while at the same time weakening the authority of mothers, the adolescent peer culture, and the sanitary products industry. However, much like the opposition to the "conspiracy of silence" that characterized early twentieth-century campaigns against prostitution and venereal disease, gynecologists in the post–Second World War era held views that were an unstable mix of progressive and traditional attitudes towards women's roles.[49] Eventually, changes during the 1960s and 1970s would expose the contradictions within gynaecologists' views on adolescent girls' sexuality, paving the way for further changes.

Two major factors helped to resolve the debates about adolescent gynaecology outlined above. The first involved changes in adolescent behaviour during the 1960s and 1970s. By the 1970s, tampon use had become so prevalent among adolescent girls (nearly one-quarter of all junior high girls and 75 per cent of high school girls used them) that opposition to their use became more of a professional liability than an asset.[50] Gynaecologists gradually realized that offering professional advice on tampon use was an excellent way to build a practice. They therefore became increasingly willing to instruct young women in how to use tampons, especially when mothers were loath to do so. Moreover, gynecologists realized that the familiarity with the body that tampons provided young women made professional objections to pelvic examinations seem silly. In fact, gynaecologists used tampon use as a way of making the gynaecological examination less threatening to their young patients. "If she states she has [used tampons] ... explain that the instruments used are smaller and better lubricated than the tampon and have been designed for the shape of the vagina and so cause less discomfort," advised one gynaecologist during the early 1970s.[51]

The debates over adolescent gynaecological exams and tampon use were further settled by a shift in the sexual behaviour of white adolescent girls during the "second sexual revolution" of the 1960s.[52] As early as 1953, Alfred Kinsey's study *Sexual Behavior in the Human Female* disclosed that over 50 per cent of the women in his sample had engaged in premarital sex, a figure that was particularly shocking given that the average age of marriage at the time was the late teens.[53] Obstetricians and gynaecologists also found that growing numbers of "nice" girls (i.e., those from white, middle-class backgrounds) were becoming sexually active – and pregnant – at increasingly younger ages, much to the dismay and embarrassment of their status-conscious parents. Jerome S. Menaker, an obstetrician from Wichita, Kansas, observed in 1958 a "marked shift of early unmarried pregnancies into the more privileged classes," a phenomenon he attributed to "the lessening of parental supervision plus the increased availability of privacy provided by the automobile." Counter to the assumption that teenage pregnancy was a problem limited to impoverished ghetto youth, physicians like Menaker found an alarming incidence of "promiscuity in the youngsters of even the most privileged and well-to-do."[54]

These changes in white adolescent sexual behaviour had two consequences: first, coitus exposed young women to a variety of new health risks, including pregnancy and sexually transmitted disease. At the same time, teenage sexuality drove a wedge between adolescents and their parents that often posed serious problems for the medical treatment of young women. Until the early 1970s, most states required parental consent for medical procedures performed on minors, except in cases of emergency, parental neglect, or legal emancipation.[55] However, many young women were afraid to tell their parents about their sexual activity, since this usually provoked parental anger at best and at worst led to severe punishment and physical abuse. Fearing parental wrath if their sexual activity was discovered, most young women chose to forego medical treatment altogether rather than submit to parental consent regulations.[56]

Within this context, objections to gynaecological examinations for adolescents seemed outdated and even dangerous. Many physicians believed it was ridiculous to withhold gynaecological examinations from girls sophisticated in both sexual knowledge and experience. As Anna L. Southam of Columbia University College of Physicians and Surgeons argued in 1966, most adolescents were quite knowledgeable about reproductive anatomy and function, and a young woman who consulted a gynaecologist would "wonder how you can know if there's anything wrong with her uterus or her ovaries if you don't examine that system as well as her heart and lungs and her breasts."[57]

Moreover, many gynaecologists began to realize that the generational rift caused by teenage sexuality prevented sexually active girls from seeking adequate medical care. Faced with the dilemma of enforcing parental consent legislation and having girls avoid medical care out of fears of parental retribution, many gynaecologists began to modify their treatment policies towards adolescents during the late

1960s and early 1970s. Privacy and confidentiality became the corner-stones of adolescent treatment. Gynaecology textbooks recommended that adolescent patients be examined without the mother in the room (instead, a female nurse or assistant was used) and advised that questions about sexual behaviour should never be asked in the presence of the mother. This position was codified by the American College of Obstetrics and Gynecology (ACOG) in 1988 in its statement concerning "Confidentiality in Adolescent Health Care," which advised ACOG members to honour the adolescent's need for privacy and confidentiality. Gynaecologists also lobbied for laws that permitted adolescents to seek gynaecological care without parental consent. By the mid-1970s, virtually all states had passed statutes permitting minors to consent to diagnosis and treatment of sensitive health issues like sexually transmitted disease, mental illness, and substance abuse. A few states had also enacted comprehensive statutes that allowed minors to consent to the full range of medical services.[58] Finally, three landmark Supreme Court decisions during the late 1970s – Planned Parenthood of Central Missouri v. Danforth,[59] Bellotti v. Baird,[60] and Carey v. Population Services International[61] – permitted young adolescents to obtain the full range of gynaecological services, including contraception and abortion, without parental consent.

The second major factor that helped resolve debates about adolescent gynaecology was the growth of the women's health movement during the 1960s and 1970s. The popular book Our Bodies, Ourselves (1971) and other feminist health-care publications promoted self-determination in women's health care and challenged traditional ideas about femininity.[62] Gynaecologists trained in the 1970s, many of whom were women, were exposed to this new feminist message about women's bodies. Consequently, many of them began to challenge traditional views about adolescent sexuality, particularly the notion that adolescent gynaecological problems were rooted in conflicts over feminine role identity.[63] Yet the women's health movement did not entirely abandon biomedical approaches; it continued to support many of the same preventive health measures as had gynaecologists in the 1940s and 1950s.

As a result of these forces, by the early 1980s, gynaecological examination for adolescents had become a routine procedure. Rather than avoiding the adolescent pelvis under the pretense of protecting virginity, most gynaecologists realized that the pelvic examination was necessary to prevent disease and provide young women with vital information about their developing bodies. These changing attitudes towards adolescent female sexuality were reflected in the new vocabulary that was used to describe teenage sexual behaviour. Until at least the mid-1960s, most physicians used morally charged terms such as "promiscuity" and "sexual delinquency" to describe sexual activity among teenagers. By the early 1970s, physicians were increasingly using the term "sexually active" to describe girls who engaged in extramarital sexual intercourse. As Brumberg observes in her history of adolescent girls and their bodies, the term "sexually active" was "an important semantic innovation because it described a social state without reference to morality." There were economic motives behind this change in vocabulary: physicians did not want to drive adolescent girls away from their practices by using morally laden language. However, Brumberg also demonstrates that this semantic shift represented physicians' recognition that the "family claim" to a daughter's virginity was no longer viable. Although parents continued to ask gynaecologists to "see if my daughter is a virgin," most gynaecologists by the late twentieth century realized that this request was completely inappropriate.[64]

This study of adolescent gynaecology shows that the relationship between women and gynaecologists in the twentieth century was a complex one that entailed both gains and losses for girls and their parents. I have demonstrated how gynaecologists seized control over a particular area of expertise, but I have also shown how medical intervention affected different family members in different ways. It is true that both mothers and their teenage daughters surrendered a certain amount of control to gynaecologists. In the case of mothers, gynaecologists' claims to expertise in adolescent problems served to weaken mothers' authority over their daughters' developing bodies. Rather than permitting parents to use the gynaecologal checkup as a means of verifying and protecting their daughters' sexual virtue, gynaecologists gradually adopted a position that recognized the rights of young women to sexual autonomy and self-determination. This clinical approach implied that parents and children could not resolve generational conflicts over sexuality without expert intervention. Moreover, by eliminating parental consent laws and selling their services directly to adolescents, gynaecologists socialized young women to turn to medical professionals rather than to family members, peers, or other experts for guidance along the difficult path to adulthood. By encouraging mothers and daughters to turn to gynaecologists for help with adolescent gynaecological problems, physicians gained control over issues that had formerly been the responsibility of the "female world of love and ritual."[65]

Medical intervention into adolescent gynaecological problems did not affect mothers and their teenage daughters in the same way.

Although gynaecologists weakened parents' authority over their daughters' bodies, the relationship between gynaecologist and adolescent patient did not always mean a similar loss of control for the adolescent patient. Indeed, the therapeutic style employed by gynaecologists ultimately served to give adolescents a greater voice in medical decision-making than they had enjoyed before.

This essay has also attempted to provide a more complex image of twentieth-century gynaecologists than is usually provided by feminist scholars, who tend to focus only on the most invasive surgical procedures and overlook larger developments in the field of gynaecology.[66] Although it is true that gynaecologists of the 1940s and 1950s tended to reinforce conservative views about women's proper place at that time, many were actually moving away from surgical solutions, especially in the area of adolescent gynaecological care. Gynaecologists in the mid-twentieth century advocated preventive health measures such as pelvic examinations, emphasized the normality of menstruation, and encouraged women to have a healthy relationship with their bodies. It was this message of health and prevention that was later picked up by the women's health movement of the late 1960s and 1970s. Although the women's health movement rejected the sexism inherent in mid-twentieth-century gynaecological theory and stressed female empowerment rather than professional control, they drew upon ideas and medical techniques that were already being promoted by members of the gynaecological profession. While it would be an exaggeration to say that male gynaecologists "got it right" before the feminists did, it is important to keep in mind that progressive social ideas can have unexpected roots.

Finally, it should be noted that there are limitations to the model of prevention outlined above in terms of race and class. Both gynaecologists and women's health activists have tended to emphasize biomedical models of prevention, such as the annual pelvic examination, which depend upon an individual's access to health care. Although the issue of availability and affordability of reproductive health care was part of the feminist health message of 1970s, reactionary politics of the past three decades have undercut these efforts. Indeed, even recent editions of *Our Bodies, Ourselves* have played up the importance of personal responsibility and lifestyle choices for women's health and overlooked the role that education and access to health-care services play in women's decisions about their health.[67] Therefore, until there is a greater social commitment to meeting the health needs of uninsured and under-insured women, a disproportionate number of whom are from racial minorities, these women will lack the routine preventive care more privileged women take for granted.

NOTES

1 This desire to protect young women from premature sexual awakenings
  extended well beyond the profession of gynaecology. See Joan Jacobs
  Brumberg, *The Body Project: An Intimate History of American Girls* (New York:
  Random House 1997); and Constance Nathanson, *Dangerous Passage: The
  Social Control of Sexuality in Women's Adolescence* (Philadelphia: Temple
  University Press 1991).

2 For example, see William Easterly Ashton, *A Textbook on the Practice of
  Gynecology* (Philadelphia: W.B. Saunders 1906); J.M. Baldy, *An American
  Textbook of Gynecology* (Philadelphia: W.B. Saunders 1896); W. Blair Bell, *The
  Principles of Gynecology* (New York: Longmans, Green and Co. 1910; reprint
  by Classics of Obstetrics and Gynecology Library 1990); Harry Sturgeon
  Crossen, *Diagnosis and Treatment of Diseases of Women* 3rd ed. (St Louis:
  C.V. Mosby 1915).

3 Herman E. Hayd, "Retrodisplacements of the Uterus in Young Girls and
  Unmarried Women – Their Frequency and Best Method of Treatment,"
  Transactions of the American Association of Obstetricians and Gynecologists 14
  (1901): 69–73.

4 For more on this transition in female sexual behaviour during this period,
  see Brumberg, *The Body Project*, 153–7; Paula S. Fass, *The Damned and the
  Beautiful* (New York: Oxford University Press 1977); Ellen K. Rothman,
  Hands and Hearts: A History of Courtship in America (New York: Basic Books
  1984); Kathy Peiss, *Cheap Amusements: Working Women and Leisure in Turn-of-
  the-Century New York* (Philadelphia: Temple University Press 1986); Beth
  Bailey, *From Front Porch to Back Seat: Courtship in Twentieth-Century America*
  (Baltimore: Johns Hopkins University Press 1988); John Modell, *Into One's
  Own: From Youth to Adulthood in the United States, 1920–1975* (Berkeley:
  University of California Press 1989); and Ruth Alexander, *The "Girl
  Problem": Female Delinquency in New York, 1900–1930* (Ithaca, N.Y.: Cornell
  University Press 1995).

5 G. Stanley Hall, *Adolescence: Its Psychology and Its Relation to Physiology,
  Anthropology, Sociology, Sex, Crime, Religion, and Education* (New York:
  D. Appleton and Co. 1904).

6 Alexander, *The "Girl Problem,"* chaps 2 and 4.

7 For more on the history of the premarital gynaecological exam and the
  hymenectomy, see Brumberg, *The Body Project*, 158–60.

8 Ibid., 159–60.

9 Nathanson, *Dangerous Passage*; Rickie Solinger, *Wake Up Little Susie: Single
  Pregnancy and Race before Roe v. Wade* (New York and London: Routledge
  1992).

10 Brooke M. Anspach, *Gynecology* (Philadelphia: J.B. Lippincott 1934), 700.

11 Hilary Millar, *Approaches to Adolescent Health Care in the 1970s* (U.S. Department of Health, Education, and Welfare 1975), 1.

12 R.W. Johnstone, "The New Physiology of Menstruation and Its Practical Implications in Obstetrics and Gynecology," *Transactions of the American Association of Obstetricians, Gynecologists, and Abdominal Surgeons* 42 (1930): 138–50.

13 Howard C. Taylor, "Presidential Address: Competition and Cooperation," *American Journal of Obstetrics and Gynecology* 76, no. 5 (November 1958): 931.

14 Pamela S. Summey and Marsha Hurst, "Ob/Gyn on the Rise: The Evolution of Professional Ideology in the 20th Century," *Women and Health* 11 (1986): 104.

15 Somers H. Sturgis, "Blueprint for Organization of a Gynecologic Unit in the Department of Surgery of Harvard Medical School at the Peter Bent Brigham Hospital," October 1950, Commonwealth Fund Archives, Grant Series, Rockefeller Archive Center, North Tarrytown, N.Y. (hereafter referred to as CFA), box 122, folder 1118.

16 Sturgis, *First Annual Report, 1952–53*, Gynecologic-Psychiatric Unit, Peter Bent Brigham Hospital, p. 15, CFA, box 122, folder 1119.

17 Elaine Tyler May, *Homeward Bound: American Families in the Cold War Era* (New York: Basic Books 1988), 3–14.

18 Goodrich C. Schauffler, *Pediatric Gynecology* (Chicago: Year Book Publishers 1942), 7.

19 Ibid., 15.

20 Schauffler, *Guiding Your Daughter to Confident Womanhood* (Englewood Cliffs, N.J.: Prentice-Hall 1964), 65, 96. For similar views, see Edward D. Allen, "Gynecological Problems of the Adolescent Girl," *Medical Clinics of North America* 27 (1943): 17–25; idem, "Examination of the Genital Organs in the Prepubescent and in the Adolescent Girl," *Pediatric Clinics of North America*, February 1958: 19–34; and Laman Gray, "Gynecology in Adolescence," *Pediatric Clinics of North America*, February 1960: 43–63.

21 Schauffler, *Pediatric Gynecology*, 17–18.

22 John W. Huffman, "Gynecologic Examination of the Premenarchal Child," *Postgraduate Medicine* 25 (1959): 169.

23 Edward D. Allen, "Examination of the Genital Organs in the Prepubescent and in the Adolescent Girl," *Pediatric Clinics of North America*, February 1958: 21–2.

24 Somers H. Sturgis et al., *The Gynecologic Patient: A Psycho-Endocrine Study* (New York: Grune and Stratton 1962), 67.

25 Huffman, "Gynecologic Examination of the Premenarchal Child," 169.

26 J. Roswell Gallagher, *Medical Care of the Adolescent* (New York: Appleton-Century Crofts 1960), 196–7.

27 For more on this point, see Solinger, *Wake Up Little Susie*, 214–15. I describe
    the impact of these attitudes on pregnancy-prevention programs in further
    detail in *A Doctor of Their Own: The History of Adolescent Medicine* (Cambridge,
    Mass.: Harvard University Press 1998), 149–50.

28 Middle-class blacks' use of social purity as a means of racial uplift dates
    back to the beginning of the twentieth century. See Christina Simmons,
    "African Americans and Sexual Victorianism in the Social Hygiene Move-
    ment, 1910–1940," *Journal of the History of Sexuality* 4 (July 1993): 51–75;
    and Susan L. Smith, *Sick and Tired of Being Sick and Tired: Black Women's
    Health Activism in America, 1890–1950* (Philadelphia: University of
    Pennsylvania Press 1995).

29 George Engelmann, *The American Girl of To-day: Modern Education and
    Functional Health* (Washington, 1900), 9–10, quoted in Carroll Smith-
    Rosenberg and Charles Rosenberg, "The Female Animal: Medical and
    Biological Views of Woman and Her Role in Nineteenth-Century America,"
    in *Women and Health in America*, ed. Judith Walzer Leavitt (Madison:
    University of Wisconsin Press 1984),12.

30 The primary and secondary literature on this subject is quite large. Some
    good introductions to the subject include Smith-Rosenberg and Rosen-
    berg, "The Female Animal"; Vern Bullough and Martha Voght, "Women,
    Menstruation, and Nineteenth-Century Medicine," in ibid., 28–37; and
    Louise Michelle Newman, ed., *Men's Ideas/Women's Realities: Popular Science,
    1870–1915* (New York: Pergamon Press 1985).

31 Summey and Hurst, "Ob/Gyn on the Rise," 137–43. Summey and Hurst
    argue that this "interventionist" strategy grew out the need to distinguish
    gynaecology and obstetrics from general practice. See also R.A.H. Kinch,
    "Dysmenorrhea: A Historical Perspective," in *Premenstrual Syndrome and
    Dysmenorrhea*, ed. M. Yusoff Dawood, John L. McGuire, and Laurence
    M. Demers (Baltimore-Munich: Urban & Schwarzenberg 1985): 79–80.

32 Margot Elizabeth Kennard, "The Corporation in the Classroom: The
    Struggles over Meanings of Menstrual Education in Sponsored Films,
    1947–1983" (PhD dissertation, University of Wisconsin, Madison, 1992);
    and Louise Lander, *Images of Bleeding: Menstruation as Ideology* (New York:
    Orlando Press 1988).

33 Schauffler, *Guiding Your Daughter,* 94. See also Elizabeth Woodward, "Do
    You Scare Her to Death?" *Parents Magazine* 24 (1949): 52–3; Marjory
    Nelson, "What a Mother Should Tell Her Daughter," *Parents Magazine* 25
    (1950): 36, 66–8, 70, 72, 74; and Margaret Albrecht, "What to Tell Your
    Daughter," *Parents Magazine* 30 (1955): 38–9, 70–6.

34 Joan Jacobs Brumberg, " 'Something Happens to Girls': Menarche and the
    Emergence of the Modern Hygienic Imperative," *Journal of the History of
    Sexuality* 4 (1993): 99–127.

35 Helene Deutsch, *The Psychology of Women*, vol. 2: *Motherhood* (New York: Grune & Stratton 1944), 321.

36 J. Roswell Gallagher, "Dysmenorrhea and Menorrhagia in Adolescence," *Connecticut State Medical Journal* 19, no. 6 (1955): 470.

37 Somers H. Sturgis, "Management of Congenital Defects," in *Adolescent Gynecology*, ed. Felix P. Heald (Baltimore: Williams and Wilkins 1966), 66–7.

38 Madeline J. Thornton, "The Use of Vaginal Tampons for the Absorption of Menstrual Discharges," *American Journal of Obstetrics and Gynecology* 46 (1943): 260.

39 Robert Latou Dickinson "Tampons as Menstrual Guards," *Journal of the American Medical Association* 7, no. 128 (16 June 1945): 494.

40 For more on the history of the tampon, see Kennard, "The Corporation in the Classroom"; Nancy Friedman, *Everything You Must Know about Tampons* (New York: Berkeley Boos 1981), 33–60; and Madeline J. Thornton, "The Use of Vaginal Tampons for the Absorption of Menstrual Discharges," *American Journal of Obstetrics and Gynecology* 46 (1943): 259–65.

41 Brumberg, *The Body Project*, 161–3.

42 Ibid., 162–3.

43 Kennard, "The Corporation in the Classroom."

44 J. Milton Singleton and Herbert F. Vanorden, "Vaginal Tampons in Menstrual Hygiene," *Western Journal of Surgery, Obstetrics, and Gynecology* 51 (1943): 146–9.

45 Dickinson, "Tampons as Menstrual Guards," 490. For more on Dickinson's research, see Jennifer Terry, "Lesbians under the Medical Gaze: Scientists Search for Remarkable Differences," *Journal of Sex Research* 27, no. 3 (1990): 317–40; and idem, "Anxious Slippages between 'Us' and 'Them': A Brief History of the Scientific Search for Homosexual Bodies," in *Deviant Bodies: Critical Perspectives on Difference in Science and Popular Culture*, ed. Jennifer Terry and Jacqueline Urla (Bloomington and Indianapolis: Indiana University Press, 1993), 129–69.

46 Schauffler, *Pediatric Gynecology*, 4th ed. (Chicago: Yearbook Publishers 1958), 89.

47 Dickinson, "Tampons as Menstrual Guards," 494.

48 Karl John Karnaky, "Vaginal Tampons for Menstrual Hygiene," *Western Journal of Surgery, Obstetrics, and Gynecology* 51 (1943): 150–2.

49 For more on the "conspiracy of silence," see Allan Brandt, *No Magic Bullet: A Social History of Venereal Disease in the United States Since 1880* (New York: Oxford University Press 1987).

50 Statistics on tampon use by adolescents are from Jeanne Brooks-Gunn and Diane Ruble, "Psychological Correlates of Tampon Use in Adolescents," *Annals of Internal Medicine* 96, no. 6 (June 1982): 962–5.

51 Hugh R.K. Barber, "Her First Pelvic Exam: When and How to Do It," *Consultant* 19 (July 1979): 33–7.

52 Beth Bailey, "Sexual Revolution(s)," in *The Sixties: From Memory to History*, ed. David Farber (Chapel Hill: University of North Carolina Press 1994), 235–62.

53 Alfred Kinsey, *Sexual Behavior in the Human Female* (Philadelphia: Saunders, 1953).

54 Jerome S. Menaker, "Teenage Obstetrics," *Pediatrics Clinics of North America*, February 1958: 141–2.

55 J.M. Morrissey, A.D. Hofmann, and J.C. Thrope, *Consent and Confidentiality in the Health Care of Children and Adolescents* (New York: Free Press, 1986).

56 Heather Munro Prescott, "Legislating Family Values: An Historical Commentary on the Parental Consent Requirement in the Casey Decision," *Trends in Health Care, Law, and Ethics* 8, no. 3 (Summer 1993): 32–6.

57 Anna L. Southam, "Metropathia Hemorrhagia and Nonpsychogenic Amenorrhea," in Heald, *Adolescent Gynecology*, 51.

58 Wilkins, L. "Children's Rights: Removing the Parental Consent Barrier to Medical Treatment of Minors," *Arizona State Law Journal* 1975: 31–92.

59 428 U.S. 52 (1976).

60 443 U.S. 622 (1979).

61 431 U.S. 678, 685 (1977).

62 Boston Women's Health Book Collective, *Our Bodies, Ourselves: A Book by and for Women* (New York: Simon and Schuster 1971). For more on this publication, see Sara Elaine Hayden, "Twenty-three Years of 'Our Bodies, Ourselves': Individualism, Community and Social Change in the Work of the Boston Women's Health Book Collective" (PhD dissertation, University of Minnesota, 1994).

63 S. Jean Emans and Donald Peter Goldstein, *Pediatric and Adolescent Gynecology* (Boston: Little, Brown and Co. 1982), 10.

64 Brumberg, *The Body Project*, 171–92.

65 For more on this issue, see Carol Smith-Rosenberg's classic essay of the same title in her *Disorderly Conduct: Visions of Gender in Victorian America* (New York: Oxford University Press 1985).

66 For an overview of this scholarship, see Judith M. Roy, "Surgical Gynecology," in *Women, Health, and Medicine in America: A Historical Handbook*, ed. Rima D. Apple (New Brunswick, N.J.: Rutgers University Press 1990), 173–95.

67 For more on this rhetorical shift in later editions of *Our Bodies, Ourselves*, see Hayden, "Twenty-three Years of 'Our Bodies, Ourselves.'"

11

Nursing and Colonization: The Work of Indian Health Service Nurses in Manitoba, 1945–1970

Kathryn McPherson

In the final years of the twentieth century, two unrelated events drew public attention to the otherwise unobserved lives of nurses working for Canada's Aboriginal health services. The first event unfolded in April 1999, when Aboriginal leaders in Sioux Lookout, Ontario, mounted a hunger strike, protesting the shortage of staff at the local hospital and demanding improvements to nursing and medical services for the sixteen thousand residents of the remote region's twenty-eight communities. A year later, northern nurses were once again in the news, this time because a nurse in the northeastern Manitoba community of Berens River had been violently raped by a patient in her nursing station. When improved security was not provided in the following weeks, nurses at Berens River refused to continue working there, leaving the northern nursing station without adequate staff.[1]

Together, these episodes from the end of the century expose the complex intersection of gender, professionalism, and colonialism that defined nurses' much-understudied location in the realm of state-sponsored health programs in Canada.[2] This essay examines one particular chapter in the history of women, medicine, and the state: the work of nurses employed by the Canadian government's Indian Health Services (IHS) between 1945 and 1970.[3] These years were transitional ones, defined by the 1945 reorganization of IHS and the creation in 1968–70 of a national health-insurance program that covered Native and non-Native Canadians alike. In focusing on these transitional years, this essay considers how gender, professionalism, and colonialism together shaped the ability of nurses to bring biomedical services

to rural and northern Aboriginal communities in IHS's Manitoba
Zone. This essay will first review the historical approaches to the relationship between gender, professionalism, and colonialism, paying
particular attention to the work of nurses in American and Canadian
Indian health services in the years before 1945. It will then focus on
the work of nurses in the Manitoba Zone of Canada's Indian Health
Services after 1945, showing how nurses contributed to the ongoing
colonial system of health care and how their gender and professionalism helped determine their position within that system.

A rich historical scholarship explores the ambiguous relationship between gender and professionalism in the history of modern nursing.[4]
Recent scholarship in the social history of North American nursing has
shown that the dramatic extension of medical and hospital services
initiated in the late nineteenth century depended upon the availability
of skilled, inexpensive nursing staff. Mirroring wider social and sexual
divisions, as women, nurses received less education than doctors,
earned lower wages, and were entrusted with less responsibility or authority in the provision of health-care services. One strategy that nursing leaders used to improve the occupation's standing was to push for
professional licensing and educational standards. In the early twentieth
century, provincial and state nursing organizations across North America struggled (often against patriarchal opposition) to win the legal authority over their occupation that local legislatures had already granted
the medical profession.

The gendered nature of the occupation often worked against nursing leaders' efforts to win the legal and educational autonomy that
other professionals enjoyed, but the female-dominated occupation
could also use femininity to enhance its social authority. Nurses publicly celebrated the superior care that nurses, as women, brought to
medical service. In public health work especially, being female gave
nurses a distinct advantage. Public health nurses were considered
uniquely able to forge meaningful relationships with immigrant and
working-class women who might otherwise find the male-dominated
world of doctors and medicine intimidating or irrelevant. The limits
of those cross-class and cross-race alliances have been explored by
socialist-feminist and anti-racist scholars; these researchers have analysed the power wielded by nurses over clients, the middle-class ideologies that defined much public health work, and the exclusion of
non-white women from nursing organizations, leadership, and even
training. In these analyses, professionalism may have served to improve the social standing of trained nurses in relation to doctors or
untrained community caregivers, but it also relied on the class and
race privileges that white, formally trained nurses held over working-

class and non-white women. This rich body of scholarship now eluci-
dates how race and class, not just gender, defined the terrain on which
nurses claimed occupational solidarity and social power.[5]

If gender and professionalism have been widely analysed by nursing
scholars, much less attention has been paid to nurses' role in the process of colonization and decolonization of North American indigenous
peoples. What does "colonization" mean? Scholarship in Aboriginal
history – in Canada also termed First Nations or Native history and in
the United States called Native American history – has emphasized
how a white government and society used the usual tools of imperialism (military and legal force) to conquer indigenous peoples and mar-
ginalize them on small, precisely demarcated parcels of land. Whether
examining the early imperial enterprises of European nations of the
fifteenth and sixteenth centuries or the colonization of western North
America by federal governments of Canada and the United States in
the nineteenth and twentieth centuries, recent international scholarship in post-colonial studies has complemented, and complicated, this
traditional view of imperial conquest. Post-colonial scholars emphasize
that the colonization of indigenous peoples around the world has not
only occurred through physical force, but also through the processes
whereby the cultures and institutions of indigenous peoples were de-
meaned, made illegal, or replaced. Women, as well as men, participated both as colonizers and colonized, ensuring that gender, like
class, became a necessary tool of colonization. And as scholars like
Laura Ann Stoler have shown, while sexual relations between European men and indigenous women could at times facilitate imperialism, such relations simultaneously complicated the clear boundaries
between colonizer and colonized – what Stoler and others have termed
the "fictions" of race, or class, or gender – that imperial authorities
sought to preserve.[6] With such complications now clearly on the scholarly agenda, colonization is now understood to include not only the
tools used in the forcible acquisition of land and resources, such as
military supremacy and law enforcement, but also the other "technologies of power," such as Western religion, education, laws, sexual norms,
and family relations.

Medicine and disease are considered technologies of power. Many
scholars have explored colonization's negative impact on indigenous
health, especially how European diseases devastated Aboriginal societies.[7] European health systems came to indigenous communities
along with the diseases. Critical new scholarship demonstrates how
colonizers tried to replace indigenous health practices with European
ones and in the process undermined a key source of indigenous
peoples' cultural power and knowledge. Medicine was, in the words of

one historian, a "'tool' of empire" that "enabled Europeans to conquer distant corners of the globe and, in certain areas, to remain."[8]

Canada was one such place where medicine helped Europeans "remain," as historian Mary-Ellen Kelm has shown. In her acclaimed study *Colonizing Bodies*, Kelm focuses on the western Canadian province of British Columbia in the 1900–50 period to delineate how the Indian Health Service contributed to the colonizing apparatus of Canada's federal government. In British Columbia, IHS personnel tried to undermine traditional medical personnel and customs but themselves provided limited and often ineffectual medical and nursing services to Aboriginal communities. Kelm documents the process whereby Western medical diagnoses pathologized Aboriginal bodies as "diseased," while Euro-Canadian medical personnel depicted their services as a key part of the superior "civilization" that the Canadian state would bring to the "backward" Aboriginal societies. Through these strategies, IHS was an active participant in legitimizing white colonization of Native peoples and cultures. Kelm concludes: "Ultimately, it is clear that when government and church officials sought to provide medical services to Native people, they did so not just to improve Aboriginal quality of life, but to justify, legitimate, and sustain Canada's internal colonial relations with the First Nations."[9]

The British Columbia experience was replayed with minor variations across Canada and the United States in the early twentieth century. Federal health services for Aboriginal people provided by Canada's Department of Indian Affairs (DIA) or the American Bureau of Indian Affairs (BIA) brought "Western" nursing, medical, and hospital services to often-isolated reserves and communities. While these federal health services frequently conformed to the colonizing discourses identified by Kelm – that is, Euro–North American health providers undermined traditional healers and at the same time emphasized the civilizing impact of Western medicine – in practice, DIA and BIA health programs and personnel were as much colonizers by omission as by commission. The persisting lack of funding, personnel, and programs meant that while Western medicine may have promised a superior system of medical care, rarely were sufficient resources available to fulfil that promise.

In Canada, for example, the federal government maintained that it had no legal or treaty-based obligation to provide medical services to First Nations communities. Indeed, only one treaty included any mention of health, and even there the "medicine chest" clause was interpreted narrowly by the federal authorities to refer to supplies, not to an extensive system of health service. Federal intervention in the health of Treaty or "Status" Indians instead stemmed from concern over high rates of communicable diseases (especially tuberculosis) among First Nations communities and how those diseases might threaten white settlements. Such concerns prompted DIA to forge contractual and/or administrative arrangements with medical practitioners and dentists[10] who would travel to and service rural and northern Aboriginal communities.[11] As well, IHS appointed in each community a dispenser – a local missionary, store owner, or wife of a white resident – to be responsible for housing and the distribution of the basic first aid and medical supplies that the federal agency provided First Nations people. And finally, IHS hired field matrons and nurses who offered local women, especially, education in nutrition, domestic hygiene, and health. Most dispensers, field matrons, and nurses had no formal training in health services.

Throughout the 1900–1945 era, IHS was chronically underfunded and understaffed, with high rates of staff turnover. Conflict often erupted among local whites over who should get the job (and pay) of the local dispenser. In response, Aboriginal leaders, sometimes motivated and assisted by local missionaries or priests, forwarded to IHS administrators requests for improved medical and nursing services and qualified personnel; on occasion, they even named the nurse they wanted hired.[12] Ongoing difficulties with the administration and efficacy of IHS programs led to the transfer of IHS in 1945 to the newly established federal Department of National Health and Welfare (DNHW), with the hope that an exclusive focus on health would improve the health of Canada's First Nations' peoples.

Around the same time, a similar story was emerging in the United States, where Indian health programs were in the domain of the Bureau of Indian Affairs. In the years after 1900, BIA tried to address the appalling health conditions among American Indians, but underfunding and erratic staffing plagued the service throughout the first half of the century. The 1928 Meriam Report, commissioned by the Department of the Interior to evaluate the quality of federal programs for American Indians, concluded that "practically every activity undertaken for the promotion of the health of the Indians is below a reasonable standard of efficiency."[13] The Meriam Report, combined with New Deal policies, did increase financial and professional resources available to BIA health programs, though many of those gains were quickly eroded when U.S. entry into the Second World War drained medical and nursing personnel from all civilian services.[14] The overall result was that throughout the early twentieth century BIA health programs and personnel were unable to produce significant improvements in the health status of American Indian communities. High rates of communicable diseases, especially tuberculosis, and infant mortality continued to devastate indigenous people in the United States. When as late as 1953 American Indian people registered death rates 42 per cent higher than the general American population and more than double the national average for infant and child mortality, health services were finally removed from BIA to the federal Public Health Service.[15]

Whether in Canada or the United States, the role of nurses in these disorganized and underfunded programs is open to interpretation. On the one hand, few dispensers or field matrons or even "nurses" were registered nurses (RNs) or, indeed, could boast medical training of any sort.[16] It is tempting to suggest that it was the *absence* of qualified nursing personnel that contributed to the weakness of the system. From the perspective of contemporary nursing history (at least the way it is written now), untrained and unqualified women are not considered part of the occupation's history, except insofar as their replacement by professional nurses is a good thing. Indeed, by the 1920s IHS officials realized that when married women with RN training assumed the position of dispenser or field matron, IHS received superior service in return for the small monthly stipend. Similarly, BIA viewed the introduction of public health nurses after 1930 as a significant reform of the existing system.

Yet it is not quite so easy to exempt nursing from the system of colonization in this early period if we shift our focus to what the "non-professional" field nurses, dispensers, and matrons were actually doing. In addition to providing some obstetrical care, basic first aid, and medical supplies, they were also responsible for health instruction. Here the non-professional personnel borrowed a page directly from the public health nurses' book, teaching First Nations women the same lessons of personal, familial, and domestic hygiene then being taught in urban centres by trained and licensed public health nurses. The gospel of hygiene and nutrition, which was difficult enough to put into effect in crowded urban working-class tenements or neighbourhoods, was nigh impossible to implement in impoverished rural and northern reserves, where houses often had dirt floors, windows without panes, no heat, and no electricity and where the community water supply was often polluted.[17] Public health instruction thus served to emphasize and even stigmatize the "flaws" in Native women's mothering and housekeeping skills without taking into account the poverty, disease, and cultural disruption that First Nations women faced. Because Aboriginal women did not conform to the standards of cleanliness, methods of feeding, or models of parenting that public health dogma prescribed, government officials felt justified in removing children from their families to attend residential school or, in a later era, in ensuring that adopted Native children were placed in white families who lived far from the children's home community.[18] Thus, in the early twentieth century, the materials and ideas developed by "professional" nurses and endorsed by RNs across the continent were embraced by non-professional nurses and other IHS personnel. In this way, then, the history of professional nursing of the 1900–45 period must be reinterpreted within the larger colonizing project whereby Euro-Canadian and bourgeois cultural values were imposed on First Nations people.

The 1945 transfer of Canadian health services from the Department of Indian Affairs to the Department of National Health and Welfare represented, in part, the recognition of the poor quality and insufficient quantity of care being provided to First Nations people in Canada. In the transfer, most of the medical personnel were retained, most importantly Dr Percy Moore, a Manitoba Indian Health doctor who had rapidly risen to the position of chief medical officer of IHS. For Moore and his medical staff, moving from DIA, with its legacy of colonial domination and neglect, opened up the possibility of creating a more extensive and effective system of health service for First Nations people. Central to what IHS officials called their new "active approach" was the extension of trained nursing services throughout the rural and northern communities. RNs would staff field hospitals that were to be built in local towns; nursing stations would offer on-site health services to large reserves; and field nurses would travel to smaller reserve communities. Thus, a small and predominantly male cadre of medical doctors travelled around rural and northern communities supervising the health work undertaken by the much larger group of female nurses who provided the on-site services. As such, IHS replicated the basic gender division of labour and authority that defined the wider health-care system.

Getting this "active" system in place was not easy, not least because IHS had to recruit nurses to work in isolated, under-serviced communities where nursing stations or hospitals were often still under construction or in states of tremendous disrepair. Nurses assigned to communities in the Manitoba Zone (which included all of the province of Manitoba and the northwestern section of Ontario) serviced approximately twenty thousand Status Indians living in fifty bands and in a diverse range of communities.[19] Unlike the nursing stations in the "far north" of the Canadian Arctic, most of the communities in the Manitoba Zone were accessible by road or rail. The southern Manitoba communities were an hour's drive from small regional centres, like Brandon or Portage la Prairie, or from the city of Winnipeg, Canada's third-largest urban centre. Western Ontario centres like Sioux

Lookout were located on the rail line. In the middle and northern regions of Manitoba, rail service and winter roads over ice meant that during much of the year, after getting to the region by rail, nurses could travel on the ground (either on dogsled or snowmobile), and the rest of the year fly in and out of the communities. That said, the largest urban centre north of Winnipeg was The Pas, which had fewer than ten thousand citizens. Thus, although transportation into and within the Manitoba Zone was relatively easier than that experienced by nurses working in the far north, Manitoba's IHS nurses worked primarily in rural settings. As a result, IHS had to recruit nurses who were willing to work well beyond the city limits.[20]

Such recruiting efforts were complicated by the continent-wide nursing shortage of the post-1945 years and federal government efforts at that time to keep civil service salaries down.[21] As well, the real or perceived threat of contracting disease (especially tuberculosis), combined with the prospect of inadequate living and working conditions, discouraged many RNs from applying, and among those who did take up IHS work, turnover was fairly high. Where possible, IHS officials took advantage of RNs who had married local Indian Agents or game wardens. Thus, while at least one IHS doctor questioned married nurses' commitment to their professional charge, declaring "I am never in favour of appointing a married woman to such a position as I know what comes first,"[22] IHS, like other postwar welfare state agencies, welcomed married women.

Once on the job, IHS nurses undertook a range of health activities. Monthly reports reveal that nurses provided on-the-spot attendance for illness, injury, or other conditions, such as miscarriage. Nurses dispensed medication, administered vaccinations, decided which patients needed to be seen by the doctor on the next visit, and determined whether a patient should be transferred to a local hospital. IHS nurses were also charged with public health instruction, especially for pregnant women and new mothers. The public health duties were expanded in the early 1960s when a community health worker (CHW) program was introduced. An Aboriginal community member was elected as CHW and, in cooperation with the local nurse or nursing staff, charged with undertaking community education on sanitation. Finally, nurses were expected to provide health authorities with information pertaining to the health of the community; they accomplished this by, among other things, collecting vital statistics and identifying families who were disrupted by illness.[23]

As Judith Zelmanovits's essay (Chapter 8) in this volume nicely shows, work in the North permitted nurses workplace autonomy not possible in southern Canadian centres. IHS positions also facilitated tremendous geographic mobility, as nurses could be transferred into and out of communities ranging from the Eastern Arctic to the British Columbia coast. The career of Manitoba nurse Ruth Hiam is illustrative of this larger trend. Hiam pursued her RN education at the Winnipeg General Hospital in the early 1940s and a few years later completed a diploma in public health from the University of Toronto. From metropolitan Toronto, Hiam travelled to the northern Manitoba community of Alonsa, where, according to family lore, she worked out of a railway car on the Hudson Bay Railroad Line, establishing nursing services in remote communities. In subsequent years, Hiam worked on the Quebec shores of James Bay, on Manitoba's Fairford Reserve, in a fishing village on the Nass River, B.C., on a reserve at The Pas, on an assignment at Hay River, Northwest Territories, and finally on the Sagkeeng (Fort Alexander) Reserve fifty miles north of Winnipeg.[24] At some point during these moves, Hiam married, a fact that did not seem to impede her mobility or her career.

With skilled and experienced nurses like Hiam at its disposal, IHS extended its services throughout northern and rural Canada. By 1960 the program boasted twenty-two hospitals, thirty clinics, thirty-seven nursing stations, and eighty-three community health centres nationally. Those figures would continue to grow, so that by 1976 fifty nursing stations and a hundred health centres were serving approximately 300,000 Status Indians in Canada.[25] In 1970 the annual expenditures allotted to IHS programs "exceeded $28 million compared to just $4 million in the late 1940s."[26] Over the same period, the number of active-treatment facilities for tuberculosis initially increased but was then reduced, reflecting the successes medical personnel had in bringing the rampant epidemic of tuberculosis among Aboriginal people under control.[27]

There is no question that IHS did provide some meaningful services, but many of its successes lay in treating First Nations patients who suffered from diseases that, like tuberculosis and polio, were the result of the penetration and extension of white society.[28] Throughout the post–Second World War era provincial and federal governments grew increasingly interested in exploiting the natural resources of Canada's North, even as the older economy of the fur trade provided less and less employment for First Nations women and men. New hydroelectric projects, like pulp and paper mills, were accompanied by new white settlements, some jobs for Aboriginal men, and, too often, tremendous environmental change.

While historians have yet to map out the gendered dimensions of the postwar economic and social upheaval in Manitoba's Aboriginal communities, IHS records do reveal some of the changes that were affecting First Nations women during these years. For example, the national

Family Allowance program established in 1945 provided mothers a regular cheque each month. The federal government placed particular restrictions on how First Nations families could receive and spend that money; First Nations women were supposed to be "at home" and their children in school for the cheque to be issued, for example.[29] In restricting women's mobility, the program also restricted their ability to work a family trapline or travel to seek work, which in turn exacerbated the poverty many Native families faced. Sedentary living, furthermore, produced new health and nutritional problems for women already confronting the dramatic change in their daily lives.[30] Such social disruptions may also have accounted for the growing demand among Manitoba Aboriginal women for medical attendance during childbirth. According to Dr Yule's 1956 annual report, more women in Split Lake, Manitoba, were requesting that "a medical doctor look after them during their confinement," a trend which he thought was related to "the passing of the old midwives and the reluctance of the younger women to do this work."[31]

Amid these substantial social changes, IHS personnel were able to offer some specific services that met the needs of Aboriginal people, but whatever value the biomedical technologies, IHS was not successful in divorcing itself from its legacy of colonialism. IHS remained embedded in colonial practices and ideologies in four specific ways. First, while IHS records contain little mention of traditional Aboriginal healing, the available evidence suggests that the agency's personnel believed that traditional practices were on the decline and that the advent of Western medicine was not responsible for that decline. For example, Dr Yule credited the demise of Native midwifery to the reluctance of the new generation of women to take on the work, but he stopped short of acknowledging how institutions like residential schools ruptured the inter generational transfer of skills such as midwifery. Likewise, Dr Cameron Corrigan blamed "civilization," specifically "the church," for undermining traditional health remedies. Corrigan noted that in the 1550s the European explorer and trader Jacques Cartier had his men cured of scurvy by "Indian medicine." Indeed, Corrigan continued, Native medicine "while essentially harmless had many good points" but "the church has relegated it to the realm of witchcraft, so that even such a simple thing as the brewing of spruce needles has disappeared."[32]

This backhanded compliment to Aboriginal knowledge was not sufficient to propel IHS officials to endorse Native healing practices in a more formal way; rather, IHS pursued a second element of colonial medicine, linking Western medical services to the superior moral and cultural values that Euro-Canadians supposedly possessed. After all,

Corrigan's appreciation of the "simple things" that Aboriginal knowledge offered could not compare with technologies like x-ray machines, BCG, or penicillin that Western doctors used to identify, prevent, or treat tuberculosis. The most prominent symbols of "civilization" were the IHS buildings themselves, the nursing stations and hospitals that stood as beacons of progress, progress made possible through an adherence to Euro-Canadian values and practices. Echoing a public health nursing prescription of an earlier age that had equated moral purity with physical cleanliness and good health,[33] IHS supervisor of nursing Mrs Helen Snary extolled the virtues of the "spotlessly clean, warm and modern dwelling" that was the nursing station: "These stations are a boon to the north country and stand out as a shining example of the future objective and goal in teaching and assisting the Indian to a better standard of living."[34] Likewise, on his fifteenth, and possibly final, trip through his northern Manitoba Zone, Dr Yule bemoaned the housing standards at Churchill and Duck Lake: "How can we hope to elevate the moral tone of our Indians if we will allow them to exist under such conditions."[35]

The link made between health and morality relates to the third element of colonizing medical practices, IHS's contradictory policies regarding provision of service. Throughout the post–Second World War era, IHS bureaucrats enthusiastically extended health services to Aboriginal communities, while zone administrators and agency doctors continued to press their superiors for more staff and new facilities. At the same time, IHS and DNHW officials insisted that the government had no legal obligation to provide any services at all. The treaties signed in the 1870s between the Canadian government and Manitoba's Aboriginal peoples included provisions for education and welfare, but not medical supplies or service. Thus, despite the fact that the federal government had been providing health services to First Nations people in Manitoba for over fifty years, federal authorities maintained that such services were a courtesy, or a charity, not a right. The growing demand for services by Aboriginal communities prompted Dr Wood, regional superintendent for the Manitoba Zone, to reiterate federal policy. In his January 1958 bulletin to all "Chiefs and Councillors" of Manitoba's First Nations communities, Wood articulated what IHS would provide and why. He explained that IHS offered health services because so many Native people were poor. Thus, as soon as individuals were self-sufficient they should join other Canadians in paying for medical services themselves.

For men, economic self-sufficiency meant: "If an Indian leaves the reserve and has a house in a town or municipality which he owns or rents we will pay for doctor and hospital services for one year if he

cannot afford them." After a year, the man had to join the ranks of
other Canadians, either paying doctor and hospital fees himself or
through an insurance plan or asking his municipal government for
charitable coverage. For women, the rules of entitlement were even
less forgiving, stipulating: "If an Indian woman lives 'common law'
with a non-Indian away from a reserve we will not pay for her treatment." Here, IHS authorities were building on, and even exceeding,
the discrimination all Native women faced under the law. The Canadian government's Indian Act dictated that if a Status Indian woman
married a non-Status or white man, she and her children, by that man,
were disentitled from their treaty rights. Even if the woman subsequently divorced that man, her rights were permanently forfeited.
Draconian as this was, IHS policy was in some ways worse: status Indian
women living common-law with non-Indian men were immediately
disentitled, though perhaps the woman's IHS coverage would resume
if the woman returned to her home reserve.[36] For Aboriginal women
and men, IHS programs were defined not as a right accorded to
people who had a treaty relationship with the state, but as welfare, a
charitable service that the federal government was not obliged to
provide.

The coercive dimensions of this "charity" constitute the fourth
element of the colonizing practices. Because many Aboriginal people
supported themselves through trapping and fishing, as well as
through seasonal wage labour, IHS personnel found administering
preventive services to the whole community difficult. Because reserve
members assembled once a year to receive their treaty payments from
the Department of Indian Affairs agent, IHS doctors and nurses
accompanied Indian agents to Treaty Days, where they did x-ray
"plating," tuberculin tests, and inoculations. A 1948 instruction sheet
from IHS regional superintendent W.J. Wood reminded doctors and
nurses that "if an x-ray survey is being conducted during treaty every
assistance should be given to ensure that every person is plated." He
further advised them that in doing this, "it is strongly recommended
that x-ray of Indians be done before they are paid treaty money. This
also applies to immunization."[37] In using the Indian agent to withhold treaty payments until the Native person complied with the particular medical procedure, IHS personnel employed the coercive
power of the colonial state and wedded biomedical practices to the
political apparatus of colonialism.

Like the doctors and bureaucrats, IHS nurses were implicated in this
system of colonial medicine, a set of services that neither recognized
Aboriginal custom and culture nor granted First Nations people any
formal entitlement to quality care.[38] And although in these years the

Canadian Nurses' Association (CNA), a national organization, adopted a formal policy of anti-discrimination and worked to eliminate racial barriers in nursing, which before 1945 had kept African-Canadian and other visible minority women out of Canadian nursing schools, the association did little to counteract the absence of Aboriginal women from nursing education or registration.[39] Privileged by race, white nurses travelled to isolated First Nations communities, where they enjoyed relative workplace autonomy and authority. Once they were there, though, their racial and cultural differences were tested and opposed by local social forces that complicated the nurses' role as representatives of colonial medical practices. Tempering the actions and activities of all IHS nursing personnel were their obligations to provide services that were meaningful to community members, their need to focus particularly on the health of Aboriginal women and children, and their commitment to the benefits of medical science. In countering, or at least working around, the colonizing structures of the IHS system, these on-the-ground relations between nurses and Aboriginal people provided opportunities, however partial and local, for Aboriginal people to assert their own definition of good health and good health care.

As the front-line workers for IHS, nurses were expected to make IHS services relevant to Aboriginal people's needs. Chief Medical Officer Percy Moore and his medical staff wanted to extend IHS services to as many First Nations communities as possible. So too did First Nations leaders, who pressed IHS officials for qualified personnel to service their communities. In 1945, for instance, chiefs and councillors of the St Martin Reserve on the east shore of Lake Manitoba, faced with two recent deaths and no doctor working in the nearest town at the time, petitioned for "a qualified nurse to take charge of the Welfare of the Reserve *at once.*" They wrote: "The Band are anxious and Willing that if her services are not required on any of the other Reserves that she is welcome to make her headquarters on Lake St Martin Reserve," but wherever posted, "a nurse is required immediately."[40]

It was essential that nurses, as the on-the-ground representatives of the IHS project, win the support of the community. In her study of U.S. Bureau of Indian Affairs public health nurses working in South Dakota's Sioux communities during the 1930s through 1950s, Nancy Reifel compiled oral histories that revealed that Native Americans used those Western medical services they deemed useful, but they "only used advanced medical services if they judged that such use would be more beneficial than traditional home care." As well, Sioux clients "accepted and appreciated the nurses as healers, holding them to the rigorous standards applied to the American Indian healers."[41] That nurses were "left so much alone to work out our own problems"[42] shifted the balance of colonial relations slightly, making it all the more important for IHS nurses to work with the community and with community leaders in order to be effective.

Tensions between nurses and community members occasionally made their way into IHS reports. In 1949 H. Snary, supervisor of public health nurses, went on record to say that "criticism of the nurse, Mrs Raynor, by the chief, the local assistant superintendent and Mr Davis are in Dr Yule's and my opinion unjustified."[43] On another occasion, Dr Yule observed that in the community of Split Lake "the atmosphere between the Indians and the nurse has changed for the better. I am told that she has been quite different since she returned last fall. She, on the other hand, says it is the Indians who have changed, not her. Be that as it may, I had no complaints."[44] And while nurses who were unhappy with local conditions did have the option to leave (this was one cause of high rates of staff turnover), there was a strong chance that they would only be redeployed to another community where many of the same demands would be made on them.

IHS nurses were also compelled to be responsive to community needs when, in the early 1960s, the Community Health Workers program was introduced. Aboriginal communities were to nominate a local community representative who would take particular responsibility for improving local sanitation. IHS nurses were instructed that CHWs "are to work *with* the people of the community and *for* them." CHWs were "not sanitary *inspectors* but teachers of basic sanitation practices." They were not to "tell or order people to do anything"; rather their job was "one of persuasion and not dictation." The CHW answered to the IHS nurse but would develop his or her own programs appropriate to local conditions.[45] Effective collaboration with the CHW could facilitate nurses' efficacy in community work. For example, in 1962 the community health worker at the Peguis Reserve, north of Winnipeg, made thirty-six home visits on her own and a further twenty-one with the nurse to talk with "mothers and fathers about flies, food. Diarrhoea [*sic*], baby clinics, water."[46] Likewise, at St Theresa's Point, the CHW and public health nurse worked together to counteract an epidemic of viral pneumonia raging among the community's children. Together the CHW and the nurse organized health demonstration classes in two different homes, at which "the nurse spoke in English and [the CHW] interpreted into our language so everyone could understand."[47] At the very least, nurses had to trust that the CHW would translate accurately.

On some reserves, the community health worker struggled to gain the cooperation of the chief and councillors, many of whom may have seen the CHW and the IHS nurses as tools of the Indian Agent and the government or as eroding the chief's local power base.[48] On one occasion, IHS nurses had to cope with a CHW who himself was "in many ways undermining the work we are attempting to do" and furthermore was "causing disruption and abus[ing] privileges." IHS authorities agreed that if the CHW was "in fact disrupting the health work of the community, we would be better off without his services."[49] As these examples illustrate, nurses had to negotiate with patients who would accept certain services and not others, with para-professional health workers who could aid or hinder the nurses' efforts, with community leaders who might refuse to cooperate with nurses' initiatives, and with IHS officials who defined the parameters of nurses' practice.

The imperative that nurses forge positive community relations and meet community health needs had particular gendered dimensions. Like public health nurses elsewhere, IHS nurses' femaleness was deemed a critical element in the campaign to improve the outrageous rates of First Nations infant and maternal mortality.[50] In 1949 Supervisor Helen Snary reported: "In all the stations the Indians come for advise [sic] and look to the nurse for guidance re: the care of their infants and children. This would indicate the service offered will prove most satisfactory and certainly essential to them."[51] Likewise, in a 1949 monthly report, K.L Goodman, RN, field nurse in Cross Lake, Manitoba, outlined the well-baby and toxoid clinic she was initiating: the clinic was held at the home of a local woman and was designed to reach out to women living at one end of the large reserve.[52] Nurses also took special interest in infant and maternal nutrition[53] and in the thorny subject of bottle- and breast-feeding.

Some nurses went well beyond physical health issues to intervene in what they saw to be the sexual exploitation of women and its social consequences. In a report that echoed previous generations of middle-class women's "rescue" efforts with working-class girls, Supervisor Snary reported in February 1948: "While in Pine Falls a social problem was brought to the nurse's attention re four girls who had illegitimate infants each naming a particular taxi driver." The public health nurse discussed the situation with the local Indian Agent (perhaps hoping he would confront the taxi driver) and then brought in social workers from the Salvation Army and the Provincial Child Welfare Department. As a result of this intervention, the "girls have decided to board their children and work in the city or near the reserve." The social workers and the Indian Agent would take on the "supervision" of the young mothers.[54] The nurse's plan spoke to the shared gendered concerns around female sexuality that brought the "girls" and the nurses together, but the resulting solution placed Native women under the supervision of white professionals, thereby re-inscribing a hierarchy of class and race.

At the same time, nurses sometimes found that relations with local women were frustrated by nurses' limited autonomy as women workers and employees of the state. At the 1965 Indian and Metis Conference, an annual meeting of Manitoba's Native leaders held under the auspices of the province's Community Welfare Planning Council, a "special session for women" addressed issues of special concern to Manitoba's Aboriginal women. One such concern pertained to family planning. Vera Richards, a delegate from Winnipeg employed as a court worker for the Indian and Metis Friendship Centre, maintained that some Aboriginal women wanted "information about how to control the size of their families." The group then turned to the public health nurse in attendance to learn whether birth control information could be supplied by IHS nurses. She replied that "because the nurse represents the taxpayers, she cannot have a family planning program, as some taxpayers are against it." The only circumstance where a nurse could provide birth control information (and presumably supplies) was if "requested to do so by a doctor," whereas "doctors themselves can provide it for individuals." The nurse's response accurately reflected Canada's birth control and abortion laws of the early 1960s, under which abortion and the provision of birth control information and devices were illegal, except when there were health reasons defined by a licensed physician. Her response also accurately reflected the division of professional authority that preserved the act of "prescribing" for doctors alone. Still, this explanation for the failure of IHS nurses to provide such information must have seemed odd to the representatives of Manitoba's Native women. After all, public health nurses may have "represented the taxpayers" (and thus the federal state that had decreed birth control illegal), but so did the IHS doctors, who were likewise salaried employees of the federal government. Moreover, because IHS doctors visited communities so irregularly, effectively leaving nurses to represent them in specific locales, the suggestion that doctors would "provide [birth control] for individuals" must have seemed an unwieldy and unlikely proposition to the Native women attending the meeting. Gender commonalties may have brought the nurse to the "special session for women" and may have prompted the female delegates to raise the delicate issue of birth control with the nurse, but the boundaries of professionalism and colonialism undercut the nurses' ability to fully cross the bounds of culture and race that divided the women.[55]

In other circumstances, IHS nurses' professional investment in medical science was fundamentally undermined by racism and colonialism.

In an era when the federal state was proving its ability to provide welfare state services for all citizens, IHS personnel seemed to be on the leading edge of "modern" government programs; yet, for many nurses, the promise of progress offered by biomedicine and the welfare state often appeared frustratingly unfulfilled when petty politics or racism got in the way. Such was the case in February 1958 when an IHS nurse undertook the routine task of accompanying a patient to the Portage la Prairie hospital. When they arrived, the nurse learned that because of disputes with IHS over payment for Aboriginal clients, the institutional administration was refusing treatment to "Indians, unless emergencies." The nurse then had to escort the patient to the Gladstone hospital, thirty minutes away. IHS authorities tried to gloss over the event, hoping that the tighter hospital admissions policy would prove a cost-saving measure if more patients had to be treated by field nurses. But for the nurse-escorts, racist incidents like this one opened up to question their professional commitment to biomedicine and patient service.[56]

Other circumstances challenged the IHS nurses' ability to provide scientifically sound care. Throughout the Manitoba Zone, the establishment of permanent Aboriginal communities was accompanied by the problem of securing sources of safe drinking water.[57] This problem reached crisis proportions for one community in 1958. That year, nurses and doctors at Fort Alexander (now Sagkeeng) reserve, one hour north of Manitoba's capital city of Winnipeg, complained of "increasing incidences of intestinal disease in Indian children on the Winnipeg River." IHS personnel alleged that pollution dumped into the river at the local mill town of Pine Falls was causing the problem. Both the town and the mill dumped raw effluent into the river along which Fort Alexander residents lived and from which they drew their water. Given that a century earlier clean water and improved sanitation had given public health officials some of their first victories over epidemic diseases, addressing the health problems in Fort Alexander should not have proved too difficult. It did. Because "rivers and streams" were a provincial concern and Aboriginal health was a federal one, a host of jurisdictional squabbles arose over who should test the water and how the pollution could be dealt with. Among other things, provincial sanitation officials would not supply IHS nurses with the sample bottles needed to carry out regular testing. Meanwhile, drinking water had to be shipped into Fort Alexander, and since many residents could not afford the water delivery service, they had no choice but to continue to use Winnipeg River water. For the community's nurses, who could see first-hand the health costs of polluted water, scientific knowledge and technological capability failed in the

face of political and economic imperatives.[58] For members of Sagkeeng Nation, polluted natural resources underscored the reality that
colonial domination by the Canadian state gave them no control over
a natural resource base. For nurses and Aboriginal people alike, the
inability of IHS staff to put community health needs ahead of the
larger politico-economic agenda of white Canadians was proof of the
limited authority of health officials.

The 1945–70 years proved to be transitional ones for Canada's
Aboriginal health services. With its reorganization in 1945, IHS offered
First Nations people an "active" system of medical and nursing services,
one that attempted to provide more systematic and effective health
services but that did not challenge the colonial relations between
Aboriginal people and the Canadian government. The introduction of
Medicare in 1968–70 provided medical insurance for all Canadians,
promising to resolve many of the tensions over payment and entitlement for Aboriginal and non-Aboriginal people alike. Yet new conflicts
were brewing. In the 1970s and 1980s, the political campaign for Native self-government laid bare the role of medical services in the history
of colonization and placed new demands on the Canadian state that
would address the future post-colonial status of Canada's First Nations
people.[59]

This examination of nurses' work for IHS before 1970 reveals the
ongoing importance of colonizing ideas and practices to the health
services provided by the federal government to Canadian Aboriginal
peoples. IHS's bureaucratic move out the Department of Indian Affairs
and into the Department of National Health and Welfare may have resulted in increased resources for IHS but did not divorce IHS from its
colonizing functions. In a system that reinforced Aboriginal people's
dependent and "uncivilized" status, nurses stood as front-line service
providers who boasted specific professional skills. To make that system
work, however, nurses were obliged to address local health needs and
establish productive working relationships with community members,
often by forging gender-based bonds with local women. In the process,
the demands of gender, professionalism, and colonialism could easily
come into conflict. Expected to represent the Canadian government's
particular colonial position on the provision of health services, nurses
sometimes found their professional abilities and obligations undermined by the racism of Canadian society, by the imperatives of northern economic development, or by the colonialist policies themselves.

More research is required to determine to what extent individual
nurses managed to work around racism and colonialism, making the
bonds of gender, for example, a higher priority than those of profes-

sionalism or "race." There is some evidence that by the 1980s some Manitoba nurses had begun collaborating with traditional Aboriginal healers[60] and that national nursing leaders had slowly come to support the work of the Registered Nurses of Canadian Indian Ancestry, now the Indian and Inuit Nurses of Canada.[61] But the research presented here does reveal the importance of theorizing the diverse, and often oppositional, ways that North American women related to their health-care "systems." Before 1970 many women in Canada and the United States might have benefited from greater state involvement in the pro-vision of and payment for medical care, but other women found the federal government all too willing to provide medical, nursing, and hospital services, all wrapped up in the larger system of colonization and/or racism. Feminist scholars studying female health-care workers, while attending to the gender asymmetry that limited the authority granted female nurses, doctors, or midwives, must not lose sight of the power those caregivers did wield, power often based on racial, ethnic, or class privilege. Understanding women's relationships with the state and with medicine demands that we ask, which women in what histori-cal circumstances and in what relations of power?

NOTES

1 "Natives on hunger strike over health problems," CBC News, 12 April 1999; and "Northern nurses working in fear," CBC News, 10 March 2000.

2 In her memoir, *Native Blood: Nursing on the Reservation* (Canada, 1994), retired nurse Judy Smith recalls, "As I gained more respect for Outpost Nurses, I also became increasingly annoyed by the total disregard of nurses both by literature and the mass media." Citing the recent news coverage of living conditions in a northern Saskatchewan First Nations community, Smith observed that the media coverage of medical care in that community "managed to discuss [living conditions and medical care] in considerable detail without mentioning the presence of nurses ... According to the media ... the only medical care available at Black Lake was from the physi-cian who visited the reserve twice a month." Smith, *Native Blood*, 19–20.

3 In 1962, Indian Health Services were again reorganized within the Depart-ment of National Health and Welfare, under the title "Medical Health Services Branch." For the sake of consistency, the term Indian Health Services will be used throughout this paper. See T. Kue Young, "Indian Health Services in Canada: A Sociohistorical Perspective," *Social Science Medicine* 18, 3 (1984): 257–64.

4 Key works in the social history of nursing include Barbara Melosh, *'The Phy-sician's Hand': Work Culture and Conflict in American Nursing* (Philadelphia:

Temple University Press 1982); Susan Reverby, *Ordered to Care: The Dilemma of American Nursing, 1850–1945* (New York: Cambridge University Press 1987); and Kathryn McPherson, *Bedside Matters: The Transformation of Canadian Nursing, 1900–1990* (Toronto: Oxford University Press 1996).

5 Most importantly, see Darlene Clark Hine, *Black Women in White: Racial Conflict and Co-operation in the Nursing Profession, 1890–1950* (Bloomington: Indiana University Press 1989); Agnes Calliste, "'Women of Exceptional Merit': Immigration of Caribbean Nurses to Canada," *Canadian Journal of Women and the Law* 6, no. 1: 85–103; and Shula Marks, *Divided Sisterhood: Race, Class and Gender in the South African Nursing Profession* (New York: St Martin's Press 1994).

6 See, for example, Laura Ann Stoler, *Race and the Education of Desire: Foucault's History of Sexuality and the Colonial Order of Things* (Durham: Duke University Press 1995).

7 Among the most influential of such studies is Alfred Crosby's classic *The Columbian Exchange: Biological and Cultural Consequences of 1492* (Westport, Conn.: Greenwood Press 1972). See also, Maureen Lux, "Beyond Biology: Disease and Its Impact on the Canadian Plains Native People 1880–1930" (PhD dissertation, Simon Fraser University 1996).

8 Roy MacLeod, introduction to in Roy MacLeod and Milton Lewis, eds, *Disease, Medicine, and Empire: Perspectives on Western Medicine and the Experience of European Expansion* (London: Routledge 1988), 2.

9 Mary-Ellen Kelm, *Colonizing Bodies: Aboriginal Health and Healing in British Columbia, 1900–1950* (Vancouver: University of British Columbia Press 1998), 101.

10 On the history of DIA's health services, see Kue Young, "Indian Health Services in Canada"; and Pamela Margaret White, "Restructuring the Domestic Sphere – Prairie Indian Women on Reserves: Image, Ideology and State Policy, 1880–1930" (PhD dissertation, McGill University 1987).

11 Marguerita Stewart Collection, Provincial Archives of Manitoba (hereafter PAM), MG 14, C 41.

12 Letter from Martin Lajeunesse, CMI Vicar-Apostolic of Keewatin, to Honourable T.A. Crerar, Minister of Mines and Resources, 17 August 1942. National Archives (hereafter NA) RG 29, vol. 2782, file 823-1-A501.

13 Lewis Meriam et al., *The Problem of Indian Administration* (Baltimore: Johns Hopkins Press 1928), 189–90, cited in Robert A. Trennert, *White Man's Medicine: Government Doctors and the Navajo, 1863–1955* (Albuquerque: University of New Mexico Press 1998), 136.

14 On the field nurses working on American reservations in the 1930s, see Emily Abel, "'We are left so much alone to work out our own problems': Nurses on American Indian Reservations during the 1920s," *Nursing History Review* 4 (1996): 43–64. The 1957 federal review of American Indian health observed that only in the 1930s, when the Depression had

eliminated funding for many other nursing jobs, did BIA health services enjoy a sufficient supply of nurses. Trennert concludes that "America's entry into World War II devastated reservation health services, as most of the gains so laboriously achieved during the 1930s disappeared under the demand of wartime necessity." *White Man's Medicine*, 201.

15 U.S. Department of Health, Education and Welfare, Public Health Service, Office of Surgeon General, *Health Services for American Indians*, Public Health Service Publication No. 531 (Washington, D.C., 1957), 2, 90, 94.

16 White, "Restructuring the Domestic Sphere," 236.

17 These problems were acknowledged in Canadian nurses' professional journal. See A.W. Tye, "Canadian Nurses on Indian Reserves," *Canadian Nurse* 22, no. 5 (May 1926): 231–2.

18 Sarah Carter, *Capturing Women: The Manipulation of Cultural Imagery in Canada's Prairie West* (Montreal: McGill-Queen's University Press, 1997).

19 Jean H. Lagasse, *A Study of the Population of Indian Ancestry Living in Manitoba* (Winnipeg: Department of Agriculture and Immigration 1959), 31.

20 Donald Kerr and Deryck W. Holdsworth, eds, *Historical Atlas of Canada: Addressing the Twentieth Century*, vol. 3 (Toronto: University of Toronto Press 1990), plates 53 and 59.

21 J.C. Rutledge, in a letter to Dr W.J. Wood, Regional Superintendent, Indian Health Service, 2 May 1947, NA, RG 29, vol. 2782 reported that the Civil Service Commission had approved several nursing positions but had rejected IHS's request for a "Charge Allowance." '

22 Letter from Cameron Corrigan to Dr P.E. Moore, Director of Indian Health Services, 22 April 1947, NA, RG 29, vol. 2782.

23 For richly detailed descriptions of nurses' work in northern Saskatchewan, see Laurie Meijer Drees and Lesley McBain, "Nursing and Native Peoples in Northern Saskatchewan: 1930s-1950s," *Canadian Bulletin of Medical History* 18, no. 1 (2001): 43–65.

24 Ruth Ellen Evans (née Hiam), obituary, *Winnipeg Free Press*, 2 December 2000.

25 In 1981 there were over 300,000 Registered Indians in Canada. Vic Satzewich and Terry Wotherspoon, *First Nations: Race, Class and Gender Relations* (Toronto: Nelson 1993), 33.

26 Kue Young, "Indian Health Services in Canada."

27 Terry Wotherspoon, "Colonization, Self-determination, and the Health of Canada's First Nations Peoples," in B. Singh Bolaria and Rosemary Bolaria, eds, *Racial Minorities, Medicine and Health* (Halifax: Fernwood 1994).

28 Frank Tough, *"As Their Natural Resources Fail": Native Peoples and the Economic History of Northern Manitoba* (Vancouver: University of British Columbia Press 1996).

29 Dominique Jean, "Family Allowances and Family Autonomy: Quebec Families Encounter the Welfare State, 1945–1955," in B. Bradbury, ed., *Cana-*

dian Family History: Selected Readings (Toronto: Copp Clark Pitman 1992), 408, 418. See also Dr Yule, "Treaty Report 1956," 12 July 1956 (p. 3), which notes that, before the "advent of Children's Allowance and Day-schools," homes were only occupied during the summer months, "as the greater part of the population took their families and moved to the tra-pline in the early fall." NA, RG 29, vol. 3124, file 860-8-X200, pt 2A.

30 See, for example, Cameron Corrigan, "Scurvy in a Cree Indian," *Canadian Medical Association Journal* 54 (April 1946): 380–2. Corrigan was medical superintendent for the IHS's Norway House Indian Hospital in Manitoba and continued on with IHS well after its transfer to DNHW. Corrigan linked the Cree woman's scurvy to her sedentary life, itself a product of "civilization."

31 Yule, "Treaty Report 1956," 12 July 1956.

32 Corrigan, "Scurvy in a Cree Indian," 380.

33 See Mariana Valverde, *The Age of Light, Soap and Water: Moral Reform in English Canada, 1880–1920* (Toronto: McClelland and Stewart 1991); see also McPherson, *Bedside Matters*, chap. 2.

34 Mrs Helen Snary, Public Health Nurse, "Progress Report February 1949," 11 March 1949, NA, RG 29, vol. 3124, file 860-8-X200, pt 1.

35 Yule, "Treaty Report 1956," 12 July 1956.

36 W.J. Wood, MD, Regional Superintendent, "Notice to Chiefs and Council-lors," 21 January 1958, NA, RG 29, vol. 3124.

37 Dr Wood, "Memo to Doctors and Nurses on Treaty Trips," NA, RG 29, vol. 3124, file 860-8-X200, pt 1.

38 Patricia Jasen analyses Euro-Canadian colonizing attitudes to Aboriginal women's childbirth practices, arguing that efforts in the post-1945 era by health authorities to improve maternity services and infant-mortality rates perpetuated, rather than eliminated, the colonization process. Jasen, "Race, Culture, and the Colonization of Childbirth in Northern Canada," *Social History of Medicine* 10, no. 3 (1997): 383–400.

39 McPherson, *Bedside Matters*, 118–20.

40 16 January 1945 (Hamilton to Indian Affairs Branch), RG 29, vol. 2782, file 823-1-A127. These requests continued throughout the 1960s, as reflected in the "Proceedings of the Annual Indian and Metis Conference," Winnipeg, 1960–67.

41 Nancy Reifel, "American Indian Views of Public Health Nursing, 1930–1950," *American Indian Culture and Research Journal* 23, no. 3 (1999): 143–54.

42 Abel, " 'We are left so much alone to work out our own problems.' "

43 W.J. Wood, MD, Regional Superintendent, "Progress Report August 1949," 2 September 1949.

44 Dr Yule to Dr Moore, Treaty Report 1956, 12 July 1956.

45 Ethel Martens, Health Educator, to Miss Voth, Nurse in Charge, Island Lake Nursing Station, 19 March 1962, NA, RG 29, vol. 2709.

46 Mrs Dorothy Stranger, CHW, Peguis Reserve "Monthly Reports," September 1962, NA, RG 29, vol. 2709, file 804-4-X200, pt 1.

47 "Memo," Louis Wood, St Theresa Point Community Health Worker, to Regional Director, Medical Services, Central Region, July 1966 NA, RG 29, vol. 2709, file 804-4-X200, pt 1.

48 For example, in "Report from Mr. W. Green, C.H.W., Berens River of his visit to Sandy Lake to Assist Belle Kakegumich, C.H.W.," the CHW noted that in his meeting with the CHW from Big Trout Lake there was "no co-operation from the Chief as yet." 22 January 1965, NA, RG 29, vol. 2709, file 804-4-X200, pt 1.

49 Letter from O.J. Rath, MD, Regional Superintendent, to Zone Superintendent, Indian Health Services, "Personnel Matters Class A," 5 November 1962, NA, RG 29, vol. 2709, file 904-4-X200, pt 1.

50 The 1948 *Annual Report* indicated that "where possible nurses were included in treaty parties to assist the doctor, to immunize, to treat cases and visit homes, to advise mothers in infant care and nutrition."

51 Snary, "Progress Report February 1949."

52 K.L. Goodman, RN, "Monthly Report," January 1949, NA, RG 29, vol. 3124.

53 In 1958 the regional superintendent, Dr Wood, reported that public health nurses had to pay more attention to "the anemia of pregnant women which may be the cause of the high incidence of prematurity. A supplementary diet plus iron and vitamins would seem to be an excellent preventive measure." "Regional Superintendent's Monthly Report – Central Region, January and February 1958," 7 March 1958, NA, RG 29, vol. 3124, file 860-8-X200, pt 2A.

54 Snary, "Progress Report February 1949," 16 March 1949.

55 "Proceedings of the Eleventh Annual Indian and Metis Conference," Winnipeg, February 1965, p. 36. The following year the Women's Meeting recommended that "a completely equipped traveling clinic on family planning and sex education for youth be organized consisting of a doctor and a nurse and that the clinic serve all persons living in outlying areas." "Proceedings of the Twelfth Annual Indian and Metis Conference," Winnipeg, 1966, p. 32.

56 "Regional Superintendent's Monthly Report – Central Region, January and February 1958," 7 March 1958.

57 At the 1963 Indian and Metis Conference of Manitoba session on "What about Women in the Community," the "women reported lack of safe drinking water on some reserves, and a greater shortage for bathing and washing clothes. This, coupled with small, cold houses made it difficult to keep their children clean in the winter, and their diet was not of the best.

Consequently scabies and other such illnesses resulted. On some reserves pills to purify the water were being distributed." "Proceedings of the Ninth Annual Indian and Metis Conference," Winnipeg, 1963, p. 26.

58 Memo from D. Jack, Supervising Engineer with Public Health Engineering Division, Ottawa, to J.R. Menzies, 1 August 1958; also letter from W.J. Wood to Dr M.R. Elliott, Deputy Minister, Department of Health and Public Welfare, Province of Manitoba, 14 October 1955, NA, RG 29, vol. 2982, file 851-5-X200, pt 1.

59 Kue Young, "Indian Health Services in Canada."

60 David Gregory, "Traditional Indian Healers in Northern Manitoba: An Emerging Relationship with the Health Care System," *Native Studies Review* 5, no. 1 (1989): 163–74. Gregory found that although "a truly collaborative relationship was the exception, rather than the norm," 81% of Manitoba's Medical Services Bureau nurses responded to his survey and of those 52% "reported client referrals to Indian elders," while "67% were aware of traditional healing practices in their communities, and 39% reported they had initiated patient referrals to traditional healers." These figures suggest a greater willingness on the part of nurses than on the part of doctors to work with Native healers. See Yvon Gagnon, "Physicians' Attitudes toward Collaboration with Traditional Healers," *Native Studies Review* 5, no. 1 (1989): 175–85.

61 Jean Cuthand Goodwill, "Organized Political Action: Indian and Inuit Nurses of Canada," in Alice Baumgart and Jenniece Larsen, eds, *Canadian Nursing Faces the Future: Development and Change* (St Louis: C.V. Mosby 1988); McPherson, *Bedside Matters*, 258.

12

Race, the State, and Caribbean Immigrant Nurses, 1950–1962

Karen Flynn

The "state" – by which I mean governments and the diverse agencies that carry out public policy – has frequently been the focus of analysis for historical researchers on women's health.[1] Attention is paid to the way state agencies provided (or did not provide) health services; how state agencies shaped women's access to health professions; and how female occupations like nursing used the state to gain public and legal authority. However, women's experiences within the health-care system have also been shaped by other forms of state power, such as immigration regulations and policies.

In this chapter, I offer an anti-racist feminist analysis of Canadian immigration regulations that provides a useful way of understanding the ideologies of "race" and racism in nursing and how these ideologies shaped the terrain on which black nurses worked. By analysing the immigration records in the National Archives of Canada and drawing on the international scholarship on ethnicity, race, and gender in nursing, I show how race was employed and articulated by the different players involved in the migration of Caribbean nurses. I explore how race was a flexible and historically determined category used to limit the migration of black nurses to Canada. For example, although immigration officials did not consider Haitian and Caribbean nurses suitable citizens and qualified workers, they welcomed Greek nurses both as workers and migrants despite questions about their professional qualifications. At the same time, racial meanings were always contested. Immigration officials, for example, made distinctions between Afro-Caribbean and Haitian nurses. In some cases, hospital administrators

solved the problem of a severe nursing shortage by challenging exclusionary immigration policies and seeking out black nurses for employment. The individual nurses and black organizations that lobbied
immigration officials further challenged how race was constituted by
the Department of Citizenship and Immigration.

The decades following the Second World War were turbulent ones
for the Canadian health-care system, and that turbulence was intensi-
fied by the shortage of nurses that persisted throughout the 1950s and
1960s. Federal funding for hospital construction and state-funded
hospitalization insurance increased the need for hospital staff nurses
at a time when new employment opportunities for women drew many
prospective recruits away from the occupation. Thus, throughout the
postwar decades, nursing leaders and educators faced the daunting
task of ensuring that there were enough nurses to meet the demands
while at the same time maintaining the standards of the occupation.
Funds were allotted for bursaries to encourage high school girls to
choose careers in nursing, and nursing organizations introduced subsidiary programs that required less training and education. They also
attempted to reduce the turnover rate, bring twenty-five thousand
unemployed nurses back into the workforce, and lobby for increased
immigration. However, their efforts were complicated by the arrival
of immigrant nurses who had been trained and had worked outside of
North America.[2]

The postwar years also saw changes in Canadian immigration policy.
Before the war and in the years immediately thereafter, Canada had a
very restrictive immigration policy. Prospective immigrants from "preferred" countries, such as Britain and the United States, were distinguished from those from "non-preferred" countries, who could not be
as readily assimilated. Up until 1962, Canada restricted the immigration of non-whites owing to deep-seated fears that they would be unable to adapt to Canadian society. According to historian John
Schultz, Immigration Branch officials sought to safeguard Canada's
racial purity by preventing an influx of those immigrants who they
thought would erode the country's national fibre. Black migration was
restricted at the beginning of the twentieth century, Schultz continued, because "the Negro, the common wisdom went, was unassailable.
His loose habits, laziness, sexual appetites, lack of manliness and mental deficiencies would pollute the stream of Canadian morals."[3] Furthermore, the harsh Canadian weather was not suitable for blacks.

Immigration regulations became less restrictive, at least for Europeans, in the early 1950s. Labour needs and public pressure from local
and international humanitarian groups led to changes in Canadian
immigration policies with respect to whites affected by the turmoil of

war. The once-exclusionary policies that deemed only people of British stock as suitable citizens were relaxed to admit southern and Eastern Europeans as a humanitarian act to deal with the aftermath of war. These migrants included, for the most part, Polish war veterans, displaced persons from Eastern Europe, and people from Holland, Germany, Italy, and Portugal who worked primarily as farm workers, domestic workers, nurses, and nurses' aides. In 1952 a new immigration act simplified immigration administration, investing a great deal of discretionary power in the hands of government officials. Like its predecessors, however, the 1952 bill continued to severely restrict the migration of "coloured" and "partly coloured" persons to Canada. As Vic Satzewich has pointed out, "According to state policies in the 1950s, the admittance of 'partly coloured persons' was restricted to certain classes of close relatives of Canadian citizens, and cases of exceptional merit ... [and] immigrant[s] who will contribute appreciably to the social, economic, and cultural life of Canada."[4] The state allowed a small number of domestic workers from the Caribbean to enter on a quota basis in 1955. Despite these minor concessions, immigration officials continued to limit the migration of Caribbean migrants on the basis of their supposed inability to assimilate into Canadian culture and adapt to Canada's climate. Non-white non-Europeans comprised just 5 per cent of immigrants prior to 1957, increasing to 8 per cent between 1958 and 1962 and then to 14 per cent.[5]

In the early 1950s, immigration officials, in conjunction with the Department of Labour, developed a number of initiatives to meet the nation's labour shortages and assist those affected by the war. One of the strategics adopted by the state was a group movement migration scheme, the purpose of which was twofold: (1) to demonstrate the government's humanitarian response to the situation in Europe and (2) to alleviate the labour shortage in Canada. Nurses' aides and domestic workers in countries like Greece and Germany, but not those in the Caribbean, were encouraged to migrate to Canada. In 1952 the chief of operations in Ottawa issued a circular that stressed the need for "Greek nurses, nurses' aides, and domestics." This particular group "was in demand and were a continuing need and may be sent in large numbers as we can obtain until further notice." Nurses from Britain, Switzerland, Belgium, Holland, and Scandinavia were also welcomed "because they have the best nursing schools."[6]

Immigration officials, employment agencies, nursing associations, and individual nursing directors concurred on the necessity of increasing immigration to alleviate the nursing shortage and support the humanitarian cause. However, the agendas and protocols of these various bodies were often in conflict. These bodies often disagreed about the role of immigration officials in determining the qualifications of immigrant nurses and, equally important, about Canada's need for Caribbean nurses. In particular, the immigration department's decision to oversee the immigration of European nurses created some difficulties with nursing associations because of the apprehension that government officials – especially if they were stationed overseas – would be unable to assess the suitability of the nurses' professional credentials.

The Canadian Nurses' Association (CNA) and provincial associations, however, were committed to helping their European sisters find employment in Canada. As early as 1947, the Registered Nurses' Association of Ontario told the province's minister of labour that it would accept displaced European nurses. Nevertheless, nurses' associations had concerns about whether immigrant practitioners would meet North American standards, given the varied meaning behind the term "nurse" in Europe. They worried about the "reported relaxation of laws which would permit the persons calling themselves nursing assistants or nursing aides to automatically be admitted to Canada subject only to the usual health, character and passport requirement." In 1950 the CNA approached the federal Department of Citizenship and Immigration with a report on this issue. Claiming that it wanted to "safeguard standards and protect the Canadian people against unqualified practitioners," the CNA had developed a number of guidelines to help immigration officials assess the new migrant nurses. The report also urged immigration officers to inform prospective "migrants that once accepted in the rehabilitation plan of the Canadian Nurses' Association, [they] are required to spend one year as a nursing aide in hospitals." It explained that "this year of service as nursing aides is a period of orientation to the Canadian nursing way of life, to hospital routine, methods of patient care and language." Once the year had been completed, the association hoped, "the immigrant – if recommended by the Director of Nursing – would be classified as a graduate intern pending exams and registration." The CNA report also highlighted the differences among the provincial associations with respect to qualifications and training. In Manitoba, for example, nurses were not required to have obstetrical training and midwives were not recognized. Some provinces, but not all, had reciprocal arrangements with Scandinavian countries, recognizing the credentials of one another's nurses. The CNA hoped that these federal guidelines would reduce the possibility that unqualified nurses would enter the occupation.[7]

Despite the CNA guidelines, large numbers of untrained nurses from countries such as Germany and Greece were allowed to enter Canada. This disturbed the Quebec Provincial Nurses' Association (QPNA), which offered an indictment of overseas immigration officials who did not adequately evaluate immigrant nurses. The QPNA, along with the secretary of the CNA in Montreal, filed a complaint with the Eastern District superintendent (Immigration) about the numerous new arrivals "who seek employment as nurses but who were found unqualified to practice." The QPNA explained that "many of these [women] declared that they were issued visas on the strength of their nursing ability and qualifications, and they were disappointed and bewildered when refused employment." Although the QPNA attempted to assist the nurses with further training and placement, it did not hide its disappointment with immigration officials. In writing to the director of immigration in Ottawa about the QPNA's concerns, the Eastern District superintendent noted that "the association is of the opinion that if more care were exercised by our officers overseas prior to granting visas to alleged nurses, less confusion, disappointment, time and effort, and expense would prevail on the arrival of these immigrants." To solve the problem of unqualified immigrants entering the country, the QPNA suggested that instead of going through the Department of Citizenship and Immigration, prospective immigrant nurses should correspond directly with the nurses' association in the province of intended residence. The association would then ascertain whether the nurse met the necessary qualifications. The QPNA noted that a similar and satisfactory procedure was in place for nurses migrating from the British Isles and that the results were satisfactory. From the QPNA's perspective, having applicants contact the association directly would be a more effective way to determine qualifications. This process would also help the nursing profession retain control over the standards of the occupation.[8]

The experience of Greek migrant nurses reveals the tensions between immigration officials and nurses' associations. The government's scheme to assist displaced Greek women failed miserably. No sooner had the initiative been implemented than issues of professional and (especially) language qualifications came to the surface. A significant number of Greek nurses could not speak either of Canada's official languages, a fact that placed them in a precarious position. One nursing director, pointing out that a knowledge of English and French was essential for dealing with human lives, said Greek nurses were not in a position to do bedside nursing.[9] By 1961, twenty-six Greek women who had been placed in hospitals had been demoted to domestic duties or "placed as nurses' aides and ward maids as their English was insufficient to ensure they could accept and give instructions accurately." An immigration official concluded that although Greek nurses were reliable and well trained, "the language barrier makes [their] advancement slow, and few have advanced beyond the level at which they are placed as they are unable to obtain registration, certification, licensing without demonstrating their facility in the use of English." Despite attempts at language training, most Greek nurses were unable to meet the language requirements advocated by nursing organizations. Of the twenty-six nurses, only two advanced from certified nurses' aides to non-registered nurses, while another two advanced from aide to certified nursing aide. The others remained as domestics or ward maids or found other areas of employment.[10]

Frustrated with the difficulty of finding jobs for Greek nurses, the director of the National Employment Services told the immigration department that Greek nurses almost always entered employment as nurses' aides because of language difficulties. He stated: "Until each can demonstrate that she has good understanding of the English language and can take and give instructions in that language, none of the provincial nurses' associations will permit her to practice as a registered nurse."[11] The many difficulties ensuing from the lack of language training led the program to be shut down in 1961. W.R. Bakersville, director of immigration, admitted that "in view of the relatively little success we have achieved with this group, we have decided to dismantle the program as a special movement." Henceforth Greek nurses' aides were to be dealt with individually and had to go through the same channels as regular immigrants. They were also encouraged to complete the necessary language training. It is striking how little attention the Department of Immigration and its provincial counterparts paid to CNA guidelines during the years the program was in operation. Indeed, as the example of Greek immigrant nurses shows, the state maintained an almost absolute jurisdiction over immigrant nurses' entrance into Canada.[12]

While the Department of Citizenship and Immigration welcomed Greek nurses and other persons displaced by the war, it discouraged any suggestion that a similar scheme be established for Caribbean nurses. However, the economic upheaval in the Caribbean should have warranted increased immigration on humanitarian grounds. Although Canadian officials considered immigration necessary for nation-building, their notions of "whiteness" and "Canadianness" led to the privileging of immigrants who they believed could assimilate easily, that is, those from European stock. Thus, in spite of a nursing shortage, only 286 nursing assistants and 982 graduate nurses from the Caribbean – about 8 per cent of the total – gained landed immigrant status in Canada between 1954 and 1965.[13] Such low figures are a clear indication that the state attempted to restrict the migration of Caribbean nurses in direct contradiction to the needs of hospital and nursing organizations that were interested in procuring labour to meet the needs of the nursing shortage.

To curtail the migration of Caribbean nurses, the state instituted a number of regulations pertaining to whether prospective immigrants were students, nurses' aides, nursing assistants, or registered nurses (RNs). Students applying for the degree of registered nurse were given temporary visas and considered for landed status once they had upgraded (by taking courses in obstetrics or pediatrics) and had passed their exams. Nursing assistant students were granted entry only if they could prove that they had been accepted by a school that would license or certify them upon graduation. This particular policy posed considerable difficulty because only four provinces – Ontario, Alberta, Manitoba, and British Columbia – certified and licensed their students upon graduation. Given this provincial disparity, the Department of Immigration reviewed its policy on certification, concluded that it was ineffective, and abandoned it. Since there was a "continuing shortage of nurses aides in Canada," the department decided that it "no longer require[d] candidates coming forward to schools which certify or license them upon graduation."[14] The change may have been an efficiency measure so that students studying to be nursing assistants did not have to go through a prolonged immigration process during a time of nursing scarcity. However, it had economic benefits for the state because nurses' aides and assistants worked for cheap wages and did not need to be certified or licensed in order to work.

The power vested in individual immigration officers sometimes led to inconsistency. In 1956 the acting chief for the Immigration Admissions Division sent a memo advising his colleagues to refuse entry to students and nursing assistants from the British West Indies unless they had been accepted into a program that "led to a degree of Registered Nurse which could be acceptable to the Provincial Nursing Association." At the same time, the immigration department issued temporary visas to two women who had been accepted for training as nursing assistants at the Norfolk General Hospital in Simcoe, Ontario, on the grounds that "these were exceptions and must not be taken as precedents." The state's policy of admitting only those who would be eligible for registration was a reactionary measure taken to minimize the number of Caribbean nurses applying for permanent status in Canada, as demonstrated by the large number of immigration inquiries into "the increasing number of ... nurses assistants who were applying for landing" in the late 1950s.[15] The fact that two nursing assistants were allowed temporary entry on an exceptional basis confirms the contradictory nature of Canadian immigration as it dealt with the migration of Caribbean nurses and hospital demands for nursing labour.

While the migration of nursing assistants and nursing aides was limited, Caribbean nurses eligible for registration with the provincial associations had much less difficulty with immigration. "It has been the

Department's practice to authorize the landing of Negro nurses, who are eligible for registration if coming forward to assured employment and the prospective employer is aware of the racial origin." Nurses who met the criteria set out by nursing organizations would be granted RN status without necessarily having to take courses to upgrade. Not surprisingly, a 1958 investigation conducted by immigration agents into the presence of Caribbean nurses in Toronto revealed that most of them were RNs. Already trained, these nurses could meet the demand for labour immediately, unlike those who were entering Canada as students.[16]

The divergent manner in which Caribbean nurses and their Greek counterparts were treated is revealing. First, the explicit attempt by the state to encourage Greek migration was not extended to Caribbean nurses. Second, no question was raised about Greek nurses' ability to assimilate in immigration discourses. Because it was accepted that Greek immigrants would acculturate to Canadian lifestyle, they were not scrutinized in the same way as Caribbean nurses. It was never mandatory – only preferred – for Greek or other white immigrant nurses to find employment prior to their arrival, and their entrance into Canada did not have to be authorized by an Order-in-Council. Even after Orders-in-Council were no longer necessary for Caribbean immigrants, the immigration of Caribbean nurses remained minimal. This was consistent with Canada's exclusion of blacks generally.

How did nursing associations and hospitals deal with the state's reluctance to allow the immigration of Caribbean nurses? Some nursing directors downplayed their need for nurses. However, hospitals faced with a severe labour shortage often expressed their frustration with immigration restrictions. Dr F.S. Lawson, director of Psychiatric Services at the Department of Public Health in Saskatchewan, complained that his department was "having difficulty maintaining their quota of nurses" and asked the Department of Citizenship and Immigration to assist with the nursing shortage by encouraging the migration of Caribbean nurses. The long delays resulting from the extensive investigations into prospective black immigrants led at least one hospital to ignore federal policies and initiate its own employment procedures. Canadian immigration officials were displeased when they learned that several British West Indies nurses had applied to Canada's immigration office in London, England, for immigration clearance so that they could accept employment at Norfolk General Hospital in Simcoe, Ontario. They chastised hospital staff for "the manner in which they encouraged these applicants, who are not admissible without an Order-in-Council, to a course of action without first applying to this office." They further maintained "that the authorization put out by the hospital is, as far as we can make out, indiscriminate without first having reviewed the applicants' qualifications." According to immigration officials, the letters of acceptance issued by Norfolk General Hospital would have no effect on admission to Canada and created "unnecessary problems for their London officials."[17] The discrepancy between immigration policy and the hospital's need for labour is apparent. Although hospitals must have been aware of Ottawa's jurisdiction over the flow of immigration, some still issued letters of acceptance that contravened immigration policies.

Immigration officials also used the issue of qualifications as a way either to slow down the immigration of black nurses or to refuse them entrance altogether. This had grave implications for nurses who accepted employment in hospitals willing to employ those who had taken the general three-year nursing course but did not have the required training in obstetrics or midwifery. Lack of midwifery and obstetrics training was often used to delay the processing of immigration applications. The contradiction, however, is that while the immigration department used the qualifications issue to defer and, in some cases, turn down the applications of immigrant nurses, hospitals were willing to disregard the lack of midwifery training in order to meet their labour needs.

Black activists, too, challenged Canada's exclusionary policies towards Caribbean nurses. In 1956 Donald Moore, director of the Negro Citizenship Association, wrote the chief of admissions at the Department of Citizenship and Immigration to object to the situation of prospective immigrant nurses from Barbados whose applications had been delayed. According to Moore, three hospitals – the Jewish General of Montreal, Windsor General, and Toronto's Mount Sinai – had offered positions to the nurses, who not only had completed the three-year general course, but also had much practical experience. Similarly, a representative of the British Caribbean Students Liaison Office in Canada sent another immigration official the names of students who had been accepted "for training by hospital schools, [but] were not successful in obtaining student visas from the Immigration Department" because of the prolonged investigations. Despite limited success, these black organizations continued to work on behalf of black nurses and Caribbean immigrants to challenge the state's racist exclusionary policies. There is no evidence that white Canadian individuals or organizations assisted the blacks in dealing with the cases involving Caribbean nurses, but in 1960 the *Globe and Mail* published an article about discrimination against Caribbean nurses that disturbed the director of immigration. There were also a few exceptional members of Parliament who, although they did not address the issues of nurses specifically, were critical of immigration policies that they felt were discriminatory with respect to West Indians.[18]

Some individuals also challenged the state when they were refused entry into Canada. Take the case of the two women granted temporary entry to train as nursing assistants at Norfolk General Hospital. Four women had applied, but only two were issued visas; the other two were sent letters informing them that their request for entry into Canada was rejected. One woman wrote to the immigration department asking why her application was refused when the two women who were accepted had applied approximately two weeks after she had. In an internal memo, the chief of admissions suggested that, "in all fairness to Miss Husbands and her friend, I think we should authorize temporary entry in their cases."[19] He added, however, that any such decision was an exception and should not be taken as a precedent. Although it is not known whether these women actually were granted temporary entry, it is significant that they were not compliant and had convinced at least one immigration officer to take their side.

In contrast to the blatant racism of the Department of Citizenship and Immigration, medical and nursing organizations sometimes displayed a more liberal attitude towards the migration of Caribbean nurses. The CNA was willing to include Caribbean nurses in the occupation not only because of the nursing shortage, but also because the association's involvement with nursing at the international level prompted a more egalitarian approach to Canada's domestic nursing culture and a commitment to eradicate racial and ethnic barriers. In the United States, where entrenched racism had forced African-American nurses to establish their own organizations and schools, the American Nurses' Association became racially integrated in 1948. In Canada, in 1951, the nurses' association "reaffirm[ed] its policy to support the principle that there be no discrimination in the selection of students for enrollment into schools of nursing" and informed the Department of Immigration "that they do not discriminate in anyway regarding coloured nurses." Not many years before, however, black nurses were excluded from Canadian nursing schools and the immigration of blacks to Canada was almost non-existent.[20]

Faced with a severe nursing shortage, employers also expressed frustration with the racial barriers to Canadian immigration. A supervisor at the Women's Division of the National Employment Services in Toronto said that she had no objection to the recruitment of Caribbean nursing assistants and nursing aides because there is "no hope whatsoever of recruiting sufficient applicants … to meet the overall demand." Likewise, Mother Superior at St Joseph's Hospital in Hamilton, Ontario, stated that "if nurses aides had the necessary qualification and there were openings in the hospitals no other conditions would be required." The Jewish General Hospital was also willing to offer employment to Caribbean nurses, although it refused to provide the usual accommodation "due to their Nurses Quarters being filled to capacity."[21] Overall, Canadian nursing organizations generally accepted the migration of Caribbean nurses, despite the desires of the state.

Despite the CNA's opposition to discrimination, the liberalism of Canadian nurses often waned, especially when they were questioned by Immigration Canada. Although Miss Weir, director for Mount Sinai Hospital, initially claimed "that there is no discrimination whatsoever, and if the person is acceptable she is registered without regard to race or creed," immigration officials reported that she "confidentially stated that the hospitals desire to maintain a considerable majority of white nurses on staff." When immigration officials inquired about a newspaper report on the local nursing shortage, Weir said that the hospital had attempted to refute the newspaper's statements with a letter to the editor, but it had apparently gone astray and was never printed. She emphasized that "there is no shortage of nurses ... and the hospitals can make a selection from a number of applicants." If Caribbean nurses were successful in the completion of their program, they would have a "reasonable amount of opportunities to obtain employment." Implicit in Weir's response is the assumption of racial difference between white and black nurses, with only the former – by virtue of being Canadian and white – deserving their rightful place within the occupation. Despite Weir's intention to portray her hospital as inclusive, she assured immigration officials that there was a limit on the number of Caribbean nurses allowed to work at the hospital. Weir's confidential statements to the immigration department seem to be in line with racist sentiments of the time and the general insistence on keeping Canada white. However, she might have felt that the immigration officer was questioning Mount Sinai's decision to admit Caribbean nurses into their program and, being on the defensive, had given the officer the answers she thought he wanted to hear.[22]

If nursing directors and organizations expressed ambivalence about Caribbean nurses who hailed from English-speaking nations of the British Commonwealth, they were unequivocal in their racism against Haitian nurses. Their notions about the "blackness" of Haitians demonstrates how colonial ideologies operated to produce subtle distinctions between Anglo-Caribbean and Haitian nurses. Although there are no specific statistics on the number of Haitian nurses who migrated to Canada during the period under discussion, it is apparent that the majority of Haitian nurses chose to live and work in Montreal and Quebec because of the French language. Their presence there

provoked anti-Haitian sentiment, and the federal immigration department and nursing associations collaborated to promote the notion of
the undesirability of Haitians. Colonial stereotypes of black people as
greedy, aggressive, indolent, and irrational were attributed to Haitian
nurses. While immigration officials portrayed Haitian nurses and students as "outsiders" who should be kept out of the country (or monitored if they were already there), nurses' associations emphasized
Haitian nurses' "otherness" in terms of their inability to adapt to Canadian nursing and lifestyles.[23]

It is difficult to ascertain when and why the particularly antagonistic
attitude towards Haitian nurses began. However, the correspondence
between Canadian immigration officials and nursing associations suggests that the former first raised the issue of Haitian nurses' undesirability in a series of circulars requesting information about Haitian
nurses. These circulars were followed in 1958 by a round of immigration investigations. Before the state had begun its investigations into
Haitian nurses, many nursing schools were willing to accept applications from Haitian students. However, once the circulars were issued
and the investigations began, nursing associations and schools re-
acted to Haitians with skepticism and distrust. Perhaps, as Miss Weir
might have done (as discussed above), they provided immigration
representatives with the "correct" answers to their questions about the
undesirability of Haitian nurses.

Immigration investigations, although described as "discreet" and
"confidential," were an attempt to monitor the movement of Haitian
nurses. In one case, an immigration officer asked for information
about three students accepted at the Cooke Sanatorium Hospital in
Montreal. He wanted "their names and full particulars about them,
including a report from the hospital authorities respecting their conduct and attitude at the hospital, and whether or not the hospital
authorities are completely satisfied with them." Such investigations
had an adverse effect on Haitian nurses, leading not only to surveillance of their work and whereabouts, but also to several hospitals
claiming to have experienced problems with them. After interviews
with immigration officials, some nursing personnel and directors concluded that "a large portion of Haitian girls … who are nursing aides
have proven themselves unsuitable and unreliable." Haitian nurses
were also described as "lazy, negligent, and also lacking in hygiene."
The director of Quebec's BCG Clinic, which treated infants whose
mothers were infected with tuberculosis, complained that her clinic
had been unfortunate in the selection of Haitians, for "hygiene plays a
capital role and this apparently is something that most Haitian students, to date do not possess." Her assumption that Haitian nurses

lacked hygiene drew on colonial religious discourses that associated "blackness" with sin, dirt, and filth. The investigations into the performance of Haitian nurses implied that these nurses would tarnish, or blacken, the image of nursing. Cultural racism, whereby blacks are deemed by the colour of their skin to be lazy and unclean, seemed to take on special significance when applied to Haitian nurses.[24]

No hospital or nursing association defended Haitian nurses against these allegations, and by June 1958 the director of immigration was able to state that hospitals "all favored some control over these persons." Indeed, nursing organizations often corroborated the so-called findings of immigration authorities. The superintendent for the Eastern District in Montreal described Haitian nurses as the "greatest offender" in terms of using the profession as an excuse to gain entry into Canada. He said, "We have formed the opinion that their main purpose in coming forward under the pretext of being students is to gain entry to this country [rather] than to extend their academic education or learn a trade." Similarly, in another memorandum, immigration officials observed that several hospitals expressed doubts as to whether Haitians really wanted nursing training. They too concluded that "Haitian nationals appear not to be interested in the course itself but are rather interested in coming forward to Canada and finding all sorts of excuses to remain in this country once in." Another immigration officer decided to refuse entry to a Haitian applicant because, in view of the "difficulties" encountered with other Haitian women, "we feel that the subject may also be a problem once in Canada." Significantly, immigration records contain no indication that the black organizations lobbying on behalf of English-speaking Caribbean nurses provided any support to Haitians.[25]

The high turnover among Haitian nurses in Canada was also used as evidence against prospective migrants. A nursing representative told immigration officials that many nursing students changed hospitals and clinics "for no apparent reason, and most without warning." Using the BCG Clinic to make the point, an immigration official commented, "Of the 21 Haitian girls, who had proceeded to the clinic, 17 had left the institution after their arrival, 2 had not presented themselves at all, and only 2 were in attendance." In a letter to Canada's ambassador to Haiti, the director of immigration concluded that "in view of the difficulties encountered with the Haitian girls who have come forward to take the course at the [BCG] clinic ... no further applications should be accepted."[26] It is possible that the high turnover of Haitian nurses was due to racism in the Canadian hospitals, and it should be noted that Haitians were not alone in their mobility. Nursing historian Kathryn McPherson points out that "tremendous turnover rates frustrated administrators' efforts at stable staffing."[27] In this context, it is striking that the high turnover rates among Haitian nurses received specific comment.

Once the investigations of 1958 were completed, immigration officials advised hospitals that employed, or intended to employ, Haitian nurses to submit the nurses' applications to the immigration office, which would conduct a full investigation to determine whether the applicant was "deserving of favorable consideration."[28] This meant that the Department of Citizenship and Immigration determined the qualifications of immigrant nurses, even though maintaining the standards of the profession was supposedly nursing's domain.

While immigration regulations made it difficult for black nurses to enter Canada, Greek nurses were encouraged to come, even though they did not meet the profession's language requirements and therefore could not practise. According to the state's perception, Europeans, but not nurses from the Caribbean, could assimilate and adapt to Canadian lifestyles.

The failure of nurses' associations to challenge this inequity is significant. Despite the nursing shortage, nursing directors contributed to the dialogue that limited the immigration of Haitian nurses, nurses' aides, and students. Despite the CNA's 1951 statement against discrimination, the association supported the state's finding that black nurses were a problem. In spite of the need for labour, nursing directors allowed Anglo-Caribbean and especially Haitian nurses to be excluded from their occupation. Had nurses stayed true to their stated principle of non-discrimination, they might have helped to shape an inclusive, non-discriminatory immigration policy in Canada. Such a policy was not enacted until the 1960s, when new regulations emphasizing education, skills, and training – rather than country of origin – made it easier for Caribbean nurses to come to Canada. Still, the racist ideologies that shaped state policies and nurses' attitudes continue to exist.

NOTES

Author's Note: This research was funded by an AMS/Hannah Institute for the History of Medicine Doctoral Scholarship.
  1 Georgina D. Feldberg, *Disease and Class: Tuberculosis and the Shaping of Modern North American Society* (New Brunswick, N.J.: Rutgers University Press 1995).
  2 Kathryn McPherson, *Bedside Matters: The Transformation of Canadian Nursing, 1900–1990* (Toronto: Oxford University Press 1996), 206–15.

3 John Schultz, "White Man's Country: Canada and the West Indian Immigrant 1900–1965," *American Review of Canadian Studies* 21 (1982): 53; Valerie Knowles, *Strangers at Our Gates: Canadian Immigration and Immigration Policy, 1540–1990* (Toronto: Dundurn Press 1992); Alan G. Green, *Immigration and the Postwar Canadian Economy* (Toronto: Macmillan of Canada 1976), 12–36.

4 Vic Satzewich, "The Canadian State and Racialization of Caribbean Migrant Farm Labor, 1947–1966," *Ethnic and Racial Studies* 11, no. 3 (1988): 289.

5 K.W. Taylor, "Racism in Canadian Immigration Policy," *Canadian Ethnic Studies* 23, no. 1 (1991): 285.

6 National Archives of Canada (hereafter NA), RG 76, vol. 626, file 960711, pt 2, reel C-10442, CGIM, Karlsruhe, Germany, to Chief, Operations Division, Ottawa, on "Movement of domestics, nurses and nurses aids," 30 October 1952; NA, RG 76, vol. 626, file 960711, pt 3, A. Reintam, Placement Officer, to Eastern District Superintendent, "Interview with Dr. Williams Storrar, A/Superintendent of the Montreal General Hospital," 2 February 1953.

7 NA, RG 76, vol. 676, file 960711, pt 2, reel C-10442, Registered Nurses' Association of Ontario to the Honourable Jasper C. Daley, Minister of Labour for Ontario, 25 October 1950; Canadian Nurses' Association Report, ca. 1950.

8 NA, RG 76, vol. 626, file 960711, pt 2, reel C-10422, Eastern District Superintendent to Director, Ottawa, "Complaints – Immigrants coming forwards as nurses," 9 October 1951.

9 NA, RG 76, vol. 626, file 960711, pt 2, reel C-10442, Department of Citizenship and Immigration, "Nursing Assistants," 19 December, 1952.

10 NA, RG 76, vol. 847, file 555-110, pt 2, Department of Citizenship and Immigration, "Movement of nurses, nurses' aids and household workers from Greece," 6 October 1961.

11 NA, RG 76, vol. 846, file 555-110, pt 2, K.E. Marsh, Assistant Director of Employment, to Mr L.M. Hunter, Chief of Settlement Division, 16 October 1962.

12 NA, RG 76, vol. 847, file 555-110, pt 2, W.R. Bakersville, Director of Immigration, to E. Thompson, Director of Employment Service, "Greek Nurses," 6 July 1961; NA, RG 76, vol. 626, file 970711, pt 2, reel C-10442, Operations Division to All Post Abroad Excluding China, "Occupational Selection of Nurses," 25 October 1951.

13 Agnes Calliste, "Women of 'Exceptional Merit': Immigration of Caribbean Nurses to Canada," *Canadian Journal of Women and the Law* 6 (1993): 85–103.

14 NA, RG 76, vol. 553-110, pt 1, Admissions "B," to Acting Chief, "Student Nurses Assistants from the British West Indies," 4 July 1956; NA, RG 76, vol. 553-110, pt 2, Admissions Division to Acting Director, 10 April 1957.

15 NA, RG 76, vol. 553-110, pt 1, To Acting Chief, Admissions "B," "Student Nurses Assistant from the British West Indies," 4 July 1956; Director of Immigration to Deputy Minister, "Negro Male Nurses and Nurses Assistants," 9 October 1956.

16 NA, RG 76, vol. 553-110, pt 2, Director to Mr C.E.S., Assistant to the Deputy Minister, "Nurses Aids from the West Indies," 7 October 1958.

17 NA, RG 76, vol. 553-110, pt 1, A/Chief, Admissions Division, to Director, "Student Nurses – (Male)," 13 August 1956; Director, CGIS, U.K. Northern General Hospital, Simcoe, Ont., to P.T. Baldwin, Chief of Admissions Division, Ottawa, 2 August 1957.

18 NA, RG 76, vol. 553-110, pt 1, Donald Moore, Negro Citizenship Association, to P.T. Baldwin, Chief, Admissions, 14 January 1956; Owen de Vere Rowe, British Caribbean Students Liaison Officer in Canada, to W.R. Bakersville, Chief of Admissions, 17 January 1957; House of Commons Debate, Session 1953–54, vol. 6, 5687–6842; House of Commons Debate, Session 1952–53, vol. 4, 3293–4394.

19 NA, RG 76, vol. 553, pt 1, Admissions "B," to Acting Chief, Admissions Division, "Student Nurses Assistants from the British West Indies," 4 July 1956.

20 Darlene Clark Hine, *Black Women in White: Racial Conflict and Cooperation in the Nursing Oppression, 1890–1950* (Indianapolis: Indiana University Press 1989); McPherson, *Bedside Matters,* 211.

21 NA, RG 76, vol. 553-110, pt 1, Mr Fox, Acting Central District Superintendent, to Acting Chief, Admissions Division, Ottawa, 9 May 1956; Eastern District Superintendent to Director of Immigration, Ottawa, "Nurses from the British West Indies," 16 February 1956.

22 NA, RG 76, vol. 553-110, pt 1, Acting Officer in Charge to Central District Superintendent, "Nurses from the British West Indies," 24 February 1956.

23 This analysis is based on my reading of the records in NA, RG 76, vol. 553-110, pt 2.

24 NA, RG 76, vol. 553-110, pt 2, A/Eastern District Superintendent, Montreal, to Director of Immigration, Admissions Division, Ottawa, "Miss Gilda Charles – Proposed Entry," 26 February 1958; Officer-in-Charge, Trois-Rivières, to Chief, Admissions Division, "Miss Harriet Whitman of Haiti," 20 January 1958.

25 NA, RG 76, vol. 553-110, pt 2, Eastern District Superintendent, Montreal, to Director of Immigration, Ottawa, "Haitian Nurses Aides," 9 June 1958; Eastern District Superintendent, Montreal, to Director of Immigration, Ottawa, "Students – 10.83 Procedures and Follow-up," 27 March 1958; Eastern District Superintendent, Montreal, to Director of Immigration, Ottawa, "Miss Gilda Charles – Proposed Entry," 26 February 1958.

26 NA, RG 76, vol. 553-110, pt 2, Eastern District Superintendent, Montreal to Director of Immigration, Ottawa, "Students – 10.83 Procedures and

Follow-up," 27 March 1958; CES Director to Ambassade du Canada, Port-au-Prince, Haiti, 4 March 1958; Eastern District Superintendent, Montreal, to Director of Immigration, "Haitian Nurses Aids," 9 June 1958.
27 McPherson, *Bedside Matters*, 231.
28 NA, RG 76, vol. 553-110, pt 2, Eastern District Superintendent, Montreal, to Director of Immigration, "Haitian Nurses Aids," 9 June 1958.

13

Women's Work in Eclipse:
Nuns in Quebec Hospitals, 1940–1980

Aline Charles

The history of *hospitalières* (hospital nuns) in Quebec is a crossroads where women's history, the history of health care, and the history of the Catholic Church in Quebec intersect. These women were still indispensable fixtures of Quebec hospitals in the 1940s, but they had almost disappeared by the 1980s. The aim here is not so much to paint a portrait of the nuns themselves, to measure their sphere of influence, or even to trace the reasons for their disappearance; rather it is to understand the nature and the evolution of the work they performed for so long before vanishing, body and soul, from the rapidly changing hospital environment. The sisters were not only pivotal figures in Quebec's health system, they also developed a model of activity that was distinct from those of other women working in this sector, such as employees and volunteers. Between 1940 and 1980, however, this specific work model disappeared from Quebec's hospitals along with the women who were its standard-bearers. This swift eclipse is the subject of this article.

Until the 1960s, many hospitals had deep and long-standing links with female religious communities.[1] This means that the evolving nature of the *hospitalières'* work can only be understood by consulting the archives of both the hospitals and the communities. Focusing on Montreal, this article examines two cases of the relationship between hospitals and female religious communities: that between the Hôtel-Dieu Hospital and the Religieuses Hospitalières de St-Joseph; and that between Ste Justine's Hospital and the Filles de la Sagesse (Daughters of Wisdom).

Both hospitals were established exclusively as lay establishments. The Hôtel-Dieu was founded in 1642 during New France's early years, a difficult time to establish a hospital. Its founder, Jeanne Mance, was a lay missionary who believed that Montreal needed a general hospital. Over two and a half centuries later, in 1907, Ste Justine's opened its doors thanks to the efforts of a small group of upper-class Montreal women led by Justine Lacoste-Beaubien. These women believed that a children's hospital was essential in order to curb endemic infant mortality. Thus, it was two lay women who founded hospitals that today are among the largest in Quebec. Neither Hôtel-Dieu nor Ste Justine's remained secular for long, however. In the seventeenth century, as in the early twentieth century, hospitals found it difficult to make ends meet without the contribution of religious labour. In both hospitals, despite the long period between their founding dates, the first administrators invited a religious community from France to come work at their institution. Jeanne Mance called on the Religieuses Hospitalières de St-Joseph, a community that, from 1639, had been devoted to healing the sick in La Flèche, France. The Hospitalières, who came to Quebec in 1659, took possession of the Hôtel-Dieu twenty-two years later on the death of its founder. Two and a half centuries later, Justine Lacoste-Beaubien enlisted the Filles de la Sagesse, who had been involved in teaching, healing the sick, and caring for the poor since the order's founding in 1703 in Poitiers. In 1910 the community signed a service contract with the hospital's administration in which it agreed to take charge of the internal operation of Ste Justine's.

Shortly after their founding, therefore, both hospitals became associated with a female religious community that would work, live, and pray inside their very walls. Reflecting the long period separating their founding, the terms governing the two hospitals' association with their respective religious communities were very different. Hôtel-Dieu was owned in *dominio suo* by the Hospitalières de St-Joseph, and thus the order, as full owner, also took care of the hospital's administration. Ste Justine's belonged to a lay corporation that delegated the day-to-day management of the hospital to the community without assigning it any property rights. Neither hospital was exceptional in this respect. Even in the mid-twentieth century, the vast majority of francophone health, charitable, and educational institutions in Quebec operated symbiotically with an order of sisters; by contrast, a more secular model existed in those institutions belonging to the anglophone minority (and in some francophone institutions). An analysis of the work of the sisters between 1940 and 1980 thus sheds light on several important aspects of the operation of Quebec hospitals, on the characteristics of a model of feminine activity that was by no means insignificant in this sector, and on the major transformations that occurred during this period.

More theoretically, the case of the nuns allows a more refined analysis of women's work. This is one of the most popular areas of research in women's studies. The notion of work, limited at first to paid work carried out in the public sphere, has since been enlarged to include various forms of unpaid activities in both the public and private spheres. One after another, housework, volunteer work, caring for dependent parents, and the work on farms or in family businesses have been examined in historical and sociological analyses of work. The work of nuns also needs to be added to this list. Nevertheless, the model of paid work in the public sphere is so dominant that unpaid forms of work, which sometimes coexist with paid work, are often neglected. Most studies of the hospital sector focus on salaried work – which is understandable – and rapidly pass over volunteer or religious work in a few sentences or pages – which is less understandable. The presence of salaried employees working side by side with nuns and volunteers was an intrinsic characteristic of the organization of hospital work in Quebec, and each component deserves analysis.[2]

This chapter focuses on the evolution of the religious component, an evolution that reflects transformations both in the hospital sector and in women's work. The perspective adopted to analyse the sisters' work reveals a three-stage evolution. In the 1940s and 1950s, the uniqueness of the *hospitalières'* work was still very apparent. In the 1960s, the foundations of this uniqueness were profoundly shaken. Finally, the 1970s sounded the death knell for this special form of women's work.

THE 1940S AND 1950S

In the 1940s and 1950s, the Quebec hospital sector underwent a series of closely interlinked changes.[3] Health-care requirements had risen sharply in a short period of time, a rise reflected in a significant increase in the number of institutions, beds, and admissions. Hospital operating costs were skyrocketing owing to exponential growth in equipment and manpower requirements. The nursing and medical professions grew and branched off at a quickening pace, bringing along the rise of technical and paramedic staff in their wake. The unionization of lay employees, which had begun in the 1930s, continued, but at a slower pace. Lay employees were increasingly unwilling to put up with long hours, low wages, and the rigid authority structures that characterized this sector, in which women made up the vast majority. The government, on the other hand, preserved the private nature of hospitals while exerting its own influence by way of subsidies and regulations that effectively undermined the Catholic Church's hold over hospitals.

These changes resulted in the acceleration of a process begun several decades before the 1940s. Scientific and medical advances, changes in the roles of state and religious communities, and increased health-care demands progressively weakened the image of hospitals as charitable institutions. For some time, salaried employees had made up the majority of hospital personnel. More and more, monetary and other donations together constituted only a marginal source of hospital funding. Increasingly, the state assumed an important role in financing the operating and construction costs of hospitals, through funds released under the 1921 Quebec Public Charities Act.[4] Aside from those deemed indigents, patients paid a growing share of hospital costs. The tradition of charity, however, remained very influential in the mid-twentieth century. This tradition became all the more persistent as the financial problems of hospitals increased. Even taken together, fees paid by patients, government funding, and charitable gifts were insufficient to cover skyrocketing costs. For example, Ste Justine's books had been in the red continuously since 1926. Thus, despite all the changes occurring in hospitals, for the mostly female workforce, dedication remained the official keynote. On one hand, hospitals' day-to-day operations still depended on various forms of unpaid work, that of volunteers but mainly that of hospital nuns as well as student nurses (the latter provided much of the basic patient care, in exchange for their training, room, and board). On the other hand, the difficult working conditions of salaried workers represented yet another form of "obligatory gift" to these institutions, whose charitable vocation both required and justified such sacrifices – whether voluntary or not.

In this context, the *hospitalières* remained visibly present and even preponderant in hospitals. Religious orders owned over two-thirds of Quebec's public hospitals, accounting for roughly 70 per cent of total hospital beds;[5] *hospitalières* made up between 15 and 20 per cent of hospital employees[6] and monopolized most management positions. From this position of strength, they succeeded in maintaining a work ethic and organizational structure very different from those of their lay counterparts, even though lay persons had made up the great majority of those working in Quebec hospitals for several decades. During the 1940s and 1950s, therefore, several distinct characteristics still marked *hospitalières'* work.

Working: A Religious Duty

The archives of the Hospitalières de St-Joseph and the Filles de la Sagesse testify to the strong work ethic of their subjects. Idleness was deemed unacceptable. Each hour, each moment of the day, was "usefully" spent in following the Rules and Customs (*Coutumier*) of both communities. There was an insistence upon constant attention to the given task; idle chatter was strictly forbidden. Rules even stipulated that recreations must not degenerate into "complete idleness." The communities' obituaries also reflected this work imperative, speaking exclusively of "tireless workers" with their "noses always to the grindstone," of women who led "full lives" with "undaunted energy," only "laying down arms" at the very end. These texts, which traced the life of each nun from birth to death according to a model that changed little over the years, described with particular care the series of duties undertaken by the nuns and the assiduousness with which they were performed.

No *hospitalière* escaped from this work imperative, it seems, not even those weakened by age or illness. The documents tell of the convalescing nuns praying to return to work, of the sick hiding their illnesses, and of the dying drawing their last breath on the job. They also speak of ninety-year-olds still full of life or fighting to stay active. Sick or aging sisters were assigned "minor duties commensurate with their strength" or transferred to one of the congregation's "rest homes" to do light work. There, they did not get actual rest, only less work to do. They could not take time off, let alone retire. Only death brought an end to their "life of toil."[7] Until the very end therefore, every nun had a task to perform, however small it might have been. She was expected to devote her entire strength and energy to it, with the same assiduousness and determination she had shown in previous more important or more demanding tasks. A recurring image in these texts is that of an oil lamp fading slowly before being extinguished altogether. This image illustrates eloquently the life of *hospitalières*, one of unceasing activity, decreasing slowly but continuing unwaveringly until death.

Two imperatives limited the importance of work in the religious world: obedience and humility. Nuns were expected to show complete indifference to their assigned tasks and accept them with total submission. Growing attached to a specific task to the point that one regretted moving on to the next one was considered an excess. Using one's position to enhance one's prestige was equally ill-regarded. Instead, nuns had to profess a great affection for even the most common and despised ("lowly") tasks. They had to avoid seeking "tasks elevated in the eyes of the world"; should they be assigned such a task, they had to accept it with complete modesty. Nuns were also expected to accept without question their transfer to another "house" in the congregation, even if this meant a completely new working environment and life-style. Ordered by the Mother Superior for reasons ranging from organizational needs to lessons in obedience, such transfers were fairly frequent, and docile acceptance sometimes proved difficult: "Our Sr M., who was employed in the nurses' dining hall, has just left us; obedience requires her in another residence. Each one of us can expect the same fate sooner or later. May we all be very gentle and obedient to the wishes of our Blessed Master" (translation).[8]

Changes of assignments and transfers to other communities were sometimes met with surprise, regret, and "painful leave-takings." Regardless of her personal feelings or opinions, every sister had to submit to the decisions of those over her; no one would dare question the judgment of the Mother Superior. Work, therefore, was not an end in itself but rather a means of serving God; this service was the true goal to strive for. The framing of work by the demands of obedience and humility appears repeatedly in the Rules of both communities, whether explicitly or implicitly. Sometimes, but not always, the observance of religious rituals became another safeguard against placing excessive emphasis on work. This was certainly true in the case of the Filles de la Sagesse, for whom nothing was "more dangerous and more appalling in the eyes of the community" than a sister who shortened her orisons and prayers so that she could return to work faster.[9] For the Hospitalières, by contrast, hospital work took priority over spiritual exercises when the sick needed assistance.[10]

Have nuns always, in actual fact, obeyed the work imperative as ordained by their Rules? Probably not, but the accessible sources shed no light on this question. The nuns rarely spoke of themselves in an open and personal way, and their individual voices faded into that of the community speaking on their behalf. The documents, moreover, almost never reveal evidence of resistance, dereliction of duty, or dispensations, all of which presumably occurred. The individual and collective portraits that have emerged celebrate the primacy of work so unequivocally and so unanimously that they doubtless reflect the aim to edify.[11] Indeed, at the Hospitalières de St-Joseph, obituaries were read in the dining hall during meals. These texts, which recount sisters' great deeds and menial tasks alike in similar detail, seek to pass a powerful work ethic on to subsequent generations. The obituaries and Community Rules, therefore, provided the broad outlines of a religious model for work. They described the ideal to which all nuns must aspire and the yardstick by which they were to be judged.

Hospital archives also reflect this ideal on occasion. The correspondence between the administrators of Ste Justine's and the Filles de la

Sagesse often reveals cases of nuns leaving work owing to "excessive fatigue." In 1941, for example, the president of the hospital wrote the following letter to a nun, a hospital bursar who, due to exhaustion, found herself on forced leave: "You have sins for which you must seek pardon; you never wanted to submit to our recommendations and each day, you delayed in submitting yourself to the will of God by refusing to follow the treatments and by postponing the rest that was prescribed for your recovery. Everything must be paid for in this world, my dear Sr G., and you are very lucky, at this time, to have to pay [only] in holidays for the misery you had to endure last winter" (translation).[12]

Although the strength of the work imperative among the *hospitalières* was much in evidence during the 1940s and 1950s, this does not mean that nothing changed during this period. The development of a postwar leisure and consumer society and the gradual decrease in the work hours of hospital employees[13] affected even those living inside the walls of the convent. Following larger trends, several religious communities active in hospitals lightened somewhat the workload of their members. An annual vacation of at first one day, then two days, and finally four days or more was gradually instituted. During this period, Hospitalières de St-Joseph took their vacations in the camp owned by the congregation in the Laurentians, went on pilgrimages to visit their counterparts on the North Shore or in Ontario, and even indulged in tourist activities.[14] The Filles de la Sagesse also made different moves towards reducing the workload of their sisters.

Nevertheless, Mother Superiors had to be repeatedly reminded that they were the guardians of the health of the sisters under their responsibility and that they must therefore avoid overworking them.[15] The problem of overwork existed in a number of communities and affected the Catholic Church's entire personnel.[16] How, then, could this phenomenon of overwork be reconciled with the spread of the popularity of leisure time, however gradual, within religious communities? The postwar context probably accounts for part of this apparent contradiction. Religious communities, wishing to respond to the population's increased need for health care while maintaining their control over this sphere, enlarged their hospitals, developed new services, and invested in training, all the while increasing the work hours of the *hospitalières*. At the same time, given falling recruitment, increasingly caustic criticism from the outside, and more vocal questioning from inside, the nuns recognized the need to ease workloads that were viewed as too demanding. Such transformations indicate that although change occurred slowly, the traditional emphasis on the primacy of work was weakening. Work, however, was still considered to be one of the cardinal virtues of an ideal sister.

Work: A Comprehensive and Flexible Notion

With few exceptions, work remained a fundamental obligation in religious communities during the 1940s and 1950s. It should be noted, however, that this obligation relied on a very comprehensive and flexible understanding of work – the second characteristic of the *hospitalières'* work. Evidence of this flexibility can be found in the long list of "obediences" – or tasks assigned to each of her "daughters" – read by the Mother Superior to the entire community at least once a year. These lists reveal a mix of very different kinds of work. First were positions comparable, if not identical, to those filled by the laity in hospitals or the labour market in general. For example, nuns were appointed as superintendents, accountants, librarians, technicians, receptionists, chief-cobblers (*maîtresses de la cordonnerie*), laundry helpers, or vegetable aides (*légumières*). Unlike the tasks of the nuns' lay counterparts, however, these were not performed exclusively within the framework of the hospital. Religious nurses could be assigned to the wards or to the community infirmary; seamstresses could work at the hospital laundry or in the community as a wardrobe sister (*roberie communautaire*).

Other obediences differed from usual salaried work in that they involved labour of a more domestic kind. Examples include making jam, preparing morning toast, cleaning the "toilets in the Notre-Dame-de-X dormitory," cleaning up the choir stalls, or washing dishes on Sunday. These were domestic chores carried out strictly for the community, similar to those done by laywomen, in the private sphere, for their families. The distinction here has more to do with the formulation of these obediences (which evoked a kind of community intimacy) than with the nature of the tasks themselves. No clear division hermetically separated hospital work from community work. In the course of their lives or during a single day, sisters moved constantly from one activity to the other, since the hospital only functioned thanks to the order and the community lived for the hospital. For the nuns then, even more than for laywomen, no real distinction existed between domestic and professional work, between the private and public spheres.

Among the obediences listed could also be found tasks totally different from jobs in the secular world. Some of these "occupations" were almost symbolic: darning socks, decorating a holy statue, visiting the dying, keeping the clocks running, tending the tombs of deceased sisters, making scapulars or the unconsecrated wafer, sounding the morning bells, or taking care of a flowerbed. Such tasks were generally assigned to nuns whose state of health or age only allowed them to work a few hours a day. Nevertheless, these sisters were considered as active as the others. The important thing was not so much the quantity of work done, but the fact that each sister dedicated all her energy to the task at hand, no matter how small or insignificant.

Finally, the Mother Superior assigned other "tasks" of a purely spiritual nature: "offering one's sufferings to God," "praying for the community," acting as "Companion to Jesus in the Blessed Sacrament," "excitator" (*excitatrice*), or "admonisher" (*admonitrice*). The presence of these tasks in the list of obediences indicates that there was also no clear demarcation separating working life from spiritual life. Furthermore, before the reform of their constitutions in 1965, the Hospitalières de St-Joseph stopped work six times a day at fixed intervals to sing in the choir. Similarly, various prayers, orisons, and readings structured the workday of the Filles de la Sagesse. The sisters prayed while working and worked while praying, to such an extent that the two often merged together.

To sum up, caring for the sick in the hospital, doing housework in the community, decorating holy statues, and praying were all considered work by the sisters. Their conception of work encompassed domestic, spiritual, professional, and symbolic tasks. This notion included tasks that were either compartmentalized in the secular world or considered pointless by its standards of productivity. Thus, to a certain extent, everything was God's work in the world of the religious community. And precisely because everything was considered work, each sister could and had to work until she reached death's door.

While work might have encompassed everything, all work was not deemed of equal value. Work in both religious communities under study here was organized according to very real and worldly hierarchies. Some positions were more prestigious than others. Being a bursar, pharmacist, or officer in a hospital department conferred a power not enjoyed by mere nurses, sacristans, clerks, or linen maids. Caring for the sick, the raison d'être of both communities, was also far more prestigious a task than making rosaries, cooking for the sisters, or simply praying. Furthermore, until 1949 the community and hospital life of the Hospitalières de St-Joseph was structured according to a hierarchy based on three classes of sisters.[17] The so-called choir nuns (*sœurs vocales*) took a nursing course, held positions of responsibility, and elected the Mother Superior; "converse sisters" (*sœurs converses*) performed domestic or unskilled work; and *sœurs tourières* (gatekeepers) received visitors and took care of outside errands. Being a choir sister signified possessing a skilled job as well as a say in the community's affairs, things that were inaccessible to *converses* and *tourières*. But whether stemming from a sister's task or rank in the community, these hierarchical relationships did not invalidate the broad conception of

work that prevailed in women's religious orders; nor did they lessen
the importance given to work. From the bottom to the top of the
pyramid, all sisters were expected to devote all their energy to their
work.

Work: An Unpaid Activity

The fact that it was unpaid constituted the third characteristic of *hospitalières'* work. Indeed, nuns received no salary. In the early 1940s, communities owning a hospital (such as the Hôtel-Dieu) began to list
sisters' salaries as an expense in their accounts but these salaries
remained purely fictitious. This accounting sleight of hand allowed
communities to satisfy the requirements of the federal government,
which sought information on the *actual* operating costs of hospitals.
Assigning a market value to the nuns' "dedication," however, required
great caution. The operation could affect the nuns' image in the mind
of the public, most seriously with respect to their self-abnegation and
vows of poverty. For over seven years, the Catholic Hospital Association
of the United States and Canada considered, debated, and reviewed
how to calculate these fictitious salaries. The amounts in question
could not be so generous as to give the impression that the communities were profiting unduly from their work, or so low as to make the sisters appear to be an underclass of hospital workers. The wage scale
finally adopted in 1947 was based on lay salaries and depended on a
sister's position, training, and degree of responsibility. Although delicate, the operation was deemed useful, since it underscored the extent
of, and need for, the nuns' unpaid work in institutions that were pe-
rennially short of money: "The Director presented a table of unpaid
services performed by the nuns in hospitals and their value calculated
according to information from various sources. This is the amount that
the sisters could demand for their work and that they gave as a gift to
society ... It is useful sometimes to inform those concerned of the free
gifts and disinterestedness of the sisters" (translation).[18]

Even when a community did not own the hospital where its members worked, the situation remained basically the same: nuns did not
receive salaries. The service contract signed between the community
and hospital simply stipulated a lump-sum amount to be paid to the
community in exchange for the services performed by all the sisters.
For example, between 1946 and 1957, Ste Justine's paid twenty-five
dollars per month for each Fille de la Sagesse.[19] Individual nuns received nothing. The amount was a lump sum paid directly to the community, which then used the money as it saw fit. Had the amount been

divided among the relevant sisters, the remuneration paid to each one would have been so low as to be symbolic compared to the salaries of lay employees, which themselves were already low.[20]

The unpaid nature of the sisters' work was neither ignored nor denied. On the contrary, it was publicized and endowed with an important social, humanitarian, and even economic role. The Church claimed that society in general and laypersons in particular should feel indebted to all sisters for this free work and the dedication it involved. Furthermore, religious communities owning hospitals deemed it all the more necessary to make citizens aware of the extent of this "gift" to the public, since critics were beginning to examine the high costs of hospitalization.[21] A good example of this is the following "message" from a sister published in 1946 in the magazine of the Association patronale des services hospitaliers de Québec:

How many people know, that, for the cost of the unremunerated services provided by the *hospitalières*, the hospital is able to take on the rehabilitation of the nation's main resource: its human capital? Furthermore, do they think of the many civilians who achieve their social and economic ambitions thanks to the institution's efforts? Are we sufficiently aware of the cost of modern hospital organizations and administrations and the deficits that result from the services that a Catholic hospital must provide without haggling over the price? ... Society has obligations to help the hospital [translation].[22]

Even if the nuns did not receive a true salary, it could be argued that their work was not entirely free, since their community supported them in exchange for their services, paying them "in kind" rather than with a salary.[23] However, taking the vows entailed signing a lifelong contract with an order that had the right to demand any amount of work and impose any tasks. No formal restriction existed on the duration, conditions, or nature of the work required of nuns. Thus, even though nuns received room and board, they effectively worked for free, since the unpaid services they provided to others were governed by a contract of unlimited work, unlike the contracts given to lay people, which stipulated a set remuneration for precise tasks lasting for a fixed period of time.[24]

Workers without Individuality

The final characteristic of this kind of work was that the nuns' relations with a hospital were all mediated by their order; they did not work as individuals. The community "devoted" itself to a specific work of charity and assumed responsibility for supplying the requisite human resources. Sisters did not undergo job interviews before being hired, did not negotiate their working conditions, did not resign, and could not be fired. They were simply assigned to a position for as long as seen fit. With a few exceptions, lay people almost never supervised them and the hospital's personnel department had no jurisdiction over them; instead sisters answered exclusively to their Mother Superior. The personnel departments of the Hôtel-Dieu and Ste Justine's thus did not keep files on *hospitalières* as they did for salaried employees.

Service contracts signed between a community and a hospital, such as between the Filles de la Sagesse and the Ste Justine Hospital, stipulated only the number of nuns assigned to the institution and the positions that should be filled. Individuals fulfilling the prescribed offices remained anonymous and interchangeable. As noted earlier, the remuneration paid to the community was a lump sum calculated on the basis of the number of active sisters. The position, qualifications, and work schedule of any given sister were neither specified nor taken into account. This financial agreement was negotiated and drawn up without her cooperation, and it did not consider her as an individual. This nun merely performed her assigned tasks, while the community used the money received from the hospital for her work as it saw fit. From the hospital's point of view, therefore, nuns did not exist as individuals but only as members of a collective.

For *hospitalières* between the years 1940 and 1960, work was thus at once a bounden duty, a flexible notion, and an unremunerated activity carried out in a collective, not an individual, capacity. Developments during the 1960s would shake the foundation of this centuries-old notion of work.

THE 1960S: AN URGENT TRANSITION

The underlying issues that had long disturbed the hospital community emerged into the open during the decade of the 1960s. Already well underway, state control as well as the secularization and unionization of hospitals now increased at an unprecedented rate. The *hospitalières* found themselves in the midst of what turned out to be a great upheaval. In this context, they managed, more or less successfully, to stay on course for a time, maintaining clear if not particularly optimistic objectives: "[We must not] let our hospitals go too quickly without a fight; we must struggle like our founders did [and] consolidate our forces to maintain our hospitals at a high standard" (translation).[25] In the end, however, the pressure for change proved too great.

A series of laws by the federal (Canadian) and provincial (Quebec) governments played a critical role in this transition. Beginning in 1961, hospitalization insurance covered most of the fees of hospital patients after admittance. Although the law allowed hospitals to balance their budgets, it also imposed new standards regarding the quality of care and demanded annual budgets as well as detailed reports on such things as cases treated, the length of hospital stays, and equipment purchases. Barely a year later, in 1962, the Hospitals Act further tightened the government's control over hospital management. It required religious communities that owned hospitals to become legally incorporated and distinct bodies. The act also established a system of operating licences, excluded nuns from chairing boards of directors (in favour of lay people and doctors), and required approval from the lieutenant-governor for any expansion or change in the role of an institution. Four years later, in 1966, a new law was adopted under which the Quebec government assumed the role of management in any contract negotiations between hospital administrations and unions. Collective bargaining would henceforth occur at the provincial level rather than on a regional or institution-by-institution basis. In a very short period of time, religious communities lost the administrative control of their hospitals and sometimes even their right to ownership.[26] Although a few communities continued to own their institutions, they did not feel as if they were owners at all, for, in reality, they were left with almost no room for manoeuvre.

The situation of religious communities was made all the more precarious by a recruiting crisis. Beginning in the 1940s and 1950s, Quebec's religious communities recruited fewer members every year, with the result that the average age of members gradually increased. Although not yet dramatic, the phenomenon became more pronounced over time, particularly for nursing orders.[27] By the 1960s it had become a crisis situation. Female religious orders confronted plummeting recruitment rates and an unprecedented wave of exclaustrations (nuns leaving the community). In other words, fewer nuns were entering communities while growing numbers were leaving. The overall result was striking – and even more so in Quebec than in France and the United States. By 1971 communities had already lost 14 per cent of their numbers, while 40 per cent of members were over sixty.[28] Such changes soon affected hospitals. *Hospitalières* who had become fewer in number and older on average, were less able than before to meet the needs of the rapidly expanding health sector. Nuns had represented up to 15 to 20 per cent of hospital staff in 1950, but by 1965 they accounted for a mere 6 to 7 per cent.[29] Already a minority, they now became a marginal presence in hospitals, small islands surrounded by an ocean of lay employees. The secularization of hospitals was for all intents and purposes achieved.

During this time, hospital unions signed up new members at a dizzying pace. General, technical, skilled, professional, and even medical personnel were swept up in the wave of unionization. The pressing issues were wage scales, paid vacation, overtime, bonuses, seniority, fringe benefits, and strikes. Eager to make up for lost time in terms of achieving improved working conditions, hospital staff no longer hesitated to go on strike. They were encouraged by public opinion, which had become increasingly critical of hospital administrations, viewing them as old-fashioned. Strikes, hitherto infrequent, became common, and the imposed notion of dedication to one's work, once so powerful, now came under question. Female workers, always a majority in the hospital sector, were able not only to improve their working conditions, but also to make gains that strongly affirmed women's right to paid work – gains that included, for example, the principle of equal pay for equal work, maternity leaves, and the partial degendering of work.

Given this swiftly changing context, *hospitalières* now found themselves caught between tradition and modernity, resistance and adaptation, preservation of their assets and exploration of new avenues. Furthermore, they aroused a growing impatience within hospitals and outside them and would increasingly be perceived as a problematic workforce. Their spiritual commitment, once considered appropriate to the exercise of their worldly functions in hospitals, was now seen as a hindrance to the smooth running of these institutions. Changes of such magnitude could not help but have repercussions on the nature, conditions, and perception of their work.

Salaried Employment, Individualization, and Unionization

One of the first results of the profound changes that took place in the 1960s was that the non-remunerative character of nursing sisters' work came under assault. In particular, the massively unionizing workforce had difficulty dealing with the presence of unpaid "workers" who exerted a downward pressure on salaries that were already too low. But it must also be noted that the nuns themselves became less willing to provide unpaid services. Now that the state paid for both patient care and the employees dispensing it, the *hospitalières'* dedication lost most, if not all, of its raison d'être. In 1961 the Mother Superior of the Filles de la Sagesse highlighted this point when she requested a complete review of the nuns' remuneration at Ste Justine's: "The services provided by nuns since 1910 were a charitable contribution to the work of Ste Justine's and I estimate that the current staff of sixty nuns contributes roughly $130,000 annually in volunteer services to the hospital. With the advent of hospitalization insurance, charity has taken another form and the Congregation did not commit itself to being charitable to the government" (translation).[30]

In addition, many communities that owned hospitals, including Les Hospitalières de St-Joseph, gave up the traditional practice of symbolic salaries for nuns. How and when this change occurred is unclear, but the 1960s were presumably a pivotal period in this respect, since hospitals and the communities that owned them became distinct legal entities. The interests of both parties began to diverge at the same time that a number of communities started to ask for salaries for their members. Hospitals began to pay sums that were no longer purely theoretical but intended as remuneration – at least in part – for sisters' work. In general, nuns still did not have access to their salaries, turning them over instead to their community. From their perspective, their work remained unpaid. From the hospital's perspective, however, the situation was less clear.

A salary is generally associated with the hiring of an individual, and in the 1960s, hospital sisters began to be considered more as individuals and less as interchangeable members of a collectivity. They now held specific positions whose characteristics marked them as individuals (skills, seniority, and level of responsibility), according to hospital regulations and collective agreements. The Mother Superior no longer decided alone where her "daughters" would be assigned, according to her own evaluation of their skills and the needs of the hospital or order. When a position became free, she now had to ensure that the sister she wanted to fill it possessed the necessary qualifications and met certain requirements set outside the community. Moreover, some hospitals began to hire nuns from outside the order with which they were associated. As a result, the Mother Superior lost a portion of her authority and the sisters gained some measure of individuality.

In this context, the working conditions of hospital nuns began to approach those of lay workers. In all respects – position, schedule, remuneration, bonuses – the gap between the two types of workers narrowed. The unionization of nuns and unions' opposition to disparities between similar categories of workers explained this change. Nursing care represented a pocket of resistance for the sisters in the late 1960s. There were concentrated most of their dwindling numbers, mainly in management positions. There too tensions increased, since lay workers were no longer willing to accept nuns in most of the management positions. The pressure to unionize was probably greatest in the nursing sector, which would explain why the first unionized nuns were nurses. At the Hôtel-Dieu and Ste Justine's, sisters signed union cards with the Alliance des Infirmières between 1967 and 1969.

Within the communities themselves, unionization generated much doubt and discomfort. In the name of charity, an increasingly anachronistic tradition, some nuns opposed or condemned union action. Others questioned the inherent contradictions involved in belonging to both a union and a community that acted as management. Still others questioned their role as women bound by vows of poverty in organizations demanding salary increases. A few hospital sisters found a good side to unions. On the whole, however, the dominant feeling towards unions was one of unease.

Religious Work That Retained Some of Its Specificity

Still, by the end of the 1960s, the transformation of *hospitalières'* work was not entirely complete. Within the communities, little had changed. Work, whether prestigious or humble, concrete or spiritual, in the hospital or community, remained the same inescapable imperative and retained its unpaid and collective nature. Community archives are replete with portraits of sisters who remained fiercely active despite all obstacles: "This burden [of the Mother Superior's] weighed on her humble shoulders for 33 years ... At 88, it was a real sacrifice for her to be sent to the rest home; for our dear good Sister who retained all her lucidity and keenness, along with her zeal for work, it was not rest since she appeared to have chosen a life of forced labour ... Once her prayers were said, she never stopped knitting: socks, mittens, etc." (translation).[31]

In the hospitals as well, many nuns continued to work as they always had, without a real salary and strictly as members of a collectivity. This was particularly true at Montreal's Hôtel-Dieu Hospital, which remained the legal property of the Hospitalières de St-Joseph. At Ste Justine's, the service contract between the hospital and the Filles de la Sagesse, first signed in 1910, remained largely in force despite some changes. Although the community now collected salaries for each of its members according to lay wage scales, the sisters were still not treated as regular employees. They did not receive an individual paycheque, they collectively made a "donation" of part of their salary to the community, and they continued to work for free.[32] Their situation was hardly unique, since the Quebec association of religious hospitals recommended in 1962 that nuns give roughly 20 per cent of their salary to a "work of charity" and continue to provide unpaid overtime.[33] Although the unionization of *hospitalières* occurred fairly rapidly, it did not happen overnight. For instance, the unionization of nuns without professional qualifications met with some problems: their status as workers was hard to define and the labour courts handed down contradictory decisions. In some cases, courts ruled that the sisters were salaried employees and should thus be included in the bargaining unit. In other cases, courts ruled differently and thus prevented unions from adding sisters to their lists of members.[34]

Nonetheless, it is clear that nuns were well on their way to salaried and individual labour. For the moment, however, they found themselves in the shaky position of tightrope walkers balancing on the fine line that separated paid and unpaid labour.

THE 1970S: A DECADE OF CHANGE

Obviously, the hospital sisters could not maintain this tenuous position for long. Their work underwent a metamorphosis from the 1970s on. Metamorphosis is not too strong a word in this context; it aptly captures the transforming process by which an activity lost all its specificity and cohesiveness under the pressure of other changes occurring in hospitals at that time.

The provincial government, anxious to improve the accessibility of health care as well as to control costs, consolidated its position as the major actor in the hospital sector. In 1970 it enacted the Health Insurance Act, which guaranteed almost totally free care. In 1972 the province further reduced the room for manoeuvre of hospital administrations with a new law that changed the composition of hospital boards. Henceforth, boards would be chaired by hospital administrators and would include representatives of the government, socio-economic groups, users, the Council of Physicians and Dentists, professional and non-professional groups, as well as interns and residents. Within such a broad representation, the power of nuns representing communities that owned hospitals (e.g., the Hôtel-Dieu) diminished greatly. Orders once responsible for managing the internal operations of institutions like Ste Justine's soon lost the few seats they had until then occupied on hospital boards. Believing that the health system had become too costly, the government imposed tighter financial controls on hospitals and imposed sanctions on those with operating deficits. By the end of the 1970s, the provincial state had become the main purveyor of health care, the largest employer in the sector, and the owner of several hospitals purchased from religious orders. The communities – and the Catholic Church in general – had lost their status as main players on the hospital stage.

Indeed, nuns barely appeared in the cast of characters. Their withdrawal from the scene accelerated at all echelons of the hospital hierarchy during the 1970s.[35] At the same time, religious communities were decimated by the shortage of those heeding the call. The dual trend of declining recruitment and increasing exodus became so acute that it could no longer be swept under the rug. It was discussed widely in public forums,[36] and in 1973 the Canadian Religious Conference even decreed a "state of alarm" and bluntly asked if religious orders had any future,[37] thereby publicizing the conclusions of many congregations worried about the steep decline of their demographic curves. In every hospital, nursing sisters were less and less visible and less and less numerous. Large institutions, such as the Hôtel-Dieu and Ste Justine's, barely had thirty nuns each in 1969, dropping to twenty and to ten in 1980.[38] Sisters made up less than 10 per cent of salaried staff around 1960, and the percentage dropped below the 1 per cent bar during the following decade.

Meanwhile, the role of the few thousand sisters who remained in Quebec hospitals came under open attack. Their administrative and health-care methods were sharply criticized; religious life and hospital work were now said to be incompatible. This evolution was not restricted to the hospital sector. In 1976 a Dominican father described the general situation before a meeting of teaching sisters in very dramatic terms: "They want our jobs. They want us dead. It is a rejection of all traditional values"(translation).[39] Sisters, for their part, rarely commented on the turmoil they faced. Spiralling deficits in their hospitals, their small numbers, and strong trends in favour of the secularization of the entire Quebec society denied them the ability to reply effectively. The secularization of hospitals was nearly completed during the 1960s, although the process would continue for another ten years. Ironically, men – chaplains – were virtually the only official Church presence a hospital would tolerate in its midst.

During the 1970s, the unions clearly strengthened and consolidated their gains in working conditions. They also became more sensitive to an abiding feature of hospitals, the fact that women made up the majority of the workforce. Unionized female workers openly questioned the sexual division of labour, which, while less flagrant than before, still defined tasks, knowledge, levels of pay, and power in hospitals. Challenging these restrictions, hospital workers across the province won the right to discuss remuneration and to impose limits on what could be required of them in institutions that were now decidedly public rather than philanthropic.

The shock waves caused by these upheavals expanded in concentric circles that, one by one, affected the basis of the sisters' presence in hospitals. Amidst such turmoil, their work could no longer be unpaid or collective. Nor could it be an imperative, a duty for all, regardless of their performance. It could no longer be an all-encompassing activity that integrated spheres that were compartmentalized in the secular world. By the 1970s, state control, secularization, and unionization in the hospitals had reached full maturity, and nuns' work had been stripped of its uniqueness. To these transformations, of course, must be added the larger changes in Quebec society and within the Church.

Salaried and Unionized Sisters

In hospitals of the 1970s, *hospitalières* became regular salaried employees. Nothing distinguished them from their lay counterparts, except perhaps the initials of their congregation that many continued to write beside their name. All nuns now received a salary and fringe benefits as stipulated in collective agreements – without exception. They could no longer be counted on to provide free work, to work unpaid overtime, or to work at a wage scale lower than that of lay employees. A government order made this mandatory in 1971.[40] Moreover, all, apart from management, were unionized. Sisters' work in the hospitals had been divested of the main element that previously characterized it, its unpaid nature.

This development modified another aspect of *hospitalières'* work. The work imperative lost its compulsion. Now salaried and unionized, nuns had to follow hospital rules, particularly those concerning working hours. Coffee breaks, weekends, and various leaves and vacations would now punctuate their working lives as it did those of lay employees. Sick leaves and retirement would interrupt their work when they were too old or too ill to perform at a level deemed sufficient. Nuns could also be dismissed from their job for professional misconduct or other reasons. Unlike before, expressions such as "convalescing" or "retired" began to appear on communities' lists of obediences without an indication that the sister concerned had been assigned other tasks.[41] While this phenomenon alone sheds no light on new religious conceptions of work, it does admit the possibility (previously unthinkable) that nuns too old or sick to work could in fact do nothing. In other words, the sisters' old motto – work at any price, regardless of the result, as long as possible – was no longer in use.

Having earlier occupied the universe of unpaid work, the *hospitalières* now found themselves in the universe of paid work. This represented a major change, prompting fierce debates even in the muffled atmosphere of the communities. As one sister of the Hôtel-Dieu explained: "Some nuns accept [salaried work] in order to be on an equal footing with lay workers (sharing the same conditions). Society also would see it as a question of justice. For others, salaried work would allow an improvement in nuns' working conditions and maintain the Church's presence in the hospital. Others see a contradiction in salaried work for people who, by vocation, had made a free gift of themselves. Is there not the risk of losing the special character of religious life?" (translation).[42]

In these debates coexisted two trends: resistance to the new secular rules, deemed to be incompatible with spiritual commitment; and the desire to adapt outmoded religious prescriptions to current realities. Whichever side they were on, sisters had no choice but to accept salaried employment.

Individual Work

The move to salaried employment and unionization had as a necessary corollary the individualization of hiring. Perhaps the best measure of these changes is the fact that *hospitalières'* files are indiscriminately mixed with those of lay workers in the archives of hospitals of that period. This was not a new phenomenon, since the personnel departments at Hôtel-Dieu and Ste Justine's already contained several examples of such mixing in the late 1960s. During the 1970s, however, the principle was applied systematically to all sisters in all hospitals.[43] Though seemingly insignificant at first glance, the systematic mixing of these files reveals that a true metamorphosis had taken place. Nuns were now considered not only salaried workers, but also individuals.

In order to work in a hospital, each nun had to go to the personnel department to fill out a job application form, undergo an interview, and provide proof of her qualifications. Eventually, she signed a contract with the hospital that was specific to her. The time she spent at work, her tasks, and any fringe benefits were stipulated in that contract. If hired, she would receive a paycheque addressed to her personally and would have to answer to the hospital's lay hierarchy. The community no longer acted in her name or played a direct role in this transaction. The Mother Superior, who everywhere and at all times had authority over the activity of her nuns, no longer had a say regarding their professional jobs. The personnel manager now interposed himself between "Mother" and "daughters" to implement the hospital's rules and the clauses of collective agreements. *Hospitalières*, once perceived and treated as members of a group dedicated to running an institution, now became simple individuals whose spiritual commitment was a personal choice, irrelevant to their professional work. Thus, from the hospital's point of view, the situation was clear: *hospitalières'* work was no longer either free or collective.

The individual hiring of nuns led to the disintegration of the system under which the community and hospital had worked in tandem, severing the links between the two parties. Since every nun signed an individual contract with a hospital, service contracts like the one between Ste Justine's and the Filles de la Sagesse lost all meaning, substance, and purpose. Even the title of ownership that the Hospitalières de St-Joseph still possessed to the Hôtel-Dieu no longer allowed the order to act as a collectivity. As one sister who was a member of the board wrote in 1971: "It can be observed that, in the future, religious communities can no longer be identified by their charities, and in these outmoded institutions, personal participation in professional activities and teamwork have taken priority over community work" (translation).[44]

When hospitals and orders got divorced, so to speak, nuns' work lost its collective basis. This loss was exacerbated by the fact that sisters no longer performed their tasks in a closed world of religious communities and charities. When the old system broke down, nuns "went out into the world," leaving their protected universe to enter the job market. The principle of a collectivity of women dedicated solely to the operation of a specific institution disappeared. Communities became more heterogeneous. The few remaining *hospitalières'* at Hôtel-Dieu and Ste Justine's now lived with nuns employed at other hospitals, treatment centres, apostolic associations, parishes, CEGEPs (Collèges d'enseignement général et professionnel), or government agencies.[45] In 1971, the Filles de la Sagesse acknowledged the phenomenon: "We must be aware that a religious community is different from a work team" (translation).[46] Thus, to a certain extent, work and community also became "divorced" from one another.

The Disintegration of Religious Work

With hospitals and communities now constituting two very distinct worlds, the conception of work as all-encompassing became obsolete. Hospital work, domestic chores, prayers, and the small symbolic tasks no longer comprised that indissoluble whole given unto God. For sisters as for lay persons, these various kinds of activities were compartmentalized and carried out in very different ways. The nuns' vocabulary now made distinctions between paid work, volunteer work, community services, and apostolic work.

In 1970, for example, the list of obediences of the Hospitalières de St-Joseph separated "hospital activities" from "community activities." The first were done exclusively for pay in the hospital, while the second constituted a huge grab bag comprising such things as volunteer work, domestic work, culture, relaxation, religious meetings, catechism courses, and swimming lessons.[47] A similar phenomenon occurred among the Filles de la Sagesse, revealing the fragmented nature of religious work. Their records now distinguished between paid, volunteer, and community jobs. Betraying a hint of unease, internal surveys asked:

"How can we link [paid] work, personal commitment, and community commitment?"(translation).[48] Some sisters abandoned community work in favour of a salaried job, while others suggested that employed sisters pay salaries to nuns working exclusively for the community to "restore their prestige."[49] At a time when the feminist movement raised the question of wages for housework, such suggestions underscore the magnitude of the upheaval occurring among nuns.

Within the fragmenting sphere of religious work, one break appears to have been more profound than others: the dissociation of hospital work from community work. The notion of public and private spheres, which up to this time did not apply in the *hospitalières'* case, suddenly became relevant. Prayers, orisons, meals, and community life in general disappeared from the hospital scene and therefore from the public sphere; henceforth, they became associated with the private sphere, much as family life is in the secular world. Among the Filles de la Sagesse, some sisters worked "outside" (in hospitals or elsewhere), while others worked "inside" (within the community). The Hospitalières de St-Joseph spoke of a "demarcation between the workplace and the home environment" in terms that evoke the Victorian (masculine) image of a domestic world as a refuge where one regains energy and temporarily escapes the harshness of the outside world: "Faced with growing tensions in the workplace caused either by the rise of unions [or] the increasing demands of professional activities ..., you feel the need, after a day of labour, to shut the door on your work. Once you have gone through this door, you feel deeply that, to be able to meet the growing demands of tomorrow, you need to achieve a community of life that creates fraternity and love" (translation).[50]

Changes in the nature of work also caused turmoil in the overall functioning of hospital orders. The move to salaried employment not only affected what can now be called the nuns' professional life; it also had implications for what became their "private," or community, life. In the 1970s the individual acquired new importance within orders that had once placed the priority on the common good. Some orders spoke of "individual missions" and "greater freedom" and abolished the bell that forced all community members to rise, work, eat, and pray at the same time.[51] Others granted the nuns a small budget for personal expenses and equipped them with the *Livre de vie* (Book of Life), which emphasized the respect due to the "autonomy, goals, freedom, and responsibility of every person and group" – in short, a book that promoted "unity in diversity" (translation).[52] Even within the communities, nuns' work became individualized and more fragmented. Sisters performed their activities in different locations according to different schedules and with different objectives. Moreover, the distribution of tasks no longer depended solely on the judgment of the Mother Superior. Her influence on nuns already restricted in the hospital environment, she was now forced to take account of individual preferences in running the community life. Along with the names of sisters "appointed" to a particular office there now appeared the names of sisters who "accepted" rather than "submitted to" an obedience, who "requested" or "negotiated for" a position, and who "refused" a position or simply "resigned."

AN ENDURING FORM OF UNPAID WORK: NUNS' VOLUNTEERING

The many changes occurring in hospitals since the 1940s seem to add up to an irresistible force that swept everything aside in its wake. However, no revolution, no matter how profound, completely wipes away the past. Although a metamorphosis did take place, the work of nuns in the 1970s was still not identical to that of lay employees. The picture of the evolution of religious work presented here requires some qualification and nuance.

Unpaid work remained a powerful imperative for the sisters. In hospitals, volunteer work now constituted the only way to conform to this imperative. Previously irrelevant to the nuns, it thus had become a common and even requisite activity by the 1970s. For the sisters, volunteer work was a compromise, a way to reconcile their religious vocation, which implied giving of themselves, with their existence in an almost completely salaried working world. Many *hospitalières* signed up as volunteers in different hospitals, working as individuals without special status. At Hôtel-Dieu and Ste Justine's, for example, their ID tags were identical to those used by the lay volunteers with whom they worked. One searches in vain for any details, information, or comments indicating that the nuns were perceived or treated differently. Instead, they melted into the mass of volunteers, except for the abbreviation "Sr" or the initials of their congregation beside their name. Perhaps the only thing that distinguished them from their lay counterparts was the fact that their activity was dictated in large part by their religious status: for nuns, volunteering did not correspond to the uniquely personal choice made by lay individuals.

Other traces of the older value system can be detected as well. The nuns continued to avoid establishing clear demarcations between the different facets of their work. As much as possible, paid, volunteer, and community work continued to be perceived and organized as a whole. The greater importance granted to individual aspirations did not mean the loss of the principle of a common objective shared by all.

Regardless of their different tasks, every sister was expected to contribute to this objective. Achieving a common goal might prove far more difficult than before, but it remained a necessity that could not be ignored without rendering the religious commitment itself irrelevant. Significantly, the Hospitalières de St-Joseph and the Filles de la Sagesse agreed that the salaries of some of the sisters could be used to finance not only the community work of others, but also the volunteer services and missionary work of their orders. Both orders, joined in a common vow of poverty, insisted that their work remain unpaid, since they pooled resources and redistributed the surplus.[53] Were they in fact able to maintain sufficient cohesiveness of their activities and limit the impact of a new hierarchy that divided paid and unpaid sisters? Were they able to avoid the pitfalls of the consumer society to the extent that they could respond to the needs of the underprivileged and respect their own vows of poverty? These questions provoked intense debate in both communities, as in many others.[54] Throughout all this questioning, however, nuns tried to maintain an all-embracing conception of their work. For them, it might be said that work for God still encompassed everything.

As the 1980s began, nuns no longer had a special status in hospitals but were either employees or volunteers. Their work had been fragmented into paid and volunteer work, with its community component disappearing from the hospital scene. In the process, this work lost both its cohesion and its specificity. Stripped of all that set it apart from the activity of lay employees, it no longer existed in its traditional sense. The disappearance of nuns from Quebec hospitals is therefore not just a question of their plummeting numbers, as is often claimed. It also reflects the disappearance of a very specific and very old model of women's work. The few remaining traces of this model, barely visible, are confined to the volunteer and community spheres. Only there do some of the characteristics of nursing sisters' activity persist, albeit in modified form.

The transformations described in this essay are explained only in their broad outline. The analysis could be refined by comparing the work of *hospitalières* with that of nuns in sectors such as education and social services. A comparison with priests' or brothers' work would also be useful. It would point to significant similarities, particularly if nuns and brothers living in similar community settings were studied. Similar does not mean identical, though, and equally significant distinctions would no doubt also emerge; the notion of unpaid work in the religious world, for instance, is probably gender-sensitive. A gender bias in the remuneration of members of teaching orders persisted until the 1960s,[55] for example, while within the Church itself, priests and dignitaries performed tasks forbidden to women, and men received various forms of remuneration not available to sisters.[56] Since most studies comparing women's and men's activities focus on remunerated tasks, it would, therefore, be useful to submit to closer scrutiny the sexual division of labour in the religious world, astride the boundary separating paid and unpaid work. In this regard, hospitals would be a promising field of study. Studying *hospitalières*, along with the few chaplains and hospital brothers, could even explain the overwhelming preponderance of females among the religious active in Quebec's hospitals.

NOTES

Author's Note: The research for this chapter was done thanks to a post-doctoral grant from the Social Sciences and Humanities Research Council of Canada. I would like to express my profound gratitude to Lucie Piché for her thoughtful reading of the preliminary version of this text and to Talbot Imlay for his careful editing of the translation.

1 Orders of *hospitaliers* (brothers working in hospitals) were very rare in Quebec and widely eclipsed by their numerous female counterparts. B. Denault and B. Lévesque, *Éléments pour une sociologie des communautés religieuses au Québec* (Montreal: Presses de l'Université de Montréal 1975), 61–3.

2 Although *hospitalières* have disappeared from today's hospitals, volunteers, most of them women, still play an active role. Education and social services are other examples of sectors in which paid workers, nuns, and volunteers have participated together and continue to do so.

3 F. Guérard, *Histoire de la santé au Québec* (Montreal: Boréal Express 1996); N. Fahmy-Eid, A. Charles et al., *Femmes, santé et professions* (Montreal: Fidès 1997).

4 Under this provincial law, enacted in 1921, indigents' hospitalization costs were shared equally by the Government of Quebec, the municipality, and the hospital. It also provided for the payment of non-statutory grants to develop hospital infrastructures.

5 Canada, Dominion Bureau of Statistics, *Annual Report of Hospitals* (Ottawa, 1947–50); Canada, Dominion Bureau of Statistics, *Hospital Statistics. Hospital Beds* (Ottawa, 1953–59). These figures do not include hospitals that delegated the management of their operations to religious communities and therefore underestimate the extent of the nuns' presence.

6 A. Petitat, *Les infirmières* (Montreal: Boréal 1989), 54.

7 This observation concurs with the very high rate of activity in the Quebec religious communities in general. D. Juteau and N. Laurin, *Un métier et une vocation* (Montreal: Presses de l'Université de Montréal 1997), 23–5.

8 *Chroniques des Filles de la Sagesse de l'Hôpital Ste-Justine* (28 May 1946), 132, Archives of the Filles de la Sagesse (hereafter A-FDLS).

9 *Explication de la Règle des Filles de la Sagesse* (1942), unpaginated, A-FDLS.

10 Sr M. Mondoux, rhsj, *L'Hôtel-Dieu, premier hôpital de Montréal* (Montreal: Les Filles hospitalières de St-Joseph 1942), 99.

11 Some obituaries were not written until several years after a nun's death. This practice tends to confirm the hypothesis that these texts served more to edify than to describe accurately the personality of the deceased, whose memory had faded by then.

12 Letter from Mme Beaubien to Sr G.R. (1941), Archives of Hôpital Ste-Justine (hereafter A-HSJ).

13 Y. Cohen, *Profession infirmière* (Montreal, Presses de l'Université de Montréal 2000), 285; F. Rousseau, *La croix et le scalpel* (Quebec: Septentrion 1994), 2: 239.

14 Sr B. Hébert, rhsj, *Avant que ma lampe ne s'éteigne ...* (Montreal: Religieuses Hospitalières de St-Joseph 1990), 64, 168–9; Sr C. Perreault, rhsj, *Les 100 ans de l'Hôtel-Dieu d'Arthabaska, 1884–1984* (Trois-Rivières: Éditions Pourquoi Pas 1983), 366–7.

15 *Bulletin des Supérieures* (Filles de la Sagesse 1958–60), A-FDLS.

16 L. Feretti, *Brève histoire de l'Église catholique au Québec* (Montreal: Boréal 1999), 144. In 1974 a Quebec-wide enquiry still emphasized that nursing sisters had little leisure time. J.-P. Rouleau, *La religieuse hospitalière canadienne dans une société en transformation* (Quebec: Université Laval 1974), 1:270.

17 A similar hierarchical structure existed among the Filles de la Sagesse, although converses disappeared in 1954. These structure also comprised postulants, novices and professed nuns that had not yet made their perpetual vows.

18 *Procès-verbaux de la Conférence de Montréal de l'Association catholique des hôpitaux des États-Unis et du Canada* (26 August 1942), collection P-271, Archives nationales du Québec à Montréal (hereafter ANQM). Active from 1932 to 1962, the Montreal section of this association consisted mainly of hospitals staffed by sisters.

19 *Procès-verbaux de l'assemblée hebdomadaire du Conseil d'administration de l'Hôpital Ste-Justine* (1946–57), A-HSJ.

20 For example, the hospital's staff files for the 1940s show that lay nurses were paid five times as much ($130/month), clerks three times as much ($72/month), and lowly seamstresses twice as much ($47/month) as their religious counterparts.

21 *Procès-verbaux de la Conférence de Montréal* (15 April 1946), collection P-271, ANQM.

22 Sr Ste Marie-Madeleine, OSA, "L'hospitalisation au point de vue social," *Message*, January-February 1946: 14. The author was head nurse at the Hôtel-Dieu Hospital in Lévis, near Quebec City.

23 On this notion of unpaid work, see C. Delphy, "Travail ménager ou travail domestique," in A. Michel, ed., *Les femmes dans la société marchande* (Paris: Presses universitaires de France 1978), 39–54; Juteau and Laurin, *Un métier et une vocation*; A. Charles, *Travail et vieillesses féminines dans les hôpitaux québécois, 1940–1980* (PHD thesis, Université du Québec à Montréal 1997).

24 The nuns' case seems to require that women's work be reconceptualized, as it invalidates "the equation established between domestic work and unpaid work, between public sphere and salaried work" (Juteau and Laurin, *Un métier et une vocation*, 10). It should be added that volunteers also invalidate this equation, with the same theoretical consequences.

25 "Rapport du Comité des Communautés religieuses hospitalières," *Procès-verbaux de l'Association des hôpitaux catholiques de la Province de Québec* (5 March 1965), collection P-271, ANQM.

26 By 1968, religious communities only owned 35% of the public hospitals in Quebec. Canada, Dominion Bureau of Statistics, *Hospital Statistics. Hospital Beds 1968*, 1:58.

27 N. Laurin, D. Juteau, and L. Duchesne, *À la recherche d'un monde oublié* (Montréal: Le Jour 1991), 200–22.

28 Ibid., 222, 238.

29 Petitat, *Les infirmières*, 55.

30 Letter from Sr Noémi to the hospital president, Mrs Beaubien (10 July 1961), A-HSJ. Instead of the usual lump-sum amount, the Mother Superior requested that the hospital pay an amount per sister based on her position, skills, and responsibilities, as in the case of lay employees.

31 *Chroniques des Filles de la Sagesse de Nicolet* [rest home for sick or elderly nuns] (17 September 1966), A-FDLS.

32 File "Filles de la Sagesse: traités et conditions d'entente" (14 October 1960), A-HSJ; *Procès-verbaux de l'assemblée hebdomadaire du Conseil d'administration de Ste-Justine* (25 April 1962 and 19 November 1963), A-HSJ.

33 Commission Générale des Hôpitaux Catholiques de la Province de Québec, *Procès-verbaux* (13 February 1962), collection P-271, ANQM.

34 "La syndicalisation des religieuses hospitalières," *L'Hôpital d'aujourd'hui* 13, no. 10 (October 1967): 53–4, and 14, no. 1 (January 1968): 52–3; File Personnel non professionnel – grief (14 November 1967), A-HSJ.

35 D. Juteau and N. Laurin, "La sécularisation et l'étatisation du secteur hospitalier au Québec de 1960 à 1966," in Robert Comeau, ed., *Jean Lesage et l'éveil d'une nation* (Québec: Presses universitaires du Québec 1989), 155–67.

36 M.A. Lessard and J.-P. Montminy, "Les religieuses du Canada: âge, recrutement et persévérance," *Recherches sociographiques* 8, no. 1 (January-April 1967): 15–47; J. Légaré, "Les religieuses du Canada: leur évolution numérique entre 1965 et 1980," *Recherches sociographiques* 10, no. 1 (January-April 1969): 7–21; Rouleau, *La religieuse hospitalière*, 1:275–85.

37 Conférence religieuse canadienne, "Les communautés religieuses ont-elles de l'avenir?", CRC Documents (12 April 1973), A-FDLS.

38 Listes d'obédiences 1970–1980, A-RHSJ and A-FDLS.

39 "Colloque de l'Association des religieuses enseignantes du Québec," *Bulletin Information Sagesse – Québec* (December 1976), A-FDLS.

40 Order by the Department of Social Affairs addressed to all Quebec health establishments (21 July 1971), A-HSJ.

41 Listes d'obédiences, 1970–1980, A-RHSJ and A-FDLS.

42 Sr C. Perreault, rhsj, "Le rôle de la religieuse hospitalière dans l'hôpital catholique de demain," *L'hôpital catholique* 3, no. 2 (March 1972): 4.

43 The speed with which this practice was instituted varied depending on such factors as the size of the institution and the composition of its board. J.-P. Rouleau, *Situation et avenir des hôpitaux catholiques au Canada* (Quebec: Université Laval 1972), 1:56–69.

44 Sr C. Perreault, rhsj, "Le rôle de la religieuse dans l'hôpital catholique de demain," *Hôpital catholique* 2, no. 6 (November 1971): 8.

45 This change occurred in many religious communities in Quebec. Rouleau, *La religieuse hospitalière*, 2.

46 Lettres à la Province (4 November 1970), A-FDLS.

47 Liste d'obédiences, 1970, A-RHSJ.

48 Rapport de la Commission "Engagement apostolique ou travail" (1976), A-FDLS.

49 Ibid.; "Échos du Conseil provincial" (October 1977), A-FDLS.

50 Perreault, "Le rôle de la religieuse", (March 1972): 4.

51 Sr O. Lavallée, rhsj, "Renouvellement des services hospitaliers," *La religieuse dans la cité* (Montreal: Fidès, Collection "foi et liberté" 1968), 211; Hébert, *Avant que ma lampe ne s'éteigne.*

52 *Bulletin Information Sagesse-Québec* (January 1970); Filles de la Sagesse Montfortaines, *Livre de vie* (Rome, 1971).

53 Perreault, "Le rôle de la religieuse" (1972), 4; Hébert, *Avant que ma lampe ne s'éteigne*; Files "Consommation" and "Vie communautaire" (1976), A-FDLS.

54 Perreault, "La religieuse à l'hôpital," *L'Hôpital catholique* 3, no. 2 (March 1972): 4–7; Rouleau, *La religieuse hospitalière*, vol. 1; M. d'Allaire, *Vingt ans de crise chez les religieuses du Québec, 1960–1980* (Montreal: Bergeron 1983); A.-M. Labarre and R. Boutet, *Rapport Recherche-action* (Montreal: Association des Supérieurs majeurs, Frères et Sœurs du diocèse de Montréal 1971).

55 M. Dumont, *Les religieuses sont-elles féministes?* (Montreal: Bellarmin 1995): 119–20.

56 Juteau and Laurin, *Un métier et une vocation*, 46.

14

Scenes from the Psychiatric Hospital

Ann Starr

During the early and mid-1990s I was not infrequently a patient at an acute-care psychiatric hospital in Boston, Massachusetts. My stays were sometimes voluntary and sometimes not. They lasted between two and five days. There were times I would have felt much safer staying rather than being released, but I was never "authorized" to act in accordance with that personal assessment. It was always thought that longer internments would be "regressive" for me. What the institution considered infantilizing I usually considered barely at the threshold of my capabilities.

My diagnosis was bipolar disorder and clinical depression, borderline personality disorder, and intense suicidal ideation prior to menstruation. One psychiatrist named post-traumatic stress syndrome; others never mentioned it within my hearing. There is, however, no doubt that my experiences in childhood played a significant role in the loss of my ability to function as an adult.

I am now, as I was then, a visual artist. As a psychiatric patient, I am bent on recovery. As an artist, I am compelled to look at and understand my experience. When artist and mentally ill person are one, image-making is a powerful and natural resource for expression, change, and the hope of understanding – however murky that goal often remains.

My experiences of the hospital over the course of my admissions during these several years are recorded in two sets of drawings I made, each executed soon after a release. Furthermore, I kept sketchbooks during my incarcerations, filling them with drawings of the people around me and with more abstract images relating to emotional states.

Images retain worlds that disappear between words. Unlike verbal narrative, drawing can preserve many experiences coexistent either in a simultaneous moment or in an eternity of duration. Imaged experience is not vulnerable to fleeting memory or poor articulation or deficiencies of vocabulary. What goes down is fact, simply, however subject it may be to differing interpretations from artist and viewers alike. The reactions of pleasure or despair an image evokes may change or commingle without the production having changed at all. An image can contain a full spectrum of registers and communicate to many distinct audiences at once without hedging any detail. That is, the image is irrefutable but open to interpretation.

When mentally ill people tell their own stories, however, most auditors instinctively estimate the cost of engagement. Will understanding the stories mean we are mad ourselves? How do we know what is twisted, omitted, embellished? Will we be taken advantage of, threatened, or implicated? Simple compassion nearly always seems too daring. If the madman was critical of doctors, for instance, it is reasoned that some important information must have been withheld from him at the time – the sort of thing that's standard procedure for doctors but out of the ken of the afflicted. My point: there is always a retort implied within verbal statements. So, for the mentally ill, there is no such thing as a complete or sufficient statement, because the skeptical question arises from a world automatically defined in opposition – that is, from the world of "health," "truth," or "reality."

This essay is based on a talk that accompanied a presentation of my in-patient drawings. Rather than print the undiluted gouache drawings in black and white for this volume, thereby vitiating the impact of the vivid colour that carries much of their emotional and narrative power, I have written this essay around them. I commit myself, then, to the difficulties of telling episodes of my story in words in a way that I hope will convince the reader of the story's truth.

Was I deeply disturbed in the hospital? No doubt about it. But was my judgment of the world around me and of what would be good for me corrupted by that circumstance? I argue that they were not. I am convinced by my experience and by my discussions with the other sufferers among whom I lived that the severe strains psychosis lays upon communication place an obligation on the "well" to probe for the needs and wishes of the "ill." Too heavily taxed with pain for clarity and conventions, the psychotic patient remains, nevertheless, self-aware enough at a significant level to guide those able to help. The most important thing the "well" can do is not to despair of finding sense.

GETTING ADMITTED

My first admission was symptomatic of the miscarriages of communication between patients and doctors so unhappily characteristic of my experience. At best, I was admitted to the hospital and protected against urgent impulses to hurt myself. At worst, the opportunity for reassurance in human form – resting as it would on good judgment – was passed over in favour of recourse to institutional solutions, with their shifting, disembodied placement of responsibilities.

Briefly, one summer day I took an overdose of an anti-anxiety drug. While I learned much later that I had taken too little to do much harm, the knowledge that I had overdosed was certainly enough to cause me even greater anxiety than I'd felt when I'd looked to the drug for relief. I live within walking distance of a private psychiatric hospital, so, making sure my children were accounted for and safe elsewhere, I hastened on foot (careful not to drive) the quarter-mile to the reception area of the hospital, seeking help. I assumed it would take the form of reassurance or detoxification. I acted very responsibly, given the entirely tormented condition from which this episode arose.

From my current perspective, I can of course comment, "Silly me!" Surely it was a symptom of unsettled thinking to believe I would be helped, all unidentified as I was except as someone else's patient. I was handled as gingerly as radioactive material and soon found myself in an ambulance speeding towards my health centre, heart beating faster every moment, still not knowing how severely I was or was not imperilled.

Once at my health centre, I was bid to lie on a gurney in an examination room, where I encountered an internist and a psychiatrist, neither of whom I had ever seen before. Completely as a result of the escalation of fears I suffered under the confusion of agitated doctors, I fled the building when I was momentarily alone. That led to a half-hour search and my forcible return to the bitter verbal reproaches of the psychiatrist. It was inevitable, my own sympathetic physician explained with a sigh once he was located, that I would be admitted to the hospital. No one said that I had acted badly enough to deserve it, but there was no doubt about that conclusion.

I was never once reassured that I was in no danger from my impulsive action with the drug. Rather, I was allowed to develop a full-blown, generalized panic in which my sense of the proportion of the crisis was magnified at every turn. Not until the next day did I learn anything about the insignificance of my drug overdose. Having erred, recognized it, and immediately sought help, I was nevertheless punitively sent to the hospital in panic because no one "in control" took a moment either to perceive or to ask about my need. It was a fiasco.

I have since had to conclude that one is not delivered to a psychiatric hospital on any occasion without being in a state of great agitation. Any incubating fears hatch dramatically as the situation escalates towards admission. The calming gestures I once received took the form of "Calm down, damn it!" On this occasion as on many others, the doctors were disconcertingly vulnerable to my anxiety and with few exceptions reflected it directly back at me in the forms of authoritarian speech and looming body positions. They always made ad hoc decisions, thrusting onto people at the next stage of the system the responsibility for making – or avoiding – any meaningful decisions on my behalf.

DOCTORS AND NURSES

At the hospital, my HMO (Heath Maintenance Organization), which fills many of its beds, sends clinicians around to its patients daily, in teams. These people are permanently attached in memory to melamine-surfaced tables; one rarely saw them below the waist – certainly not too often perambulating the ward. In my experience, nurses were almost always female, doctors always male. Over my several stays I saw three doctors and three nurses in various combinations.

Being unable to establish a single doctor-patient relationship was very troubling for me, as I was hospitalized frequently enough for there to have been a lively memory of me and my situation. Lack of a predictable relationship was the more disconcerting, as I registered acutely that the hospital's environment was simultaneously promising and ominous. Trust is not one of the virtues that gets people into the hospital in the first place. However comforting the security of lock-up may be on one level, one's fortunes in a locked environment are always – as it is quite normal to assume they should be – a source of anxiety.

There is simply no telling how tiring and frightening it is to be mentally ill. One is caught in the irony of being very well aware that one suffers the lack of big, ill-defined, areas of self-awareness. All the evidence I gathered was that if I was not certain of the impression I was giving, it was infinitely better not to risk being misinterpreted through any attempt to be plain-spoken. Patients are forthcoming only at their own risk.

Relationships with doctors are, of course, posited on the idea that the patient speaks truthfully. Yet the doctors, who are in authority, are often quite unaware of their routine abuses of that authority. Little about them in their routine hospital presence inspires a spirit of full cooperation and trust. A doctor treating me on one visit walked unannounced – no knock or hesitation – into my room when my back was turned, then startled me not only with an unexpected hand on my shoulder, but with the peremptory announcement that he "had time for me now."

Daily interviews with the teams of doctors and nurses were conducted in small private rooms. Around these teams I sometimes felt genuinely mad, as if I were invisible before them. The revelations of their purported scrutiny never seemed to be what I thought obvious or central. For instance, none of my psychiatrists once consented to look at my sketchbooks, extensive and revealing as they were. Maybe it was because I offered them as my own idea.

I was uncomfortable around the nurses in these encounters because I sensed that they were playing a demonstrably inferior role to the doctors, under the pretense of equality. They not only helped conduct the interviews – ably – but also carried out practical work that saved steps for the doctor. This is not necessarily a prima facie indignity, but I was alive to the gender coding often implied and in conflicting significance to the small gains of efficiency. On one occasion I objected to the fact that doctor and nurse had both settled in for my interview with cups of coffee in hand. Coffee was forbidden to patients except at meals, when decaffeinated was served. It was discourteous at the simplest level that they should flaunt their exemption during my session. The doctor agreed to my having a cup as well (not to yielding theirs!) but sent the nurse to get it for me. From my point of view, he had asked his female subordinate to perform a task that could serve as an icon for the way women's jobs are assumed to include personal service to males. He had gone even a step further by sending the nurse to fetch something that would indulge not only the doctor's convenience, but also a lowly patient's aggravating insistence on an unearned display of respect.

On the floor the rest of the day, though, ward nurses (female and male), unattached to doctors in the performance of their jobs, defined kindness, justice, and strength in practical ways. Their authority derived directly from their continuous observation, calm interactions, and persistence in trying to create an atmosphere of fairness. By contrast, it was too easy to perceive the doctors as jailers, the boss, or Dad-who-will-reckon-with-you-when-he-gets-home.

This is an occupational hazard for the psychiatrists, no doubt, but I'm thinking of something that goes deeper than the obvious: that is, although doctors prescribed drugs, awarded privileges, and determined dates and conditions for release, their knowledge of individual patients appeared largely derivative. This certainly reinforced the conviction that the people who knew you best had little authority. This is squarely in the feminine tradition of mothers, secretaries, or, of course, nurses.

The doctors on my ward had little awareness of the image their standard operating procedures projected. Although I can give credit for decency and for efforts to practise well, there was clearly not enough thought given to the sociology of the floor, to its hierarchy from the least able patients through the attending doctors. The doctors weren't around enough to see the big picture that was so apparent to female-patient-me, that gender or gendered roles were an inevitable feature of that hierarchy.

This truth was especially problematic given the centrality of patient compliance as an issue. I needed to practise self-control, but not as an issue of civility in a group setting. However, I was compelled to take seriously the reasons to be good that are particular to an authoritarian institution in which one is at the bottom of the hierarchy. If I revealed any of the rage that defines borderline personality disorder – one of my central difficulties – in a place where transgression (no matter what its source) is taken very seriously, there could be severe consequences that only the most cynical could construe as therapeutic. I did not want acts of will or its lapse to land me in shock "therapy."

But I also suffer a deeply gendered awareness that "good girls must not make a fuss." This is a feminine habit thoroughly instilled in me in childhood. That it is so deeply entrenched makes me rage – it makes me furious enough to behave badly if my self-control is impaired. This is a part of my illness that mood stabilizers do not address. In short, one cannot survive with any degree of feminist or political awareness in a psychiatric hospital. It is not an asset there, where outrage and rage are not subtly diagnosed.

SEMI-PRIVATE ROOMS

The floor I am recalling was given over entirely to the care of patients with psychotic conditions. The depressions alone among the population would be a source of almost overwhelming sorrow to anyone; my heart and gratitude go out still to the nursing staff who were able to remain so caring, active, and even-spirited among us.

I recall that we were not supposed to sleep during the day, and the nurses tried to enforce the rule. I think they needed to keep everyone on a similar schedule. In this, as in most things, smooth functioning of the hospital environment was the goal, whatever the patients' individual needs. In my own experience of clinical depression, it is clear that sleep is one of the only sources of relief and, ultimately, one of the great healers.

I mention the daytime sleep ban as part of a brief physical description of the floor. It was shaped like a thick "U". Men's rooms were on one arm and women's on the other, with the nursing station, the day room where we ate, and the supply closets clustered in the broad curve. On the patient wings, bedrooms occupied the space between the outer walls and a broad common area for group meetings on the interior. In terms of natural light, only the base of the "U" was pleasant, thanks to a whole wall of double-thick windows in the day room that illuminated the nursing station as well. On either wing, however, the patient rooms each had one window along the exterior wall. Since room doors were often closed, that meant there was rarely anything other than low-wattage artificial light in the dull interior common areas. In fact, the patient rooms were long and narrow, so that the window shed most of its light on just one patient's end; the other patient, closer to the door, stayed in a gloom the natural light barely touched, illuminated only by a neon fixture marginally adequate for reading.

The architecture itself invited sleep, so dark and soporific were most of the patient spaces. People's illnesses invited sleep in and of themselves, and the considerable doses of medication among us also contributed to a phenomenal dulling of bodies and minds. But the nurses were always trying to get us up, to keep us from growing "a-socialized." This was a hospital policy; I don't think the nurses were stupid.

Unobtrusive head counts were constant. It took me a while even to notice this during the day, so adroitly was it carried out. During the night, though, I was quite aware that our rooms were visited at intervals by staff checking for our presence and safety. The beam from a flashlight would arc across the room, searching and landing briefly on each patient in turn. One of course is never able to identify the person behind the light. I often awoke from what passes for sleep in the hospital to find this event in progress, something I experienced as simultaneously reassuring and weird.

The night staff was in fact always obscure. They arrived after curfew and departed before we shuffled out in our foam slippers for morning meds. I was afraid of them; I was either being surprised by their lights or being half-awakened by their conversations and laughter at the desk. They were big. The night makes all strangers big, and sleeping poorly increases the size of one's fears. But I am confident they were indeed large people, as large people were always needed in case of emergency in a volatile population. During the day we sometimes saw large people in action.

Most personal property (jewelry down to shoelaces) is locked up upon admission as being potentially dangerous. I was always grateful to be allowed to keep my drawing pencils and sketchbooks. I felt I retained my identity through them. When not engaged in an obligatory activity, I drew or read. I devoured several good long books during hospital stays. I recall these as very serene and comfortable hours. They did me a lot of good.

There were always patients slyly revealing the matches, "sharps," and other forbidden items they managed to secrete on their persons or in their rooms. Cigarettes, next to coins for the telephone, were as precious as gold is to buccaneers. I had my small cache of change robbed a couple of times. I doubt that cigarettes were stolen because of the ease of identification by brand and the predictable fury of the owner's retribution. The staff kept the cigarettes of the smokers and passed them out when the morning and afternoon smoking outings occurred. The floor would then clear of literally everyone but a few nurses and myself as the trembling patients were shepherded to a kind of walled exterior well where they packed in and sucked up their fags. I went once, just for the outing, but found it – admitted sociological interest aside – nauseating. If there were occasions when I felt overwhelmed with sorrow, it was while witnessing the departure of the quavery smoking parties.

As many times as I was in the hospital, I cannot say that I remember much about my roommates. Occasionally there would be three of us crammed into a double room; once or twice I had a double to myself for a night or two. That was really nice.

Most people entertained themselves around the television. (I recall vividly the O.J. Simpson trial as incessant televised background to several visits.) Outside of the hospital I would have had little that was obvious in common with most people I met within it. I was one of the few educated, suburban, white women. The population was more heavily Hispanic, black, and urban. Many were homeless save for their recurrent visits to our hospital. I felt no fear or hostility towards my peers, just that our needs as personalities – not as humans – were usually different. I read; they watched TV. Sometimes I did enjoy long individual conversations with people in the lounges. These more searching conversations reaffirmed the proposition that one need not be foolish, unintelligent, or unkind to remain uneducated or thwarted in every detail of life by mental illness.

One can be rendered inscrutable and unpredictable, however, and it would be incorrect to leave the impression that there were not such people on my floor. I recall the homeless woman of indeterminate weathered age (forty? sixty?) with whom I shared a room for two days and nights. At the time we were paired, several hospitalizations had taught me not to worry much about what my roommates were doing or thinking. She muttered a good deal, but I still figured that was not much as annoyances go, given our setting and all this woman seemed up against.

I had been placed in the empty room the day before my roommate was admitted. I had installed myself in the bed by the window, in complete conformity with any idea of rational thinking at this hospital. My new roommate never addressed me directly, however commonly she addressed the walls and beings invisible to me. On our second night together, however, she broke out suddenly in physically violent and obscene apostrophe to the space and its inhabitants about "her" viciousness – mine, I finally understood – that prevented this woman access to the window. The staff came running. I feared attack. If anyone has ever scared me more, then the incident was too traumatic for memory. My fright was complicated into an even more dismal emotion by my awareness that this woman had something legitimate to be aggrieved about, and that I myself thought virtually the same thing, however "unreasonably," whenever I felt deprived of the view for a few days. I was hurried to another room, the nurses following with my effects. I suspect that my roommate got the window. Instantly. Fair enough? I got the door end in my new digs.

GROUP THERAPY

I did not receive any individual psychotherapy in the hospital, only the daily consultations with my team from the HMO. The nominally therapeutic hospital activities were group sessions. Some of these were required of everyone, though not everyone came. Despite the staff's efforts to round up the whole floor, there were those who did not attend for their own intractable reasons, those who acted out and were dismissed (a strategy used particularly effectively on many occasions), and those whose bodies were present and asleep throughout the meetings.

Because I was "high functioning" and the judgmental insinuation of my refusal to participate would have been apparent enough for repercussions, I attended routinely. While the discussions often evoked in me sorrow for my fellow-sufferers, I never felt myself equipped for the sessions. I tried to keep quiet because my "big words" and "insight" marked me unhelpfully. Only by adopting a slump and a carefully limited vocabulary could I have prevented other patients from treating me like a doctor (to the point of asking for all sorts of help). Although this was annoying, it was easier for me to accept than the staff's apparent expectation that my aptitudes would indeed elicit inoffensive and even helpful behaviour. As a result of both reactions, group therapy sessions were not only barren of help for me, but put me into an unacceptable relationship with my colleagues. I felt the need to protest that I was sick too, however doomed I felt never to be "sick enough" to get the attention I – like everyone – was desperate for.

DAY HOSPITAL

Since the period of my frequent hospitalizations, I have grown in the strength and self-awareness that encourage confidence about my ability to keep myself whole. But there have been nevertheless seizures of panic, despair, and pain severe enough for my psychotherapist to remind me of the hospital as a secure haven. Both my hospital memories and the stressed state of mind I labour under during these episodes have made the hospital's drawbacks seem insurmountable. I always vow that I'll never go back. Nevertheless, on some level, I recognize that as little as it provides, the hospital does protect me against self-destruction.

To my surprise, however, I learned at the end of a recent difficult episode that the hospital in fact is *not* a possibility for me any longer. Although the psychosis unit exists at the same facility, it is essentially closed to "someone like me," having been given over to intractable cases of psychosis. For "intractable" we may understand "homeless," I gathered. People "like me" (read: suburban, white, educated) tend to be scared of street psychotics and are now to be managed in other sorts of facilities – the less supervised houses and day hospitals. "We," as normal middle-class consumers, demand a friendlier, neater experience. So I am given to understand.

At one point, after several days of hospitalization, I had the "good fortune" (it was presented to me thus) to be admitted to the day hospital. This is a full-day program held at a non-medical site, where patients are sent for group therapies and mutual support. Patients go home at night and report back in the morning; it is likened to a job.

The day hospital is staffed by a psychiatrist-director and a good many others – nurses? clinical aides? social workers? – who organize the programs and routines for the patients. The expectation is that the patient who is given a precious space in the program will attend daily for as long as it takes to ease back into normal life. It runs on the idea that the patients take responsibility for their environment and "own" the rules.

The day I attended, I was handed over to another patient for my orientation. When I undertook to use the Quiet Room he had shown me for the purpose he noted – calming down if overtaxed – a nurse discovered me in it, reproached me for my bad behaviour, and returned me to the activity that had caused me anxiety in the first place. That the patients were in any sense genuinely in charge of the program was patently not true, but rather a sponsored myth most seemed happy to accede to.

The psychiatric hospital had offered me a locked door, good nurses, and colleagues whose pain and souls clearly showed. In the day hospital, which I attended for one long and disturbing day only, the suburban and professional population ("like me") enjoyed therapy groups where they were bolstered in the pretense that their problems were behavioural rather than rooted in the emotional issues of grief or loss, in the legacy of abuses, or in other real sources of soul pain. Among the in-patient hospital population, I had seen no such fantasies. There was not a lot of self-awareness there, but neither was there a lot of active and sponsored self-deception. I found the day hospital simplistic in what it offered and demeaning in the obviousness of its economic and class segregation.

So while I still wonder whether I could return to the psychiatric hospital, for this polite placebo alternative there is no question: I would never do it, despite my favoured demographics. The frightening superficiality of its behavioural programs and its reliance on promises of self-control were invitations tendered only for "someone like me" to violate. This Ann, in the circumstances that drive her to a need for safety, finds it chilling that she be required to "be good" and follow specific rules as a precondition of receiving sanctuary. "Don't knock if you can't sign the agreement first." When I need help, I cannot be asked to read the fine print. For more people than me, I'm sure, the day hospital is an invitation to suicide, with the waiver of institutional responsibility.

The question of the hospital is, therefore, more and more decided for me. If I could get to the hospital in the first place, I might be able to bully my way in among my homeless colleagues to get the basic, needed security. But should the time come when I am finally too tired of fighting even for externally imposed safety, this reductive system, in which I am "known" as a sum of my education, address, and deportment rather than as a particular, peculiar psychic entity, invites me only to resist such normative treatment. I do not fit the profile for those who need help.

Obviously, this situation is literally life-threatening for me. It is terrifying to be required to advocate for myself when I am in extremis:

confused and unable to cope with ambiguity, complications, or reassurances that the doctor knows best. "The doctor" has not been a
universally reassuring concept for me, as I am sure it is not for many
sufferers of mental disorders. Each encounter with the system adds to
the patient's experience and information, and thus alters her or his
ability to respond to the expectations doctors, provokingly, insist on
finding routine. For the patient, accumulated experience of hospitalizations and of disease render moot the very idea of "routine." Patients
are dynamic and smart.

If I find myself in a crisis now, I am too easily put back where I
began, crouched in a corner, hoping death will make me invisible,
scraping to be alive at the end of another infinitely protracted hour,
convinced that life has too many minutes to be survivable.

REFLECTIONS

I think my hospital did as good a job as was possible. The nurses on the
floor were extraordinarily good, the HMO showed a little flexibility in
dealing with me, and the facility was not too oppressive. I do not think
the medical professionals around me were intentionally stupid or
uncaring. The food was great.

But it is clear that holding and crisis management were the only
institutional goals. I was kept alive and my family was spared the most
severe manifestations of my depression and rage – thank God for both.
But the low level of the institutional sights put a low ceiling on the
quality of aid I could receive from the doctors.

On this level, my recollections are very painful. I hoped to be helped
in some active way and was not. I was in fact damaged by my sense that
even here, in the most protected setting, I constantly had to grind a
bone-dry self in order to adjust to expectations of conventionally ordered, shallow norms, to yield to the authorities who upheld those
norms without demonstrating the legitimate sources of their authority,
and to avoid experiencing punishment for self-expression. It was hard
work to be there, since the price of physical safety was the quashing of
most aspects of my personality, sensibilities, the very expressions of my
illnesses. At the time I wondered – and do even now – if the price was
too high. Although it is indeed impossible to know what one would do
if one were in danger of self-immolation again, I think I could never go
back to the hospital. With all due respect.

People ask if drawing and writing about my hospital experience is
"therapeutic" for me. In the most literal and clinical way, the first
value of drawing and writing is in simple expression – getting it out.
What is genuinely therapeutic is having access to the observations and

understanding that follow the expression, having documents that exist in limitless time and can be considered calmly. This is because the mentally ill person lives inside the unspeakable curse of immediacy. During acute suffering, time is a straitjacket of pain, a tunnel on fire. Then it's hard to talk about.

15

Subcutaneous Scars: A Black Physician Shares What It Feels Like to Be on the Receiving End of Racial Prejudice, despite a Successful Career

Vanessa Northington Gamble

I was frightened as I drove slowly through the winter storm. Although I had lived in New England and the Midwest for almost fifteen years, I still did not feel comfortable driving in snow. On this day my journey was particularly treacherous – the roads had not yet been plowed, visibility was severely compromised, night was falling, and I was upset from events that had occurred earlier in the day.

I was a faculty member at a midwestern university school of medicine, and the dean had invited me to give a presentation about the status of minority faculty, residents, and students at the dean's retreat, a meeting that included school administrators and representatives from all departments. I jumped at the invitation. I had been appointed to the medical school's strategic planning committee and had been working to get the school to address issues of racial and ethnic diversity. This meeting, I thought, would give me an opportunity to press my case to an influential audience.

The morning of the event I set out early for the sixty-mile drive to the resort where the meeting was to be held. It was sunny, but the forecast called for snow. As I drove, I thought about what I wanted to say to my audience, most of whom I had never met. I decided that I wanted to let them know what it was like to be a person of colour in medicine. I was one of the few black faculty members at the medical school, so minority students often came to my office to talk about their lives. They shared stories of triumph – making it through the first year, delivering a baby, getting into a residency program. They also shared stories of sadness – feeling isolated from their classmates; being mistaken

(even by medical professionals) for janitors, maids, and dietary workers; being more intensely scrutinized than their white classmates are by
security guards and attending physicians. Making myself available to
the students was time-consuming, and I often worried about the effects
on my research productivity. But I felt an obligation to these students.
If I turned them away, where would they go? Also, I felt that I was
repaying a debt; minority faculty had been there for me when I was in
medical school.

At times my minority colleagues and I talked about the difficulties
we faced at a predominantly white medical school in the Midwest. We
talked about being asked to leave the doctors' eating area because we
did not fit the picture of the typical physician, and about a female patient screaming when a black man (her physician) had walked into
her room. We realized that despite our credentials, achievements, and
white jackets, our race would make it impossible for some people to
see us as physicians. Yes, I thought, as I drove to the meeting, it was
important for those at the dean's retreat to better comprehend the
experiences of people of colour in medicine.

A LONE VOICE

I walked to the podium and looked at my audience. It was overwhelmingly male and almost exclusively white, except for one black female
administrator. For fifteen minutes I discussed the experiences of
minority faculty, residents, and students at my university and at other
medical schools. Following the style set by my grandmother, who was a
storefront minister, I am usually a very emotional, dynamic speaker. But
on this day I altered my style. I gave what I thought was a clinical, dispassionate presentation. I reported my observations about some of the
obstacles that minorities in medicine faced. I made my diagnosis: the
medical school needed to create an environment that was more hospi-
table to people of colour. I even suggested a few remedies: increase the
number of faculty of colour, augment the resources of the multicultural affairs office, add more multicultural topics to the curriculum.

I finished my talk and sat down amid polite applause. At my table sat
the acting chair of one of the departments, who made the first comments on my presentation: "I talk to a lot of minority students, and I've
not heard what we've heard here today. I doubt if it is an accurate depiction of what goes on here. I have a woman resident who will tell you
differently."

I was taken aback by the hostility of his comments. I had not expected such a response. His words hurt. He was dismissing out of hand

my experiences and those of other minority physicians. He was calling me a liar. He was saying that my words could not be trusted but that those of a white woman resident who was under his supervision could. He also was disrespecting my status as a senior faculty member. I was the first and only black woman tenured at the medical school, and I was very proud of that accomplishment. I wanted to cry, but I translated my hurt into anger. My voice rising, I retorted, "I will *not* be dismissed. Just because *you* have not heard the stories does not deny their existence."

The room went silent. My challenger went on to introduce the white resident, who said that despite some problems, being a woman resident was not difficult. "I just don't dwell on the problems," she said. Even more angrily I responded, "I will not be dismissed." Two female faculty members in the tense room tried to assist me. I don't remember their words because my emotions were so raw. I do remember that not one man attempted to help me. The dean stood up: "It's time to move on to the next topic."

I sat there for a couple of hours, feeling angry, vulnerable, and lonely. At lunch a few of my male colleagues came over to tell me that what I had to say was important. "Why didn't you speak up in the meeting?" I asked. They had no excuse to offer.

I decided not to stay for the afternoon session. As I walked to my car, the first flakes of snow began to fall. The only other black person who had been in the room tried to convince me to stay overnight because she knew that I was upset and that a storm was approaching. I thankëd her but told her that I needed to get home, where I could feel safe. As I drove home, I tried to keep my mind on the road, but the day's events made concentration difficult.

I made it home without mishap. As soon as I entered the house, I burst into tears. I cried because I was happy to have made it back without killing myself. I cried because I was in a place where I could feel vulnerable and secure. I cried because I was angry with my challenger and with myself. I was mad at him because he had been so hostile and rude. I was mad at myself because I feared that my response to him made me look like the stereotypical angry black woman – an impression that I did not want to leave on an audience who did not know me. I cried because I felt insecure in the profession that I had so long yearned to join. Although I grew up in a poor inner-city community in Philadelphia, I had decided at the age of six to become a physician. My family fought for, believed in, and nurtured my dream of becoming a doctor. I later learned that the pain associated with childhood dreams being rocked can be traumatic.

OTHER TIMES

The confrontation at the dean's retreat was not the first or the last time that an incident had wounded me professionally and personally. The first time occurred during medical school at the University of Pennsylvania. During my junior clerkship in internal medicine, wearing a lab coat and carrying a stethoscope, I walked into the room of an elderly white male patient who had been admitted for evaluation because of high blood calcium. I introduced myself as a student doctor and proceeded to ask him questions about his medical history. Later, the white male intern came out of the patient's room and announced, laughingly, "You know what that guy asked me? 'Why didn't that girl clean up while she was in here?'" My being mistaken as a maid became a joke on the ward team, all of whom, except for me, were white and male.

The next morning on rounds the attending physician said, "Let's go see Vanessa fluff some pillows." I didn't find the episode humorous. I was angry and shaken. I was a good student at an Ivy League school and had begun to define myself as an aspiring physician, and I expected others to see me the same way. I might not be welcome in the medical fraternity, but they were going to have to let me in because I was qualified. This incident shook my self-confidence and threatened to undermine not only my professional identity but also my personal one. I had spent so much of my life in pursuit of becoming a doctor. Now it became clear to me that my race and sex would be an integral part of my professional identity. I would not just be a physician, but a black woman physician. I recall thinking that if I had been a white woman, the patient would have mistaken me for a nurse rather than a maid.

As I sat in my house crying, I thought of Helen O. Dickens, a black physician then on the medical school faculty at Penn. When I was in medical school, she often provided me with comfort and encouragement. I vividly remember one conversation in which I told her that, at times, I was made to feel inferior to my classmates and that I did not belong in medical school. She looked at me sternly and said, "The way I always figure it, for me to have gotten from where I started to where I am now, I had to be better than they were. You should start thinking that way." Dr Dickens, whose father had been a slave, graduated from the University of Illinois Medical School in 1934; she was the only black woman in her graduating class of 175. Sixteen years later, in 1950, she became the first African–American woman admitted to the American College of Surgeons. Her personal integrity and professional achievements reminded me that black women had succeeded in medicine under circumstances much more difficult than the ones I had faced.

SUFFERING IN SILENCE

My talk at the dean's retreat did prompt the department chair who had challenged me to investigate my contentions. A week after our encounter he sent me a letter in which he tried to prove, once again, that I was wrong. He stated that he had looked at all of the student evaluations over a period of several years and had not found one in which a student had complained about racial discrimination. Of course not, I thought. When I was a medical student, I too suffered in silence, fearful of jeopardizing my fragile status. Although the episode that occurred during my medicine clerkship had angered me, I had said nothing to my colleagues. I had even joined in their joking. I was afraid to confront them and show my anger. I thought it was more important to get a good evaluation from the rotation. I did not want to get a reputation as a troublemaker; I wanted to get a good dean's letter for my residency applications.

The department chair's refusal to learn from my discussion and even consider that racial discrimination affected the lives of people of colour in the medical profession did not surprise me. I have often observed that physicians find it difficult to discuss racism and its impact on their patients and colleagues. Many firmly believe that medicine is a profession that is immune from the values, mores, and prejudices of the wider society. As a black woman, I know otherwise. The chair was intent on maintaining the image of medicine as a value-neutral profession. My contentions punctured that image. The gulf between us was so wide that I decided not to answer his letter. I did not see the opportunity to respond as a proverbial teachable moment, only as a source of continued anger and frustration on my part.

HEALING THE PAIN

The physician's letter made me realize that he had been right on one count: he and most other white physicians had not heard the stories about the experiences of people of colour in the medical profession. Why? Because many of the stories are painful, and revealing one's pain involves an element of trust. As my grandmother used to say, "The three most important things that you own in this world are your name, your word, and your story. Be careful who you tell your story to." Besides, one often needs to bury pain in order to make it professionally, personally, and psychically.

Another reason why the physician had not heard these stories is that up until very recently medical historians have virtually ignored black physicians' lives and contributions. At the time of the dean's retreat, I was struggling with what would be the subject of my next book. That confrontation persuaded me to write a book on the history of black female physicians, and thus I found a way to heal a painful experience. My hope is that my book will make it more difficult for these physicians' stories to be dismissed as easily as mine had been. (In tribute to my challenger, I have thought about titling the book *We Will Not Be Dismissed.*)

The history of my professional foremothers has provided me with a source of sustenance and reaffirmation. These women have had long-standing ties to the medical profession – the first black woman physician, Rebecca Lee, received her medical degree in 1864. They have also made valuable contributions to the profession and their communities. They, and I, rightfully belong in medicine. The history of black women physicians makes plain that I will face obstacles. Although I have had a very successful career, I will always bear the subcutaneous scars of racism and sexism. The stories of my professional ancestors reveal that their lives have contained not only trauma and scars, but also strength and healing. Their lives, and mine, are testaments to the Negro spiritual "Balm in Gilead." Yes, there is a balm in Gilead to make the wounded whole.

Originally published in *Health Affairs* 19, no. 1 (January/February 2000): 164–9. Reprinted with permission.

PART FIVE

Women, Activism, and the State

A large and growing body of scholarship demonstrates women's role in shaping health care and public health services in the early twentieth century. The essays in this section explore women's health activism in the years after 1945. On both sides of the border, women physicians, nurses, and activists battled for wider access to care, asked tough questions about the kind of health system women needed and wanted, and challenged the medicalization of life processes such as birth, menopause, and death.

Women used many different strategies in their struggle to transform medicine. Writing was a particularly important and versatile tool, as the documents reprinted in Chapter 16 reveal. Michele Landsberg and Suzanne Hyers, writing in the 1970s and early 1980s, used humour to criticize the arrogance and ignorance of gynaecologists. Chuck Conconi, reflecting on his mother's experience with breast cancer in the 1940s, called attention to the ways in which families as well as patients suffered from the stigma of cancer. Like the feminists' irreverent denunciations of medical sexism, Conconi's bittersweet recollections reveal the power of the pen and the significance of speaking out.

Three essays chronicle the development of women-led campaigns for palliative care and reproductive rights. Susan Smith and Dawn Nickel (Chapter 17) show how bedside nurses who cared for dying patients developed a deep appreciation of the limits of biomedicine and led the movement to reform terminal care. Leslie Reagan (Chapter 18) describes the work of California feminists who openly (and illegally) referred pregnant women to abortionists in Mexico, while Elena Gutiérrez (Chapter 19) discusses the forced sterilizations of Mexican-origin women at a Los Angeles hospital – and the class-action suit the women filed to stop them. In all three cases, efforts to help individual women led to political movements that challenged both the authority of medical doctors and conventional thinking about gender and women's bodies.

These essays also underscore the importance of the law, and of national borders, in the struggle for health care and reproductive rights. Reagan's abortion activists defied the law by distributing information on abortionists and crossing the border into Mexico for abortions. (In the 1970s, Canadians would go "south" to the United States for legal abortions not yet available in Canada.) The border had a different meaning for Mexican-origin women, however, for stereotyped representations of Mexicans – as abortion butchers or "pregnant pilgrims" – had a powerful resonance in California politics. The essays by Gutiérrez and Reagan raise important questions about the ways in which national citizenship – along with race, class, and gender – shaped women's relationships with their physicians and as a result also shaped their health activism.

Many cultural discourses – about the authority of biomedicine, for example – crossed the border. However, future research is needed on how and to what extent national differences in health-care funding and access shaped activist agendas. For example, family doctors in Canada provided basic health services that specialists such as gynaecologists provided in the United States. Did this and other national differences affect health activists' priorities?

The feminist maxim "The personal is political" runs throughout the essays in this section, as throughout the women's movement itself. Yet, as Susan Reverby reminds us in the volume's concluding essay (Chapter 20), a tension between the personal – the "body" – and the political – the "body-politic" – remains. The conflict between the goal of enhancing the health of individual women and the goal of changing the health-care system has been at the heart of feminist health activism. Understanding this history can help health activists develop new strategies for the future.

16

Writing as Activism: Three Women's Health Documents

Popular education, or consciousness-raising, has been a central tool of women's health activism since the 1970s. The three documents reprinted here – from a Canadian women's magazine, an American women's studies reader, and a Washington, D.C., magazine – provide a sampling of popular writing on women's health. Note that while all three authors address a mostly white middle-class audience, they exhibit different approaches to and concerns about women's health.

Show Me a Gynecologist and I'll Show You a Male Chauvinist (Even If She's a Woman) (1973)

Michele Landsberg

Hop up on the gynecologist's examining table, leave your shoes on when you plunk your feet in the stirrups, call him George if he calls you Mary, and remember to ask for the culture test for gonorrhea, because it's more accurate than the Gram stain. Oh, and if he offers you a white sheet to hide your blushing femininity, immediately throw it on the floor. (You're not ashamed of your body, are you?)

That's some of the women's lib advice to gynecological patients these days. It's a little tongue-in-cheek, of course – few of us can throw off the cultural shackles of modesty and deference so lightly – but it reflects a growing uneasiness on the part of many thousands of women about the health care they are getting.

Gynecologists not only mirror many of society's attitudes to women, they also have tremendous power to influence the fate of women seeking abortions, sterilization, birth control advice and even sexual guidance. As obstetricians, they can determine how women will experience childbirth. In the most critical and vulnerable areas of a woman's physical life, key decisions may rest in the hands of gynecologists … most of whom are male (94 percent in the U.S. and probably the same here).

Most gynecologists, like most doctors, are highly skilled, and most of us have had more than one occasion to feel grateful for their competence. Nevertheless, it's getting harder and harder to ignore medicine as one of the great bastions of male authoritarianism. Or worse … one U.S. gynecologist revealed in a recent book, that he never shows his patients' files to anyone because he adorns them with comments such as "Breasts – nice!" or "Pretty as hell."

What makes men choose a profession in which they will spend most of their working lives poking around female genitalia, inner and outer, or officiating over female events like childbirth, menopause and abortion? It's not a passionate dedication to women, anyway. A quick survey of a dozen Canadian gynecologists turned up a peculiar sidelight: all of them said they had chosen their specialty out of admiration for various older doctors who just happened to be ob-gyn men.

"Gynecology, you have to remember, is a surgical specialty," said one man. "We're all trained as surgeons to begin with, and then we specialize in obstetrics and gynecology during our residence [a graduate doctor's training period at a hospital]. We're surgeons first and foremost."

Another gynecologist admitted candidly, "I'm a perfectionist, and it seemed like a surgical specialty where I could learn to perform perfect operations."

CONTEMPTUOUS ATTITUDE

It's a fact that most gynecologists, by upbringing, training and early professional experience, are Typhoid Toms who carry the infection of male chauvinism and spread it more widely than most men have a chance to. Sociological surveys have frequently pointed out that it is typically the dominating, controlling, fairly uptight kind of person who goes into medical school to begin with. Then there's the lengthy training in an almost all-male environment. The females the fledgling doctors come in contact with are mostly nurses (regarded as willing lackeys or hilarious objects of sexual aggression) or scared, ill-informed women crowding into hospital clinics because they are poor. Their teachers are mostly from another generation, and the students can hardly be blamed if they absorb a contemptuous attitude toward the women who will eventually depend on them for medical advice.

A beautiful young woman gynecologist recalled that she gave up on dating medical students because so many of them said (even on the first date), "Of course, if we get married, you'll have to give up medicine." A student was horrified that in the one lecture on female sexuality given to medical students, the professor constantly referred to the women as "chicks" and patronizingly suggested that doctors should ignore many female complaints, since so many symptoms are caused by "a poor sex life."

"Surgeons, you know, are notorious for learning to treat parts of the body rather than whole people," confided a top gynecologist. In other words, they learn to think of their patients as "that hysterectomy in 303" rather than as "Mrs Jones who's worried about the operation."

They also, in this man's opinion, unlearn any sensitivity they may have had to start with, during their arduous apprenticeship. Residents are overloaded with too many patients and too long hours, and, because they do not have total responsibility for any of their cases, they learn to see people as ciphers.

The gynecological training itself seems amazingly haphazard, consisting of a series of lectures crammed into the busy hospital schedule of the resident. There is no standardized course of study that incorporates the latest findings in female sexuality, either. Dr Lionel Tanzer, a genial Toronto Gynecologist and teacher at Toronto General Hospital, says that instruction in sexuality is in its infancy in Canadian medical schools; he doubts that the stunning revelations of sex researchers William H. Masters and Virginia Johnson are even referred to in most gynecologists' training.

Masters and Johnson, whose work has been around since 1966, revolutionized the way women understood their own bodies by proving that vaginal orgasms (as distinct from clitoral) are a myth, and that the female sex drive is at least as strong as, if not stronger than, the male. Yet the standard gynaecological reference work used in Canadian medical schools (*Principles of Gynecology*, by T. Jeffcoate) states that the vaginal orgasm is the only "mature" response, and that "an important feature of sex desire in the man is the urge to dominate the woman and subjugate her to his will; in the woman, acquiescence to the masterful takes a high place." Other out-of-date texts still referred to by many students suggest that all women are naturally frigid, and should fake orgasms in order to please their husbands. Most texts still cling to the old chestnut that females have a weaker sex drive than males.

One text that we can be sure *is* universally read by Canadian ob-gyn students is the medical journal. American studies show that the *American Journal of Obstetrics and Gynecology* is the gyn's chief and often the only extracurricular reading material. According to Canadian gynecologists, the same is true here, since there is no similar Canadian publication.

It's not the articles that are horrifying; it's the ads. Overwhelmingly, in bright color and alluring type, month after month, the ads hammer home two images of women: neurotic, whining, dishonest bitches who make life miserable for their families and their doctors ... or simpering, mindless boobs who are always voluptuously naked, prancing nude behind wispy veils, or smirking out over deep cleavages.

Here's a sampler: "She is suffering from estrogen deficiency!" wisecracks the headline. A dignified old gent cowers behind his morning paper, while his harridan of a wife shrieks at him through gritted teeth.

Her hair, predictably, is wound up in grotesque curlers. The copy advises doctors that menopausal women who don't have enough estrogen "make life miserable for everyone they come in contact with."

- *"Vive la difference!"* leers the headline, over the usual bulging cleavage. That's the come-on ... the ad itself is for a new birth control pill that supposedly caters to individual hormonal differences.
- "For the Girl Who Forgot to Remember the Other Pill." This ad is for a prenatal supplement. The assumption is that only a "girl" (not woman) stupid enough to forget her birth control pills would get pregnant.
- "When she swears she eats like a bird." The illustration for this appetite-suppressant ad is possibly the grossest of all: a silly woman's face attached to a bulbous fowl's body. The copy reminds doctors that "birds gorge themselves" and so, presumably, do women "who swear they eat like birds."
- Innumerable tranquilizer ads promise to "restore emotional health" (actually impossible by drugs alone). They encourage doctors to hand out pills as the sure cure for anxiety and depression caused by any number of real problems, ranging from breast surgery to menopause. One ad, for Valium, suggests that the doctor can easily see through the brave facade put up by his worried but docile patients. But one kind of woman, says the ad, doesn't try to hide her anxiety ... this is "the anxious psychoneurotic who has crying spells and insomnia" before her hysterectomy. This ad is a real switcheroo ... it actually manages to suggest that the dishonest women are the nice ones (unlike the gorging bird) and that the ones who don't try to hide their feelings are a bunch of neurotics.
- The only ads that depict women as independent working people (rather than dependent housewives) unfailingly refer to exotic ballerinas and showbiz types. In dozens of journals, not one ad showed a woman as a professor, or a bus driver, or, God forbid, as a doctor.

The absurd stereotypes and attitudes have inevitably had their impact on the profession. Gynecology used to attract the worst students; now it draws heavily on foreign students because fewer and fewer Americans and Canadians are interested. When the top gurus of the profession did a lengthy survey of gynecology residents, they found that the students were getting the best supervision and instruction in the operating room (where everyone can be a masked technical genius) and the worst in obstetrics and outpatients (where doctors must deal with women, not helpless bodies). The survey also showed that gynecology research lags behind the other disciplines, and has more unfilled teaching posts than any other specialty.

LEGENDARY BULLYING

The negativism also shows up in the clinics and consulting rooms. Obstetrical patients particularly are bullied: a pregnant woman with small children waiting for her at home is resigned to waiting up to two hours for a prenatal visit that may last five minutes; after her long wait on uncomfortable chairs, with not even good reading material or coffee provided, she is usually afraid to "bother" the busy doctor with questions, and may even neglect to mention important symptoms. Once in hospital, the bullying is legendary. The routines, possibly even the medical management of the birth, are designed for the doctor's convenience. The woman experiencing one of her life's most important events, and the precious first days of the newborn, are almost an afterthought.

Ask any ten women about their medical experiences, and there will be at least half a dozen gynecological horror stories, ranging from medical insensitivity and callousness at the mildest, to unashamed medical malpractice at the worst. The following cases are quoted from *The Vancouver Women's Health Survey*, published by A Woman's Place, a women's liberation group, and interviews with Toronto women:

- Just before the birth control pill first came on the market, a Toronto college student consulted a gynecologist to ask for birth control advice and help for difficult periods. She was told her menstrual troubles were due to "guilt over premarital sex" and that he could not help her with birth control. She was given a prescription to "help her periods" and didn't learn for six months that she was taking an experimental birth control pill.
- A woman with two children was suffering from a rare hormonal disorder that prevented her from conceiving a third time. A top gynecologist, delighted by the challenge, treated her for a year with a series of drugs that caused distressing side effects. Finally, she studied the syndrome in a medical library and learned that it disappears without treatment in at least 50 percent of all cases. When she told her doctor that she wanted to cease treatment, and why, his usual friendly paternalism turned to rage and he exclaimed, "This is very presumptuous of you!"
- An unmarried woman who had been living with the same man for several years told her doctor she wanted to become pregnant. He did an internal examination that was unusually painful, and it wasn't until she phoned him later to complain of painful cramps that she learned he had inserted an IUD.

- A Vancouver woman whose doctor brushed off her postnatal complaints of pain and fever for weeks ... was finally taken back to hospital. A sanitary napkin had been accidentally sutured into the birth canal.
- An unmarried woman asked her doctor for birth control pills. When he handed over the prescription, he leered, "Now you can do it as much as you like!"

That male attitudes can lead to bad medical practice is increasingly accepted as a fact within the profession itself. At a medical conference in the U.S. two years ago, one doctor admitted that, for many of his colleagues, "No ovary is good enough to leave in, and no testicle is bad enough to take out," a reference to the shocking ease with which U.S. doctors were prescribing hysterectomies, but shying away from interfering with male organs.

DOCTOR AS MORALIST

Does it happen here? Possibly, though Canadian hospitals are more tightly regulated through their tissue committees, which rule on the necessity of each operation performed. Probably more threatening to women's health care is the doctor-as-moralist. Dr Lise Fortier, a Senior Assistant on Ob-Gyn at Montreal's Notre Dame Hospital, wrote angrily in *Canadian Nurse* that "Medicine is still a man's world, and men who become physicians are not entirely free of their male prejudices nor of their desire to dominate females." Medical decisions, she says (about pain relief during childbirth, for example, or hysterectomies), are often made on the basis of the doctor's belief about women's role.

Dr Fortier writes bitterly about the difficulty of getting a tubal ligation. Individual hospitals make their own rules about this procedure, even though it doesn't come under any Canadian law. Some doctors try to force the operation on poor women or women who have had a number of illegitimate children; they may also refuse to do the operation for a woman of their own social class unless she passes the rule of 120 (multiply the age of the mother by the number of children she has had ... if the total doesn't come to 120, she is ineligible for sterilization at some hospitals).

"Ninety-five percent of the doctors should be given a Victoria Cross for their medical skills, but ninety-five percent should be shot for their sociological views" on women and abortion, according to Dr W. Gifford-Jones (the pseudonym of a Niagara Falls gynecologist, author of a good medical book called *On Being a Woman*). He maintains that

women are being driven across the border for legal abortions simply
because of Canadian medical reluctance to get involved ...

Doctors and patients are, as usual, incredibly slow to perceive the
problems and to give up old attitudes. When the Vancouver Woman's
Place did their survey, questioning a cross-section of women on their
medical experiences, a high number of women told them they felt
rushed, ill at ease, embarrassed to ask questions, or even humiliated in
their doctor's offices; an equally high number said that they would recommend their doctor to others. Either they suffered from the familiar
"Daddy can do no wrong" syndrome, or they accepted the medical
put-down as inevitable.

Doctors utterly fail to grasp that there is a problem about male attitudes. One man, the very cream of the avant-garde (whose pink and
purple consulting rooms have mirrors so women can learn about their
bodies, and where the hated stirrups have been removed) was blankly
astonished. "If a woman doesn't like her doctor's attitude, she should
just tell him so," he said, blithely ignoring his own admission that if a
woman patient questioned his treatment he would be openly angry
and "tell her off," but would swallow his anger if it was a male patient.

Even Gifford-Jones, sturdy and lonely battler for women's medical
rights, slips into male smugness now and then. His chapter on venereal
disease in *On Being a Woman* warns readers (all female, presumably)
against "being led astray by a pretty skirt" or "pure-looking teenagers"
or "call-girls." No mention at all that men can give diseases to women!
Confronted with this aberration, Dr Gifford-Jones blushes and says, "I
must have been a male chauvinist pig when I wrote that!"

Whether it's fair or not, the onus will certainly be on women to get
better and less prejudiced health care for themselves. Women's medical
self-help self-examination groups have sprung up in liberationist circles
in the U.S. In Canada, it's likely that women will become more questioning about their doctor's dicta, and less embarrassed about their own
bodies. Some will make the old mistake of picking a female gynecologist
out of the phone book, on the assumption that a woman will be more
congenial. The sad fact is that many women doctors, especially of the
older generation, survived medical school by adopting, only more so,
the hard-edged, reactionary attitudes of many of the men around them.

GYNECOLOGY GUIDE

A woman gynecologist who *is* sympathetic suggests that all women can
benefit by examining the kind of health care they are getting, and by
asking themselves how much (or how little) they are demanding. As a
pocket guide she proposes the following questions:

- Did your doctor give you a completely thorough physical checkup, including taking a family and medical history, before prescribing the birth control pill? Did he explain which type he was prescribing, and why, and how it works? Did he warn you of possible side effects?
- Do you hold back information from the doctor? Many women will worry about perfectly normal things like slight vaginal discharge due to normal sexual excitement but will hide symptoms like bleeding after intercourse.
- Does your doctor do a Pap smear and breast examination at least once a year?
- Does he explain many routine procedures, or does he wordlessly jam instruments into you? No matter what the pressures on his time, a good doctor should explain, for example, what type of vaginal infection you might have, its possible causes and cure.
- Are you ashamed to express pain or fear to your doctor? Clear the air with him or find a different doctor; you may soon find yourself suppressing important symptoms.
- Does your doctor give you options? Birth control, for example, can be handled in many different ways. A good doctor may state his medical preference, but he takes your feelings into account. He does not recommend the same method to all patients.

Are you using a gynecologist when you should be using a family doctor? Gynecologists say check with your general practitioner first – for any problem, including pregnancy, menopause, tubal ligation – and he will act as the screening agent, referring you to a gynecologist if indicated. Gynecologists are surgical specialists who dote on rare cases and problems, and openly admit that they get bored with routinely doling out pills or taking blood pressure. You should be using your family GP unless he refers you to a specialist himself, or unless you feel he is not giving you good gynecological care.

Originally published as "Your Gynecologist: Show Me a Gynecologist and I'll Show You a Male Chauvinist (Even If She's a Woman)," *Chatelaine* 46 (August 1973): 42, 64–6. Reprinted with the permission of the author.

(Not Just) Another Day
at the Gynecologist (1983)

Suzanne Hyers

My doctor is a man, fiftyish, with a heavy accent; Austrian, I think. I've been seeing him for about four years. He doesn't really appear to be at ease with my body, seeming almost shy. During the breast exam, for example, he always raises his head and shuts his eyes a bit while rolling my breast in his two hands, reminding me of a fortune teller with her crystal ball. I'm usually charmed by his awkwardness. He also gives me gynecological exams, referring always to my sex partner(s) as "he." I've never corrected him. Until now.

Last week we went through the same routine, but during our requisite, impersonal discussion (*"Are you sure you don't want birth control pills?"*), I corrected the pronouns he used. He assumed I had made an error and continued. I corrected him again and he just looked at me.

"That's right. I sleep with women." (*Long pause.*) Again, "I'm with women. I don't go out with men. I go to bed with women, a woman." He sat down.

"What exactly do you do?" he asked. (*My turn to pause, spitting out nervous laughter.*)

"What do you mean 'what do we do'? What do *you* do? It's not all that different." (*I lied.*)

He thought about that for a while and said, "I don't understand how one of you plays boy without a penis."

Wishing desperately for, but just as desperately lacking, the wit of Dorothy Parker after being handed such a line, I could only (*with a smile recognizing that this is what is meant by "the real world"*) look him in the eye and say, "We don't try to play boy."

"Then what exactly do you do?" he said. I began to get impatient.

"Well, what do *you* do whcn you don't have intercourse with your wife?" His face was a total blank. Another long pause. "Well, there's the whole area of oral sex, for example." Again, his face was a total blank – as must be, I began to think, his sex life. He sat with his head down for a while, looked up at me a few times, and said, "man-to-man,"

"I knew a homosexual once. In the war. POW camp. He always went to young boys. I never really knew what they did. I never asked."

He asked if there was anything else he could do for me; he said it was good seeing me again. And, for the first time, he shook my hand, thanking me for answering his questions.

(*I hope his wife thanks me.*)

Originally published in Laurel Richardson and Verta Taylor, eds, *Feminist Frontiers: Rethinking Sex, Gender and Society* (New York: Random House 1983), 116. Reprinted with the permission of the author.

Mom's Secret: She Was One
of the Lucky Ones – A Survivor.
But No One Was Ever to Know (1998)

Chuck Conconi

There was a festive air at last year's Race for the Cure even though the June morning was cold and overcast. I was shivering as I watched more than 35,000 runners, rollerbladers, walkers, and some people in wheelchairs head up Constitution Avenue from Washington Monument. There were even dogs – Labradors, goldens, and a pit bull wearing a yellow race T-shirt.

There were the breast-cancer survivors, proud and happy in pink T-shirts, and delegations from the military. But I was caught by the runners wearing makeshift signs in memory of "Aunt Wanda," "My daughter Jill," "Mom."

My mom had died six years earlier from lung cancer. But when I was a little boy, breast cancer almost took her, scaring me so much that it made me insecure about all my future relationships.

She had been one of the lucky ones, a breast-cancer survivor who lived on for another 45 years. She could have been at the race wearing a pink T-shirt, though the fact that she had undergone a mastectomy was a taboo subject in our family.

It was the summer of 1945. I was looking forward to my seventh birthday. It was the final months of World War II, and I had my own Army, Air Cadet, and Navy uniforms. I fought the Nazis and the Japs on the back porch of our flat behind Mom's La Frantz Beauty Shoppe. She came up with that name because someone told her a French name was good in the beauty business. I don't know where she came up with the spelling.

In my war games, I had a shiny brass whistle, an official one my Uncle Joe Menapace had brought home from the Army. My mother was close to her brother Joe, and the bond between them had grown stronger after their father died of cancer the previous winter.

In one of my earliest memories of my mother's breast cancer, we are riding with Uncle Joe in his pickup truck. I loved that truck. It was light blue and always covered with road dust. The left front fender was dented and rusting. A metal toolbox rattled around in the truck bed. We didn't own a car, so I was enjoying a rare ride along a country road, a warm breeze coming in through the open windows.

We rode in silence. While I was enjoying the passing trees and fields, I was aware of the tension in the cab. Mom, only 30 at the time, seemed distracted, unhappy about the summer ride. Uncle Joe seemed to be smoking more than usual.

The truck slowed down. "I think this is the road," he said as he shifted gears and turned into a narrow dirt lane with weeds growing between the tire tracks. Heavy brush slapped at the sides of the truck. I didn't like the spooky closeness of the undergrowth and moved closer to my mother.

We drove for another ten minutes until we came to a small clearing. Uncle Joe directed us to a path that worked its way up a hill through a grove of pine trees. The ground was padded with fallen needles. I gripped my mother's hand as we followed my uncle until we came to a small, weathered house. A black crow, perched on the porch railing, was flapping its wings and making a lot of noise. A man stepped out of the shadow of the doorway. He was wearing gray work clothes, his long sleeved shirt buttoned to the neck. He looked old and had several days' growth of beard. I pulled closer to my mother.

The man smiled at me, revealing tobacco-stained teeth. He seemed friendly. He crumbled pieces of bread into a jar lid and directed me over to the crow. He placed the lid on the porch floor, and the bird hopped down to eat. I had never been so close to a bird before.

Then the three of them sat a few feet away on wooden kitchen chairs and talked. I could hear some of the conversation. Mom told him about what she described as a "pea-size lump" she had discovered in her right breast. Her doctor, she said, thought she needed surgery. She had heard this man was an herb doctor and had ointments that could dissolve the cancer.

My uncle sat quietly smoking his Camels. He frequently ran his fingers through his thick black hair. I left the crow to stand beside Mom, leaning against her. The man went into the house and returned carrying a small, flat, round tin. He opened it: inside was a black goo that smelled like tar and sulphur. Mom was to rub it on the tumor three times a day and it would dissolve.

On the ride home, Mom clutched the tin as Uncle Joe pleaded with her to trust her doctor. Though he had taken her to who he called the "witch doctor," he was opposed to it. He warned her that she wasn't facing reality, that she was risking her life. The word "witch" got my attention. I had seen *The Wizard of Oz* and knew what witches were. Mom said she just wanted a few weeks to try the ointment.

It didn't work. The attempt to avoid surgery failed. There were constant discussions in subdued voices. But we lived in four small rooms behind the beauty shop, so I heard more of the conversations than I should have. My father and Uncle Joe and Mom's younger sister Irene, her partner in the beauty shop, argued with her. I liked having Irene around. She was a lively, fun person. But she was very serious when she warned Mom not to delay in getting the problem resolved, reminding her that she had a son to raise.

One morning a few weeks later while we were having Sunday breakfast before church, Mom told Dad, "I'm going to go through with the operation. I had a dream last night and Daddy was there. He said, 'Mary, if you don't get the operation you'll end up where I am.'"

It always scared me when my parents talked about visions and messages from the dead. They believed in the supernatural, and so did I.

I was sent to live with my Grandmother Conconi and my Uncle Mike and Aunt Erma Tamborini in Roswell, a nearby coal-mining town where my father had grown up. I loved it there. I had a big yard to play in and Uncle Mike's rabbit hound, Queenie. She was a working dog, not a pet, but she loved the attention I gave her and I loved her. It was, I decided, where I would live if I became an orphan. I thought a lot about what might happen to me, but I didn't feel there was anyone with whom I could share those fears.

I don't remember exactly how soon it was after her decision that Mom had her operation at Mercy hospital in Canton, Ohio, some 35 miles away. I also don't remember how long she was at the hospital. It seems like it was a couple of weeks. There were times I would be consumed with her and other times where a couple of days would go by that I didn't think of her at all.

I knew it was in the late summer. Next door was another boy, Albert Amicone, who was almost two years older than I and who protected me from the bigger boys. I was small for my age and had mostly spent time with my mother or playing alone. Albert and I fought the Axis powers together on the coal-mine slag heaps behind the two houses.

I know the time of year because one morning I came outside to see Albert breaking his toy gun against the apple tree that grew between the two houses. "The Japs have surrendered," he shouted. "The war is over." It was August 14, 1945.

Breast-cancer surgery was different then. There were not lumpectomies or partial mastectomies. It is possible that she went for a biopsy. As Washington surgeon Dr Katherine Alley recently told me, women had to sign a release to permit the biopsy or surgery: "They never knew when they went under if they would awaken without a breast."

Mom did wake up without a breast. They removed her right breast in what Dr Alley says was probably the Halsted radical procedure prevalent at that time. It included removal of lymph nodes and chest muscle. "It was a very mutilating operation," Dr Alley explains. "The muscle removal was down to the rib cage. But they got a better cure rate that way and saved lives."

The surgery left a disfiguring scar and caved in the right side of Mom's chest, but it did save her life. I now realize that no matter how bad the surgery was, the emotional scar for her was even deeper.

There was no reconstructive breast surgery in the 1940s. There were no prostheses, not even padded bras to help my mother mask the loss of her right breast. It was a daily struggle for her to pad her own bras and face herself in the mirror.

Mom was always meticulous about her appearance. No one saw her without makeup: her dark hair was always perfectly combed and sprayed. She was slender and was always dressed in the latest fashions available in New Philadelphia, Ohio, a town of some 17,000.

No one would ever notice that she had lost her right breast. I remember once, about a year after the surgery, rushing into the bathroom without knocking and seeing my mother in the tub. She was wearing a bra.

Throughout my childhood and most of my adult years, my mother's denial of the surgery was an unbreachable wall. If the subject came up, it was discussed in whispers and only when Mom wasn't present.

Mom changed other things in her life. We attended Mass on Sundays, usually at the 10 o'clock or 11:30 services. After her surgery, she went alone to 6:30 Mass. I slept in a small room off the kitchen and was awakened one Sunday morning by the sound of something breaking in the sink and my father trying to comfort my mother. As I listened quietly, I heard her saying with a catch in her voice, "How did she know? How did she know?"

A friend of the family – a Mrs Sciarini – had approached Mom outside the church to tell her that she had had a similar operation and to assure her that it would be all right. Dad was saying, "But Mary, she was being nice."

"I don't care," Mom shouted. "How did she know? I don't want anyone to know. Ever!"

The family was a conspiracy of silence. We respected her wishes throughout the radiation treatments that left burn scars under her arm, and throughout the periodic checkups to see if the cancer had returned. What was especially frustrating for her was her doctor saying she would have only limited use of her right arm. Mom was an artist with a comb and scissors. She had only an eighth-grade education, but her dexterity in shaping a head of hair was something to behold.

But while she desperately needed to get back to work, her right arm was failing her. As I would sit playing alone in the apartment living room, there were times I would hear her drop her scissors in the beauty shop. She would come back into the apartment and I could see that her eyes were red and she would angrily rub her arm. I pretended not to notice.

Through sheer stubbornness, Mom returned time after time to the beauty shop and eventually found that the dexterity and skills were returning. As that happened, she became more involved with her work, and what she had been through and what it had done to her emotionally slipped from my day-to-day consciousness.

I buried most of my memories about that period of my life, and it wasn't until I had left home and was married with a family of my own that I began to realize how much my father and I were also victims of her disease.

I can only guess at what the surgery did to my parents' relationship. My father adored my mother. He ran a small pool hall and had seasonal work in a nearby steel mill. Mom was the major success of his life. Once when I was in my thirties he confided that after the operation he never again saw my mother without her bra. I hated being an only child, but Dad said the doctors warned after the surgery that a pregnancy would endanger her life.

One Sunday evening in 1975, I was talking with my parents on the phone. I usually called them a couple of times a week. Mom was now 60. Her surgery was half a lifetime away. That week First Lady Betty Ford announced to the world that she had had a double mastectomy.

I wondered if my mother had noticed, but I didn't dare introduce the subject as we talked about the usual family things.

Mom seemed unusually upbeat. Then she blurted out, with a touch of pride in her voice: "Did you see the news about Mrs Ford? She had an operation just like I had."

It took me a few moments to steady my voice. "Yes, Mom. Mrs Ford is a wonderful woman." I didn't know what else to say.

"She's a brave woman," she added.

"Just like you," I said.

Originally published in *The Washingtonian*, June 1998: 43–5. Reprinted with the permission of the author.

17

Nursing the Dying in
Post–Second World War Canada and
the United States

Susan L. Smith and Dawn Dorothy Nickel

In the mid-1960s, a student nurse in California sought to understand her emotional reaction to a female patient with terminal cancer. The nurse recalled that when the patient said, "I want to die," she had kept thinking, "Well, *I* don't want to die – you *couldn't* want to die." The nurse continued: "I was always thinking that she *can't* mean that, and tighten up … In some ways, I guess it was a drain on me because I got to like her so much, maybe more than I should have, and I just felt too much I *wish* there were some way I could help her, but I didn't know how. She wanted some answers, and I couldn't give them to her."[1] This student nurse's personal and professional frustration with death and dying was echoed by other nurses. They, along with a range of health and welfare professionals, patients, and family members, concluded that the dying had become the hospital's forgotten patients.[2]

The post–Second World War era was a time of rising public and professional expectations for the health-care system. New developments, including advances in medical technology, wonder drugs like penicillin, the expansion of hospitals, and new surgical procedures like heart surgery, seemed to suggest the limitless powers of science and medicine to control and cure illness.[3] In this optimistic age, who cared about the dying – those people who could not be rescued by scientific medicine?

This essay examines the gendered nature of terminal care in the years following the Second World War, and it does so by investigating the work of nurses, most of whom were women. As historian Gerda Lerner pointed out years ago, "since so much of the actual care of the sick fell on the women, this relationship to death and illness forms an important part of the historical experience of women."[4] Women, as family members and professional health providers, directly affected the dying experience because they provided the bulk of home and institutional care. Although the issue of what to do for the dying was a concern for doctors, nurses had a greater responsibility and burden in dealing with the dying process because of their close relationship to and daily interactions with patients. Nurses were more likely than doctors to learn about patient distress.[5]

Thus, terminal care presented particular problems for nurses. "Nurses themselves need to face the reality that care for the dying is essentially a nursing problem, not a medical problem," argued American nurse Jeanne Quint (Benoliel). In the 1960s Quint conducted research on nursing students and their dying patients in California. The results of her study, *The Nurse and the Dying Patient*, presented a powerful critique of the nursing profession's failure to provide appropriate terminal care.[6]

Postwar demographic trends affected the type of nursing care required in North America. As Canadian nurse Pamela Poole explained in 1960, "Because there is a marked increase in the number of older people in our society there is also a proportionate increase in chronic and long-term illness. We live longer and we live longer with our diseases."[7] Consequently, deaths in North American hospitals were not just cases of sudden death, but of patients with chronic, long-term illnesses and degenerative diseases, such as cancer and heart disease. As sociologist Victor Marshall observed, in the modern age "death now typically comes as the culmination of a protracted period of time when the person can be viewed as 'dying.' By this, I mean that death follows a period of chronic illness in a much larger proportion of cases than in earlier times."[8] Historically, diseases such as tuberculosis had also resulted in a long dying process. However, in the postwar era, biomedical advances meant that health professionals experienced their inability to cure chronic diseases even more sharply as failure.[9]

Although there were national differences in how nurses and other professionals in Canada and the United States provided care for the dying, the similarities were more striking. Canadians focused on establishing palliative-care units within hospitals, while Americans often focused on creating free-standing hospice centres; yet they shared a similar philosophy of care. Even the terms "palliative care" and "hospice care" were used interchangeably. Palliative care is a term that may have originated in Canada in order to escape the image of poverty connoted by the term hospice.[10] Palliative care is a philosophy of terminal care that focuses on the person and not just the disease. It promotes a comfort-oriented approach to improving the quality of life for patients and family members during the dying process. It attempts to ease pain and suffering, promote dignity, provide social support, and return control to the dying person.[11] Similarly, in the words of two American writers, "hospice is a humane and caring approach to a meaningful death that begins where technology ends."[12]

Canadian and American nurses shared not only a similar philosophical approach to end-of-life care, but also a commitment to changing the status quo. Canadian nurse Sheila O'Neill, reporting on a 1973 study, emphasized that "the traditional goals of acute care hospitals – to investigate, to diagnose, to cure, to prolong life – are simply inappropriate to the individual whose need is to live as fully and as comfortably as possible until death comes."[13] American nurse Thelma Ingles stressed in 1974 that "the quality of care which dying patients receive, wherever they are – in hospitals, nursing homes, or their own homes – can be significantly influenced by nurses."[14] The growing concerns of nurses and other health and welfare professionals in the postwar years helped to launch the widespread reform efforts of the 1970s.

Nurses sought to improve end-of-life care in order to help patients through the dying process and to rectify their own sense of ineptitude and professional unease.[15] Their bedside experience led them to see first-hand the necessity for change, for their sake as well as the patients'. "The suffering, loss of self respect and self image [of the dying] witnessed by caring professionals was wrenching and caused them anguish," explained a team of American health professionals.[16]

In reforming care of the dying, nurses argued for increased autonomy and recognition as equal members of the health-care team.[17] In a field like terminal care, where the caring versus curing dichotomy was so obviously meaningless, nurses questioned a health-care hierarchy that privileged medical authority.[18] Consequently, nurses addressed the problem of dying by finding better ways to manage it.

HOSPITALIZATION OF THE DYING: A NEW SET OF PROBLEMS

Hospitals are one of North Americans' most cherished community institutions and the foundation of today's health-care system. By mid-twentieth century, hospitals had become the dominant location for acute health-care services, as they increasingly promised hotel-like qualities, excellence in care, and the benefits of modern science. People entered hospitals because they expected staff there to do something to preserve life.[19] However, as more people were admitted to hospitals, the possibility that some would die there increased. As we have pointed out elsewhere, changes in women's caregiving labour in the interwar years contributed to the dying moving out of the home and into the hospital. Thus, by 1950 half of all deaths in Canada and the United States took place in hospitals, and by the 1990s the figure was 70 per cent.[20]

In the post–Second World War years, both Canadians and Americans gained increased access to hospital care through government funding. The extraordinary growth of hospitals, both in number and in services, was inspired by government efforts to "ward off death."[21] The Hill-Burton Act of 1946 in the United States and the Federal Hospital Grant Programme in 1948 in Canada dramatically expanded hospital construction across North America, especially in small towns and rural areas.[22] At this time, differences in government support for the Canadian and American health systems were slight.

By the end of the 1950s, national differences in government funding began to affect access to health care. Throughout the decade, expanded insurance programs made it possible for more people to gain access to hospital services. A growing number of Americans purchased hospital insurance or had health insurance provided through their employers. By 1950 nearly half of all Americans had some type of private hospital insurance.[23] At the same time in Canada, millions of Canadians purchased private hospital and medical insurance. Most significantly, however, in Canada in 1957 the Hospital Insurance and Diagnostic Services Act provided publicly funded hospital coverage; this coverage was extended to all Canadian residents by 1961.[24]

Modern health care in the affluent postwar years was invested in saving lives, not in improving end-of-life care. This emphasis is clearly illustrated by the invention of the field of critical care in the 1950s. As historians Julie Fairman and Joan Lynaugh explained, "critical care accentuates and enables a tendency long noted in American health care ideology – the supremacy of curing disease and prolonging life over all other considerations. The invention of and massive investment in critical care and critical care nursing was, one could argue, simply a manifestation of the power of that ideology. Even now, critical care remains the most expensive and fastest growing type of care offered in hospitals."[25] Nurses, physicians, and hospital leaders created critical-care (or intensive-care) programs for those in danger of dying.[26] These programs "extolled the salvage rather than the failure" and therefore often excluded patients with terminal illness.[27] Although the postwar growth of intensive care for the critically ill exceeded health-care experts' expectations, programs for the terminally ill were largely absent from health-policy agendas.[28]

Within the hospital, staff time was geared more towards the workings of technology and less towards personalized care. Patients often suffered from a lack of personal attention and tactless behaviour from some personnel. For example, birthing women complained that obstetric nurses were so focused on technology that they showed a distinct lack of sympathy and compassion for them. So, too, family members and dying patients questioned the pointless, often stressful, heroic measures to prevent death.[29] Consider the case of Robert, a twenty-one-year-old student dying from leukemia in a Chicago hospital in the early 1960s. He faced his last hours with "tubes hanging out of his mouth, lips cut, infusion bottles running, the tracheotomy, the respirator – the whole works." He lay in bed bothered by a "strong light shining into his eyes" because that was one of the rules of the intensive-care unit. Furthermore, his parents were permitted only five minutes per hour for visiting. When he died, he was "alone, with tubes in his mouth, with infusion and respirator going, the light shining in his eyes – and with parents sitting outside in the waiting room."[30] As a U.S. congressional report from the mid-1980s explained, "while hospitals were once feared as 'places to die' because so little could be done to avert death, some people now fear hospitals as places to die because so much can be done."[31]

The hospital created a new set of problems for nurses, as well as patients. In the postwar years, hospitals became the standard locale for nursing services, yet too often they were impersonal and alienating institutions. Instead of providing private nursing care for a single patient in the home, as most graduate nurses had done in previous decades, nurses became part of the paid hospital workforce.[32] Although professionalizing trends meant that many "personal-care tasks" were now relegated to aides and subsidiary workers, nurses were frustrated by the hospital's stress on rationalization, efficiency, and scientific management. Nurses reported that they wanted more time for personal interactions with patients and more time to provide psychosocial bedside care.[33]

In the postwar years, health professionals frequently commented on the need to address the psychological health of patients. For example, in 1947 a Canadian doctor described the type of care needed by dying cancer patients: "Much of it must be psychotherapeutic and its success may depend on the nurse more than on any other person."[34] In the 1960s Jeanne Quint reported on "the newer psychiatric emphasis on nurse-patient relationships and communication skills."[35] The impact of psychological and psychiatric theories on the major social issues of the day affected professionals' claims for the value of caregiving and emotional support. Those who provided social services and professional care in relation to family violence, unwed motherhood, abortion, and lesbianism all turned their attention to questions of mental health and illness in defining these "social problems."[36] Indeed, ultimately so much attention was focused on the mental health needs of the dying that in 1977 a Canadian doctor warned, "We mustn't make death into a psychiatric illness."[37]

AVOIDING THE DYING PATIENT

The first voices of concern about terminal care in health-care literature appeared in the 1940s and 1950s, and suggested that nursing and medical procedures were often inappropriate. For example, in 1943, as part of a report discussing the need for national health insurance, the Canadian Medical Association indicated that hospital care for the dying must be improved.[38] In the 1950s the *Canadian Medical Association Journal* contained several articles by physicians drawing attention to the needs of dying patients and urging other physicians to coordinate care with nurses and ministers.[39] In the 1940s the *Canadian Nurse* published articles about the unique challenge of care for the dying.[40] Among American nurses, Esther L. Brown, Florence S. Wald, and Catherine M. Norris were at the forefront of raising issues of death and dying in the 1950s.[41]

Yet, because of the general cultural avoidance of death, many nurses developed ways to avoid the issue.[42] While conducting a research project on dying in the 1960s, Elisabeth Kubler-Ross, a psychiatrist at the University of Chicago, approached nurses working in a six hundred–bed Chicago hospital in order to interview dying people. She was dismayed by the nurses' denial of death. As Kubler-Ross explained, "I had gone from ward to ward, asking politely to talk to a dying patient, always receiving the answer: 'Nobody is dying on our ward.'" As she noted, "The staff really did not like to be reminded that patients were dying in their hospital."[43] According to American hospice advocates, "the nurse urgently monitored sophisticated apparatus, and because the rule was that the doctor was the one to answer questions, she learned to escape the repeated, direct, and urgent questions of patients and families by referring them to the doctor or by avoiding patient and family."[44]

In fact, nurses learned this avoidance model in nursing school.[45] Student nurses, for example, learned from experienced staff about "riding patients out" in order to avoid dealing with a death. Quint found that "nurses might make every effort to keep a patient alive until the change of shift to avoid the tedious and time-consuming task of postmortem care."[46] One student she interviewed explained how she felt about caring for a man who "was only given three or four weeks at the longest." According to the student, "He was extremely frightened and was always asking to talk about his feelings. I couldn't let him ... Every time he brought up feelings I would change the subject. If he mentioned the word *death*, I would practically walk right out of the room without giving him any warning."[47] In order to avoid this uncomfortable issue, student nurses avoided dying patients.

Students quickly learned from observation that when nurses were unsure about how to help family members, they hid from them. One student nurse, on a case in which a newborn baby was not breathing properly, remembered that "the father was walking down the hall, pacing around, asking what it was. One nurse was avoiding him, and this bothered me a lot because nothing could make him more apprehensive, you know, unless there was something the matter. Yet as a decision, I didn't know what to do, and I don't know that I would know what to do right now as to what to tell him. So I stayed in the nursery because I felt I was safer. I didn't want to go out there and be confronted by him."[48] Her nursing education left her unprepared for such encounters.

Nurses often did a poor job in caring for the dying because they were neither emotionally prepared nor practically trained in what to do. The curriculum taught them how to save lives, not how to care for the dying.[49] Another student nurse described a difficult experience caring for a critically ill patient: "I just remember feeling so helpless and not knowing. I did not know what to do, yet I knew that there had to be something that could have been done, but I was just standing there watching him die. I think this hit me hardest of all, just to stand there and look at him as if he were a guinea pig. I remember just going into the room, picking up objects and moving them around."[50]

Experiences like these could be haunting events for student nurses, for they would have felt so incompetent. However, even if they wanted to, nurses could not fully escape encounters with dying patients. Another student described an awkward caregiving situation in which she had a patient who was having convulsions as he lay dying: "The wife was crying and was going in and out of the room, and the doctor had just told the wife that nothing more could be done, and she took this well at first, but then she did finally break down and she told her husband that things weren't quite as well as he made them out to be, and I just remember feeling so helpless. I did not know what to do."[51] In such intimate, emotional situations, students repeatedly felt inadequate to the task of nursing the dying and comforting family members. Critics within nursing began to challenge the ambivalent response of nurses to dying patients.

ACCEPTING AND MANAGING DEATH

Given that no one profession had specialized knowledge about death, it became apparent that management of terminal illness required a multidisciplinary team.[52] Nurses concluded that accepting death as a fact of life had to become an underlying philosophy of their work. In turn, the issue of terminal care highlighted nurses' frustrations with their limited autonomy, a characteristic of their work that seemed especially unfair in cases where the limits of medical practice were most apparent. Thus, nurses came to question both their avoidance of death and their subordinated role in the health-care hierarchy.

The rise of hospital employment for graduate nurses in the postwar years resulted in not only a more impersonal type of patient interaction, but also greater doctor supervision of nurses' work. Historians debate whether nurses gained or lost autonomy in the transition from private duty nursing to hospital employment; however, the history of end-of-life care suggests nurses felt constrained by the hospital workplace. Although hospital work was more prestigious than home care and thus enhanced nursing's status, the gendered division of labour in the hospital environment meant that female nurses had to be obedient and closely follow male doctors' orders or face dismissal.[53]

Given the medical hierarchy, it was disillusioning for nurses to see that doctors did not have all the answers. It was a disturbing lesson, a student nurse explained to Quint. The student recalled that she had overheard physicians discuss an emergency case in which the patient had died. "The thing that struck me as a sign of weakness was the way they tried to reassure themselves that they had used the right choice of drugs. They were saying that, 'It was right, wasn't it?' and, 'Oh, yes, I'm sure that this was the correct choice.' I knew that I could not help this patient, and if anybody could it had to be the doctors. I could not, at this time, tolerate their indecision and the feelings that perhaps they were not omnipotent."[54]

After 1965, physician authority began to decline. The public grew more critical of medicine and science and questioned whether they could solve the nation's social and health problems. Biomedicine lost credibility because of what some saw as the abuse of power and trust. For example, in the wake of mounting evidence of unethical medical experiments, lawyers, judges, legislators, and academics raised questions about ethics in medical decision-making and called for increased patient autonomy. Historian David Rothman identified this transformation of medicine that occurred from 1965 to 1975 as the "loss of doctors' authority at the bedside and the expanded prerogatives of outsiders."[55]

The post-1965 transformation of medicine, along with the resurgence of the women's movement, created a fertile ground for the hospice movement. These changes meant that both the public and nurses were more willing and able to question medical authority, including in the area of terminal care. Nursing leaders and staff began to insist that nurses needed more independence and the right to do more than merely carry out doctors' orders. They believed that nurses had to talk to dying patients and should not accept doctors' claims that patients should not be told of their terminal illness.[56] In order to do so, nurses had to challenge male authority. As Quint explained in 1967, nursing's difficulties were connected to issues of sexism and "stem directly from societal norms for male-female relationships – male dominance and assumed male superiority. The nurse's historical role of 'handmaiden' serves to reinforce the subordinate female position and has been perpetuated in the minds of many practicing physicians."[57] Thus, patient care would be improved only when nurses gained more power in relation to doctors as a consequence of women in general gaining more power in relation to men.

In addition to the enormous task of addressing gender inequality within the health-care system, some nurses also began to question the cultural avoidance of death. Nurses, among other health reformers, argued that health professionals should provide patients with a peaceful death, rather than constantly attempting to avert death through the use of technology. They wanted to refocus attention on quality of life rather than on delaying death at all costs.[58] Postwar reformers were not trying to produce a "natural death" in that they still emphasized the value of the health sciences. As one nurse explained, death should be treated as a normal, human event, but "most patients need help with the dying process."[59] The actions of health reformers constituted a redefinition rather than rejection of science – one that incorporated the therapeutic value of caring, whether in the hospital, the hospice, or the home. According to early movement participants, the goal was to unite "science, faith, and caring."[60] In an era of rising rates of specialization, health reformers helped to create yet another area of expertise.[61]

Reformers focused on what could be done to alleviate suffering of the dying. They advanced a team approach to deal with pain and fear. Many physicians worried that ending curative treatment was an admission of failure and therefore resisted the new hospice philosophy.[62] However, as England's hospice leader Dr Cicely Saunders explained, the point was to challenge the notion expressed in modern medicine's lament, "there is nothing more to be done."[63] Medicine, therefore, sought to "defeat" physical pain, when it could not conquer the disease. Saunders criticized the medical profession's obsessive concern with drug addiction and urged physicians to use strong narcotics for pain relief in terminal cases. Meanwhile, nursing was to provide comfort by addressing the emotional and mental health needs of patients. Physicians, led by Saunders, created "treatment for terminal distress" and nurses emphasized the therapeutic value of "psychological nursing."[64]

Given the professional imperative to do something for the patient, nurses found that accepting death provided them with the best path to humane care. In "surrendering" to death, nurses found ways to redefine the meaning of their work. Some nurses learned these lessons during wartime service. For example, during the Vietnam War, American nurses often provided comfort to the dying, those patients dismissed by doctors who had to focus their attention on the lives that could be saved. "In Vietnam, and in other wars, women learned that nursing was more than healing," explained historian Elizabeth Norman. "The women learned to measure death and soothe the way" so that soldiers did not die alone.[65] These were lessons equally important to civilian nurses. As a Canadian nurse explained in 1963, "Even though the battle for life has been lost, the nurse who has succeeded in supporting the spirit to the end should derive lasting satisfaction."[66]

Nurses looked for ways to offer comfort and psychological support to both patients and family members, despite the protocols that called for professional distance. Ironically, Quint found that "very frequently the beginning, inexperienced nurse student in her spontaneous and human interactions with dying patients is more apt to make a positive contribution to the psychological well-being of the patients than is the more experienced nurse."[67] In one case, a nursing student began to cry while attending to a patient who kept calling out that she just wanted to die. The student did not know what to do and so she fled the room in tears. However, she soon returned and told the woman she would stay with her and hold her hand, which seemed to give the woman some satisfaction.[68] Nurses also learned to help family members by listening to them and helping them to grieve.

Nurses were inspired by and contributed to an emerging criticism of the bureaucratic ways in which modern society dealt with social problems, including death and dying. Along with reformers in childbirth, mental-health care, and health education, they joined those who were dissatisfied with authoritarian institutions and raised questions about quality of life.[69] Most notably, in 1959 Herman Feifel published *The Meaning of Death*, an influential anthology of major psychological and philosophical writings on death in Western culture.[70] Sociological analysis of death and dying expanded throughout the 1960s and included studies by nurses.[71] Throughout the postwar era, there were new publications, organizations, and conferences on the topic, including a symposium on "Death, Grief, and Bereavement" at the University of

Minnesota in 1967, international seminars in Montreal in the 1970s, and the International Work Group on Death and Dying.[72]

SAUNDERS, KUBLER-ROSS, AND
THE MODERN HOSPICE MOVEMENT

Despite nurses' bedside experiences with the dying and interest in reforming patient care, it was not until doctors, albeit women, spoke to the issue that the problem gained widespread attention. Drs Cicely Saunders and Elisabeth Kubler-Ross, two charismatic leaders, helped to identify the inappropriate treatment of the dying as a social problem in North America.

Saunders and Kubler-Ross, active medical researchers, were able to gain prominence because of their unusual backgrounds and caregiving interests. In particular, they developed their approaches by listening to patients and encouraging health professionals to learn from them. Saunders, who trained as a nurse, social worker, and physician in the 1940s and 1950s, but established her name in medicine, made patient rounds with a tape recorder. She explained in 1961: "It is a very great help, both to get permanent records of them talking about their pain and its relief, but also about their attitudes towards their illness; what they know about it, and what they find particularly hard, and it is very revealing, both for them, and about myself too when I play it back."[73] Similarly, in the early 1960s, Kubler-Ross interviewed hundreds of patients and "sat on beds, held hands and talked for hours." Out of this attention to the patient's perspective, something nurses had long encountered, Saunders developed her theory about "total pain" and Kubler-Ross her theory of the "stages of dying."[74]

Saunders became well known in the death and dying movement as the founder of the first modern hospice and the leader of an international hospice movement.[75] She visited Yale–New Haven Medical Center in 1963, and according to some in attendance, she "touched deep feelings and compelling needs in her audience. Medical students, nurses, clergy, and social workers, feeling as cut off and helpless as the patient and families, now were brought to a common mission around which they could rally. Dr Saunders's approach emphasized loving care from expert caregivers, an involved interdisciplinary staff, pain relief, spiritual help, and concern for the family during the illness and after death."[76] In 1966 Saunders and Kubler-Ross gave a set of historic lectures on death and dying at Yale University Hospital at the invitation of Florence S. Wald, who was then dean of the Yale University School of Nursing.[77] Their spark set the American hospice movement in motion.

AMERICAN HOSPICE CENTRES

American nurses and other professionals interested in reforming terminal care built a movement in the United States that drew explicitly on the approach of Cicely Saunders. In 1967 Saunders launched the St Christopher's Hospice in London, England, the first teaching and research hospice centre. Partly funded by the National Health Service and partly by foundations and patients, it was, and still is, a Christian, in-patient facility for mostly cancer patients that also provides home care.[78]

There were, of course, hospices before the 1960s, most of which were established by religious orders. Saunders herself spent time at St Joseph's Hospice in London, founded by the Irish Sisters of Charity in 1905, where she learned from the nuns about care of the dying. Saunders worked there from 1958 to 1965 studying how to control the pain of cancer patients.[79] Hospices were a phenomenon of medieval Europe that re-emerged in the nineteenth century in Europe as centres for care of the terminally ill. In the United States, by the late nineteenth century religious groups founded and maintained hospice facilities, especially for people with cancer, and as in Europe, some of these facilities survived well into the twentieth century.[80]

In the 1960s Americans experienced renewed interest in hospice care and turned to St Christopher's as the model. Thelma Ingles, a professor at the Duke University School of Nursing and a consultant with the Rockefeller Foundation, worked as a volunteer at St Christopher's in 1974 for three weeks to learn more. "I never saw 'last stand' measures used to prolong the dying process – no IV's, no respirators, no emergency surgical procedures. Temperatures, pulse, respirations, and blood pressures are not taken. But great care is directed toward keeping patients comfortable – frequent changes of position, back rubs, tucked in pillows, bathing, good mouth care, attention to the small details that mean so much."[81] Partly as a result of such visits, St Christopher's Hospice became an inspiration to programs in the United States throughout the 1970s and 1980s.

Like Saunders's hospice program, most American programs operated outside of the hospital environment, often in the form of freestanding hospice centres. In 1971 health professionals from Yale University launched the first modern hospice centre in the United States, Hospice Incorporated in New Haven. It began with a home-care service in 1973 and by 1979 opened an in-patient facility. It was funded by private foundations, including the National Cancer Institute, and received some government support. Members of an interdisciplinary group visited St Christopher's Hospice numerous times to gather ideas.[82]

American hospices, however, took many forms. In 1978 the National Hospice Organization was established with plans for hospice programs in a hundred communities, including free-standing hospice centres and independent agencies that provided hospice care for patients, whether they were at home or in a hospital. Furthermore, a few programs were located in hospitals and provided care to patients either in a hospital bed or at home. Some programs had no doctors and some no nurses. Finally, there were those programs, such as at Green Bay, Wisconsin, that operated as a separate unit within a hospital, patterned after a Canadian program.[83]

CANADIAN PALLIATIVE-CARE UNITS

Canadians were also inspired by the work of Saunders, but in contrast to the free-standing hospice centre model, they developed mostly hospital-based palliative-care programs.[84] The distinction seems to have derived from the different methods of funding health care. The American health-care system was an expensive private system, with means-tested government funding only for the needy. Meanwhile, Canada's health-care system was a provincially based government-run insurance plan. Inspired in part by the United Kingdom National Health System, the Canadian government passed the Medical Care Act in 1966, which went into effect in 1968. By 1972, once all provinces and territories had joined the program, Canadians had universal access to hospital care and medical services.[85] Therefore, health reformers in Canada tried to work within the publicly funded, hospital-based health-care system.

Reforming care of the dying within the Canadian hospital system meant that physicians were prominent in the field of palliative care. In contrast, extensive research by social scientist Cathy Siebold suggests that physicians played a minimal role in the United States.[86] The most famous Canadian physician in this field was Dr Balfour Mount, who is credited with establishing Canada's first hospital-based palliative-care unit. Focused on cancer patients, the unit opened in January 1975 at the Royal Victoria Hospital in Montreal. According to Mount, it was "a specialized unit within the general hospital, staffed by an interdisciplinary team and designed with goals aligned to the specific needs of the dying."[87] Mount argued that such units were more economically feasible than the creation of numerous hospice centres.[88] According to one physician, the success of the program at the Royal Victoria Hospital "can be at least partially attributed to Dr Balfour Mount's well-established position on the hospital's medical staff and his intimate knowledge of its power structure."[89] Furthermore, as a surgeon in one of Canada's major cities, Mount was able to attract a great deal of national attention to the project.[90]

Doctors may have played a greater leadership role in Canada than in the United States, as suggested by Siebold, but nurses in both countries were nonetheless key members of the multidisciplinary palliative-care team. Sheila O'Neill, a leader in the Canadian Nurses' Association and nursing director at the Royal Victoria Hospital, reported that the Department of Nursing at the hospital "has been actively involved in the development of the Palliative Care Service." As she explained, "no one discipline incorporates all of the skills which need to be mobilized" and so nurses worked with doctors, physiotherapists, dietitians, social workers, chaplains, and legal advisers to meet patient needs. Volunteers, many of whom had lost husbands or wives, also formed part of the caregiving team.[91]

In addition to the well-known program at Royal Victoria Hospital, there were several palliative-care programs across Canada in the 1970s. For example, the St Boniface Hospital in Winnipeg also opened a palliative-care unit under the direction of Dr Paul Henteleff. Like the unit in Montreal, it too was located in a teaching hospital.[92] In the 1970s and 1980s, over three hundred palliative-care units opened, at least half of which were affiliated with hospitals, including one in the Edmonton General Hospital in 1982.[93] Furthermore, there were other approaches to terminal care in Canada. For example, since 1980 the Victoria Hospice Society has run a hospice with its own in-patient beds and home-care programs on the grounds of the Royal Jubilee Hospital.[94]

Although reformers in Canada and the United States looked to a range of options for terminal care, certain models predominated in each nation. Americans focused on free-standing centres and Canadians on hospital units. Americans required more private funding than Canadians because of the differences in the health systems. However, despite different administrative structures for the provision of terminal care, Canadian and American nurses participated in a multidisciplinary, international movement with a shared philosophy of care.

THERE'S NO PLACE LIKE HOME

Finally, nurses' promotion of the home for end-of-life care cut across national boundaries. "In North America, one of the primary goals of palliative care is to support people to die in the comfort of their own home," explained two Canadian nurses.[95] The assumption was that home care for the dying was not only cheaper, but it allowed greater freedom and control for both patients and nurses.[96] Home care was also desired by those concerned about the limitations of hospice centres and palliative-care units, which had begun as alternative programs but increasingly assumed many of the drawbacks of bureaucratized care. While such programs promised family and friends accessibility to patients, some nurses were concerned that "death continued to be an institutionalized experience."[97]

Although female caregiving has long been a staple of the home, there was renewed interest in access to professional home care beginning in the 1950s. "Responding to rising hospital costs, an increase in chronic illness, and a rapidly growing elderly population," explained nursing historian Karen Buhler-Wilkerson, "the home was once again considered as a less costly and more appropriate locus of care."[98] Indeed, one of Canada's first funded home-care programs was established by the Herbert Reddy Memorial Hospital in Montreal in 1950, a program that purchased visiting nursing services from the Victorian Order of Nurses (VON).[99] The VON, which has a long history in home care, has been an integral part of the development of insured programs in Canada. The goal of the Memorial Hospital's program was to bring the hospital to the home for former hospital patients. The VON nurses worked under the doctor's instructions. By 1960 there was a growing awareness and interest in the development of organized home-care programs. The Canadian Nurses' Association, for example, sponsored a conference in Ottawa on home care in 1960.[100] In the United States, there was renewed interest in home care in the 1950s, and federal legislation for Medicare in 1965 increased home-care options for the elderly.[101]

Home care was also promoted by specialists in palliative care. For example, in 1976 Dr Balfour Mount argued that "the health care system should support, facilitate and assist the terminally ill in their desire to be at home while that is feasible, and to die at home if that is possible."[102] Some proponents argued that home care was cost-effective and that hospital systems continued to provide inappropriate terminal care because they were too invested in prolonging life. Some argued that home death contributed to quality of life because of the significance of personal relationships and the family in nursing the dying.[103] Dr David Skelton at the University of Alberta reported in 1982 that "in a study I did of more than 100 patients who were fully aware of their imminent death, almost 80% expressed a deep desire to die in their own homes. For many this was the home in which they had lived and loved and coped with the problems that life had previously dealt to them. It should be hardly surprising to us that so many therefore would choose to remain there to die."[104] Thus, home care seemed preferable to some dying people and health professionals.

However, dying at home still required that family caregivers be available to provide assistance. In both Canada and the United States, public funding of home care proved to be insufficient and so there were drawbacks for family members. The shift from hospital to home meant that costs were transferred from the public to the private domain with little recognition of where the burden often fell. In calculating the real costs of providing home care for the dying, one had to include the physical, emotional, social, and financial problems that could be experienced by family caregivers, many of whom were women.

Family caregivers often made personal sacrifices to provide care at home, sometimes at great cost to their own health and well-being.[105] For example, it can be emotionally very difficult for adult children to provide palliative care for their parents.[106] At times caretakers may find nursing a dying family member to be very isolating, since other relatives and friends may be uncomfortable visiting the person who is dying.[107] Consequently, although some nurses believed that there were benefits to home deaths, they recognized that there were "circumstances in which death at home may impose undue pressures on the family."[108]

In sum, the gendered dimensions of terminal care were apparent in the home, the hospice, and the hospital. In all sites, women remained closest to the bedside. Indeed, it is the continuity of women's labour that is most striking, whether family members or nurses provided care. Men, as doctors, may have been "the dominant figures in the management of health and illness," but women retained their responsibility for caregiving. Furthermore, nursing the dying revealed that gender inequality hindered patient care and led nurses to try to carve out increased power for themselves in the health-care system.[109]

WHOSE "GOOD DEATH"?

Since the Second World War, North Americans have been, in the words of Victor Marshall, "bombarded with verbiage about how people should die properly and the barriers to the good death."[110] What have been the results of the efforts of nurses and other professionals to help us to "die well"? From the 1940s through the 1960s, Canadian and American nurses joined a small reform effort to build a death and dying movement. Fully launched in the 1970s and 1980s, the movement has been known by several names, including the hospice movement, palliative-care movement, good death movement, happy death movement, and death with dignity movement.[111] The overall goal was an acceptance of death as a part of life.

Although the death and dying movement was not as visible a mass movement as the childbirth, abortion-rights, and birth control movements, its impact has been widespread. Death and dying became the topic of numerous self-help books, magazines, and support groups, as well as of professional conferences and publications. "Death control," like reproductive control, did have professional and public appeal for those people affected by terminal illness.[112]

What is the legacy of this movement? On the one hand, terminal care in Canada and the United States remains in the hands of experts whose interests still shape the experience of dying. The choices of the dying are still circumscribed and their lives affected by the needs of the caregivers who manage their bodies. From this perspective, in responding to the postwar medicalization of dying, reformers simply created "a new mode of surveillance and an extension of medical dominion."[113]

On the other hand, terminal care within institutions has become gentler and more empathetic than it was at mid-twentieth century. By addressing their own discomfort, health professionals became more open to involving patients in decisions regarding end-of-life care. Nurses, especially, saw their professional interests as linked to those of their patients. The patients benefited, they felt, from whatever increased autonomy nurses were able to secure.

Ultimately, the promotion of hospice/palliative care has implications for health care well beyond the dying. As one physician observed, "Hospice units within hospitals have a capacity – which is largely untapped – to change the very nature of hospital treatment. The essential humanism of hospice care and the value placed on an interdisciplinary network can only enhance hospital care."[114] An emphasis on continuity of care, holistic, family-centred care, and sensitivity and compassion on the part of caregivers can benefit all patients.[115]

The history of terminal care, however, reminds us of the limits of caregiving. As historian Gerda Lerner wrote in 1978 in her poignant account of her husband's death, "No one knows the experience of the dying. Even the most sympathetic observation can capture only its paltry outward manifestations." Consequently, despite the best intentions and efforts of caregivers, a person's final act remains "a death of one's own."[116]

NOTES

Authors' Note: This research was an outgrowth of a larger study on the history of palliative care and the dying in twentieth-century Canada, funded by Health Canada through the National Health Research and Development Program.

We thank the project director, Donna Wilson, for her inspiration. We also wish to thank the following for their helpful comments on earlier versions: the audiences at the Canadian Society for the History of Medicine Conference in Edmonton, Canada (2000); the Fifth International Conference on the Social Context of Death, Dying and Disposal in London, England (2000); and the reviewers and editors of this anthology.

1 Student nurse quoted in Jeanne C. Quint, *The Nurse and the Dying Patient* (New York: Macmillan 1967), 99–100 (emphasis in the original). In this and the following cases, Quint did not report the names of student nurses.

2 Ibid., x.

3 Paul Starr, *The Social Transformation of American Medicine* (New York: Basic Books 1982), 335–67; James H. Cassedy, *Medicine in America: A Short History* (Baltimore: Johns Hopkins University Press 1991), 125, 135, 139; Kathryn McPherson, *Bedside Matters: The Transformation of Canadian Nursing, 1900–1990* (New York: Oxford University Press 1996), 76, 220; Julie Fairman and Joan Lynaugh, *Critical Care Nursing: A History* (Philadelphia: University of Pennsylvania Press 1998), 22, 29.

4 Gerda Lerner, *The Female Experience: An American Documentary* (New York: Oxford University Press 1977; reprinted 1992), 148.

5 Cicely Saunders and Mary Baines, *Living with Dying: The Management of Terminal Disease* (New York: Oxford University Press 1983), 57; Quint, *The Nurse and the Dying Patient*, xii, 7, 15, 196; David Clark, " 'Total Pain,' Disciplinary Power and the Body in the Work of Cicely Saunders, 1958–1967," *Social Science and Medicine* 49 (1999): 732. On death as a problem for doctors, see August M. Kasper, "The Doctor and Death," in *The Meaning of Death*, ed. Herman Feifel (New York: Blakiston Division, McGraw-Hill 1959), 259–70.

6 Jeanne C. Quint, "When Patients Die: Some Nursing Problems," *Canadian Nurse* 63, no. 12 (December 1967): 33–6, quote 36; Quint, *The Nurse and the Dying Patient*. She published in the 1960s under the name Jeanne C. Quint and from 1970 on as Jeanne Q. Benoliel. Our attention was drawn to her research by Donna Wilson, who was principal investigator of a study in which we participated on death and dying in Canada. Donna M. Wilson et al., "Twentieth-Century Social and Health Care Influences on Location of Death in Canada," *Canadian Journal of Nursing Research* (forthcoming 2002).

7 Pamela E. Poole, "Patient Care at Home," *Canadian Nurse* 56, no. 2 (February 1960): 141.

8 Victor W. Marshall, "A Sociological Perspective on Aging and Dying," in *Later Life: The Social Psychology of Aging*, ed. Victor W. Marshall (Beverly Hills: Sage Publications 1986), 132, courtesy of Herb Northcott. See also Cassedy, *Medicine in America*, 129; and Fairman and Lynaugh, *Critical Care Nursing*, 28.

9 Sheila M. Rothman, *Living in the Shadow of Death: Tuberculosis and the Social Experience of Illness in American History* (Baltimore: Johns Hopkins University Press 1994).

10 Helen Hays, "Palliative Care: History and Impact in Canada," *Bioethics Bulletin* 2, University of Alberta Hospitals (April 1989): 2; Harry Van Bommel, *Choices: For People Who Have a Terminal Illness, Their Families, and Their Caregivers* (Toronto: NC Press 1987), 60; Mary Pickett, Mary E. Cooley, and Debra B. Gordon, "Palliative Care: Past, Present, and Future Perspectives," *Seminars in Oncology Nursing* 14, no. 2 (May 1998): 87.

11 David A.E. Shephard, "Principles and Practice of Palliative Care," *Canadian Medical Association Journal* 116 (5 March 1977): 522–6; Marshall, "A Sociological Perspective on Aging and Dying," 135–6, 143; Hays, "Palliative Care," 1.

12 Joseph R. Proulx and Elizabeth J. Colerick, "The Hospice Movement: A Management Perspective," in *Hospice U.S.A.*, ed. Austin H. Kutscher et al. (New York: Columbia University Press 1983), 27.

13 Sheila O'Neill, "Palliative Care at the Royal Victoria Hospital," *Canadian Nurse* 74, no. 10 (November 1978): 3.

14 Thelma Ingles, "St Christopher's Hospice," *Nursing Outlook* 22, no. 12 (December 1974): 759.

15 Quint, *The Nurse and the Dying Patient*, 66, 70, 108, 164, 165, 196; Vivian Smith, "Going Gently," *Canadian Living* 21, no. 8 (August 1996): 54.

16 Zelda Foster, Florence S. Wald, and Henry J. Wald, "The Hospice Movement: A Backward Glance at Its First Two Decades," *New Physician* 27, no. 5 (May 1978): 21–2, quote 22.

17 Cathy Siebold, *The Hospice Movement: Easing Death's Pain* (New York: Twayne Publishers 1992), 85.

18 Dianne Dodd and Deborah Gorham, eds, *Caring and Curing: Historical Perspectives on Women and Healing in Canada* (Ottawa: University of Ottawa Press 1994).

19 Cassedy, *Medicine in America*, 138; McPherson, *Bedside Matters*, 187.

20 Susan L. Smith and Dawn D. Nickel, "From Home to Hospital: Parallels in Birthing and Dying in Twentieth-Century Canada," *Canadian Bulletin of Medical History* 16, no. 1 (1999): 50, 55; Wilson et al., "Twentieth-Century Social and Health Care Influences on Location of Death in Canada."

21 Marshall, "A Sociological Perspective on Aging and Dying," 126.

22 Cassedy, *Medicine in America*, 138; McPherson, *Bedside Matters*, 187, 208.

23 Fairman and Lynaugh, *Critical Care Nursing* 22, 27–8, 39; Cassedy, *Medicine in America*, 131.

24 Eugene Vayda and Raisa B. Deber, "The Canadian Health-Care System: A Developmental Overview," in *Canadian Health Care and the State: A Century of Evolution*, ed. C. David Naylor (Montreal and Kingston: McGill-Queen's University Press 1992), 125–40, esp., 127; Meluccia M. Di Marco and Janet

L. Storch, "History of the Canadian Health Care System," in *The Canadian Health Care System*, ed. Donna M. Wilson (Edmonton: Donna M. Wilson 1995), 9.

25 Fairman and Lynaugh, *Critical Care Nursing*, 114.

26 Ibid., 1–3, 11, 13. On the development of emergency medicine in the postwar years, see Mickey S. Eisenberg, *Life in the Balance: Emergency Medicine and the Quest to Reverse Sudden Death* (New York: Oxford University Press 1997).

27 William Mosenthal and David D. Boyd, quoted in Fairman and Lynaugh, *Critical Care Nursing*, 14.

28 Fairman and Lynaugh, *Critical Care Nursing*, 2–3, 14.

29 Judith Walzer Leavitt, " 'Strange Young Women on Errands': Obstetric Nursing between Two Worlds," *Nursing History Review* 6 (1998): 3; Cassedy, *Medicine in America*, 139, 145, 146.

30 Elisabeth Kubler-Ross, "Dying with Dignity," *Canadian Nurse* 67, no. 10 (October 1971): 35.

31 Congressional Office of Technology Assessment report, quoted in Cassedy, *Medicine in America*, 146.

32 Barbara Melosh, *"The Physician's Hand": Work Culture and Conflict in American Nursing* (Philadelphia: Temple University Press 1982), chap. 5; McPherson, *Bedside Matters*, chap. 6; Fairman and Lynaugh, *Critical Care Nursing*, 68.

33 McPherson, *Bedside Matters*, 223, 227–30; Fairman and Lynaugh, *Critical Care Nursing*, 41, 49, 50; Cassedy, *Medicine in America*, 139; Leavitt, " 'Strange Young Women on Errands,' " 8–10.

34 George S. Young, "The Late Cancer Case," *Canadian Nurse* 43, no. 3 (March 1947): 196.

35 Quint, *The Nurse and the Dying Patient*, 29. See also Fairman and Lynaugh, *Critical Care Nursing*, 96.

36 Linda Gordon, *Heroes of Their Own Lives: The Politics and History of Family Violence* (New York: Viking 1988), 226; Donna Penn, "The Meanings of Lesbianism in Post-War America," *Gender and History* 3 (Summer 1991): 190–203; Rickie Solinger, *Wake Up Little Susie: Single Pregnancy and Race before Row V. Wade* (New York: Routledge 1992), chap. 3; Leslie J. Reagan, *When Abortion Was a Crime: Women, Medicine, and Law in the United States, 1867–1973* (Berkeley: University of California Press 1997), chap. 8.

37 John Scott of Royal Victoria Hospital in Montreal, quoted in Shephard, "Principles and Practice of Palliative Care," 523.

38 Canadian Medical Association, "A Submission Respecting Health Insurance," *Canadian Medical Association Journal* 48, no. 5 (1943): 383–94.

39 See, for example, F. Hebb, "The Care of the Dying," *Canadian Medical Association Journal* 65 (1951): 261–3.

40 R. Ostic, "Nursing Care of the Chronically Ill," *Canadian Nurse* 36, no. 2 (1940): 97–9; J.C. Meakins, "The Future of Nursing," *Canadian Nurse* 41, no. 10 (1945): 784–7.

41 Catherine M. Norris, "The Nurse and the Dying Patient," *American Journal of Nursing* 55 (October 1955): 1214–17; Quint, *The Nurse and the Dying Patient*, 11; Siebold, *The Hospice Movement*, 57.

42 Quint, *The Nurse and the Dying Patient*, 247–8.

43 Kubler-Ross, "Dying with Dignity," 31.

44 Foster, Wald, and Wald, "The Hospice Movement," 21.

45 Quint, *The Nurse and the Dying Patient*, 45, 73.

46 Ibid., 34.

47 Student nurse quoted in ibid., 191.

48 Student nurses quoted in ibid., 45.

49 Ibid., 20, 37, 176.

50 Student nurse quoted in ibid., 31.

51 Student nurse quoted in ibid., 130.

52 Siebold, *The Hospice Movement*, 36; Pickett, Cooley, and Gordon, "Palliative Care," 87.

53 Melosh, "The Physician's Hand," chap. 5; Susan M. Reverby, *Ordered to Care: The Dilemma of American Nursing, 1850–1945* (Cambridge: Cambridge University Press 1987), chap. 10; McPherson, *Bedside Matters*, chap. 6; Leavitt, " 'Strange Young Women on Errands,' " 13, 18; Fairman and Lynaugh, *Critical Care Nursing*, 71, 73; Margarete Sandelowski, *Devices and Desires: Gender, Technology, and American Nursing* (Chapel Hill: University of North Carolina 2000), chap. 5.

54 Student nurse quoted in Quint, *The Nurse and the Dying Patient*, 127.

55 David J. Rothman, *Strangers at the Bedside: A History of How Law and Bioethics Transformed Medical Decision Making* (New York: Basic Books 1991), 1–3, quote 4.

56 Quint, *The Nurse and the Dying Patient*, 80, 224, 232, 248, 249.

57 Ibid., 233.

58 Ibid., 134; Foster, Wald, and Wald, "The Hospice Movement," 22; Daniel Callahan, "Death and the Research Imperative," *New England Journal of Medicine* 342, no. 9 (2 March 2000): 655, courtesy of Dorothy Tovell; Sandelowski, *Devices and Desires*, 9.

59 Ingles, "St Christopher's Hospice," 762.

60 Foster, Wald, and Wald, "The Hospice Movement," 21.

61 Shephard, "Principles and Practice of Palliative Care," 523; Starr, *The Social Transformation of American Medicine*, 356; Cassedy, *Medicine in America*, 136; David Field, "Awareness and Modern Dying," *Mortality* 1, no. 3 (November 1996): 255+, retrieved 28 February 2000 from the University of Alberta Library Databases (Academic Search Fulltext Elite) on the World Wide Web: http://www.library.ualberta.ca/library_html/databases/elite.html.

62 Siebold, *The Hospice Movement*, 125, 152.

63 Clark, "'Total Pain,' Disciplinary Power and the Body," 733.

64 Saunders and Baines, *Living with Dying*, v; Quint, *The Nurse and the Dying Patient*, 11, 29, 40, 245; Clark, "'Total Pain,' Disciplinary Power and the Body," 731; Sandelowski, *Devices and Desires*, 116.

65 Elizabeth Norman, *Women at War: The Story of Fifty Military Nurses Who Served in Vietnam* (Philadelphia: University of Pennsylvania Press 1990), 38.

66 L. Richardson, "Nursing Care of the Patient with Advanced Cancer," *Canadian Nurse* 59, no. 4 (1963): 355–9.

67 Quint, *The Nurse and the Dying Patient*, 206.

68 Ibid., 98.

69 Emily K. Abel, "The Hospice Movement: Institutionalizing Innovation," *International Journal of Health Sciences* 16, no. 1 (1986): 71–85; Marshall, "A Sociological Perspective on Aging and Dying," 133.

70 Feifel, *The Meaning of Death*.

71 Raymond G. De Vries, "Birth and Death: Social Construction at the Poles of Existence," *Social Forces* (June 1981): 1074–93; Janet Harvey, "The Technological Regulation of Death: With Reference to the Technological Regulation of Birth," *Sociology* (November 1997): 719–35, courtesy of Herb Northcott; Quint, *The Nurse and the Dying Patient*.

72 Barney G. Glaser and Anselm L. Strauss, *Awareness of Dying* (Chicago: Aldine 1965); Robert Blauner, "Death and Social Structure," *Psychiatry* 29 (1966): 378–94; Quint, "When Patients Die," 36 n. 12; Robert J. Lifton, *Death in Life: Survivors of Hiroshima* (New York: Random House 1967); Elisabeth Kubler-Ross, *On Death and Dying* (New York: Macmillan 1969); Gerda Lerner, *A Death of One's Own* (New York: Simon and Schuster 1978; reprint, University of Wisconsin Press 1985); Lynn H. Lofland, *The Craft of Dying: The Modern Face of Death* (Beverly Hills, Calif.: Sage 1978); Shephard, "Principles and Practice of Palliative Care," 522; Foster, Wald, and Wald, "The Hospice Movement," 24; Philip Aries, *The Hour of Our Death* (New York: Knopf 1981); Marshall, "A Sociological Perspective on Aging and Dying," 131, 133, 135.

73 Saunders quoted in Clark, "'Total Pain,' Disciplinary Power, and the Body," 729.

74 Clark, "'Total Pain,' Disciplinary Power, and the Body," 729. See also Kubler-Ross, "Dying with Dignity," 31; and Saunders and Baines, *Living with Dying*, v.

75 Gill Oliver, "Hospice Pioneer," *Nursing Standard* 13 (11 August 1999): 18; Clark, "'Total Pain,' Disciplinary Power and the Body," 729. Clive Seale argues that "the phenomenon is largely one of the English speaking world." Clive Seale, *Constructing Death: The Sociology of Dying and Bereavement* (Cambridge: Cambridge University Press 1998), 114.

76 Foster, Wald, and Wald, "The Hospice Movement," 22.

77 Siebold, *The Hospice Movement*, 56–7.

78 Saunders, *The Hospice Movement*, v; Foster, Wald, and Wald, "The Hospice Movement," 23.

79 Clark, " 'Total Pain,' Disciplinary Power and the Body," 729; Hays, "Palliative Care," 1.

80 Siebold, *The Hospice Movement*, 3–4, 14, 21, 23; Foster, Wald, and Wald, "The Hospice Movement," 23.

81 Ingles, "St Christopher's Hospice," 759–63, quote 760.

82 Foster, Wald, and Wald, "The Hospice Movement," 21, 23, 24.

83 Ibid.; De Vries, "Birth and Death," 1086; Pickett, Cooley, and Gordon, "Palliative Care," 87; Hays, "Palliative Care," 1.

84 Shephard, "Principles and Practice of Palliative Care," 525; Kelli I. Stajduhar and Betty Davies, "Death at Home: Challenges for Families and Directions for the Future," *Journal of Palliative Care* 14, no. 3 (1998): 8–14, esp. 9.

85 Vayda and Deber, "The Canadian Health-Care System," 125, 126, 128, 137; Di Marco and Storch, "History of the Canadian Health Care System," 10.

86 Siebold, *The Hospice Movement*, 74, 125, 152.

87 Balfour M. Mount, "The Problem of Caring for the Dying in a General Hospital; The Palliative Care Unit as a Possible Solution," *Canadian Medical Association Journal* 115 (17 July 1976): 120.

88 Balfour Mount letter to the editor, *Canadian Medical Association Journal* 117 (9 July 1977): 14–15.

89 A. Abyad, "The Hospice Movement: Growth as an Alternative, Not Integrated Movement," *Medical Interface*, June 1994: 130.

90 Thanks to Dr Peter Warren, University of Manitoba, for this observation.

91 Ingles, "St Christopher's Hospice," 763; O'Neill, "Palliative Care at the Royal Victoria Hospital," 3.

92 Hays, "Palliative Care," 1.

93 Ibid., 2; Siebold, *The Hospice Movement*, 183; Smith, "Going Gently," 53–4.

94 Ibid., 55.

95 Stajduhar and Davies, "Death at Home," 8.

96 Ibid., 9.

97 Ibid.

98 Karen Buhler-Wilkerson, "Home Care the American Way: An Historical Analysis," *Home Health Care Services Quarterly* 12, no. 3 (1991): 5–17, quote 12. See also Karen Buhler-Wilkerson, *No Place Like Home: A History of Nursing and Home Care in the United States* (Baltimore: Johns Hopkins University Press 2001), chaps 8 and 9.

99 Dorothy Pringle and Donna Roe, "Voluntary Community Agencies: VON Canada as Example," in *Canadian Nursing Faces the Future*, ed. Alice J.

Baumgart and Jenniece Larsen (St Louis: Mosby-Year Book 1992), 611–26; Wilma A. Howes, "Taking the Hospital Home," *Canadian Nurse* 47, no. 10 (October 1951): 721–2.

100 "What Is the V.O.N.?" *Canadian Hospital* 39 (September 1943): 23–5, 52; Pamela E. Poole, "Patient Care at Home," *Canadian Nurse* 56, no. 2 (February 1960): 141.

101 Buhler-Wilkerson, "Home Care the American Way," 12.

102 Mount, "The Problem of Caring for the Dying," 120.

103 Stajduhar and Davies, "Death at Home," 9; S. Malkin, "Care of the Terminally Ill at Home," *Canadian Medical Association Journal* 115 (17 July 1976): 129–30; Abyad, "The Hospice Movement," 131.

104 David Skelton, "The Hospice Movement: A Human Approach to Palliative Care," *Canadian Medical Association Journal* 126 (1 March 1982): 556–8, quote 557.

105 Gail O'Neill and Margaret M. Ross, "Burden of Care: An Important Concept for Nurses," *Health Care for Women International* 12 (1991): 111–21; Margaret M. Ross, "Spousal Caregiving in Later Life: An Objective and Subjective Career," *Health Care for Women International* 12 (1991): 123–35, esp. 129.

106 Janice Thibodeau, "Caring for a Parent: A Phenomenologic Inquiry," *Nursing Outlook* 41, no. 1 (January/February 1993): 15–19.

107 Anna O'Kinsky, "Grandmom's Blessing," *American Journal of Nursing* 96, no. 1 (1996): 5–57, esp. 57.

108 Stajduhar and Davies, "Death at Home," quote 9, see also 11.

109 Starr, *The Social Transformation of American Medicine*, 22. See also Emily K. Abel, "A 'Terrible and Exhausting' Struggle: Family Caregiving during the Transformation of Medicine," *Journal of the History of Medicine and Allied Sciences* 50 (October 1995): 478–506; and Seale, *Constructing Death*, 115.

110 Marshall, "A Sociological Perspective on Aging and Dying," 136.

111 Ibid., 135; De Vries, "Birth and Death," 1086; Foster, Wald, and Wald, "The Hospice Movement," 21–4.

112 Quint, "When Patients Die," 35; Barbara J. Logue, "Taking Charge: Death Control as an Emergent Women's Issue," *Women and Health* 17, no. 4 (1991): 97–121; Callahan, "Death and the Research Imperative," 654.

113 Clark, "'Total Pain,' Disciplinary Power and the Body," 734. See also Tony Walter, *The Revival of Death* (London and New York: Routledge 1994); Field, "Awareness and Modern Dying"; Bethne Hart, Peter Sainsbury, and Stephanie Short, "Whose Dying? A Sociological Critique of the 'Good Death,'" *Mortality* 3, no. 1 (March 1998): 65+, retrieved 28 February 2000 from the University of Alberta Library Databases (Academic Search Fulltext Elite, renamed Academic Search Premier) on the World

Wide Web: http://www.library.ualberta.ca/library_html/databases/ elite.html.

114 Abyad, "The Hospice Movement," 131
115 Quint, *The Nurse and the Dying Patient*, 252; Saunders and Baines, *Living with Dying*, 2; Pickett, Cooley, and Gordon, "Palliative Care," 87, 91.
116 Lerner, *A Death of One's Own*, 8.

18

Crossing the Border for Abortions: California Activists, Mexican Clinics, and the Creation of a Feminist Health Agency in the 1960s

Leslie J. Reagan

After five years of organizing for abortion rights, Patricia Maginnis decided to break the law. In June 1966, she passed out a leaflet in San Francisco that named physicians in Mexico and Japan who performed abortions. With this daring act, Maginnis inaugurated the first open (and illegal) abortion referral service in the United States.[1] What began in protest of a new anti-abortion campaign instigated by California authorities resulted in the development of an underground feminist health agency for women's rights and women's health. The list of abortion providers took on a life of its own. As demand for the "List" soared, Maginnis and her comrades created mechanisms for regulating illegal abortion practices in order to ensure that they were sending women to safe practitioners. To carry out these illegal activities, they founded a new organization, the Association to Repeal Abortion Laws (ARAL).

American women were indeed desperate for abortions, but as ARAL's success demonstrates, that did not preclude them from wielding collective clout in the underground world of illegal abortion – even across an international border. The criminal status of abortion, which left the practice open to anyone, skilled or not, and patients unprotected and fearful, made the regulation of practitioners essential. The vacuum created by the lack of state and professional regulation combined with the availability of Mexican providers contributed to the power of ARAL as a feminist, non-governmental organization in the United States.

Historians of the 1960s neglect the rich history of health-care activism and the rise of alternative medical institutions, of which Maginnis and ARAL are prime examples.[2] ARAL was a forerunner of the women's health movement, which by 1974 consisted of over one thousand women's health services. As an early and outspoken advocate for women's right to abortion, Maginnis helped shape the feminist perspective on abortion law and practice. Moreover, ARAL's openly illegal activities contributed to the growing national awareness that the law was helpless to stop the practice of abortion. In 1969, when activists from around the country founded the National Association for Repeal of Abortion Laws (NARAL), they adopted ARAL's name and political perspective.[3]

As the California activists took on unanticipated bureaucratic functions, they acted in essence as a feminist health agency that combined the responsibilities of a medical licensing board and a public health office. On the one hand, ARAL educated practitioners and monitored the quality of illegal abortionists. On the other hand, it provided women with information about the prevention of pregnancy and the names of competent abortion specialists and established clinics that offered inexpensive laboratory and medical services.

Yet the feminist vision of this "agency," its opposition to century-old criminal abortion law, and its commitment to the transformation of the health-care system made it unlike a conventional state-run public health agency. This effort to obtain adequate medical services was embedded within a militant movement for women's rights and sexual freedom. In the eyes of ARAL and its precursor and educational counterpart, the Society for Humane Abortion (SHA), women's rights and good health care went hand in hand; one was not more important than the other. One of SHA-ARAL's goals was the normalization of abortion in medical practice; the activists sought to drain abortion of politicized and stigmatized meanings, to make it a medical procedure like any other. At the same time, they pressed for a reversal in the power of physicians and patients: female patients rather than (male) physicians or hospital committees should make decisions about abortions and other health-care issues affecting women.

American law forced hundreds of thousands of law-abiding women to cross the line into the illegal world to find an abortion; ARAL's "List" pointed them to Mexico. Women crossing the border for abortions underlines an important point about the historical relationship between Mexico and the United States: Mexico served as a resource for Americans. ARAL is an example of the nearly unexamined tradition of Americans seeking health services across the border. Mexico provided more than illegal medical services, however; it also provided symbols for American political debates and contributed to changing abortion law in the United States. The scholarly literature on the

Mexican-American border since the 1970s concentrates on the economic relationship between the two countries and the use of Mexican workers by American manufacturing industries, as do recent studies of Mexican women on the border.[4] Yet Mexico also attracted masses of Americans who sought solutions to personal problems and access to medical and other services unavailable in the United States. Furthermore, the advantages of living next door to a poor, subordinate neighbour were available to all Americans, not just those who lived literally on the border. In this case, the "border" stretched to Iowa, Virginia, Oklahoma, and New York; women from all over the United States crossed into Mexico for abortions.

At a time when the topic of abortion was nearly completely suppressed in the public arena, Maginnis moved discussion of abortion law reform from professional meetings to the streets.[5] In 1961 Assemblyman John T. Knox presented the first reform bill in California to permit therapeutic abortions for a broader range of reasons, including rape, incest, and congenital fetal defects.[6] Maginnis initiated a petition supporting the bill and collected a thousand signatures. She and her partner, Robert Bick, also surveyed a cross-section of the San Jose population and discovered the general public's underlying support for "good medical care for abortion."[7] Despite her legwork on behalf of the Knox bill, Maginnis soon repudiated reform laws because of their restrictiveness. She appraised proposed legal reforms from the perspective of women who needed abortions, particularly women who were not wealthy; in this, she was unique in the early 1960s. She became the first to demand complete repeal of the nation's criminal abortion laws.[8] In 1962 she founded the Citizens' Committee for Humane Abortion Laws (later renamed the Society for Humane Abortion), which advocated repeal.[9] Maginnis's activism developed within a larger countercultural political milieu and radical health movement in the San Francisco Bay Area, but she was singular in her untiring commitment to legal abortion for women.[10] By 1965 SHA had two hundred members,[11] two of whom – Rowena Gurner and Lana Clarke Phelan – joined Maginnis in devoting themselves to the cause.

The leaders of this California effort were white working women who had all had illegal abortions. Their backgrounds remind us that second wave feminism arose from the working class as well as the middle class. Patricia Maginnis was from a large, not very well off Catholic family from Oklahoma, attended San Jose State College on the GI bill, and supported herself as a laboratory technician. Indeed, Maginnis's manner and look were the opposite of the privileged woman, although she learned to wear "demure" pastel dresses as demanded by "the strategist" Gurner. Maginnis was a militant renegade and outspoken, particularly against the Catholic Church in which she was raised. Not only was she not a member of the respected medical, legal, or clerical professions, but she also regularly attacked the hypocrisy and sexism of all three. Gurner was from a Jewish family in New York. When she had her abortion, she had to rush back to her job as a bookkeeper or lose it. Phelan, who joined Maginnis in 1965, grew up poor in the South during the Depression; at the time she joined SHA, she was married to a police officer and working as a secretary in Los Angeles.[12]

Maginnis moved from collecting petitions and lobbying to breaking the law in 1966, when California state medical authorities accused nine highly respected San Francisco physicians who had performed therapeutic abortions of participating in a criminal act.[13] Maginnis and Gurner then decided to publicize their secret referrals to Mexican abortionists in order to provoke an arrest and generate a test case challenging the criminal abortion laws. The activists did not undertake lawbreaking lightly but felt driven to act by political events. Like everyone else who publicly urged revision of the nation's abortion laws in the early 1960s, Maginnis and Gurner were regularly approached by women and men searching for abortionists. Gurner "had a few names of people in Tijuana that she would write down on a piece of paper, and stick it in an envelope with no return address, and she would go to another town, and mail it."[14] The secrecy of these early mailings reveals the activists' anxiety about the law. By the mid-1960s, however, bolder action seemed necessary.

The political conditions of the period produced similar strategies around the country, nearly simultaneously. What became known as Jane in Chicago and the Clergy Consultation Service (CCS) in New York developed similar abortion referral services the year after Maginnis hit the streets with her "List." Jane activists, however, never sought arrest, were more secretive, and, eventually, performed abortions themselves. CCS, in contrast, was as public as ARAL but used its religious base to assert the legitimacy of abortion and the need for legalization. Furthermore, CCS required that women speak with individual clergy first about their "problem" pregnancies before being given referrals, a practice Maginnis labelled "patronizing." CCS chapters dotted the country, including Atlanta, Cleveland, Detroit, and Los Angeles. Within a year or two, local chapters of Planned Parenthood, the Young Women's Christian Association, the National Organization for Women, and other groups all made abortion referrals.[15]

In June 1966 Maginnis passed out the first "List of Abortion Specialists" in San Francisco.[16] In July she escalated the attack on California law by offering to teach women how to perform their own abortions. Teaching the classes, Maginnis recalled, was one of Gurner's "brilliant" ideas. Furthermore, hoping to goad police into arresting her, Maginnis advertised her plan to give this information during an official hearing of two of the physicians under investigation for performing therapeutic abortions.[17] Maginnis passed out leaflets, a "do-it-yourself" kit, and began conducting "classes."[18]

Prosecutors did not pursue Maginnis in the way that she wished, but media attention garnered an immediate influx of new "sympathizers" and attracted hundreds of women clamouring for classes and the "List."[19] By November, Maginnis and Gurner had taught twenty-five classes in the San Francisco Bay Area and soon offered classes elsewhere in California and in Ohio, New Mexico, and Washington, D.C. Class size ranged from "15 women of various ages and race" in Berkeley to 150 in Washington, D.C. Women predominated among the "students," but men also attended. Students included people seeking abortions, reporters, and police officers; the activists welcomed all.[20]

Although the racial, class, and educational backgrounds of the women who went to ARAL classes or used the "List" cannot be reconstructed, there was multiracial and cross-class support for both. The women who used ARAL represented "a very widespread cross-section of economic strata," Maginnis reports, "from destitute to rich. Poor women saved their grocery money" to pay for abortions. At an early press conference advocating legalization, Maginnis, a white woman, was joined by Audrey Smith, an African-American organizer among poor blacks in San Francisco.[21] A Spanish-language leaflet advertised classes to San Francisco's Latina community, and Chicanas used the "List."[22]

The ARAL abortion class was a model of feminist health and political education. Maginnis argued for repeal of the nation's abortion laws, taught female anatomy and reproduction, and passed around contraceptives while explaining their proper use and effectiveness. Finally, as promised, she passed out materials detailing how a woman could induce an abortion using her own fingers, gauze, syringes, and other items. However, Maginnis was never a romantic about these methods. In fact, she strongly advised against self-inducing an abortion. Foreshadowing the emphasis of the women's liberation movement on "the personal is political," Maginnis told audiences of her own self-induced abortions and subsequent hospitalizations. Not only had she had three illegal abortions, but Maginnis had also seen women injured as a result of illegal abortions and women forced to carry unwanted pregnancies to term. Furthermore, Maginnis advised women to remain silent about their abortions and to demand a lawyer if interrogated by hospital staff or police.[23] If a woman pursued the self-induced route, Maginnis warned, she was almost guaranteed a week in the hospital. "The cost is as much as going to Mexico," she observed.[24] Maginnis urged her students to go to an abortion specialist instead and passed out the "List" in her classes. Plenty of women took her advice and used the "List" to find a trustworthy specialist; some met at an abortion class and went to Mexico together.[25]

ARAL asked women who used the "List" to help with the work at the office, to write letters to their legislators, and to monitor the specialists. By asking women who had had abortions to contribute in both practical and political ways, ARAL helped teach women that their need for an abortion was not only a personal problem but a political one as well. For women to get the "List," initially given freely, ARAL began to ask for a five-dollar contribution or two hours of work at the San Francisco office.[26]

The mimeographed "List of Abortion Specialists" included names of abortion providers, directions for contacting them, fees, descriptions of the procedure, and instructions on how the woman should prepare herself beforehand (not eating eight hours before the scheduled procedure, cutting her pubic hair, etc.). Although the "List" included information on abortion specialists in Japan, Canada, Sweden, and elsewhere, most women went to Mexico. The 1968 "List" advised American travellers to Mexico to "carry with you a toothbrush, Spanish-English dictionary, oral fever thermometer, sanitary napkins and belt … sturdy walking shoes," and a "map."[27] Maginnis and her comrades constantly updated the information based on reports received from women who used the "List" and distributed it nationwide.

American women had been travelling to Tijuana for abortions since at least the early 1950s. Maginnis herself used a practitioner there.[28] The abortion business apparently grew in Mexico during the 1940s and 1950s when police and prosecutors in the United States cracked down and closed established abortion clinics across the country.[29] American authorities even reached across the border to impose their laws. In the early 1950s, the San Diego district attorney identified abortionists in Mexico and pressed his Mexican counterparts to arrest them. San Diego police also restricted access to abortion by refusing to allow young women (under eighteen years) to cross the border without parental permission.[30] Although Americans had long gone to Mexico for abortions, Tijuana symbolized danger. As one woman who wrote ARAL in 1967 declared, "I am not willing to submit myself to the dangers of the renown 'abortion mills' of Tijuana." She asked instead for a "licensed physician."[31] The "List" helped women like her find the competent and avoid the dangerous.

Abortion, like prostitution and quick divorces, was a service that Americans wanted but could not obtain legally or easily at home. Since the 1930s, Americans had travelled to Mexico for medical treatments banned in the United States, including cancer cures and operations for sexual renewal.[32] At the end of the twentieth century, the medical business across the border continued to flourish. Mexican border towns sell pharmaceutical drugs, which require prescriptions in the United States, over-the-counter at greatly reduced prices. Historically, Americans crossed into Mexican border towns for more mundane services as well. San Diego residents went to Tijuana to have their hair cut and styled, clothing made, and cars fixed at half the price.[33] Like haircuts, illegal abortions cost less in Mexico than in the United States. And providing abortions, like other services, brought needed dollars into the Mexican border economy.

ARAL built precisely on the traditional relationship between Americans and Mexican border towns, teaching women how to obtain illegal abortions in Mexico and how to use the image of the tourist to protect themselves from arrest. Avoiding trouble in Mexico, according to ARAL, depended on one's appearance. ARAL advised women to make themselves look like tourists. The 1968 "List" thus advised readers in capital letters to, first, "CARRY AS LITTLE LUGGAGE AS POSSIBLE. Border guards are extremely suspicious." Second, they should "buy a souvenir or two while in Mexico to put border police minds at ease." Officials expected tourists travelling to border towns like Ciudad Juarez to buy trinkets to remember the fantasy version of Mexico. Serapes, sombreros, plaster statues, paper flowers, and piñatas were not mementos for the traveller in the ARAL drama but props "to show [the] border guards."[34]

The "tourist's" appearance was as important as what she carried. "Put on make-up," advised ARAL. By the late 1960s, the woman wearing makeup was seen as "conservative" and police were likely to ignore her. In contrast, tourists who imported marijuana were identified by their long hair and funky clothing, as well as the fragrance that surrounded them. At the El Paso border, ARAL reported, tourists with long hair were subjected to strip searches by U.S. border agents.[35]

Americans who crossed the border for abortions risked being caught by Mexican police, but they might escape the full consequences of breaking the law. ARAL reported in one "List" that a Tijuana doctor "was arrested in the middle of an operation" on an American woman. Despite the arrest, "the police permitted him to complete the abortion. The aborted woman (from the United States) was arrested with the doctor and paid $1,200 bail which she forfeited in order to leave Mexico."[36] The raid during the procedure matched U.S. police methods for suppressing illegal abortion exactly.[37] The Mexican police, however, kindly let the doctor finish the abortion and let the American woman get away. Although not all patients could have afforded such an arrest, in this case, the financial advantage that the U.S. woman had by virtue of crossing from an affluent First World nation into a poor Third World nation protected her. Furthermore, the border itself served as protection. Once she recrossed it, Mexican police could not easily pursue her.

One would like to read this information alongside a woman seeking an abortion in 1968 and hear her thoughts. Was she scared? Did she reconsider the abortion? Did she review her options: find someone to perform the abortion in the United States, where she could also be arrested; self-induce an abortion at great risk of physical injury; or continue the pregnancy, give birth, and keep the child or place it for adoption? Or did she tell herself, arrest is unlikely and, just in case, I know how to get the thousand dollars if needed? Fear of police, prison, and physical harm surely kept some away, but others knew that women before them had survived, weighed the competing dangers, and drove, flew, or walked across the border for help.

ARAL did more than provide tourist tips and collate and distribute a list of names of abortion "specialists"; its primary task was monitoring the specialists in order to protect the women who sought their services. ARAL had its own rules for practitioners, and it inspected clinics and effectively "licensed" specialists by giving them special handwritten cards signed by Patricia Maginnis.[38] These cards offered a measure of protection to the women whom ARAL sent to Mexico. The "List" instructed women to ask the specialist to show them the ARAL card that gave specialists ARAL's stamp of approval and assured patients of their qualifications. The "List" and the card served as an underground "licence," akin to a state licence or a specialty certificate distributed, accepted, and displayed by members of the medical profession. Maginnis or a comrade inspected nearly thirty of the specialists on their lists, including fourteen in Mexico.[39]

ARAL established simultaneously friendly and regulatory relationships with the abortion specialists. The group made four demands: excellent medical care, humane treatment, low prices, and, when the specialists failed, refunds for incomplete abortions.[40] In return, ARAL promised to send them paying patients. Correspondence between a Ciudad Juarez doctor (No. 55) and ARAL provides an example of how a relationship developed and the extended negotiations over practice and price. After *Playboy* covered efforts in California to legalize abortion, Dr No. 55 wrote to inform the California activists about his clinic. "I am a M.D.," he wrote; "my clinic is small but with all the necessary things to perform perfect minor surgery in it." Furthermore, he had ob-gyn training in American hospitals.[41] Gurner wrote back describing the "List," how he could get his name included, and how ARAL monitored the specialists. "The women who use our service," she explained, are asked "to send us letters after the surgery is over describing the doctor, his office, [and] the quality of the care they received ... In this way we are able to keep track of the behavior of the specialist and judge whether he is giving excellent, humane, professional treatment." The doctor did not pay a fee to be listed, but if he failed to comply, his name would be removed and women would be warned to avoid him. "The specialist who gives excellent care for a low fee," Gurner promised, "will have a steady flow of customers." She told the doctor that if he wanted his name on this demanding but lucrative list, he must send her a copy of his medical licence and information about prices charged, anaesthesia, antibiotics, operating procedure, staffing, and nearby hotels. The doctor soon responded with copies of his diploma and certificates showing he had interned at St Luke's Hospital in Pittsfield, Massachusetts, and el Hospital Juarez.[42]

Once safety was assured, echoing the tradition of generations of women, ARAL spent a lot of energy trying to lower the prices for abortions. ARAL and Dr No. 55 had disputes by mail and phone over fees. Gurner reminded the physician of their "bickering" and his agreement to accept $200 for abortions for pregnancies up to eleven weeks. His local competitors, Gurner pointed out, accepted less. She also reminded him of his moral duties: "As a physician, you should certainly keep in mind *your vow of service* as well as your personal desire to make money fast."[43] Many of the specialists wanted to give ARAL kickbacks for the referrals, but Gurner said no. Instead, she told them, "You give free abortions for women who are poor." "And," Maginnis recalled, "they did."[44]

A twenty-point "List of Minimum Requirements" sent to specialists reveals that ARAL's expectations were not minimal at all. ARAL aimed to ensure emotional and physical comfort, safety, and equal treatment for all women. The requirements ranged from advice about personnel to procedure to prices. This list began with "a nurse ... day and night, who speaks and understands English," a requirement that reflected the importance of creating an atmosphere that calmed anxious Americans.[45] One woman's report points to the importance of English speakers. She went to Nogales for an abortion but ended up having surgery for a tubal pregnancy and staying in a Mexican public hospital for five days. As she remarked, "Since I spoke no [S]panish, this was a lonely experience ... And it was impossible to request anything even a bedpan because of the language barrier." Without a trained health professional who could explain procedures and respond to symptoms and complaints in English, American patients could not communicate or feel safe.[46]

Requirements two, three, and four were more recognizable as medically significant: disinfection of operating rooms; "the doctor should scrub his hands"; and "all operating equipment sterilized." (MDs no doubt found these requirements patronizing but went along with it because they wanted patients.) ARAL described the ideal hospital/clinic atmosphere, which included "extra blankets" and a "pitcher of water" in every bedroom, nurses who automatically put clean sheets on the beds, and food ("hot tea or coffee and possibly toast" were suggested). Toast rather than tortillas was an Americanism that would, like English-speaking staff, reassure American clients. The last two "minimum requirements" concluded with financial concerns and statements of principle: "Your prices should remain low" and "*All* women should receive excellent care. This includes the women we send, the women other people send, and Mexican women."[47]

As the final requirement reveals, these activists hoped that their regulation of medical practices would benefit Mexican as well as American women. Mexican women had high abortion rates, and at least some of the clinics performed abortions for patients from both sides of the border. At one clinic that housed recovering Mexican and American patients in separate sections, Gurner insisted on inspecting and approving the Mexican women's quarters as well.[48] ARAL's ability to monitor the treatment of Mexican patients was limited, however. Interestingly, given Gurner's willingness to send outraged letters demanding refunds, the ARAL list of minimum requirements ended not on an authoritative note but on a weak one: "If we find out that you are not providing *all* women with excellent care, we will be very disturbed." Still, the unspoken message was that if the clinic failed to follow the directions of U.S. feminists, ARAL would stop sending patients.[49]

As Gurner had informed Dr No. 55, ARAL's main method of monitoring abortion specialists was through the collection of evaluations by patients. Through the "List" and the evaluation form given to women, ARAL defined the kind of care that women should expect and alerted them to their responsibility to help others in similar circumstances. The hundreds of evaluations and letters preserved in the records of the Society for Humane Abortion and the Association to Repeal Abortion Laws at the Schlesinger Library show the seriousness with which women took this responsibility. These evaluations, written at the time rather than retrospectively and thus not coloured by the controversy over abortion since the 1973 *Roe v. Wade* Supreme Court decision, reveal individual experiences in Mexico, expectations, and reactions to abortion. The evaluation form shows that ARAL looked for cleanliness, safe aseptic medical procedures, and sympathetic treatment. After identifying the specialist, the form asked about travel, motels, and "any problems crossing the border"; the specialist's practice, including fees and "the condition of the office (clean, dirty, crowded, etc.)"; and "How were you treated … (coldly, sympathetically, neglectfully, etc.)?"

The form also asked about sterilization of instruments, anaesthesia, and post-abortion advice. The forms generated detailed responses on all counts. Women (or sometimes a parent, boyfriend, or husband) recorded the clinical atmosphere, the number of patients and nurses, medications and IVs used, as well as their emotional responses to the entire experience. In addition to feeling that they helped others by submitting evaluations, doing so made women feel empowered and protected. They knew a bad report could put a practitioner out of business and that the specialists realized that ARAL patients observed and reported on their practices.[50]

Unfortunately, the ARAL regulatory system was not perfect, as the activists knew it could not be. "There's nothing safe in the underground," Maginnis observed when interviewed thirty years later. Some women's abortion experiences were terrible. Occasionally someone wrote in fury of fake or failed abortions. A Santa Barbara woman wrote, "the doctor in Agua Prieta should be shot! – [Pretended?] to do the operation – charged us $300.00 – Now there's going to be another unwanted child ... PLEASE TAKE THIS MAN OFF YOUR LIST."[51] One man wrote that his wife and three other patients agreed that the specialist "was quite intolerant, ruthless, and ... mean."[52]

In at least one case, a specialist named on the "List" raped a woman, but it was not until ARAL received a second letter telling of an attempted rape that Gurner believed it. The incident offers a reminder of the distance Americans, including feminists, have come in their thinking about sex and violence. "We had received another report several months ago from a woman who claimed you raped her," Gurner wrote the man, "but doubted the truth of it until now." Gurner first demanded a refund to cover the hospitalization costs of the second woman, then told him "we shall have to warn people about your unprofessional conduct. We fervently hope there will be no such attempts at seduction or rape on your part in the future."[53] It is surprising to see a women's-rights organization first treat a woman's rape charge as dubious and then handle it as a business matter. In 1967 these feminists were slow to believe a woman who said she was raped and reluctant to eliminate a practitioner from their "List."[54]

Nonetheless, women who went to Mexico generally had satisfactory experiences. Of the several hundred post-abortion letters and evaluations sent to ARAL analysed thus far, most expressed relief and wellbeing. Only a few expressed guilt about their abortions. In the main, women told ARAL that they were grateful and wanted to help others in the same situation.[55] One woman used the evaluation system to send a message back to the Mexican specialist warning him to protect himself better.[56]

The evaluations women sent ARAL concerning their experiences underline the importance that women and their families attached to kindness and sensitivity during the abortion process. Several patients of a Nogales doctor (No. 49) remarked on how "understanding" he was. They were treated "very tenderly," "very sympathetically," and "very kind[ly]" by the doctor and his staff. One woman called him "humanitarian."[57] In contrast, another informant, who believed her doctors were "competent" and the clinic "clean," thought they lacked "a humanitarian attitude towards their patients. Though perhaps," she mused, "that is asking too much."[58] Raising expectations, however, was precisely part of the SHA-ARAL project. Another wrote of her clinic that "all were superlatively kind, gentle, courteous, careful, concerned," and "*far* more 'humane' than what one encounters in aseptic U.S. hospitals!"[59]

Some women managed to transform their abortion trip into a traditional tourist excursion; when they showed border guards their souvenirs, it was not an act. An Oregon woman reported that after her abortion she went "immediately to a restaurant and ate a big Mexican dinner. The next day I saw the sights of the town and ... made a holiday of it."[60] Indeed, she expressed some sorrow that she would probably never repeat the experience. Another woman thought that ARAL should advise people to go with a friend because it could be "lonely," and as she said, "I felt good after the operation and wanted to see some of the city. Hard to enjoy alone."[61] One woman who stopped at an Arizona museum remarked, "It's such a simple procedure the most difficult thing is the expense and breaking the law!"[62] These comments about the pleasures of indulging in a Mexican meal and exploring cities indicate some jubilation on the part of women who went to Mexico in crisis and succeeded in obtaining an illegal abortion.

Although Mexican physicians and other abortion specialists may have gone along with the demands of Maginnis and Gurner because the pair came from Mexico's powerful and wealthy northern neighbour, ARAL's scrutiny and regulation of Mexican abortion providers cannot simply be attributed to racism or American imperialism. In the postwar period, the press consistently represented abortion as deadly and abortionists as "back-alley butchers," a frightening image that underlined the necessity of ensuring safety. Without medical licences, specialty board certifications, and open practices to guarantee practitioners' skills, ARAL took on the job of a state agency and regulated the illegal practice. Jane, the feminist underground abortion group based in Chicago, also assessed the qualifications and safety of the abortionist to whom it sent women.[63] Negotiations between the California activists and Mexican abortionists were two-way, however. Indeed, the first clinic inspection done by Maginnis and Gurner was at the specialist's urging. Specialists asked ARAL to "insist," as one put it, that the women be honest about the length of their pregnancies and that they bring enough money to pay the full fee (ARAL did the former but not always the latter). Furthermore, a camaraderie developed between ARAL and some of the Mexican specialists.[64]

Finally, ARAL used the evaluation system developed to regulate practitioners outside the United States on practitioners at home. Activists collected information and then broadcast their assessments of physicians and clinics in the United States. The Abortion Communication Center handled this domestic work. When New York legalized abortion in 1970, ARAL activists used their years of experience to evaluate newly opened abortion clinics, warning women of New York "fleecers." ARAL's assessment of the situation was succinct and surprising to American physicians, who assumed they were better than Mexican and illegal practitioners. ("We are only referring a few women now to New York, as most of the physicians performing abortions there are not properly trained in abortion technique.")[65] ARAL also gave advice on how to obtain therapeutic abortions in San Francisco and alerted women to the availability of state welfare assistance to pay for them.[66]

ARAL further challenged mainstream medicine by establishing related health centres in San Francisco. The San Francisco clinics did not provide illegal abortions but offered two necessary services as part of the underground illegal abortion effort: pregnancy testing and post-abortion care. On Wednesday evenings, the Post Abortion Care Center, opened by ARAL in 1968, provided pregnancy tests, contraceptive information and prescriptions, and, as a service to the women sent across the border for abortions, post-abortion checkups. The centre usually saw eight women for post-abortion examinations and did ten pregnancy tests a night.[67] Four doctors volunteered their services, an attorney donated office space, and the American Humanist Association funded the activity.[68]

Today, when home pregnancy test kits are readily available, some readers may not realize that confirming a suspected pregnancy was no simple matter. Access to pregnancy tests and the confidentiality required by a single woman or any woman considering an abortion posed a serious problem. Without confirmation of pregnancy, women sometimes underwent and paid for unnecessary procedures. Obtaining a pregnancy test meant not only paying for a trip to a physician and waiting for the results, but possibly enduring sermons, misinformation, or tricks from physicians who lied to patients whom they suspected would seek abortions. Some women found the fees prohibitive.[69]

When Patricia Maginnis and Robert Bick set up their pregnancy-testing service at the Post Abortion Care Center and later at the Abortion Communication Center, they created alternative health-care institutions designed to meet women's need for inexpensive, quick, and honest test results. Both Bick and Maginnis were laboratory technicians; thus, not only were they well aware of the problems faced by women who feared pregnancy, but they also had the skills to interpret the tests. A leaflet announcing the availability of pregnancy tests highlighted the problems and hostility encountered by women trying to determine whether they were pregnant. The leaflet listed the advantages: "results in less than an hour; At cost ($5) or less if you cannot afford it; no physical examination; no red tape – no moral lecture; confidential."[70] Once pregnancy was confirmed, women could make travel plans for an abortion with the help of ARAL's "List" and centre volunteers.

The San Francisco clinics, like the "List" of specialists, served several purposes: each was part of a political project intended to radically change American law and medical practices, a response to a real need, and envisioned as a way to raise women's political consciousness. Particularly striking, when one considers that present-day pro-choice activism for many has been reduced to writing cheques to national organizations or voting for the least objectionable candidate, are the opportunities ARAL created for people to express their support actively. ARAL asked professionals, including gynaecologists, lab technicians, and nurses, to use their expertise on behalf of a political movement. The Post Abortion Care Center provided services with volunteer help for nearly two years but ended when the activists concluded that the centre had failed to inspire women to join the movement.[71] It was difficult to get women to overcome their desire for personal secrecy and go public with their abortions.

Like a conventional public health agency, SHA-ARAL was dedicated to both protecting the public and improving health through the education of professionals and patients. ARAL was involved in illegal activities, not part of any recognized medical institution, and founded by iconoclasts; yet the medical profession used ARAL activists as educational resources. Physicians borrowed movies on abortion methods from ARAL, attended classes, and invited ARAL to provide a speaker for a weekly educational series for residents and physicians at one hospital.[72] SHA produced a newsletter with a national readership of fifteen thousand by 1970 and advertised a lending library.[73]

Maginnis and her colleagues originally encouraged women to go to Mexico for abortions in order to contest existing laws in the United States. They did not plan to create an alternative feminist health system, but the numerous requests from ordinary women resulted in its creation. The "List" grew out of the quiet practice of helping individual women; publicizing it was a political strategy. As ARAL worked to protect the health of women through the inspection, supervision, and correction of practitioners, as it established clinics to provide basic services to the public, and as it educated the public and the medical profession on pregnancy and abortion, the organization became what I have called a feminist public health agency, one that always had a political purpose. In 1970, four years after the initial leafletting, the organizers observed that "the abortion laws ... remain unrepealed, and ARAL, which was envisioned ... as a temporary organization, is still in existence." By then, more than twelve thousand women had obtained illegal abortions outside the country with ARAL's help.[74]

Thousands of Americans returned home safely after an abortion in Mexico, yet the image of the deadly Mexican abortionist loomed in the minds of many.[75] "All we ever heard," Maginnis recalled, was that "many [an American] girl lies in a shallow grave in Mexico."[76] "The stories we always got in this country were these 'dirty Mexicans doing all these dirty abortions on these poor girls.' "[77] Maginnis knew differently, however, and defended the Mexican specialists. Yet the stories taught women to fear for their lives if they needed an abortion, while simultaneously teaching and reinforcing American contempt for Mexico and Mexicans. The label "dirty" concisely differentiated between the good, clean American sanitation system and the bad Mexican one, between the good, safe country and its infectious neighbour.

Although individual experiences in Mexico frequently contradicted American ideology, ultimately the deadly representation of Mexican abortionists served as a politically useful symbol. Indeed, the symbol advanced legal reform in the United States. *People v. Belous*, a California case decided in 1969, was one of the pivotal cases leading up to *Roe v. Wade*. At its centre was a story about Tijuana abortionists. Dr Leon Belous of Los Angeles was arrested in 1966 and prosecuted for referring a young unmarried couple to a physician-abortionist in the San Diego area. Belous referred to the "Tijuana abortionist" in his defence. After first refusing to help the college couple who contacted him, Belous gave in when they told him that they would go to Tijuana. "Dr Belous testified that he ... knew that women who went to Tijuana were taking their lives in their hands"; he recommended the physician-abortionist in order to protect his patient from "butchery in Tijuana." The representation was powerful, if disingenuous; the abortionist to whom Belous sent his patient was a Mexican physician who had moved to the San Diego area.[78] In *People v. Belous*, the California

Supreme Court ruled that the state's criminal abortion law was unconstitutional, a decision that inspired attorneys nationwide to challenge
the constitutionality of state criminal abortion laws.

While lawyers challenged the law in the courtroom, ARAL defied the
law publicly and daily. This feminist health organization taught women
that together they could challenge and change both law and medicine,
two of the most powerful social structures and professions in America.
Mexican abortion clinics were one site in which American women
learned to exert their power as patients. Feminists paid close attention to
the safety and quality of illegal medical services. "By joint effort in demanding excellent care and insisting on sterile conditions, we," ARAL
urged, can "improve standards."[79] The activists sought superb medical
care for all. ARAL's vision of a health-care system in which women, and all
patients, were empowered to make decisions and were treated with respect continued in the women's health movement. In 1975 SHA-ARAL
transferred its work of teaching abortion techniques and guarding the
health of female patients to the Women's Center in Oakland.[80] In 1999,
as she approached her seventy-first birthday, Patricia Maginnis was defending access to legal abortion clinics every Saturday at 7 a.m.

When ARAL monitored illegal abortion services, however, it aimed for
more than access or safety. Maginnis and her partners wanted the medical service of abortion to be given in a caring and "humane" manner.
The word "humane" was central to their vision and their activism. SHA
and ARAL helped to create an expectation among women that abortion
care and, by extension, all medical care should be provided in a sensitive
fashion. Compassion was as important as expertise. In some Mexican
clinics women found both. Sustaining a humane atmosphere and feminist vision in abortion clinics once the procedure was legal in the United
States would prove to be equally or even more difficult than monitoring
illegal practices and challenging the criminal law.[81]

Originally published in *Feminist Studies* 14, no. 3 (Summer 2000): 323–438. Reprinted with permission.

NOTES

Author's Note: I am grateful for the Radcliffe College Schlesinger Library
Research Grant, which made the research for this essay possible.
  1 See *San Francisco Chronicle*, 17 June 1966, folder 59, box 3, Records of
    the Society for Humane Abortion and the Association to Repeal Abortion
    Laws (hereafter SHA-ARAL), Schlesinger Library, Radcliffe College,
    Cambridge, Mass.

2 For previous discussions of Patricia Maginnis, see Kristin Luker, *Abortion and the Politics of Motherhood* (Berkeley: University of California Press 1985), 95–100; Nina Baehr, *Abortion without Apology: A Radical History for the 1990s*, pamphlet, no. 8 (Boston: South End Press 1990), 7–20; Leslie J. Reagan, *When Abortion Was a Crime: Women, Medicine, and Law in the United States, 1867–1973* (Berkeley: University of California Press 1997), 222–4; David J. Garrow, *Liberty and Sexuality: The Right to Privacy and the Making of "Roe v. Wade"* (New York: Macmillan 1994), chap. 5; and Lawrence Lader,
Abortion II: Making the Revolution (Boston: Beacon Press 1973), 26–34. On the 1960s movements, see Linda Gordon, *Woman's Body, Woman's Right: Birth Control in America* rev. ed. (New York: Penguin Books, 1990), 436–46; Bruce J. Schulman, "Out of the Streets and into the Classroom? The New Left and the Counterculture in United States History Textbooks," *Journal of American History* 85 (March 1999): 1527–34; David Farber, introduction to *The Sixties: From Memory to History*, ed. David Farber (Chapel Hill: University
of North Carolina Press 1994), 1–10; and Philippa Levine and Judith DeGroat, "Teaching Medical History: Introduction," *Radical History Review*, no. 74 (Spring 1999): 137–9.

3 On massive lawbreaking as a source of legal change, see Rosalind Pollack Petchesky, *Abortion and Woman's Choice: The State, Sexuality, and Reproductive Freedom*, rev. ed. (Boston: Northeastern University Press 1990), 125–32; on NARAL, see Garrow, *Liberty and Sexuality*, 350, 358–61; and Lader, *Abortion II*, 88–97.

4 Oscar J. Martinez, *Border Boom Town: Ciudad Juarez Since 1848* (Austin: University of Texas Press 1975); idem, ed., *U.S.-Mexico Borderlands: Historical and Contemporary Perspectives* (Wilmington, Del.: Scholarly Resources 1996); idem, *Border People: Life and Society in the U.S.-Mexico Borderlands* (Tucson: University of Arizona Press 1994); Lawrence A. Herzog, *Where North Meets South: Cities, Space, and Politics on the U.S. Mexico Border* (Austin, Tex.: CMAS Books, Center for Mexican American Studies at the University of Texas 1990); Milo Kearney and Anthony Knopp, *Border Cuates: A History of U.S.-Mexico Twin Cities* (Austin, Tex.: Eakin Press 1995); John A. Price, *Tijuana: Urbanization in a Border Culture* (South Bend, Ind.: University of Notre Dame Press 1973); Jorge A. Bustamante, "Demystifying the United States-Mexico Border," *Journal of American History* 79 (September 1992): 485–90; Maria Patricia Fernandez-Kelly, *For We Are Sold, I and My People: Women in Mexico's Frontier* (Albany: SUNY Press, 1983); Vicki L. Ruiz and Susan Tiano, eds, *Women on the U.S.-Mexico Border: Responses to Change* (Winchester, Mass.: Allen & Unwin 1987). Debbie Nathan, a journalist, analyses very different issues, including contemporary abortion practices on the border, in *Women and Other Aliens: Essays from the U.S.-Mexico Border* (El Paso, Tex.: Cinco Puntos Press 1991), 74–83. Debra A. Castillo et al. reach the same conclusions about the state of Mexican research on the border. See their

"Border Lives: Prostitute Women in Tijuana," *Signs* 24 (Winter 1999): 387–422, esp. 398–9.

5 Mildred Schroeder, "One Woman's Abortion Crusade," *San Francisco Examiner*, 26 September 1966, folder 59, box 3, SHA-ARAL.

6 California, like most states, permitted physicians to perform legal thera-peutic abortions only when pregnancy threatened the life of the woman. (When an abortion was considered necessary, however, varied historically and among practitioners.) The Knox bill was the American Legal Insti-tute's (ALI) model law on abortion, written in 1959. In 1967 Governor Ronald Reagan signed an abortion reform bill into law. By 1970 twelve states had passed the ALI model law. See Luker, *Abortion and Politics*, 69–73; Garrow, *Liberty and Sexuality*, 296–7, 330–2, chap. 5; Reagan, *When Abortion Was a Crime*, 218–22.

7 Patricia Maginnis Oral History (hereafter PMOH), interview by Jeannette Cheek, November 1975, 79–81, 83–4, quotation on 93, Schlesinger-Rockefeller Family Planning Oral History Project, Schlesinger Library.

8 Schroeder, "One Woman's Abortion Crusade." The reform laws were restrictive in two ways: they permitted abortion for a set of specified indica-tions, which would exclude most women who sought abortions; and they required the approval of a medical committee.

9 PMOH, 87.

10 Schulman, "Out of the Streets," 1530–2; Kenneth Cmiel, "The Politics of Civility," 268–73, George Lipsitz, "Who'll Stop the Rain? Youth Culture, Rock 'n' Roll, and Social Crises," 206–34, and Beth Bailey, "Sexual Revolu-tions," 235–62, all in Farber, *The Sixties*. On the New Left health movement and San Francisco free clinics, see Sheryl Burt Ruzek, *The Women's Health Movement: Feminist Alternatives to Medical Control* (New York: Praeger 1978), 61–3.

11 Joan McKinney, "A Step toward Legality," *San Francisco Chronicle*, 20 May 1965, folder 59, box 3, SHA-ARAL.

12 Susan Berman, "The Abortion Crusader," *San Francisco Magazine* 12 (July 1970), folder 60, box 3, SHA-ARAL; PMOH, 77; Baehr, *Abortion Without Apology*, 8–13; Patricia Maginnis, telephone interview with author, 28 May 1999, Oakland, Calif.

13 PMOH, 105–6; "Doctors Backed in Abortion Clash," *New York Times* (12 March 1967); Keith Monroe, "How California's Abortion Law Isn't Working," *New York Times Magazine*, 29 December 1968; Luker, *Abortion and Politics*, 86–7; Garrow, *Liberty and Sexuality*, 300–1, 306–7, 354; Reagan, *When Abortion Was a Crime*, 61–7, 142–4, 173–81, 200–8.

14 Quotation from PMOH, 106. See also Lader, *Abortion II*, 26; Allan F. Guttmacher correspondence, 26 September 1968, 18 November 1968, and 16 January 1969, in Allan F. Guttmacher Papers, Countway Library of Medicine, Harvard University, Cambridge, Mass.; Heather Booth, interview

with Paula Kamen, 1 September 1992, Paula Kamen Collection, C.D. McCormick Library of Special Collections, Northwestern University Library, Evanston, Ill.

15 On Jane, see Laura Kaplan, *The Story of Jane: The Legendary Underground Feminist Abortion Service* (New York: Pantheon Books 1995); Pauline Bart, "Seizing the Means of Reproduction: An Illegal Feminist Abortion Collective – How and Why It Worked," *Qualitative Sociology* 10 (Winter 1987): 339–57; and Reagan, *When Abortion Was a Crime*, 224–5. On abortion referral services, see Lader, *Abortion II*, 27, 42–55; Judith Hole and Ellen Levine, *Rebirth of Feminism* (New York: Quadrangle Books 1971), 299–302; and Arlene Carmen and Howard Moody, *Abortion Counseling and Social Change from Illegal Act to Medical Practice: The Story of the Clergy Consultation Service on Abortion* (Valley Forge, Penn.: Judson Press 1973).

16 When Maginnis began leafletting, she did so as an individual, not as president of SHA. To protect SHA's non-profit status as an educational organization, she and Gurner very soon founded ARAL as a parallel organization to carry out illegal activities.

17 Quotation on Gurner is from Maginnis telephone interview with author. See also "Seeks Arrest for Anti-Abortion Cause [sic]," *Berkeley Barb*, 15 July 1966, folder 59, box 3, SHA-ARAL; "Tijuana Doctors Are Closed," flyer [June 1966], Guttmacher Collection.

18 Maitland Zane, "A Do-It-Yourself Kit on Abortions," *San Francisco Chronicle*, 22 July 1966, folder 59, box 3, SHA-ARAL.

19 "The State of ARAL," *Society for Humane Abortion Newsletter* (hereafter *SHA Newsletter*) 6 (Winter 1970–71), C.D. McCormick Library of Special Collections, Northwestern University Library. Maginnis was arrested twice: for leafletting in San Francisco and with Gurner for teaching their abortion class in Redwood City in 1967. See *San Francisco Chronicle* clippings, 18 and 19 August 1966, Guttmacher Collection; "Women Lose Second Abortion Trial," *San Francisco Chronicle*, 2 November 1971, and "Two Abortion Crusaders Convicted," *San Francisco Chronicle*, 3 November 1971, both in folder 20, box 2, Family Planning Oral History Project Records (hereafter FPOHP), Schlesinger Library.

20 Carolyn Lund, "Abortion Crusader Dares the Police to Arrest Her," *Santa Rosa Press Democrat*, 17 November 1966, folder 20, box 2, FPOHP. For a summary of existing class lists, see Archivist's Note (Zephotene L. Stickney), August 1979, folder 66, box 4, SHA-ARAL; "Auditorium Refused for Abortion Classes," newspaper clipping, no pub., 26 April 1968, folder 20, box 2, FPOHP. Quotation from Mildred Schroeder, "Abortions and the Law," *San Francisco Examiner*, 27 September 1966, folder 59, box 3, SHA-ARAL. Newspaper coverage and controversy over the use of a room no doubt contributed to the size of the Washington, D.C., class. Carol Honsa, "Abortion Class Draws Crowd," *Washington Post*, 6 September 1967;

"Gynecology: Disease of Unwanted Pregnancy," *Time* 15 September 1967, both clips in folder 20, box 2, FPOHP.

21 Maginnis quotation is from telephone interview with the author; reporting on Audrey Smith is from Zane, "A Do-It-Yourself Kit." See also the supportive column by African-American commentator Thomas C. Fleming's Weekly Report, *Sun-Reporter,* 6 August 1966, folder 59, box 3, SHA-ARAL; and Berman, "The Abortion Crusader," 38. An SHA "Progress Report," March and April 1966, reported a talk and discussion "with an enthusiastic group of 15 Negro women in Richmond," Guttmacher Collection.

22 Clases de aborto, folder 62, box 4, SHA-ARAL; Maginnis, interview with author.

23 "Sixteen women attend abortion instruction," *Palo Alto Times* 1 September 1966, folder 59, box 3, SHA-ARAL; Schroeder, "One Woman's Abortion Crusade"; Post Abortion Care Center leaflet [1968], folder 52, box 3, SHA-ARAL.

24 Quotation in Schroeder, "Abortions and the Law."

25 Honsa, "Abortion Class Draws Crowd"; "Dear Pat," evaluation of No. 36, 6 November 1966, folder 119, box 6; evaluation of No. 30, 12 May 1968, folder 137, box 7. Letters in SHA-ARAL requesting abortion information and evaluations of abortion specialists have had all names and addresses removed and are identified only by the town and/or zip code of the writer and the number of the abortion specialist. The names of specialists have all been replaced with code numbers by the Schlesinger Library.

26 "How to obtain the list of abortion specialists," n.d., folder 65, box 4, SHA-ARAL; Baehr, *Abortion without Apology,* 10.

27 Quotations from "List of Abortion Specialists" [1968], folder 70, box 4, SHA-ARAL. Most of the specialists were in Mexico; travelling to Japan or Sweden was very expensive; and the Canadian physician, No. 54, took few patients and was described as "very temperamental, gruff … and frightening." For location of specialists, see Archivist's Note (Zephorene L. Stickney), August 1979, folder 81, box 4, SHA-ARAL.

28 Berman, "The Abortion Crusader."

29 Reagan, *When Abortion Was a Crime,* chap. 6.

30 Price, *Tijuana,* 60–1.

31 Quotation in Los Angeles, 90029 to ARAL, 8 July 1967, folder 107, box 6, SHA-ARAL. Initiatives like the San Diego district attorney's no doubt helped produce such fears.

32 Each of these topics deserves greater historical attention. See Gene Fowler and Bill Crawford, *Border Radio: Quacks, Yodelers, Pitchmen, Psychics, and Other Amazing Broadcasters of the American Airwaves* (Austin: Texas Monthly Press 1987). On sex workers, pornography, and drugs, see Price, *Tijuana, 106–13, 61–2.* On divorces, see Martinez, *Border Boom Town,* 126.

33 Ronald J. Vogel, "Crossing the Border for Health Care: An Exploratory Analysis of Consumer Choice," *Journal of Borderlands Studies* 10 (Spring 1995): 19–44; Robert Pear, "Online Sales Spur Illegal Importing of Medicine to U.S.," *New York Times*, 10 January 2000: A1, A12; Price, *Tijuana*, 87.

34 "List of Abortion Specialists," 18 February 1968, folder 70, box 4, SHA-ARAL.

35 "List of Abortion Specialists," n.d., folder 70, box 4, SHA-ARAL; "U.S. Border Guards Assault People," *SHA Newsletter 4* (September 1968). On border patrol searches for drugs, see Price, *Tijuana*, 103, 108–9.

36 "List of Abortion Specialists," [1968].

37 Reagan, *When Abortion Was a Crime*, chap. 6.

38 "Specialist Listing," 1 April 1968, folder 70, box 4, SHA-ARAL.

39 Over 130 specialists were included on the "List" over the years. ARAL inspected eight clinics in Japan, two in Puerto Rico, two in the United States, and one other. See Archivist's Note regarding specialists.

40 Rowena Gurner to No. 55, 15 November 1967, folder 89, box 5, SHA-ARAL.

41 No. 55 to F.H. Kirkpatrick, folder 89, box 5, SHA-ARAL.

42 Rowena Gurner to No. 55, 15 November 1967; No. 55 to Rowena, November [1967], both in folder 89, box 5, SHA-ARAL.

43 No. 55 to Rowena, 3 April 1968; Rowena Gurner to No. 55, 10 April 1968, both in folder 89, box 5, SHA-ARAL.

44 Maginnis, telephone interview with author.

45 "List of Minimum Requirements," Rowena Gurner to No. 30, 17 September 1967, folder 86, box 5, SHA-ARAL.

46 Abortion Report, 7 September 1968, folder 144, box 7, SHA-ARAL.

47 "List of Minimum Requirements." For a description of one Mexican clinic, see Donald W. Ball, "An Abortion Clinic Ethnography," *Social Problems* 14 (Winter 1967): 243–301.

48 On abortion in Latin America, see Henry Giniger, "Birth Curb Gains in Mexican Study," *New York Times*, 30 April 1967: 26; Juan do Onis, "Mexican Official Opposes the Pill," *New York Times*, 9 November 1969: 26; Paul L. Montgomery, "Birth Curbs and Illegal Abortion Are Increasing in Latin America," *New York Times*, 18 September 1967: 6. Maginnis reported Mexican women's use of the specialists and Gurner's inspection in our telephone interview.

49 Quotation from "List of Minimum Requirements." For examples of letters demanding refunds and warning specialists of the consequences of incompetent practices, see Rowena Gurner to No. 67, 18 April 1968, folder 84, box 5; Patricia Maginnis to No. 35, 20 March 1968, folder 87, box 5, SHA-ARAL. ARAL often succeeded in getting refunds, PMOH, 147.

50 "Information on Specialists," evaluation of No. 30 from Greeley, Colo.,
   1 October [1968], folder 146, box 7, SHA-ARAL.
51 Maginnis, telephone interview; evaluation of Agua Prieta (no code number)
   from Santa Barbara, 10 October 1968, folder 146, box 7, SHA-ARAL.
52 Evaluation of No. 10 to Mrs P.T. Maginnis, 10 December 1966, folder 118,
   box 6, SHA-ARAL.
53 Rowena Gurner to No. 53, Agua Prieta, 31 October 1967, and letter from
   Palo Alto to "Dear Pat," [n.d.], both in folder 84, box 5, SHA-ARAL.
54 PMOH, 140.
55 Crystal River, Fla. 32629, Questions and Answers on No. 12, folder 117,
   box 9; evaluation of No. 35 [?] from Goleta, Calif., 2 May 1968, folder 137,
   box 7, SHA-ARAL. For the exceptional letter from a woman who wrote that
   she felt "ashamed and I even regret it now ... [but] I really had no alternative," see evaluation of No. 3 from San Mateo, Calif., 28 March 1969, folder
   157, box 8, SHA-ARAL.
56 See evaluation of No. 5 from Escondido, Calif., 16 August 1969, folder
   167, box 8, SHA-ARAL.
57 First four quoted phrases in evaluation of No. 49 from Berkeley,
   19 October 1968, folder 147, box 7; last quotation in evaluation of No. 49
   from San Francisco, 22 October 1968, folder 147, box 7, SHA-ARAL.
58 Evaluation of No. 30 from Greeley, Colo., 1 October [1968], SHA-ARAL.
59 This writer had an abortion and sterilization. (First sentence was also
   underlined in original.) Evaluation of No. 5, [1966?], folder 120, box 6,
   SHA-ARAL.
60 Evaluation of No. 35 from Portland, Ore., 8 May 1968, folder 137, box 7,
   SHA-ARAL.
61 Evaluation of No. 4 from San Diego, 21 March 1969, folder 157, box 8,
   SHA-ARAL.
62 "Dear Mrs Maginnis," evaluation of No. 42, 17 December 1966, folder 119,
   box 6, SHA-ARAL.
63 Kaplan, *The Story of Jane*; Bart, "Seizing the Means."
64 Maginnis, telephone interview; No. 55 to Rowena, 3 April 1968, folder 89,
   box 5; No. 35 to Patricia, 1 August 1968, folder 87, box 5, SHA-ARAL;
   PMOH, 138–9, 142. ARAL encouraged all women to keep the fees for
   abortion down. See "List of Abortion Specialists," 29 March 1968,
   folder 70, box 4, SHA-ARAL; PMOH, 138–9, 143.
65 Resource Notebook, folder 76, box 4, SHA-ARAL. Quotation in ARAL to Private Shelter for Unwed, Expectant Mothers, 17 August 1970, Abortion–Association to Repeal Abortion Laws, Women's Ephemera Folders (hereafter
   cited as WEF), C.D. McCormick
   Library of Special Collections, Northwestern University Library.
66 Resource Notebook, folder 74, box 4, SHA-ARAL. On welfare, see R. to
   A.R.A.L. Girls, 22 July 1971, and San Jose, Calif. to friends, 2 March 1971,

both in folder 78, box 4, SHA-ARAL. See also Resource Notebook: "Reports received by A.R.A.L. on 'therapeutic' abortions in California," 1969, Association to Repeal Abortion Laws Folder, Abortion, WEF.

67 The centre served 300 clients in the first six months. "S.F. Abortion Care Center Announced," *San Jose Mercury*, 31 October 1968, folder 60, box 3; Virginia K. Anderson form letter, 30 September 1969, folder 63, box 4, both in SHA-ARAL.

68 Sharon McCahon to Mr Richard Kirschman, 30 April 1968; "A Post-Abortion Aid Center," *San Francisco Chronicle*, 31 October 1968; American Humanist Association News Release [1968], all in folder 52, box 3, SHA-ARAL.

69 See form letter to "Dear Dr." from ARAL, 9 January 1971, folder 52, box 3, SHA-ARAL; PMOH, 146.

70 "Where to Obtain a Pregnancy Test," folder 74, box 4, SHA-ARAL; PMOH, 146; "Repeal Repressive Abortion Laws" leaflet, [1968], folder 52, box 3, SHA-ARAL.

71 PMOH, 147; *SHA Newsletter* 6, no. 1 (1969–70).

72 No. 61 to Miss Patricia T. Maginnis, 8 February 1968, and Patricia T. Maginnis to No. 61, 23 February 1969, both in folder 90, box 5, SHA-ARAL. Sixty doctors attended one class on abortion procedures, *SHA Newsletter* 6 (Summer 1970). Virginia K. Anderson to San Jose, Calif., 13 February 1969, folder 63, box 4, SHA-ARAL.

73 Berman, "The Abortion Crusader," 18; "Society for Humane Abortions Lending Library," bibliography, n.d., folder 55, box 3, SHA-ARAL.

74 "The State of ARAL."

75 Newspaper reports of an occasional abortion-related death in Mexico confirmed this image of Mexico. In our telephone interview, Maginnis recalled the death of an eighteen-year-old California woman after an abortion in Nogales. The woman had been referred by another group, but Maginnis observed that it could have happened to ARAL. She reiterated the dangers and remarked, "I figured there would be casualties; there's nothing safe in the underground." "California Teenager's Death Uncovers Giant Abortion Mill," 1 November 1968, and "Mystery Abortion Mill," 13 November 1968, both in *Nogales Herald*; these and related newspaper clippings in microfilm, m-100, SHA-ARAL.

76 "American" replaces "U.S." here because it would have been used in the original according to Maginnis. In 1975 Maginnis objected to both terms in "American Girl," for slighting the peoples of the rest of the Americas and for slighting women. See PMOH, 143.

77 PMOH, 144. For an example of the pervasive use of the term "dirty" to describe Mexico, see "Merry Christmas Pat MaGinnis [*sic*]," evaluation of No. 53, 22 December 1966, folder 119, box 6, SHA-ARAL. On the early twentieth-century construction of Mexico as "dirty," see Alexandra Minna Stern, "Buildings, Boundaries, and Blood: Medicalization and

Nation-Building on the U.S.-Mexico Border, 1910–1930," *Hispanic American Historical Review* 79 (February 1999): 41–81.

78 *People v. Belous*, 80 Cal. Rptr. 354, 458 P. 2d 194, quotations on 196; Garrow, *Liberty and Sexuality*, 354–6, 377–9. ARAL also advised avoiding Tijuana (Specialist Listing, 1 April 1968, folder 70, box 4, SHA-ARAL).

79 Supplemental Sheet No. 2, 27 November 1967, 18, folder 69, box 4, SHA-ARAL.

80 Before and after *Roe v. Wade*, SHA-ARAL ran conferences teaching doctors how to perform abortions. Maginnis, telephone interview; PMOH, 92.

81 For observations on the clinic atmosphere by women who worked both in Jane and in post-*Roe* clinics, see Kaplan, *The Story of Jane*, 283–93.

19

Policing "Pregnant Pilgrims": Situating the Sterilization Abuse of Mexican-Origin Women in Los Angeles County

Elena R. Gutiérrez

Spanning the late nineteenth and twentieth centuries, the formidable history of sterilization abuse in the United States is well documented.[1] Early campaigns labelled various groups genetically, mentally, or otherwise "inferior" and advocated their sterilization, but it was during the late 1960s and early 1970s that the most massive sterilization campaign the country has seen targeted poor women of colour. Although Native American, Mexican-origin, and Puerto Rican women were also affected by this egregious medical practice, the extant social history about this particular period of sterilization abuse predominantly documents the forced sterilization of poor African-American women.[2]

While it has provided persuasive documentation of how racial, class, and gender ideologies can fundamentally endanger the reproductive experiences of women, this focus upon the experiences of African-American women has also resulted in an overly generalized understanding of how sterilization abuse occurred and operated. For example, in the extant literature on coercive sterilization during the late 1960s and early 1970s, racialized class interests, expressed as concern about overpopulation and rising welfare rolls, are generally seen as having provided the ideological impetus behind the massive sterilization abuse of poor women and women of colour across the nation. As Federal District Judge Gerhard Gessel acknowledged in his 1974 decision in the case of *Relf v. Weinberger*, a class-action suit crucial to establishing the requirement of informed consent and federal regulations regarding sterilization, "there is uncontroverted evidence in the record that ... an indefinite number of poor people have been improperly coerced into accepting a sterilization operation under the threat that various federally supported welfare benefits would be withdrawn unless they submitted to irreversible sterilization."[3]

However, while sterilization abuse during this period was undeniably class based and justified by the ideologies of population and welfare control, the coercive sterilization of African-American women in the South and northeast, Puerto Rican and Dominican women in New York, Mexican-origin women in Los Angeles, and Native American women in Indian Health Service clinics across the nation cannot be universally explained by these forces. Although a widespread national practice during the late 1960s and early 1970s, sterilization abuse assumed different characteristics in diverse institutional and regional circumstances and was directed at women of various racial backgrounds.

In this essay I examine the sterilization abuse of Mexican-origin women at the Women's Hospital of the University of Southern California (USC)–Los Angeles County Medical Center (LACMC) during the late 1960s and early 1970s. Largely overlooked in the social history of sterilization abuse is the fact that, just as with other women of colour, there were social reasons, rather than justified medical rationale, behind the coerced sterilization of these women. However, beyond the rhetoric of overpopulation and rising welfare roles, additional social concerns about increasing Mexican immigration and, in particular, the perceived undue costs of delivering the children of Mexican immigrant women made Mexican-origin women the target group for sterilization in Los Angeles County.[4] These converging popular discourses not only propelled the massive sterilization abuse of Mexican-origin women at the Medical Center, but also became codified ideological tools utilized by individual medical practitioners to coercively sterilize their patients.

AN "EPIDEMIC" OF STERILIZATION ABUSE REVEALED

According to sociologist Thomas Shapiro, two events directly precipitated the coercive sterilization of poor women of colour across the nation during the early 1970s, both of which were manifestations of a newly established federal interest in issues of family-planning policy.[5]

First, previously stringent medical regulations restricting sterilization options for most women were significantly loosened in 1960–70, substantially expanding the procedure's availability. Formerly, sterilization was guided by an age-parity formula designed to ensure that women of child-bearing age did not "prematurely" terminate their child-bearing; sterilization was only allowed if a woman's age multiplied by the number of her children amounted to at least 120 and if two physicians and a psychiatrist advised the procedure. In 1970 the American College of Obstetrics and Gynecology withdrew this standard, offering millions of women access to the procedure.[6]

Second, governmental financial assistance for reproductive services to the poor increased substantially after 1965, most notably through passage of the Family Planning Services and Population Research Act in 1970. Signalling a dramatic reversal of federal policy on issues of reproduction, which were previously considered a "private" matter outside of the realm of governmental interest, the act committed significant resources to promote research in the areas of reproduction and population growth, and to provide funding for family-planning services.[7] While in 1965 only $5 million of federal money was allocated for family-planning services to the poor, by 1979 this amount had reached $260 million.[8] Augmented funding of sterilization procedures was particularly substantial. Prior to 1969, federally supported family-planning services were prohibited from subsidizing sterilization and abortion services. Funds for sterilization became available in 1971, with Medicaid covering 90 per cent of the cost of a sterilization procedure. Most of these federal monies were offered through the Office of Economic Opportunity (OEO), established to fight the war on poverty.[9]

Following the increased availability of federal funding and relaxed requirements for the procedure, sterilization rapidly advanced to become the most popular contraceptive in the United States.[10] By 1973 sterilization was the method of birth control most used by people thirty to forty-four years of age, and in 1976 nearly one-third of American couples reported that they had been sterilized.[11] Despite the skyrocketing of sterilization rates, the procedure remained unmonitored by medical boards or governmental officials for the first few years of its more widespread practice.[12] Although OEO-funded family-planning clinics were not to go ahead with the sterilizations until a set of guidelines was in place, no other safeguards to prevent widespread abuses were implemented for the first three years that publicly funded sterilization procedures were available. Such negligent circumstances allowed many coerced sterilizations to occur unhindered before the infamous case of the Relf sisters was brought to public attention.

During June of 1973 twelve-year-old Mary Alice and fourteen-year-old Minnie Lee, two African-American sisters, were unknowingly sterilized in a Montgomery, Alabama, hospital. The hospital covered the cost of these operations using OEO funds. Although Mrs Relf signed an "X" to a consent form that she could not read, neither she nor her daughters were advised of the specific nature of the procedure that the nurse advised was necessary. When they learned that their daughters were permanently sterilized, the parents of the two girls enlisted the aid of the Southern Poverty Law Center, and a class-action lawsuit demanding the cessation of federal funding for sterilization proce- dures was filed. Subsequent investigation revealed a striking trend of similar abuses in clinics and federally funded hospitals in the South. Judge Gerhard Gessel, who decided the *Relf* case, estimated that in the South alone 100,000 to 150,000 poor women annually were sterilized through federally funded programs.[13]

Following publicity of the *Relf* case, several in-depth investigations revealed a national trend of sterilization abuse against the poor, and many other lawsuits were filed. One major study, conducted and co- authored by Dr Bernard Rosenfeld and Dr Sidney Wolfe and pub- lished in 1973 by the Ralph Nader Health Research Group, exposed an "epidemic of sterilization" in teaching hospitals between 1971 and 1973.[14] Pointing to glaring class differentials in medical care, the study found that in nearly every major medical teaching hospital in the country the number of elective tubal ligations had at least doubled in those two years. According to the authors, "such abuses ... historically have found fertile climates in the nation's giant, core-city teaching complexes such as the USC-Los Angeles County Medical Center, where medicine is high volume, often impersonal – and practiced on patients who are generally poor, frightened and uneducated."[15] While Califor- nia had long held the highest rates of sterilization in the nation, these rates increased even more during this time.[16]

Statistics from the Women's Hospital of the Los Angeles County Medical Center exemplify the extraordinary upsurge in the numbers of women obtaining surgical sterilization. During the two-year period between July 1968 and July 1970, the number of elective hysterecto- mies increased by 742 per cent, elective tubal ligation experienced a 470 per cent increase, and post-delivery tubal ligation rose by 151 per cent.[17] Most of these women were not adequately informed of alterna- tive birth control options available and of the permanency of the oper- ation, or even aware of their sterilization. Finding that of the thousands of victimized women throughout the nation most were low-income minorities, the report's authors charged that racist attitudes regarding overpopulation and rising welfare costs provided strong motivation for the large push in sterilization.

THE POPULATION "EXPLOSION" AND WELFARE "BACKLASH"

Changes at this time in federal policy relating to family planning were in part a governmental response to mounting concerns that population growth threatened national well-being. Public anxiety about the disas- trous consequences of unchecked population growth escalated during the late 1960s, largely sparked by the efforts of environmentalists who feared that the earth's resources were endangered by unencumbered birth rates in the nation and across the globe.[18] Members of the population control lobby and the nation's highest governmental officials both adamantly called upon professionals to turn their efforts towards the elimination of excess population growth. For example, President Nixon's science advisor, Dr Lee A. DuBridge, declared that "the prime task of every human institution should be to halt population growth ... Every human institution, school, university, church, family, government and institutional agency should set this as its prime task."[19]

Many professional individuals and organizations took this charge seriously, including medical practitioners. Those in the medical community felt a particular call to duty. Many considered that their professional responsibilities rendered the problem of overpopulation explicitly theirs to remedy. Not only was the so-called population bomb hotly debated by the highest-ranking officials and institutions in the health-care profession, it influenced a major reversal of medical policy on issues of reproduction.

While previously it had left matters of family planning to the individual practitioner, in 1966 the American Medical Association (AMA) adopted an official policy regarding population control. Believing that "the medical profession should accept a major responsibility in matters related to human reproduction as they affect the total population and the individual family," the AMA expected all physicians to be prepared to counsel patients on matters of family planning no matter his or her specialty.[20] The espousal of such a policy was, of course, controversial, but many doctors agreed that it was in fact their duty to resolve the problem of overpopulation, as issues of human reproduction and birth control fell squarely within their professional obligation. As one wrote in the *Journal of the American Medical Association*, "Historically, physicians have been leaders in medicine and in the furtherance of human welfare, and only if the medical profession recognizes its opportunity and responsibility can it meet its clear obligation to help solve what is now widely regarded as the world's number one problem."[21]

During this time, the problem of overpopulation was closely linked to concerns about rising welfare rolls, a trend that also emerged during the 1960s. Owing to the liberalization of eligibility requirements for welfare during the 1960s, the numbers of recipients rose significantly during this period.[22] Moreover, the increase in recipients was noticeably racialized; as Gwendolyn Mink notes, "by 1967, a welfare caseload that had once been 86 percent white had become 46 percent nonwhite."[23]

This increase in the rates of welfare recipiency, not unnoticed by working and middle-class taxpayers, resulted in a piercing racialized discourse on the program's (and its clientele's) legitimacy.[24] A 1965 Gallup poll, initiated by the Population Council, demonstrated that by and large the general public believed that welfare recipients were deceitful, lazy, and lacking in initiative. Sixty-three per cent favoured federal funding of state and city family-planning programs, while 20 per cent of respondents were in favour of the sterilization of unwed mothers.[25] Decrying rising public assistance expenditures due to increased welfare rolls and "illegitimate" pregnancies, several states considered bills legitimizing the compulsory sterilization of welfare recipients, and in sentencing many women, judges gave them the choice of sterilization or a jail term. Many physicians echoed these sentiments, often even more vociferously. A 1972 survey of physician attitudes about family planning found that by far the most "punitive" medical practitioners were obstetrician-gynaecologists, 94 per cent of whom favoured compulsory sterilization or the withholding of welfare support for unwed mothers who already had three children.[26]

Thus, for some lay activists, policy-makers, and health-care professionals, birth control appeared to be the most effective panacea for both of the imagined social ills of overpopulation and welfare dependency. The comments of Dr Curtis Wood, president of the Association for Voluntary Sterilization, provide one example of how overpopulation, welfare, and sterilization became linked in the medical mind. In an article published in *Contemporary Obstetrics and Gynecology* in 1973, Wood wrote: "People pollute, and too many people crowded too close together cause many of our social and economic problems. These, in turn, are aggravated by involuntary and irresponsible parenthood. As physicians we have obligations to our individual patients, but we also have obligations to the society in which we are a part. The welfare mess, as it has been called, cries out for solutions, one of which is fertility control."[27] As his statement indicates, decreased fertility became the primary way in which advocates envisioned controlling both the impending population bomb and the welfare dependence of poor women. These women's fertility (and thus, their bodies) was placed at the centre of national interest.

In addition to the targeting of indigent African-American women in the South, Native American women suffered from rampant sterilization abuse at Indian Health Service (IHS) clinics. A study requested by Senator James Abourzek and conducted by the General Accounting Office (GAO) revealed that many Native women were coercively sterilized by the Indian Health Service; most of them believed that their welfare benefits would be retracted if they did not agree to the operation. In the four IHS areas examined in the GAO study, 3,406 sterilizations were performed between 1973 and 1976, approximately one-quarter of all Native Americans sterilized during those years.[28] Many of these coercive sterilizations were conducted on women under the age of twenty-one, some of them in violation of the moratorium called by the U.S. Department of Health, Education and Welfare (HEW) in 1974.

FORCED STERILIZATION AT LOS ANGELES COUNTY MEDICAL CENTER

Prior to the promulgation of the 1974 HEW guidelines, there was no official policy regulating the practice of sterilization at the Women's Hospital at the USC-Los Angeles County Medical Center.[29] During the late 1960s, the Women's Hospital received substantial federal funds for the development and strengthening of the Department of Obstetrics and Gynecology; these funds were in large part funnelled towards the rebuilding of the hospital within which these specialist services were housed. During this period several prestigious doctors joined the Women's Hospital staff under the direction of newly appointed Dr Edward James Quilligan. With these changes in facilities, staff, and funding, the upsurge in the promotion of birth control for the women whom the hospital serviced began.[30]

As commonly occurred in teaching hospitals across the nation, students at the Los Angeles County Medical Center were encouraged to conduct surgical procedures to refine their skills. According to Dr Bernard Rosenfeld, co-author of the Health Research Group report and a resident in the obstetrics-gynaecology department at Los Angeles County Medical Center, staff doctors would often congratulate residents on the number of postpartum tubal ligations accomplished within a week's time.[31] Similarly, residents reportedly encouraged interns to press women into agreeing to a sterilization procedure. In one instance, a resident whose solicitations for sterilization were refused by a patient was told by his supervisor: "Talk her into it. You can always talk her into it." In June 1973 a resident told new interns: "I want you to ask every one of the girls if they want their tubes tied, regardless of how old they are. Remember everyone you get to get her tubes tied means two tubes [i.e., an operation] for some resident or intern."[32] Rosenfeld estimated that 10 to 20 per cent of the physicians at the Los Angeles County Medical Center "actively pushed sterilization on women who either did not understand what was happening to them or who had not been given all the facts regarding their options."[33]

Women were most often approached for sterilization while in the last stages of labour, during their wait in the active labour room, where they stayed until actual delivery. Here, women in the most painful stages of labour were placed on beds side by side, attached to fetal monitors. Dr Karen Benker, who was a student at the University of Southern California Medical School and employed by the Women's Hospital when the sterilization abuses occurred, described a typical scene: "The general picture ... was of crowding, screams of pain, bright lights, lack of sleep by patients and staff, and an 'assembly-line' approach so that many women were literally terrified of what was happening at the time they signed the consents. Of course, this was especially true of non-English-speaking mothers who were left with no explanation of what was happening."[34]

Dr Benker's recognition that "of course" Spanish-speaking women were more likely to experience medical mistreatment points to the critical role of language in perpetuating the sterilization abuse occurred at USC–Los Angeles County Hospital. Residents and doctors were not bilingual; most knew but a few obstetrical-related words. There was "virtually no one available" to interpret for Spanish-speaking women, and often "these women were sterilized on the basis of the question, 'More babies?' said in either English or broken Spanish."[35] While some nurses or translators tried to communicate with Spanish-speaking women, as illustrated below, doctors often took advantage of their patients' inability to understand English to manipulate them into consenting to sterilization.[36]

Women needing a Caesarean-section delivery were most at risk of coercive sterilization. According to Dr Benker,

Once it became clear that a C-section was going to be necessary the resident staff was extremely aggressive in pushing for sterilization, virtually without exception ... On almost a daily basis I saw the following types of coercion being used: the doctor would hold a syringe in front of the mother who was in labor pain and ask her if she wanted a pain killer; while the woman was in the throes of a contraction the doctor would say, "Do you want the pain killer? Then sign the papers. Do you want the pain to stop? Do you want to have to go through this again? Sign the papers."[37]

Nurses or residents often approached women to sign consent forms while she was in active labour and sedated, usually immediately before or after childbirth. Women in labour were given a shot of Valium in preparation for the operation, and consent forms were shoved into their hands while they were too groggy to understand or notice that they were granting permission for their own sterilization.[38]

Moreover, often the hospital staff did not fully explain the irreversible nature of the sterilization procedure. Many women agreed to the surgery believing that their tubes were being tied and that their fertility could easily be restored when they decided to reverse the procedure. María Figueroa specifically recalled that the doctor described sterilization as the "tying" of a woman's tubes that could later be untied. Although she initially refused the procedure, after being loaded with painkillers, tired of the doctor's pressuring, and on the basis of her own understanding of the operation, Mrs Figueroa agreed to sterilization if she delivered a boy. Even though she later delivered a baby girl, she was sterilized.[39]

Women at the hospital were also browbeaten and continually harassed by nurses and doctors until they signed consent forms for the sterilization procedure, usually under the duress of the pain and exhaustion of childbirth. Elena Orozco declined the option to be sterilized several times during her prenatal care at the county hospital. However, after numerous solicitations and while crying from intense pain while in labour, Mrs Orozco signed the consent for sterilization because "I just wanted them to leave me alone, sign the papers and get it over with ... I was in pain on the table when they were asking me all those questions, and they were poking around my stomach, and pushing with their fingers up there. I just wanted to be left alone."[40] Mrs Orozco also agreed to the operation because she "thought he meant tying tubes only. Then they could be untied later."[41] She was sure that "What I was signing, I understood it to tie my tubes, not to sterilize. If they would have put the word 'sterilization' there, I would not have signed the papers."[42] Based on her comprehension of the reversibility of the procedure, Mrs Orozco planned to untie her tubes in three years, and she did not find out until a year and a half after the procedure that she could never again have children.

Hospital personnel also limited communication between labouring women and their husbands. When a delivering patient adamantly resisted sterilization, some doctors would warn her husband that her health was in danger, hoping that he would then convince her to submit to the procedure.[43] Such tactics are apparent in the experience of Dolores Madrigal, who refused sterilization from the outset of her stay at Los Angeles County Hospital. Talking with Mr Madrigal in a separate room, doctors gave him the false impression that his wife would die if she had another child. Ten minutes later, a nurse returned to Mrs Madrigal, laughingly told her that her husband had agreed to her sterilization, and threw a consent form at her.[44]

As evident in the case of Dolores Madrigal, doctors sometimes told women that they would die if they weren't sterilized.[45] Upon the delivery of her third child by Caesarean section, Consuelo Hermosillo was advised by her doctor that a sterilization procedure would be necessary because a fourth pregnancy would most likely put her life at risk. As Mrs Hermosillo recounts, "He told me, in these words: 'Lady, the limit for cesarean are three by law. So, you have to decide whether you want to risk the next one, because I think the next one you can die because you are rated here in the history as a patient of high risk.' "[46]

Estela Benavides similarly took seriously her doctor's warnings that another delivery by Caesarean section could threaten her life, and she consented to a tubal ligation while hemorrhaging during labour. In her words: "They told me the reason was that if I got pregnant again the baby would probably be in the same position, and something else could happen serious ... I thought maybe I could die ... I thought if I had another child something could happen to me." Moreover, she testified that her only concern was for the daughters she already had: "The only thing I thought about was the girls. That is why I asked the question, that if I accepted that operation, I want it to be all right for my girls."[47]

Some physicians violently mistreated and harassed their patients. One doctor slapped a patient and told her to shut up as she cried out in labour pains. Often moralistic references to the woman's sexual activity were expressed (i.e., if you hadn't had sex you wouldn't be in pain right now). Many doctors falsely told women that the state law only allowed a woman three Caesarean sections (see above testimony by Consuelo Hermosillo) and that their sterilization was subsequently required. Maria Hurtado recalled that her doctor "brought someone from outside and explained to her to ask me why I wanted so many children since the State of California only permitted three Cesareans."[48] While unconscious following the delivery of her child, Mrs Hurtado was given a tubal ligation without her consent. She recalled that it was not until she requested contraceptives during her six-week postpartum visit that a receptionist at the hospital told her, "Lady, forever you will not be able to have any more children."[49]

The physicians' attitudes towards the clientele served at Los Angeles County Medical Center and their perceptions of their own role in providing a panacea for overpopulation and rising welfare rolls were intricately linked. Dr Rosenfeld recalled that in a discussion with another doctor about coercing patients into sterilization, his colleague told him: "Well, if we're going to pay for them we should control them."[50] While under partial anaesthesia in preparation for her Caesarean-section delivery, Jovita Rivera was approached by a doctor who told her that she should have her "tubes tied" because her children were a burden on the government. Ironically, Ms Rivera was not receiving public assistance; nor were any of the other plaintiffs in the *Madrigal* case (this case will be discussed below).[51] However, it was because the doctors perceived these women as poor welfare recipients that they were deemed to require sterilization.

The doctors would also make use of the patients' race and immigrant status to coerce them into sterilization. Many physicians "would express very prejudiced remarks about patients who did not speak English – Mexican-American patients" and referred to them as "beans."[52] After remaining in the delivery room in advanced labour for four hours, Georgina Hernández was approached by her doctor. After talking to her about how Mexicans were very poor and couldn't provide for a large family, he suggested that she be sterilized. Although Mrs Hernández resisted her doctor's urgings and did not recall signing a consent form, she was surgically sterilized during the delivery of her fourth child.[53] Other women were threatened with deportation if they didn't consent to be sterilized. According to one newspaper account, at a San Diego hospital "one resident would be so furious if a woman declined [sterilization] that he would say, 'We know you're here illegally and if you don't consent to have a tubal, we'll call the feds [immigration officials] and get you deported.'"[54]

The experiences described above provide a telling glimpse into the multiple manipulations of power and privilege that converged at the USC–Los Angeles County Medical Center to rob Mexican-origin women of their reproductive liberty. As was done in other instances of sterilization abuse across the country, Medical Center personnel employed patriarchal, class-based, and racial ideologies to coerce Mexican-origin women into sterilization. However, it is also clear that an ideology of U.S. citizenship was another prominent force in the sterilization abuse of Mexican-origin women. The centrality of this factor is clearly evidenced in the report that USC–Los Angeles County Medical Center doctors often commented that their patients "weren't really 'American' and [that they] had come from Mexico pregnant on the bus just so that they could have their baby born a U.S. Citizen so they can't be deported themselves."[55] Because ideas like this provide new insight into the ways in which sterilization abuse was justified, they are further examined below.

POLICING "PREGNANT PILGRIMS": THE IDEOLOGIES OF CITIZENSHIP

Like many feminist analyses of health politics in the United States, this examination of the sterilization abuse of Mexican-origin women asserts that institutional aspects of the delivery of medical care converged with ideological forces to influence medical practice. Undeniably, certain structural factors were in place that enabled doctors to conduct the coercive sterilization surgery easily. The absence of any guidelines to monitor physician behaviour in a large urban teaching hospital, federal funding that could be funnelled towards paying for the operations, and a poor, non-English-speaking clientele all facilitated the sterilization abuse that occurred at Los Angeles County Medical Center.

However, I have also demonstrated that underlying the social concerns were operative forces that not only fuelled a proactive medical policy, but were in the forefront of the minds of many doctors who practised coercive sterilization. During the 1970s a confluence of concerns about overpopulation, welfare, and dwindling social services generated a proliferation of discourses that defined poor women of colour and their child-bearing as a problematic public charge. While these concerns were differently applied to different groups of women of colour, for pregnant Mexican immigrant women in California during the 1970s, the issue of welfare and overpopulation were immutably tied to larger questions of citizenship and of who was rightfully deserving of social benefits such as medical care.

Such connections are evident in the public uproar about undocumented immigrants illegally receiving welfare benefits. In 1973, 8 to 9 percent of recipients in California were found to be "aliens," and this group reportedly received $100 million a year in welfare and other social services.[56] Concerned that "there are far too many illegal welfare recipients among our citizens," people across the nation called for an end to the "problem[, which is] so big we don't know where to start."[57] Indeed, this imagined problem was considered so menacing in Los Angeles County that a special report on the impact of welfare payments to "illegal aliens" was commissioned and a project designed to "weed out" aliens on local welfare rolls instituted.[58] This study found that, surprisingly, the actual numbers of illegal immigrants on welfare were negligible. Ironically, a previous report had shown that, in fact, Spanish-speaking Californians were being discriminated against by state welfare agencies.[59]

Similar concerns arose over the numbers of Mexican immigrant women who reportedly crossed the Mexican-U.S. border to have their children. A host of exposés documenting the lives of these "pregnant pilgrims" flourished in the early to mid-1970s. As one emblematic story on the impact of this "problem" on Los Angeles County hospitals depicts, many Mexican women allegedly expended great effort to cross the border illegally, often times while in labour, in order for their children to be born American citizens at U.S. taxpayers' expense. The exposé begins:

A woman in labor groans with pain, and a nurse tries to comfort her.
"What do you think it will be," the nurse asks, "a boy or a girl?"
The woman smiles, relaxing slightly.
She knows what the baby will be.
An American.

In one Los Angeles County hospital alone [the story continued], some 45 per cent of all maternity cases involve illegal alien women giving birth to brand-new U.S. citizens. And, according to a recent survey, Los Angeles County Hospitals cost taxpayers nearly $51 million per year in health services for illegal or "undocumented" aliens, as some bureaucrats prefer to call them.[60]

Reportedly growing in numbers as the decade progressed, by 1977 deliveries of the children of immigrant women in Los Angeles county hospitals were considered only part of the costs of health services for illegal immigrants that "cost taxpayers" $51 million per year. According to a hospital administrator who had surveyed hospitals in other border counties, "every one of them has exactly the same problem" – paying for the childbirth of hundreds of undeserving Mexican women.[61] According to media reports, Mexican women were equally duplicitous about their child-bearing in other ways. While some were said to have had their babies falsely registered as U.S. born, others reportedly abandoned their newborn babies on the United States side of the U.S.-Mexico border.[62] Widely published articles in major newspapers across the nation suggested that Mexican-origin women were becoming an increasingly threatening mass of problematic child-bearers necessitating regulation. The publication of such stories demonstrates that public concern about the ever-present hyper-fertile immigrant woman crossing the border to secure free prenatal care, American citizenship for her children, and the chance to live on the public dole emerged at the very same time that stringent efforts to limit her reproductive autonomy were mounted. While such efforts did not go unchallenged, issues of citizenship continued to undermine the legal redress sought by those coercively sterilized.

MADRIGAL V. QUILLIGAN AND CHICANA RESISTANCE[63]

The legal struggle on behalf of the women sterilized at the Los Angeles County Medical Center began in August of 1974, when lawyers at the Los Angeles Center for Law and Justice were provided with information about the abuses by Dr Bernard Rosenfeld. After hearing of the incidents of sterilization abuse, Antonia Hernández, then just two months out of law school, and others from Comisión Femenil, a Chicana activist group, attempted to locate the women in the Los Angeles area whom Dr Bernard Rosenfeld's records indicated had been sterilized, most likely without their knowing consent.

Following a year of interviewing dozens of women, Hernández and other lawyers were convinced that there was in fact a distinct pattern of coercive sterilization taking place at Los Angeles County Medical

Center. Funds raised through educational outreach efforts, demonstrations, and the fundraising efforts of Comisión Femenil enabled
the filing of a class-action civil-rights lawsuit on behalf of the women
coercively sterilized at the Medical Center.[64] Although data showed
that hundreds of Mexican-origin women were forcibly sterilized at
the facility, only ten represented the plaintiff class at the trial. For
many of the women, the expiration of the statute of limitations
barred their participation in the lawsuit; others were simply not interested in becoming involved in the judicial process or were afraid to
take part in such an action. Others were wary of the judicial process
and doubtful that their case would be believed. For those who were
undocumented or whose family members were not yet documented,
however, legal redress was not a viable option. Most were hesitant to
even talk to the lawyers or make any formal complaint to the hospital for fear of being located and deported by the Immigration and
Naturalization Service.[65]

On 18 June 1975, a class-action civil-rights suit was filed in the federal district court in Los Angeles.[66] The suit, *Madrigal v. Quilligan*,
named USC–Los Angeles County Medical Center, twelve doctors
(including the head of the Department of Obstetrics and Gynecology and of the Medical Center itself), the State of California, and
the U.S. Department of Health, Education and Welfare as defen-
dants. In addition to financial compensation, the plaintiffs requested that the Department of Health, Education and Welfare
require federally funded hospitals to provide thorough sterilization
counselling and consent forms in Spanish.[67]

Following over three years of preparation, the attorneys for the
plaintiffs in *Madrigal v. Quilligan*, Charles Nabarette and Antonia
Hernández, began their case in court on 31 May 1978. The lawyers
argued that the sterilization of the women without their informed
consent was a violation of their civil rights and their constitutional
right to bear children. Over the course of the two-and-a-half-week
trial, Hernández and Nabarette called upon the plaintiffs, hospital
personnel, and several expert witnesses to establish that the custom
and practice of the doctors at the USC–Los Angeles County Medical
Center was to approach women during labour and "push" them into
giving their consent to sterilization.[68] However, after hearing extensive testimony, on 8 June 1978 Judge Jesse Curtis handed down his decision in favour of the defendant doctors, concluding that they were
acting in "good faith" and with a "bona fide belief" that they were performing the sterilization operation with the knowledge and voluntary
consent of each patient. The judge attributed the sterilization of the
plaintiffs to a "communication breakdown" between the doctors and

their patients rather than to any improper conduct by the staff at Los Angeles County Medical Center. In his extensive opinion, Judge Curtis stated: "There is no doubt that these women have suffered severe emotional and physical stress because of these operations. One can sympathize with their inability to communicate clearly, but one can hardly blame the doctors for relying on these indicia of consent which appeared to be unequivocal on their face and are in constant use in the Medical Center."[69]

Despite the ultimate judgment of the court against the *Madrigal* plaintiffs, because of the mobilization by community members, significant gains towards the reproductive freedoms of all women were won.[70] As a direct result of Dr Rosenfeld's complaints, the organizing efforts of Chicana activists, and public media attention given to the alleged abuses, the Los Angeles County Medical Center began to enforce compliance with the federal sterilization regulations.[71]

Additionally, as a direct result of the lawsuit, significantly revised regulations and guidelines for sterilization surgery were established at the state level. Working together, the Chicana Rights Project of the Mexican American Legal Defense and Education Fund and the Coalition for the Medical Rights of Women filed a petition with the California State Department of Public Health calling for the implementation of more strenuous regulations guaranteeing the uncoerced, informed consent for every person undergoing sterilization in California.[72] Members of both organizations drafted what eventually became the state's official guidelines for the procedure. They mobilized a coalition of organizations and individuals that travelled to the sterilization regulations hearings across the state to voice their experiences of forced sterilization and other medical mistreatment to state officials, ensuring that the process surrounding the establishment of the state guidelines was accountable to and addressed the concerns of Mexican-origin and other poor women of colour in the state. These efforts led to the eventual acceptance of guidelines that required that consent forms be written in the woman's native language and at the sixth grade reading level.

Moreover, as a result of the *Madrigal* case and similar trials across the nation, new regulations issued by the Department of Health, Education and Welfare ensured that a patient opting for sterilization would be supplied with sufficient information to make a decision under "legally effective informed consent."[73] These guidelines required that surgical sterilization candidates be formally advised that federal benefits would be available to them regardless of their choice to sterilize or not, that patients be thoroughly informed of the procedure, its risks, and its permanence, and that they be counselled on the range of birth control alternatives available. Moreover, a waiting period of seventy-two hours – to allow the woman to change her mind – was established and a federal ban on sterilization of girls under the age of eighteen was implemented.[74]

Perhaps most importantly, the plaintiffs' lawsuit and the Chicana activists' political activism at the community level brought public attention to the severe infringements upon the reproductive freedoms of Mexican-origin women.[75] Prevailing despite the ignorance of the nationalist Chicano movement and the mainstream women's movement on issues of sterilization abuse, Chicana feminist activists argued that "it is minority women who must take it upon themselves to insure that their right to determine whether or not to bear children be preserved" and must organize to take control of their reproductive lives.[76]

The lawsuit was a particularly significant moment in Chicana and Latina campaigns for reproductive freedom, because perhaps for the first time health professionals, lawyers, community activists, and other concerned individuals were brought together to fight for the recognition and redress of abuses against the reproductive freedom of Mexican-origin women. Members of Comisión Femenil, the Chicana Welfare Rights Organization, and the Chicana Rights Project of the Mexican American Legal Defense and Education fund, as well as other Chicana and Chicano health activists, all played a critical role in organizing against forced sterilization. The organization of public marches and rallies, the legal battle, and other efforts to publicize the abuses that occurred were spearheaded by the Chicana leadership.[77] Combining both community-based organizing techniques and the legal means available to them, Chicanas were at the forefront of a very public battle to gain social redress for the medical mistreatment that Mexican-origin peoples encountered in the United States. As so eloquently stated by Georgina Torres-Rizk, a lawyer for the *Madrigal* plaintiffs until just before the trial, the case "resulted in a growing awareness among Chicanas ... that they themselves are the most qualified to address themselves to these issues."[78]

CONCLUSION

The forced sterilization of Mexican immigrant women at the USC–Los Angeles County Medical Center during the late 1960s and early 1970s not only provides rare insight into the medical abuses poor women of colour faced during this period, but uniquely demonstrates how particular cultural and regional issues like language – and, even more importantly, issues of citizenship – crucially shaped their reproductive health experiences. Often overshadowed by racist, classist, and sexist ideologies operating in the sterilization abuse of poor women of colour during the 1960s and 1970s, conceptions of citizenship (and non-citizenship) worked at multiple levels to fundamentally influence the reproductive health experiences of Mexican immigrant women.

First, presuming that their Mexican-origin patients were in the United States illegally, many doctors predicated their coercion on the women's citizenship status, threatening patients with deportation if they did not succumb to irreversible sterilization surgery. Second, for those women coercively sterilized who were indeed undocumented or who had family who were undocumented, the lack of citizenship status left them without access to the legal means to redress the violence done to them. Third, questions of citizenship and contestation of the rights that it "guaranteed" operated at a more amorphous ideological level to provide a justification for the coercive sterilization of Mexican-origin women. In all of these ways, citizenship was used as a clear marker of those who were "undeserving" of proper medical care and, in effect, of membership in the national community. Not only a means of punishing Mexican women who were believed to be "illegally" utilizing public health care services, sterilization abuse also served as a means to eliminate future "undesirable" citizens.

In addition to highlighting another significant axis upon which reproductive health matters turn, public concerns about citizenship, spoken through the discourses of "illegal" immigration, welfare, and population control, demonstrate how social interests operate in medical practice, often with devastating results for poor recipients of health care. The attitudes expressed by doctors at the Los Angeles County Medical Center cannot be dismissed as individual personal attitudes, but must be recognized as reflective of a particular socio-political context that engendered, and at times even advocated, the reproductive abuse of Mexican-origin women.

Such histories must be examined further, since Mexican-origin and other immigrant women still face coercive efforts to limit their reproductive autonomy. The ideas and events documented here remain eerily resonant in the increasingly hostile politics surrounding the child-bearing of today's Mexican-origin women. Public concern about the child-bearing of Mexican immigrant women has vociferously re-emerged during the past decade in concert with equally aggressive attempts to control their reproductive behaviour.[79] Several members of Congress have recently proposed legislation abrogating birthright citizenship, arguing that if their children were not guaranteed citizenship upon birth in the United States (and thus their right to a host of social services), Mexican women would no longer illegally cross the border.[80] Efforts to repeal the fourteenth amendment, as well as to deny immigrant women prenatal care (this was one of the primary concerns of Proposition 187, a referendum on barring undocumented immigrants from public entitlements and services such as non-emergency health care, welfare, and public school education; it was passed in California in 1994 but was overturned in 1996), have revitalized the image of the "pregnant pilgrim."

During the heyday of Proposition 187's advocates, dozens of major metropolitan newspaper accounts attested to the "widespread" phenomenon of Mexican women illegally crossing the border to deliver their children on United States soil, surreptitiously planning their migration around their upcoming delivery. For example, in February 1994 the *San Diego Union-Tribune* ran a multi-article series titled "Born in the USA" that looked into the purportedly common occurrence of Mexicans delivering their children in California hospitals with the expectation that the state would pay for it.[81] Together the articles accentuated the problematic nature of the issue, running under headlines such as "Births to Illegal Immigrants on the Rise: California Taxpayers Finance Soaring Numbers of Foreigners' Babies" and "Blockade at Border Hasn't Cut Births." The prevalence of these images in the mainstream media helped to circulate a stereotype in the larger public domain.

As we continue to live this history, equal attention must also be paid to the continued efforts of Mexican-origin women to secure their procreative freedom. As important as it is to document and analyse the atrocious abuses that have occurred, it is also incumbent upon us to remember that Mexican-origin women have been more than mere victims of efforts to construct and constrain their reproductive practices. Their willingness to bear witness and seek redress for their coerced sterilization and the grassroots organizing of Chicana activists have been fundamental to the implementation of safeguards that, if complied with, will help ensure that other women will never confront such violent intrusions upon their reproductive lives.

NOTES

1 Although it is focused on the first half of the twentieth century, the most comprehensive account of sterilization abuse is Philip R. Reilly's *The Surgical Solution: A History of Involuntary Sterilization in the United States* (Baltimore: Johns Hopkins University Press 1991). During the 1950s Puerto Rican women also suffered a disproportionate amount of sterilization abuse at the hands of the U.S. government; 33% of Puerto Rican women living on the island were sterilized. See Annette B. Ramirez de

Arellano and Conrad Seipp, *Colonialism, Catholicism and Contraception* (Chapel Hill: University of North Carolina Press 1983). See also Iris Lopez, "Agency and Constraint: Sterilization and Reproductive Freedom among Puerto Rican Women in New York City," *Urban Anthropology* 22, nos 3–4 (1993): 299–323.

2 For overviews of late twentieth-century sterilization abuse that largely focus on the sterilization of poor African-American women, see Dorothy Roberts, *Killing the Black Body: Race, Reproduction, and the Meaning of Liberty* (New York: Vintage Books 1997), 89–98; Linda Gordon, *Woman's Body, Woman's Right: Birth Control in America* (New York: Penguin Books 1990): 431–6; Rosalind Petchesky, *Abortion and Woman's Choice: The State, Sexuality and Reproductive Freedom* (Boston: Northeastern University Press 1990): 178–82; Angela Davis, "Racism, Birth Control and Reproductive Rights," in Angela Davis, *Women, Race and Class* (New York: Vintage Books 1981), 202–21; Thomas B. Littlewood, *The Politics of Population Control* (Notre Dame: University of Notre Dame Press 1977); and Thomas M. Shapiro, *Population Control Politics: Women, Sterilization and Reproductive Choice* (Philadelphia: Temple University Press 1977). Of the many cases of coercive sterilization reported during this period, none documented abuses against middle-class white women. Gordon, *Woman's Body, Woman's Right*, 433.

3 *Relf et al. v. Weinberger et al.*, Civil Action (hereafter Civ. A.) No. 73-1557, U.S. Dist Ct, Washington, D.C., 15 March 1974.

4 Throughout this essay, Mexican-origin women and Mexican immigrant women are used interchangeably to refer to the women coercively steril-ized at Los Angeles County Medical Center. While it is not known if all of the women who were ever sterilized there were indeed immigrant women, all of the plaintiffs in the trial of *Madrigal v. Quilligan*, from which I have drawn my primary data, are Mexican immigrants. I use the term Chicana, which designates women of Mexican origin born in the United States, only in reference to the activists who organized against sterilization abuse, as this was their chosen self-referent.

5 Shapiro, *Population Control Politics*, 87.

6 Ibid.; Elaine Tyler May, *Barren in the Promised Land: Childless Americans and the Pursuit of Happiness* (New York: Basic Books 1995).

7 Donald T. Critchlow, *Intended Consequences: Birth Control, Abortion, and the Federal Government in Modern America* (New York: Oxford University Press 1999), offers a thorough account of the federal government's change in family-planning policy between 1965 and 1974.

8 Shapiro, *Population Control Politics*.

9 A 1967 study conducted by the OEO determined birth control as the most cost-effective method of poverty prevention. In 1968 Congress declared family planning a "special emphasis" program of the War on Poverty. James Reed, "Public Policy on Human Reproduction and the Historian," *Journal*

of Social History 18 (1985): 383. Also see Simone M. Caron, "Race, Class and Reproduction: The Evolution of a Reproductive Policy in the United States, 1800–1989" (PHD dissertation, Clark University 1989), chap. 5.

10 U.S. Department of Health and Human Services, National Center for Health Statistics, *Trends in Contraceptive Practice: United States, 1965–76* (Hyattsville, Md: Office of Health Research, Statistics and Technology 1982).

11 "28% of Married Couples Surgically Sterile in 1976," *Los Angeles Times*, 22 August 1978: pt 1, 6.

12 While guidelines were printed in 1972, they remained undistributed until 1974. Les Payne, "Forced Sterilization of the Poor," *San Francisco Chronicle*, 26 February 1974.

13 *Relf v. Weinberger.*

14 Health Research Group, *A Health Research Group Study on Surgical Steriliza-tion: Present Abuses and Proposed Regulation* (Washington, D.C. 1973); Robert Kistler, "Women 'Pushed' into Sterilization, Doctor Charges: Thousands Victimized at Some Inner-City Teaching Hospitals, Report Claims," *Los Angeles Times*, 2 December 1975: 1.

15 Health Research Group, *Study on Surgical Sterilization.*

16 Reilly, *Surgical Solution.*

17 Health Research Group, *Study on Surgical Sterilization.* Comparable data for hospitals across the nation show that at Mt Sinai hospital in New York City sterilizations increased 200% from 1970 to 1974 and that at a "large hospi-tal" in St Paul, Minnesota, the ratio of tubal ligations to births increased from 1:9.2 in 1968–69 to 1: 4.3 in 1973. L. Edwards and E. Hakanson "Changing Status of Tubal Sterilization: An Evaluation of Fourteen Years' Experience," *American Journal of Obstetrics and Gynecology*, 1973: 115, 347, cited in Antonia Hernández, "Chicanas and the Issue of Involuntary Sterilization: Reforms Needed to Protect Informed Consent," *Chicano Law Review* 3, no. 1 (1976): 25.

18 Charles F. Westhoff, "Recent Developments in Population Growth and Policy in the United States," in Charles F. Westhoff, ed., *Toward the End of Growth: Population in America* (Englewood Cliffs, N.J.: Prentice-Hall 1973), 165.

19 James S. Rummonds, "The Role of Government in Population Policy," *Pro-ceedings of the Conference on Population Growth and Public Policy (8–9 February 1975)* (Berkeley, Calif.), 24b, c.

20 "AMA Policy on Human Reproduction, Including Population Control," as quoted in "Population Policy and the Values of Physicians," in Robert M. Veatch and Thomas Draper, eds, *Population Policy and Ethics: The American Experience* (New York: Irvington Publishers 1977), 377–408.

21 Richard K. Anderson, "Obstacles to Population Control," *Journal of the American Medical Association* 197, no. 8 (22 August 1966): 126.

22 For example, from 1966 to 1967 the number of welfare recipients rose from 7.4 to 8.4 million. "Why the Welfare Bill Is Stuck," *Newsweek*, 7 December 1970: 23, cited in Jill Quagdagno, *The Color of Welfare: How Racism Undermined the War on Poverty* (New York: Oxford University Press 1994).

23 Gwendolyn Mink, "Welfare Reform in Historical Perspective," *Connecticut Law Review* 26 (1994): 879, 891, quoted in Roberts, *Killing the Black Body*, 207.

24 See Dorothy Roberts, "The Welfare Debate: Who Pays for Procreation," in Roberts, *Killing the Black Body*, 202–45.

25 *Washington Post*, 27 January 1965: 2A; "Ahead of Washington," *Time* 87 (25 February 1966): 25.

26 "Physician Attitudes: MDs Assume Poor Can't Remember to Take Pill," *Family Planning Digest* 3 (January 1972): 3–4.

27 *Contemporary Obstetrics and Gynecology* 1 (1973): 31–44.

28 See the three-piece discussion of the IHS sterilizations by Brint Dillingham: "Indian Women and IHS Sterilization Practices," *American Indian Journal* 3 (1977): 27–8; "Sterilization of Native Americans," *American Indian Journal* 3 (1977): 16–19; and "Sterilization Update," *American Indian Journal* 3 (1977): 25.

In-depth research by Dr Connie Uri, who investigated beyond those four IHS areas, indicates that even more Native women were sterilized. See Joan Burnes, "Shocking Sterilization Statistics Surface," *Indian Country Today* 14, no. 9 (24 August 1994): 8; and "Sterilization of Native Women to IHS Charged," *Akwesasne Notes* (Early Winter 1974): 6–7. For narrative accounts of sterilization abuse of Native American women, see Janet Larson, "And Then There Were None," *Christian Century*, 26 January 1977: 61; and Richard Lou, "The Sterilization of American Indian Women," *Playgirl Magazine* 4, no. 12 (May 1977): 43, 51, 57, 100. For accounts of legal action taken on behalf of Native women who were coercively sterilized, see Richard M. Harley, "Indian Women Plan to Sue U.S. in Sterilization Cases," *Christian Science Monitor*, 27 May 1977: 6; and "Killing Our Future: Sterilization and Experiments," *Akwesasne Notes* (Early Spring 1977).

29 Not until 22 February 1974 was it specified that "patients will not be approached for the first time concerning sterilization when they are in active labor"; this instruction was given in a memo dispersed to all staff by Dr Quilligan. Deposition of Roger Freeman, 29 June 1977, 12, *Madrigal v. Quilligan*, No. CV-75-2057-EC. I am indebted to Carlos Vélez-Ibañez, who generously shared his personal collected materials from the *Madrigal* case. Documents from his personal collection will be acknowledged as Carlos Vélez Personal Collection (hereafter Vélez Personal Collection).

30 While definitive statistics are unavailable, it was reported by the head of obstetrics/gynaecology, Dr Quilligan, that the "predominate race" that frequented LACMC was Mexican American. *Madrigal v. Quilligan*, trial

transcript, 740. The trial transcript and other case pleadings are available in the Carlos Vélez Sterilization Archive, Chicano Studies Library, University of California, Los Angeles (hereafter Vélez Papers).

31 Rosenfeld documented his personal observations while a resident at Los Angeles County Medical Center, and his accounts were utilized by the attorneys for the Southern Poverty Law Center in the *Relf* case against HEW over the adoption of sterilization guidelines.

32 Health Research Group, *Study on Surgical Sterilization*, 7–8.

33 Narda Zacchino and Kris Lindgren, "Plaintiffs Lose Suit over 10 Sterilizations," *Los Angeles Times*, 1 July 1978.

34 Karen Benker Statement, 5, Vélez Personal Collection.

35 Ibid.; Deposition of Dr Karen Benker, 6 September 1977, 32, Vélez Personal Collection.

36 Juan Nieto, an intern at LACMC, reported that he had observed similar treatment – "particularly of Mexican-Americans" – at a hospital in Colorado, where he had completed his medical training. Suggesting a pattern of abuse of Mexican-origin women throughout the Southwest, Nieto was sure that Spanish-speaking patients "had no idea the procedure urged on them was permanent." Quoted in Mariana Hernandez, "L.A. Women Protest Forced Sterilizations," *Militant*, 20 December 1974: 17.

37 Karen Benker Statement, 3.

38 Ibid.

39 Georgina Torres-Rizk, "Sterilization Abuses against Chicanas in Los Angeles," 2 December 1976: 1–2, in RG 9, box 95, folder 4, Mexican American Legal Defense and Education Fund, Stanford University Special Collections, Palo Alto, Calif. (hereafter MALDEF Archives).

40 Trial transcript, 370. All following quotes from the women involved in the *Madrigal* case are taken directly from the court transcript. During the trial the women all testified in the Spanish language, with their words translated by a court translator, then transcribed by the court reporter.

41 Ibid., 368.

42 Ibid., 383.

43 Karen Benker Statement, 4.

44 Trial transcript, 453–4.

45 Karen Benker Statement, 3.

46 Trial transcript, 665.

47 Ibid., 126–9.

48 Ibid., 406.

49 Ibid., 416.

50 Ibid.

51 Antonia Hernández, "Chicanas and the Issue of Involuntary Sterilization: Reforms Needed to Protect Informed Consent," *Chicano Law Review* 3, no. 1 (1976): 9.

52 Karen Benker Deposition, 58–9.

53 Torres-Rizk, "Sterilization Abuses against Chicanas," 2; interview of Georgina Hernández, 9 May 1978, 10, Vélez Personal Collection.

54 Kistler, "Women 'Pushed' into Sterilization," 2.

55 Karen Benker Statement, 5

56 See "The Aliens Who Get Welfare Aid," *San Francisco Chronicle*, 27 January 1973, and "Aliens Reportedly Get $100 Million in Welfare," *Los Angeles Times*, 27 January 1973. Both articles are located in the collection of the Comite de Mexico y Aztlán, News Clippings Service (Oakland, Calif.) (hereafter COMEXAZ clippings).

57 Robert M. Lewis, "Illegal Welfare Recipients," *Arizona Republic*, 7 September 1975, and "Aliens Reportedly Get $100 Million," both in COMEXAZ clippings.

58 See Frank Del Olmo, "Few Aliens on Welfare Illegally, Study Indicates," *Los Angeles Times*, 1 July 1975; "A Ruling on Aliens and Welfare," *San Francisco Chronicle*, 25 December 1974; and "Study of Alien Welfare Ruling on County's Finances Sought," *Los Angeles Times*, 27 December 1974, all in COMEXAZ clippings.

59 Jim Wood, "Report on Bias against Latinos in Welfare," *San Francisco Chronicle*, 2 July 1972, in COMEXAZ clippings.

60 Steve Kline, "Aliens: Victims or Victimizer?" *San Antonio Express*, 23 August 1977, in COMEXAZ clippings. See also "Pregnant Pilgrims Make Trips to U.S. Hospitals," *El Paso Times*, 23 November 1972; Steven M. Eames, "Mexico's Pregnant Women Wish to Give Birth in the U.S.," *El Paso Times*, 15 June 1975; Phil Kimball, "Juarez Mothers-to-Be Using El Paso Hospitals Have Financial Impact," *El Paso Times*, 1 August 1975; Tom Kuhn, "Aliens Give Birth at State's Expense," *Arizona Republic*, 27 April 1975; and "Hospital Told to Refuse Alien Births," *Arizona Republic*, 1 November 1975, all in COMEXAZ clippings.

61 Kuhn, "Aliens Give Birth."

62 "False Registration of Alien Babies Alleged," *El Paso Times*, 12 May 1977; and "Born on Border, Twins Left behind by Mexican Mother," *Los Angeles Times*, 8 July 1977, both in COMEXAZ clippings.

63 The *Madrigal* suit was not the only one filed against the USC–LACMC for the sterilization abuse of Mexican-origin women. In *Andrade et al. v. Los Angeles County–USC Medical Center*, six other women and their husbands sued the Medical Center and Los Angeles County for permanent sterilization without the women's knowledge or consent. For a short account of the case, refer to Patti Garcia, "Forced Sterilization of Third World Women," *Razón Mestiza*, Summer, special edition (1975). In an article published in the *Militant*, Mariana Hernandez writes of a $6-million suit filed by five women against the Medical Center, but it is unclear whether this is a different case than that filed by Andrade et al. Mariana

Hernandez, "L.A. Women Protest Forced Sterilizations," *Militant*, 20 December 1974: 17.

64 Virginia Espino, "Women Sterilized as You Give Birth: Forced Sterilization and Chicana Resistance in the 1970s," in Vicki Ruiz, ed., *Las Obreras: Chicana Politics of Work and Family* (Los Angeles: UCLA Chicano Studies Research Center Publications 2000), 75.

65 According to Hernández, "We could have had many, many more plaintiffs on the lawsuit, but the women were afraid of the Immigration and Naturalization Service." Antonia Hernández, personal interview.

66 Robert Rawitch, "11 Latin Women File Suit on Sterilization: Claim They Were Coerced or Deceived into Having Operation at Medical Center," *Los Angeles Times*, 19 June 1975.

67 Plaintiffs' Proposed Findings of Fact and Conclusions of Law, *Madrigal v. Quilligan*, C.D. Cal., 22 June 1978.

68 Trial transcript, 789.

69 *Madrigal v. Quilligan*, court opinion, 19. I examine the trial proceedings in this case, which were as laden with racial, class-based, and gendered dynamics as the events that occurred in the hospital, elsewhere.

70 Based on the contention that Judge Curtis erred in his application of the law to the case, the decision was taken to the Ninth Circuit Court of Appeals. The appeal claimed that Judge Curtis abused his judicial authority in his decision by unilaterally overlooking the testimony of several key witnesses for the plaintiffs. When the Ninth Circuit Court of Appeals denied the appeal, lawyers involved with the case decided not to take the appeal to the U.S. Supreme Court. See Narda Zacchino and Kris Lindgren, "Plaintiffs Lose Suit over 10 Sterilizations," *Los Angeles Times*, 1 July 1978; and Narda Zacchino, "10 Women Will Appeal Ruling on Sterilization," *Los Angeles Times*, 8 July 1978: 26.

71 Diane Ainsworth, "Mother No More," *Los Angeles Reader* 1, no. 13 (26 January 1979): 1, 4–9.

72 See *California Coalition for the Medical Rights of Women et al. v. California Department of Health*, "Petition for Regulations to Prevent Coerced Sterilizations in All Licensed Health Facilities," n.d., in RG 5, box 10, folder 6, MALDEF Archives.

73 For the legal aspects of the debate over the regulations, see *Relf et al. v. Weinberger et al.* and *National Welfare Rights Organization v. Weinberger, et al.*, Civ. A. Nos 73-1557, 74-243 372 F. Supp 1196, 15 March 1974; *Relf et al. v. Mathews et al.* and *National Welfare Rights Organization v. Mathews et al.*, Civ. A. Nos 1557-3, 74-243 403 F. Supp 1235, 22 October 1975; and *Relf et al. v. Weinberger et al.* and *National Welfare Rights Organization v. Weinberger, et al.*, 13 September 1977. For an excellent and thorough analysis of the debate as it developed in the public arena, see Rosalind Pollack Petchesky, "Reproduction, Ethics, and Public Policy: The Federal

Sterilization Regulations," *Hastings Center Report* 9, no. 5 (October 1977): 29–42.

74 Despite the promulgation of these guidelines by HEW, however, a 1975 study found "gross noncompliance" with the regulations. Elissa Krauss, "Hospital Survey on Sterilization Policies" (American Civil Liberties Union 1975).

75 Theresa Aragon de Valdez, "Organizing as a Political Tool for the Chicana," *Frontiers* 5, no. 2, (1980): 7–13. For a more in-depth analysis of Chicana activism against sterilization abuse during this time and how it demonstrates a distinct Chicana ideology that differs from that of the Chicana/o and women's rights movements, see, Espino, "Women Sterilized as You Give Birth."

76 Torres-Rizk, "Abuses against Chicanas," 13.

77 On 23 November 1974 the Committee to End Forced Sterilization, a coalition of "feminists and community groups," staged a 250-people demonstration against the sterilization of minority women. Protesters held placards reading "Que se ponga fin a la esterilización involuntaria" (Stop forced sterilization) and "Que paren las practicas experimentales de medicina con la gente pobre" (Stop medical experimentation with poor people). Hernandez, "L.A. Women Protest Forced Sterilizations."

78 Torres-Rizk, "Abuses against Chicanas," 13.

79 See Dorothy E. Roberts, "Who May Give Birth to Citizens? Reproduction, Eugenics, and Immigration," in Juan P. Perea, ed., *Immigrants Out! The New Nativism and the Anti-Immigrant Impulse in the United States* (New York: New York University Press 1997), 205–19.

80 See Jonathon P. Decker, "Lawmakers Look to Revoke Automatic Citizenship Law," *Christian Science Monitor,* 27 December 1995: 3.

81 See Nancy Cleeland, "Births to Illegal Immigrants on the Rise: State Paid Pre-natal Care for Undocumented Moms Depends on Residency" and "Blockade a Border Hasn't Cut Births," A23; Rex Dalton, "Births to Illegal Immigrants on the Rise: California Taxpayers Finance Soaring Numbers of Foreigners' Babies," A1 – all in *San Diego Union-Tribune,* 20 February 1994: A1.

20

Thinking through the Body and the Body Politic: Feminism, History, and Health-Care Policy in the United States

Susan M. Reverby

Feminism and health care have had a long, if complicated, relationship. I would even dare to claim that every contemporary feminist movement has had something to say, in rhetorical language and political struggles, about women's health care, sexuality, and the body. The critical roles played by science, medicine, and nursing in defining the "normal," in deciding what was even "humanness," have forced feminists who fight for any form of equality to confront science and the health-care system.

In doing so, feminists have sought a language with which to speak to health-care providers; they have also sought to identify the issues they should focus upon and the political battles they should wage. We have attempted to understand the differences between sex and gender (and the social construction of both) and to explore the "intersectionality" of race, gender, sexuality, and class as it shapes our experiences. All of these efforts required remaking women as subjects, not just objects, of health policy and care, and finding a way to navigate the possibilities for making our differing needs both "matter and not matter" at the same time.[1] As another historian of welfare policy has noted, however, we have done this under the conditions where "policy is as much constructed by denials of needs as by meeting them."[2]

As a historian of women and health care in the United States, I want to reflect upon the changes that have occurred over the last half-century and to focus on the importance of a historical understanding for the shifting ground of health policy. To do this I want to trace some familiar ground, to suggest some of the dilemmas historians face in trying to speak to those who set policy and provide care, and to create a historical typology for understanding the experience in the United States.

The last fifty years have seen a wild expansion of the health-care industry with new forms of government funding for access to health care, continued financial crises and denials of care, enormous increases in privatization, and the failed attempt at national health reform (yet again). Welfare reforms, new jobs without health insurance, inflationary spirals and recessions, and the shift to managed care have left increasing numbers of Americans without health-care coverage. Millions of others pay huge out-of-pocket expenses for prescription drugs, nursing home care, and even basic services as our aging population (increasingly female) struggles to meet daily needs. More recently, with the trumpeting of biomedicine's apparent successes, especially with the promises of success to come from the decoding of the humane genome and the use of stem cells, there has been the vocal questioning of biomedicine's power and legitimacy.[3]

In the context of these enormous changes, women's experiences have been dramatic. We have struggled to make issues of the body and health central to a second wave women's movement and then watched some of the movement's great successes either get taken for granted or eroded. We have seen the legalization of contraception and abortion, but have continued to endure sometimes even murderous attacks on every form of what we came to call reproductive rights. Many of us are painfully aware that if a presidency can be decided by the vote of one of our "Supremes," then so can reproductive control over women's bodies. Our efforts to provide specific care for women have resulted in the commercialization of women's health care in the mainstream institutions, while the failure to deal with the needs of immigrants, low-income women, the poor, elderly, and minorities has continued. We have witnessed the expansion of the technosciences, new reproductive technologies, and increasingly contentious debates over whether we are pre-twenty-first-century humans or (increasingly) post-twenty-first-century cyborgs.[4]

Obviously, larger economic and political forces have been the underlying foundations upon which these changes in health care were constructed. Social movements, organized by shifting alliances of consumers, reformers, providers, state officials, and lawyers, created the actual shape of the system.[5] Thus, no explanation for the changes in health care in the United States could be written without an effort to explore the agency of health activists in the making of change.[6]

Yet the form that such a history would take if it were to prove meaningful for policy-makers is not clear. For if we historians do our jobs right, we rarely do what many policy-makers, health-care providers, or even women's health activists want. We rebuff demands to predict the future or to practise what one scholar labelled preventive history – "drawing on the past to highlight for us potentially undesirable and avoidable consequences of future decisions."[7] We tell complicated stories about the past, refusing often to name individual enemies or to perceive their victims as only powerless. We talk about fluidity in meaning and refuse to create static categories.[8] We choose subjects and analytic styles that follow current historiographic debates. The result is that those who make policy, in the government, in the health-care industry, or in consumer advocacy groups, tend to ignore us.[9]

Policy-makers at every level, however, need a past as a touchstone. To gain such a place, they often create the histories they want, finding safety in uncomplicated historical narratives, journalist accounts, or the mining of parts of what historians have written to serve their purposes. Historian S. Ryan Johansson has argued that "rhetorical methods" have been critical to the way "history is often used to justify social policy," since "the transformation of historical 'facts' into policy 'facts' is not a straight forward scientific process."[10] Thus, how the story gets told reflects the way facts get chosen and organized into a coherent narrative.

As scholars, we may think we have come closer to historical truths. When it comes to policy formation, however, the better story or narrative, the one that seems to reflect what others have experienced or want, often wins out.[11] As historian and health-policy administrator Daniel Fox noted over a decade ago, "beliefs about history have had an enormous influence on health policy in the United States and abroad. Historians may have a subordinate role in public affairs, but historicism – the notion that history teaches, that the past is prologue – retains enormous power."[12]

There is an extant narrative of sorts about the changes that women have wrought in the American health-care system over the last fifty years. It is all but impossible to deny the importance of the grassroots, multiple-constituency women's health movement, although the growth of gay men's AIDS activism in the 1980s has sometimes obscured the beginnings of the initial women's efforts in the decades before.

The women's health movement in the United States began with the birthing movements of the 1950s. With the advent of the second wave of the American women's movement, it expanded into the broader areas of abortion, reproductive rights, and general women's health care in the late 1960s and early 1970s. Today the women's health movement exists in differing interests groups that range from breast cancer community organizations to the recently formed American College of Women's Health Physicians.

The women's health movement has done many things. It made demands for individual choice. It challenged the sexist, economic elitist, and racist social practices embedded in supposedly neutral medical care. It expanded the demands for reproductive rights. It shifted the focus towards what has come to be called women's health rather than just maternal and child health policy. It opened up new options for providers, from nurses to abortion counsellors and from allopathic doctors to alternative healers. And it created highly visible organized consumer groups around issues ranging from birthing practices to breast implants. By the end of the twentieth century, more women entered the ranks of policy-makers, providers, and researchers. This gave us the power to demand answers to larger questions about how gender, race, sexuality, and class affect every aspect of health and medical care, from double-blind research studies to the use of alternative therapies.

Our movement in the decades between the 1950s and the end of the century was built, in part, on a very American demand often denied to women: that individual choice had to be the basis for the consideration of what we needed for our health. But it was not just individualism as a core value of a particular social group that shaped the focus on individual need and choice. It was also how many of us, although never all, thought about history, health, and our bodies.

I realize that many of us create the history of our relationship to health care through the memory of our bodies and those of our mothers, grandmothers, sisters, lovers, and friends. Our knowledge of what has happened in our bodies and in those we have loved becomes our mnemonic device, our way to remember the elements in a historical story, our belief that "history teaches, that the past is prologue ..."[13] Our demands for policy and for change are in part shaped by what we remember and the way we tell our stories.[14] Our stories can be, for some, about the kindness of an illegal abortionist who made it possible for us to feed the children we did have. For others, the stories are about the heartbreak when our ovaries and womb were removed without our knowledge by a paternalistic physician; or a breast taken, when a lump might have sufficed, by medical tradition that did not question or even statistically measure the great Halstead's dictum. We remember when a sign of heart disease was ignored because it did not fit clinical norms established for men. We recall the stories of bodies that were stolen and used for research. We experience an aberrant mental moment taken to label us as crazy for all time.

These historically embodied memories contribute and shape our clinical judgments and policy concerns. Fifty years ago such memories were kept mostly in silence. If heard, they were whispered perhaps in quiet, desperate moments among friends or female family members. These memories, our histories, were often more secrets than silences, as historian Leslie Reagan so eloquently argued in her study of the illegal abortion era.[15]

More than anything else, the rapid expansion of the women's health movement (in both its grassroots and professionalized forms) was fuelled by allowing, even demanding, this explosion in remembering.[16] Some of our secrets became public and ultimately the basis for policy demands. Our seemingly transgressive stories became the way we made identity and survived, or became the reasons we were labelled so dangerous.[17] Thus, the changes we have seen over the last half-century are the results of the broader political-economy reorganization in health-care delivery, the triumph and questioning of biomedicine's promises, and the interlinking power of medical, state, and legal surveillance. The changes are also about what we remembered, and then organized for, won and compromised on, remain attacked for, and often failed to understand.[18]

As we write the history of feminism and health policy, we will have to do what historians have always done. We will examine policy-makers' decisions, "read dead people's mail" (as one of my friends so succinctly put it),[19] look through legal documents, newspapers, journals, congressional reports, and hearings, and so on. We will have to read what patients have written. We will have to ask different groups of women more about what they experienced, how it affected them, what they remembered, what changed or did not change their lives, what choices they thought possible, what ones they did not have. We will have to consider how differing experiences of history shape bodily memory and political action.[20] We need to historicize how the differing representations of our bodies have shaped our sense of selves.[21]

I would argue that this kind of "body history knowledge" was foundational to much of past women's health politics and policies. But it was not the only bedrock. This is where a more nuanced understanding of our history would be helpful. I first came to understand this thirty years ago. As a leftist feminist critic of the health-care system, I was working in the early 1970s with an organization in New York City called the Health Policy Advisory Center (commonly known as Health/PAC before the word PAC took on its political, soft-money connotations). We had what later became a standard criticism of the interlocking powers and priorities of the health industry and the structures of health empires (large hospital complexes that controlled both private and public sectors), drug and insurance companies, and federal funding.

The solutions we suggested built on the traditions of other twentieth-century U.S. health reformers – improved access, lower costs through a single-payer and state-run system, price controls, and changing priorities towards prevention rather than expensive tertiary care. Being good new leftists, we also added democratic decision-making, asking the people what they wanted, and "boring from within" to change the priorities and power structures of the health-care institutions. Our precepts were not so much about individual choice as they were about community-based planning and prevention strategies.

However, whenever I gave the Health/PAC rap (as we so affectionately referred to our critique) to groups of women, I had a problem. I would run into what I came to call, to use the much-abused trope, the body/body politic difficulty. No matter what I said, the questions after my talk were always bipolar in their distribution. Half would be about how we should take on United States capitalism *in toto*; the other half would be about what advice I would give about a vaginal itch or the latest breast cancer treatment.[22] One set of questions was too broad a query about the body politic, leaving no way for us to think about strategies or tactics short of revolution. The questions in the other set were too specific about individual bodies, failing to get us beyond requests for information about what we then called "seizing power." At the time, the activist in me was often stymied by this repeated experience and stumbling to figure out how these divisions could be reconciled.

Now, however, the historian in me thinks that this problem was not so much a division as a tension, a tension that all of us trying to think about health policy and feminism will have to consider. In other words, I think we have to look historically at how the connections between body and body politic have been felt and expressed by different groups of women, providers, and policy-makers. To do this, I will first briefly suggest a typology of how we might understand this by looking at the focus in the United States on our bodies and our historical sense of victimization. Second, I will examine forms of resistance that used body knowledge in medical/health-care encounters. Third, I will discuss overt attacks against institutions that did not converge on individual bodies. Finally, I will consider where that leaves us in terms of the struggles we now face and the histories we must write.

In the 1970s context of a growing critique of medical power and social control, feminist histories of women's health care were written with a very didactic focus on precedents for contemporary difficulties. These histories had as their dominant rhetorical concern the increased medicalization of women's lives and our victimization by the health-care system. This view played with supporting claims about our lack of knowledge (the extent to which our bodies were not ourselves), our position as maternal objects for rapacious doctors, the paternalistic policies of the state, and the suppression of female healing traditions, crushed by the seeming juggernaut of biomedicine.

Histories, whether of contemporary problems or of vast stretches of human history, emphasized these themes within the rhetoric of outrage, even as they often ignored contradictory evidence or complex historical forces.[23] Medical sociologists and anthropologists added resonance to these accounts by following women home from their doctors' offices to ask them what they understood, or by studying the talk between physicians and their patients. They explicated the narratives of women's experiences of illness, providing more evidence of "the sexual politics embedded in conceptions of sickness and beliefs about appropriate care."[24]

At first, all of this led to a wide questioning of the power of physicians, to the death (at least ideologically) of the "MD-iety" as activist Belita Cowan once labelled it. As public knowledge grew of what we had *not* been told about the pill, about DES, about the Dalkon shield, about illegal abortions and enforced sterilizations, about unnecessary hysterectomies and mastectomies, and more recently about the AIDS epidemic, our historical knowledge became embedded in stories about ourselves and our bodies. Many women began to trust what we thought we knew and could learn – not what "they" could or would tell us. For some groups of women, our "cherished precepts," as feminist activist and sociologist Sheryl Ruzek noted, became our demand for individual choices and knowledge. It was often assumed that more knowledge would provide women with power over our physicians and our own bodies.[25]

When I began to think about women and health policy in the early 1970s, however, I too thought through the bodies of those who were hurt, maimed, or left to die. As an early abortion activist, I knew the stories of those who had been harmed. I witnessed the transformations in women who came to New York for legal abortions when the state law changed in July of 1970, two and a half years before the historic *Roe v. Wade* Supreme Court decision that legalized abortion across the country. I understood our victimization and our need for more knowledge. I believed that armed with information we could gain better care. I helped, as did many other activists across the country, to write the endless pamphlets we produced to provide women with information. "Know your vaginal infections," we wrote. "Find your cervix," other women said as they guided one another in self-help groups. "Our bodies, ourselves," the women in Boston told us as their mimeo-graphed pamphlets became larger and larger best-selling information guides. We thought that with more knowledge and information we were in our own ways making and demanding new policies.

I knew then in a more inchoate way than I know now that more information was never enough, however. I believed that a history of victimization would neither tell the full story nor help us really think about change. I saw, as we researched the public clinics in New York City (in order to write a pamphlet with the pithy title "How to Get through the Maze with Your Feet in the Stirrups,"), that class attitudes and racism shaped what happened to women who had to rely upon publicly funded care.[26] The work we did to combat sterilization abuse in the public hospitals that served minority communities, that others did on this issue in Puerto Rico, and that the federally funded health services provided to Native American women, for example, proved to me that more knowledge was not enough to make change. I worried aloud and in print about whether looking inward at our cervixes, or creating menstrual extraction groups, or even establishing alternative feminist health centres would teach us how to challenge power and eliminate the pervasive racism, class oppression, and homophobia that structured the delivery system and research centres.[27]

Groups in the women's health movement began to fall apart over such issues, drowning in trying to meet the need that individual women had for services, care, and information, which left little time to make the connections to strategies for change, or little energy to organize for it. Nor could many women find the language or experience to confront class, sexuality, or racial conflicts in their own midst. As in other places in the second wave of the women's movement, the essentialism of a gender-only argument proved to be unstable ground as an earthquake of demands hit us broadside.

In the women's health movement, a number of groups and individual leaders understood quite early that more information and gender alone had their limitations. Many women activists did think through the history of their bodies and made the connections to larger political structures. They saw that resistance and agency could happen. They found ways to make knowledge become the power to transform medical and other health-care encounters when that knowledge is not just limited to more physiological or medical information.[28] Thinking through bodies to larger political forces became a second way to structure both history and political action.

Interestingly, much of this approach took the forms of fiction, art, films, and stories. These genres have been most powerful as histories written out of the body into resistance and change. Memoirs of illness, from Audre Lorde's iconic *The Cancer Journals* to Judith Helfand's film of her DES experience, *A Healthy Baby Girl,* made body politics emotionally accessible and powerful, helping women to see the racial, class, and sexuality specificity of the embodied gendered experience.[29] In England, photographer-feminist Jo Spence used her art to explore the experience of breast cancer and to gaze back at those who gazed at her, reshaping, as sociologist Susan Bell argues, the very "narrative of illness" itself.[30] Or consider how Byllye Avery explained that the National Black Women's Health Project learned to provide a space for African-American women to discuss the realities of their lives before health information could be exchanged. In this way, these women did not just gain knowledge about diets or health habits, but acceptance and a way to understand how the structures of racism, poverty, and sexism were linked to everyday lives.[31] In sum, all of these examples show how the lived body experience and social structures are intimately connected.

We have much to gain from understanding the differing stories that individual women have told about how this body/resistance connection is made, what attachments to historical events they develop, what meanings for resistance and struggle they create. Sociologist Susan Bell's careful narrative analysis of two DES daughters who have had vaginal cancers demonstrated the connection between an individual's experience and the rhetoric and politics of the women's health movement as it changed over time. Historians can make use of the work of sociologists like Bell. We can apply the model she provides of narrative analyses in both stories and art to oral histories and written narratives to understand how the differing "language and logic of feminism" as well as specific historical experiences can become the basis for resistance.[32]

In a third part of this typology, we can look at how other groups of women ignored the individual modes of resistance or knowledge to imagine an assault on given health policy through collective actions. Some of us stormed the doors of the Senate when hearings on the pill kept women out, demanding that future meetings of the U.S. Food and Drug Administration be made open to the public and that consumers as well as industry representatives and scientist/practitioners be on the expert panels. We formed the National Women's Health Network in order to have an organized voice speaking out in Washington, combining the power of the law and feminist expert testimony. We used publicity to catch drug companies or device manufacturers in their lies and overzealous medicalizing as well as to provide critical information to the public. Some of us struggled to make sure that state and federal regulations required that access to abortion was not bought at the price of an unwanted sterilization. We formed organizations that forced changes in research priorities and study protocols at the National Institutes of Health.

Finally, we have learned through long and painful discussions how much our strategies and priorities could or could not have meaning beyond the borders of the United States. We need a more comparative historical analysis of how these ideas have either been translated or informed or ignored by women in other parts of the world. Those of us who have gone on to work with women from other cultures and countries have realized how much new terminologies and strategies are necessary to make any change possible.

From international conferences and connections, we have learned that our strategies and language cannot travel or make policy without what political activist and theorist Rosalind Petchesky calls the linking of "the ethics of women's bodily self-determination to the materiality of their bodies in the world."[33] Many American health activists have been humbled by our contact with women across the globe. We have seen how rhetoric of "bodily integrity" is becoming attached by other feminists to issues of human rights. This provides us, as Petchesky claims, with the language with which to "challenge the moral arsenal" of various fundamentalists, one that closes the division between body and body politic, private and public, and demands rights as it also understands duty and collective responsibility.[34]

Ironically, the AIDS pandemic has forced many of us worldwide to think about the connections between self-determination and health. In the spring of 2001, Kofi Annan spoke at the United Nations about the necessity for better education of women and improvement in our lives if AIDS is to be prevented. We have to be on guard, as always, to make sure that analysis that points to women's lack of power and illiteracy does not turn into blaming us for the spread of AIDS, as it often has with any sexually transmitted disease. Nevertheless, the growing discussion worldwide of the links among poverty, gender, health, societal inequality, and human rights provides us with a clear moment that we can use to make broader demands for action on behalf of women and their families.[35]

This brief typology – from the focus on knowledge about the individual body, to political action through the body, to more collective political actions that are culturally specific – is not meant to suggest a hierarchy of better politics; rather it is to begin to lay out a research agenda for historians of this recent past in the making of health policy. The task for historians will be to chronicle and explain why some women, but not others, would see the political work of the women's health movement change through a connection of knowledge and power. It will require us to explain what was seen as political and

culturally possible within different groups at various points in the
recent past. We will have to explore how much of this came from a
deeply remembered embodied history, or explore other sources for
political motivations, strategies, and tactics.

We will have to see how the threads of these differing strategies spun
out over the decades from the 1960s onward. Some of the history of
this period should explore the deadends of the differing strategies and
the working out of the body/body politic tensions. Sociologist Kathy
Davis's new work on the history of the Boston Women's Health Book
Collective, the writers of the multiple editions of *Our Bodies, Ourselves*,
may help us to understand, for example, when knowledge making
could lead to a basis for political action and when it could not. Her
analysis of the changes made in the book as it was translated, or
adapted, into dozens of languages from across the globe should give us
a sense of how a focus on individual choice and knowledge "travels"
into other societies.[36]

Davis's analysis should also force us to consider how a strategy for
knowledge, so powerful in the early 1970s, could become useless in
the new century. The call for individual choice has become, in part,
the ideological cover for a thousand new websites on women's health
all competing for our attention as sources of knowledge, not as the basis for an assault on the health-care system, as we expected. It should
make us see how learning more about what could happen to our bodies could become depoliticized and the source of the reinscription of
control by those selling us women's health "information."[37] It should
make us understand how a political language that works for some
groups in one culture often provides the wrong words in another,
forcing us to listen to the very specificity of differing struggles in their
cultural contexts.

It would of course be convenient in telling these stories if these
differing strategies and understandings of the body/body politic
tension would fall neatly into historical periods we could wall off with
dates and major events, even within specific cultural and racial groups.
But the reality is that they will not. Some of us were storming office
doors at the same moment that others were climbing onto their
couches to look for their cervixes. Some women took this visioning of
their inner self into self-help groups and alternative feminist health
centres; others just kept the information to themselves. Some women
saw new technologies as their saviour and the U.S. Food and Drug
Administration's approval process as an impediment to their survival;
others, remembering the experiences of the Dalkon shield or DES,
were much more fearful of quick approval and reliance on a "technological fix."[38] While some of us struggled against the state, others first

had to confront the demands of their own racial political groups and religious practices.

Sometimes class or race or sexual identity can explain the differing strategies and beliefs women brought to their health-care struggles. But other times we need to explore the idea that differing bodily experiences are the basis for political action on health care.[39] We will have to look at the dangers of relying on only one way of understanding our histories, of seeing our precepts as coming from only one dominate discourse.

There is much we can do. We will need to know what memory and understanding meant to different women as they moved from individual health experiences to various forms of political and collective action. We will need to know how women's bodies were experienced, imagined, and represented and whether this linked them to a history of the politically possible. Whether we write the history of the National Institutes of Health's Women's Health Initiative on women as research subjects or whether we write about the period when greater global links began to be made, for examples, we will need to see if this embodied understanding affected policy change.[40] We will have to determine whether the voices of women patients/consumers, spoken out loud in individual confrontations, collective demonstrations, or conveyed in the starkness of a morbidity and mortality report, affected those who made policy or provided care.[41] We will have to consider how to periodize the shifting concerns even in this recent past. We will have to understand the international and comparative aspects of what feminism and health care have meant across the multiple cultures of this world.

I worry that we have been very bad historians of our own life times. Many students have a better sense of the women who wanted water cures in the nineteenth century than they do of the struggles within the New York Women's Health and Abortion Project of the early 1970s or of what happened to the feminist health centres.

We cannot answer the questions that policy-makers want answered now if we do not attempt a sophisticated look at what we have all been doing over the last fifty years and if we do not settle on the kind of historical analysis we will bring to this project. We cannot make policy unless we understand what kinds of histories, representations, and cultural experiences shaped our underlying principles, made some strategies possible, and limited others.

I do think that historians have much to say to those who will make policy and practise health-care delivery in the future. In thinking about this, I considered the haunting final words in an article on women and health policy by feminist sociologist and health reformer

Sheryl Burt Ruzek. She concluded: "It is only when we let go of uncritical attachment to precepts that might have served women well in the past that new visions will emerge to shape our futures."[42] Ruzek was offering up a clarion call, a demand, that we let go of cherished past beliefs so that we might shape a feminist policy future that takes equality and justice as its baseline. But first we will need a more complete understanding of what these beliefs have been and how they have survived over time and for whom.

We can use the tension between body and body politic in its multiple forms to examine the kinds of demands women have made in the past on the health-care system and how they have made them. We can explore how various groups of women remember and use differing histories to make meaning, find ways to resist, sort out the possibilities for challenge. We desperately need to understand the policy dead ends that certain beliefs take us to. We do need to know when knowledge together with a demand for more care for ourselves means we are not thinking enough about cost and cost containment, about the implications of what counts as feminist policy for all women, about what makes us relevant to the real issues of contemporary policy.[43] We do need to understand when embodied knowledge can lead to power, and when it can lead to a failure to understand difference and political change.

I suspect we may never end the tension between the body and the body politic, nor do I think it will be possible. We will never, I am sure, find one way to explain the past. We will have to listen to those who are willing to tell us in multiple forms about their claims, concerns, and needs. We may never be heroes to policy-makers and providers. We can, however, write histories of the recent past with a commitment to theory that provides us with the richest historical analysis possible as we search for justice.

NOTES

Author's Note: I wish to thank Susan Bell, Kathy Davis, and Bill Quivers for the hours they spent listening to me agonize over aspects of this paper. They are wonderful friends and colleagues. Any failures to heed their advice are mine. A different version of this essay appeared as "Feminism and Health," *Health and History: Journal of the Australian Society of the History of Medicine* 4, no. 1 (2002): 3–17.

1 Nancy Cott uses the terms "matter and not matter" to refer to gender as the central focus of feminism in her *The Grounding of American Feminism* (New Haven: Yale University Press 1987).

2 Linda Gordon, "The New Feminist Scholarship on the Welfare State," in
   Women, the State and Welfare, ed. Linda Gordon (Madison: University of
   Wisconsin Press 1990), 10.
3 See Ruth Hubbard and Elijah Wald, *Exploding the Gene Myth* (Boston:
   Beacon Press 1993).
4 See Sheryl Burt Ruzek et al., eds, *Women's Health: Complexities and Differences*
   (Columbus: Ohio State University Press 1997); and Carol S. Weisman,
   Women's Health Care: Activist Traditions and Institutional Change (Baltimore:
   Johns Hopkins University Press 1998).
5 See Daniel M. Fox, *Power and Illness: The Failure and Future of American Health
   Policy* (Berkeley: University of California Press 1994).
6 I am grateful to Evelynn M. Hammonds for reminding me how important
   the problem of the erasure of our activism is to a proper historical account-
   ing. For another of view on this from the labour history perspective, see
   James Green, *Taking History to Heart: The Power of the Past in Building Social
   Movements* (Amherst: University of Massachusetts Press 2000).
7 Paul Sanazaro, "Historical Discontinuity, Hospitals and Health Services," in
   Medical History and Medical Care, ed. Gordon McLachlan and Thomas
   McKeown (London: Oxford University Press 1971), 131; quote in Susan
   Reverby and David Rosner, "Beyond the Great Doctors," in *Health Care
   in America: Essays in Social History,* ed. Susan Reverby and David Rosner
   (Philadelphia: Temple University Press 1979), 12.
8 For an excellent example of this kind of history, see Leslie J. Reagan,
   *When Abortion Was a Crime: Women, Medicine and Law in the United States,
   1867–1973* (Berkeley: University of California Press 1997).
9 See Daniel Fox, "History and Health Policy: An Autobiographical Note on
   the Decline of Historicism," *Journal of Social History* 18 (Spring 1986):
   349–64. I am grateful to Dan Fox for sending me a copy of this article and
   his willingness to discuss the issues with me.
10 S. Ryan Johansson, "Food for Thought: Rhetoric and Reality in Modern
   Mortality History," *Historical Methods* 27 (Summer 1994): 101.
11 For a discussion of narratives vs truths, see Margaret Talbot, "The Journalist and the Lawyer," *New York Times Book Review,* 7 February 1999: 6.
   On the role of the creation of history and myth, see David Blight, *Race
   and Reunion: The Civil War in American Memory* (Cambridge: Harvard
   University Press 2000).
12 Fox, "History and Health Policy."
13 On the use of objects as mnemonic devices to create historical memory,
   see Mary Nooter Roberts and Allen F. Roberts, eds, *Memory: Luba Art and
   the Making of History* (New York: Museum for African Art 1996). On the
   body and history, see Ruth Behar, "The Body in the Woman, The Story in
   the Woman: A Book Review and Personal Essay," in *The Female Body: Figures,*

Styles, Speculations, ed. Laurence Goldstein (Ann Arbor: University of Michigan Press 1991), 267–311.

14 On the transgressive nature of women's stories of birthing, for example, see Della Pollock, *Telling Bodies, Performing Birth* (New York: Columbia University Press 1999).

15 Reagan, *When Abortion Was a Crime*, 21.

16 Sheryl Burt Ruzek and Julie Becker, "The Women's Health Movement in the United States: From Grass-Roots Activism to Professional Agendas," *Journal of the American Medical Women's Association* 54 (Winter 1999): 4–8.

17 On the complex use of women's birth stories as both sites of identity and danger, see Pollock, *Telling Bodies*. As Pollock argues in the conclusion to a chapter on secrets told in birth stories, "These stories are born in risk. Not so much in the physical dangers of birth but in *narrative* risk, in the process of subjecting *knowing* to the perils of *not knowing* or *unknowing*, even undiscovering the truths and facts that science covets, in the exigencies and im/mediacies of re-membering birth" (248).

18 Our body knowledge included the shifting language of the women's health movement as well as that of medicine; indeed they have become embedded in one another. See Susan E. Bell, "Narratives and Lives: Women's Health Politics and the Diagnosis of Cancer for DES Daughters," *Narrative Inquiry* 9, no. 2: 1–43.

19 I am grateful to Harry Marks for this comment.

20 For as sociologist Susan E. Bell has argued in writing about the narratives of DES daughters with cancers, "embedded in these accounts is information which shows how historical events as well as dominant and emerging cultural discourses play a role in sense making." See Bell, "Narratives and Lives," 2.

21 See Evelynn M. Hammonds, "Black (W)holes and the Geometry of Black Female Sexuality," *differences* (1994): 127–45.

22 For an earlier discussion of this problem, see Susan Reverby, "The Body and the Body Politic: Towards a History of Women and Health Care," Bunting Institute Fellows Colloquium, 11 May 1988, unpublished paper.

23 For some of the early histories, see for example Ellen Frankfort, *Vaginal Politics* (New York: Vintage 1970); and Deirdre English and Barbara Ehrenreich, *For Her Own Good* (Garden City: Anchor Press 1978).

24 Quote is from Catherine Riessman, "Women and Medicalization: A New Perspective," *Social Policy* 11, no. 1: 3. For an overview, see Judith D. Auerbach and Anne E. Figert, "Women's Health Research: Public Policy and Sociology," *Journal of Health and Social Behavior* (extra issue 1995): 115–31.

25 We did all of this, of course, well before the Internet and Web made health information available to anyone who could access a computer terminal and a connection. As the current maze of health-care information now widely available grows daily (the very information we struggled so hard to find

thirty years ago), I am again reminded that knowing more still does not translate directly into the power to do anything about the issues. Indeed, the welter of information (often provided by the pharmaceutical and medical-device multinational companies) leaves out as much as it informs, providing disconnected body information that can be mind numbing and stripped of its political possibilities.

26 Women's Health and Abortion Project, "How to Get through the Maze with Your Feet in the Stirrups," pamphlet (New York: Women's Health and Abortion Project 1971). Pamphlet in the Rachel Fruchter Collection in the Women's Studies Department, Wellesley College.

27 Susan M. Reverby, review of *Our Bodies, Ourselves, University Review*, no. 28 (April 1973): 25–7.

28 For a discussion of how this political aspect of the women's movement is often left out in the histories, see Rosalyn Baxandall and Linda Gordon, "Second-Wave Soundings," *Nation* 271 (3 July 2000): 28–30.

29 Audre Lorde, *The Cancer Journals* (San Francisco: Aunt Lute Press 1980, 1992); Judith Helfand, *A Healthy Baby Girl*, video recording (New York: Women Make Movies 1996).

30 Susan E. Bell, "Photo Images: Jo Spence's Narratives of Living with Illness," *Health* 6, no. 1: 5. I am grateful to Susan Bell for helping me understand the textuality of photography and art as well as for our many discussions on the topics this essay covers.

31 Byllye Y. Avery, "Breathing Life into Ourselves: The Evolution of the National Black Women's Health Project," in *The Black Women's Health Book*, ed. Evelyn C. White (San Francisco: Seal Press 1994), 4–10.

32 Bell, "Narratives and Lives," 7. See also Pollock, *Telling Bodies*.

33 Rosalind P. Petchesky, "Spiraling Discourses of Reproductive and Sexual Rights: A Post-Beijing Assessment of International Feminist Politics," in *Women Transforming Politics*, ed. Cathy J. Cohen, Kathleen B. Jones, and Joan C. Tronto (New York: New York University Press 1997), 587.

34 Ibid., 589.

35 See Timothy Evans et al., *Challenging Inequities in Health: From Ethics to Action* (New York: Oxford University Press 2001).

36 Kathy Davis's new work on the history of the Boston Women's Health Book Collective will focus on this problem directly. I am grateful for the great discussions we had on the problems that this essay is exploring.

37 For the last five years, students in my health history course have been evaluating women's health-care websites. We have all been amazed by what is passing for "information" and how the "facts" differ from site to site.

38 See Susan M. Reverby, "What Does It Mean to Be an Expert? A Health Activist at the FDA," *Advancing the Consumer Interest* 9 (Spring 1997): 34–6.

39 Several years ago some of my students led a discussion on breast cancer and started the class by talking about how they felt about their breasts. As a

teacher I did not think I could begin the class that way. But their leadership suggested the importance of the issue to them and the way they came to understand our readings and discussions on cancer.

40 For a good example of how we might consider problematizing the body in feminist theory, see Alison Caddick, "Making Babies, Making Sense: Reproductive Technologies, Postmodernity, and the Ambiguities of Feminism," in *Troubled Bodies: Critical Perspectives on Postmodernism, Medical Ethics, and the Body*, ed. Paul A. Komesaroff (Durham, N.C.: Duke University Press 1995), 142–67.

41 Leslie Reagan's history of abortion does an excellent job of showing the link between what women said and what they experienced and how this changed what many physicians thought about abortion reform and repeal. See Reagan, *When Abortion Was a Crime*.

42 Sheryl Burt Ruzek, "Rethinking Feminist Ideologies and Actions: Thoughts on the Past and Future of Health Reform," in *Revisioning Women, Health and Healing*, ed. Adele E. Clarke and Virginia L. Olesen (New York: Routledge 1999), 319.

43 Ibid., 303–23.

Contributors

ALINE CHARLES is assistant professor in the Department of History at Laval University. She has authored *Travail d'ombre et de lumière: Le bénévolat féminin à l'hôpital Ste-Justine 1907–1960* (1990) and co-authored *Femmes, santé et professions 1930–1980* (1997). She is preparing her dissertation, "Travail et vieillesses féminines dans les hôpitaux québécois 1940–1980" (1997), for publication.

BARBARA CLOW is a social historian of medicine whose areas of interest and expertise include alternative medicine, doctor-patient relations, lay perspectives, disease, stress, pharmaceuticals, infertility, and gender. She recently published a book on the history of cancer care in Canada, *Negotiating Disease: Power and Cancer Care, 1900–1950,* and is currently working on a history of thalidomide in North America.

LAURA E. ETTINGER is an assistant professor of history at Clarkson University in Potsdam, New York. She has published several articles on the history of American nurse-midwifery and is currently completing a book on this subject. Her interests include the culture of childbirth, gender and the professions, and the structure of American health care.

GEORGINA FELDBERG, an associate professor of social science at York University, teaches in graduate programs in history and women's studies. As director of the York University Centre for Health Studies and academic director of the National Network on Environments and Women's Health, she has focused her research and teaching on women and health in North America. Her publications include *Disease and Class: Tuberculosis and the Shaping of Modern North*

American Society and several articles. A book on *Defining Women's Health* in twentieth-century Canada is in progress.

KAREN FLYNN, a doctoral candidate in Women's Studies at York University, teaches in the Department of Women' Studies at St Cloud State University. Her research interests include women, work, family, health, racism, feminism, and post-colonial theory. She also writes a regular column for the community newspaper *Share.*

VANESSA NORTHINGTON GAMBLE, a physician and medical historian, is an internationally recognized expert on the history of race and racism in American medicine, cultural competence, and diversity. Her positions have included vice-president of the Division of Community and Minority Programs at the Association of American Medical Colleges, director of the Center for the Study of Race and Ethnicity in Medicine, and associate professor of history of medicine and family medicine at the University of Wisconsin School of Medicine. Her book *Making a Place for Ourselves: The Black Hospital Movement, 1920–1945* was named an outstanding academic book by *Choice,* the journal of academic librarians. Dr Gamble is a recipient of a Robert Wood Johnson Foundation Health Investigator Award to write a book of essays on race and racism in American medicine. She is also writing a biography of Virginia M. Alexander, an African-American woman physician and social activist.

ELENA R. GUTIÉRREZ is an assistant professor in the programs in gender and women's studies and Latin American and Latino studies at the University of Illinois at Chicago. She is currently completing a book manuscript entitled *Fertility Matters: The Racial Politics of Mexican-Origin Women's Reproduction.*

MOLLY LADD-TAYLOR teaches American history at York University in Toronto. Her publications include *Mother-Work: Women, Child Welfare and the State;* '*Bad' Mothers: The Politics of Blame in 20th Century America* (co-edited with Lauri Umansky), and "Saving Babies and Sterilizing Mothers: Eugenics and Welfare Politics in the Interwar US," *Social Politics* (1997).

ALISON LI is the author of *Endocrines and Enterprise: J.B. Collip, A Life in Medical Research,* forthcoming from McGill-Queen's University Press. She is also co-author of a study of Internet regulation and the non-profit sector, part of the Nonprofit Sector Research Initiative, Queen's University School of Policy Studies.

MAUREEN MCCALL practised family medicine in Ontario and Alberta for nine years before returning to graduate school. She completed a master's in public health with a specialization in international health at Harvard University in 1997. Since then, she has continued part-time clinical practice while providing technical advice to numerous health and development- projects around the world. Dr McCall's international work has focused on improving women's health through efforts ranging from grassroots village development to the government of Nepal's Safer Motherhood program, which includes the implementation of a liberalized abortion policy. She and her husband are currently living and working in Nepal.

MICHELLE L. McCLELLAN received her PhD in American history from Stanford University in 2000, with a prize-winning dissertation entitled "'Lady Lushes': Women Alcoholics and American Society, 1880–1960." She currently teaches medical history at the University of Georgia and coordinates educational programs for the Georgia Trust for Historic Preservation.

KATHRYN McPHERSON teaches women's and Western Canadian history at York University in Toronto and is chair of York's School of Women's Studies. Her publications include *Bedside Matters: The Transformation of Canadian Nursing 1900–1990*; *Gendered Pasts: Historical Essays in Femininity and Masculinity in Canada* (co-edited with Cecilia Morgan and Nancy Forestell); and "Was the Frontier 'Good' for Women?" *Atlantis* (2000).

DAWN DOROTHY NICKEL is a PhD candidate in history at the University of Alberta. Her doctoral dissertation focuses on home care of the dying in the North American West, 1900 to 1950. Her publications include an article co-authored with Susan L. Smith, "From Home to Hospital: Parallels in Birthing and Dying in Twentieth-Century Canada," *Canadian Bulletin of Medical History* (2000).

HEATHER MUNRO PRESCOTT is a professor in and chair of the Department of History at Central Connecticut State University. During the fall 2001 semester she served as the A. Lindsay O'Connor Distinguished Visiting Associate Professor of American Institutions in the Department of History at Colgate University. She is the author of *"A Doctor of Their Own": The History of Adolescent Medicine* (Harvard University Press, 1998). She is currently working on a history of college health tentatively entitled *Student Bodies*.

LESLIE J. REAGAN is associate professor of history and medical humanities and social sciences at the University of Illinois, Urbana-Champaign. Her book, *When Abortion Was a Crime: Women, Medicine, and Law in the United States, 1867–1973*, won the Willard Hurst Prize, among others. Her essay on miscarriage, motherhood, and the making of emotions, "From Hazard to Blessing to Tragedy: Representations of Miscarriage in Twentieth-Century America," is forthcoming in *Feminist Studies*.

SUSAN M. REVERBY is professor of women's studies at Wellesley College and a historian of American women, medicine, and nursing. She is the author or editor of numerous volumes on women's history, the history of medicine, and the history of nursing. From 1993 to 1997 she served as the consumer representative on the U.S. FDA's Obstetrics and Gynecology Devices Advisory Panel. Her latest edited book is *Tuskegee's Truths: Rethinking the Tuskegee Syphilis Study* (2000), and she is currently writing a book on the ways the stories of that study are told.

SUSAN L. SMITH, an associate professor of history at the University of Alberta in Canada, is the author of *Sick and Tired of Being Sick and Tired: Black Women's Health Activism in America, 1890–1950*. She is currently writing a book on the history of Japanese-American midwifery.

ANN STARR, a visual artist and writer interested in medicine and medical history, shows her painting and drawing internationally. She has lectured on art and medicine at the National Portrait Gallery in London, Cambridge University, Northwestern, Yale, the University of Chicago, the University of Illinois at Chicago, and many conferences. Her publications include "Choosing My Own Doctor," *Yale Journal for Humanities in Medicine* (2001).

JUDITH BENDER ZELMANOVITS is trained as a physiotherapist and holds a master's degree in Canadian history from York University. She is a PhD candidate in York University's School of Women's Studies and teaches courses for the School of Women's Studies and the Faculty of Education. Her chapter in this volume is based on research for her dissertation, a study of the work of nurses hired by the federal government to provide health services in isolated Subarctic and Arctic communities in the post–Second World War period.

Index

86–90; rejection of government support, 93, 94; as a woman reformer, 85, 94–5. *See also* alcoholism

mastectomy, 324, 327–9

Masters, William H., and Virginia Johnson, 316

Maternal Health Center (Santa Fe), 145, 147

maternal mortality, 20, 130, 132, 146, 154, 237

maternity care: of Latina women at the Catholic Maternity Institute, 144–55; in northern Canada, 161–79. *See also* Aboriginal communities in northern Canada; midwifery; outpost nurses

Maternity Center Association (New York), 149

Medicaid (U.S.), 24–5, 381; and abortion, 30

Medical Care Act (Canada): 1966, 342; 1968, 24

medical hierarchy, 19, 22, 197–8, 319, 388. *See also* doctors

Medical Mission Sisters, 144, 145, 147, 148, 154, 156n5, 157n12. *See also* Catholic Maternity Institute

medical research, 44–5; funding of, 21–2, priority of "male" over "female" diseases, 22; and voluntary/charity sector, 21–2

Medical Research Council of Canada, 21

Medical Services Branch (Canada), 164; orientation program for nursing leaders, 186n73

medical specialties: growth in numbers of, 22; representation of women in, 22. *See also* gynaecology; obstetrics

Medicare (Canada), 4, 15; and Aboriginal health issues, 240; alternative forms of service delivery, 34; delisted services, 34; growing weakness in, 34; guiding principles of, 24; imposition of "caps" on

physicians' earnings, 34; increased spending on, 34; "two-tier" system, 35

Medicare (U.S.), 24–5

"medivac," 162, 181n7

Menagh, Nancy, 168

menopause: as a "deficiency disease," 101–2, 105–6; as a normal phase of life, 104; socio-economic impact of, 116, 120n57; symptoms of, 104. *See also* estrogen replacement therapy; hormone replacement therapy; Premarin

menstruation, 210; gynaecologists' views on, 207–9, 210; as a pathological process, 207

mental hospitals: environment of, a source of anxiety, 295; expectations of patients within, 303; institutional goals of, 303; population within, 299–300; the psychiatric floor, 298–9; regulations in, 297, 298; staff at, 296, 297, 298

mental illness, 292–304; care for white middle class vs care for "intractable" ("homeless"), 301; communications between the "well" and the "ill," 293–5; credibility of the mentally ill, 293

mental retardation, 77, 79

Meriam Report (1928), 227

Mexican-origin women. *See* reproductive rights; coercive sterilization: of Mexican-origin women

Mexico: abortion destination, 355–70; economic relationship with U.S., 357; as health resource for U.S. citizens, 356–7, 360

midwifery, 161, 148–9, 178, 241, 255; Aboriginal, 169, 173–4, 175, 178, 179, 232; alegality of, 165, 183n22; countenanced by doctors in remote areas, 167; teaching manuals, 170; training

in, 165, 166, 167–8, 184n41; unrecognized in Manitoba, 250. *See also* CMI nurse-midwives

Migrant Health Act (U.S., 1962), 24

modern alcoholism movement, 84, 85

Moore, Donald, 255

Moore, Dr Percy, 164, 229, 235

Morgentaler, Dr Henry, 29–30

morning sickness, 52–3; perceived as psychosomatic, 53, 54

mothering: and child behaviour, 22; in northern Aboriginal communities, 175–6

Mother Superior, 269, 270, 271, 279; authority of, 275, 278, 283; and list of "obediences," 271–2, 286; restricted authority of, 286

Mount, Dr Balfour, 342–3

Mudd, Emily, 72

Myles, Margaret (*A Textbook for Midwives*), 170

Nabarette, Charles, 392

Nader, Ralph, 28

narcotics, and pain relief, 338

Nation, Carry, 92, 93, 99n24

National Action Committee on the Status of Women (NAC), 29

National Association for the Repeal of Abortion Laws (NARAL), 356. *See also* Association to Repeal Abortion Laws

National Black Women's Health Project, 412

National Committee for Education on Alcoholism (NCEA), 84–5, 89, 90, 91–3

National Council on Alcoholism and Drug Dependence, 85, 91

National Hospice Organization (U.S.), 342